Shojo Beat

honey and clove

Vol. 1

Story & Art by
Chica Umino

honey and clover

Volume 1
CONTENTS

honey and clover™

chapter 1

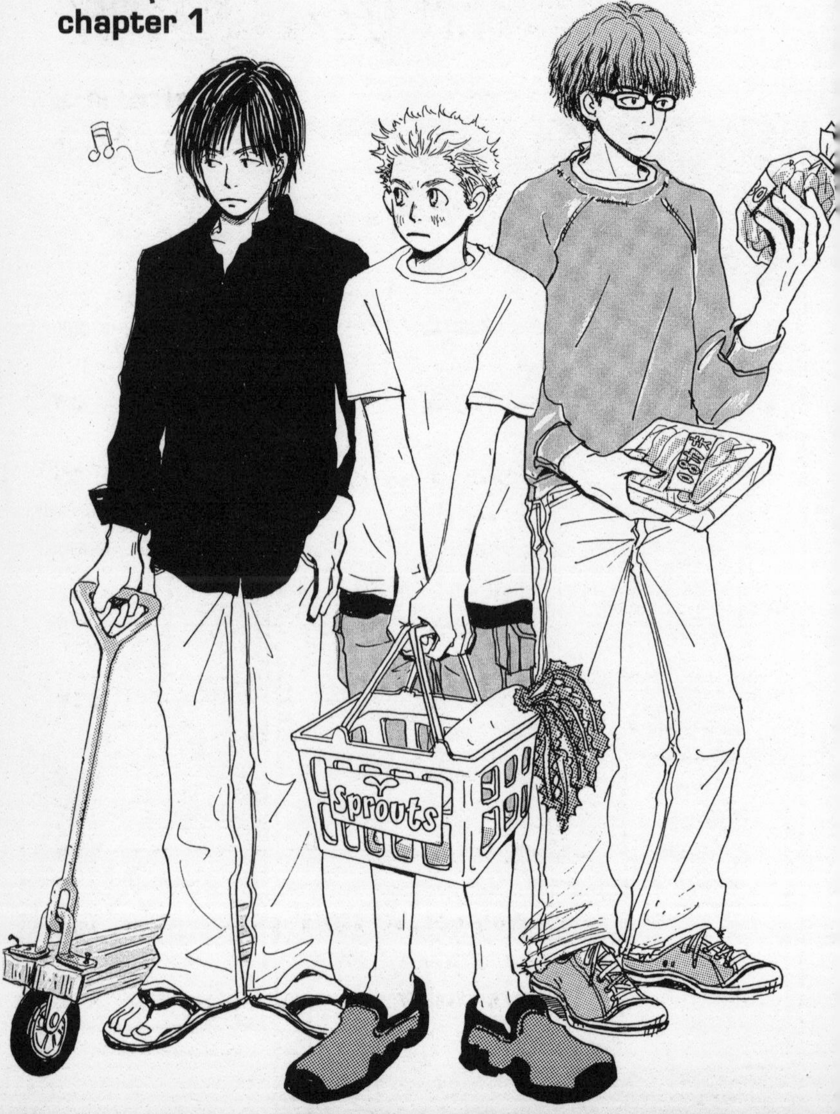
Sprouts

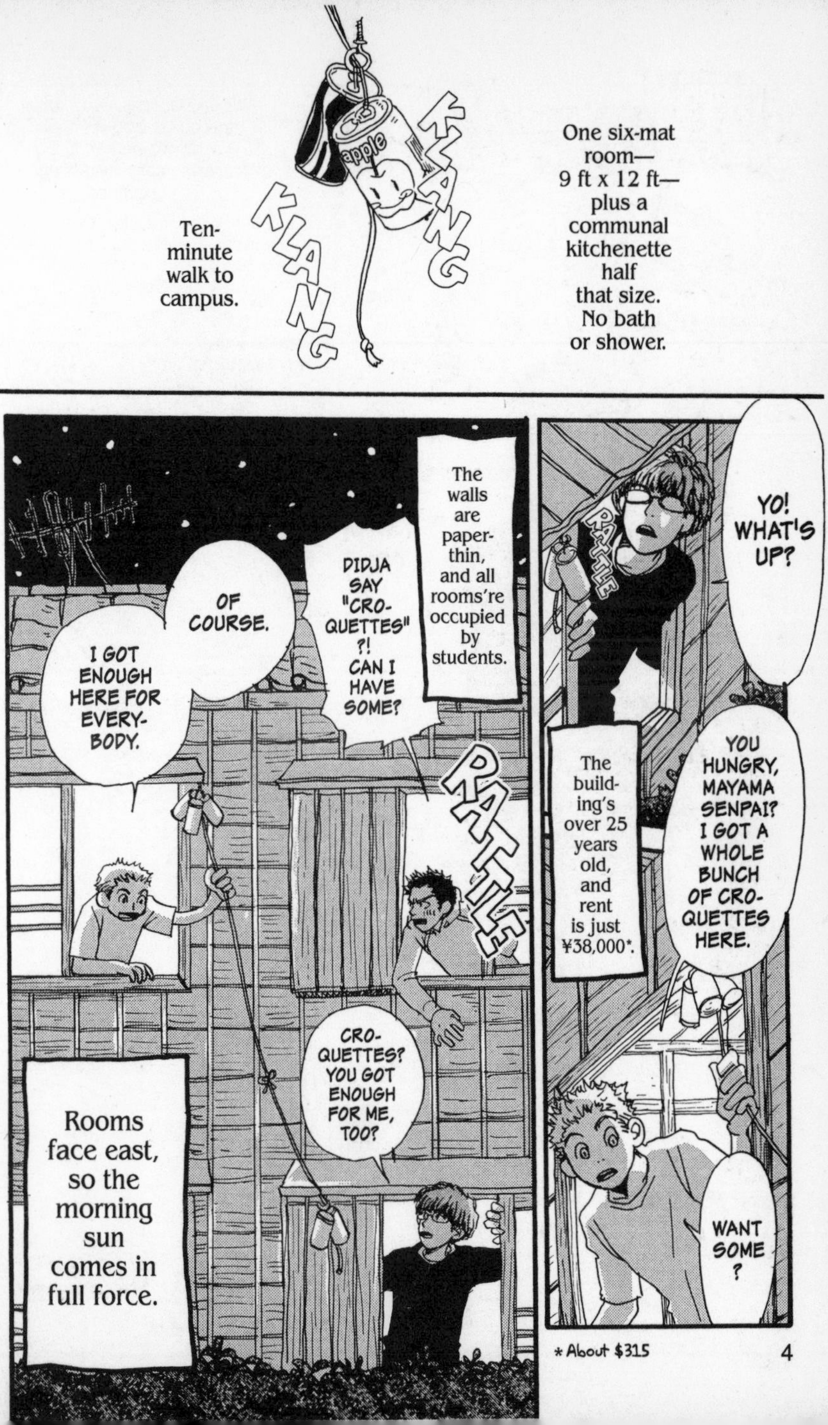
One six-mat room—9 ft x 12 ft—plus a communal kitchenette half that size. No bath or shower.
KLANG
KLANG
apple
Ten-minute walk to campus.
YO! WHAT'S UP?
RATTLE
The building's over 25 years old, and rent is just ¥38,000*.
YOU HUNGRY, MAYAMA SENPAI? I GOT A WHOLE BUNCH OF CROQUETTES HERE.
WANT SOME?
The walls are paper-thin, and all rooms're occupied by students.
DIDJA SAY "CROQUETTES"?! CAN I HAVE SOME?
OF COURSE.
I GOT ENOUGH HERE FOR EVERYBODY.
RATTLE
CROQUETTES? YOU GOT ENOUGH FOR ME, TOO?
Rooms face east, so the morning sun comes in full force.

* About $315

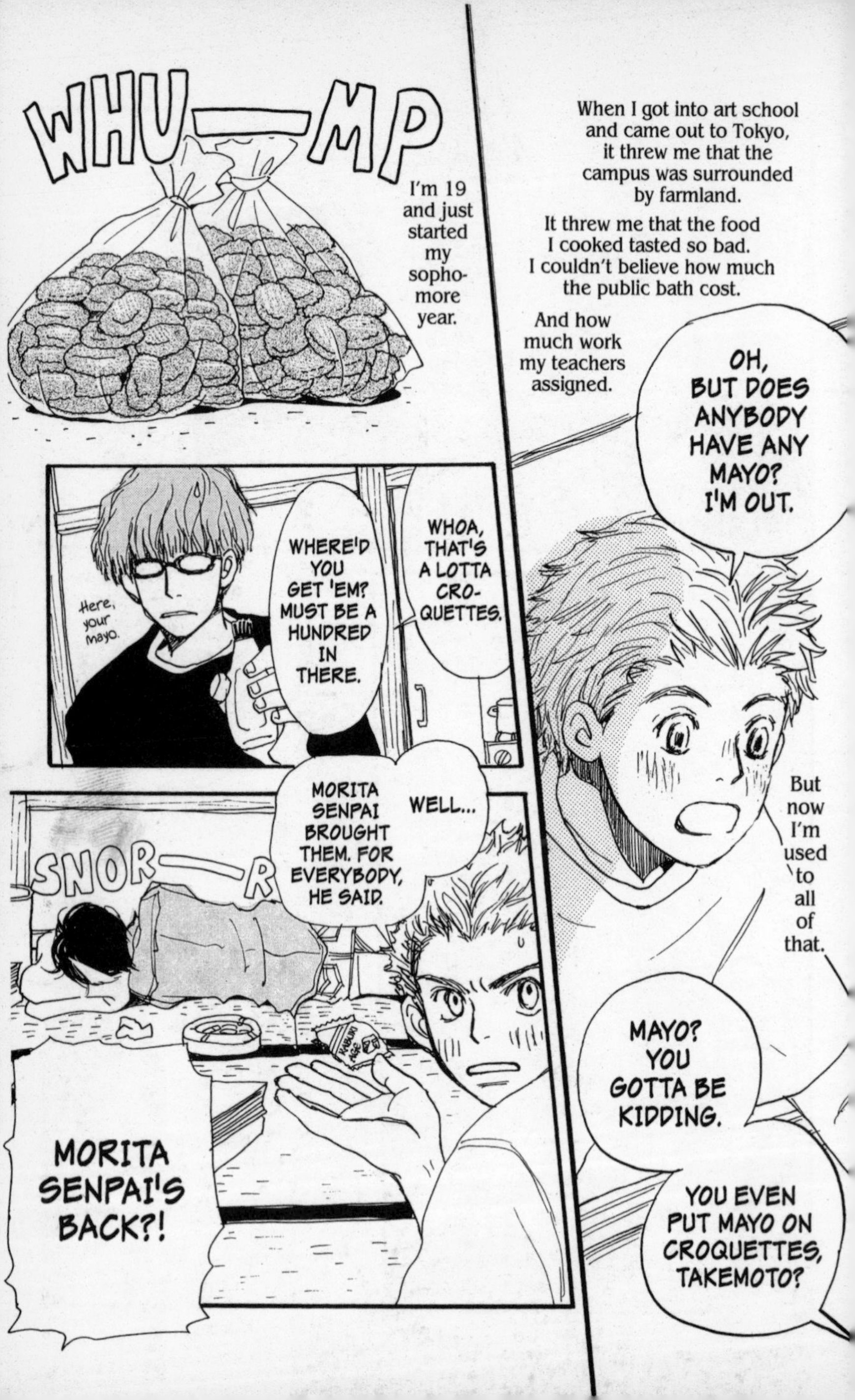
When I got into art school and came out to Tokyo, it threw me that the campus was surrounded by farmland.
It threw me that the food I cooked tasted so bad. I couldn't believe how much the public bath cost.
And how much work my teachers assigned.
OH, BUT DOES ANYBODY HAVE ANY MAYO? I'M OUT.
But now I'm used to all of that.
MAYO? YOU GOTTA BE KIDDING.
YOU EVEN PUT MAYO ON CROQUETTES, TAKEMOTO?
WHU—MP
I'm 19 and just started my sophomore year.
WHOA, THAT'S A LOTTA CROQUETTES.
WHERE'D YOU GET 'EM? MUST BE A HUNDRED IN THERE.
Here, your mayo.
WELL...
MORITA SENPAI BROUGHT THEM. FOR EVERYBODY, HE SAID.
SNOR—R
KABUKI AGE
MORITA SENPAI'S BACK?!

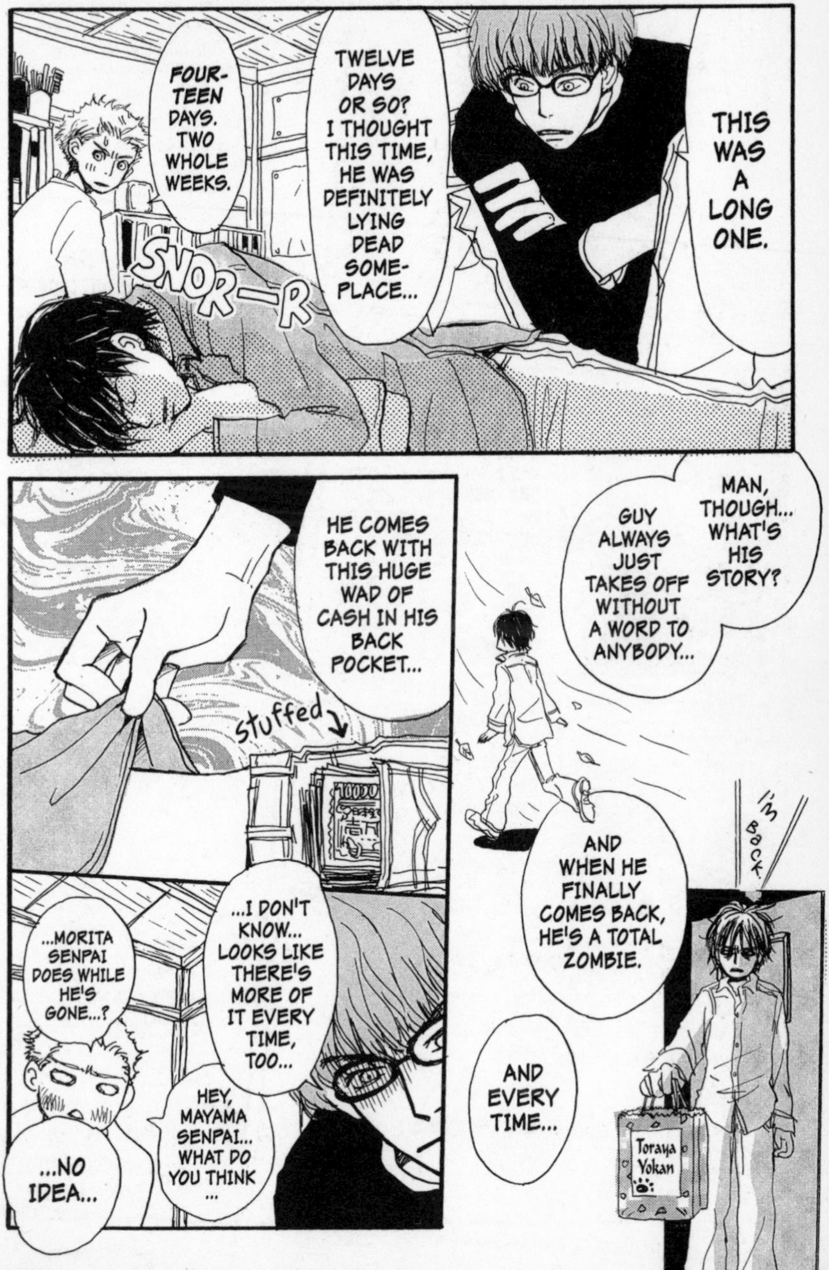
THIS WAS A LONG ONE.
TWELVE DAYS OR SO? I THOUGHT THIS TIME, HE WAS DEFINITELY LYING DEAD SOMEPLACE...
FOURTEEN DAYS. TWO WHOLE WEEKS.
SNOR—R
MAN, THOUGH... WHAT'S HIS STORY?
GUY ALWAYS JUST TAKES OFF WITHOUT A WORD TO ANYBODY...
AND WHEN HE FINALLY COMES BACK, HE'S A TOTAL ZOMBIE.
I'M BACK.
Toraya Yokan
AND EVERY TIME...
HE COMES BACK WITH THIS HUGE WAD OF CASH IN HIS BACK POCKET...
Stuffed
...I DON'T KNOW... LOOKS LIKE THERE'S MORE OF IT EVERY TIME, TOO...
HEY, MAYAMA SENPAI... WHAT DO YOU THINK ...
...MORITA SENPAI DOES WHILE HE'S GONE...?
...NO IDEA...

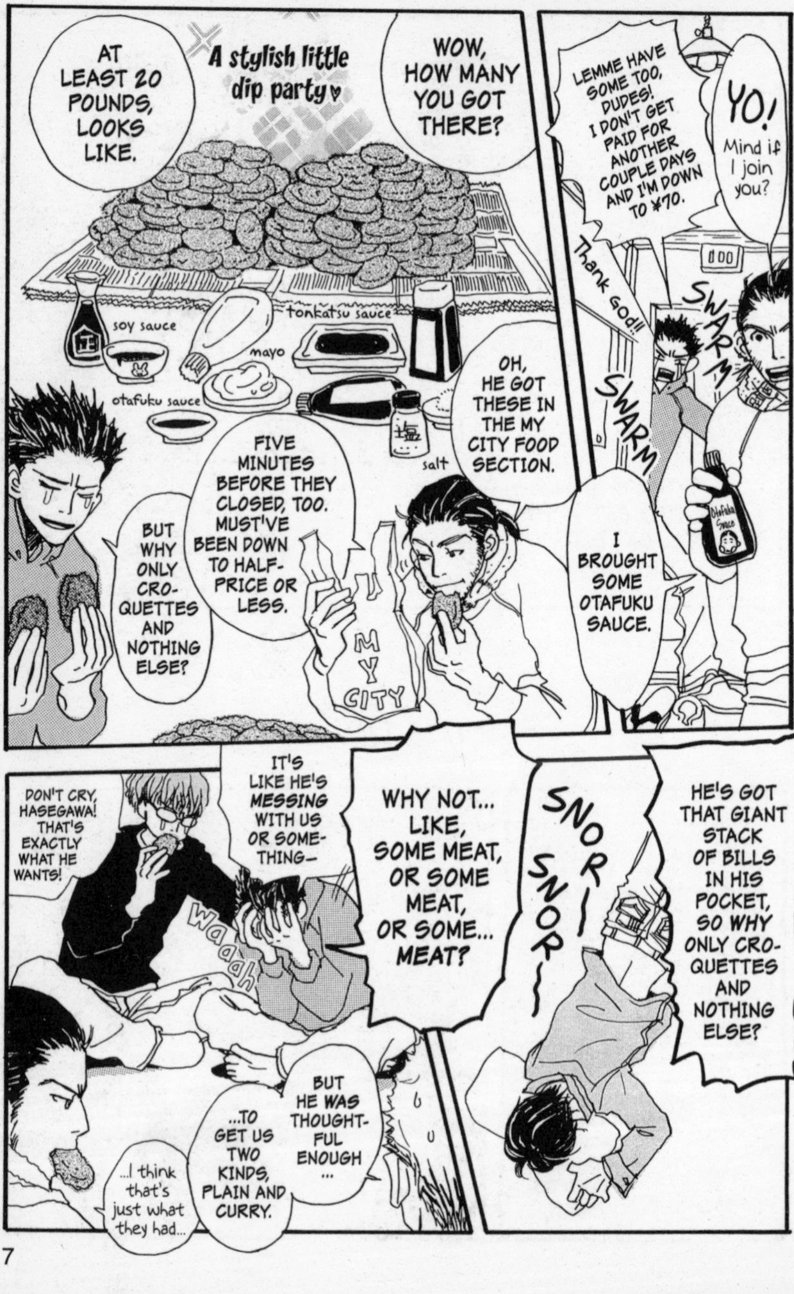
YO! Mind if I join you?
LEMME HAVE SOME TOO, DUDES! I DON'T GET PAID FOR ANOTHER COUPLE DAYS AND I'M DOWN TO ¥70.
Thank God!!
SWARM
SWARM
I BROUGHT SOME OTAFUKU SAUCE.
Otafuku Sauce
WOW, HOW MANY YOU GOT THERE?
A stylish little dip party♥
AT LEAST 20 POUNDS, LOOKS LIKE.
tonkatsu sauce
soy sauce
mayo
otafuku sauce
salt
OH, HE GOT THESE IN THE MY CITY FOOD SECTION.
FIVE MINUTES BEFORE THEY CLOSED, TOO. MUST'VE BEEN DOWN TO HALF-PRICE OR LESS.
BUT WHY ONLY CRO-QUETTES AND NOTHING ELSE?
MY CITY
HE'S GOT THAT GIANT STACK OF BILLS IN HIS POCKET, SO WHY ONLY CRO-QUETTES AND NOTHING ELSE?
SNOR
SNOR
WHY NOT... LIKE, SOME MEAT, OR SOME MEAT, OR SOME... MEAT?
IT'S LIKE HE'S MESSING WITH US OR SOME-THING–
DON'T CRY, HASEGAWA! THAT'S EXACTLY WHAT HE WANTS!
Waaah
BUT HE WAS THOUGHT-FUL ENOUGH...
...TO GET US TWO KINDS, PLAIN AND CURRY.
...I think that's just what they had...

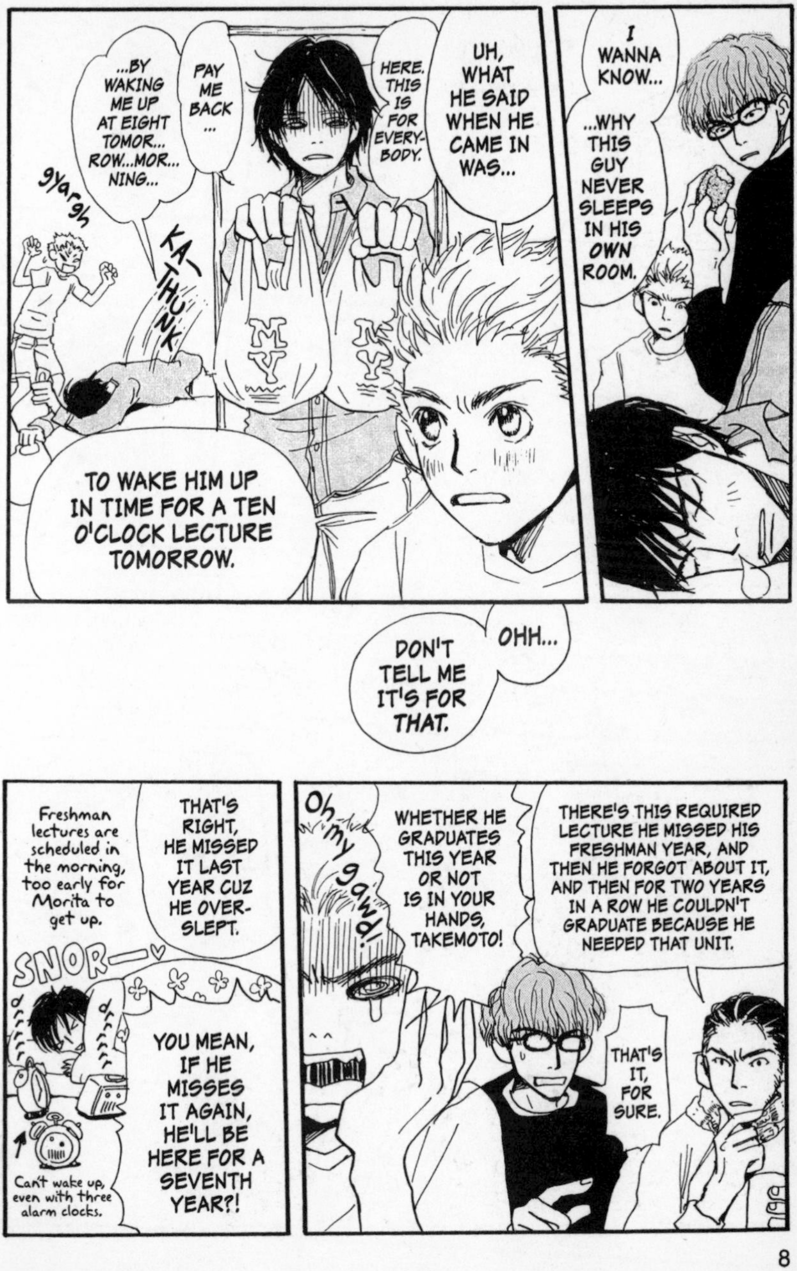
I WANNA KNOW...
...WHY THIS GUY NEVER SLEEPS IN HIS OWN ROOM.
UH, WHAT HE SAID WHEN HE CAME IN WAS...
HERE. THIS IS FOR EVERYBODY.
PAY ME BACK...
...BY WAKING ME UP AT EIGHT TOMOR... ROW...MOR... NING...
gyargh
KA-THUNK
TO WAKE HIM UP IN TIME FOR A TEN O'CLOCK LECTURE TOMORROW.
OHH...
DON'T TELL ME IT'S FOR THAT.
THERE'S THIS REQUIRED LECTURE HE MISSED HIS FRESHMAN YEAR, AND THEN HE FORGOT ABOUT IT, AND THEN FOR TWO YEARS IN A ROW HE COULDN'T GRADUATE BECAUSE HE NEEDED THAT UNIT.
WHETHER HE GRADUATES THIS YEAR OR NOT IS IN YOUR HANDS, TAKEMOTO!
Oh my gawd!
THAT'S IT, FOR SURE.
THAT'S RIGHT, HE MISSED IT LAST YEAR CUZ HE OVERSLEPT.
Freshman lectures are scheduled in the morning, too early for Morita to get up.
SNOR—♥
drrrrr
drrrrr
YOU MEAN, IF HE MISSES IT AGAIN, HE'LL BE HERE FOR A SEVENTH YEAR?!
Can't wake up, even with three alarm clocks.

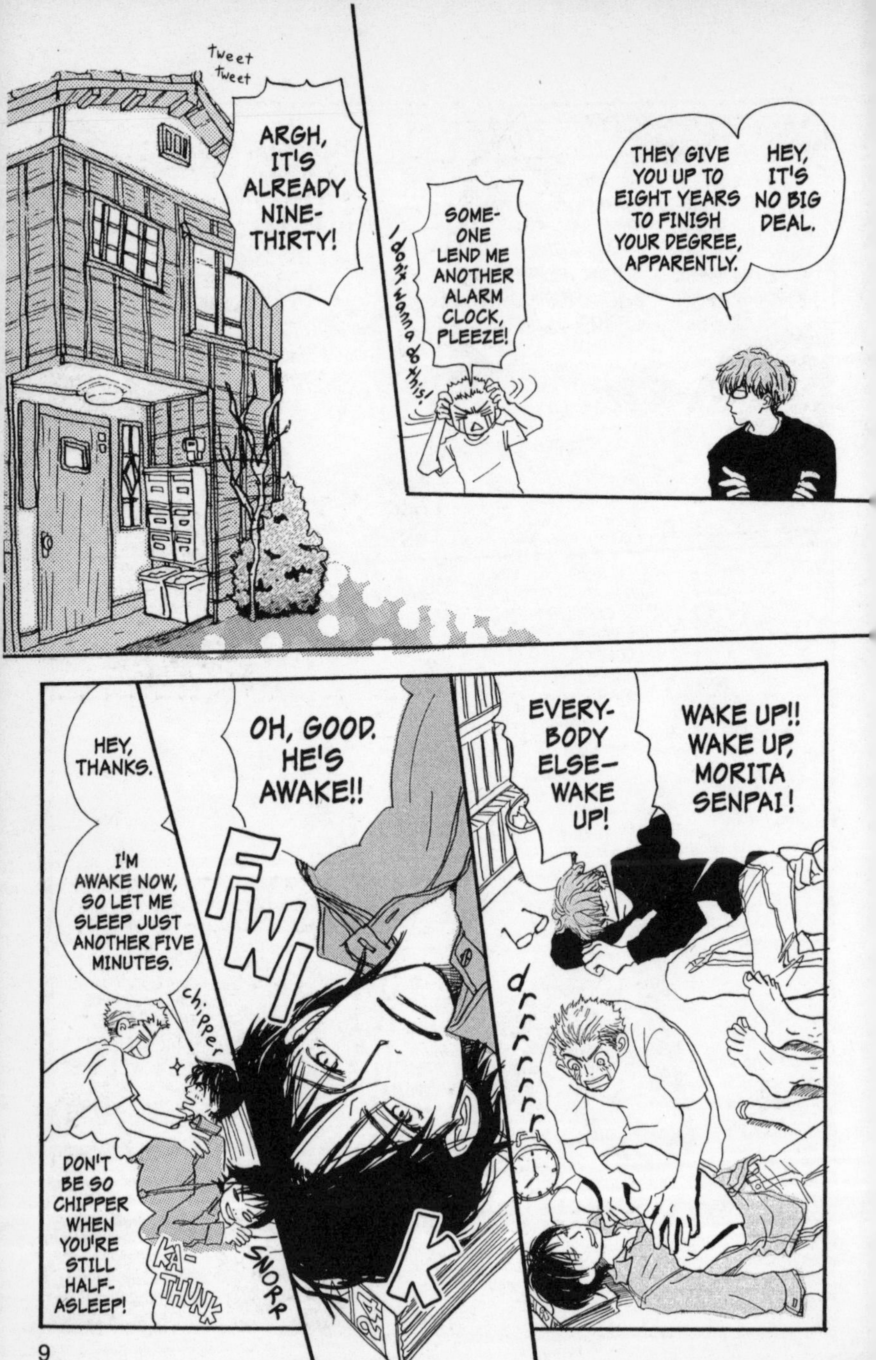
HEY, IT'S NO BIG DEAL.
THEY GIVE YOU UP TO EIGHT YEARS TO FINISH YOUR DEGREE, APPARENTLY.
SOME-ONE LEND ME ANOTHER ALARM CLOCK, PLEEZE!
I don't wanna do this!
tweet tweet
ARGH, IT'S ALREADY NINE-THIRTY!
WAKE UP!! WAKE UP, MORITA SENPAI!
EVERY-BODY ELSE—WAKE UP!
drrrrrrr
OH, GOOD. HE'S AWAKE!!
FWIK
SNORR
HEY, THANKS.
I'M AWAKE NOW, SO LET ME SLEEP JUST ANOTHER FIVE MINUTES.
chipper
DON'T BE SO CHIPPER WHEN YOU'RE STILL HALF-ASLEEP!
KA-THUNK

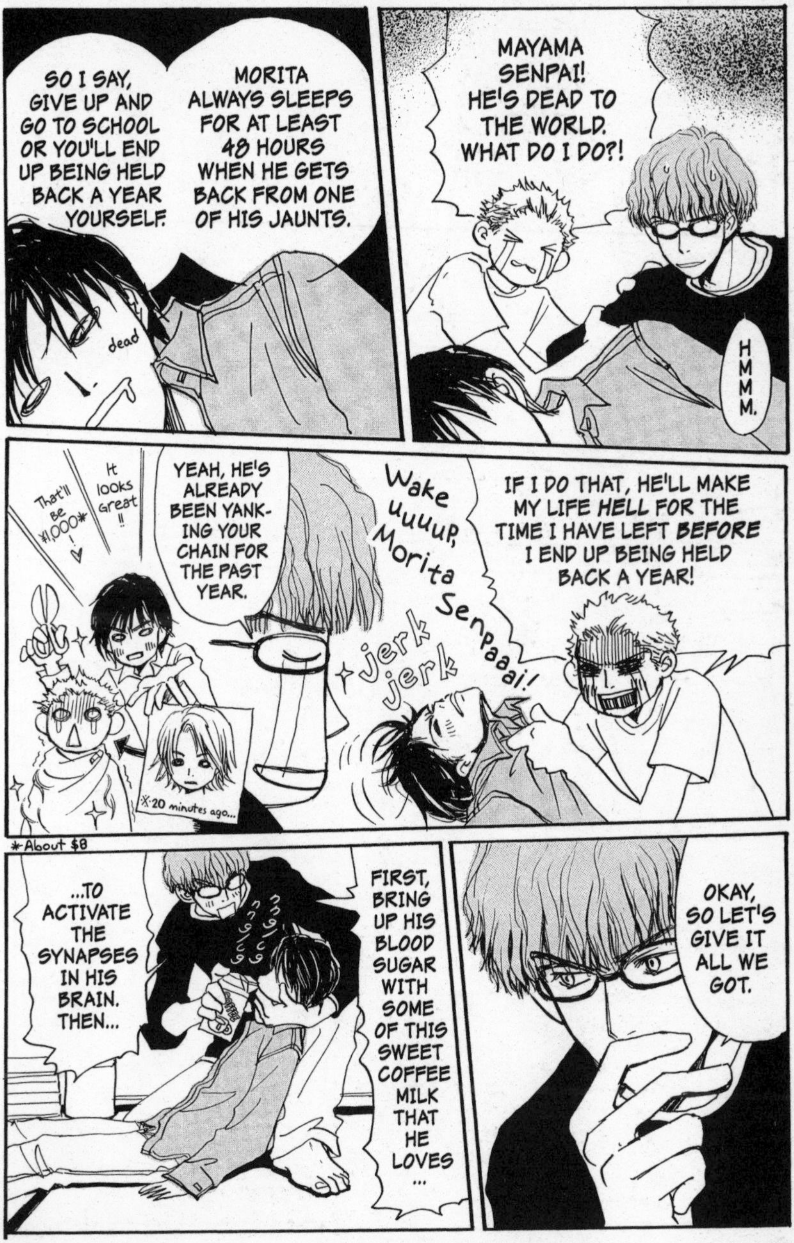
MAYAMA SENPAI! HE'S DEAD TO THE WORLD. WHAT DO I DO?!
HMMM.
MORITA ALWAYS SLEEPS FOR AT LEAST 48 HOURS WHEN HE GETS BACK FROM ONE OF HIS JAUNTS.
SO I SAY, GIVE UP AND GO TO SCHOOL OR YOU'LL END UP BEING HELD BACK A YEAR YOURSELF.
dead
IF I DO THAT, HE'LL MAKE MY LIFE **HELL** FOR THE TIME I HAVE LEFT **BEFORE** I END UP BEING HELD BACK A YEAR!
Wake uuuup, Morita Senpaaai!
jerk jerk
YEAH, HE'S ALREADY BEEN YANKING YOUR CHAIN FOR THE PAST YEAR.
It looks Great!!
That'll be ¥1,000*! ♥
※20 minutes ago...
*About $8
OKAY, SO LET'S GIVE IT ALL WE GOT.
FIRST, BRING UP HIS BLOOD SUGAR WITH SOME OF THIS SWEET COFFEE MILK THAT HE LOVES ...
...TO ACTIVATE THE SYNAPSES IN HIS BRAIN. THEN...

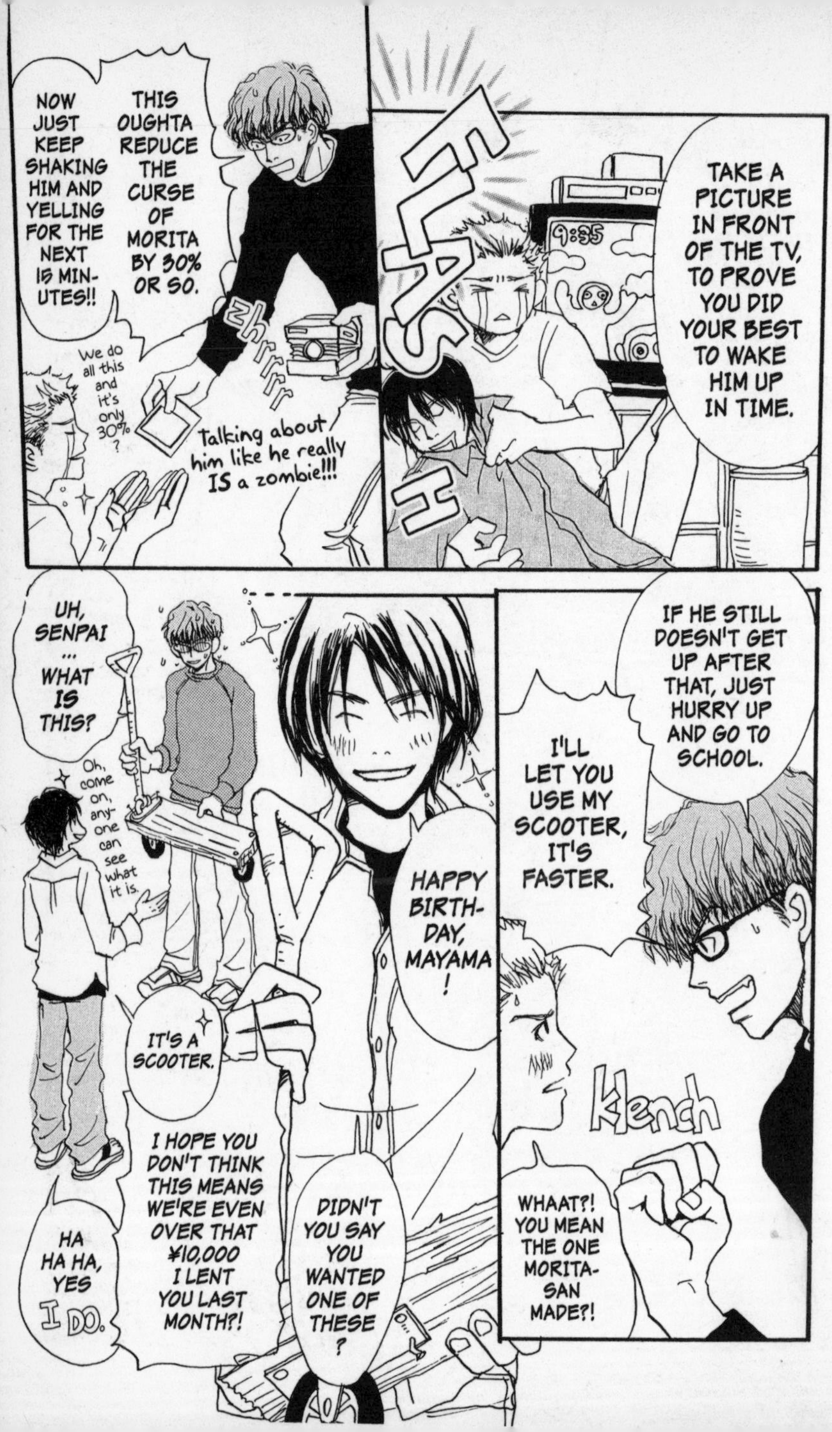
FLASH
TAKE A PICTURE IN FRONT OF THE TV, TO PROVE YOU DID YOUR BEST TO WAKE HIM UP IN TIME.
9:35
THIS OUGHTA REDUCE THE CURSE OF MORITA BY 30% OR SO.
NOW JUST KEEP SHAKING HIM AND YELLING FOR THE NEXT 15 MINUTES!!
zhrrrr
We do all this and it's only 30%?
Talking about him like he really IS a zombie!!!
IF HE STILL DOESN'T GET UP AFTER THAT, JUST HURRY UP AND GO TO SCHOOL.
I'LL LET YOU USE MY SCOOTER, IT'S FASTER.
klench
WHAAT?! YOU MEAN THE ONE MORITA-SAN MADE?!
HAPPY BIRTHDAY, MAYAMA!
DIDN'T YOU SAY YOU WANTED ONE OF THESE?
UH, SENPAI... WHAT IS THIS?
Oh, come on, anyone can see what it is.
IT'S A SCOOTER.
I HOPE YOU DON'T THINK THIS MEANS WE'RE EVEN OVER THAT ¥10,000 I LENT YOU LAST MONTH?!
HA HA HA, YES I DO.

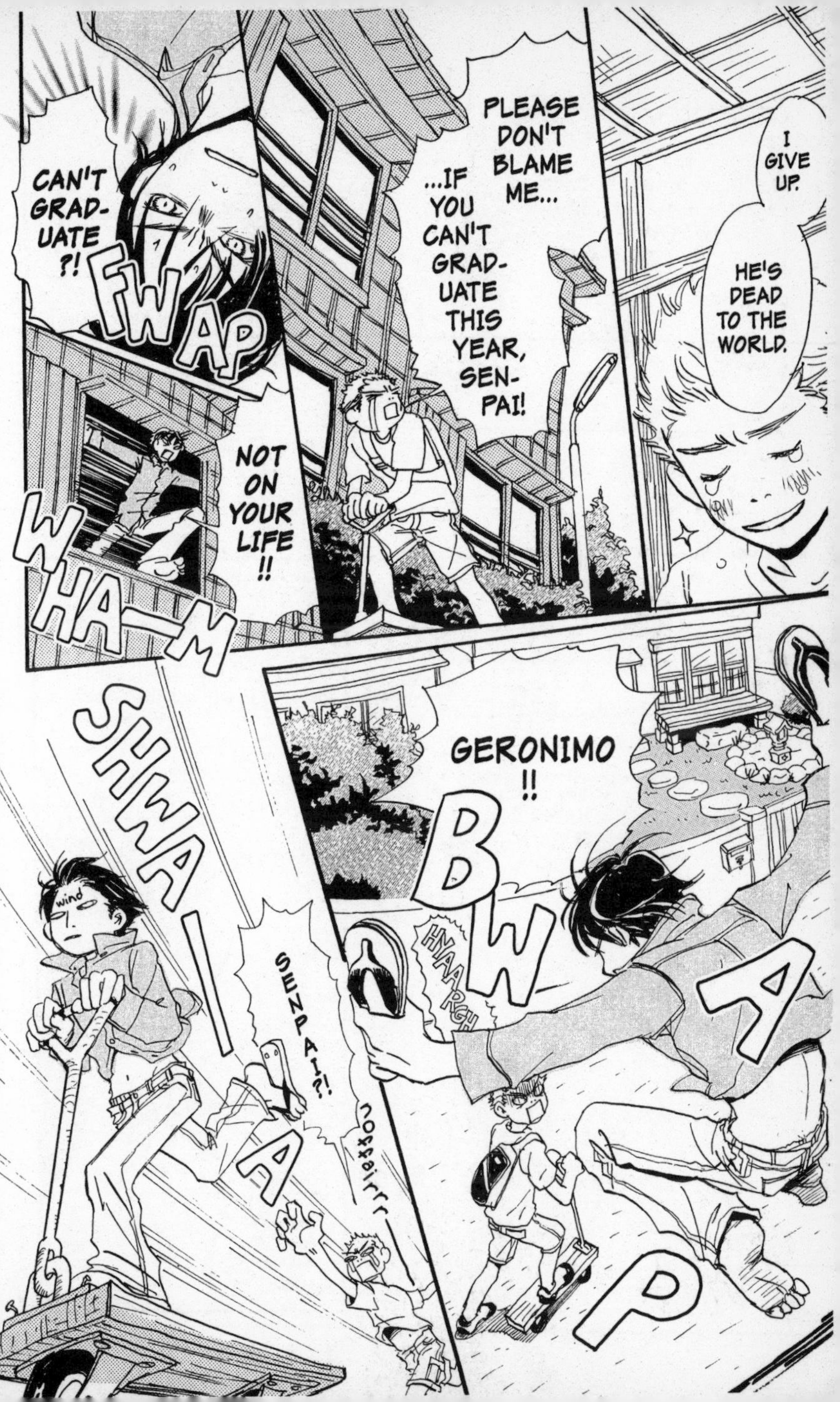
I GIVE UP.
HE'S DEAD TO THE WORLD.
PLEASE DON'T BLAME ME...
...IF YOU CAN'T GRAD-UATE THIS YEAR, SEN-PAI!
CAN'T GRAD-UATE ?!
FWAP
NOT ON YOUR LIFE !!
WHA-M
GERONIMO !!
BWAAP
HYAAARGH
SHWAAA
wind
SENPAI?!

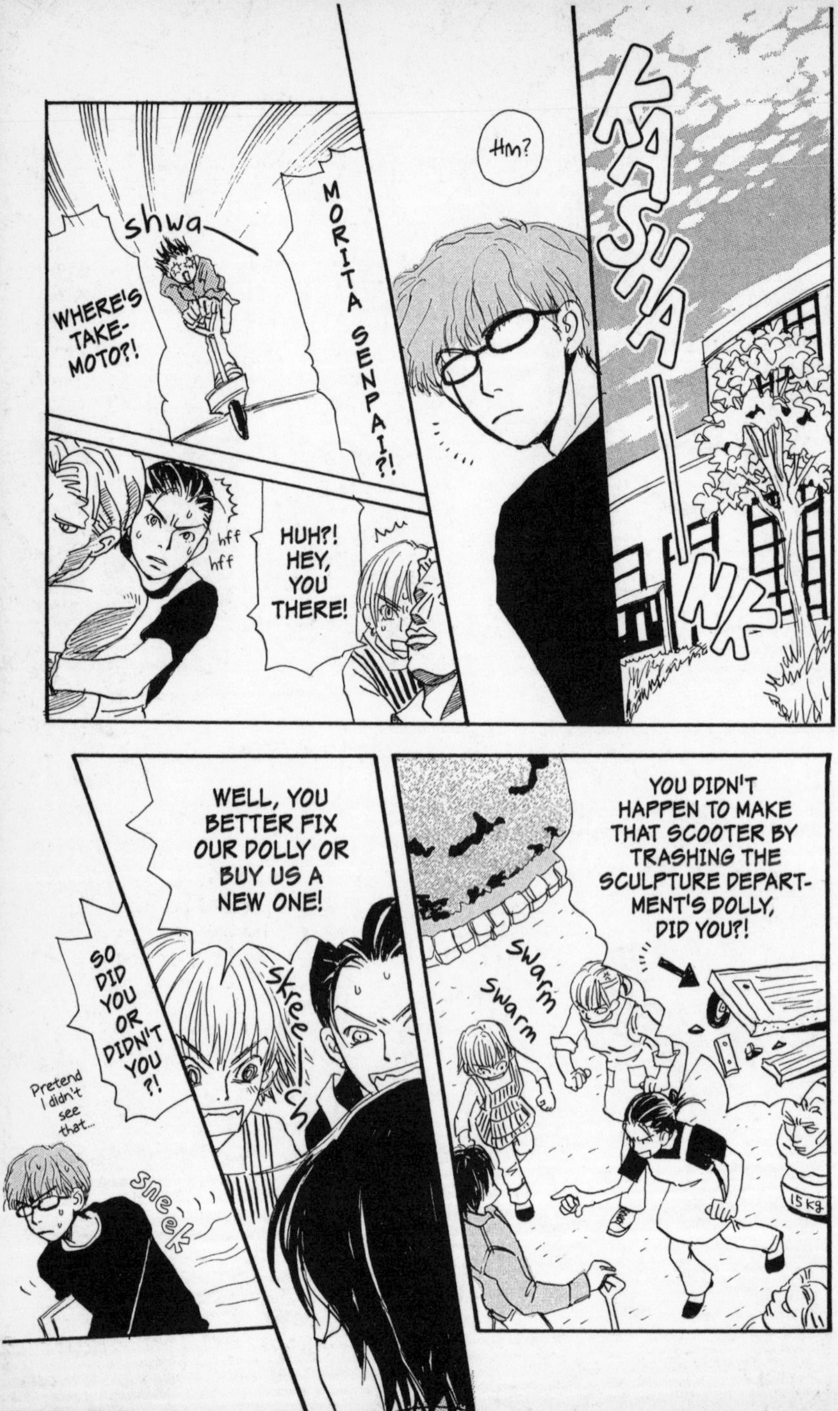
KASHA—NK
Hm?
MORITA SENPAI?!
shwa—
WHERE'S TAKE-MOTO?!
HUH?! HEY, YOU THERE!
hff hff
YOU DIDN'T HAPPEN TO MAKE THAT SCOOTER BY TRASHING THE SCULPTURE DEPARTMENT'S DOLLY, DID YOU?!
Swarm Swarm
15kg
WELL, YOU BETTER FIX OUR DOLLY OR BUY US A NEW ONE!
skree—ch
SO DID YOU OR DIDN'T YOU?!
sneek
Pretend I didn't see that...

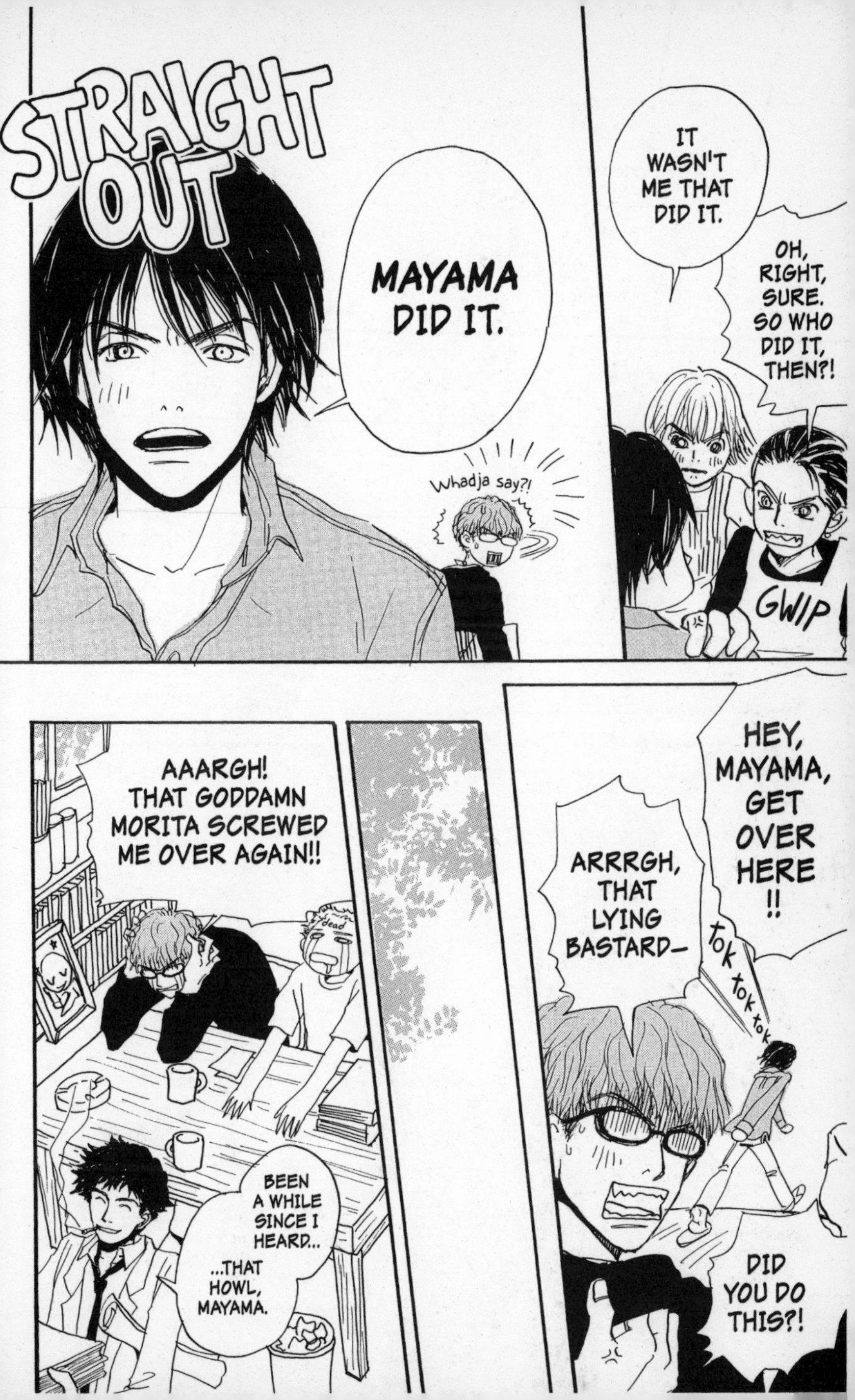
IT WASN'T ME THAT DID IT.
OH, RIGHT, SURE. SO WHO DID IT, THEN?!
GWIP
STRAIGHT OUT
MAYAMA DID IT.
Whadja say?!
HEY, MAYAMA, GET OVER HERE!!
ARRRGH, THAT LYING BASTARD—
tok tok tok
DID YOU DO THIS?!
AAARGH! THAT GODDAMN MORITA SCREWED ME OVER AGAIN!!
dead
BEEN A WHILE SINCE I HEARD...
...THAT HOWL, MAYAMA.

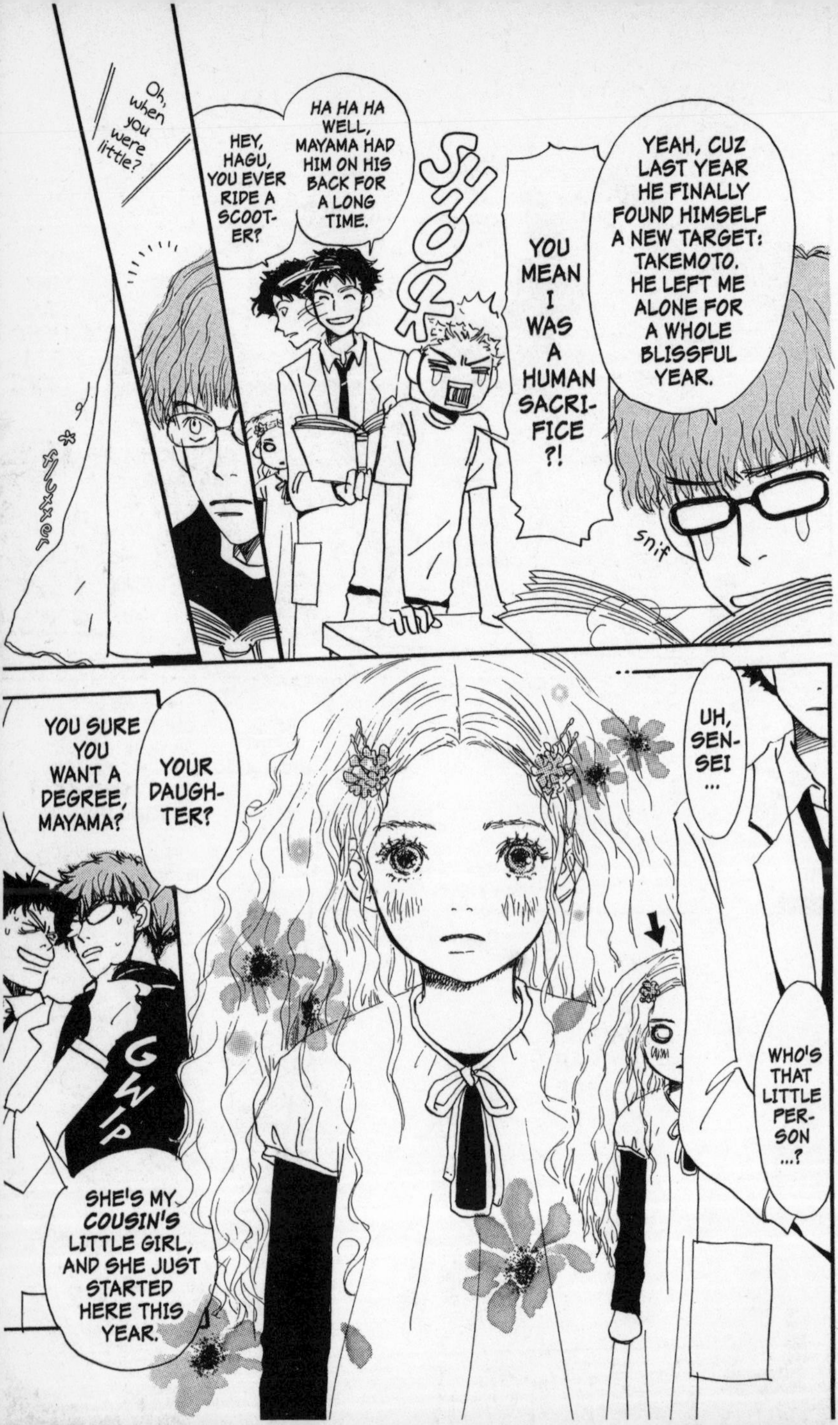
YEAH, CUZ LAST YEAR HE FINALLY FOUND HIMSELF A NEW TARGET: TAKEMOTO. HE LEFT ME ALONE FOR A WHOLE BLISSFUL YEAR.
snif
YOU MEAN I WAS A HUMAN SACRIFICE?!
SHOCK
HA HA HA WELL, MAYAMA HAD HIM ON HIS BACK FOR A LONG TIME.
HEY, HAGU, YOU EVER RIDE A SCOOTER?
Oh, when you were little?
flutter
UH, SENSEI...
WHO'S THAT LITTLE PERSON...?
YOUR DAUGHTER?
YOU SURE YOU WANT A DEGREE, MAYAMA?
GWIP
SHE'S MY COUSIN'S LITTLE GIRL, AND SHE JUST STARTED HERE THIS YEAR.

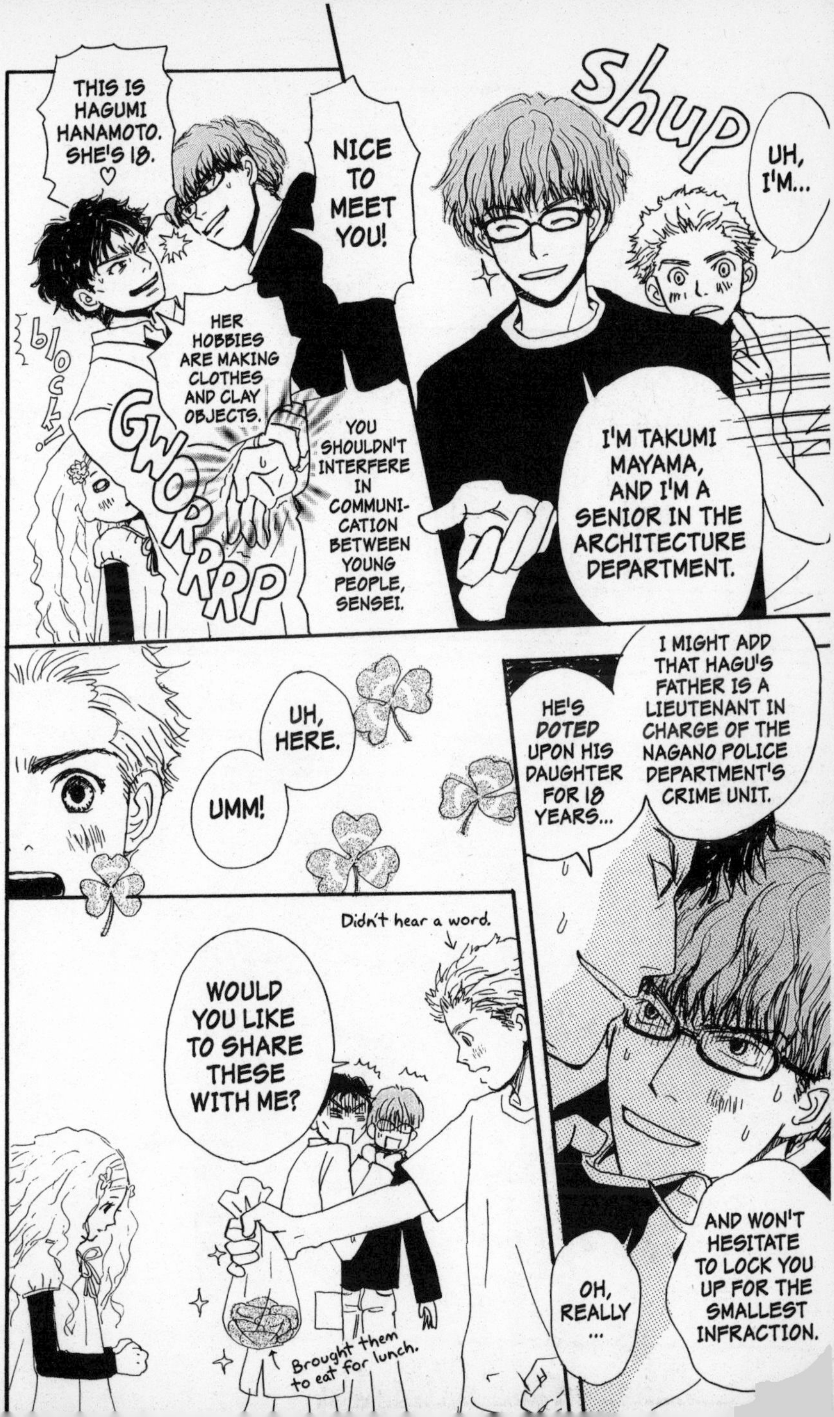
Shup
UH, I'M...
I'M TAKUMI MAYAMA, AND I'M A SENIOR IN THE ARCHITECTURE DEPARTMENT.
NICE TO MEET YOU!
THIS IS HAGUMI HANAMOTO. SHE'S 18. ♡
HER HOBBIES ARE MAKING CLOTHES AND CLAY OBJECTS.
YOU SHOULDN'T INTERFERE IN COMMUNICATION BETWEEN YOUNG PEOPLE, SENSEI.
GWORRRP
block!
I MIGHT ADD THAT HAGU'S FATHER IS A LIEUTENANT IN CHARGE OF THE NAGANO POLICE DEPARTMENT'S CRIME UNIT.
HE'S DOTED UPON HIS DAUGHTER FOR 18 YEARS...
AND WON'T HESITATE TO LOCK YOU UP FOR THE SMALLEST INFRACTION.
OH, REALLY...
UH, HERE.
UMM!
Didn't hear a word.
WOULD YOU LIKE TO SHARE THESE WITH ME?
Brought them to eat for lunch.

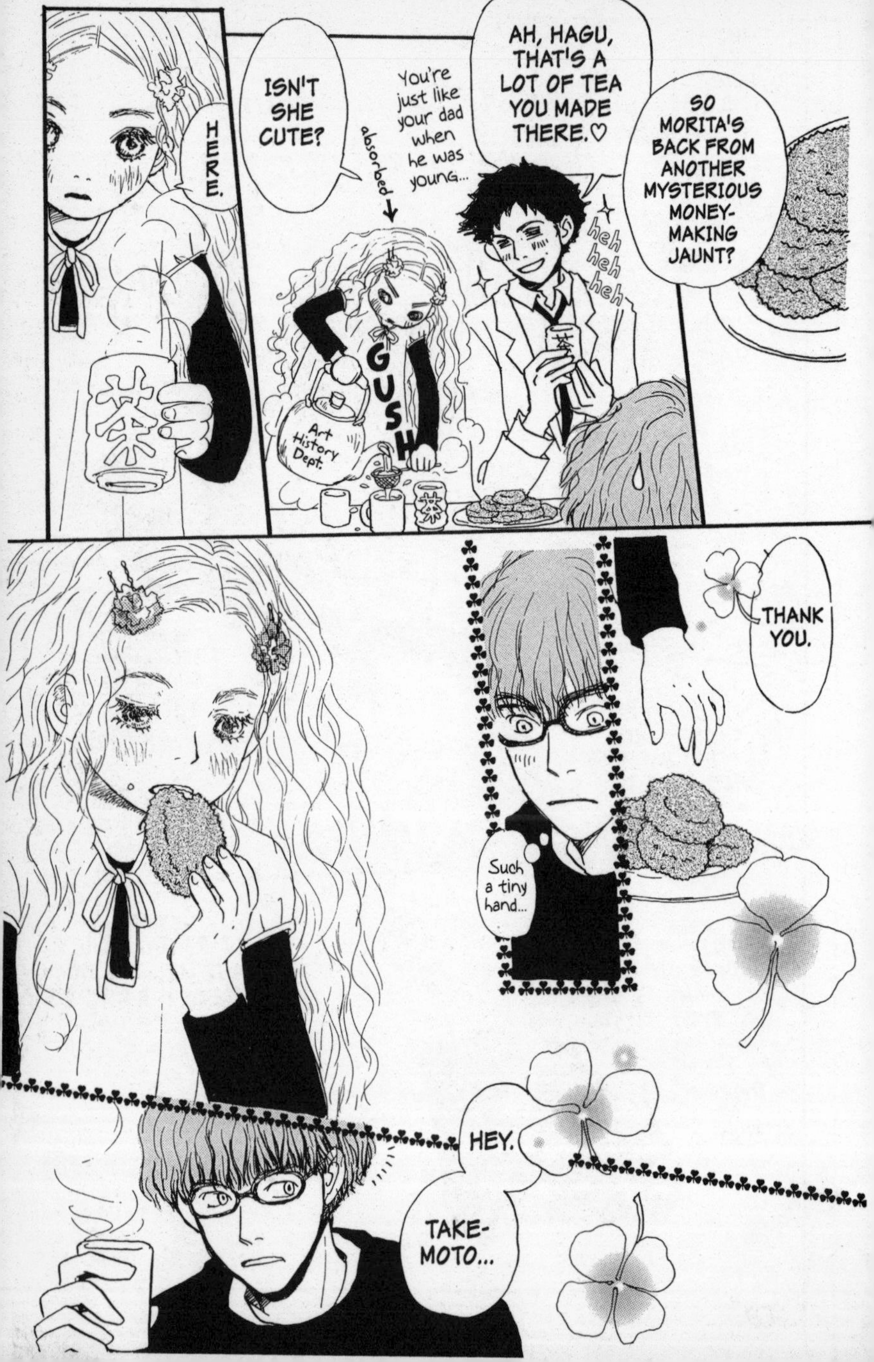
SO MORITA'S BACK FROM ANOTHER MYSTERIOUS MONEY-MAKING JAUNT?
AH, HAGU, THAT'S A LOT OF TEA YOU MADE THERE.♡
heh heh heh
You're just like your dad when he was young...
absorbed
ISN'T SHE CUTE?
GUSH
Art History Dept.
HERE.
THANK YOU.
Such a tiny hand...
HEY.
TAKE-MOTO...

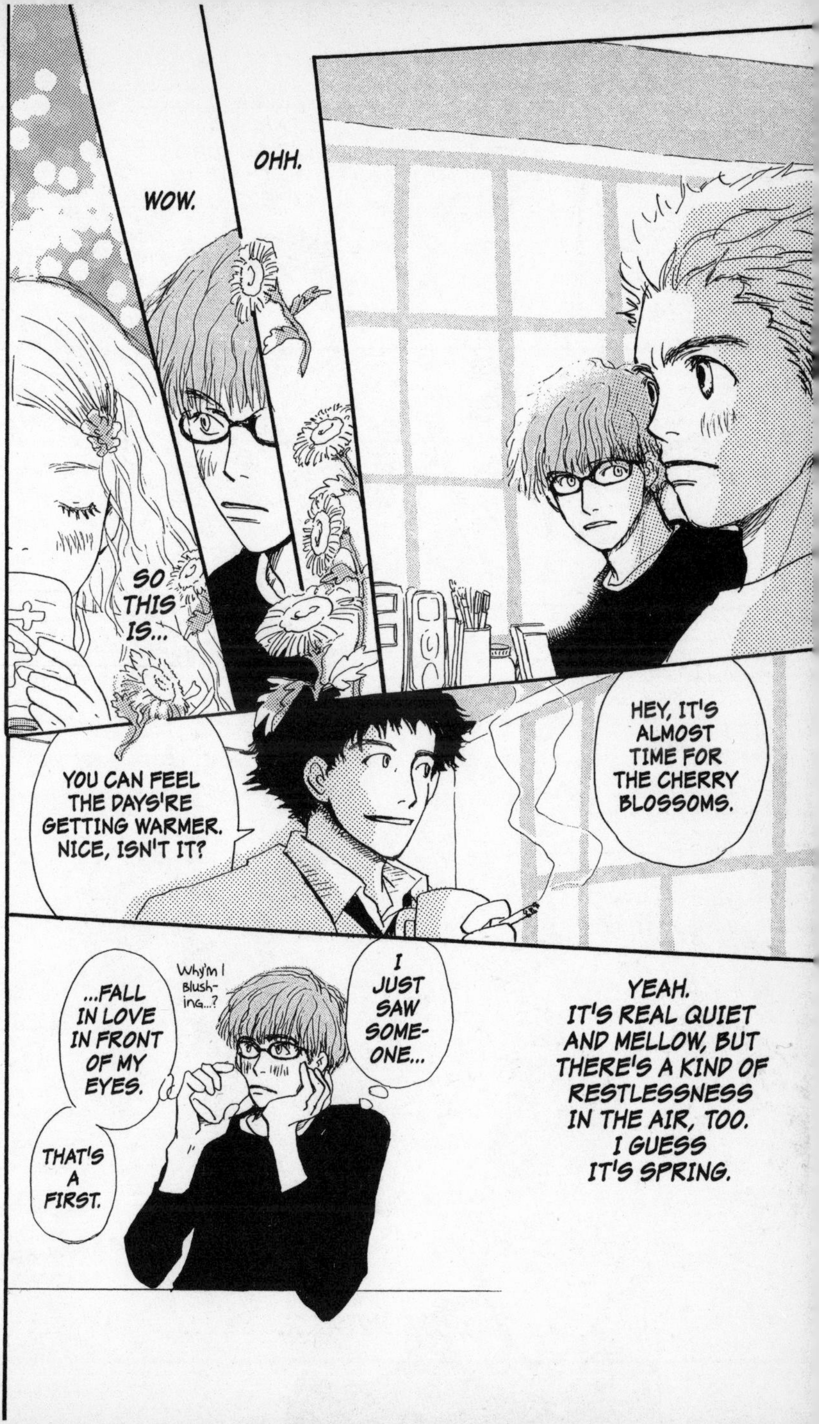
OHH.
WOW.
SO THIS IS...
HEY, IT'S ALMOST TIME FOR THE CHERRY BLOSSOMS.
YOU CAN FEEL THE DAYS'RE GETTING WARMER. NICE, ISN'T IT?
YEAH. IT'S REAL QUIET AND MELLOW, BUT THERE'S A KIND OF RESTLESSNESS IN THE AIR, TOO. I GUESS IT'S SPRING.
I JUST SAW SOME-ONE...
Why'm I blush-ing...?
...FALL IN LOVE IN FRONT OF MY EYES.
THAT'S A FIRST.

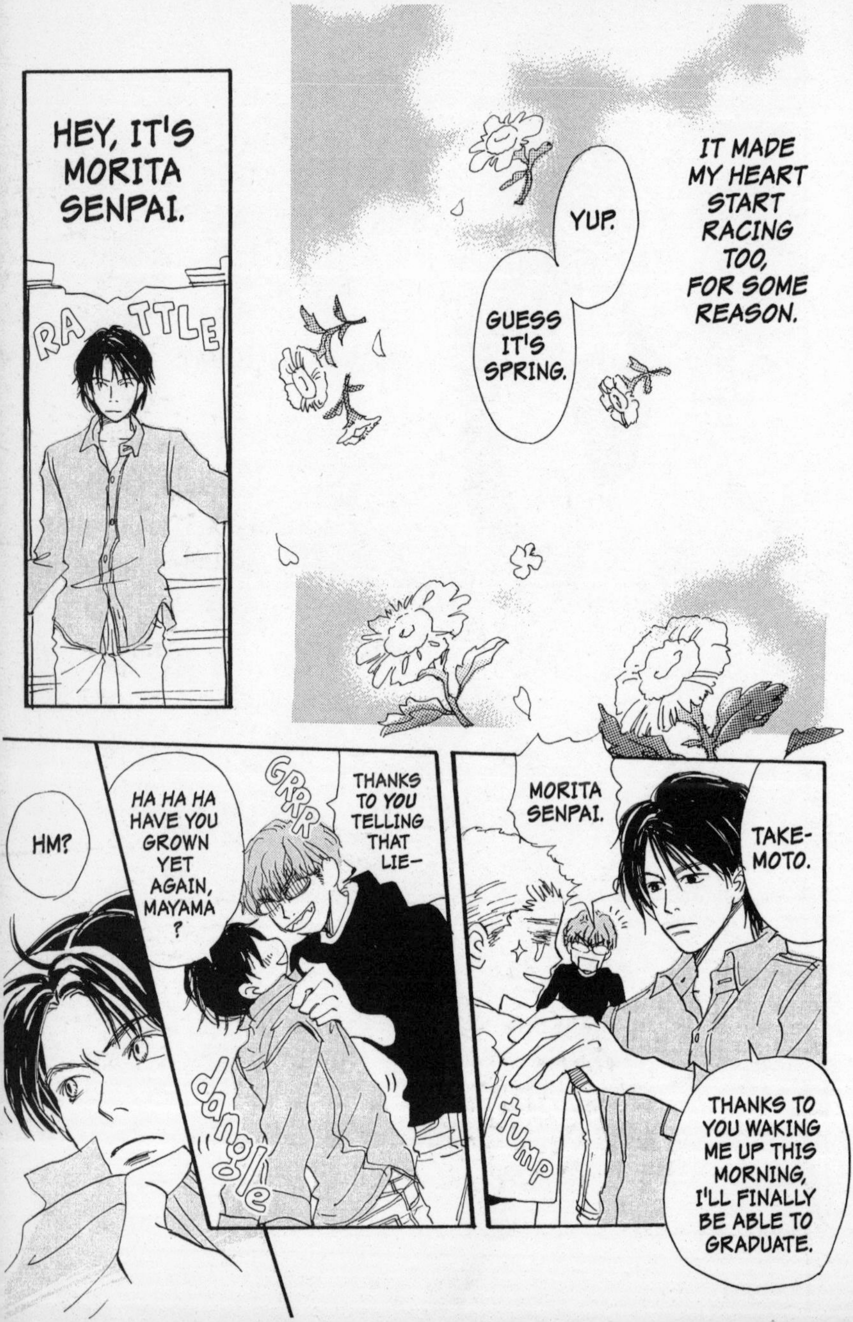
IT MADE MY HEART START RACING TOO, FOR SOME REASON.
YUP.
GUESS IT'S SPRING.
HEY, IT'S MORITA SENPAI.
RATTLE
TAKE-MOTO.
MORITA SENPAI.
THANKS TO YOU WAKING ME UP THIS MORNING, I'LL FINALLY BE ABLE TO GRADUATE.
tump
THANKS TO YOU TELLING THAT LIE—
GRRR
HA HA HA HAVE YOU GROWN YET AGAIN, MAYAMA?
dangle
HM?

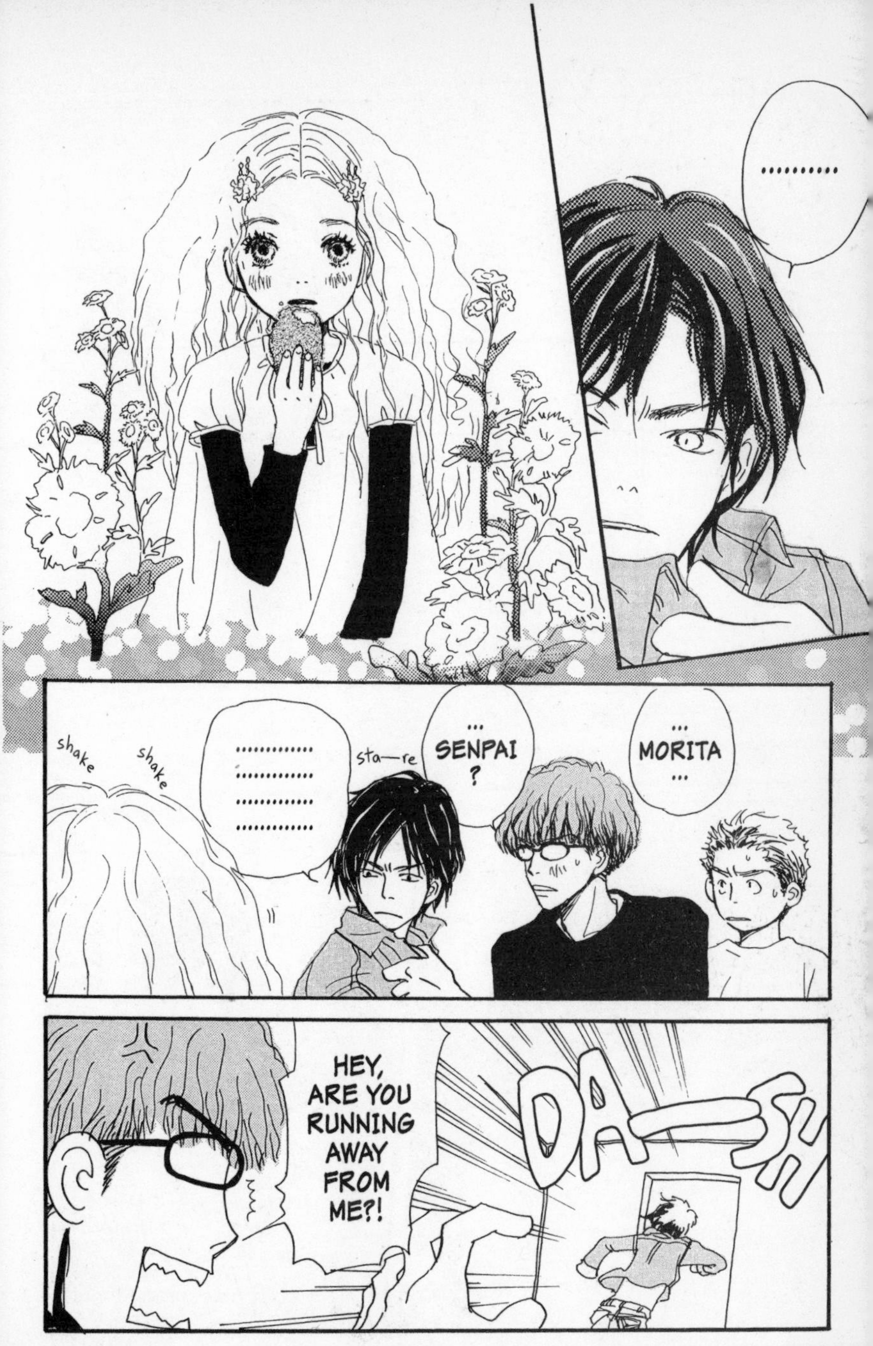

....
... MORITA ...
... SENPAI ?
sta—re
....
....
....
....
shake
shake
DA—SH
HEY, ARE YOU RUNNING AWAY FROM ME?!

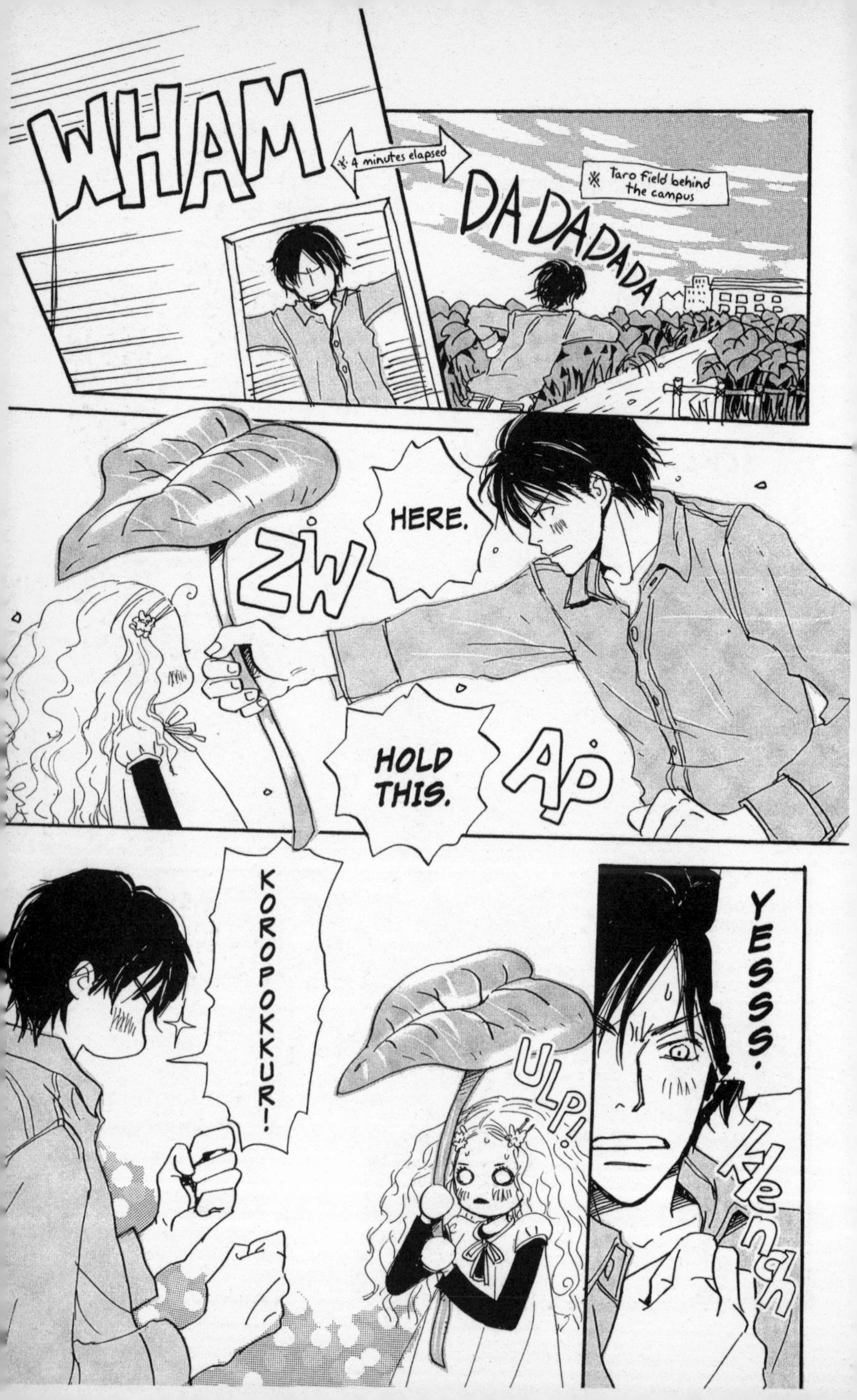
※ taro field behind the campus
DADADADA
※ 4 minutes elapsed
WHAM
HERE.
ZW
Ap
HOLD THIS.
YESSS.
klench
ULP!!
KOROPOKKUR!

In fact, someone else fell in love in front of Mayama's eyes that day.

But it manifested in such an unconventional way (see picture below)...

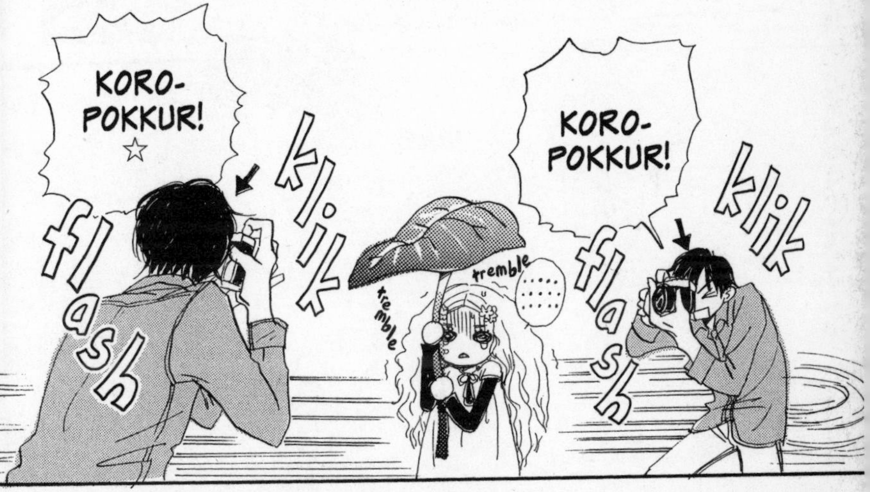
klik
flash
KORO-POKKUR!
tremble
tremble
klik
flash
KORO-POKKUR! ☆

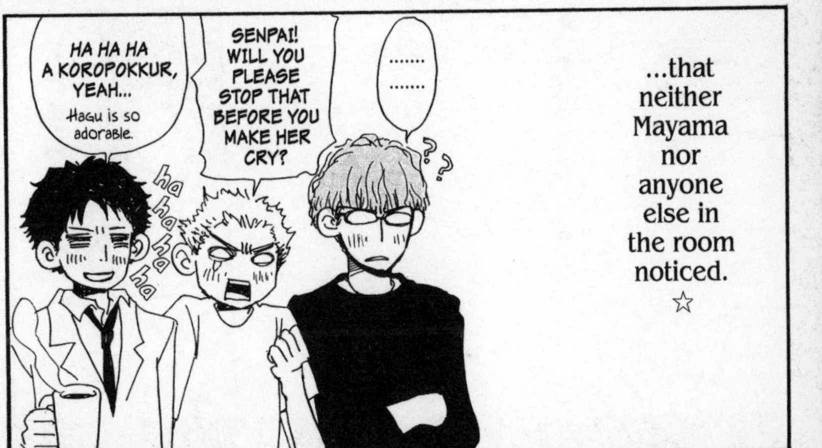
...that neither Mayama nor anyone else in the room noticed. ☆
....
....
??
SENPAI! WILL YOU PLEASE STOP THAT BEFORE YOU MAKE HER CRY?
HA HA HA A KOROPOKKUR, YEAH...
Hagu is so adorable.
ha ha ha ha ha

chapter 1—the end—

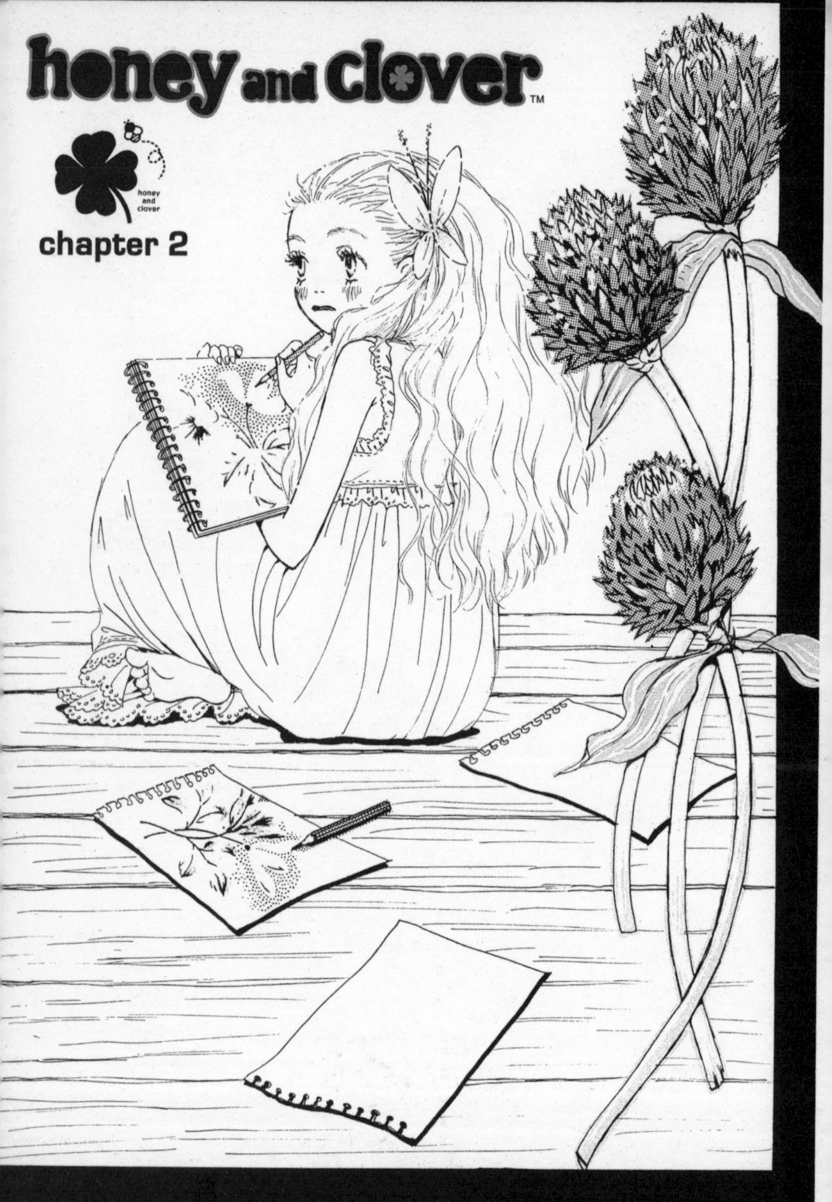
honey and clover™
honey and clover
chapter 2

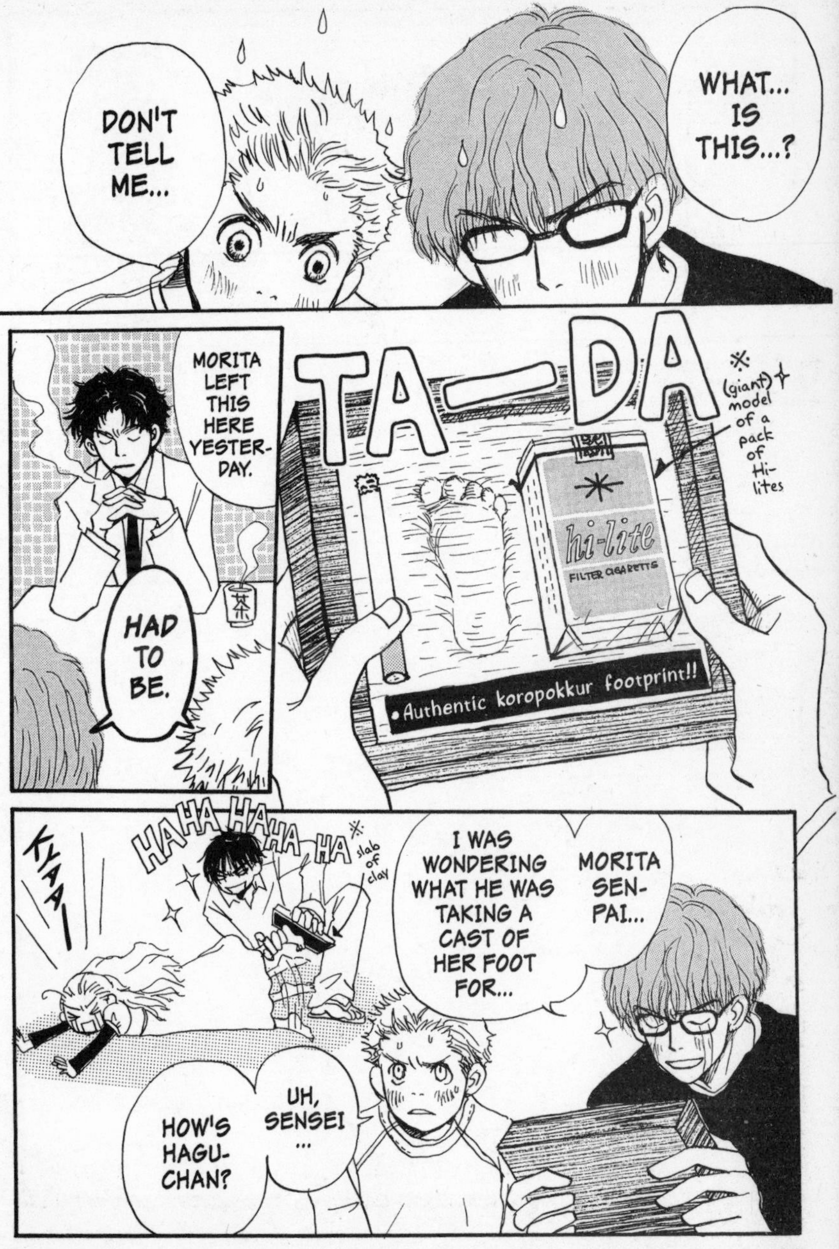
WHAT... IS THIS...?
DON'T TELL ME...
TA—DA
※ (giant) model of a pack of Hi-lites
hi-lite
FILTER CIGARETTS
• Authentic koropokkur footprint!!
MORITA LEFT THIS HERE YESTER-DAY.
HAD TO BE.
MORITA SEN-PAI...
I WAS WONDERING WHAT HE WAS TAKING A CAST OF HER FOOT FOR...
※ slab of clay
HAHA HAHA HA HA
KYAA!
UH, SENSEI ...
HOW'S HAGU-CHAN?

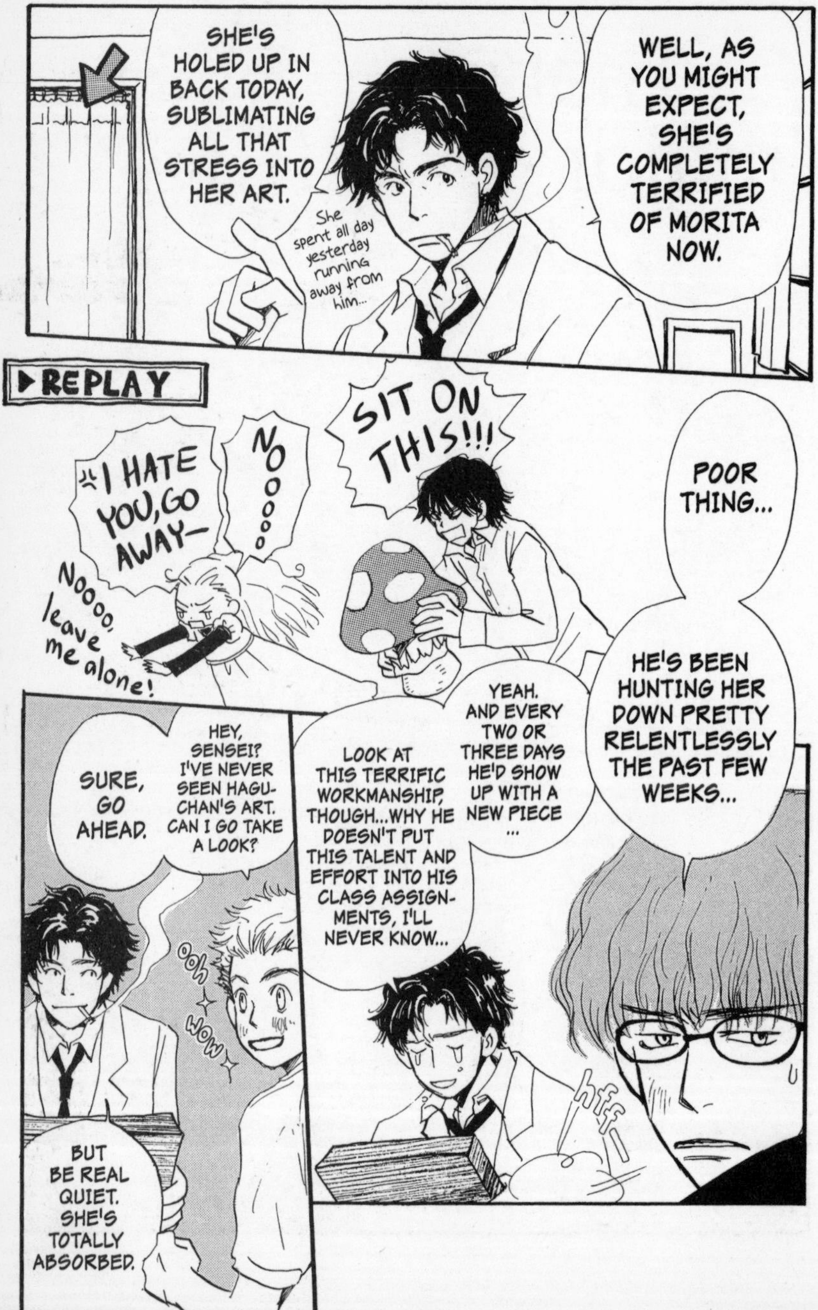
WELL, AS YOU MIGHT EXPECT, SHE'S COMPLETELY TERRIFIED OF MORITA NOW.
SHE'S HOLED UP IN BACK TODAY, SUBLIMATING ALL THAT STRESS INTO HER ART.
She spent all day yesterday running away from him...
REPLAY
POOR THING...
SIT ON THIS!!!
NOOOOOO
I HATE YOU, GO AWAY—
Noooo, leave me alone!
HE'S BEEN HUNTING HER DOWN PRETTY RELENTLESSLY THE PAST FEW WEEKS...
YEAH. AND EVERY TWO OR THREE DAYS HE'D SHOW UP WITH A NEW PIECE ...
LOOK AT THIS TERRIFIC WORKMANSHIP, THOUGH...WHY HE DOESN'T PUT THIS TALENT AND EFFORT INTO HIS CLASS ASSIGNMENTS, I'LL NEVER KNOW...
hff
HEY, SENSEI? I'VE NEVER SEEN HAGU-CHAN'S ART. CAN I GO TAKE A LOOK?
SURE, GO AHEAD.
ooh
wow
BUT BE REAL QUIET. SHE'S TOTALLY ABSORBED.

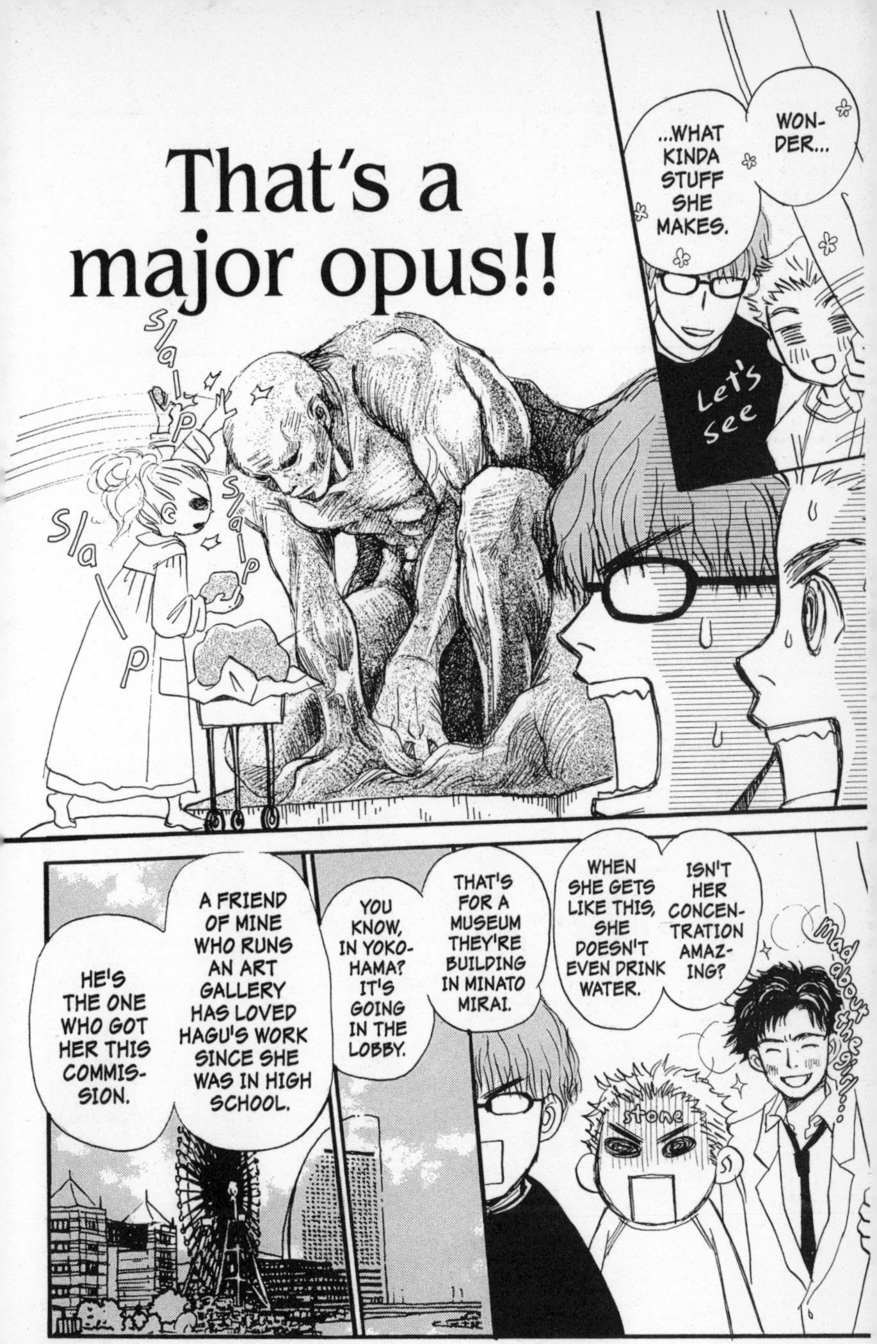
WONDER...
...WHAT KINDA STUFF SHE MAKES.
Let's see
That's a major opus!!
slap
slap
slap
ISN'T HER CONCENTRATION AMAZING?
WHEN SHE GETS LIKE THIS, SHE DOESN'T EVEN DRINK WATER.
mad about the girl...
stone
THAT'S FOR A MUSEUM THEY'RE BUILDING IN MINATO MIRAI.
YOU KNOW, IN YOKOHAMA? IT'S GOING IN THE LOBBY.
A FRIEND OF MINE WHO RUNS AN ART GALLERY HAS LOVED HAGU'S WORK SINCE SHE WAS IN HIGH SCHOOL.
HE'S THE ONE WHO GOT HER THIS COMMISSION.

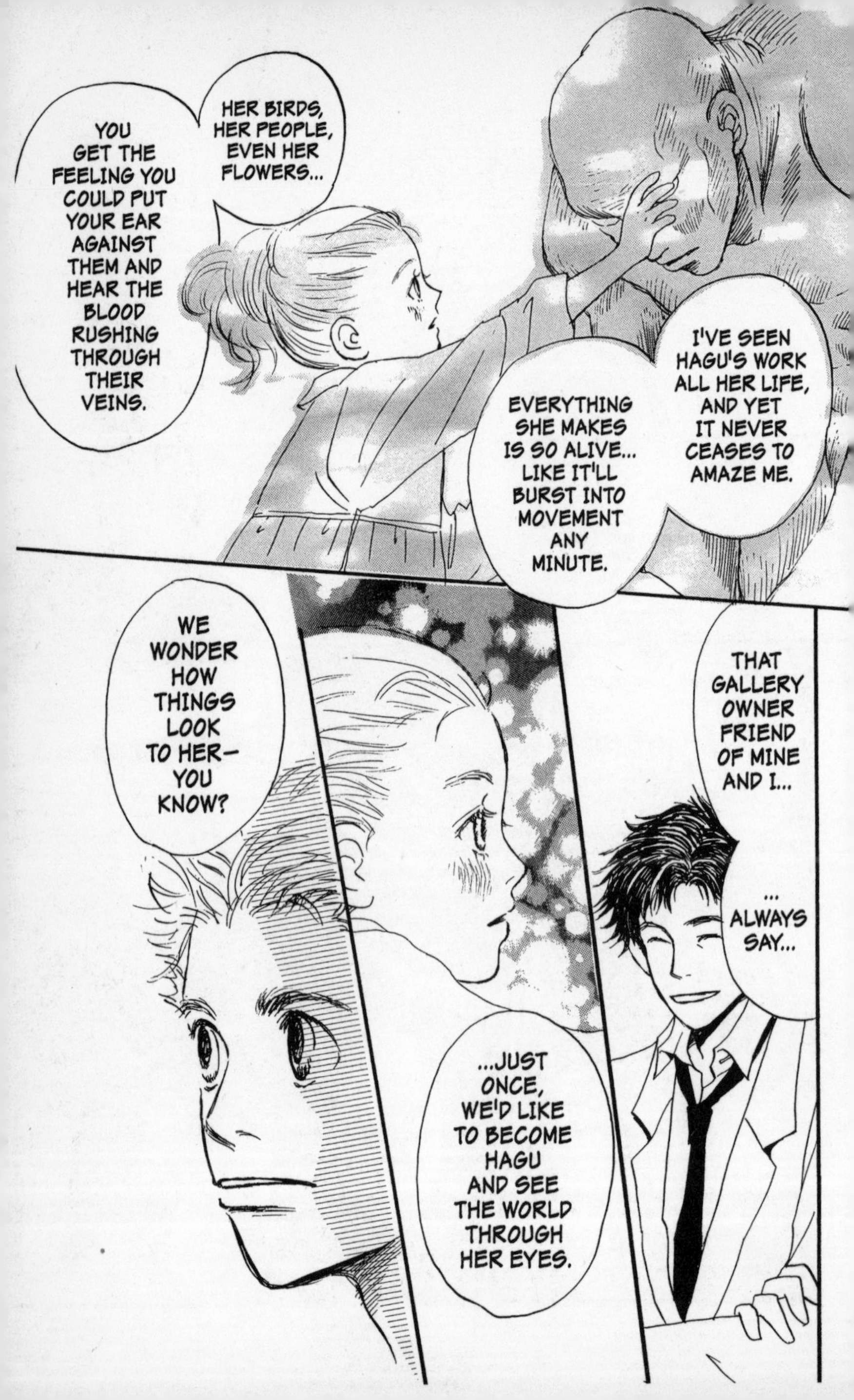
I'VE SEEN HAGU'S WORK ALL HER LIFE, AND YET IT NEVER CEASES TO AMAZE ME.
EVERYTHING SHE MAKES IS SO ALIVE... LIKE IT'LL BURST INTO MOVEMENT ANY MINUTE.
HER BIRDS, HER PEOPLE, EVEN HER FLOWERS...
YOU GET THE FEELING YOU COULD PUT YOUR EAR AGAINST THEM AND HEAR THE BLOOD RUSHING THROUGH THEIR VEINS.
THAT GALLERY OWNER FRIEND OF MINE AND I...
...ALWAYS SAY...
...JUST ONCE, WE'D LIKE TO BECOME HAGU AND SEE THE WORLD THROUGH HER EYES.
WE WONDER HOW THINGS LOOK TO HER— YOU KNOW?

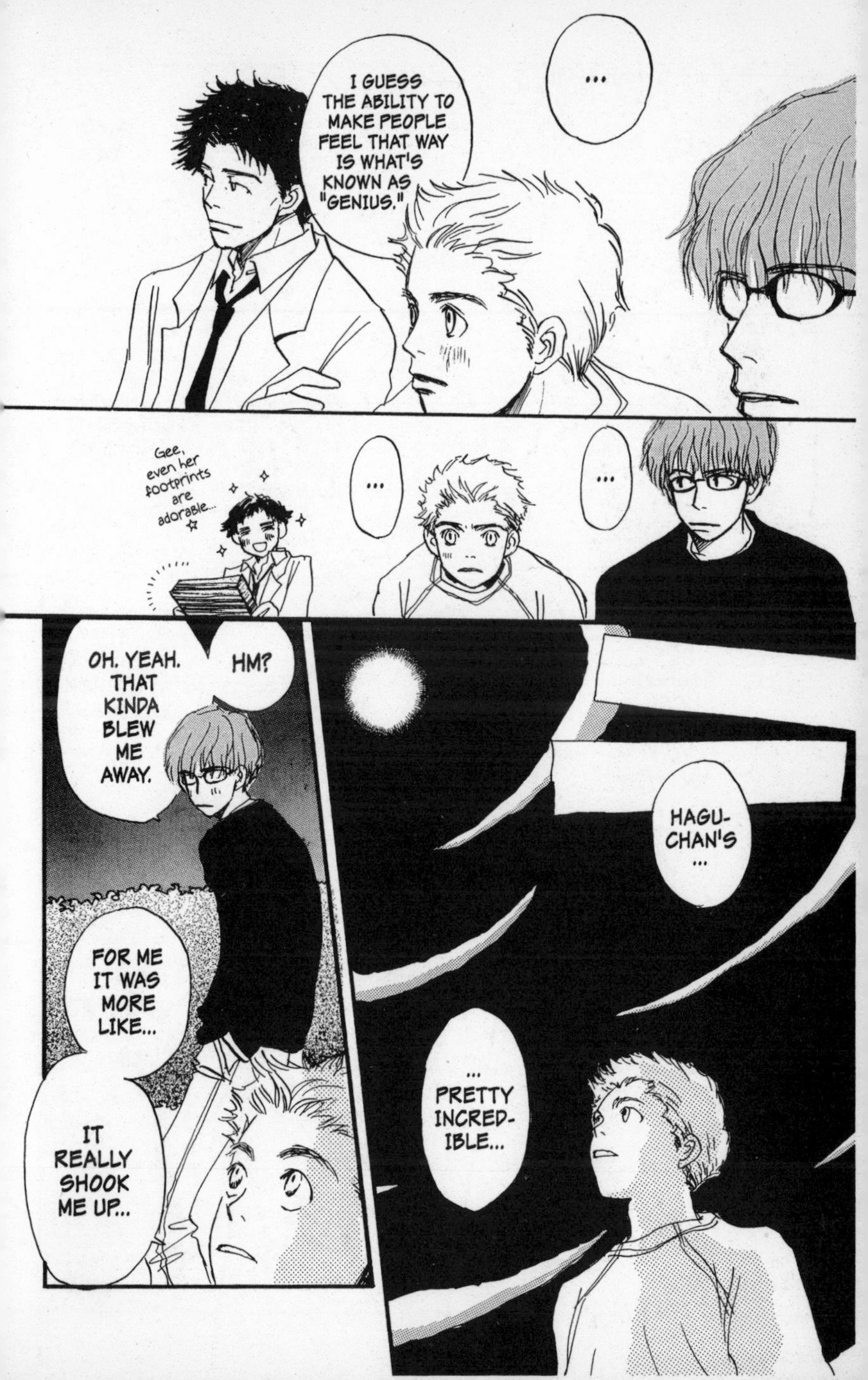
...
I GUESS THE ABILITY TO MAKE PEOPLE FEEL THAT WAY IS WHAT'S KNOWN AS "GENIUS."
...
...
Gee, even her footprints are adorable...
HAGU-CHAN'S ...
... PRETTY INCRED-IBLE...
HM?
OH. YEAH. THAT KINDA BLEW ME AWAY.
FOR ME IT WAS MORE LIKE...
IT REALLY SHOOK ME UP...

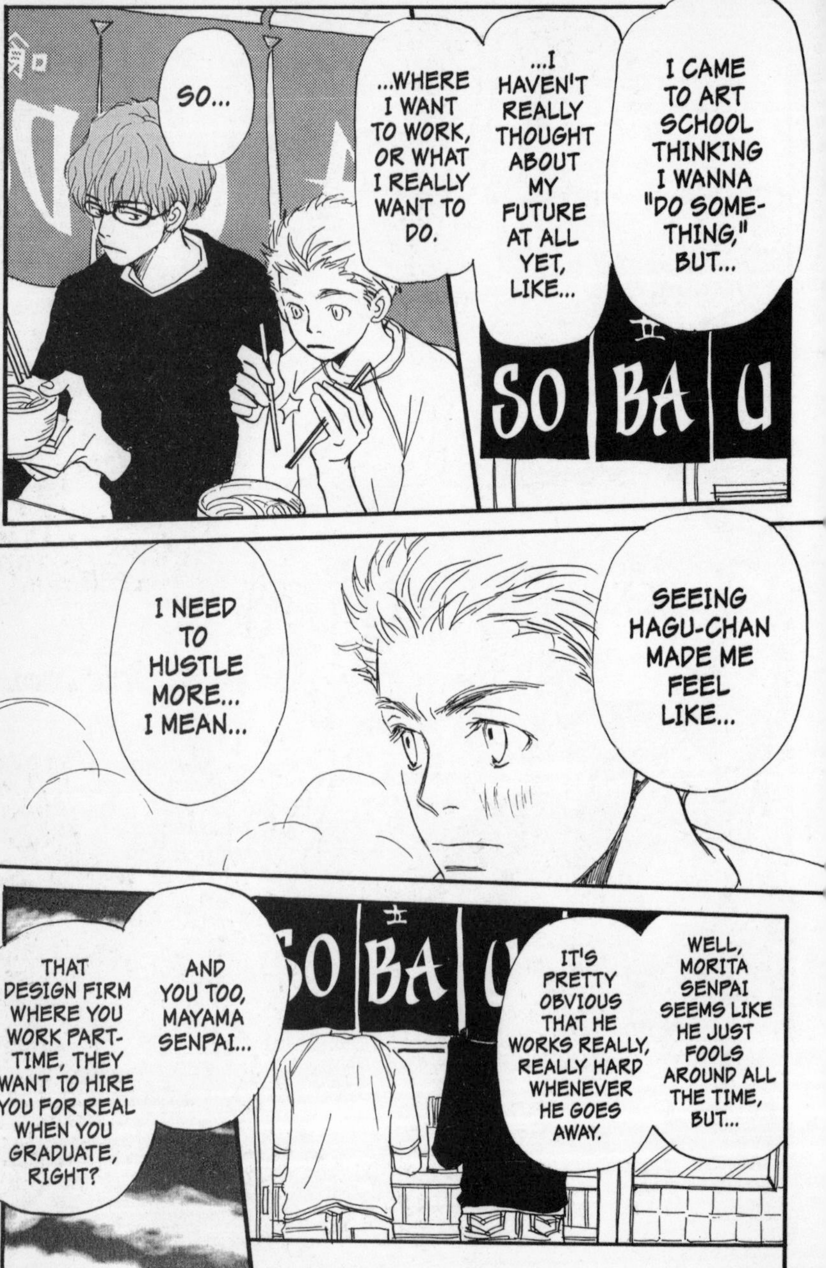
I CAME TO ART SCHOOL THINKING I WANNA "DO SOMETHING," BUT...
...I HAVEN'T REALLY THOUGHT ABOUT MY FUTURE AT ALL YET, LIKE...
...WHERE I WANT TO WORK, OR WHAT I REALLY WANT TO DO.
SO...
SO BA U
SEEING HAGU-CHAN MADE ME FEEL LIKE...
I NEED TO HUSTLE MORE... I MEAN...
SO BA U
WELL, MORITA SENPAI SEEMS LIKE HE JUST FOOLS AROUND ALL THE TIME, BUT...
IT'S PRETTY OBVIOUS THAT HE WORKS REALLY, REALLY HARD WHENEVER HE GOES AWAY.
AND YOU TOO, MAYAMA SENPAI...
THAT DESIGN FIRM WHERE YOU WORK PART-TIME, THEY WANT TO HIRE YOU FOR REAL WHEN YOU GRADUATE, RIGHT?

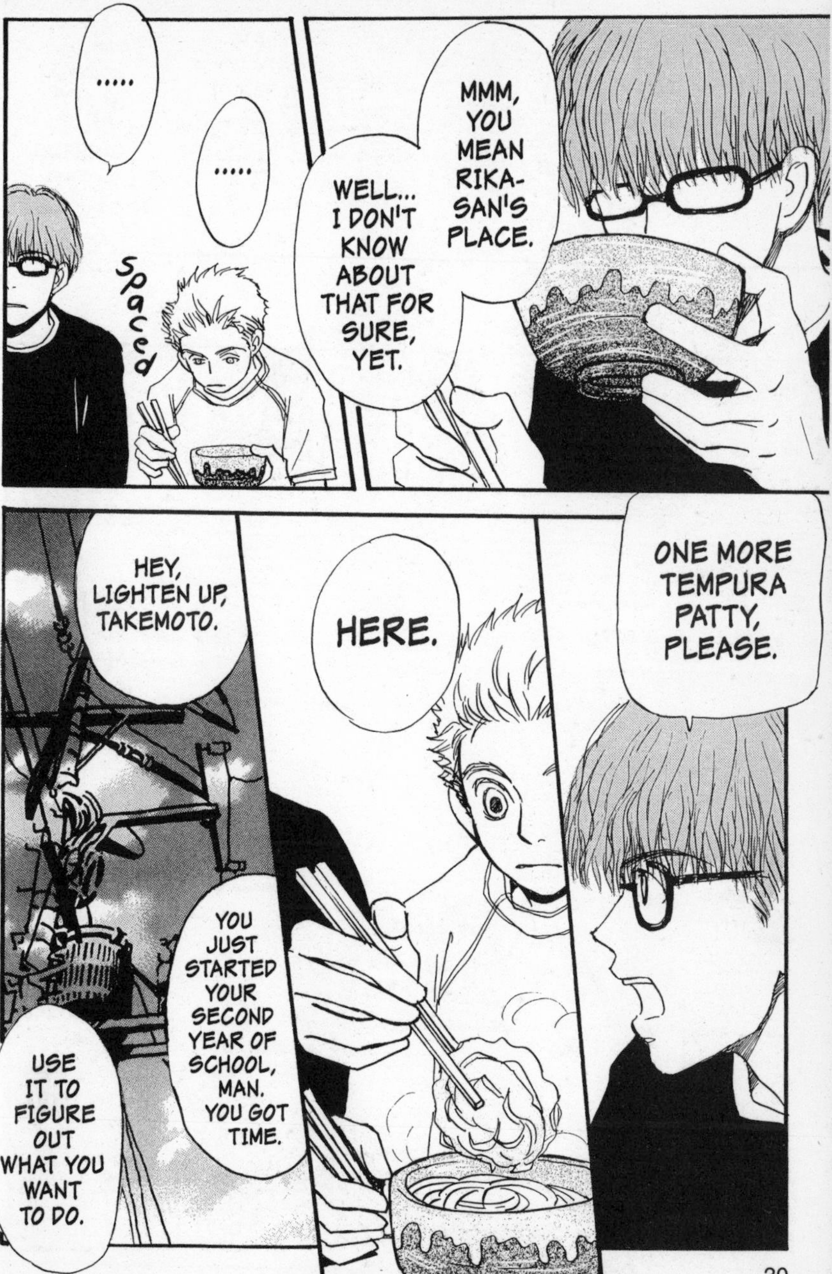
MMM, YOU MEAN RIKA-SAN'S PLACE.
WELL... I DON'T KNOW ABOUT THAT FOR SURE, YET.
......
......
Spaced
ONE MORE TEMPURA PATTY, PLEASE.
HERE.
HEY, LIGHTEN UP, TAKEMOTO.
YOU JUST STARTED YOUR SECOND YEAR OF SCHOOL, MAN. YOU GOT TIME.
USE IT TO FIGURE OUT WHAT YOU WANT TO DO.

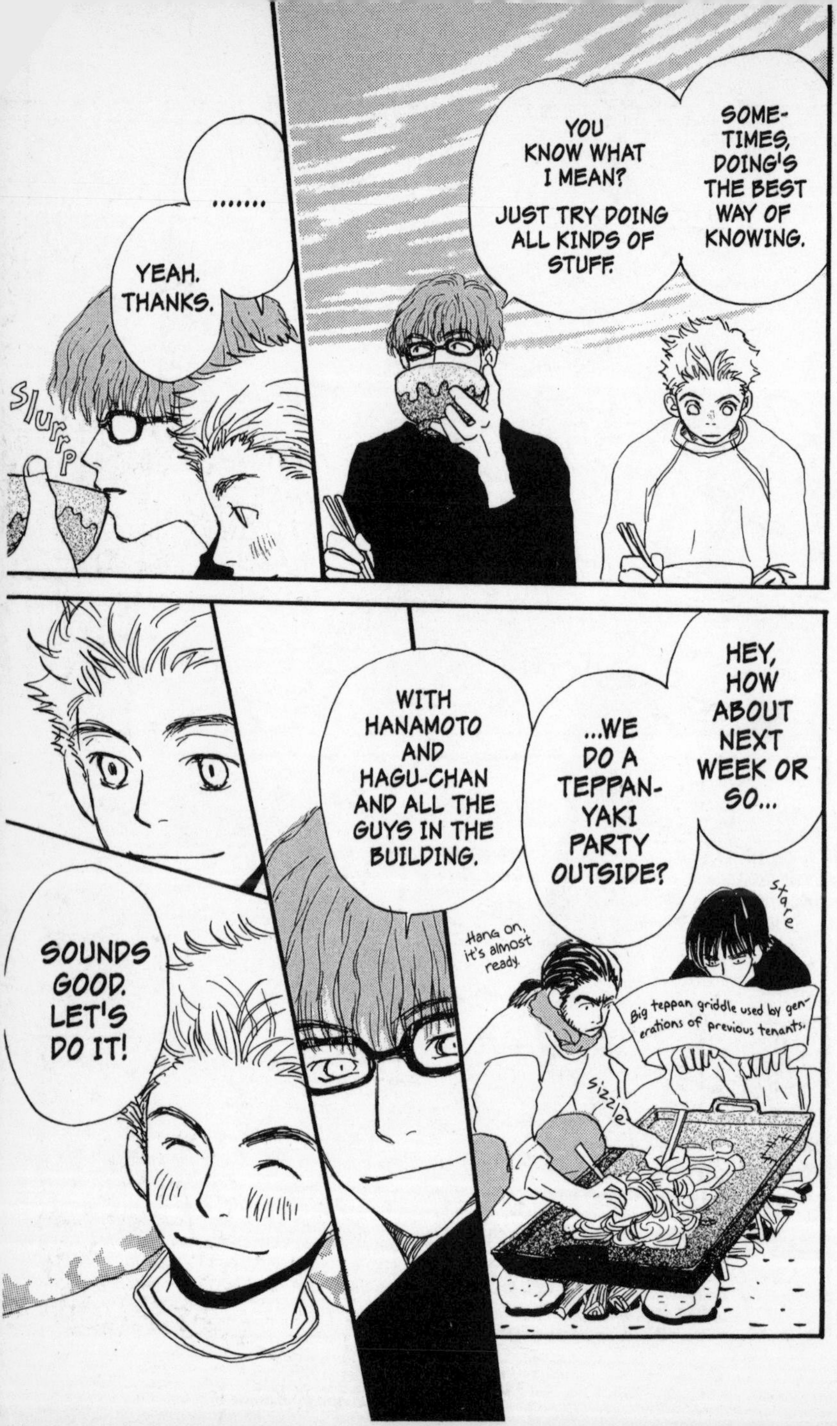
SOME-TIMES, DOING'S THE BEST WAY OF KNOWING.
YOU KNOW WHAT I MEAN?
JUST TRY DOING ALL KINDS OF STUFF.
....
YEAH. THANKS.
Slurrp
HEY, HOW ABOUT NEXT WEEK OR SO...
...WE DO A TEPPAN-YAKI PARTY OUTSIDE?
WITH HANAMOTO AND HAGU-CHAN AND ALL THE GUYS IN THE BUILDING.
Stare
Hang on, it's almost ready.
Big teppan griddle used by generations of previous tenants.
sizzle
SOUNDS GOOD. LET'S DO IT!

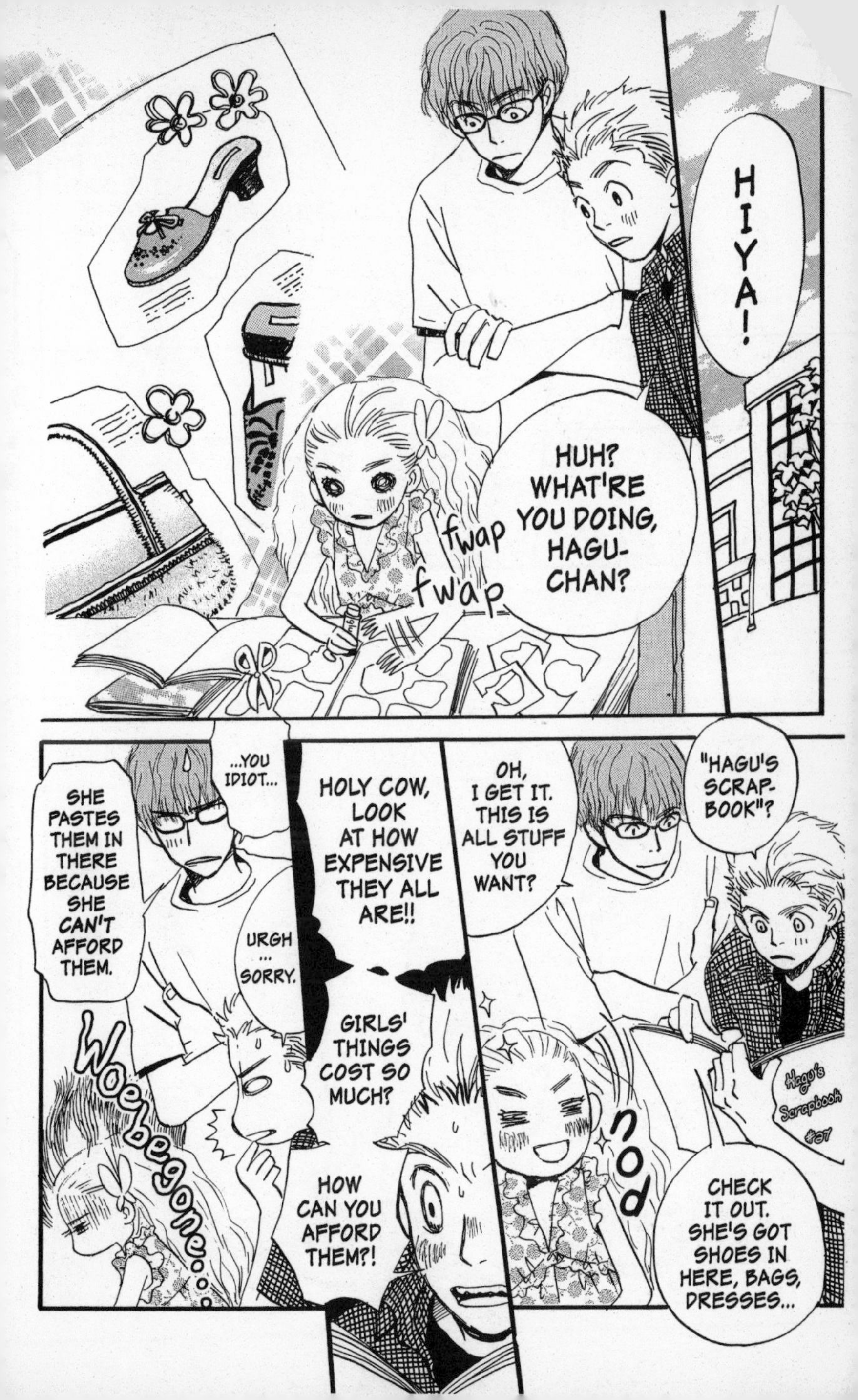
HIYA!
HUH? WHAT'RE YOU DOING, HAGU-CHAN?
fwap
fwap
"HAGU'S SCRAP-BOOK"?
OH, I GET IT. THIS IS ALL STUFF YOU WANT?
Hagu's Scrapbook #37
nod
CHECK IT OUT. SHE'S GOT SHOES IN HERE, BAGS, DRESSES...
HOLY COW, LOOK AT HOW EXPENSIVE THEY ALL ARE!!
GIRLS' THINGS COST SO MUCH?
HOW CAN YOU AFFORD THEM?!
...YOU IDIOT...
SHE PASTES THEM IN THERE BECAUSE SHE CAN'T AFFORD THEM.
URGH ... SORRY.
Woebegone...

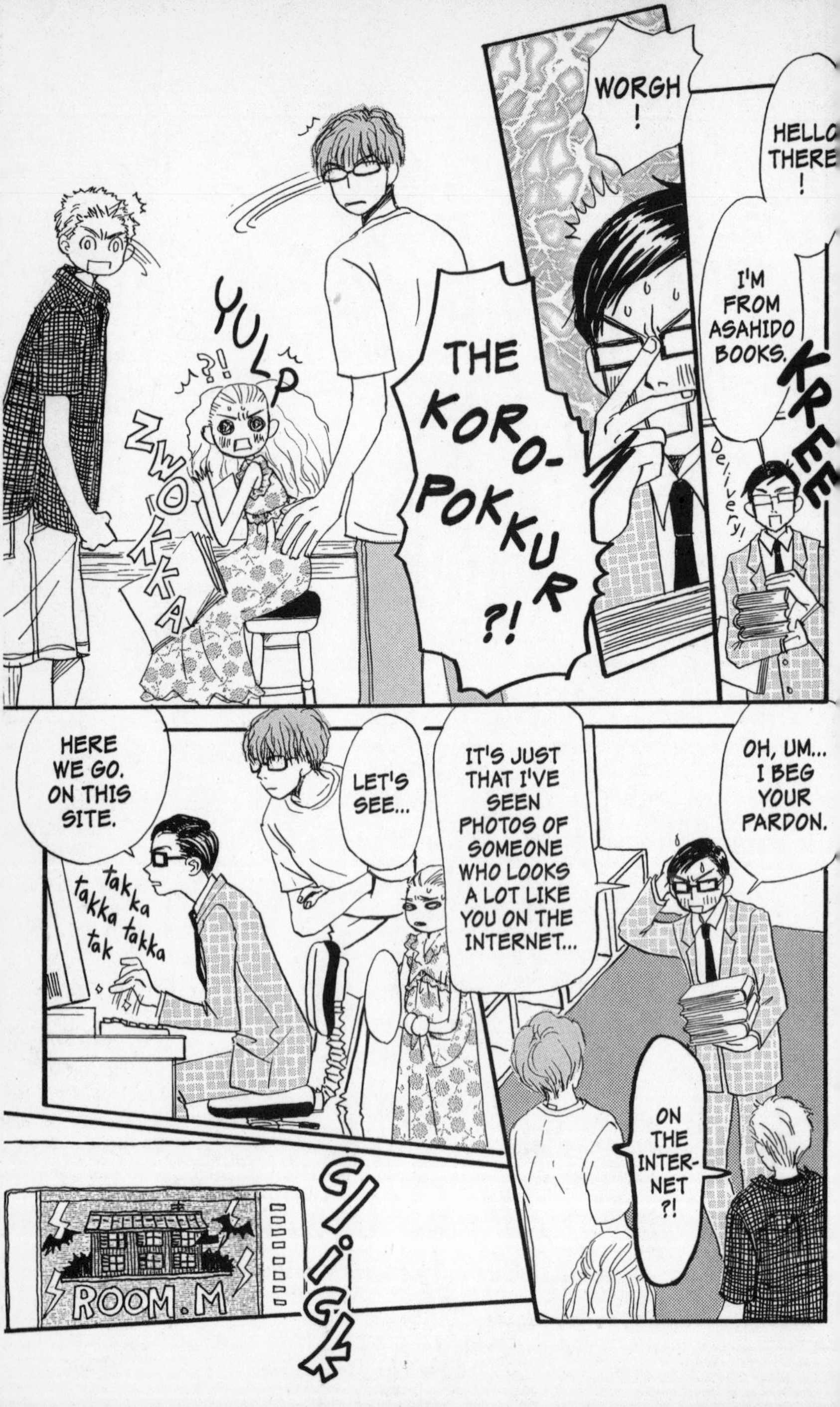
HELLO THERE!
I'M FROM ASAHIDO BOOKS.
KREE
Delivery!
WORGH!
THE KORO-POKKUR?!
YULP
?!
ZWOKKA
OH, UM... I BEG YOUR PARDON.
IT'S JUST THAT I'VE SEEN PHOTOS OF SOMEONE WHO LOOKS A LOT LIKE YOU ON THE INTERNET...
ON THE INTER-NET?!
LET'S SEE...
HERE WE GO. ON THIS SITE.
takka takka takka tak
ROOM.M
CLICK

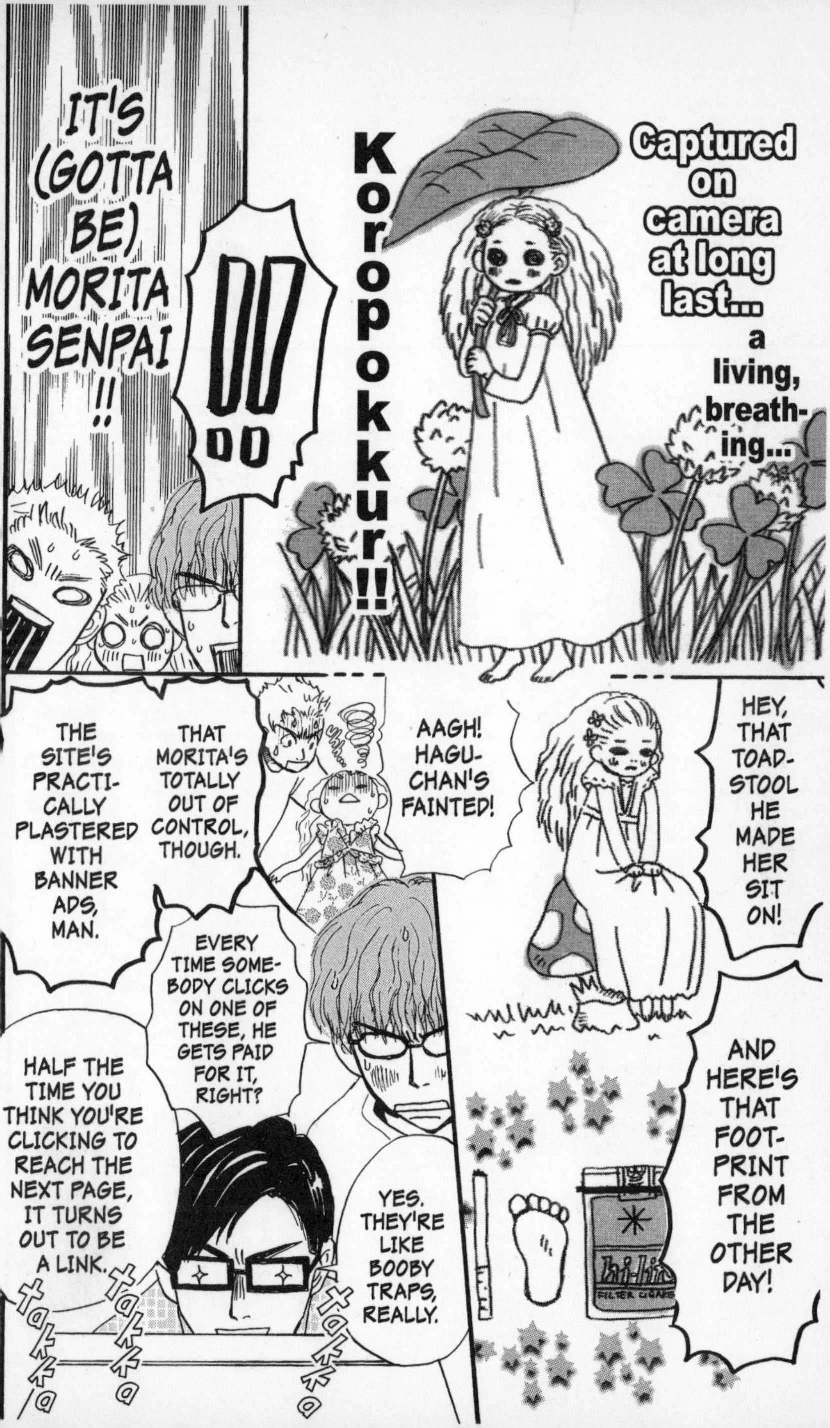
Captured on camera at long last... a living, breathing...
Koropokkur!!
IT'S (GOTTA BE) MORITA SENPAI!!
HEY, THAT TOADSTOOL HE MADE HER SIT ON!
AND HERE'S THAT FOOTPRINT FROM THE OTHER DAY!
AAGH! HAGU-CHAN'S FAINTED!
THAT MORITA'S TOTALLY OUT OF CONTROL, THOUGH.
THE SITE'S PRACTICALLY PLASTERED WITH BANNER ADS, MAN.
EVERY TIME SOMEBODY CLICKS ON ONE OF THESE, HE GETS PAID FOR IT, RIGHT?
YES. THEY'RE LIKE BOOBY TRAPS, REALLY.
HALF THE TIME YOU THINK YOU'RE CLICKING TO REACH THE NEXT PAGE, IT TURNS OUT TO BE A LINK.
takka takka
takka
takka

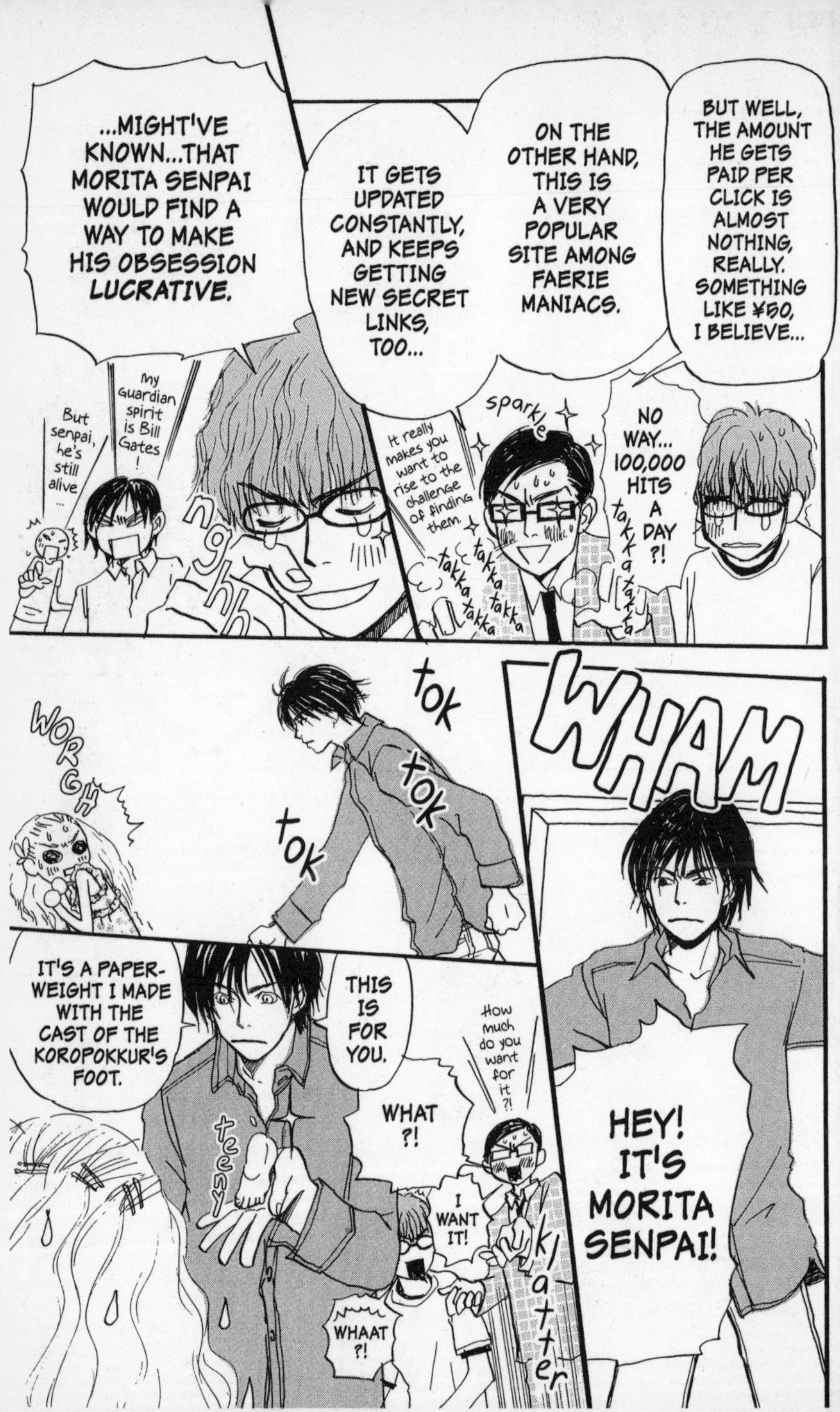
BUT WELL, THE AMOUNT HE GETS PAID PER CLICK IS ALMOST NOTHING, REALLY. SOMETHING LIKE ¥50, I BELIEVE...
NO WAY... 100,000 HITS A DAY?!
takka takka
ON THE OTHER HAND, THIS IS A VERY POPULAR SITE AMONG FAERIE MANIACS.
IT GETS UPDATED CONSTANTLY, AND KEEPS GETTING NEW SECRET LINKS, TOO...
sparkle
It really makes you want to rise to the challenge of finding them.
takka takka takka takka
...MIGHT'VE KNOWN...THAT MORITA SENPAI WOULD FIND A WAY TO MAKE HIS OBSESSION LUCRATIVE.
My Guardian spirit is Bill Gates!
But senpai, he's still alive...
nghhh
WHAM
HEY! IT'S MORITA SENPAI!
tok
tok
tok
WORGH
How much do you want for it?!
WHAT?!
klatter
I WANT IT!
THIS IS FOR YOU.
IT'S A PAPER-WEIGHT I MADE WITH THE CAST OF THE KOROPOKKUR'S FOOT.
teeny
WHAAT?!

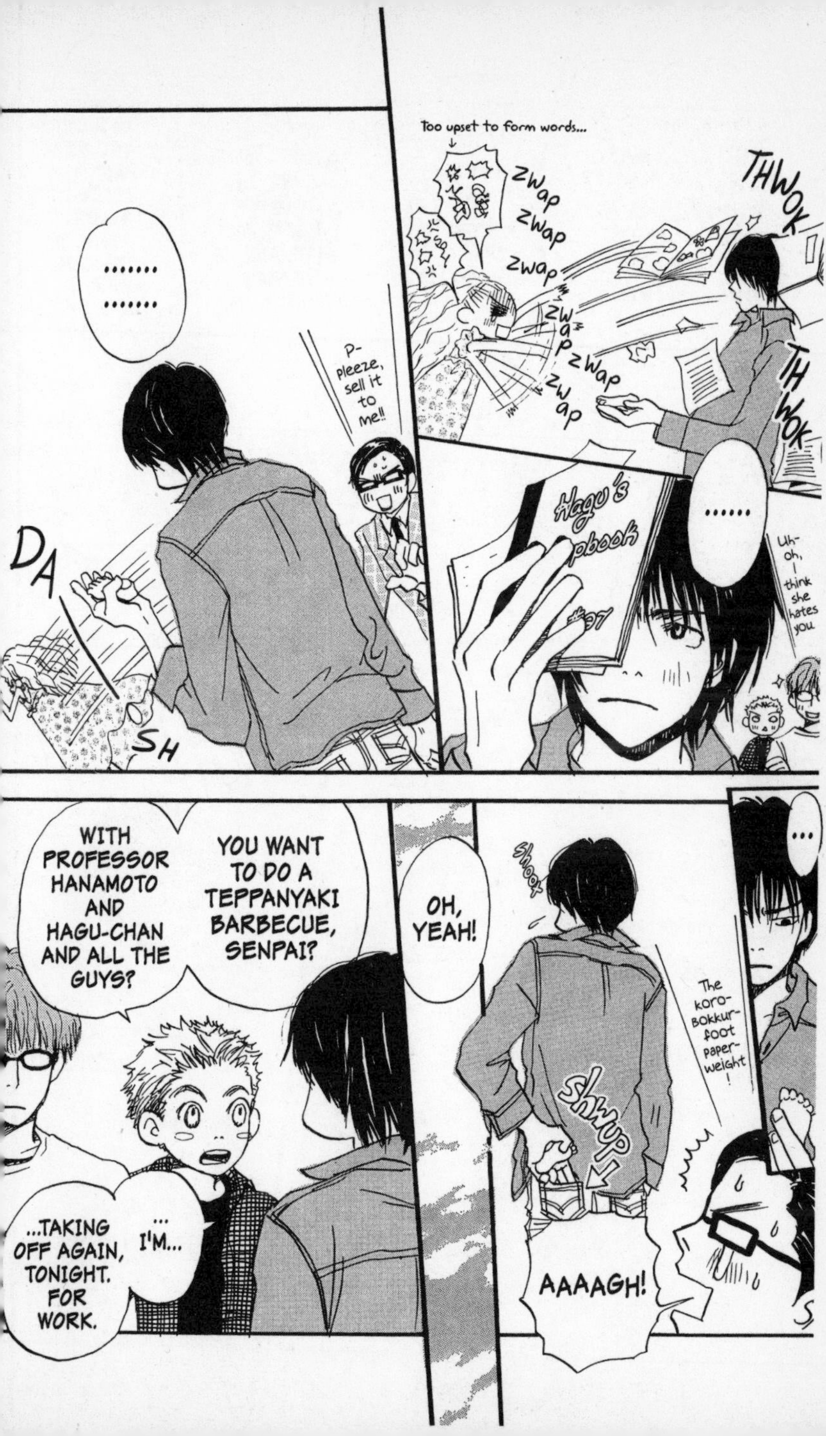
Too upset to form words...
ZWAP
ZWAP
ZWAP
ZWAP
ZWAP
ZWAP
THWOK
THWOK
......
Uh-oh, I think she hates you
P-pleeze, sell it to me!!
....
....
DA
SH
...
The koro-bokkur-foot paper-weight!
Shoot
OH, YEAH!
SHWUP
AAAAGH!
YOU WANT TO DO A TEPPANYAKI BARBECUE, SENPAI?
WITH PROFESSOR HANAMOTO AND HAGU-CHAN AND ALL THE GUYS?
... I'M...
...TAKING OFF AGAIN, TONIGHT. FOR WORK.

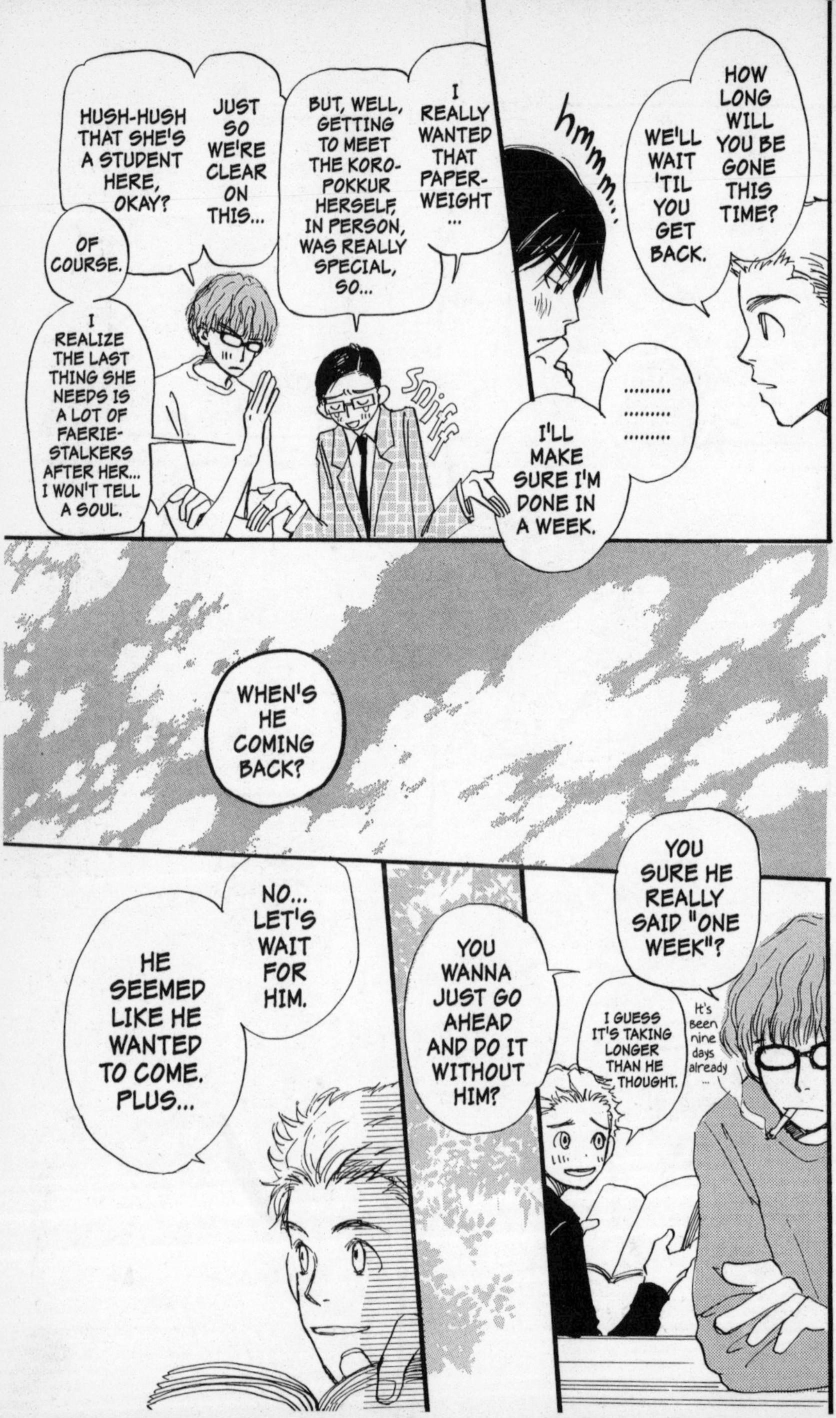
HOW LONG WILL YOU BE GONE THIS TIME?
WE'LL WAIT 'TIL YOU GET BACK.
hmmm...
....
I'LL MAKE SURE I'M DONE IN A WEEK.
I REALLY WANTED THAT PAPER-WEIGHT...
BUT, WELL, GETTING TO MEET THE KORO-POKKUR HERSELF, IN PERSON, WAS REALLY SPECIAL, SO...
Sniff
JUST SO WE'RE CLEAR ON THIS...
HUSH-HUSH THAT SHE'S A STUDENT HERE, OKAY?
OF COURSE.
I REALIZE THE LAST THING SHE NEEDS IS A LOT OF FAERIE-STALKERS AFTER HER... I WON'T TELL A SOUL.
WHEN'S HE COMING BACK?
YOU SURE HE REALLY SAID "ONE WEEK"?
It's been nine days already...
I GUESS IT'S TAKING LONGER THAN HE THOUGHT.
YOU WANNA JUST GO AHEAD AND DO IT WITHOUT HIM?
NO... LET'S WAIT FOR HIM.
HE SEEMED LIKE HE WANTED TO COME. PLUS...

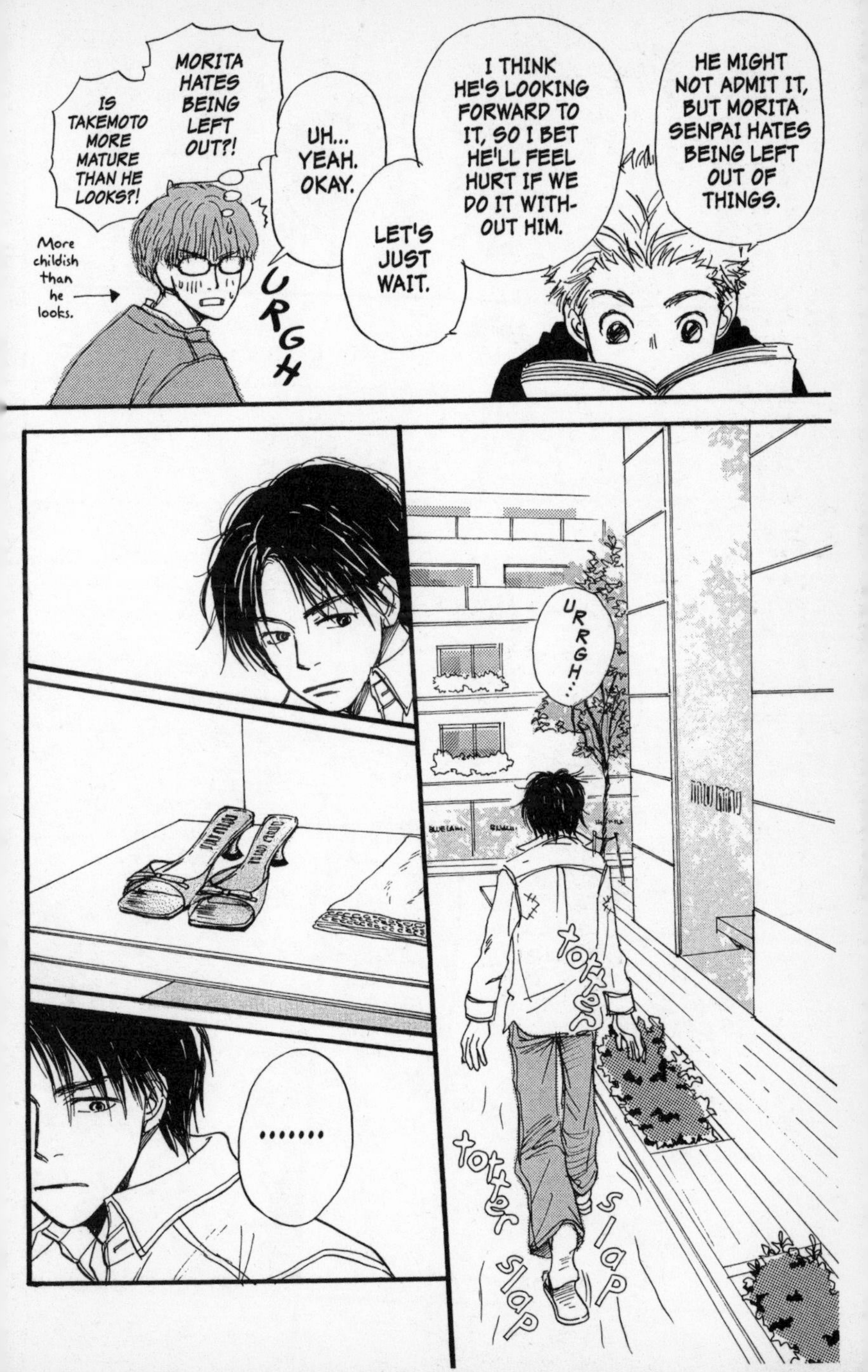
HE MIGHT NOT ADMIT IT, BUT MORITA SENPAI HATES BEING LEFT OUT OF THINGS.
I THINK HE'S LOOKING FORWARD TO IT, SO I BET HE'LL FEEL HURT IF WE DO IT WITH-OUT HIM.
LET'S JUST WAIT.
UH... YEAH. OKAY.
URGH
MORITA HATES BEING LEFT OUT?!
IS TAKEMOTO MORE MATURE THAN HE LOOKS?!
More childish than he looks.
URRGH...
totter
totter
slap
slap
....

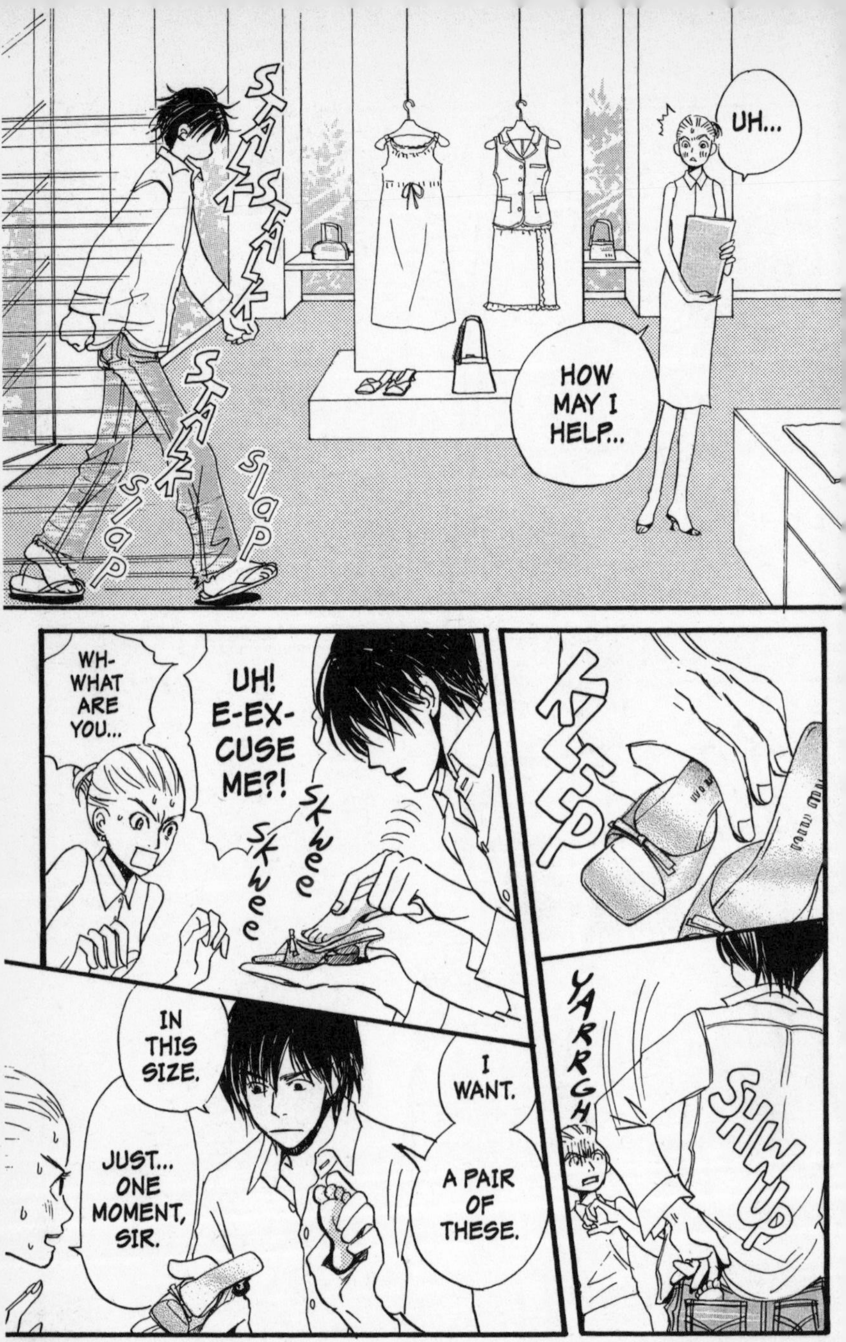

UH...
HOW MAY I HELP...
STALK STALK
STALK STALK
slap slap
KLIP
UH! E-EX-CUSE ME?!
WH-WHAT ARE YOU...
SKWEE SKWEE
YARRGH
SHWUP
I WANT.
A PAIR OF THESE.
IN THIS SIZE.
JUST... ONE MOMENT, SIR.

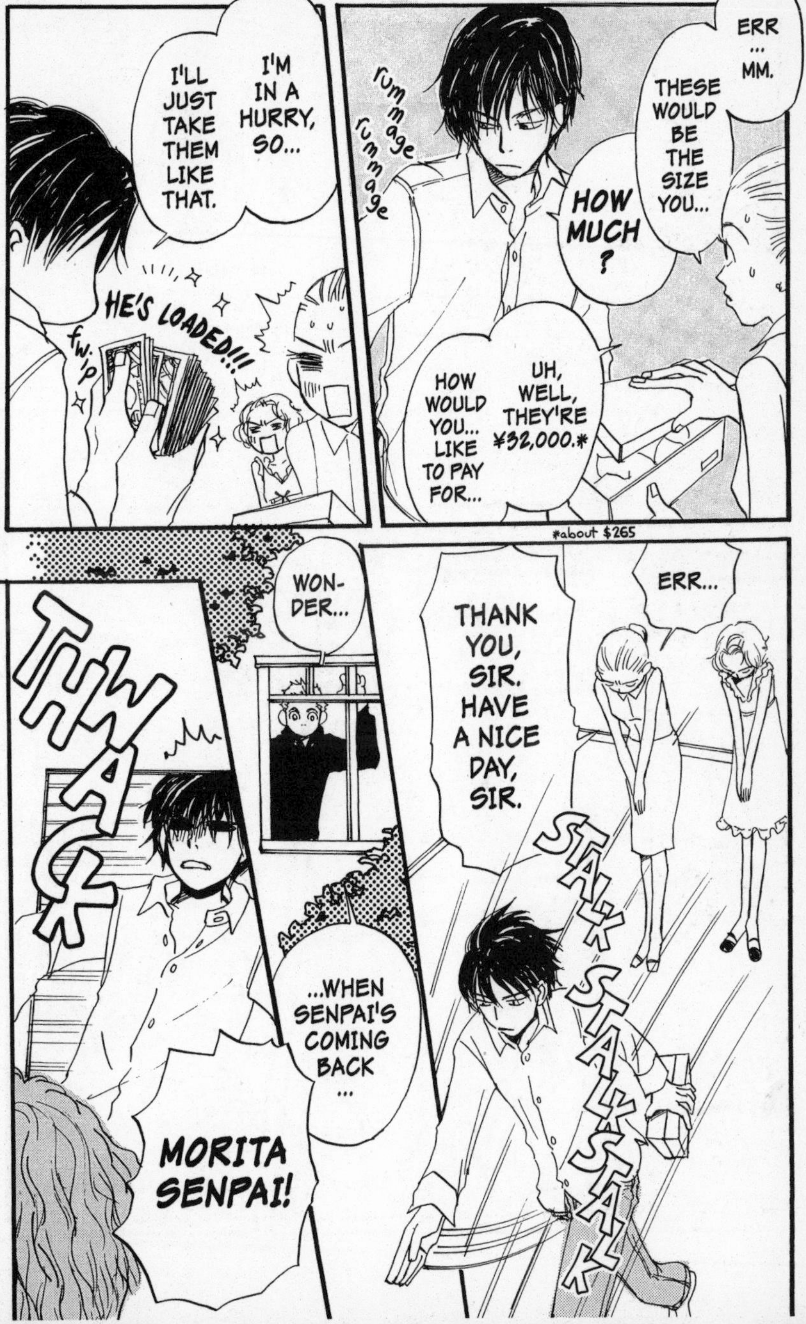
ERR ... MM.
THESE WOULD BE THE SIZE YOU...
rummage rummage
HOW MUCH?
UH, WELL, THEY'RE ¥32,000.*
HOW WOULD YOU... LIKE TO PAY FOR...
I'M IN A HURRY, SO...
I'LL JUST TAKE THEM LIKE THAT.
HE'S LOADED!!!!
fwip
ERR...
THANK YOU, SIR. HAVE A NICE DAY, SIR.
STALK STALK STALK
WON-DER...
...WHEN SENPAI'S COMING BACK...
THWACK
MORITA SENPAI!

*about $265

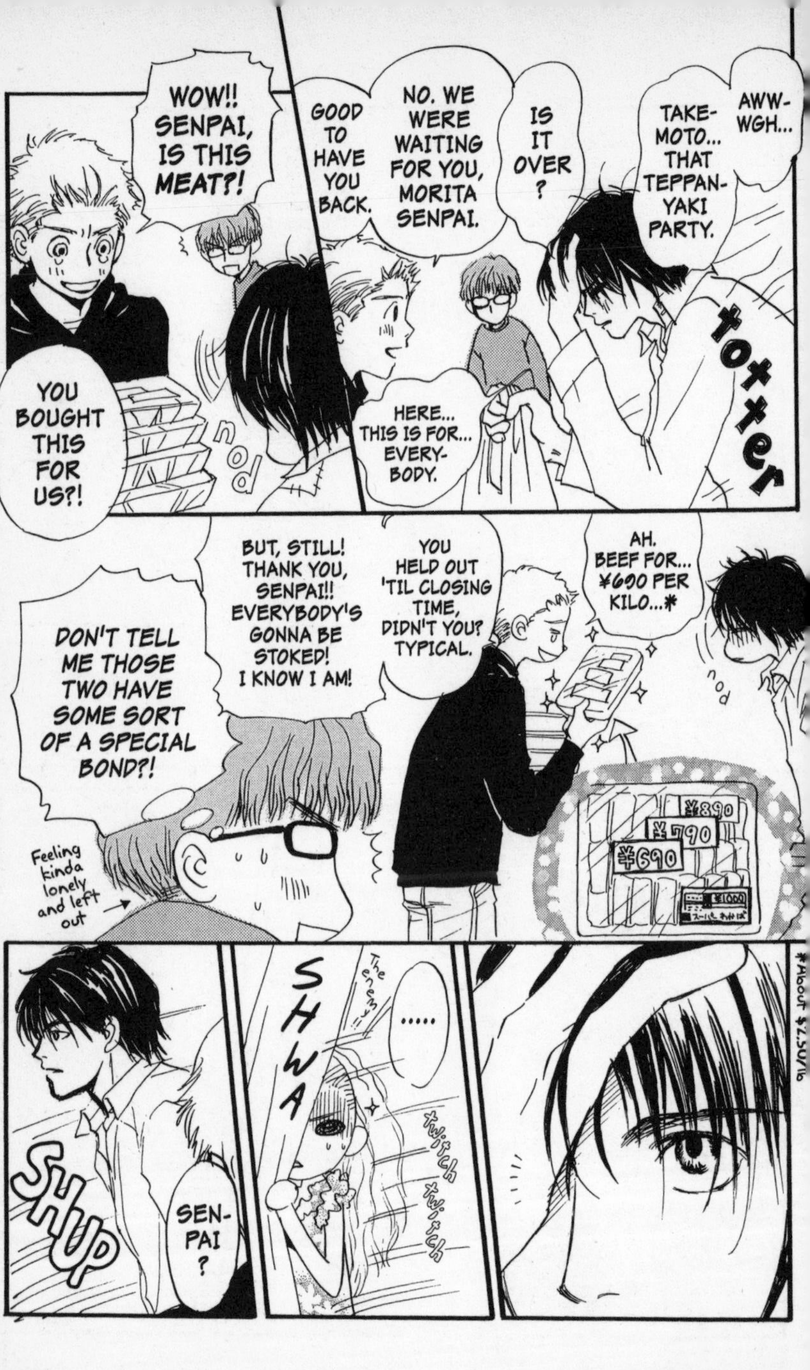
AWW-WGH...
TAKE-MOTO... THAT TEPPAN-YAKI PARTY.
IS IT OVER?
NO. WE WERE WAITING FOR YOU, MORITA SENPAI.
GOOD TO HAVE YOU BACK.
totter
HERE... THIS IS FOR... EVERYBODY.
WOW!! SENPAI, IS THIS MEAT?!
nod
YOU BOUGHT THIS FOR US?!
AH. BEEF FOR... ¥690 PER KILO...*
nod
¥890
¥790
¥690
¥1000
YOU HELD OUT 'TIL CLOSING TIME, DIDN'T YOU? TYPICAL.
BUT, STILL! THANK YOU, SENPAI!! EVERYBODY'S GONNA BE STOKED! I KNOW I AM!
DON'T TELL ME THOSE TWO HAVE SOME SORT OF A SPECIAL BOND?!
Feeling kinda lonely and left out
*About $2.50/lb
......
The enemy!!
SHWA
twitch twitch
SEN-PAI?
SHUP

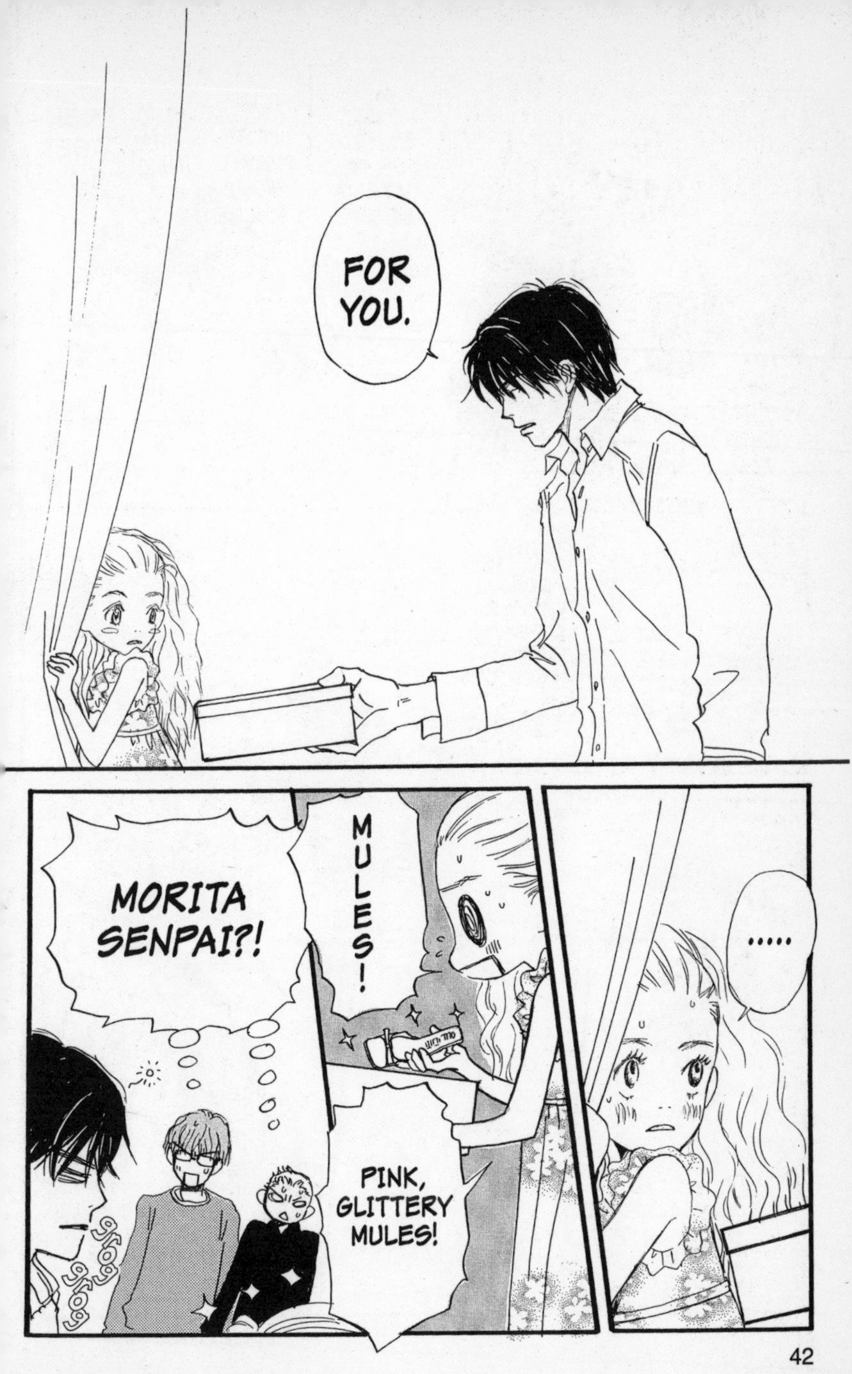
FOR YOU.
.....
MULES!
PINK, GLITTERY MULES!
MORITA SENPAI?!

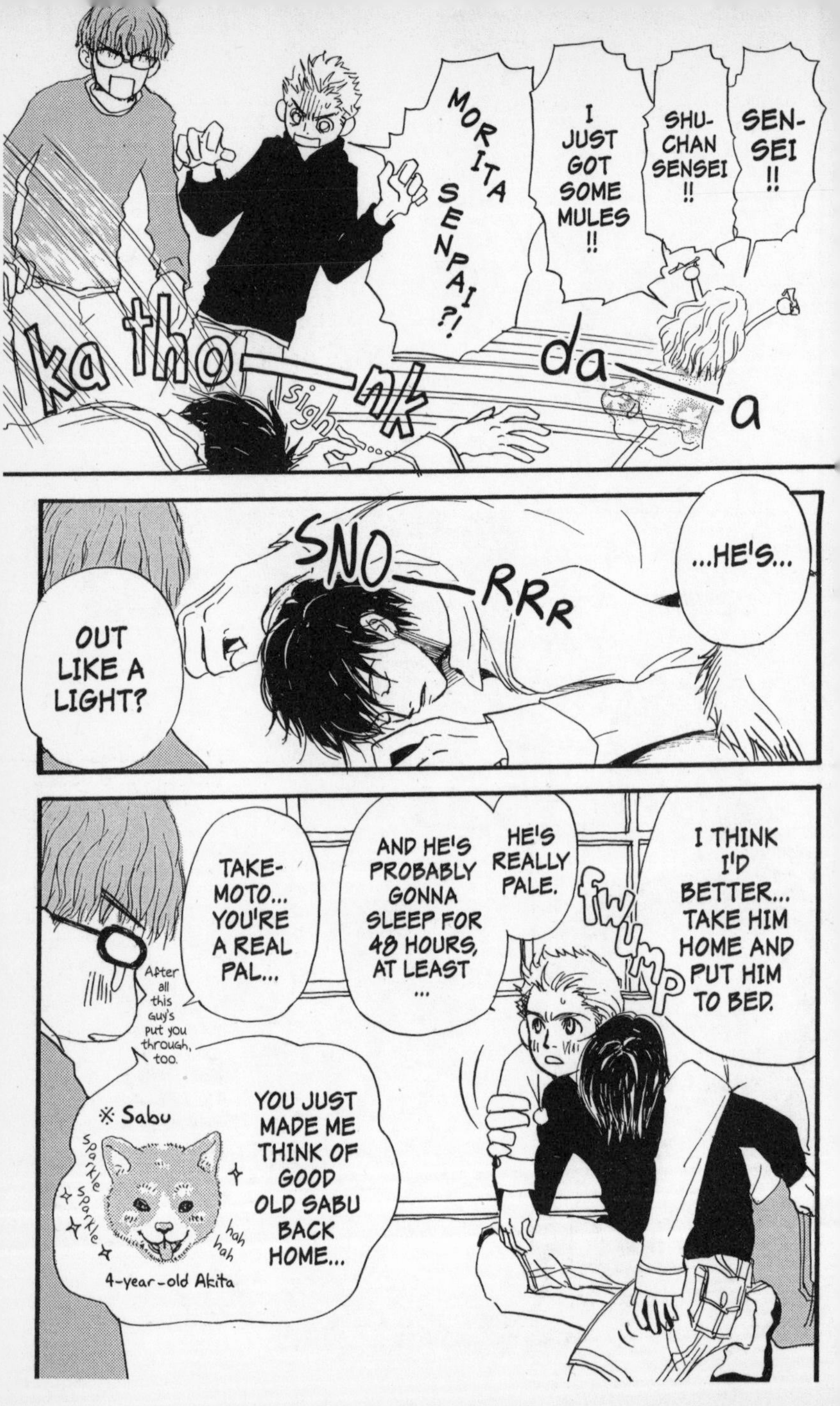
SEN-SEI !!
SHU-CHAN SENSEI !!
I JUST GOT SOME MULES !!
MORITA SENPAI ?!
da—a
ka tho—nk
sigh....
...HE'S...
SNO—RRR
OUT LIKE A LIGHT?
I THINK I'D BETTER... TAKE HIM HOME AND PUT HIM TO BED.
fwump
HE'S REALLY PALE.
AND HE'S PROBABLY GONNA SLEEP FOR 48 HOURS, AT LEAST ...
TAKE-MOTO... YOU'RE A REAL PAL...
After all this guy's put you through, too.
YOU JUST MADE ME THINK OF GOOD OLD SABU BACK HOME...
※ Sabu
sparkle sparkle
hah hah
4-year-old Akita

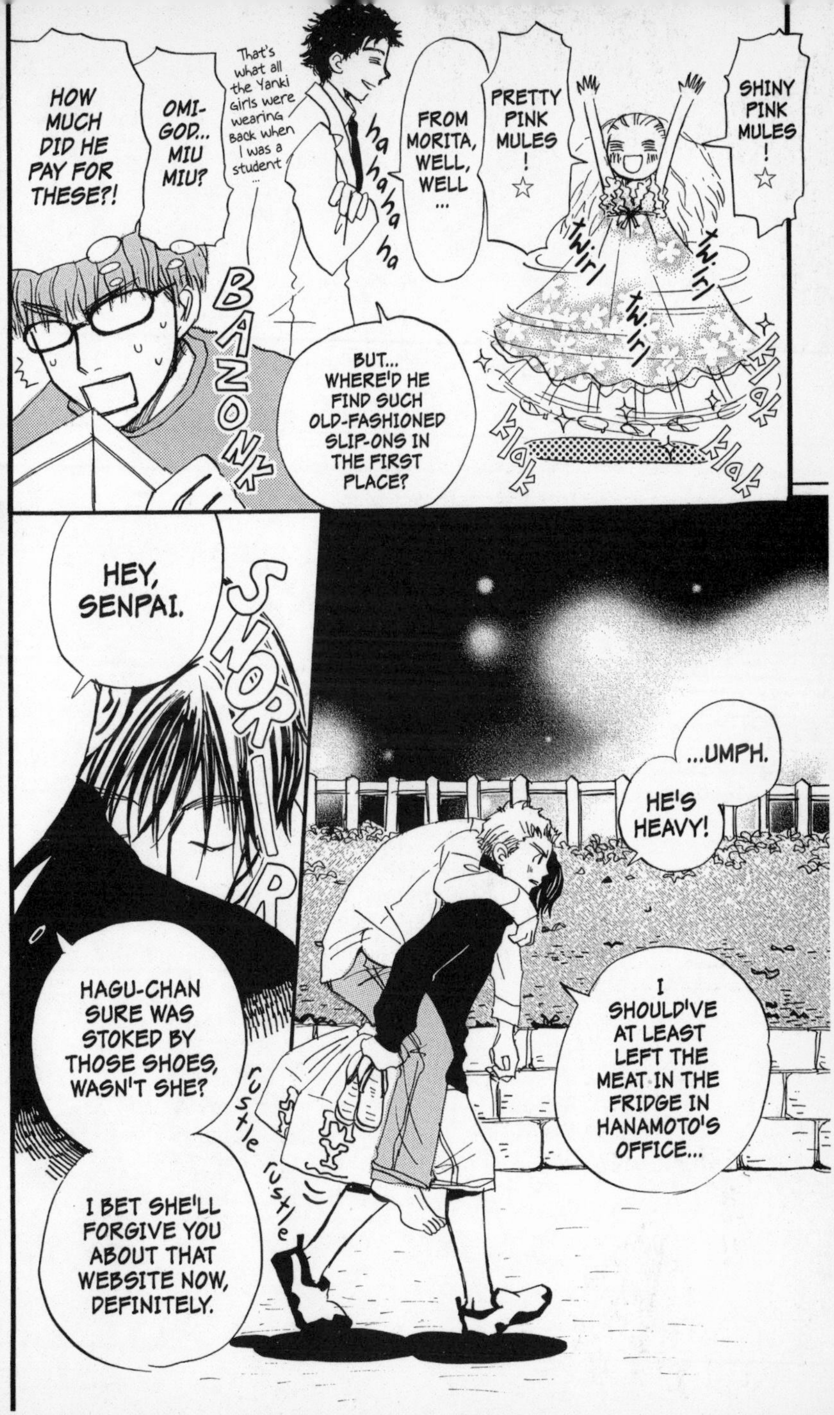
SHINY PINK MULES! ☆
PRETTY PINK MULES! ☆
twirl
twirl
twirl
klak klak
klak klak
FROM MORITA, WELL, WELL...
ha ha ha ha ha
That's what all the Yanki Girls were wearing back when I was a student...
OMI-GOD... MIU MIU?
HOW MUCH DID HE PAY FOR THESE?!
BAZONK
BUT... WHERE'D HE FIND SUCH OLD-FASHIONED SLIP-ONS IN THE FIRST PLACE?
...UMPH.
HE'S HEAVY!
I SHOULD'VE AT LEAST LEFT THE MEAT IN THE FRIDGE IN HANAMOTO'S OFFICE...
rustle
rustle
HEY, SENPAI.
SNORRR
HAGU-CHAN SURE WAS STOKED BY THOSE SHOES, WASN'T SHE?
I BET SHE'LL FORGIVE YOU ABOUT THAT WEBSITE NOW, DEFINITELY.

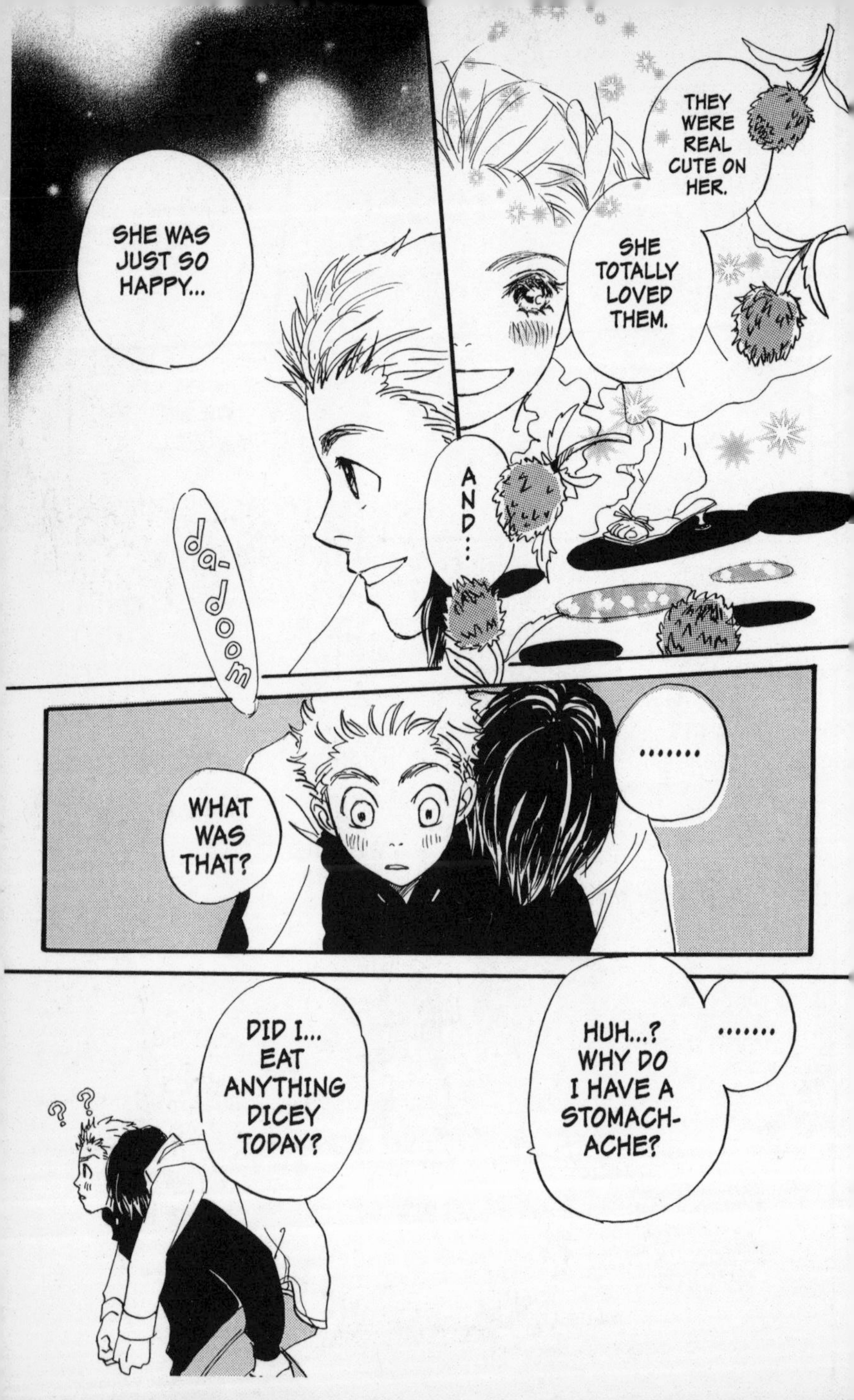
THEY WERE REAL CUTE ON HER.
SHE TOTALLY LOVED THEM.
SHE WAS JUST SO HAPPY...
AND...
da-doom
....
WHAT WAS THAT?
....
HUH...? WHY DO I HAVE A STOMACH-ACHE?
DID I... EAT ANYTHING DICEY TODAY?
? ?

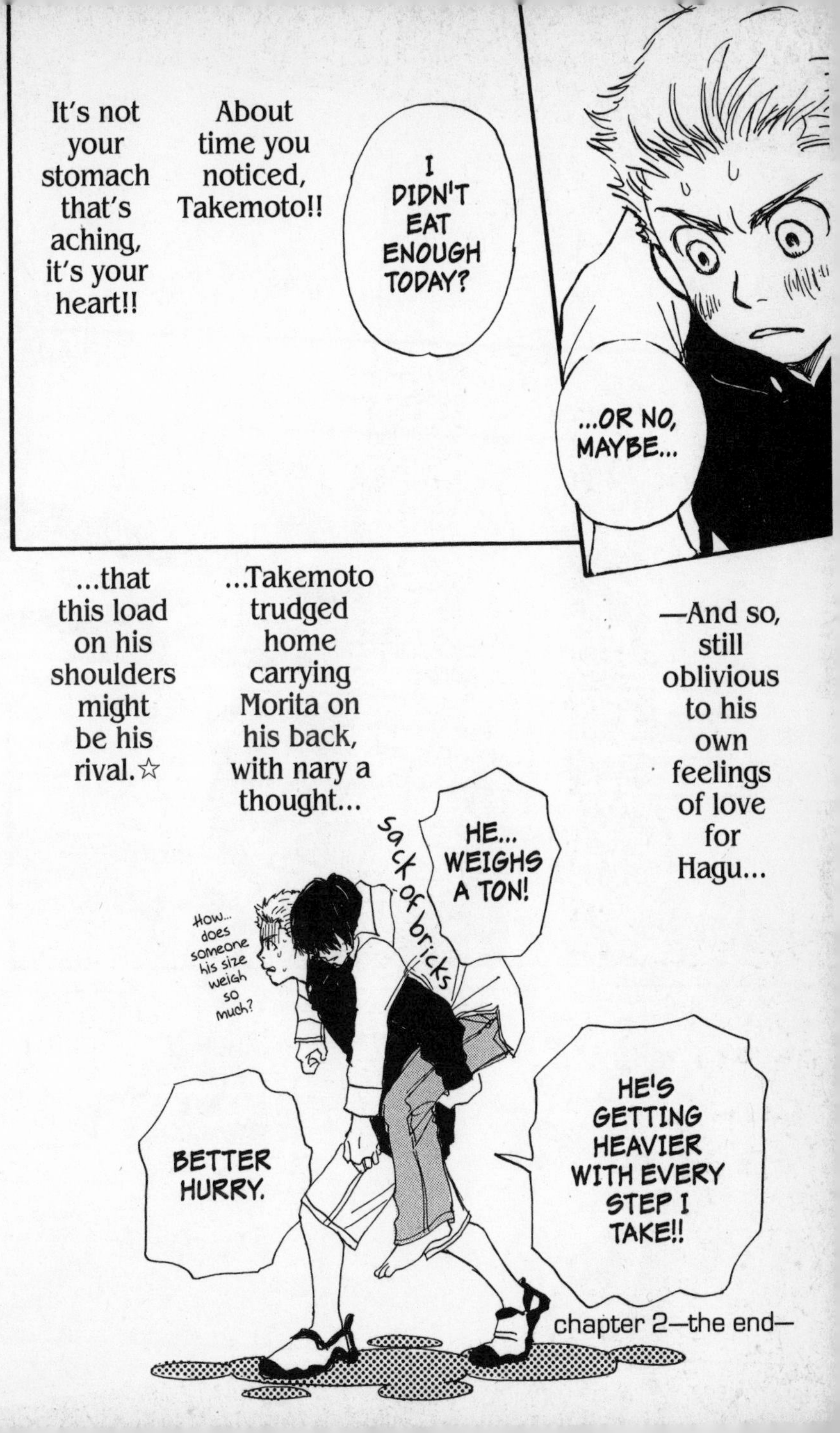
I DIDN'T EAT ENOUGH TODAY?
...OR NO, MAYBE...
About time you noticed, Takemoto!!
It's not your stomach that's aching, it's your heart!!
—And so, still oblivious to his own feelings of love for Hagu...
...Takemoto trudged home carrying Morita on his back, with nary a thought...
...that this load on his shoulders might be his rival.☆
HE... WEIGHS A TON!
sack of bricks
How... does someone his size weigh so much?
HE'S GETTING HEAVIER WITH EVERY STEP I TAKE!!
BETTER HURRY.
chapter 2—the end—

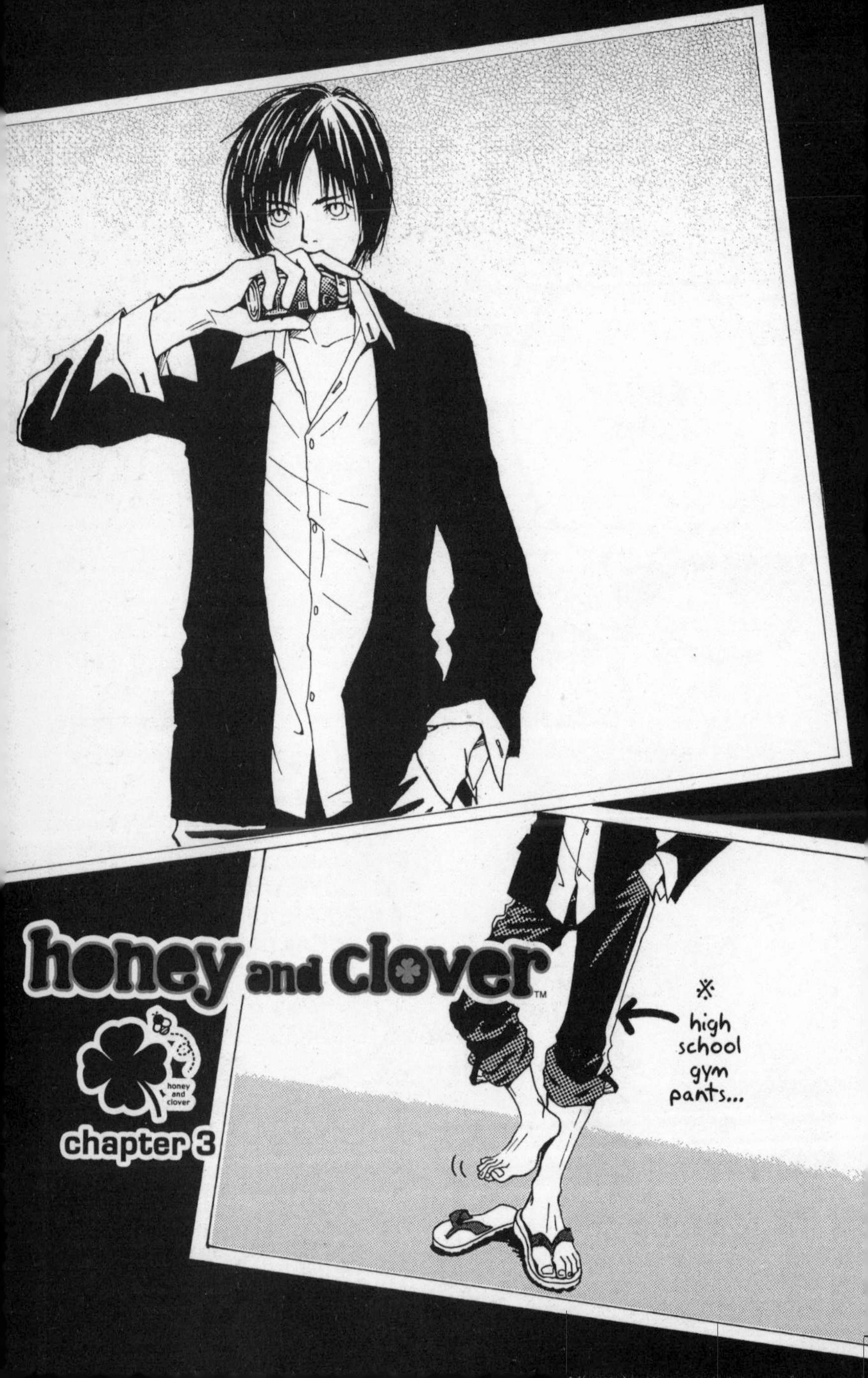

honey and clover
honey and clover
chapter 3
※ high school gym pants...

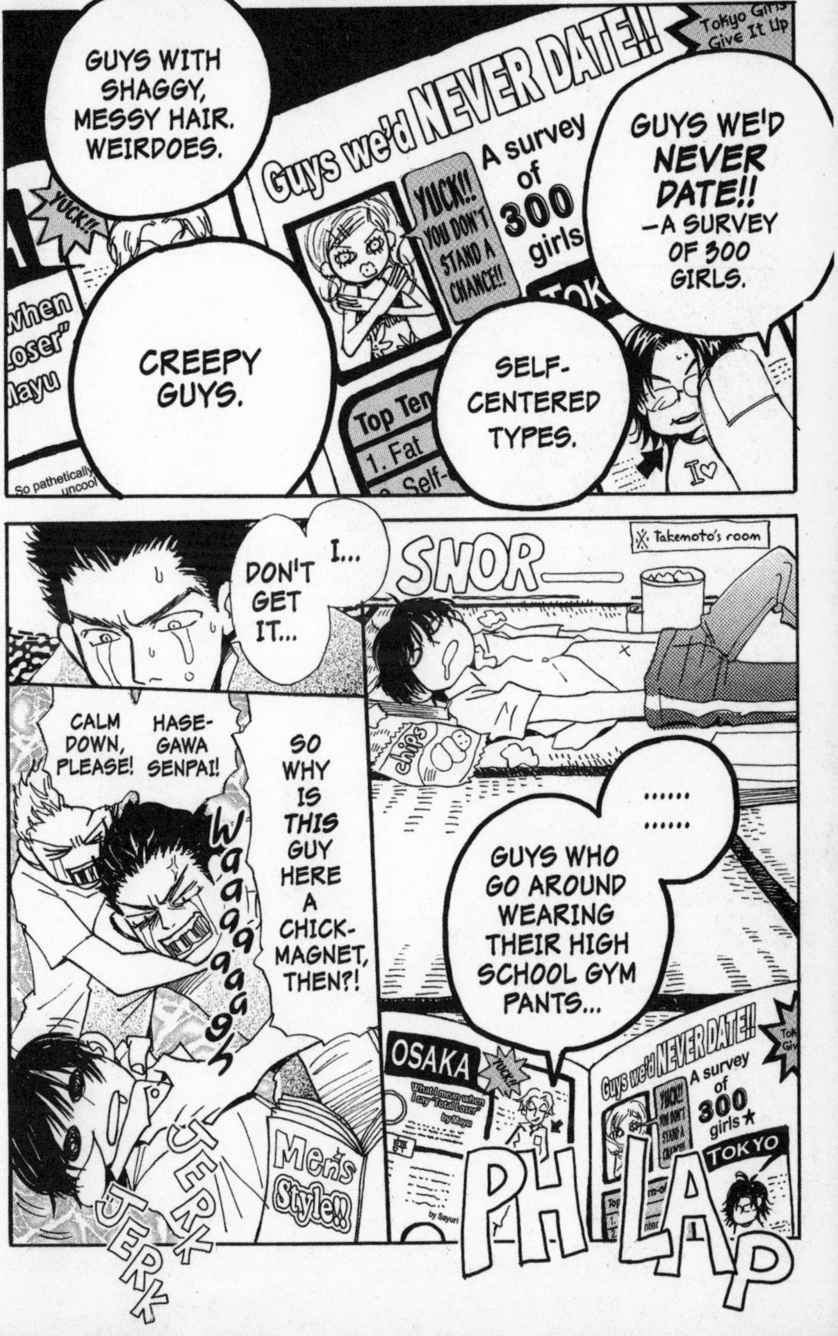
Tokyo Girls Give It Up
Guys we'd NEVER DATE!!
A survey of 300 girls
GUYS WE'D NEVER DATE!! —A SURVEY OF 300 GIRLS.
YUCK!! YOU DON'T STAND A CHANCE!!
Top Ten
1. Fat
SELF-CENTERED TYPES.
CREEPY GUYS.
YUCK!!
So pathetically uncool
GUYS WITH SHAGGY, MESSY HAIR. WEIRDOES.
※ Takemoto's room
SNOR—
chips
....
GUYS WHO GO AROUND WEARING THEIR HIGH SCHOOL GYM PANTS...
Guys we'd NEVER DATE!!
A survey of 300 girls★
TOKYO
OSAKA
YUCK!!
What I mean when I say "Total Loser" by Mayu
by Sayuri
PHLAP
I... DON'T GET IT...
SO WHY IS THIS GUY HERE A CHICK-MAGNET, THEN?!
HASE-GAWA SENPAI!
CALM DOWN, PLEASE!
Waaaaaaaagh
Men's Style!!
JERK JERK

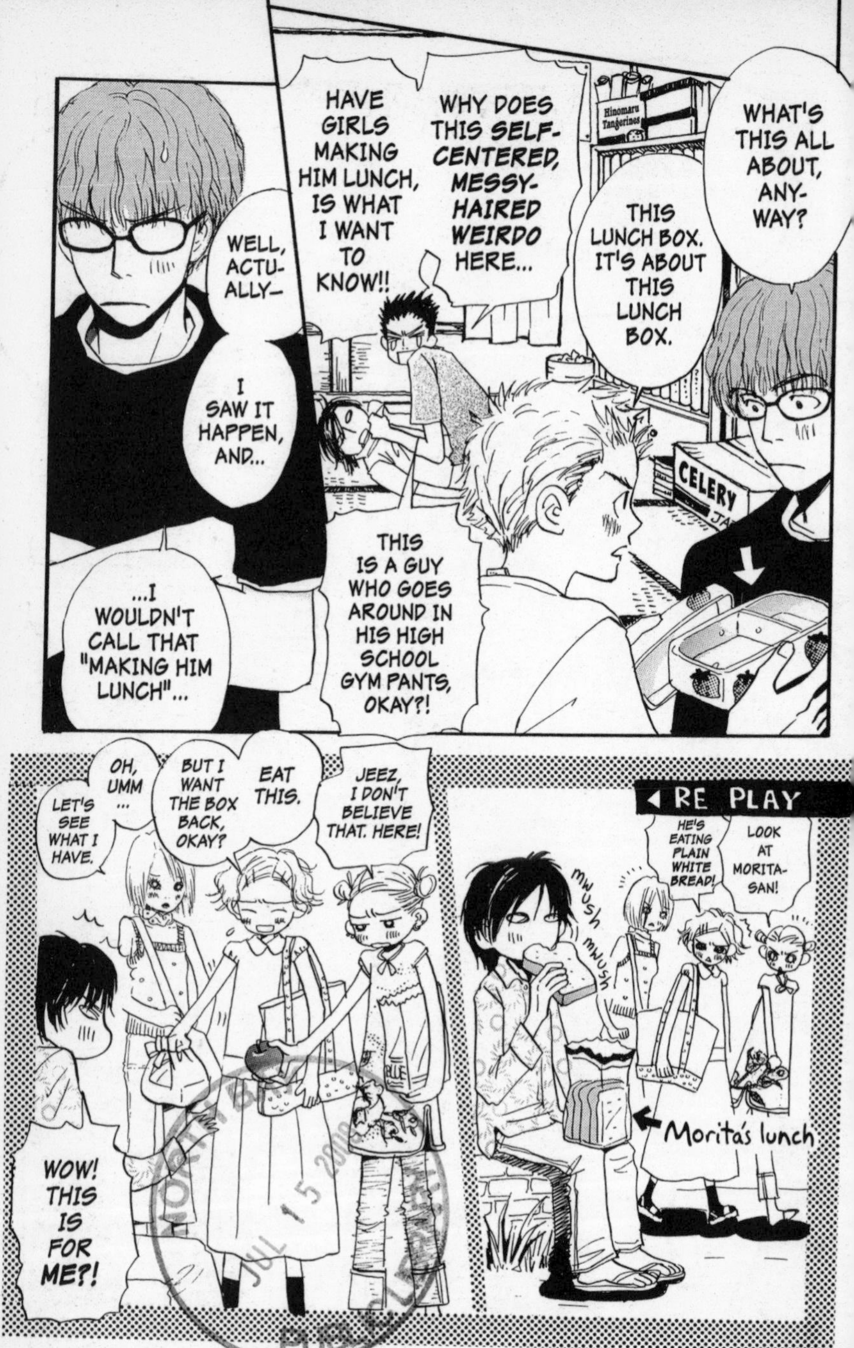
WHAT'S THIS ALL ABOUT, ANY-WAY?
THIS LUNCH BOX. IT'S ABOUT THIS LUNCH BOX.
Hinomaru Tangerines
CELERY
WHY DOES THIS SELF-CENTERED, MESSY-HAIRED WEIRDO HERE...
HAVE GIRLS MAKING HIM LUNCH, IS WHAT I WANT TO KNOW!!
THIS IS A GUY WHO GOES AROUND IN HIS HIGH SCHOOL GYM PANTS, OKAY?!
WELL, ACTU-ALLY—
I SAW IT HAPPEN, AND...
...I WOULDN'T CALL THAT "MAKING HIM LUNCH"...
RE PLAY
LOOK AT MORITA-SAN!
HE'S EATING PLAIN WHITE BREAD!
mwush mwush
Morita's lunch
JEEZ, I DON'T BELIEVE THAT. HERE!
EAT THIS.
BUT I WANT THE BOX BACK, OKAY?
OH, UMM ...
LET'S SEE WHAT I HAVE.
WOW! THIS IS FOR ME?!

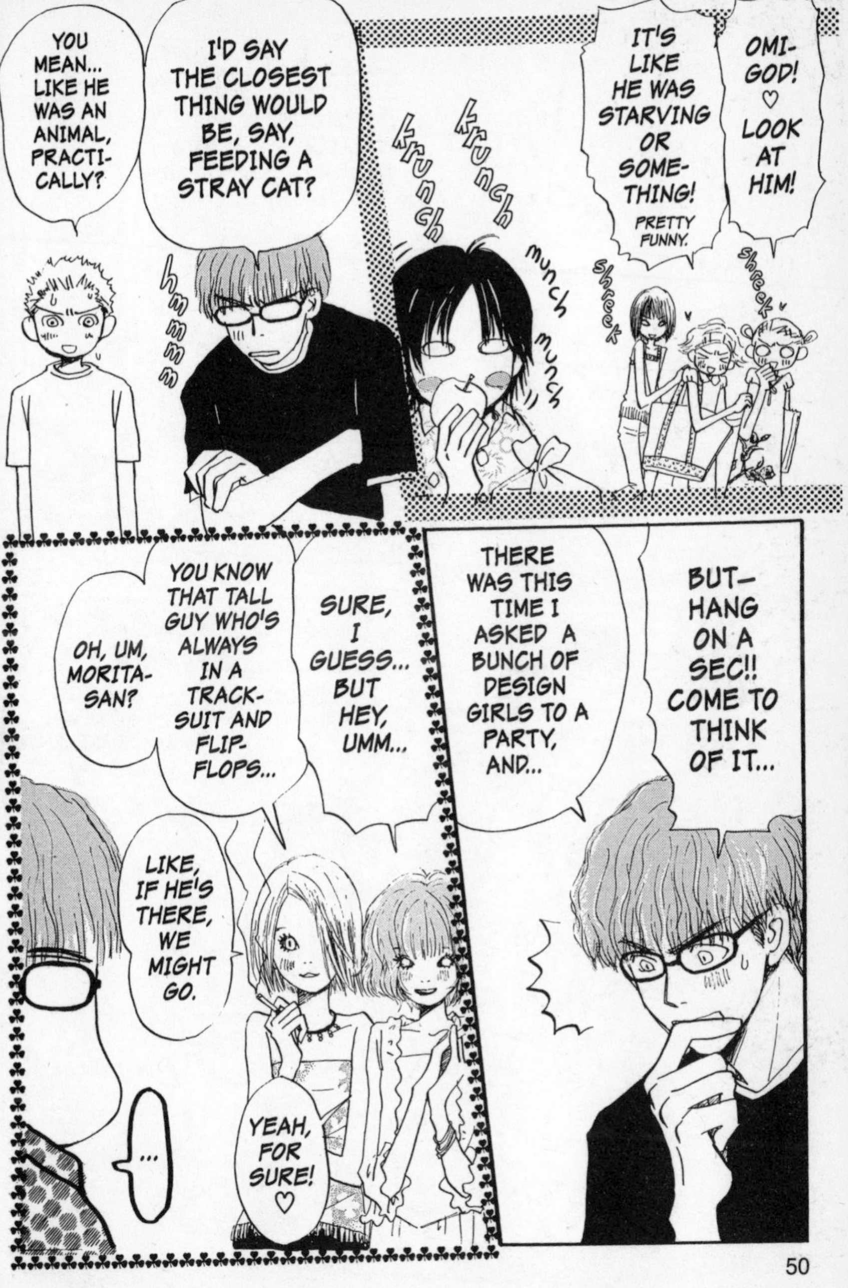
OMI-GOD! ♡ LOOK AT HIM!
IT'S LIKE HE WAS STARVING OR SOMETHING!
PRETTY FUNNY.
shreek
shreek
krunch
krunch
munch
munch
I'D SAY THE CLOSEST THING WOULD BE, SAY, FEEDING A STRAY CAT?
hmmmm
YOU MEAN... LIKE HE WAS AN ANIMAL, PRACTICALLY?
BUT— HANG ON A SEC!! COME TO THINK OF IT...
THERE WAS THIS TIME I ASKED A BUNCH OF DESIGN GIRLS TO A PARTY, AND...
SURE, I GUESS... BUT HEY, UMM...
YOU KNOW THAT TALL GUY WHO'S ALWAYS IN A TRACK-SUIT AND FLIP-FLOPS...
OH, UM, MORITA-SAN?
LIKE, IF HE'S THERE, WE MIGHT GO.
YEAH, FOR SURE! ♡
...

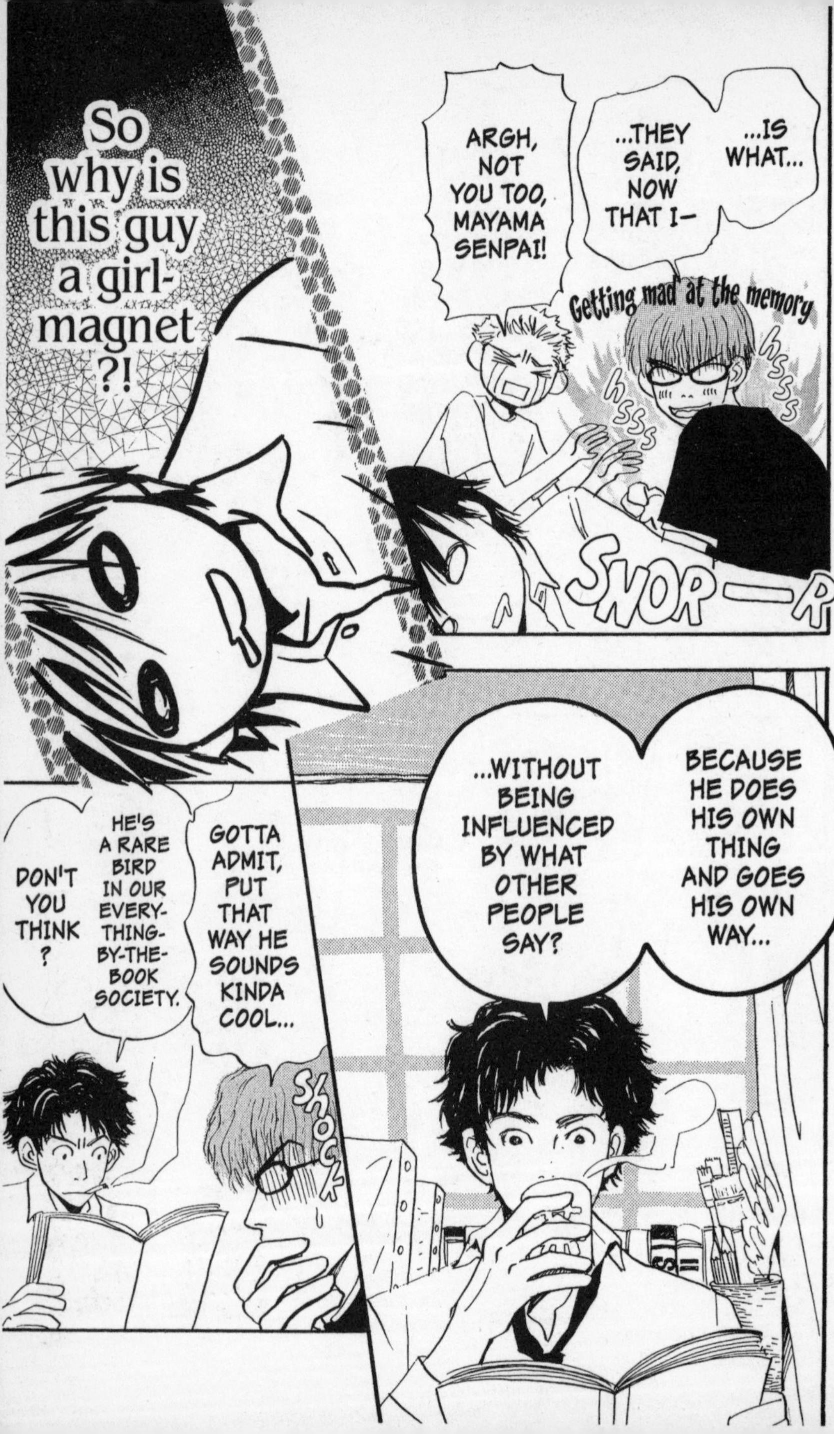
...IS WHAT...
...THEY SAID, NOW THAT I—
ARGH, NOT YOU TOO, MAYAMA SENPAI!
Getting mad at the memory
hsss
hsss
SNOR—R
So why is this guy a girl-magnet?!
BECAUSE HE DOES HIS OWN THING AND GOES HIS OWN WAY...
...WITHOUT BEING INFLUENCED BY WHAT OTHER PEOPLE SAY?
GOTTA ADMIT, PUT THAT WAY HE SOUNDS KINDA COOL...
SHOCK
HE'S A RARE BIRD IN OUR EVERY-THING-BY-THE-BOOK SOCIETY.
DON'T YOU THINK?

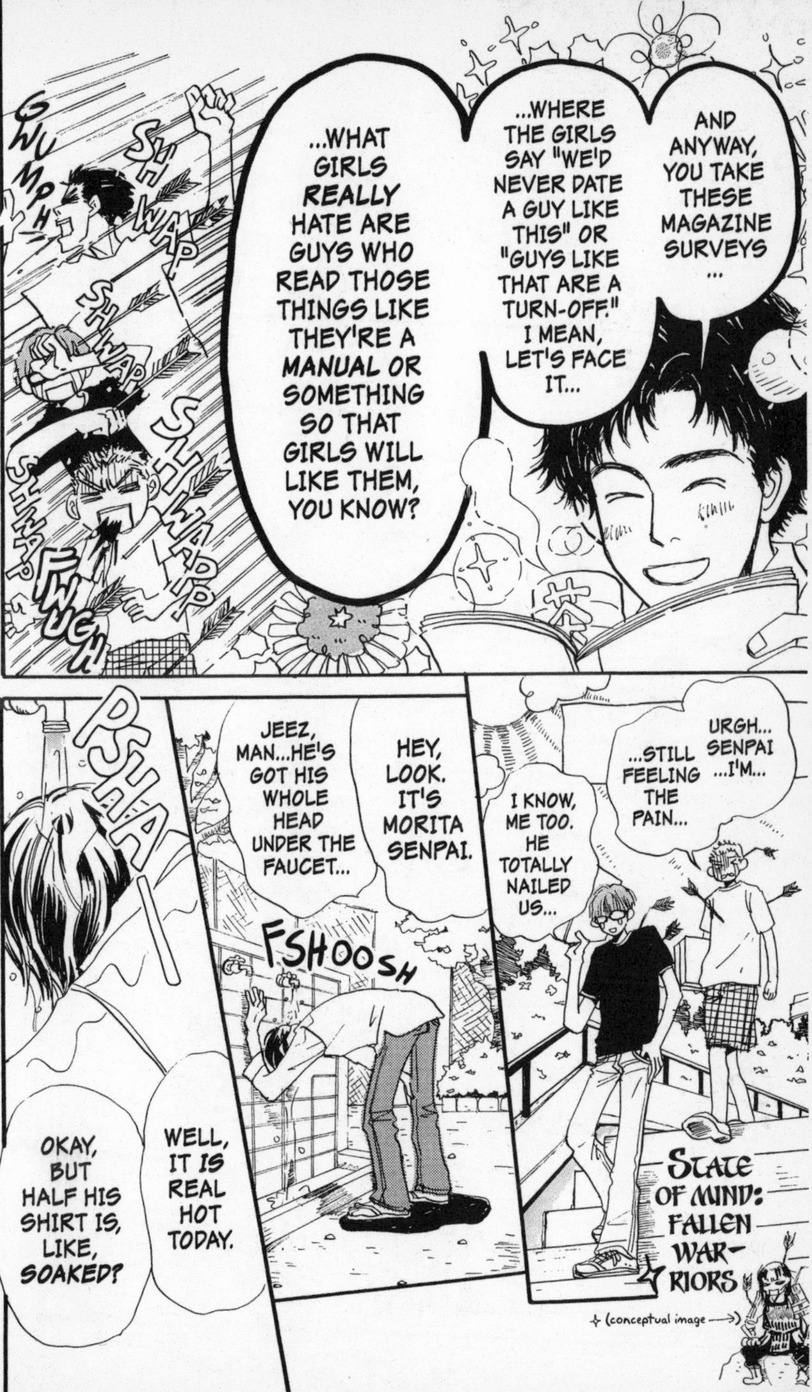
AND ANYWAY, YOU TAKE THESE MAGAZINE SURVEYS...
...WHERE THE GIRLS SAY "WE'D NEVER DATE A GUY LIKE THIS" OR "GUYS LIKE THAT ARE A TURN-OFF." I MEAN, LET'S FACE IT...
...WHAT GIRLS REALLY HATE ARE GUYS WHO READ THOSE THINGS LIKE THEY'RE A MANUAL OR SOMETHING SO THAT GIRLS WILL LIKE THEM, YOU KNOW?
SHWAP
GWUMPH
SHWAP
SHWAP
SHWAP
SHWAP
FWUCH
URGH... SENPAI ...I'M...
...STILL FEELING THE PAIN...
I KNOW, ME TOO. HE TOTALLY NAILED US...
STATE OF MIND: FALLEN WAR-RIORS
(conceptual image →)
HEY, LOOK. IT'S MORITA SENPAI.
JEEZ, MAN...HE'S GOT HIS WHOLE HEAD UNDER THE FAUCET...
FSHOOSH
PSHAA
WELL, IT IS REAL HOT TODAY.
OKAY, BUT HALF HIS SHIRT IS, LIKE, SOAKED?

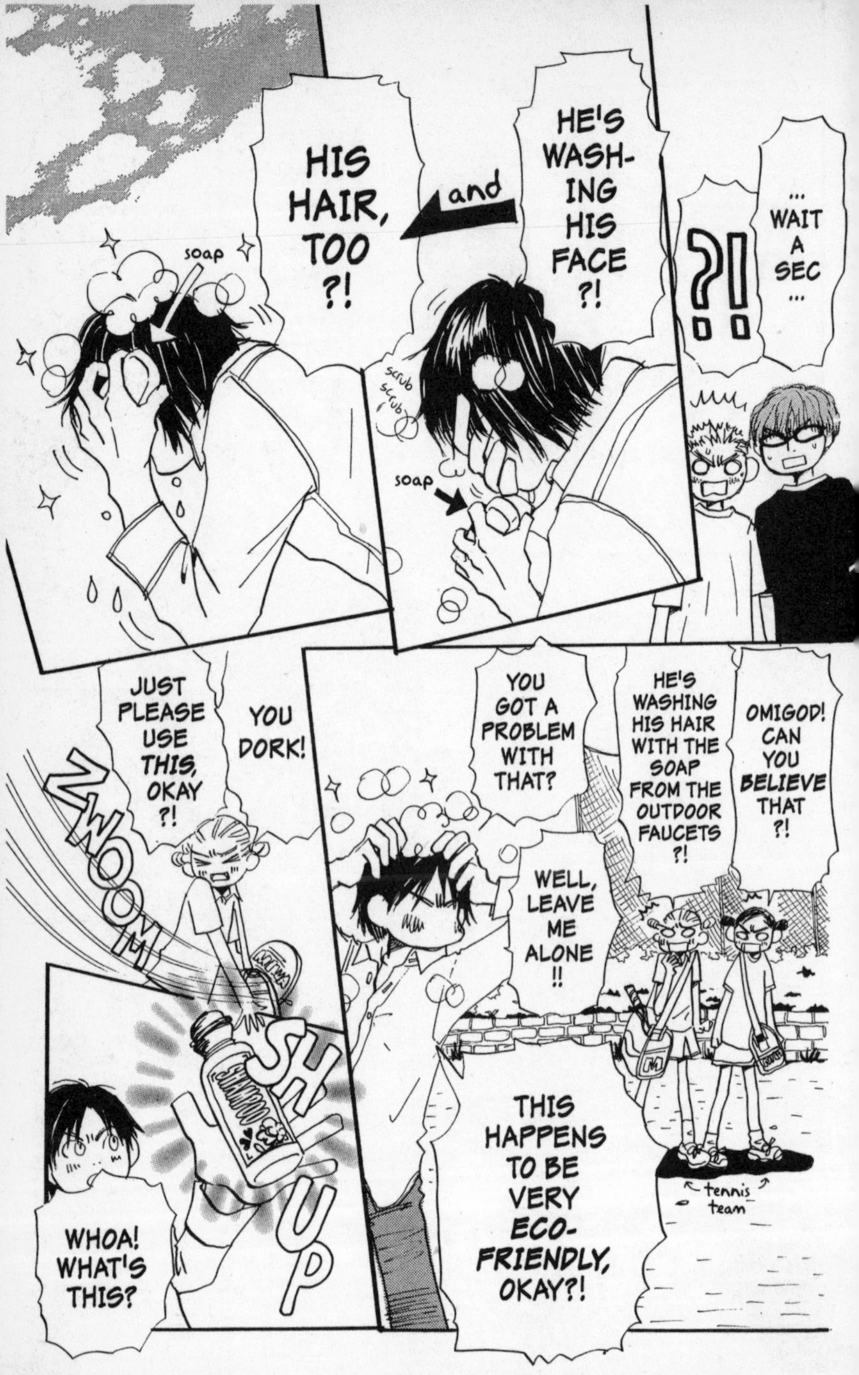

... WAIT A SEC ...
?!
HE'S WASHING HIS FACE ?!
scrub scrub
soap
and
HIS HAIR, TOO ?!
soap
OMIGOD! CAN YOU BELIEVE THAT ?!
HE'S WASHING HIS HAIR WITH THE SOAP FROM THE OUTDOOR FAUCETS ?!
YOU GOT A PROBLEM WITH THAT?
WELL, LEAVE ME ALONE !!
tennis team
THIS HAPPENS TO BE VERY ECO-FRIENDLY, OKAY?!
YOU DORK!
JUST PLEASE USE THIS, OKAY ?!
ZWOOM
SHUP
WHOA! WHAT'S THIS?

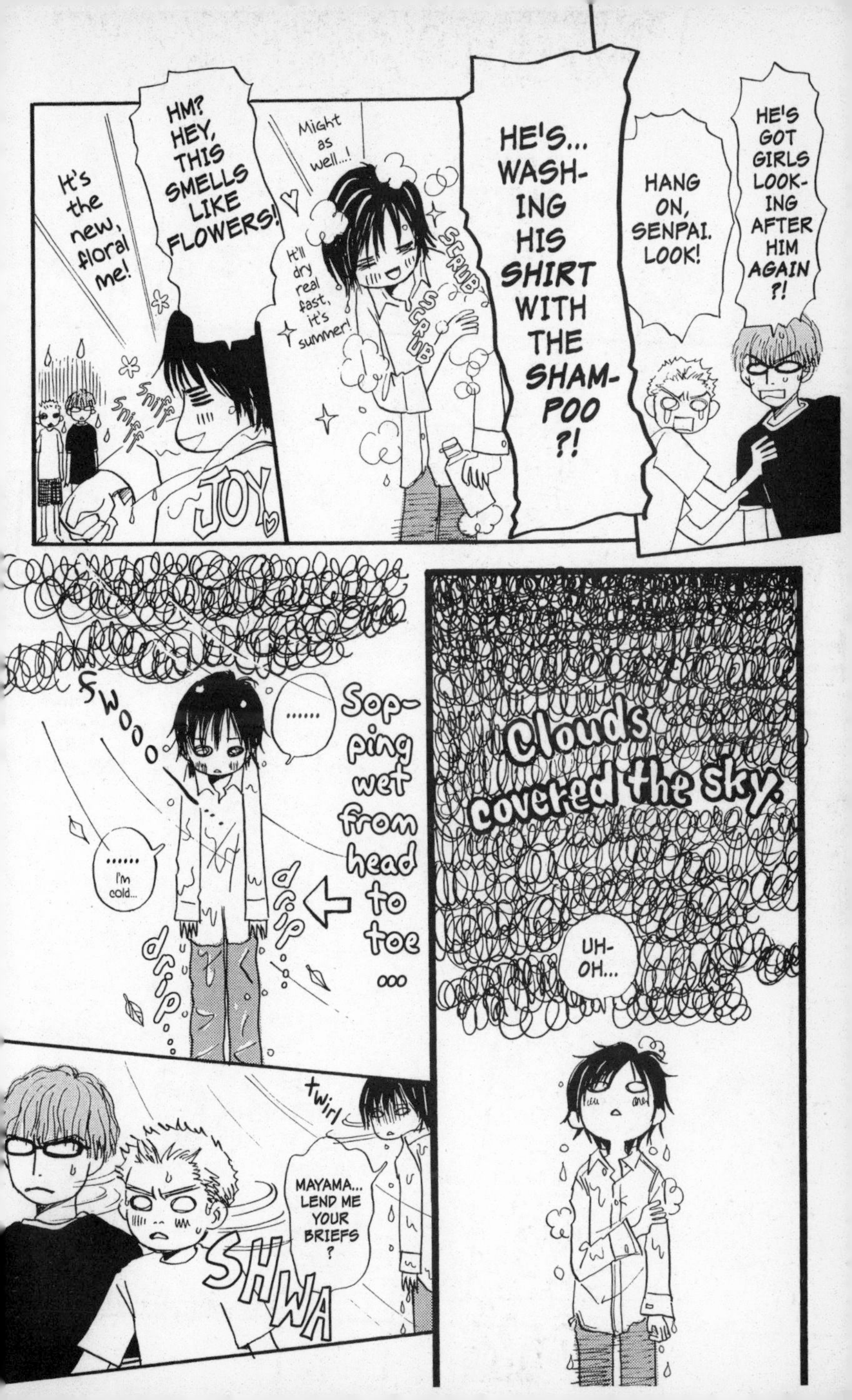
HE'S GOT GIRLS LOOKING AFTER HIM AGAIN?!
HANG ON, SENPAI. LOOK!
HE'S... WASHING HIS SHIRT WITH THE SHAMPOO?!
Might as well...!
SCRUB SCRUB
It'll dry real fast, it's summer!
HM? HEY, THIS SMELLS LIKE FLOWERS!
It's the new, floral me!
Sniff Sniff
JOY
Clouds covered the sky.
UH-OH...
Sopping wet from head to toe...
......
FWOOO
......
I'm cold...
drip drip
twirl
MAYAMA... LEND ME YOUR BRIEFS?
SHWA

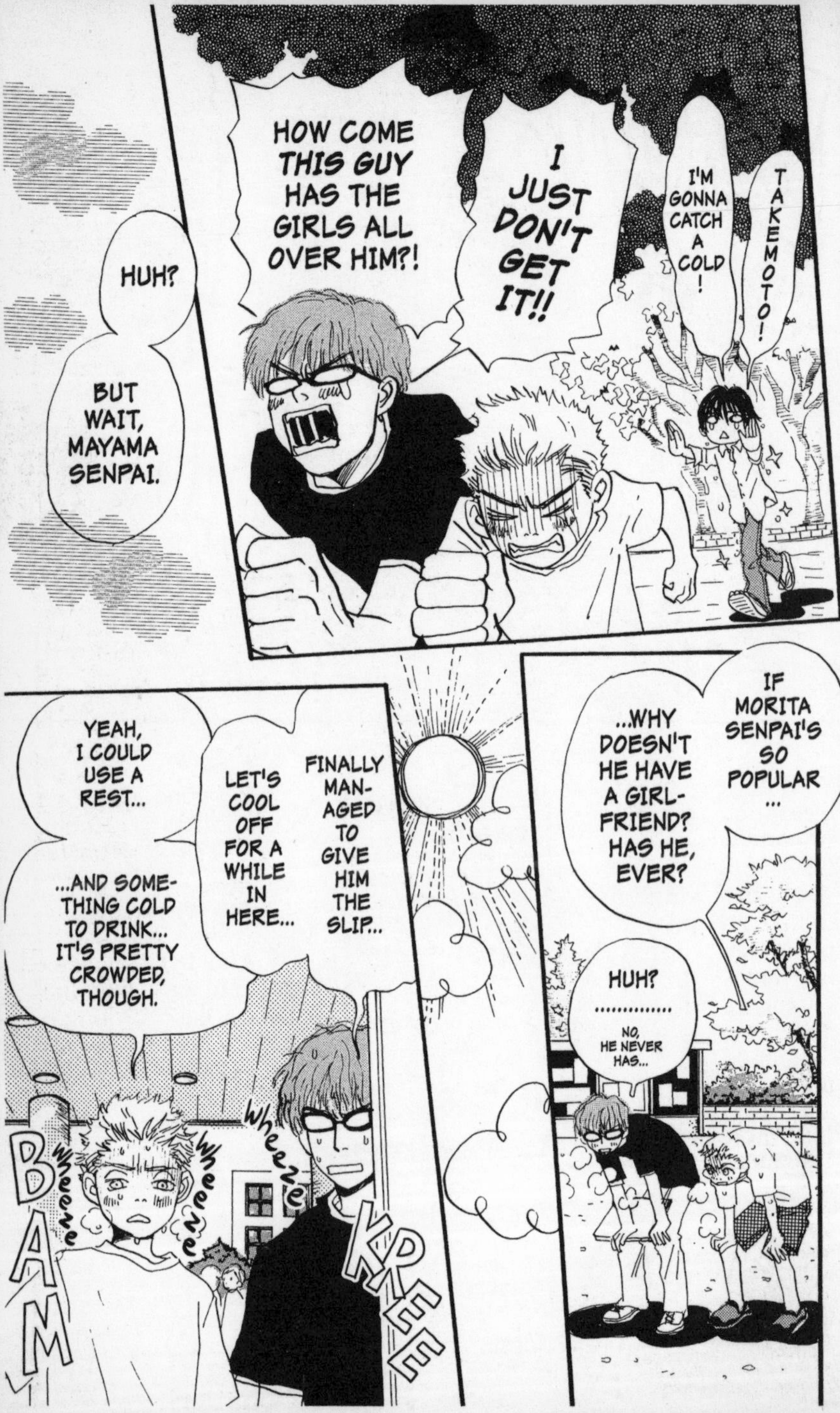
TAKEMOTO!
I'M GONNA CATCH A COLD!
I JUST DON'T GET IT!!
HOW COME THIS GUY HAS THE GIRLS ALL OVER HIM?!
HUH?
BUT WAIT, MAYAMA SENPAI.
IF MORITA SENPAI'S SO POPULAR...
...WHY DOESN'T HE HAVE A GIRL-FRIEND? HAS HE, EVER?
HUH? ....
NO, HE NEVER HAS...
FINALLY MAN-AGED TO GIVE HIM THE SLIP...
LET'S COOL OFF FOR A WHILE IN HERE...
KREE
wheeze
wheeze
YEAH, I COULD USE A REST...
...AND SOME-THING COLD TO DRINK... IT'S PRETTY CROWDED, THOUGH.
wheeze
BAM

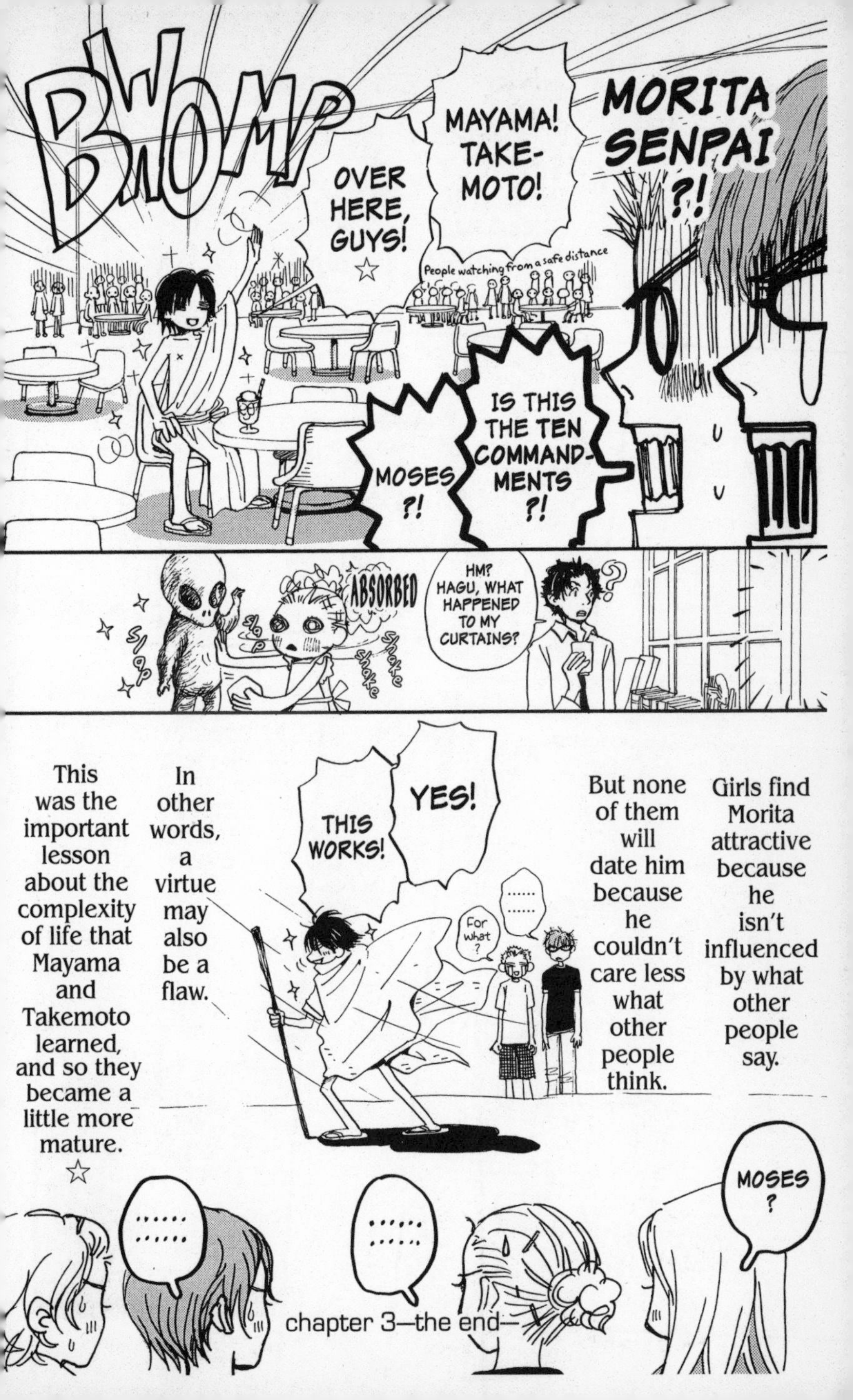

MORITA SENPAI ?!
MAYAMA! TAKE-MOTO!
OVER HERE, GUYS! ☆
BWOMP
People watching from a safe distance
IS THIS THE TEN COMMAND-MENTS ?!
MOSES ?!
HM? HAGU, WHAT HAPPENED TO MY CURTAINS?
ABSORBED
shake shake
slap slap
Girls find Morita attractive because he isn't influenced by what other people say.
But none of them will date him because he couldn't care less what other people think.
......
......
For what?
YES!
THIS WORKS!
In other words, a virtue may also be a flaw.
This was the important lesson about the complexity of life that Mayama and Takemoto learned, and so they became a little more mature. ☆
MOSES?
......
......
......
......
chapter 3—the end—

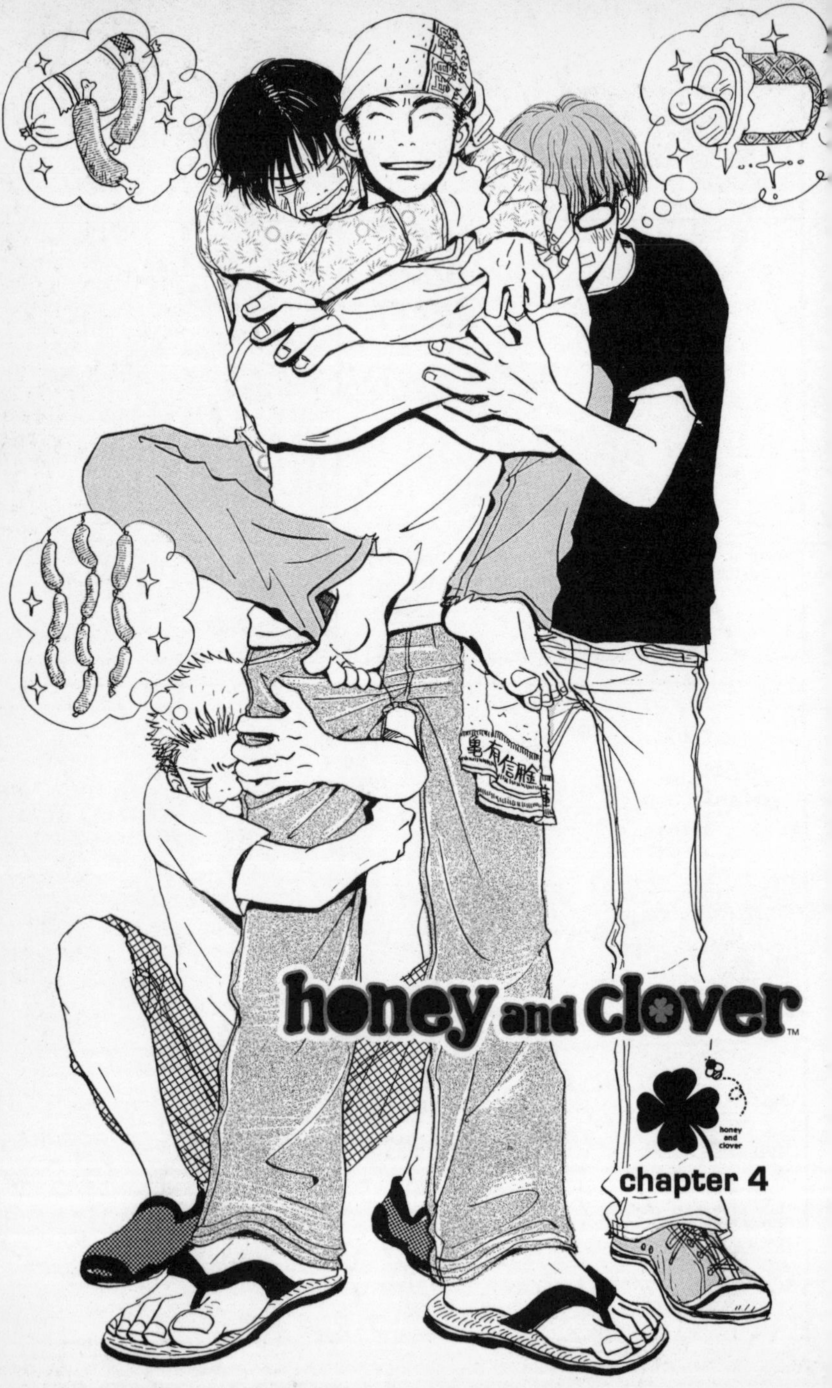
honey and clover™
honey and clover
chapter 4

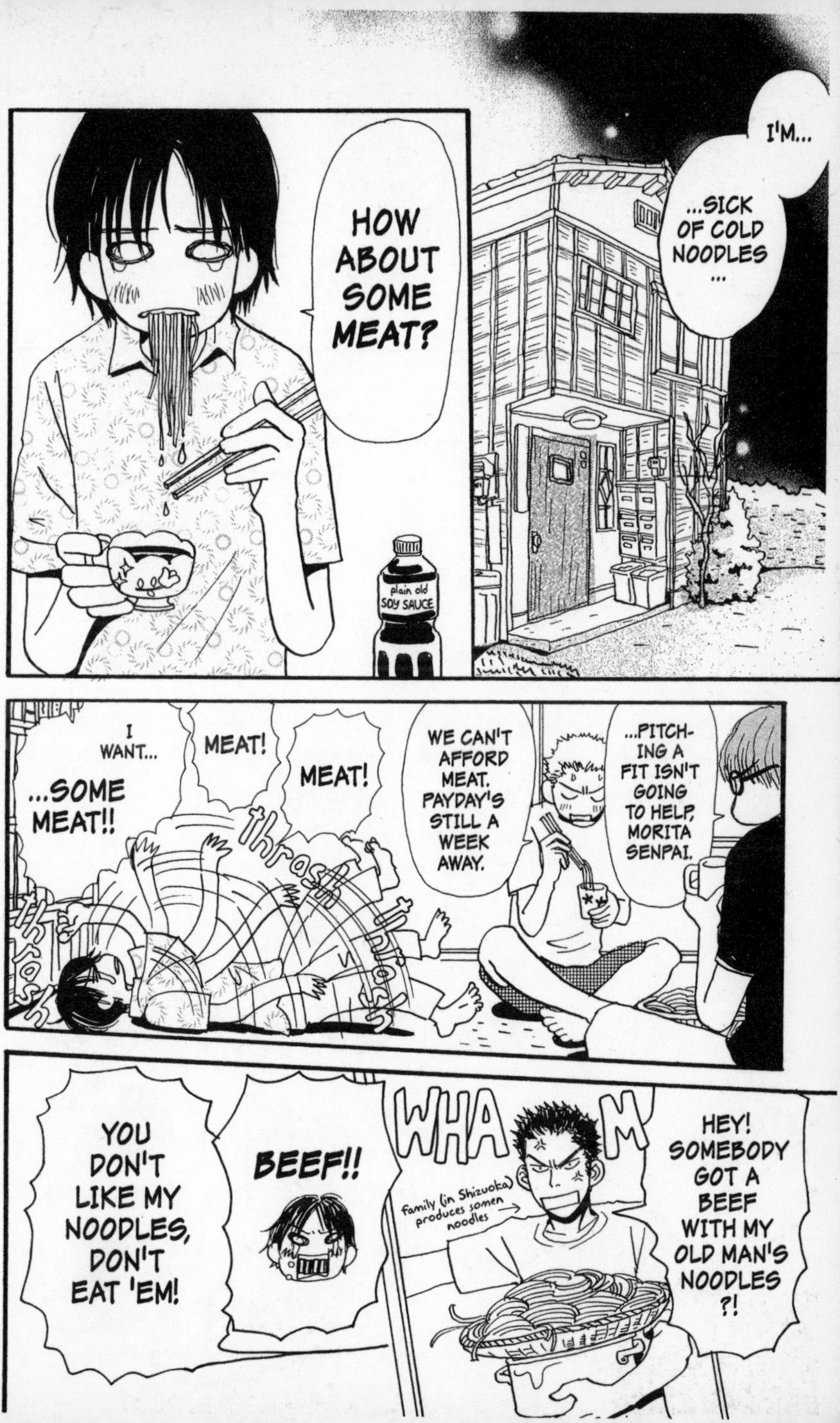
I'M...
...SICK OF COLD NOODLES ...
HOW ABOUT SOME MEAT?
plain old SOY SAUCE
...PITCHING A FIT ISN'T GOING TO HELP, MORITA SENPAI.
WE CAN'T AFFORD MEAT. PAYDAY'S STILL A WEEK AWAY.
MEAT!
MEAT!
I WANT...
...SOME MEAT!!
thrash thrash thrash
HEY! SOMEBODY GOT A BEEF WITH MY OLD MAN'S NOODLES ?!
WHAM
family (in Shizuoka) produces somen noodles
BEEF!!
YOU DON'T LIKE MY NOODLES, DON'T EAT 'EM!

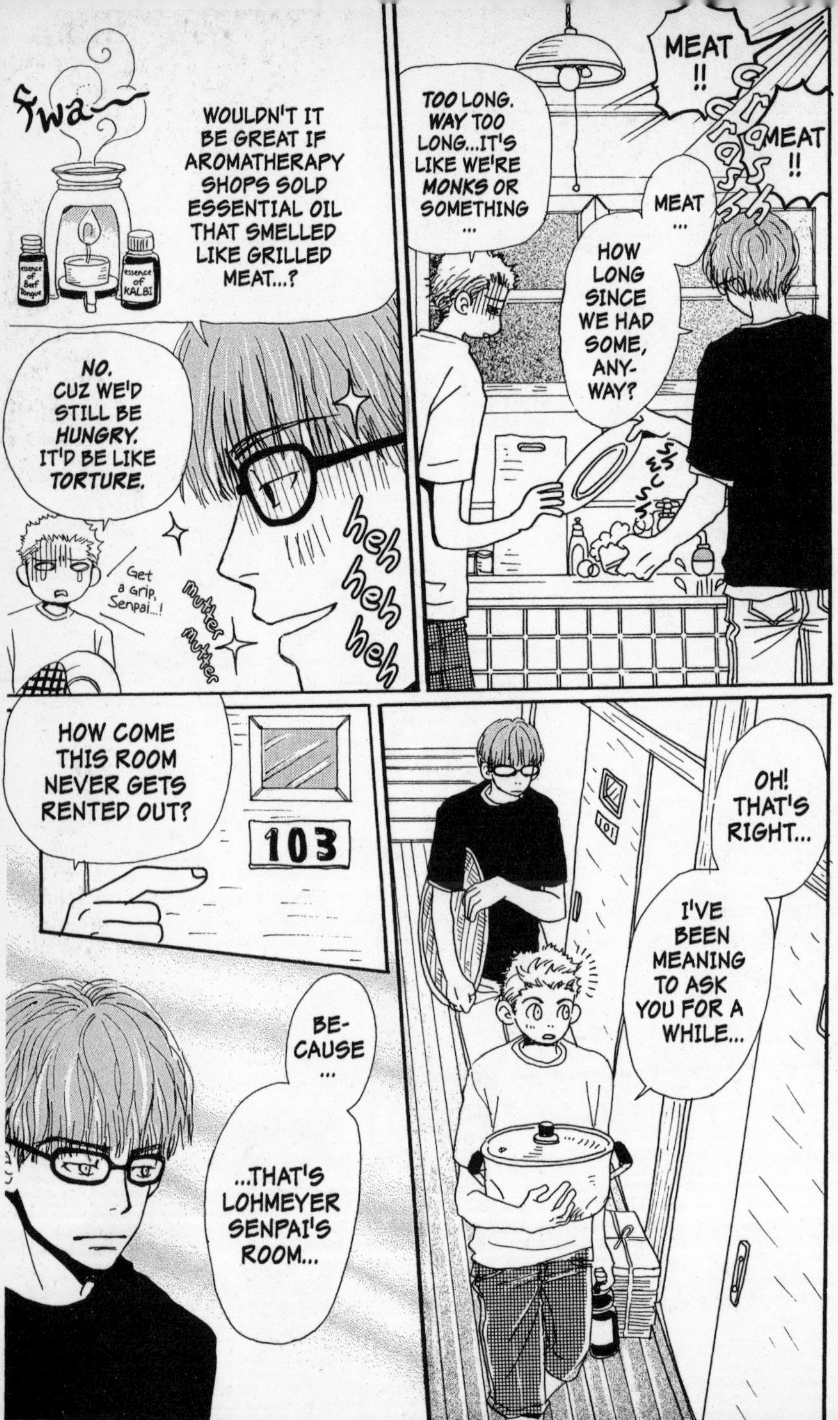
MEAT !!
crash
MEAT !!
MEAT ...
HOW LONG SINCE WE HAD SOME, ANY-WAY?
TOO LONG. WAY TOO LONG...IT'S LIKE WE'RE MONKS OR SOMETHING ...
fwa~~
WOULDN'T IT BE GREAT IF AROMATHERAPY SHOPS SOLD ESSENTIAL OIL THAT SMELLED LIKE GRILLED MEAT...?
essence of Beef Tongue
essence of KALBI
NO. CUZ WE'D STILL BE HUNGRY. IT'D BE LIKE TORTURE.
heh heh heh
mutter mutter
Get a Grip, Senpai...!
OH! THAT'S RIGHT...
I'VE BEEN MEANING TO ASK YOU FOR A WHILE...
101
HOW COME THIS ROOM NEVER GETS RENTED OUT?
103
BE-CAUSE ...
...THAT'S LOHMEYER SENPAI'S ROOM...

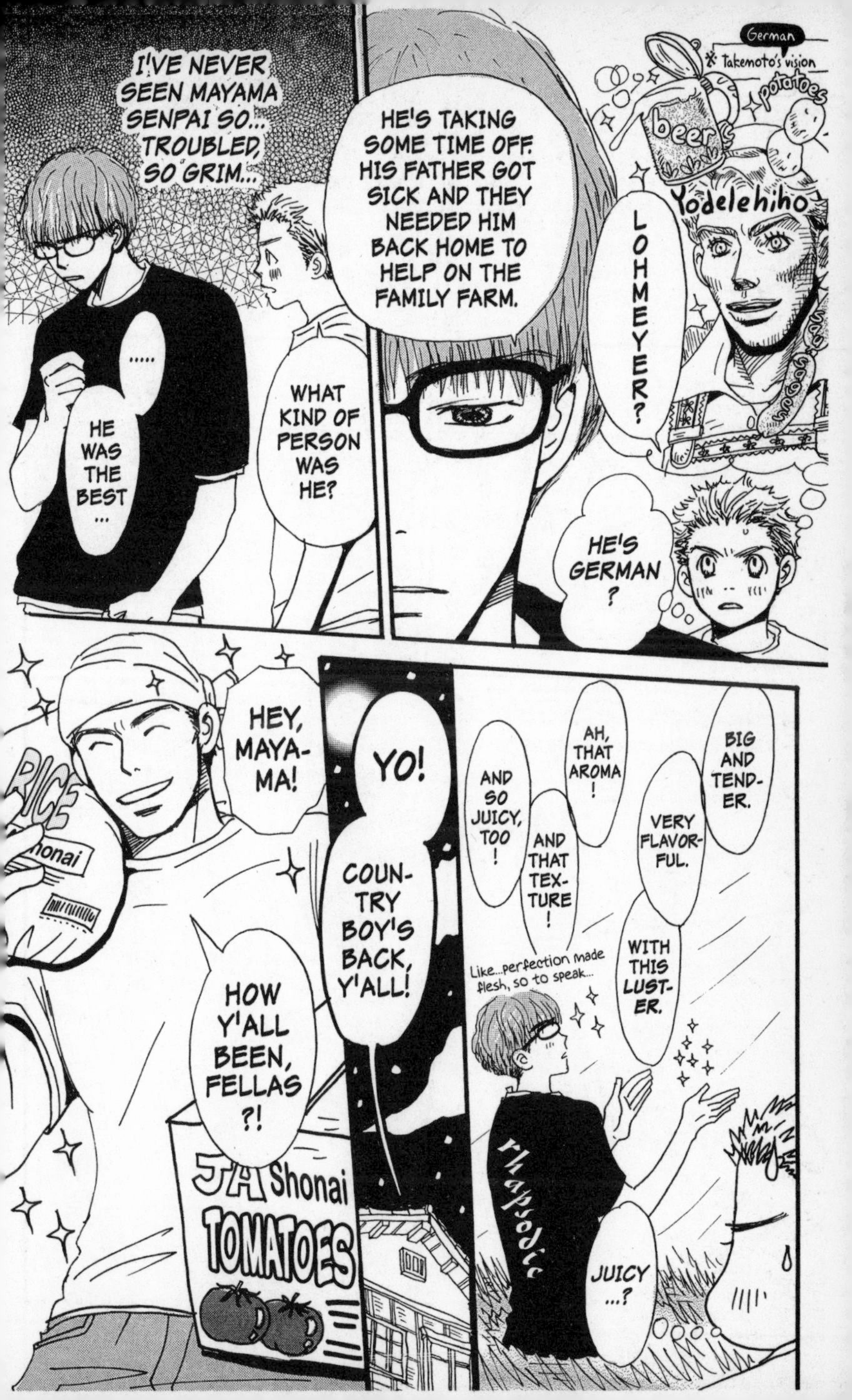
German
※ Takemoto's vision
beer
potatoes
Yodelehiho
sausages
LOHMEYER?
HE'S GERMAN?
HE'S TAKING SOME TIME OFF. HIS FATHER GOT SICK AND THEY NEEDED HIM BACK HOME TO HELP ON THE FAMILY FARM.
I'VE NEVER SEEN MAYAMA SENPAI SO... TROUBLED, SO GRIM...
WHAT KIND OF PERSON WAS HE?
.....
HE WAS THE BEST...
BIG AND TENDER.
AH, THAT AROMA!
VERY FLAVORFUL.
AND SO JUICY, TOO!
AND THAT TEXTURE!
WITH THIS LUSTER.
Like...perfection made flesh, so to speak...
rhapsodic
JUICY...?
YO!
COUNTRY BOY'S BACK, Y'ALL!
HEY, MAYAMA!
RICE
Shonai
HOW Y'ALL BEEN, FELLAS?!
JA Shonai
TOMATOES

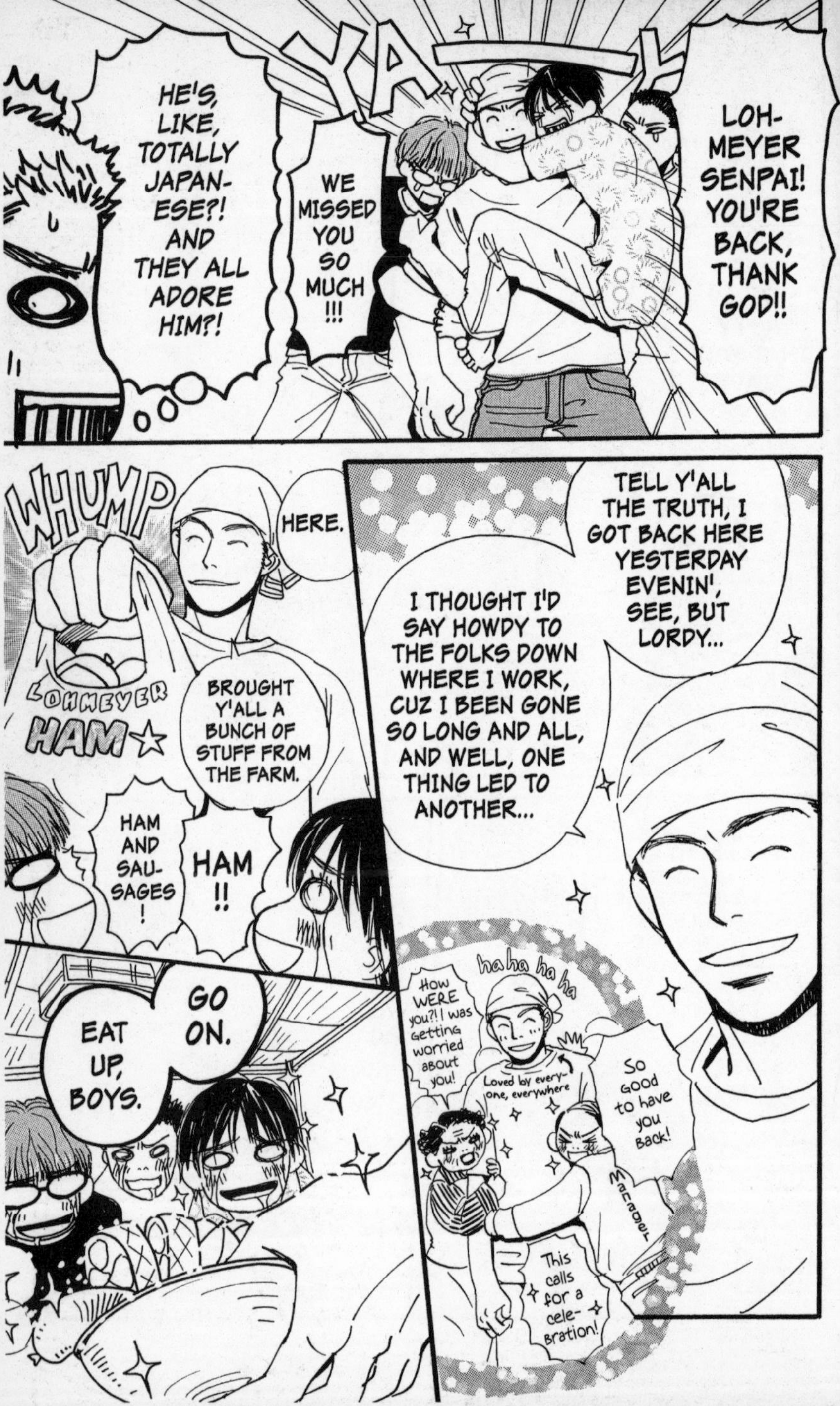
LOH-MEYER SENPAI! YOU'RE BACK, THANK GOD!!
YAY
WE MISSED YOU SO MUCH!!!
HE'S, LIKE, TOTALLY JAPANESE?! AND THEY ALL ADORE HIM?!
TELL Y'ALL THE TRUTH, I GOT BACK HERE YESTERDAY EVENIN', SEE, BUT LORDY...
I THOUGHT I'D SAY HOWDY TO THE FOLKS DOWN WHERE I WORK, CUZ I BEEN GONE SO LONG AND ALL, AND WELL, ONE THING LED TO ANOTHER...
ha ha ha ha
How WERE you?! I was Getting worried about you!
Loved by everyone, everywhere
So Good to have you Back!
Manager
This calls for a celebration!
WHUMP
HERE.
BROUGHT Y'ALL A BUNCH OF STUFF FROM THE FARM.
LOHMEYER HAM☆
HAM!!
HAM AND SAUSAGES!
GO ON.
EAT UP, BOYS.

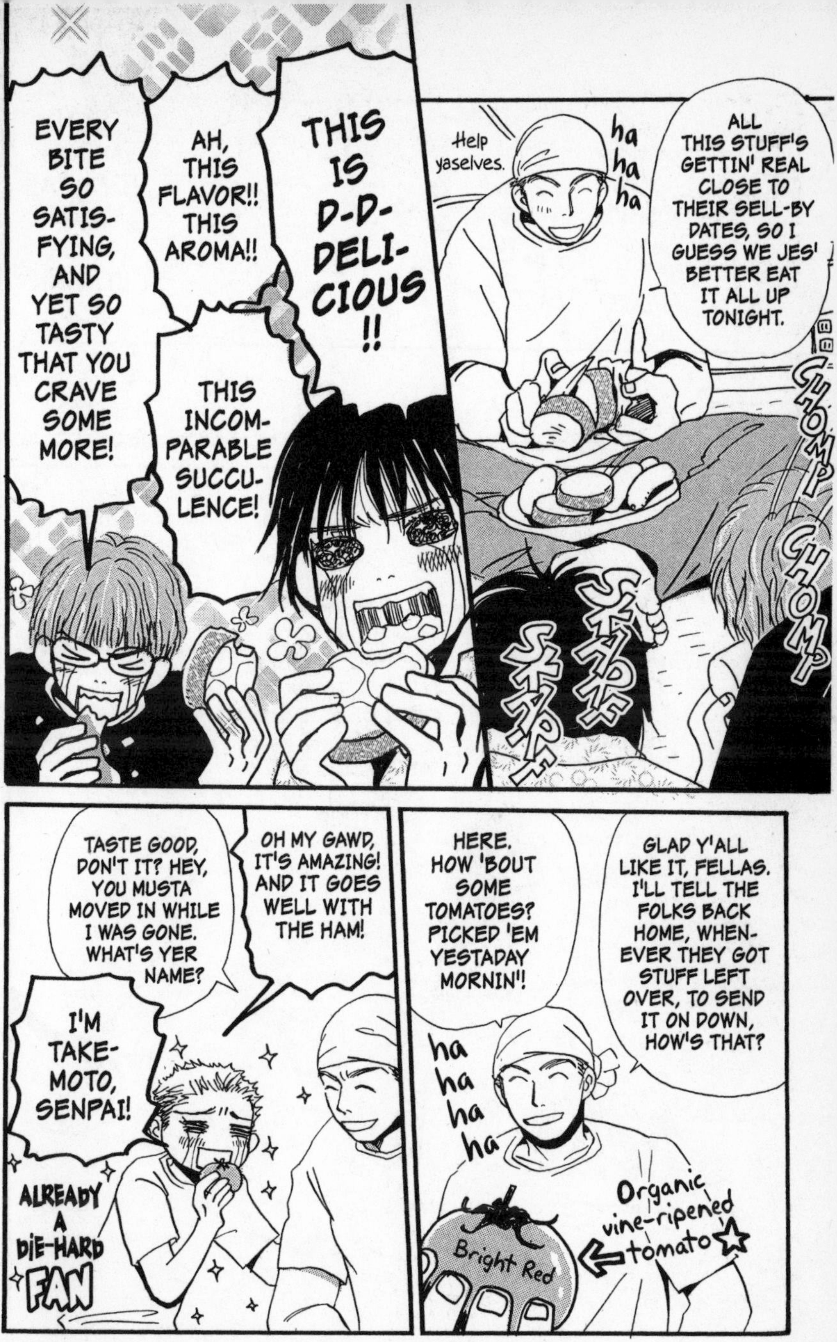
ALL THIS STUFF'S GETTIN' REAL CLOSE TO THEIR SELL-BY DATES, SO I GUESS WE JES' BETTER EAT IT ALL UP TONIGHT.
ha ha ha
Help yaselves.
CHOMP CHOMP CHOMP
THIS IS D-D-DELICIOUS!!
AH, THIS FLAVOR!! THIS AROMA!!
THIS INCOMPARABLE SUCCULENCE!
EVERY BITE SO SATISFYING, AND YET SO TASTY THAT YOU CRAVE SOME MORE!
GLAD Y'ALL LIKE IT, FELLAS. I'LL TELL THE FOLKS BACK HOME, WHENEVER THEY GOT STUFF LEFT OVER, TO SEND IT ON DOWN, HOW'S THAT?
HERE. HOW 'BOUT SOME TOMATOES? PICKED 'EM YESTADAY MORNIN'!
ha ha ha ha
Organic vine-ripened tomato☆
Bright Red
TASTE GOOD, DON'T IT? HEY, YOU MUSTA MOVED IN WHILE I WAS GONE. WHAT'S YER NAME?
OH MY GAWD, IT'S AMAZING! AND IT GOES WELL WITH THE HAM!
I'M TAKEMOTO, SENPAI!
ALREADY A DIE-HARD FAN

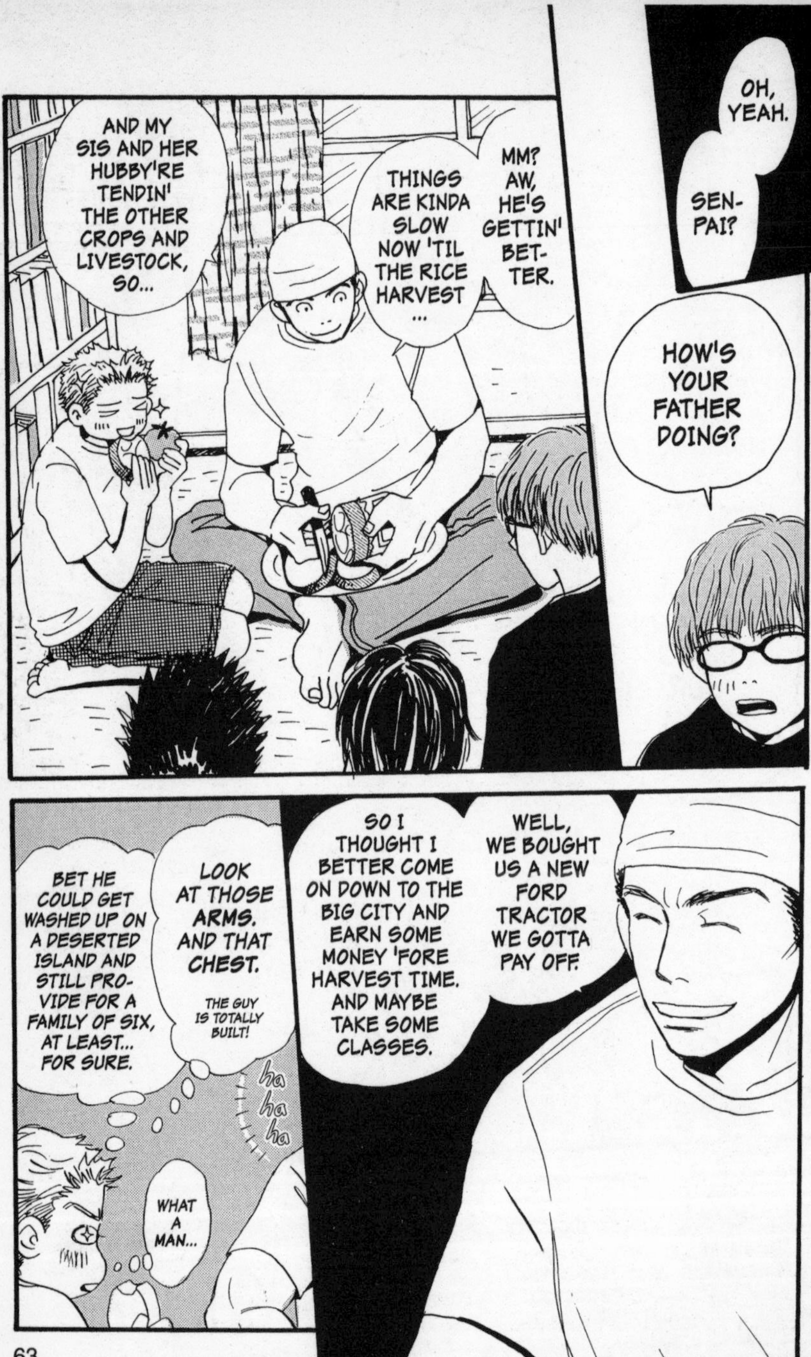
OH, YEAH.
SEN-PAI?
HOW'S YOUR FATHER DOING?
MM? AW, HE'S GETTIN' BET-TER.
THINGS ARE KINDA SLOW NOW 'TIL THE RICE HARVEST ...
AND MY SIS AND HER HUBBY'RE TENDIN' THE OTHER CROPS AND LIVESTOCK, SO...
WELL, WE BOUGHT US A NEW FORD TRACTOR WE GOTTA PAY OFF.
SO I THOUGHT I BETTER COME ON DOWN TO THE BIG CITY AND EARN SOME MONEY 'FORE HARVEST TIME. AND MAYBE TAKE SOME CLASSES.
ha ha ha
LOOK AT THOSE ARMS. AND THAT CHEST.
THE GUY IS TOTALLY BUILT!
BET HE COULD GET WASHED UP ON A DESERTED ISLAND AND STILL PRO-VIDE FOR A FAMILY OF SIX, AT LEAST... FOR SURE.
WHAT A MAN...

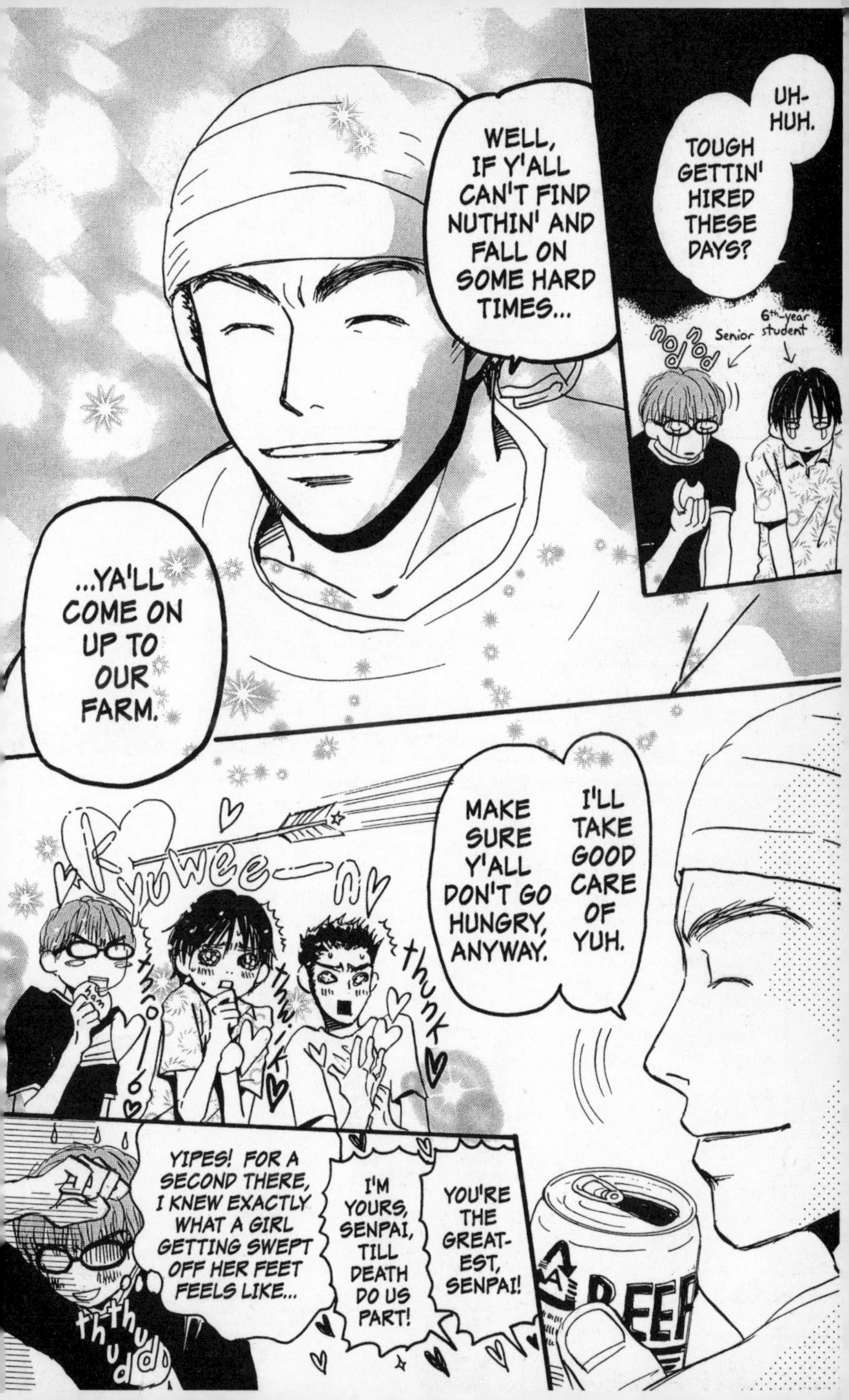
UH-HUH.
TOUGH GETTIN' HIRED THESE DAYS?
Senior
6th-year student
WELL, IF Y'ALL CAN'T FIND NUTHIN' AND FALL ON SOME HARD TIMES...
...YA'LL COME ON UP TO OUR FARM.
I'LL TAKE GOOD CARE OF YUH.
MAKE SURE Y'ALL DON'T GO HUNGRY, ANYWAY.
Kyuwee—n
thunk
YOU'RE THE GREAT-EST, SENPAI!
I'M YOURS, SENPAI, TILL DEATH DO US PART!
YIPES! FOR A SECOND THERE, I KNEW EXACTLY WHAT A GIRL GETTING SWEPT OFF HER FEET FEELS LIKE...
thud thud
BEER

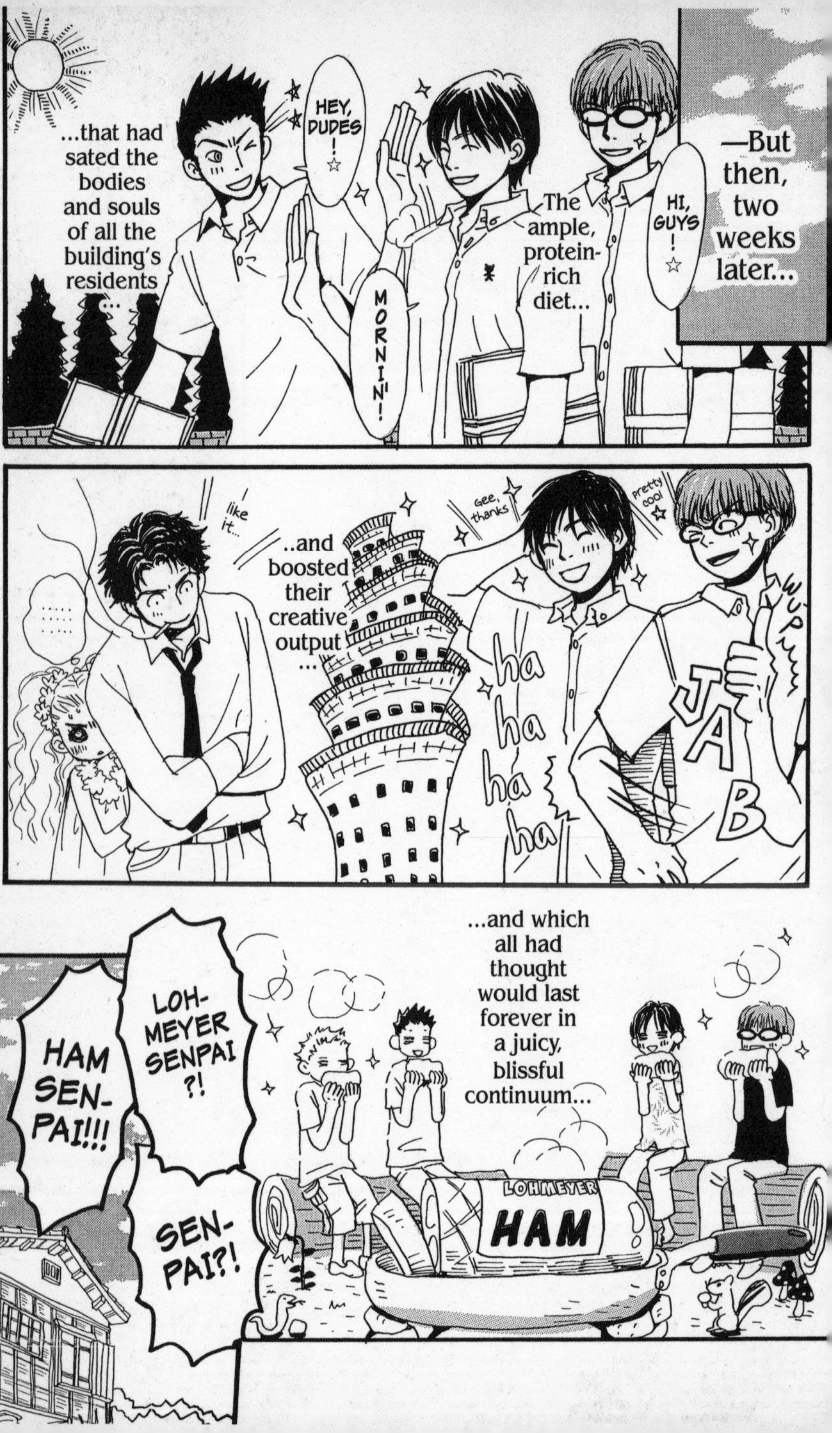
—But then, two weeks later...
HI, GUYS! ☆
The ample, protein-rich diet...
MORNIN'!
HEY, DUDES! ☆
...that had sated the bodies and souls of all the building's residents...
WUP
JAB
pretty cool ☆
ha ha ha ha
Gee, thanks
..and boosted their creative output...
I like it...
......
...and which all had thought would last forever in a juicy, blissful continuum...
LOHMEYER
HAM
LOH-MEYER SENPAI?!
SENPAI?!
HAM SEN-PAI!!!

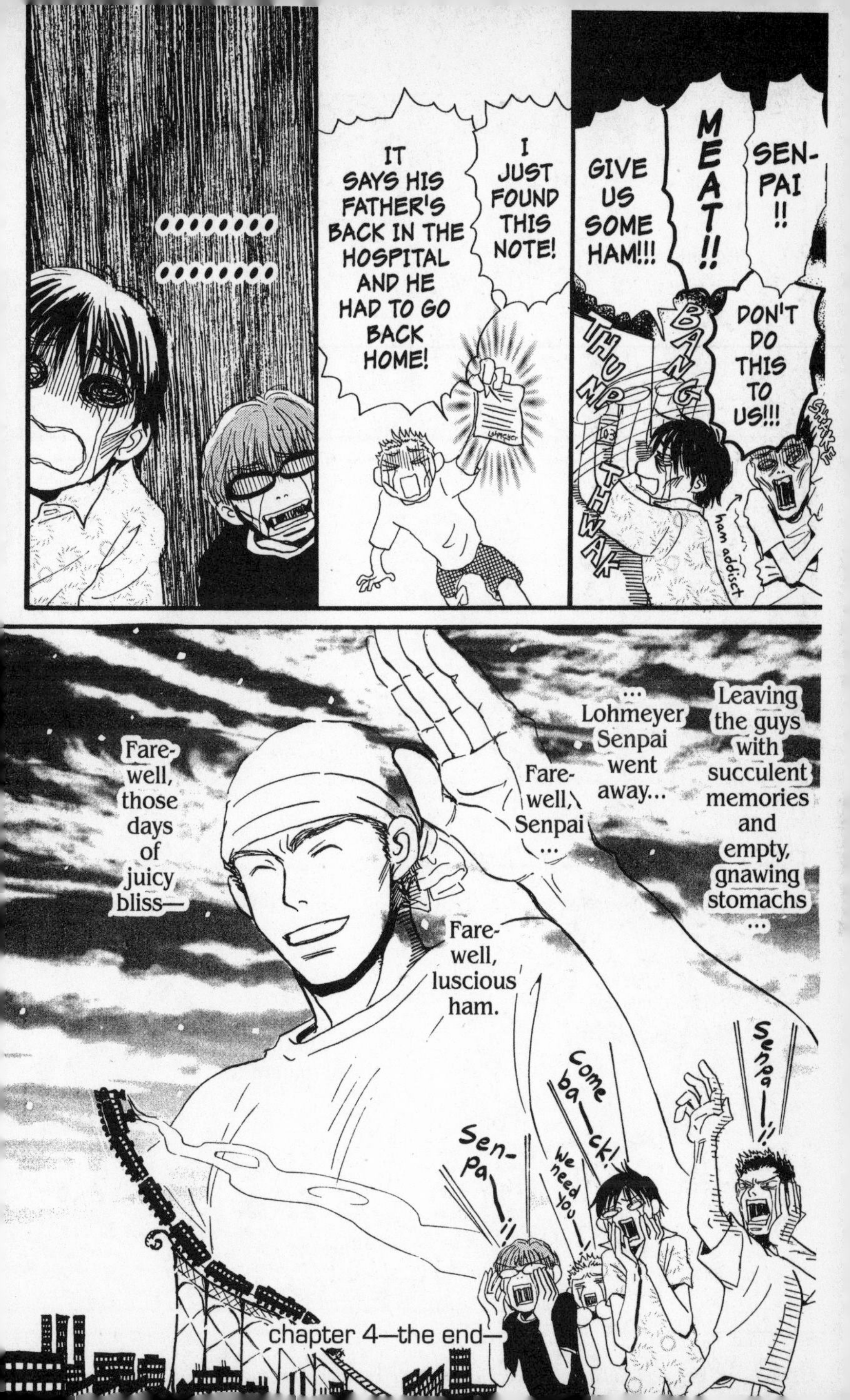
SEN-PAI !!
MEAT!!
GIVE US SOME HAM!!!
DON'T DO THIS TO US!!!
SHAKE
BANG
THUNP
THWAK
ham addict
I JUST FOUND THIS NOTE!
IT SAYS HIS FATHER'S BACK IN THE HOSPITAL AND HE HAD TO GO BACK HOME!
....
....
Leaving the guys with succulent memories and empty, gnawing stomachs...
... Lohmeyer Senpai went away...
Fare-well, Senpai...
Fare-well, those days of juicy bliss—
Fare-well, luscious ham.
Senpa—i!!
Come ba—ck!
we need you—!
Sen-pa—i!!
chapter 4—the end—

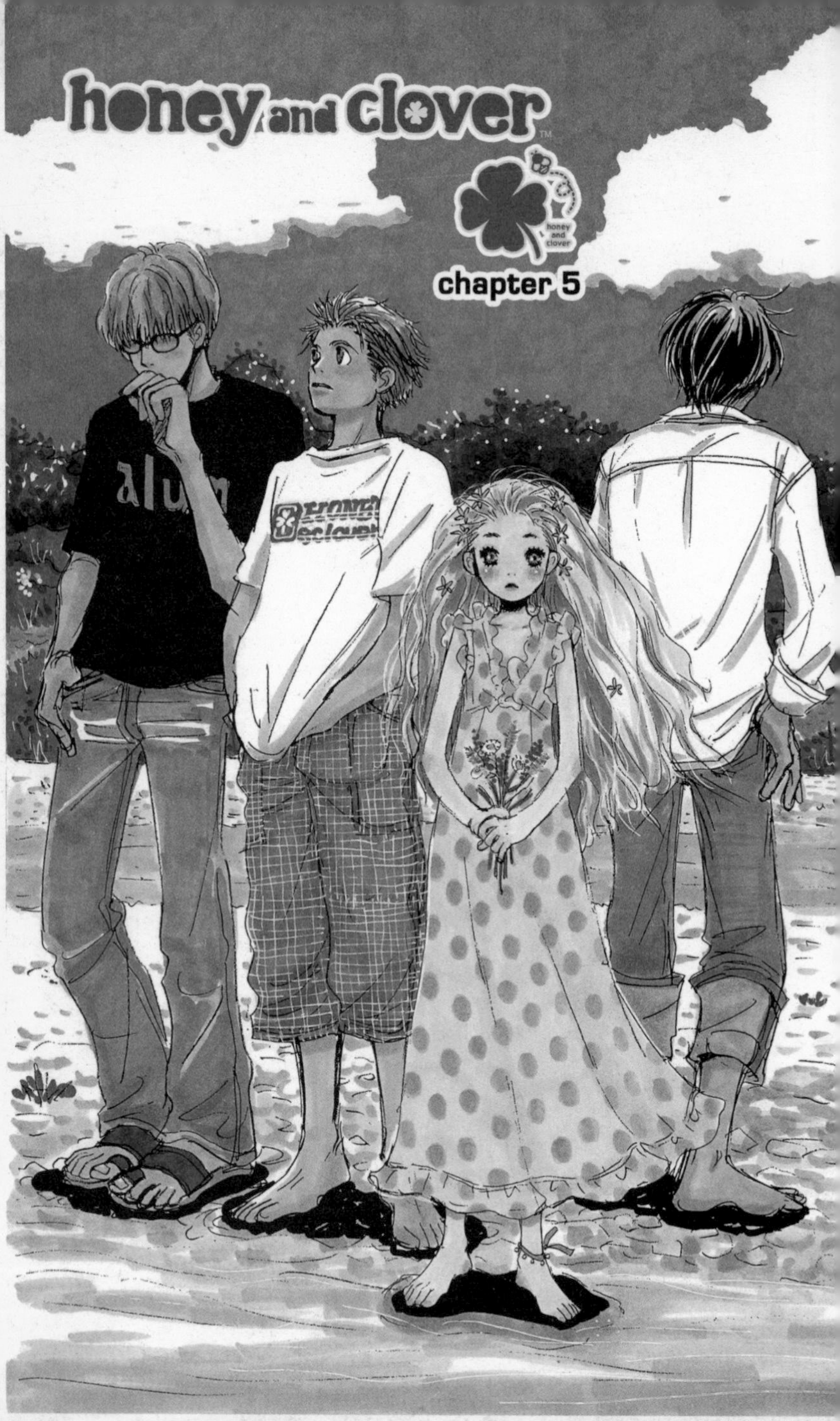
honey and clover™
honey and clover
chapter 5

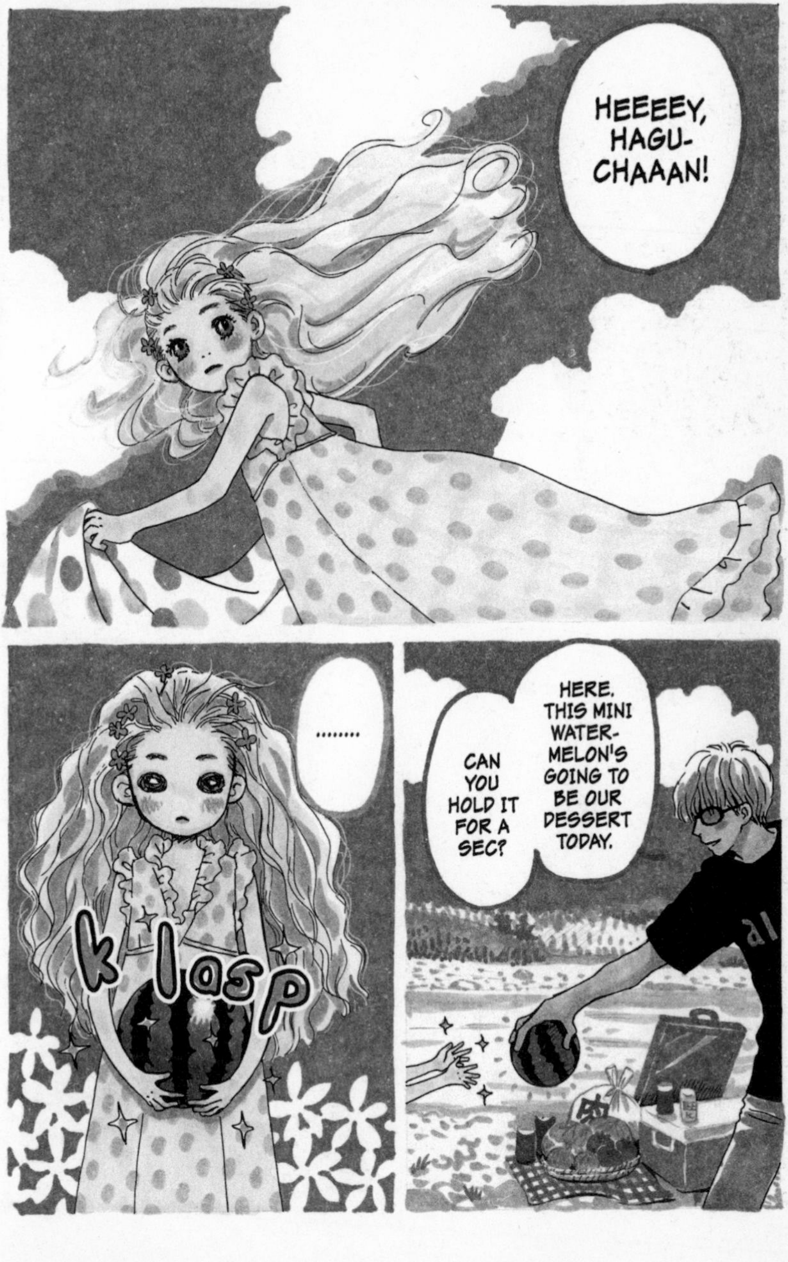
HEEEEY, HAGU-CHAAAN!
HERE. THIS MINI WATER-MELON'S GOING TO BE OUR DESSERT TODAY.
CAN YOU HOLD IT FOR A SEC?
....
klasp

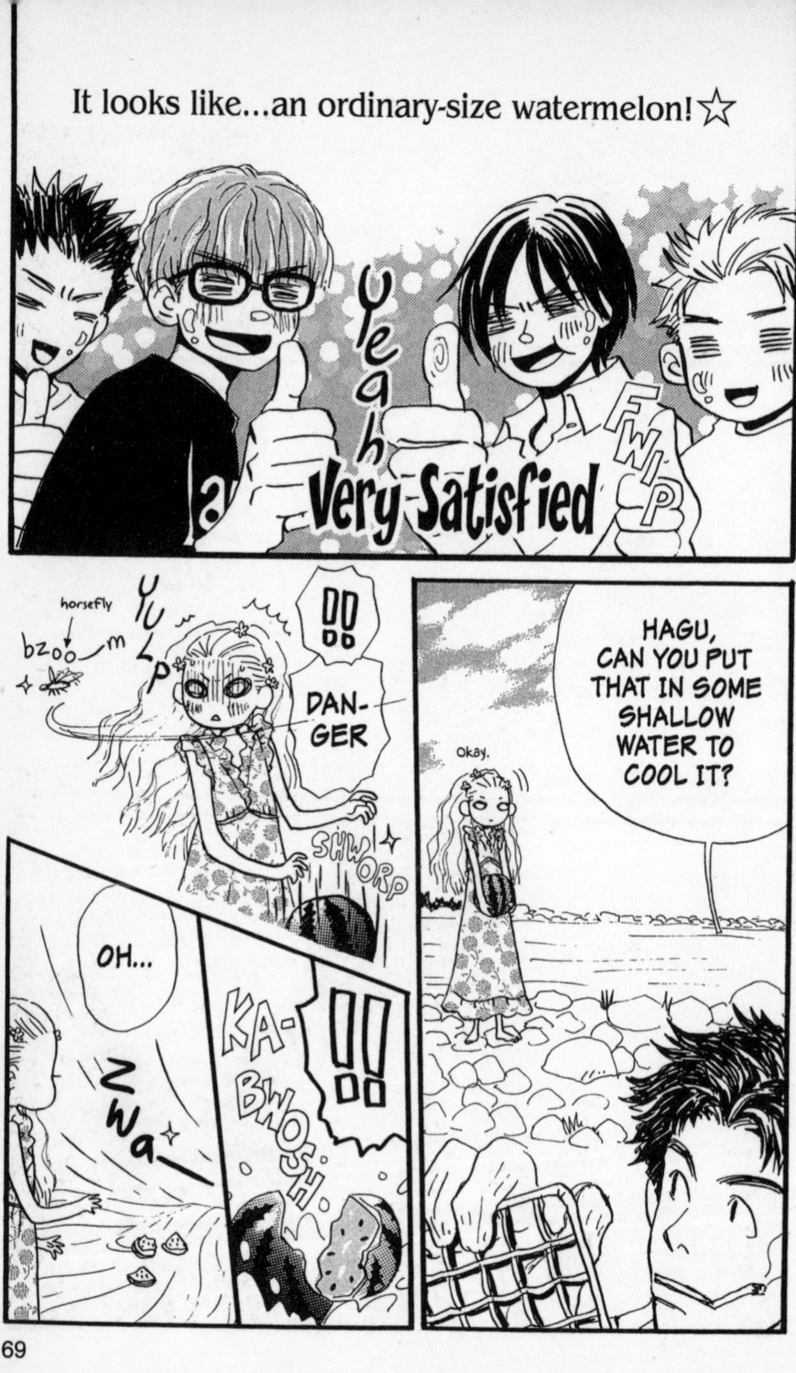
It looks like...an ordinary-size watermelon!☆
Yeah
Very Satisfied
FWIP
HAGU, CAN YOU PUT THAT IN SOME SHALLOW WATER TO COOL IT?
Okay.
!!
DAN-GER
YULP
horsefly
bzoooom
SHWORP
!!
KA-BWOSH
OH...
Zwa

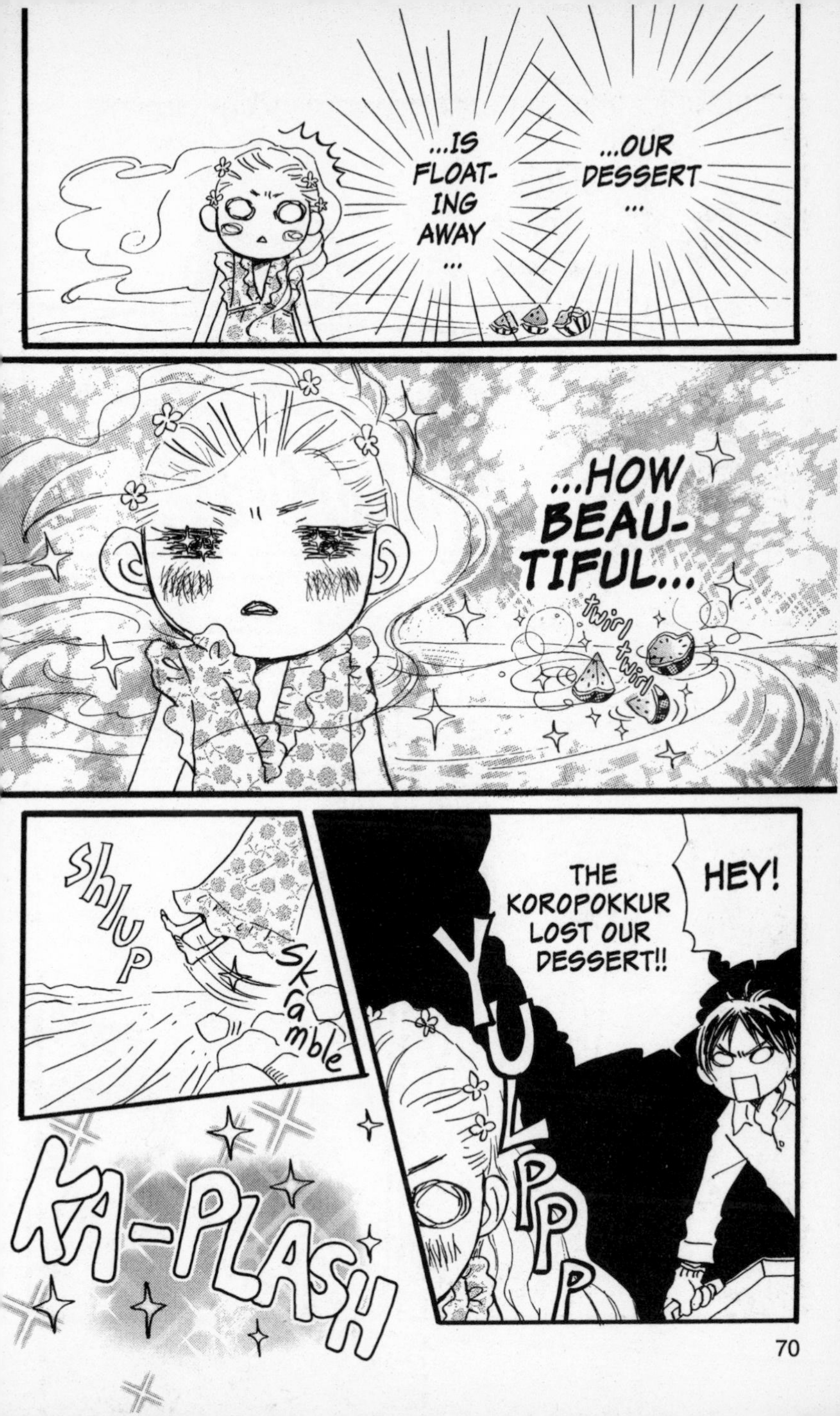
...OUR DESSERT...
...IS FLOAT-ING AWAY...
...HOW BEAU-TIFUL...
twirl twirl
HEY!
THE KOROPOKKUR LOST OUR DESSERT!!
YULPPPP
SHLUP
SKRAMBLE
KA-PLASH

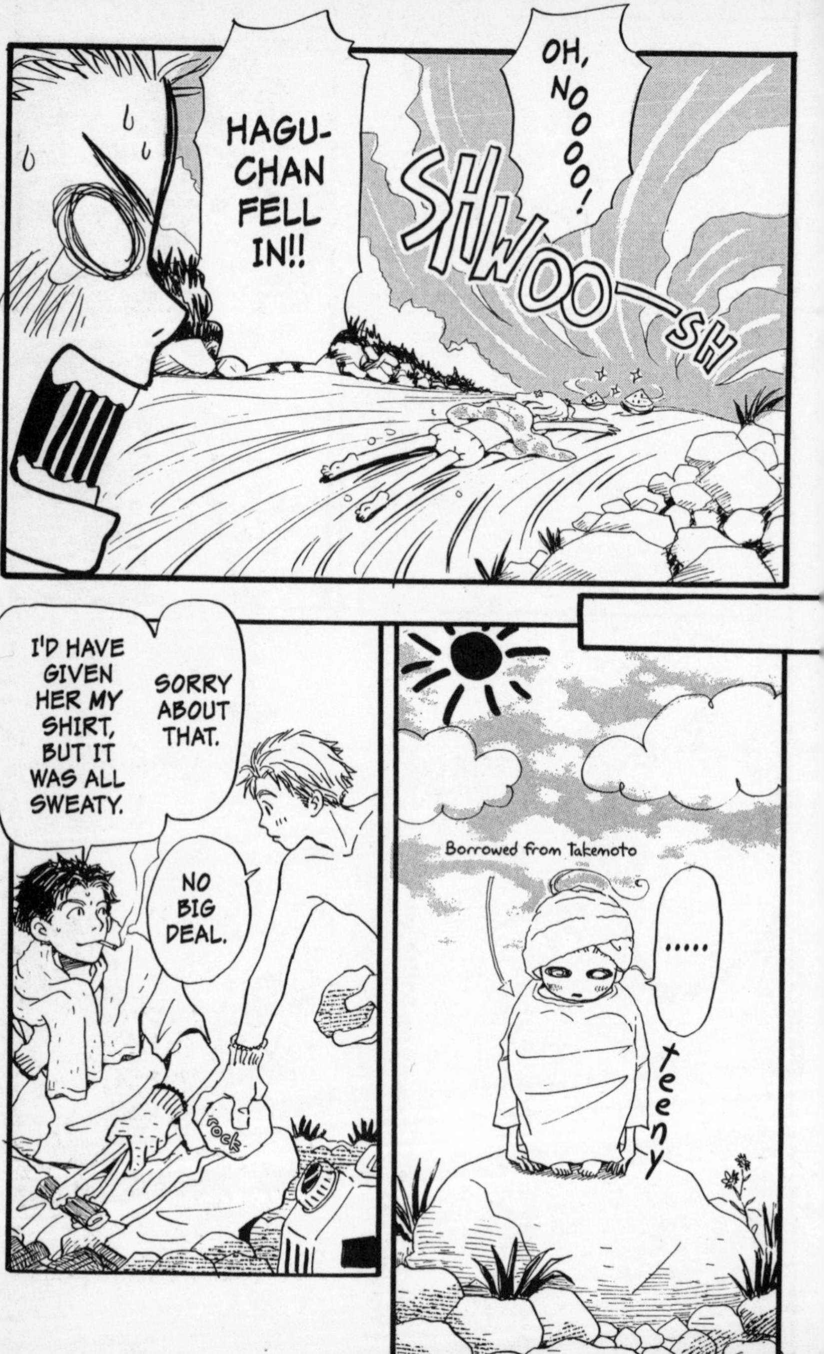
OH, NOOOOO!
SHWOO—SH
HAGU-CHAN FELL IN!!
Borrowed from Takemoto
......
teeny
SORRY ABOUT THAT.
I'D HAVE GIVEN HER MY SHIRT, BUT IT WAS ALL SWEATY.
NO BIG DEAL.
rock

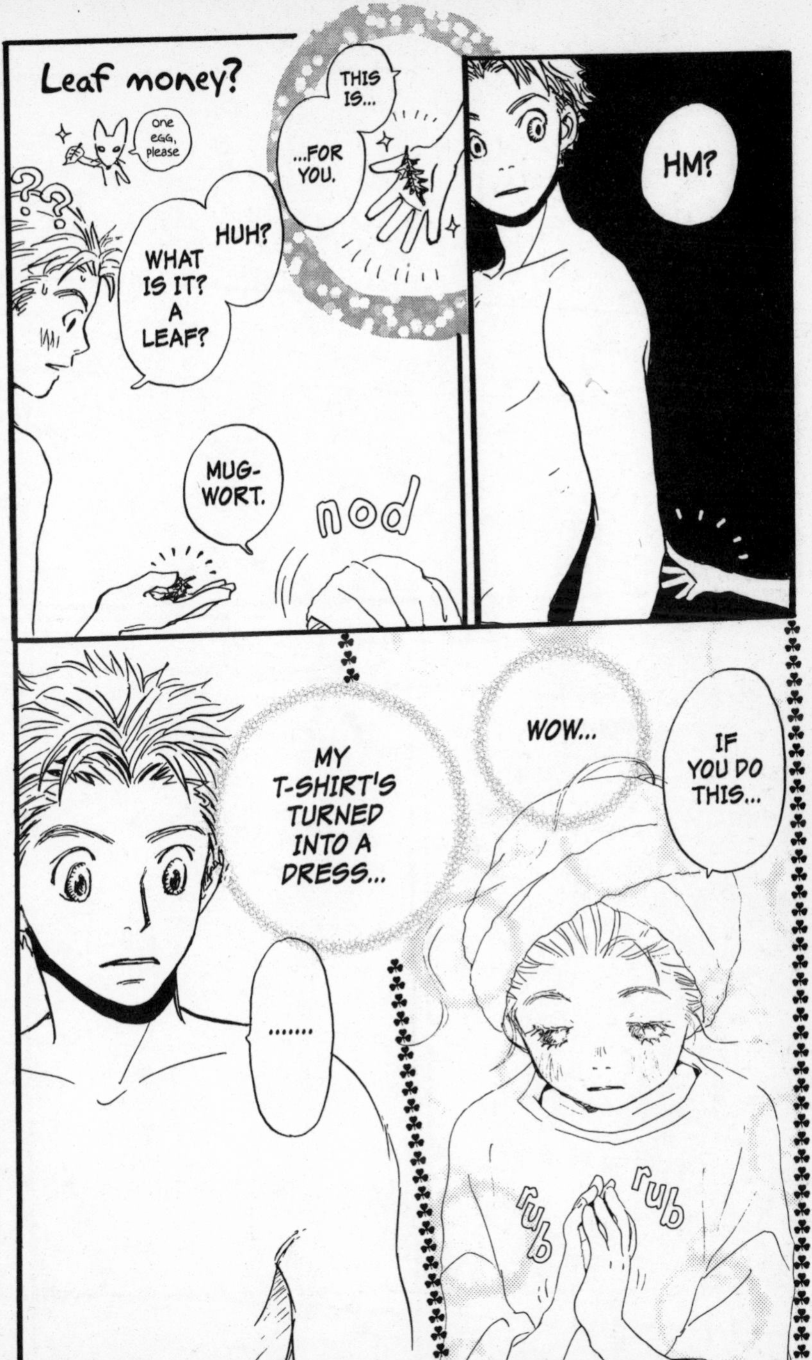
HM?
THIS IS...
...FOR YOU.
Leaf money?
one egg, please
HUH?
WHAT IS IT? A LEAF?
MUG-WORT.
nod
IF YOU DO THIS...
WOW...
MY T-SHIRT'S TURNED INTO A DRESS...
....
rub
rub

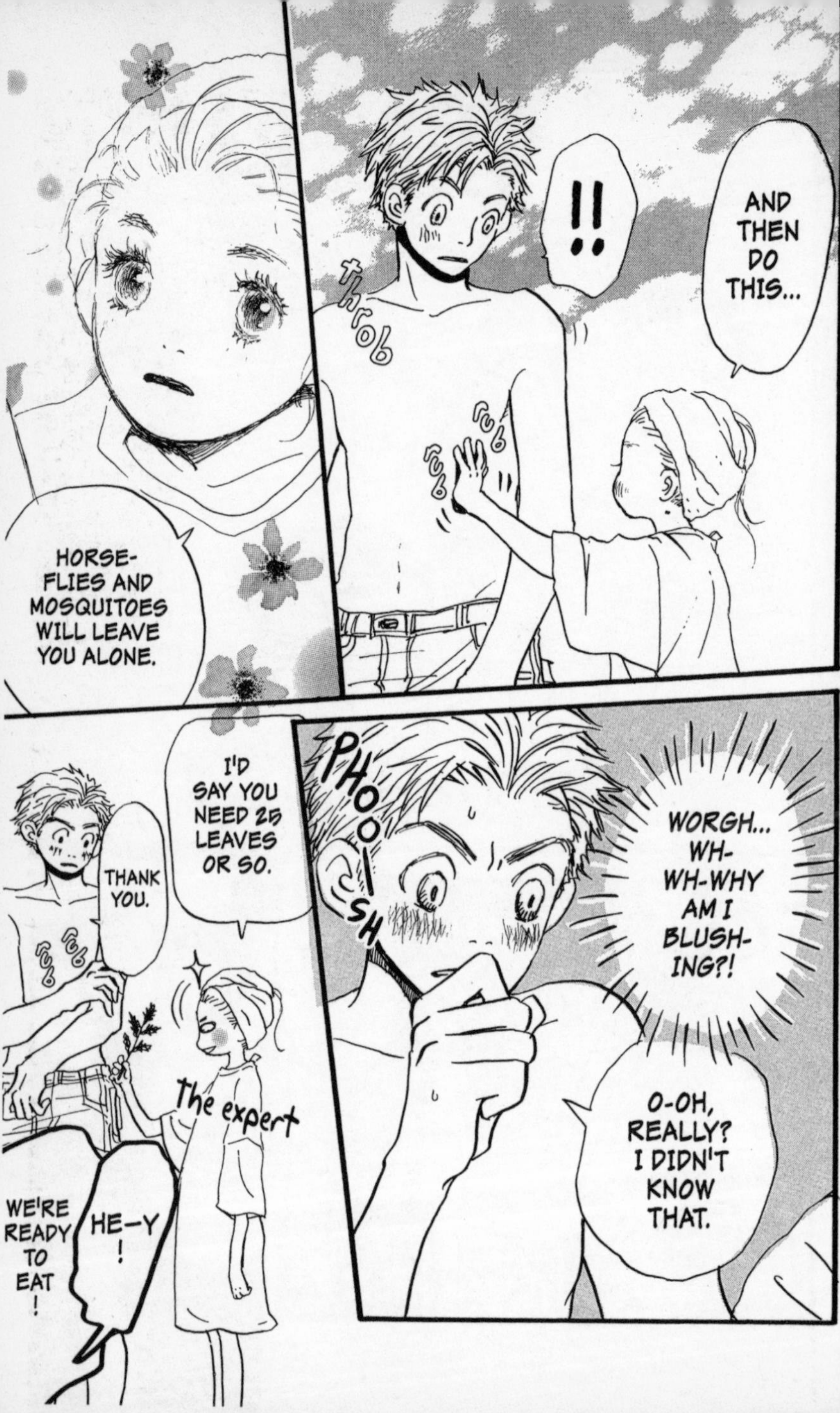
AND THEN DO THIS...
!!
throb
rub rub
HORSE-FLIES AND MOSQUITOES WILL LEAVE YOU ALONE.
PHOOOSH
WORGH... WH-WH-WHY AM I BLUSH-ING?!
O-OH, REALLY? I DIDN'T KNOW THAT.
I'D SAY YOU NEED 25 LEAVES OR SO.
THANK YOU.
rub rub
The expert
HE-Y!
WE'RE READY TO EAT!

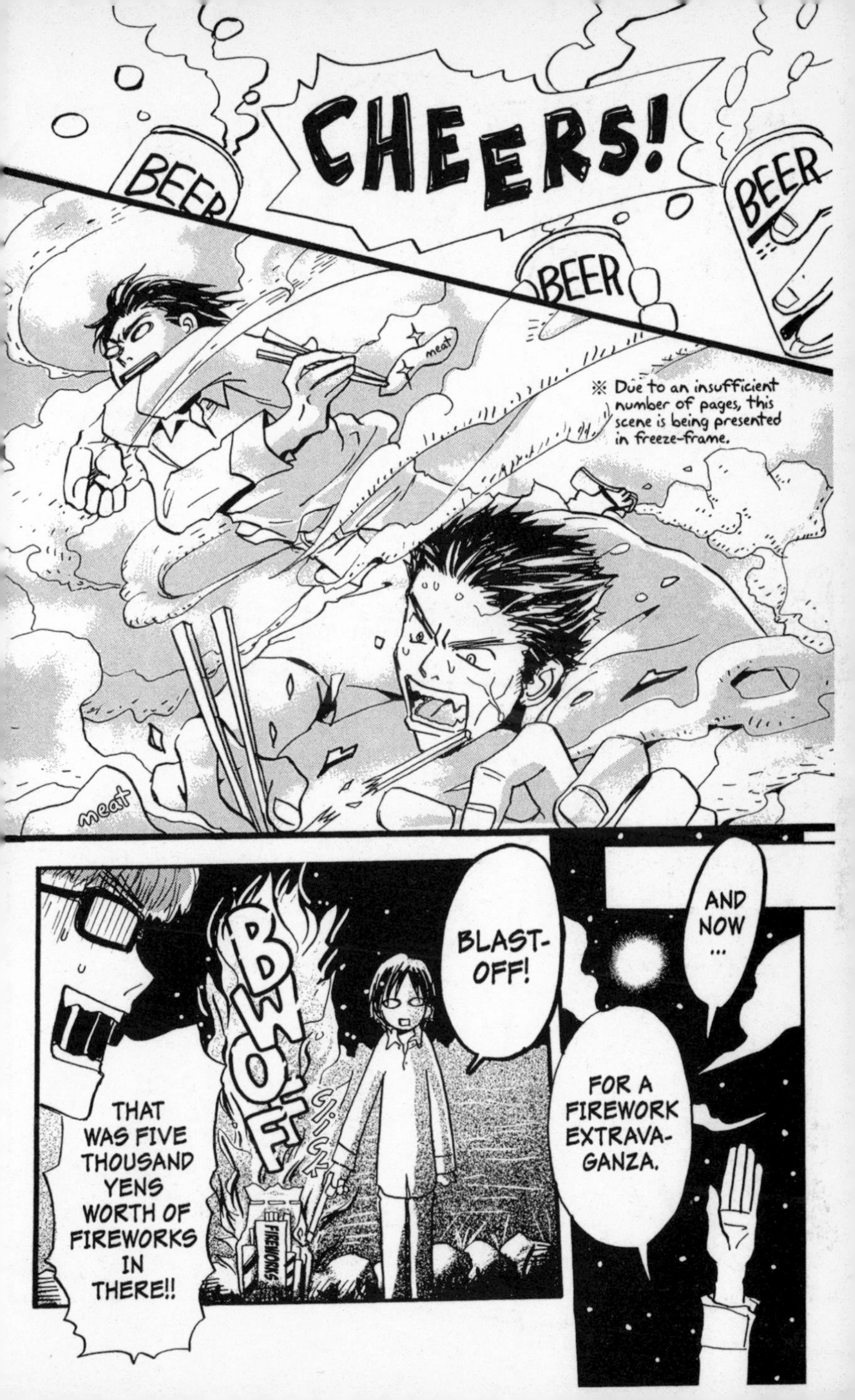
BEER
CHEERS!
BEER
BEER
meat
※ Due to an insufficient number of pages, this scene is being presented in freeze-frame.
meat
AND NOW ...
FOR A FIREWORK EXTRAVA-GANZA.
BLAST-OFF!
BWOOF
GLICK
FIREWORKS
THAT WAS FIVE THOUSAND YENS WORTH OF FIREWORKS IN THERE!!

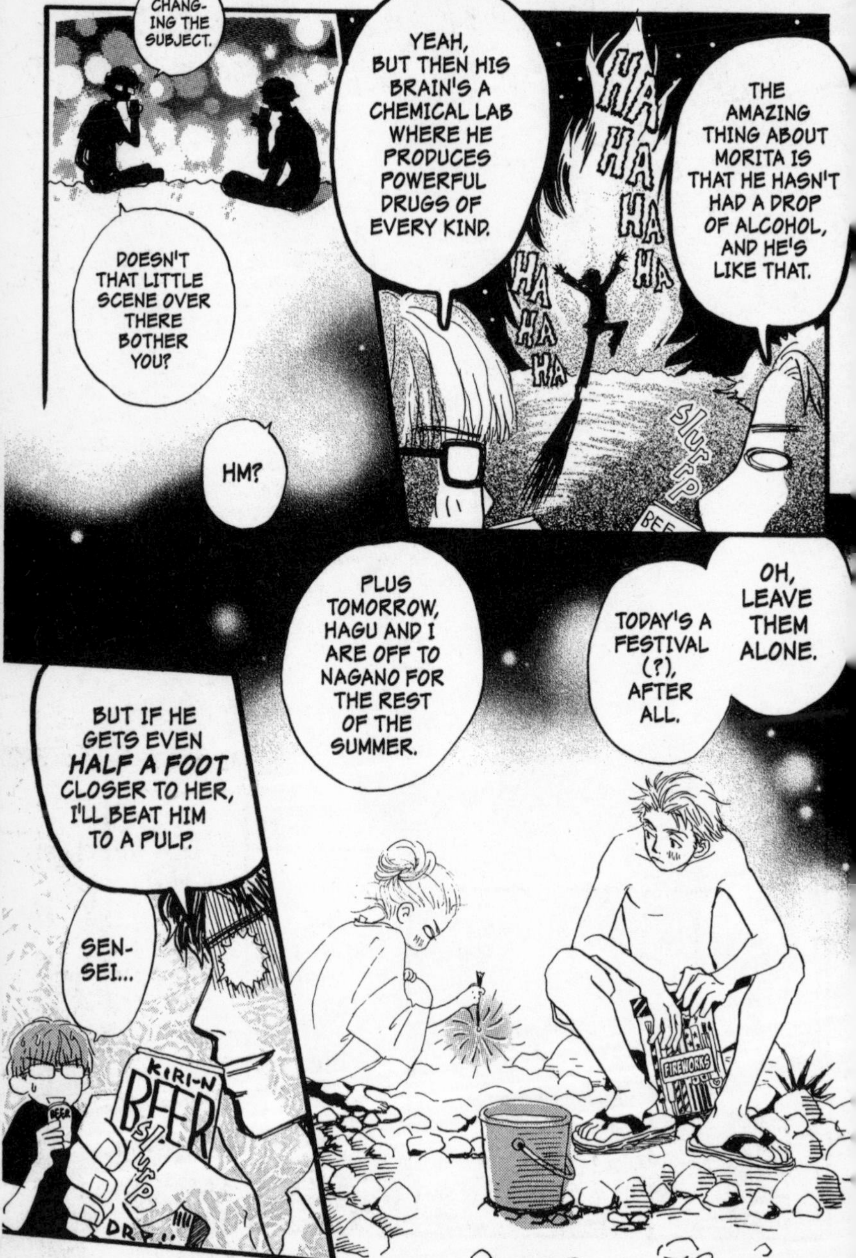
THE AMAZING THING ABOUT MORITA IS THAT HE HASN'T HAD A DROP OF ALCOHOL, AND HE'S LIKE THAT.
YEAH, BUT THEN HIS BRAIN'S A CHEMICAL LAB WHERE HE PRODUCES POWERFUL DRUGS OF EVERY KIND.
HA HA HA HA
HA HA HA HA
slurp
CHANG-ING THE SUBJECT.
DOESN'T THAT LITTLE SCENE OVER THERE BOTHER YOU?
HM?
OH, LEAVE THEM ALONE.
TODAY'S A FESTIVAL (?), AFTER ALL.
PLUS TOMORROW, HAGU AND I ARE OFF TO NAGANO FOR THE REST OF THE SUMMER.
FIREWORKS
BUT IF HE GETS EVEN **HALF A FOOT** CLOSER TO HER, I'LL BEAT HIM TO A PULP.
SEN-SEI...
KIRI-N BEER
slurp
BEER

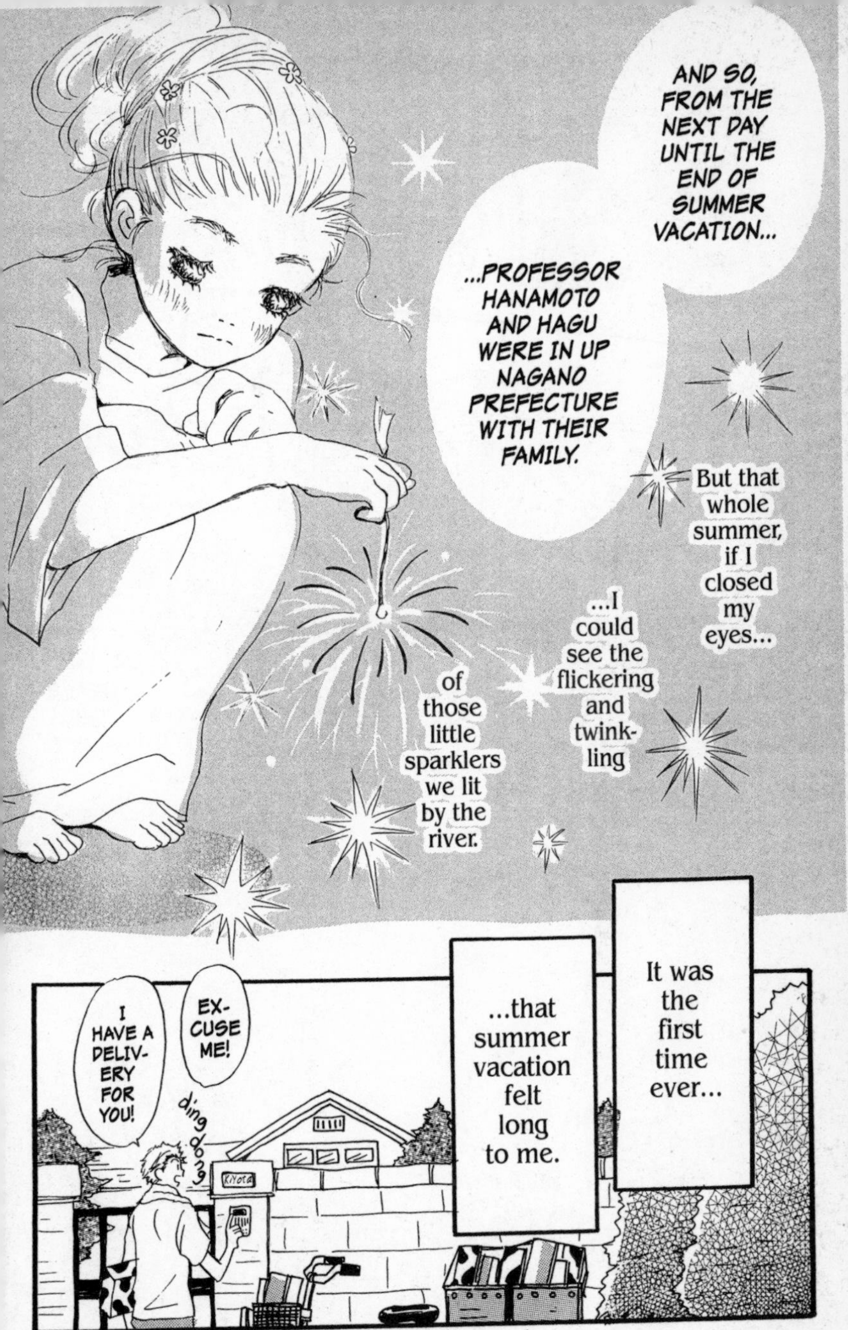
AND SO, FROM THE NEXT DAY UNTIL THE END OF SUMMER VACATION...
...PROFESSOR HANAMOTO AND HAGU WERE IN UP NAGANO PREFECTURE WITH THEIR FAMILY.
But that whole summer, if I closed my eyes...
...I could see the flickering and twinkling
of those little sparklers we lit by the river.
It was the first time ever...
...that summer vacation felt long to me.
EX-CUSE ME!
I HAVE A DELIV-ERY FOR YOU!
ding dong
Kiyota

chapter 5—the end—

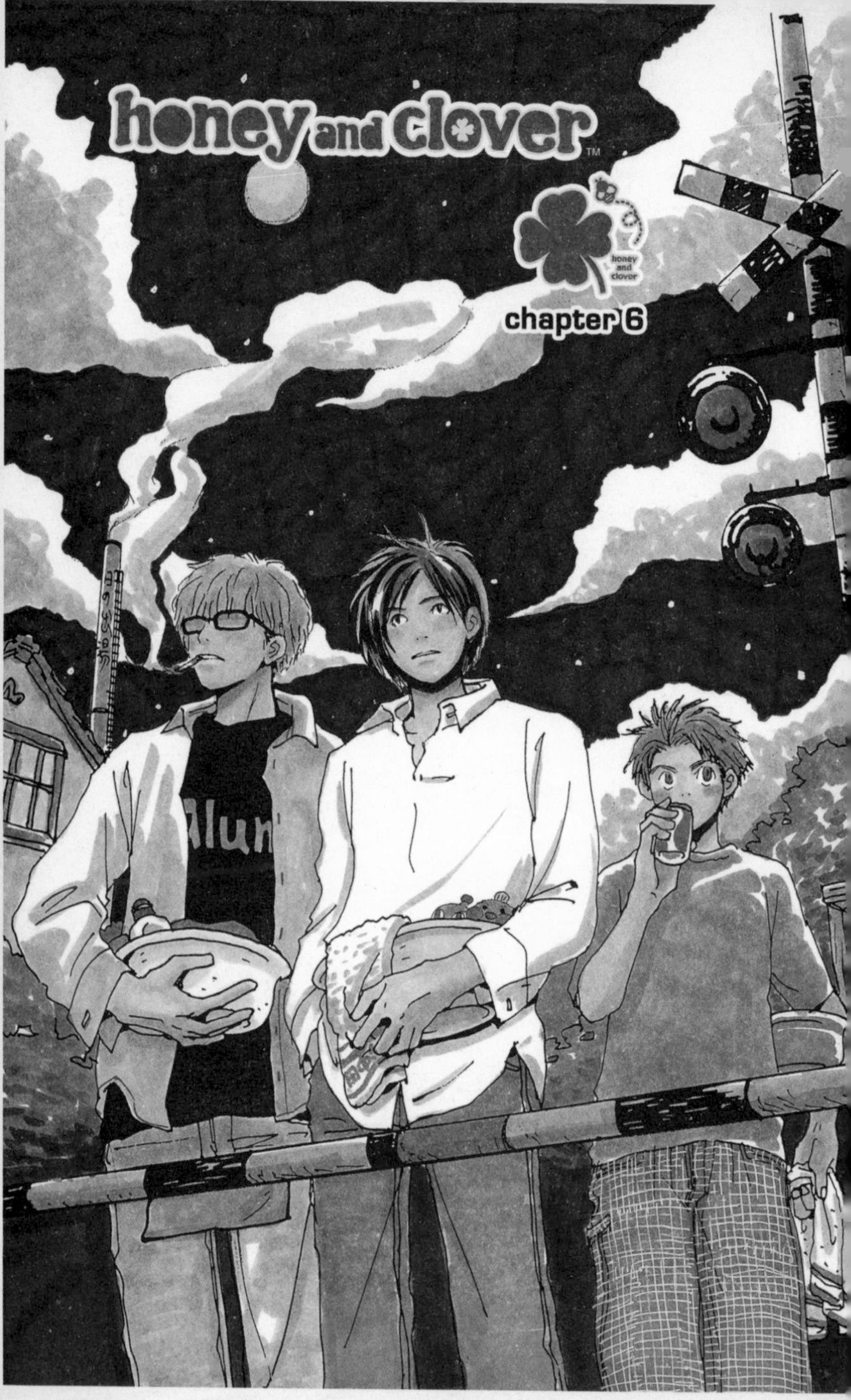
honey and clover™
honey and clover
chapter 6

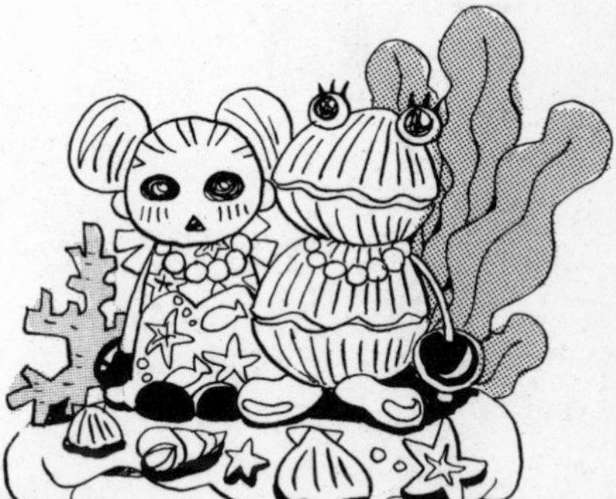
Enoshima Souvenir

made by Shinobu Morita

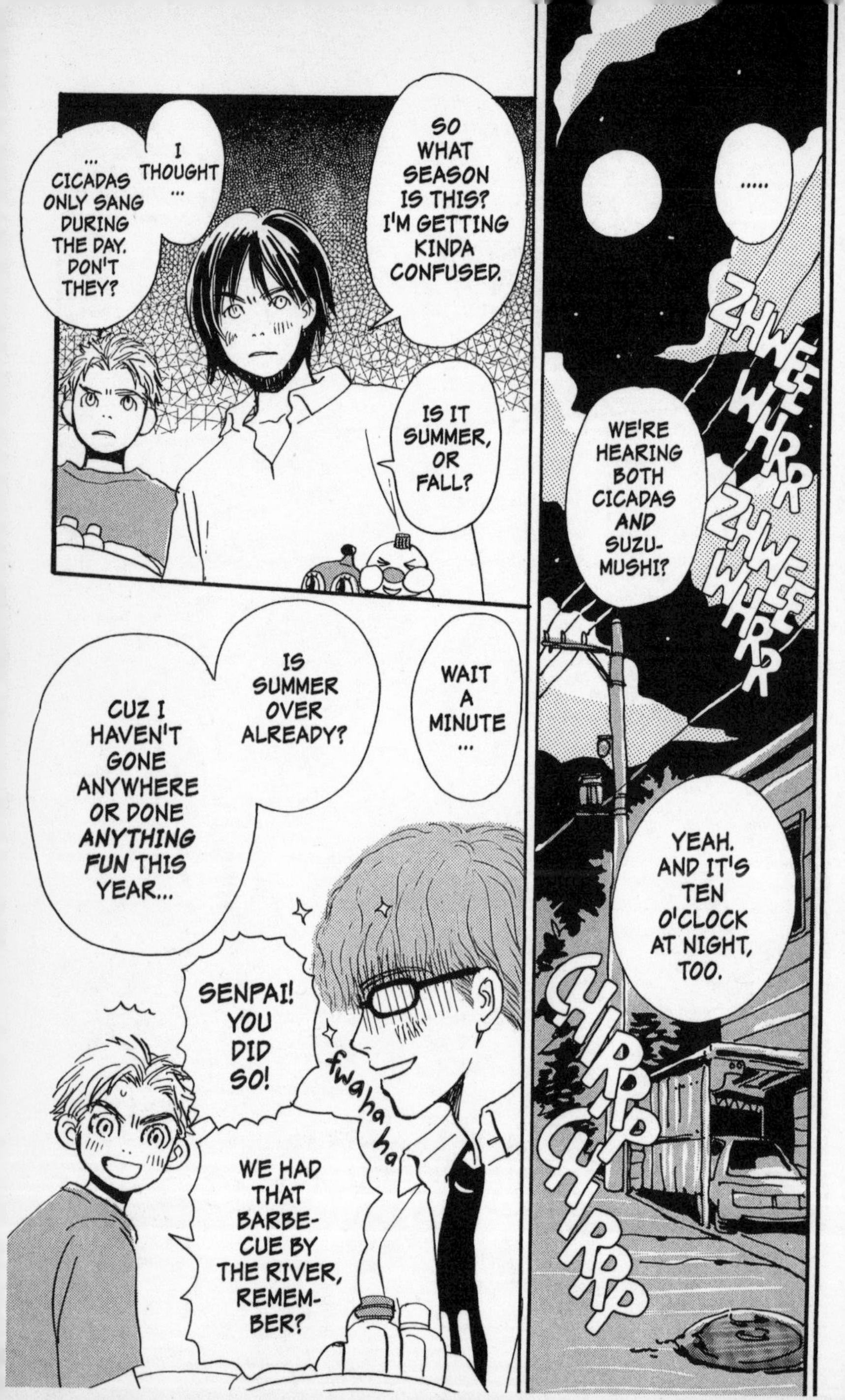
.....
ZHWEE WHRR
WE'RE HEARING BOTH CICADAS AND SUZU-MUSHI?
ZHWEE WHRR
YEAH. AND IT'S TEN O'CLOCK AT NIGHT, TOO.
CHIRRP CHIRRP
SO WHAT SEASON IS THIS? I'M GETTING KINDA CONFUSED.
IS IT SUMMER, OR FALL?
I THOUGHT ...
... CICADAS ONLY SANG DURING THE DAY. DON'T THEY?
WAIT A MINUTE ...
IS SUMMER OVER ALREADY?
CUZ I HAVEN'T GONE ANYWHERE OR DONE ANYTHING FUN THIS YEAR...
SENPAI! YOU DID SO!
fwahaha
WE HAD THAT BARBECUE BY THE RIVER, REMEMBER?

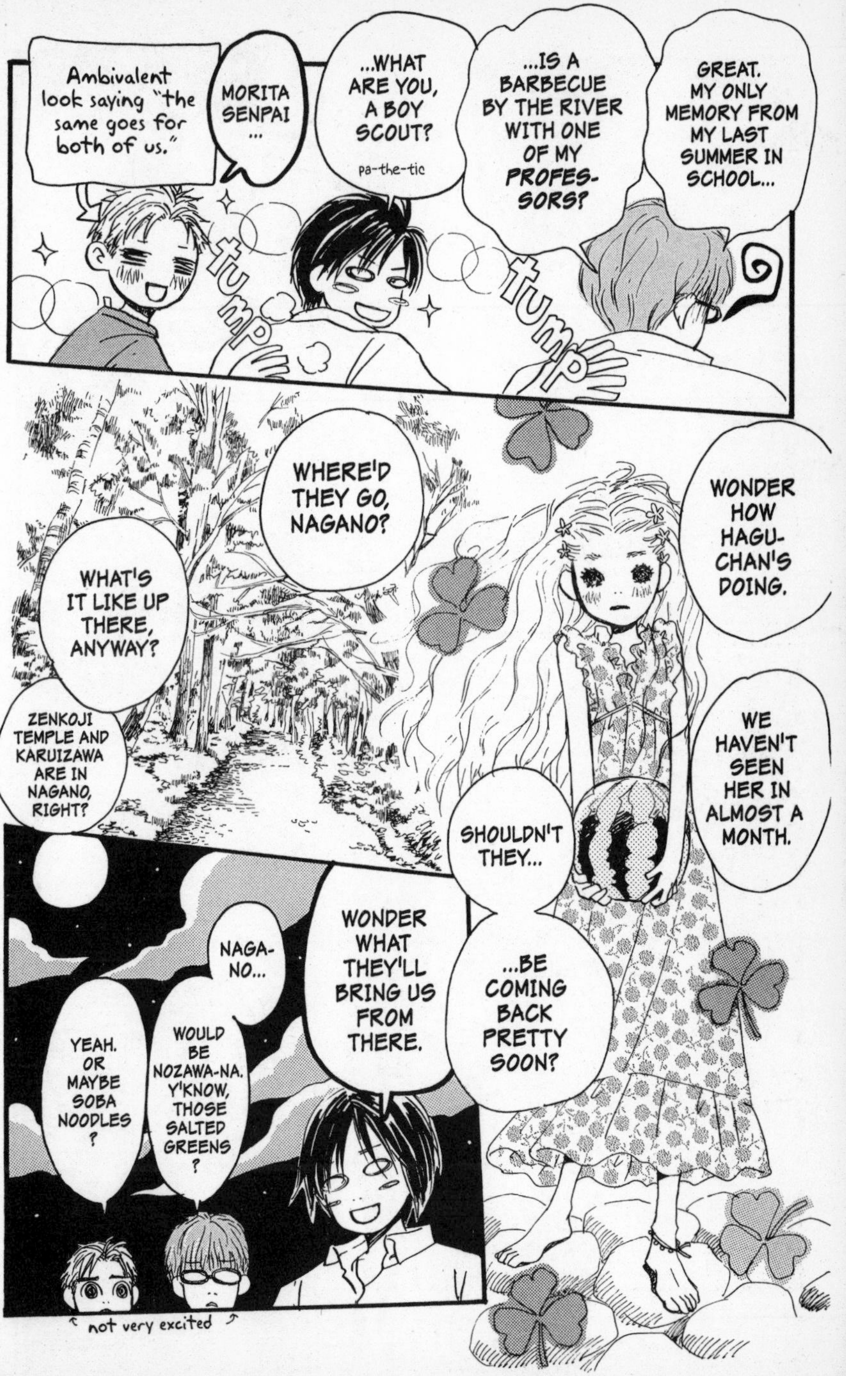
GREAT. MY ONLY MEMORY FROM MY LAST SUMMER IN SCHOOL...
...IS A BARBECUE BY THE RIVER WITH ONE OF MY PROFESSORS?
...WHAT ARE YOU, A BOY SCOUT?
pa-the-tic
tump
tump
MORITA SENPAI ...
Ambivalent look saying "the same goes for both of us."
WONDER HOW HAGU-CHAN'S DOING.
WE HAVEN'T SEEN HER IN ALMOST A MONTH.
SHOULDN'T THEY...
...BE COMING BACK PRETTY SOON?
WHERE'D THEY GO, NAGANO?
WHAT'S IT LIKE UP THERE, ANYWAY?
ZENKOJI TEMPLE AND KARUIZAWA ARE IN NAGANO, RIGHT?
WONDER WHAT THEY'LL BRING US FROM THERE.
NAGA-NO...
WOULD BE NOZAWA-NA. Y'KNOW, THOSE SALTED GREENS?
YEAH. OR MAYBE SOBA NOODLES?
not very excited

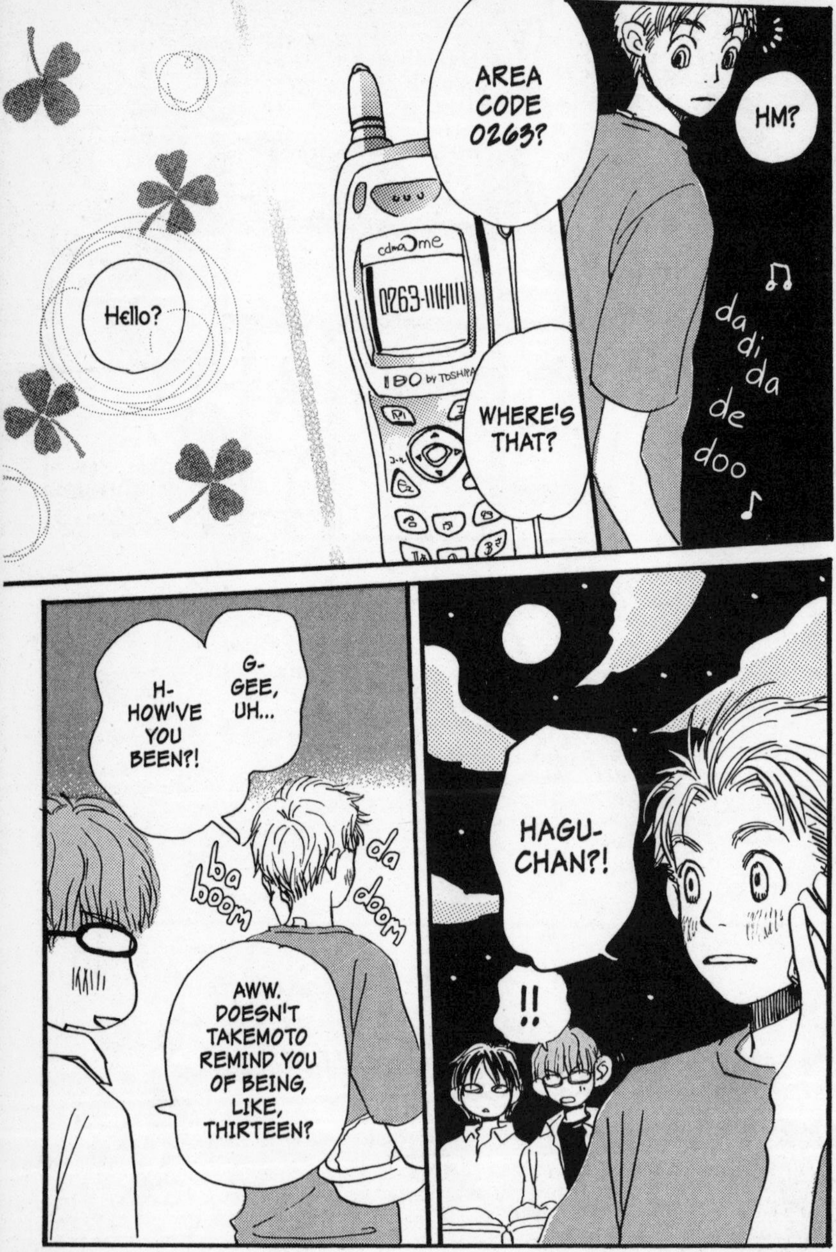
HM?
AREA CODE 0263?
dadida de doo
WHERE'S THAT?
0263-
Hello?
HAGU-CHAN?!
!!
G-GEE, UH...
H-HOW'VE YOU BEEN?!
da doom
ba boom
AWW. DOESN'T TAKEMOTO REMIND YOU OF BEING, LIKE, THIRTEEN?

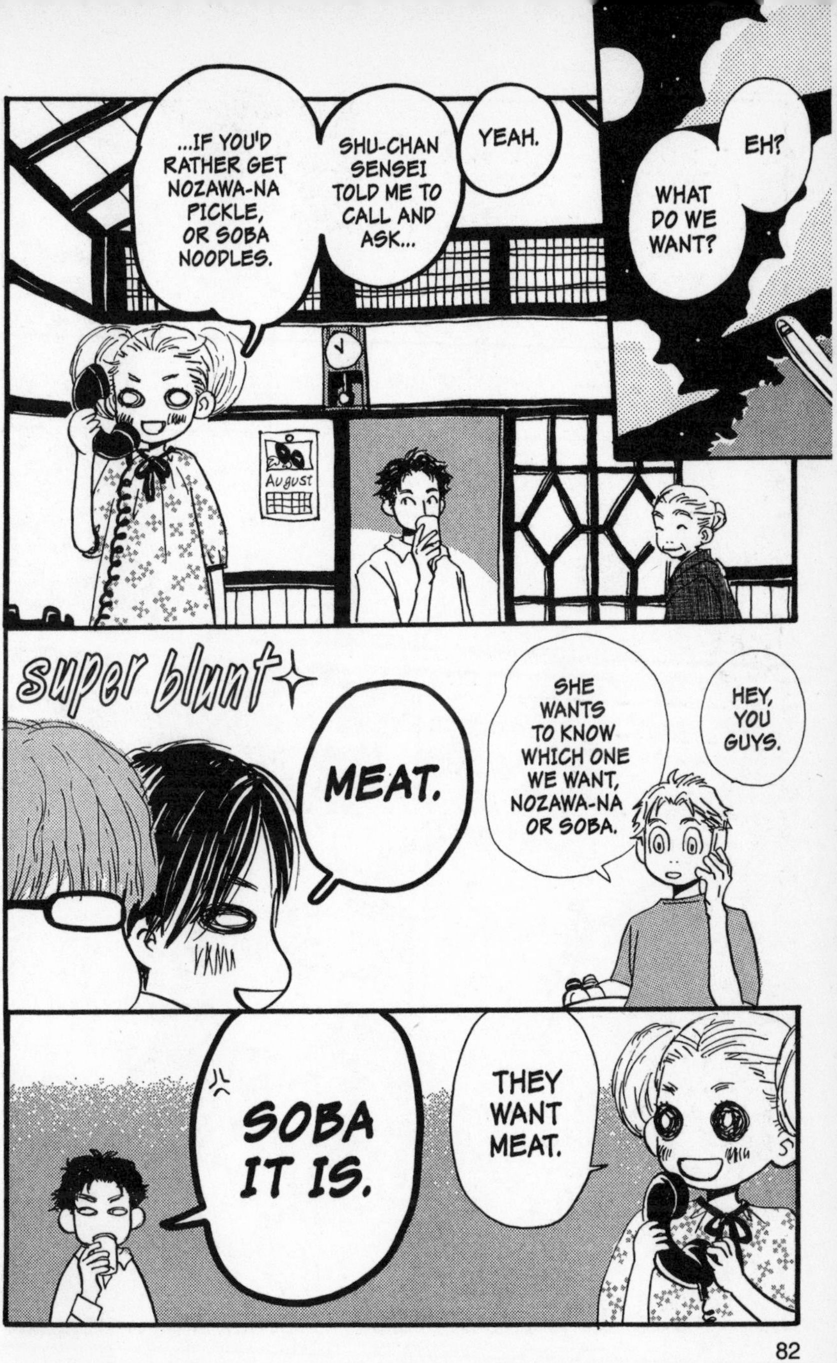
EH?
WHAT DO WE WANT?
YEAH.
SHU-CHAN SENSEI TOLD ME TO CALL AND ASK...
...IF YOU'D RATHER GET NOZAWA-NA PICKLE, OR SOBA NOODLES.
August
super blunt
HEY, YOU GUYS.
SHE WANTS TO KNOW WHICH ONE WE WANT, NOZAWA-NA OR SOBA.
MEAT.
THEY WANT MEAT.
SOBA IT IS.

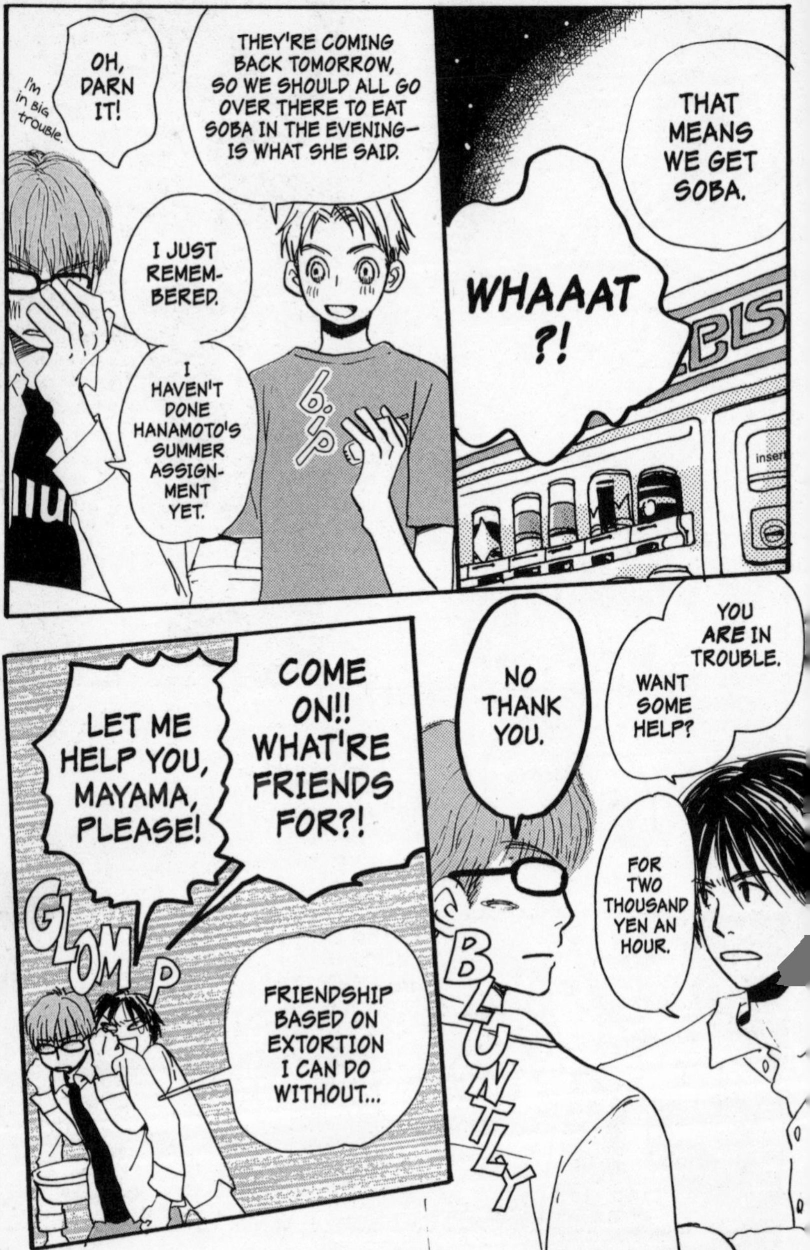
THAT MEANS WE GET SOBA.
WHAAAT ?!
THEY'RE COMING BACK TOMORROW, SO WE SHOULD ALL GO OVER THERE TO EAT SOBA IN THE EVENING—IS WHAT SHE SAID.
OH, DARN IT!
I'm in big trouble.
I JUST REMEMBERED.
I HAVEN'T DONE HANAMOTO'S SUMMER ASSIGNMENT YET.
YOU ARE IN TROUBLE.
WANT SOME HELP?
NO THANK YOU.
FOR TWO THOUSAND YEN AN HOUR.
BLUNTLY
COME ON!! WHAT'RE FRIENDS FOR?!
LET ME HELP YOU, MAYAMA, PLEASE!
GLOMP
FRIENDSHIP BASED ON EXTORTION I CAN DO WITHOUT...

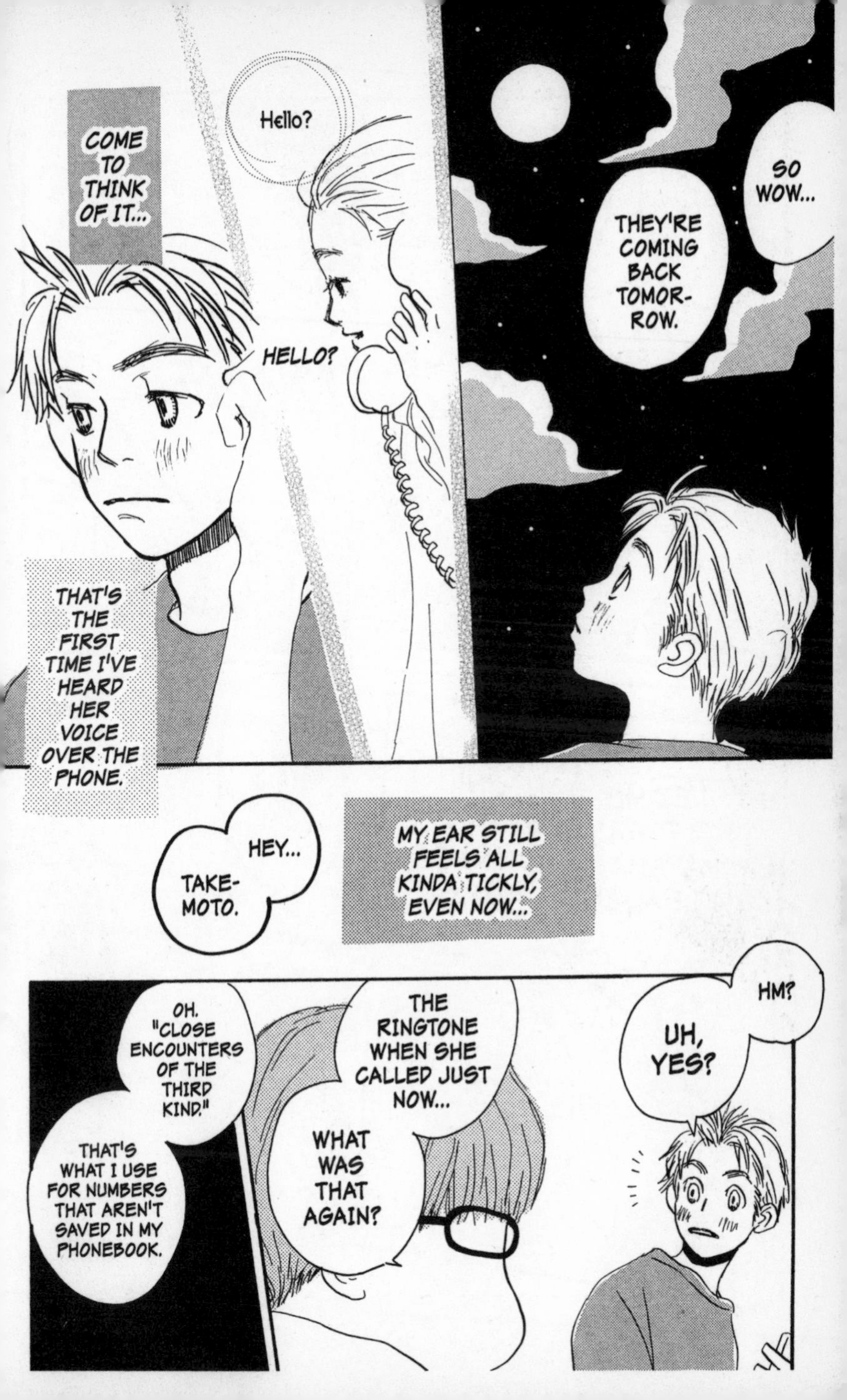
SO WOW...
THEY'RE COMING BACK TOMORROW.
Hello?
COME TO THINK OF IT...
HELLO?
THAT'S THE FIRST TIME I'VE HEARD HER VOICE OVER THE PHONE.
MY EAR STILL FEELS ALL KINDA TICKLY, EVEN NOW...
HEY...
TAKEMOTO.
HM?
UH, YES?
THE RINGTONE WHEN SHE CALLED JUST NOW...
WHAT WAS THAT AGAIN?
OH. "CLOSE ENCOUNTERS OF THE THIRD KIND."
THAT'S WHAT I USE FOR NUMBERS THAT AREN'T SAVED IN MY PHONEBOOK.

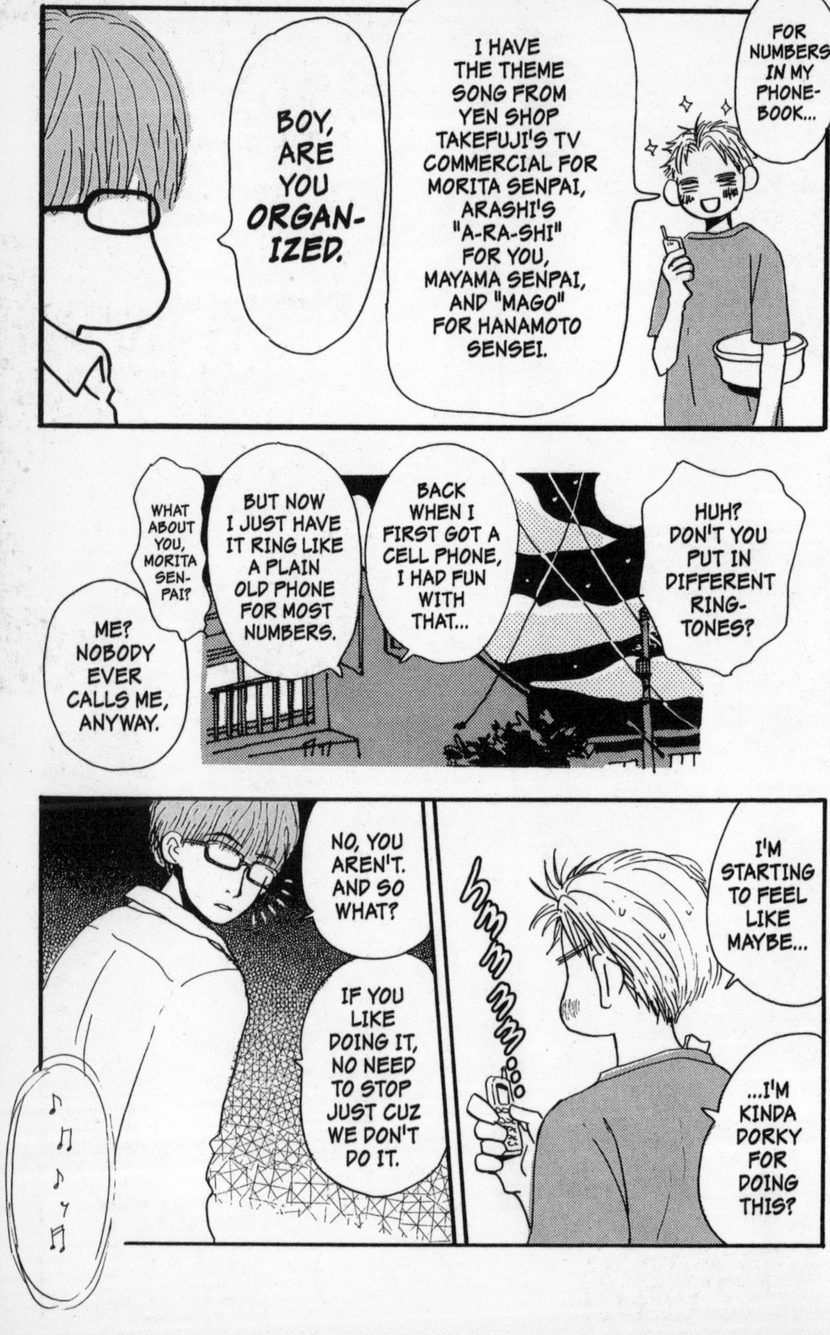
FOR NUMBERS IN MY PHONE-BOOK...
I HAVE THE THEME SONG FROM YEN SHOP TAKEFUJI'S TV COMMERCIAL FOR MORITA SENPAI, ARASHI'S "A-RA-SHI" FOR YOU, MAYAMA SENPAI, AND "MAGO" FOR HANAMOTO SENSEI.
BOY, ARE YOU ORGANIZED.
HUH? DON'T YOU PUT IN DIFFERENT RING-TONES?
BACK WHEN I FIRST GOT A CELL PHONE, I HAD FUN WITH THAT...
BUT NOW I JUST HAVE IT RING LIKE A PLAIN OLD PHONE FOR MOST NUMBERS.
WHAT ABOUT YOU, MORITA SEN-PAI?
ME? NOBODY EVER CALLS ME, ANYWAY.
I'M STARTING TO FEEL LIKE MAYBE...
...I'M KINDA DORKY FOR DOING THIS?
NO, YOU AREN'T. AND SO WHAT?
IF YOU LIKE DOING IT, NO NEED TO STOP JUST CUZ WE DON'T DO IT.

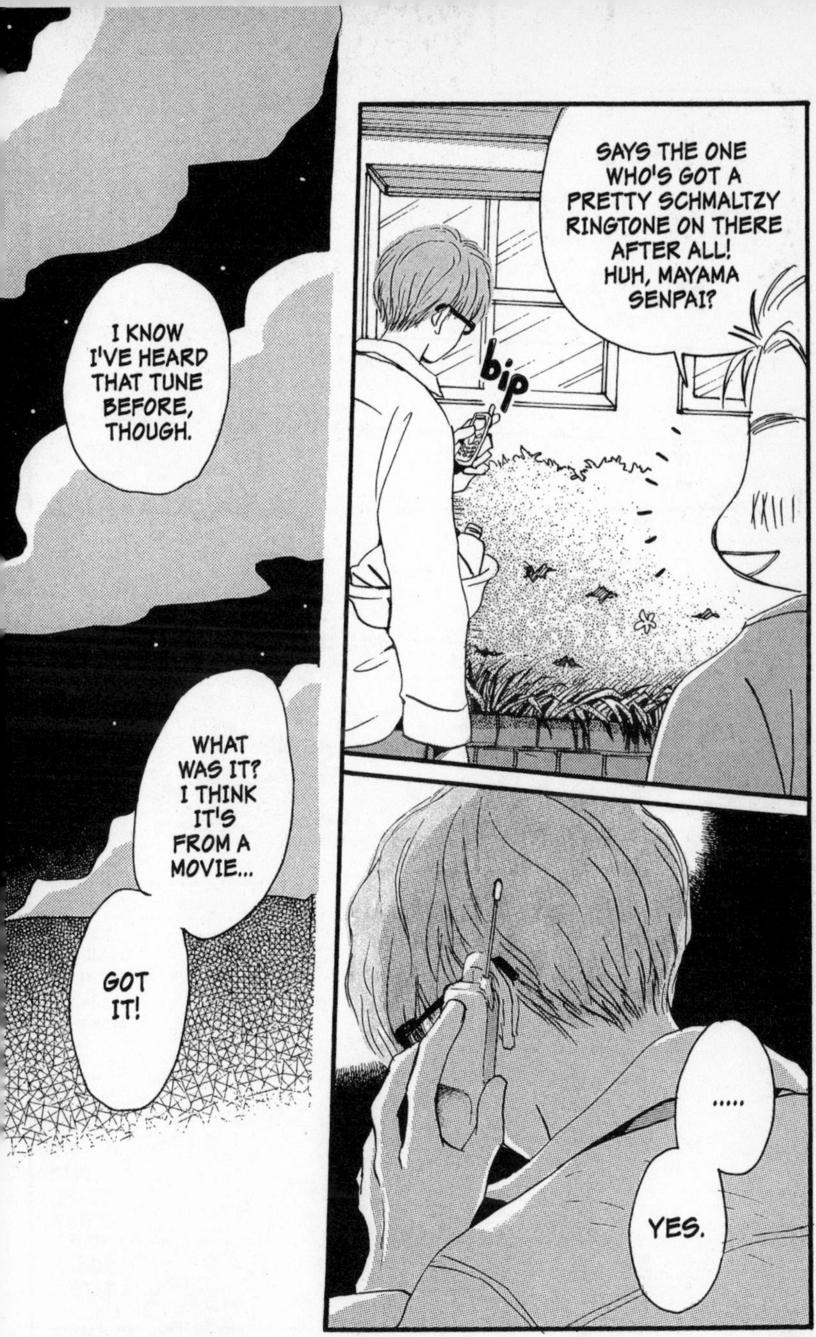
SAYS THE ONE WHO'S GOT A PRETTY SCHMALTZY RINGTONE ON THERE AFTER ALL! HUH, MAYAMA SENPAI?
bip
.....
YES.
I KNOW I'VE HEARD THAT TUNE BEFORE, THOUGH.
WHAT WAS IT? I THINK IT'S FROM A MOVIE...
GOT IT!

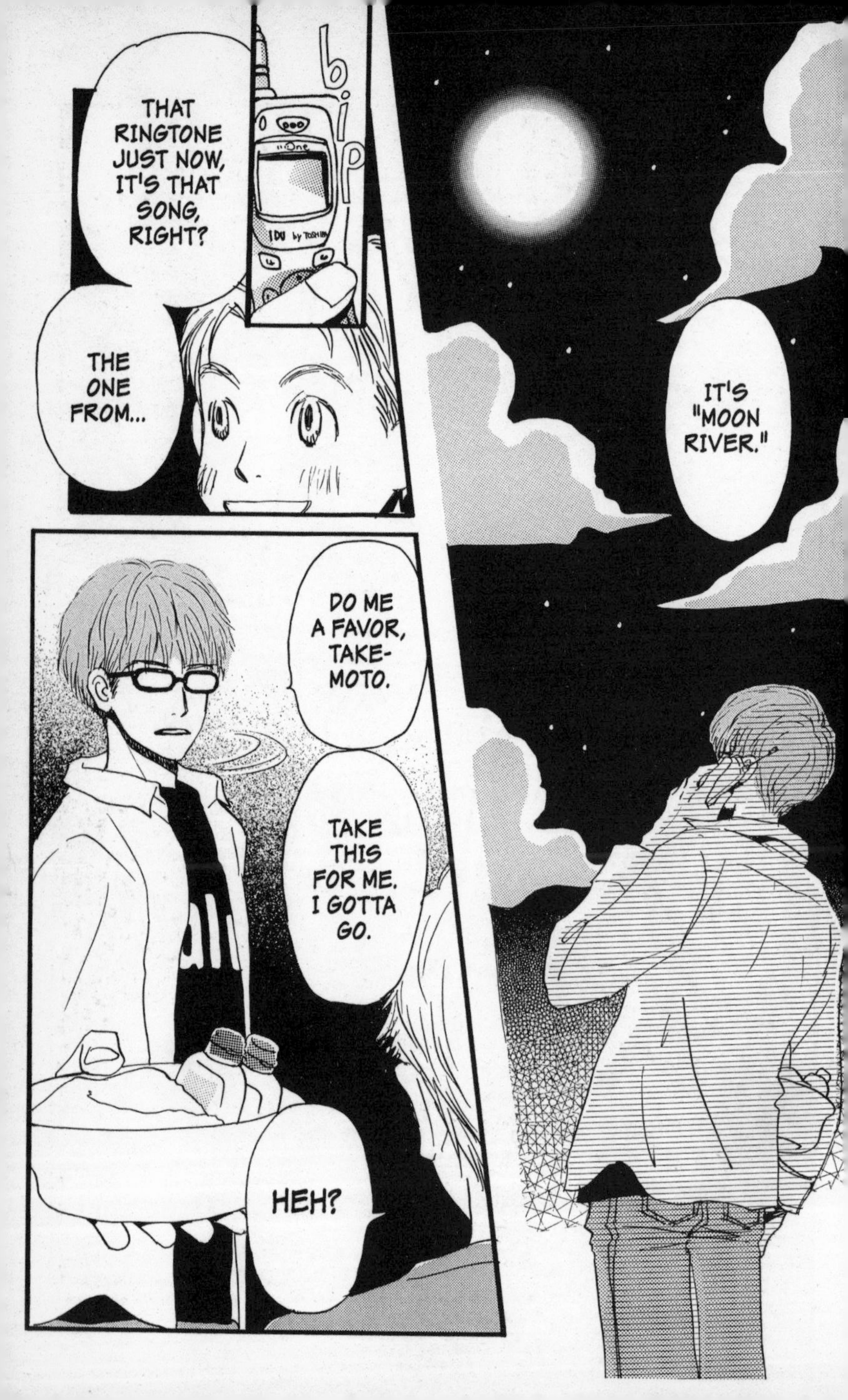
bip
THAT RINGTONE JUST NOW, IT'S THAT SONG, RIGHT?
THE ONE FROM...
IT'S "MOON RIVER."
DO ME A FAVOR, TAKE-MOTO.
TAKE THIS FOR ME. I GOTTA GO.
HEH?

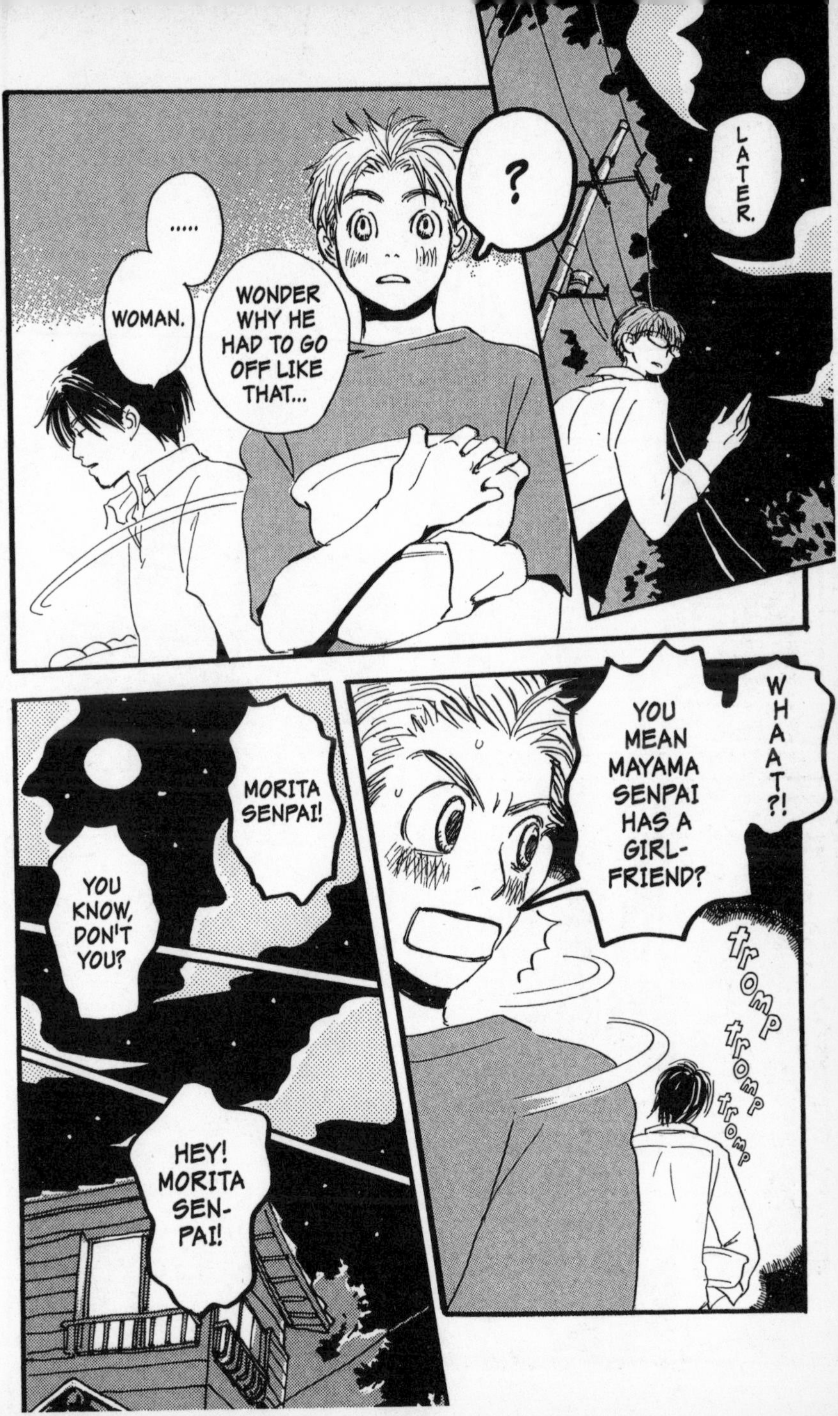
LATER.
?
WONDER WHY HE HAD TO GO OFF LIKE THAT...
.....
WOMAN.
WHAAT?!
YOU MEAN MAYAMA SENPAI HAS A GIRL-FRIEND?
tromp tromp tromp
MORITA SENPAI!
YOU KNOW, DON'T YOU?
HEY! MORITA SEN-PAI!

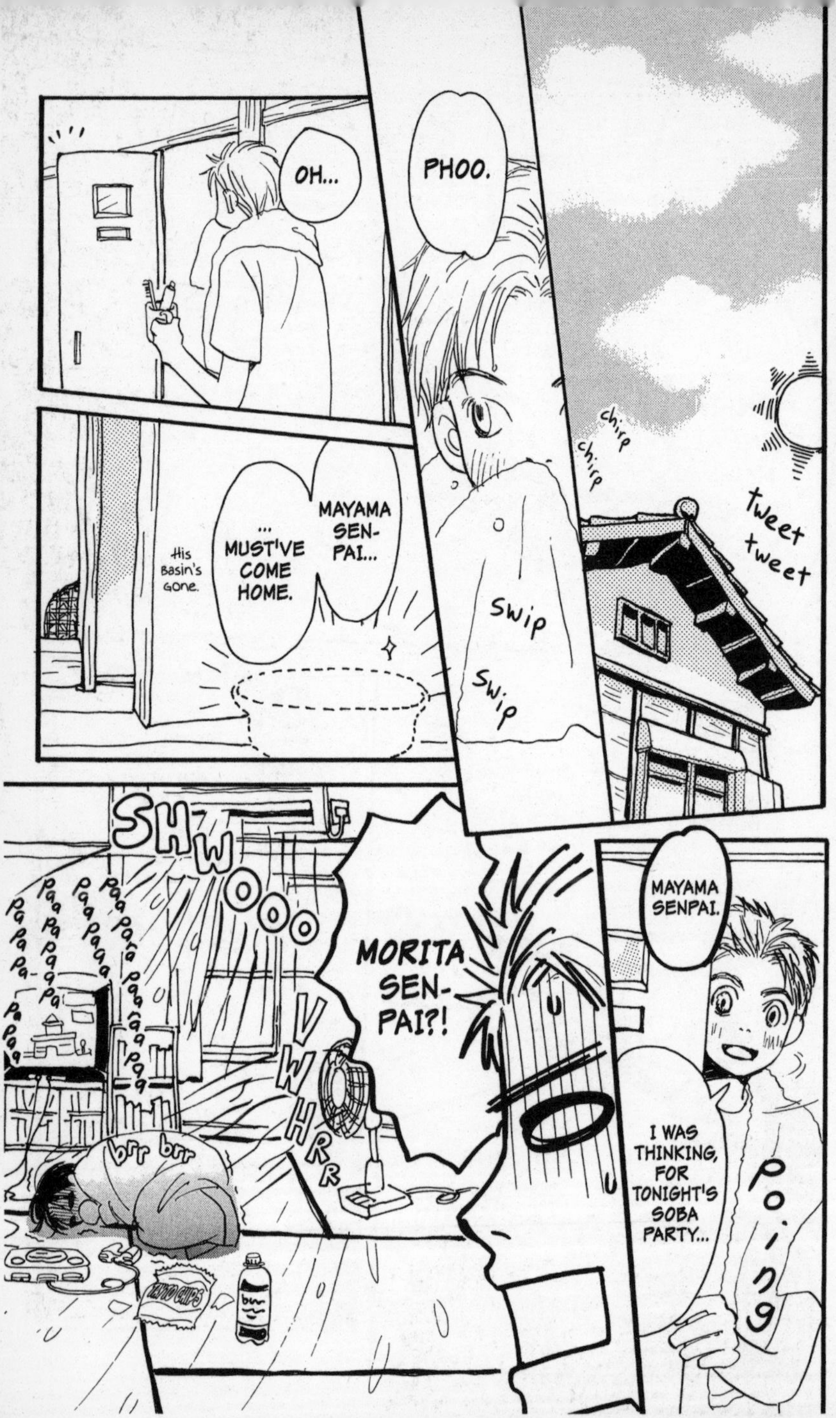
chirp
chirp
tweet
tweet
PHOO.
swip
swip
OH...
MAYAMA SENPAI...
... MUST'VE COME HOME.
His Basin's Gone.
MAYAMA SENPAI.
I WAS THINKING, FOR TONIGHT'S SOBA PARTY...
Poing
MORITA SEN-PAI?!
SHWOOO
VWHRR
Paa Paa Para Paa raa Paa Paa
Paa Paa Paaa
Pa Pa Pa Pa Pa
Pa Pa Pa Pa-
Pa Paa
brr brr

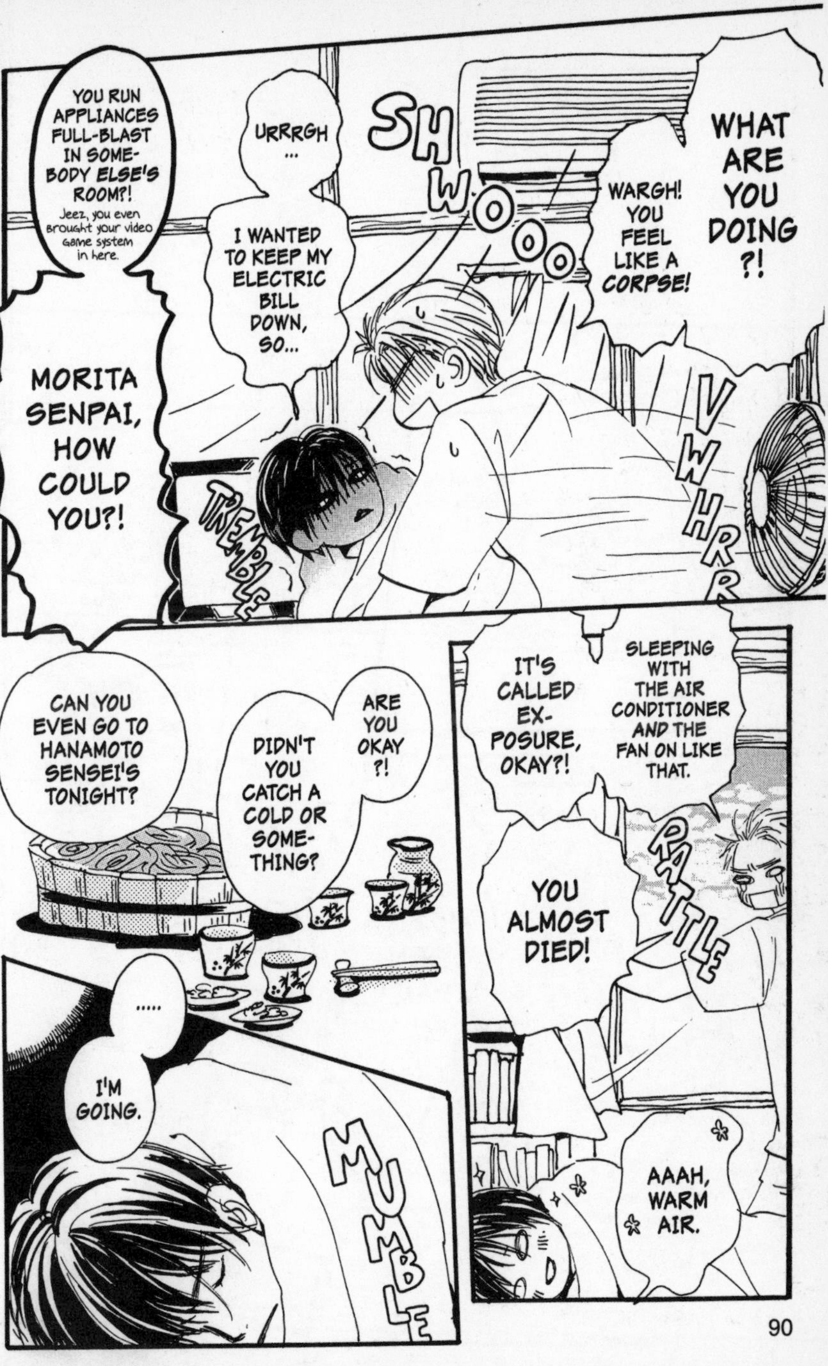

WHAT ARE YOU DOING?!
WARGH! YOU FEEL LIKE A CORPSE!
SHWOOOO
URRRGH...
I WANTED TO KEEP MY ELECTRIC BILL DOWN, SO...
VWHRR
TREMBLE
YOU RUN APPLIANCES FULL-BLAST IN SOMEBODY ELSE'S ROOM?!
Jeez, you even brought your video game system in here.
MORITA SENPAI, HOW COULD YOU?!
SLEEPING WITH THE AIR CONDITIONER AND THE FAN ON LIKE THAT.
IT'S CALLED EX-POSURE, OKAY?!
RATTLE
YOU ALMOST DIED!
AAAH, WARM AIR.
ARE YOU OKAY?!
DIDN'T YOU CATCH A COLD OR SOME-THING?
CAN YOU EVEN GO TO HANAMOTO SENSEI'S TONIGHT?
.....
I'M GOING.
MUMBLE

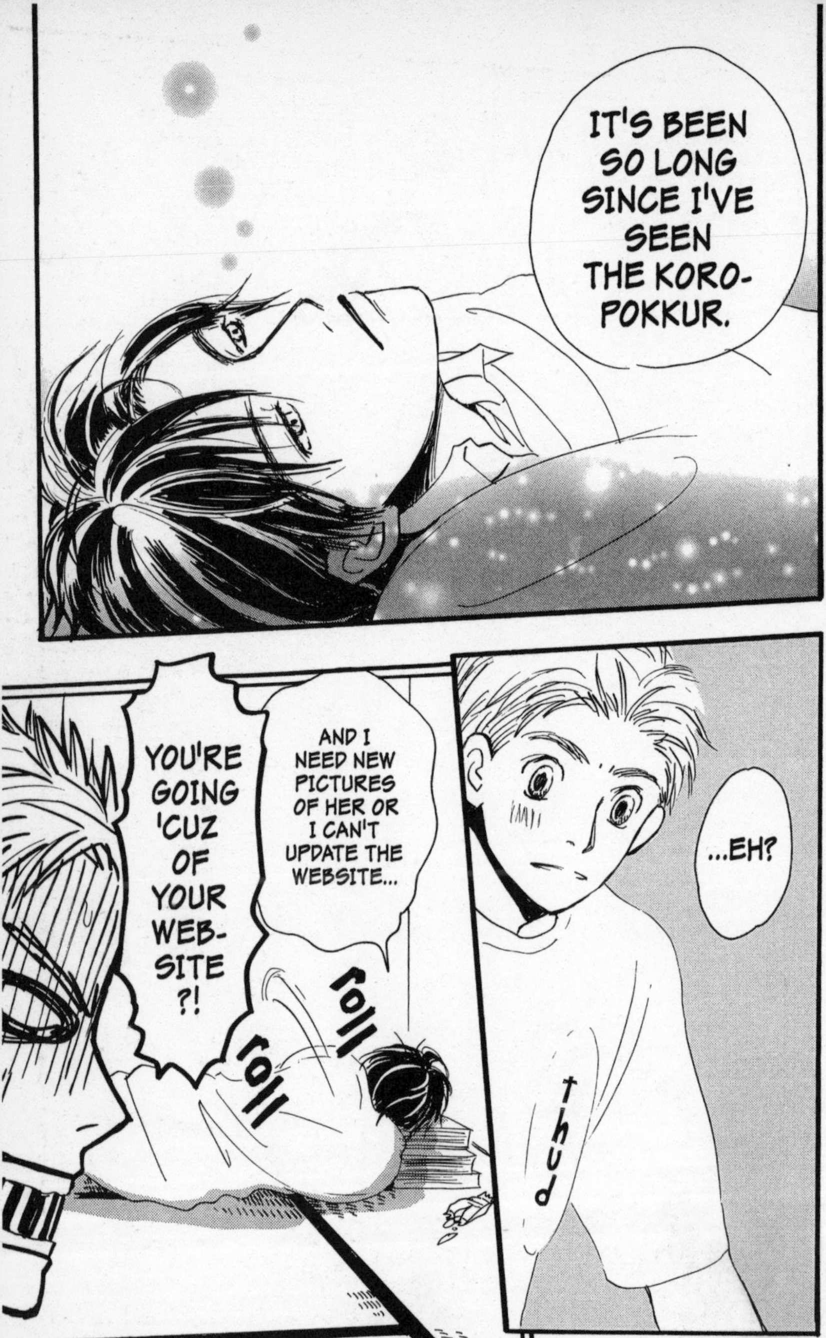
IT'S BEEN SO LONG SINCE I'VE SEEN THE KORO-POKKUR.
...EH?
thud
AND I NEED NEW PICTURES OF HER OR I CAN'T UPDATE THE WEBSITE...
YOU'RE GOING 'CUZ OF YOUR WEB-SITE ?!
roll
roll

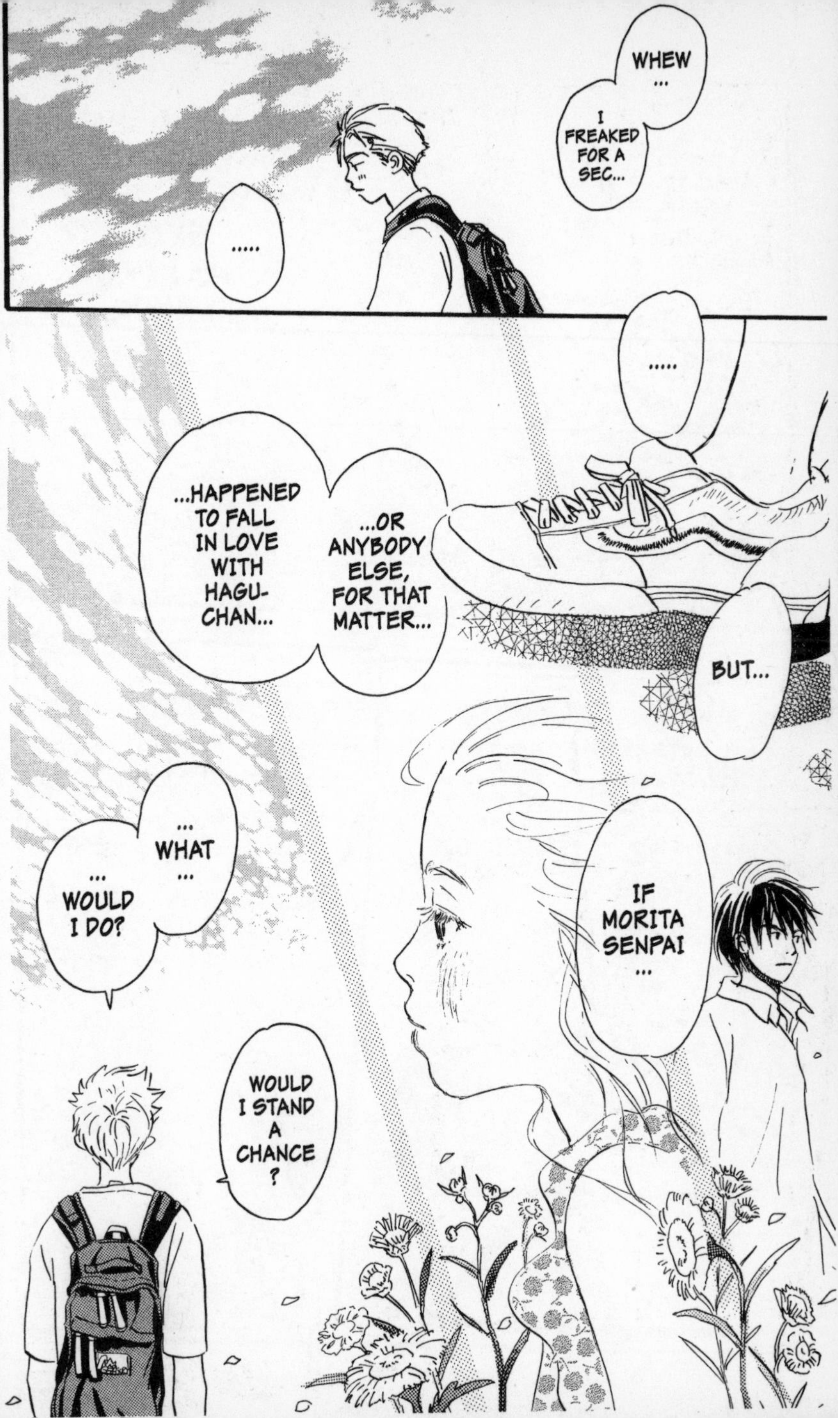
WHEW ...
I FREAKED FOR A SEC...
.....
.....
BUT...
IF MORITA SENPAI ...
...HAPPENED TO FALL IN LOVE WITH HAGU-CHAN...
...OR ANYBODY ELSE, FOR THAT MATTER...
... WHAT ... ... WOULD I DO?
WOULD I STAND A CHANCE ?

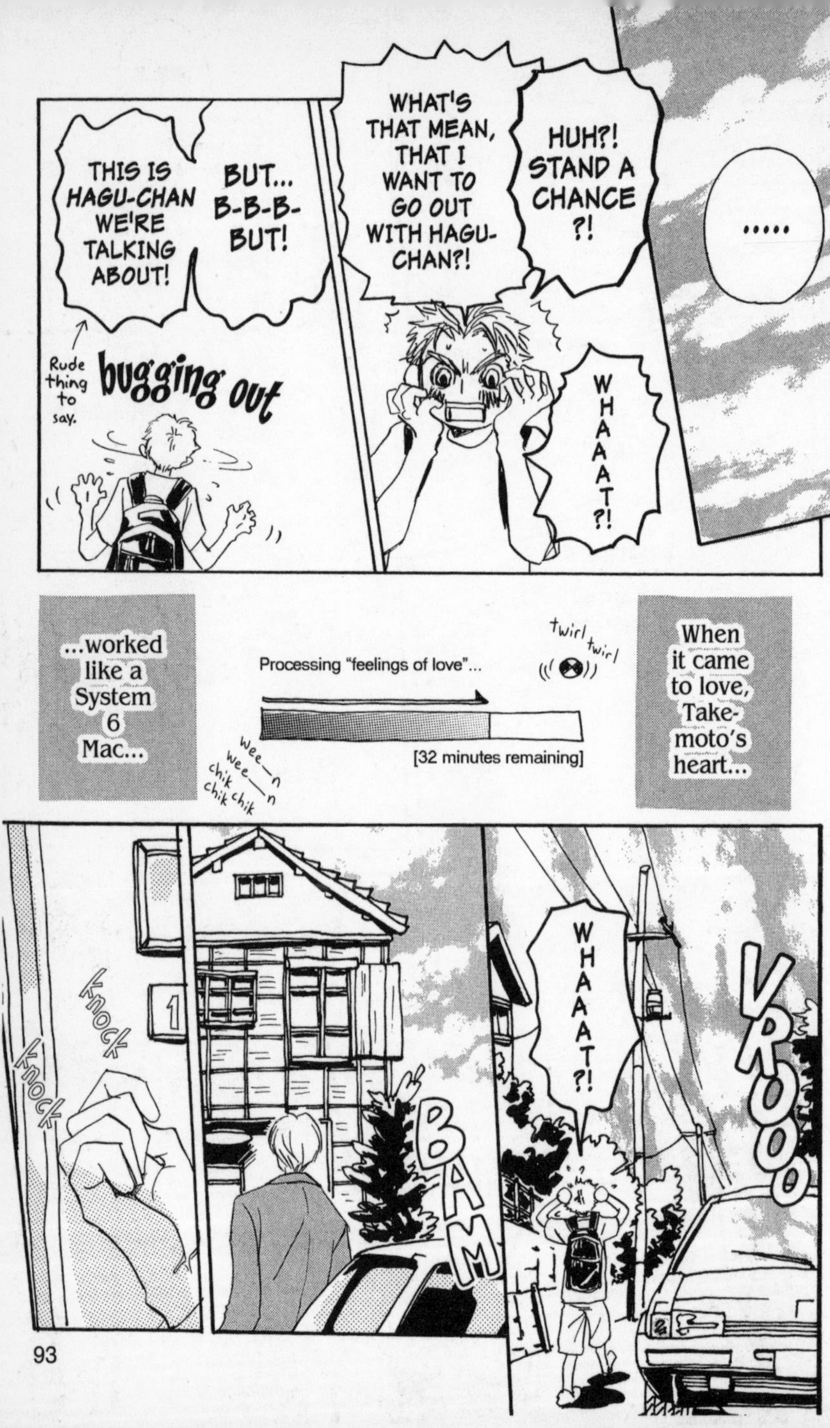
.....
HUH?! STAND A CHANCE?!
WHAT'S THAT MEAN, THAT I WANT TO GO OUT WITH HAGU-CHAN?!
WHAAAAT?!
BUT... B-B-B-BUT!
THIS IS HAGU-CHAN WE'RE TALKING ABOUT!
Rude thing to say.
bugging out
When it came to love, Take-moto's heart...
twirl twirl
Processing "feelings of love"...
[32 minutes remaining]
wee—n wee—n
chik chik chik chik
...worked like a System 6 Mac...
VROOO
WHAAAAT?!
BAM
knock knock

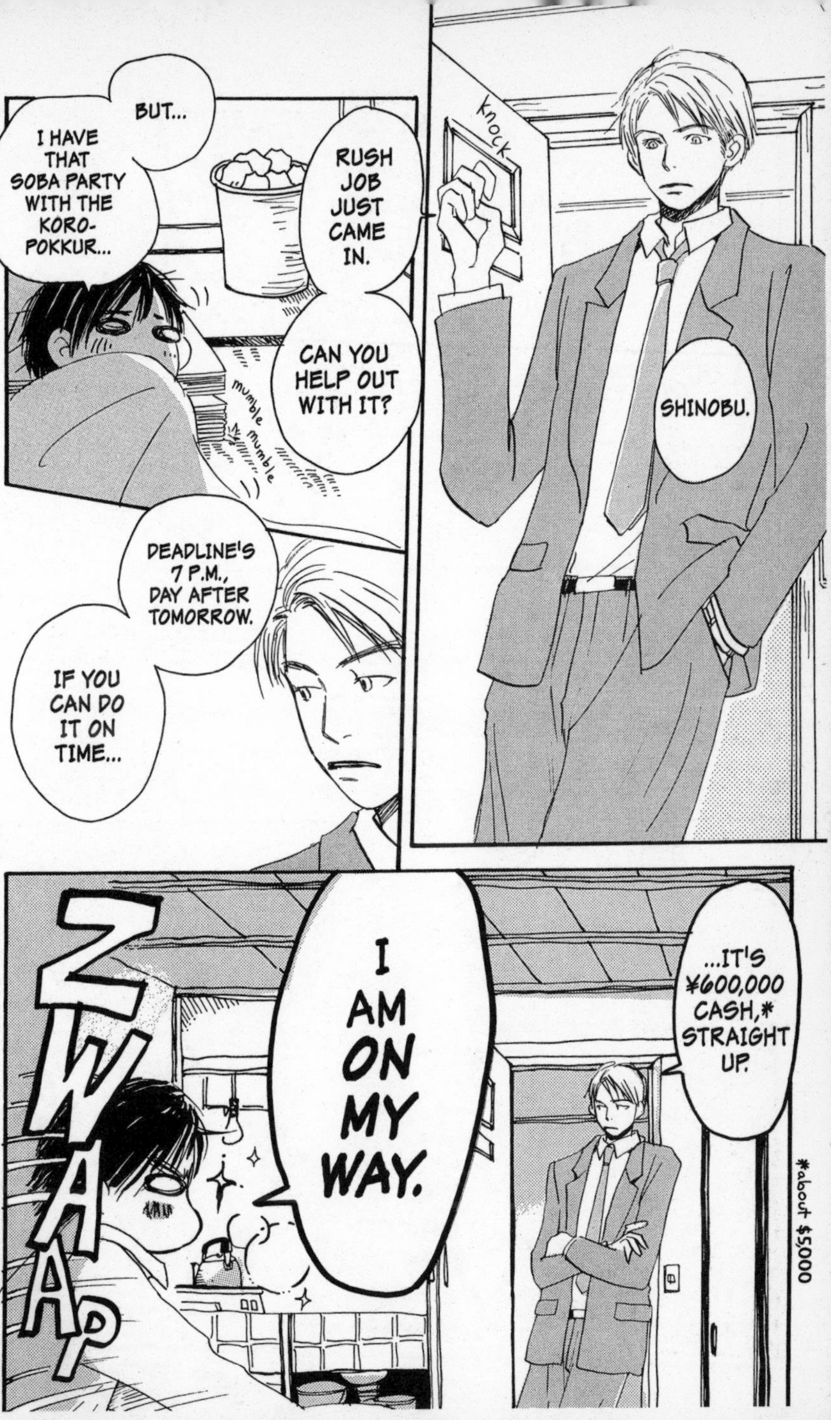
knock
SHINOBU.
RUSH JOB JUST CAME IN.
CAN YOU HELP OUT WITH IT?
BUT...
I HAVE THAT SOBA PARTY WITH THE KORO-POKKUR...
mumble mumble
DEADLINE'S 7 P.M., DAY AFTER TOMORROW.
IF YOU CAN DO IT ON TIME...
...IT'S ¥600,000 CASH,* STRAIGHT UP.
I AM ON MY WAY.
ZWAAP
*about $5,000

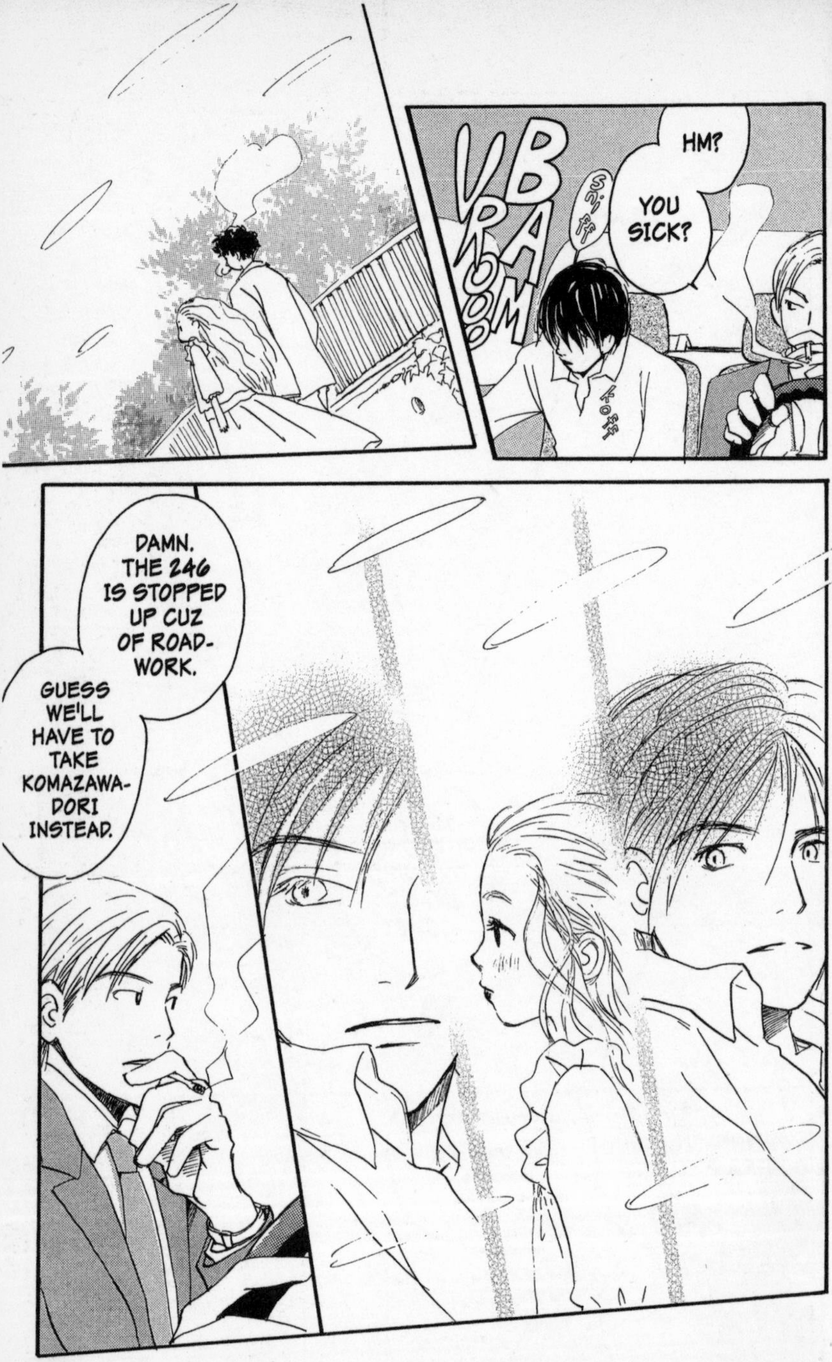
HM?
YOU SICK?
sniff
BAM
VROOO
koff
DAMN. THE 246 IS STOPPED UP CUZ OF ROAD-WORK.
GUESS WE'LL HAVE TO TAKE KOMAZAWA-DORI INSTEAD.

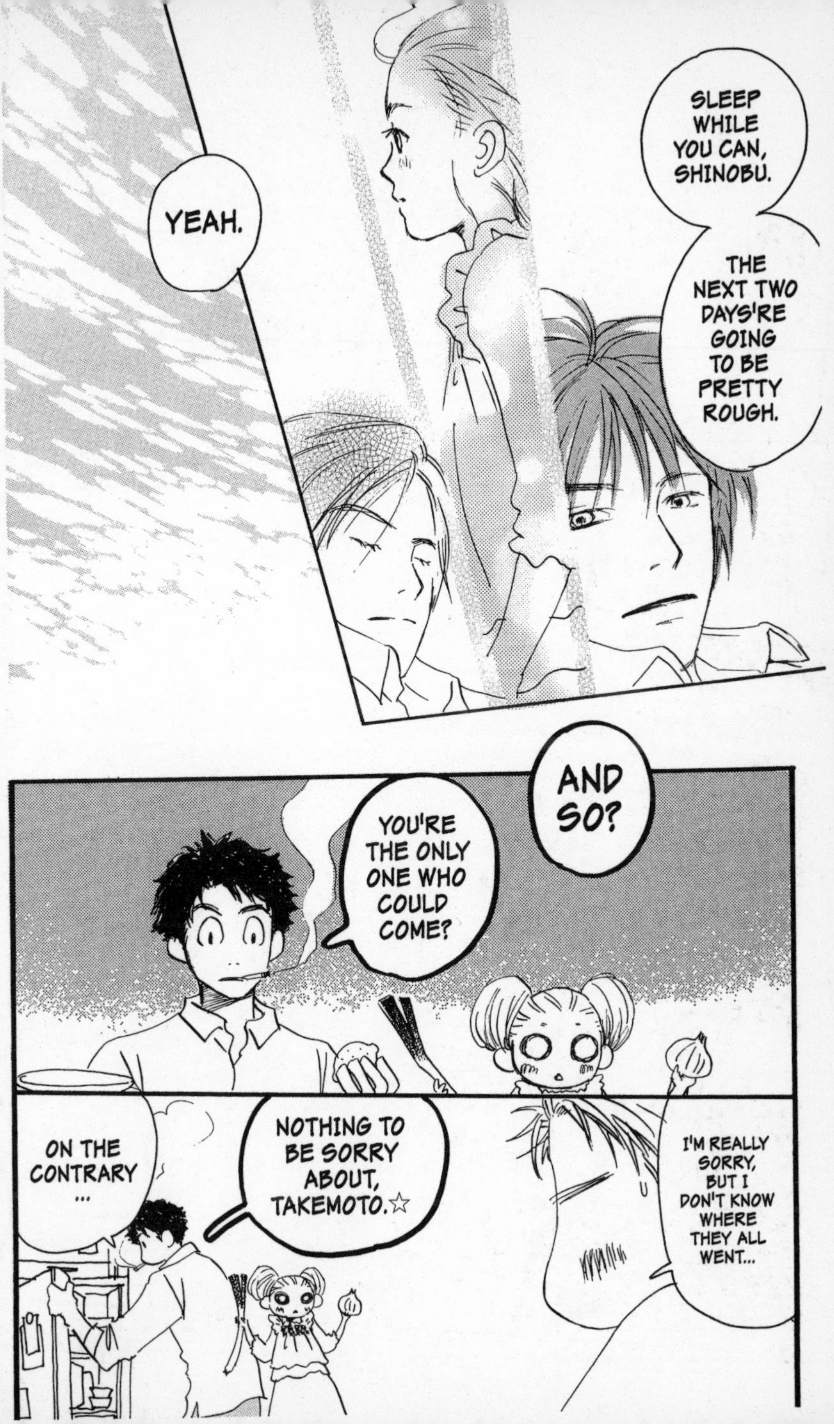
SLEEP WHILE YOU CAN, SHINOBU.
THE NEXT TWO DAYS'RE GOING TO BE PRETTY ROUGH.
YEAH.
AND SO?
YOU'RE THE ONLY ONE WHO COULD COME?
I'M REALLY SORRY, BUT I DON'T KNOW WHERE THEY ALL WENT...
NOTHING TO BE SORRY ABOUT, TAKEMOTO.☆
ON THE CONTRARY ...

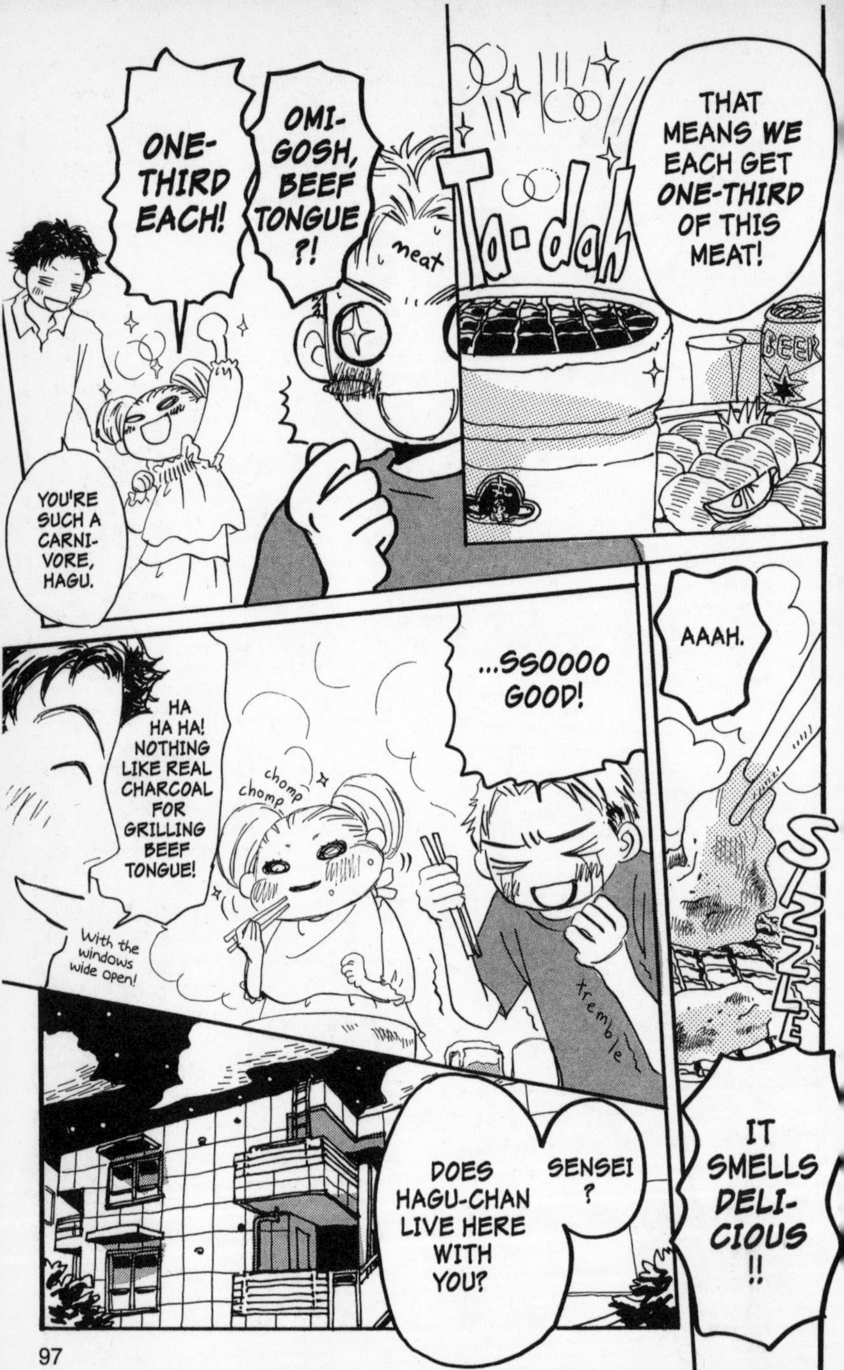
Ta-dah
THAT MEANS WE EACH GET ONE-THIRD OF THIS MEAT!
OMI-GOSH, BEEF TONGUE ?!
meat
ONE-THIRD EACH!
YOU'RE SUCH A CARNI-VORE, HAGU.
AAAH.
SIZZLE
IT SMELLS DELI-CIOUS !!
...SSOOOO GOOD!
tremble
chomp chomp
HA HA HA! NOTHING LIKE REAL CHARCOAL FOR GRILLING BEEF TONGUE!
With the windows wide open!
SENSEI ?
DOES HAGU-CHAN LIVE HERE WITH YOU?

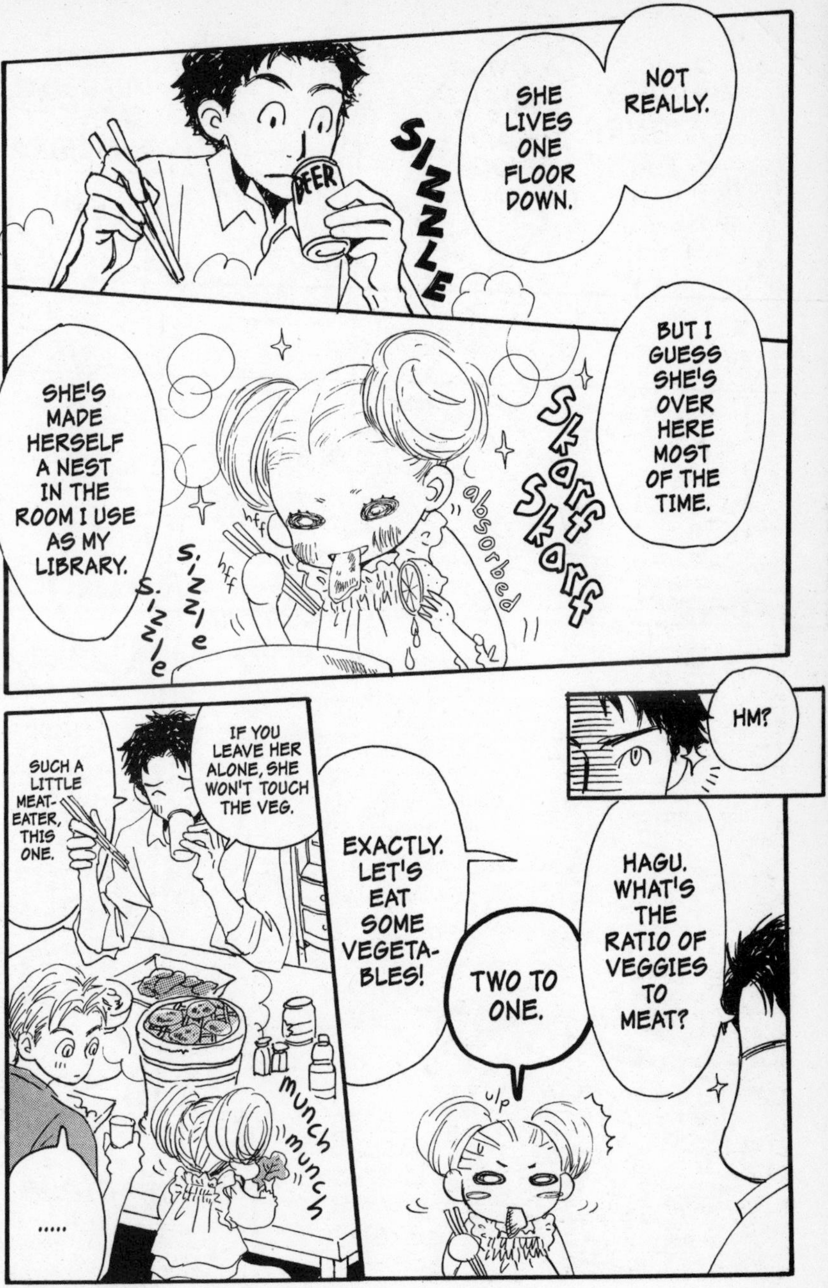
NOT REALLY.
SHE LIVES ONE FLOOR DOWN.
SIZZLE
BUT I GUESS SHE'S OVER HERE MOST OF THE TIME.
Skarf Skarf
absorbed
hff
hff
sizzle sizzle
SHE'S MADE HERSELF A NEST IN THE ROOM I USE AS MY LIBRARY.
HM?
HAGU. WHAT'S THE RATIO OF VEGGIES TO MEAT?
TWO TO ONE.
ulp
EXACTLY. LET'S EAT SOME VEGETA-BLES!
IF YOU LEAVE HER ALONE, SHE WON'T TOUCH THE VEG.
SUCH A LITTLE MEAT-EATER, THIS ONE.
munch munch
.....

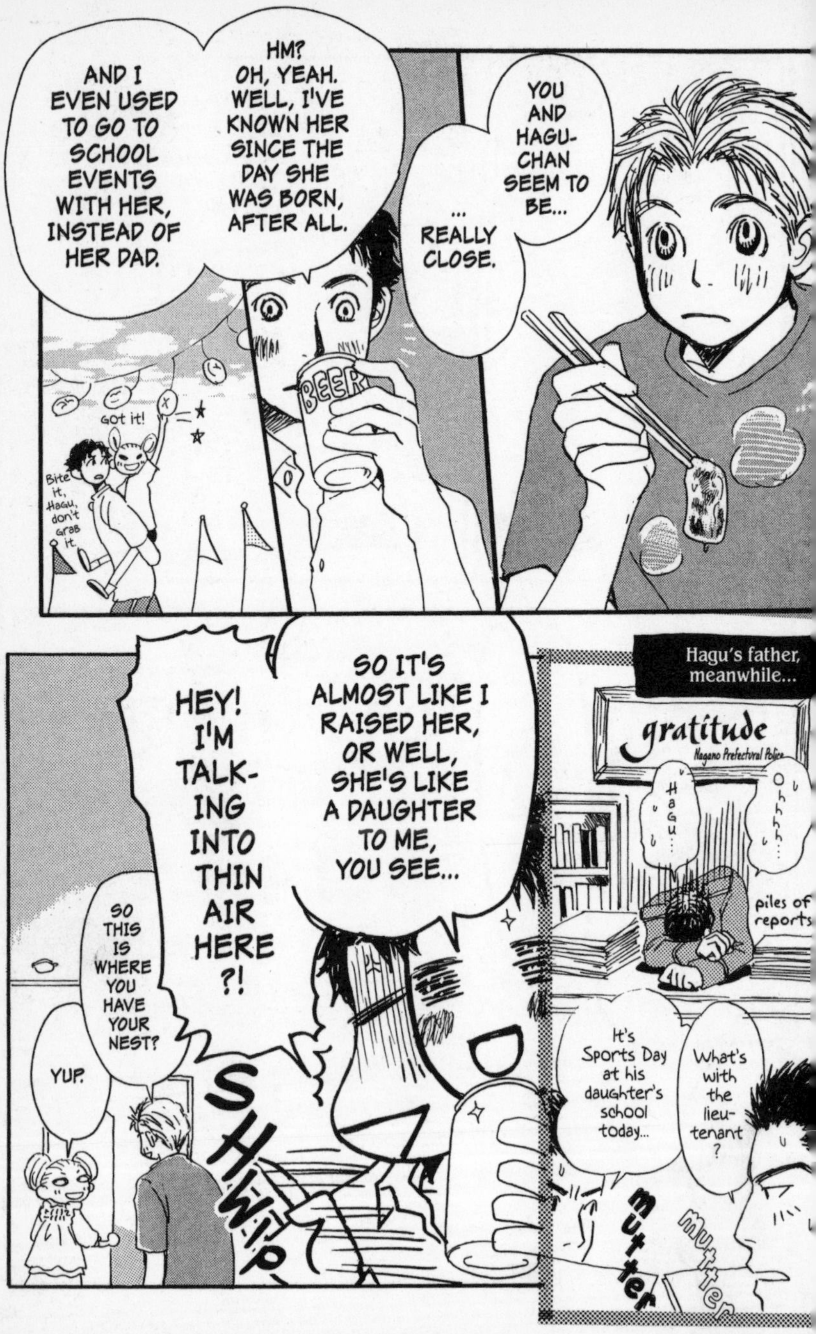
YOU AND HAGU-CHAN SEEM TO BE...
... REALLY CLOSE.
HM? OH, YEAH. WELL, I'VE KNOWN HER SINCE THE DAY SHE WAS BORN, AFTER ALL.
AND I EVEN USED TO GO TO SCHOOL EVENTS WITH HER, INSTEAD OF HER DAD.
Got it!
Bite it, Hagu, don't grab it.
BEER
Hagu's father, meanwhile...
gratitude
Nagano Prefectural Police
Hagu...
Ohhhh...
piles of reports
What's with the lieutenant?
It's Sports Day at his daughter's school today...
mutter
mutter
SO IT'S ALMOST LIKE I RAISED HER, OR WELL, SHE'S LIKE A DAUGHTER TO ME, YOU SEE...
SHWIP
HEY! I'M TALKING INTO THIN AIR HERE?!
SO THIS IS WHERE YOU HAVE YOUR NEST?
YUP.

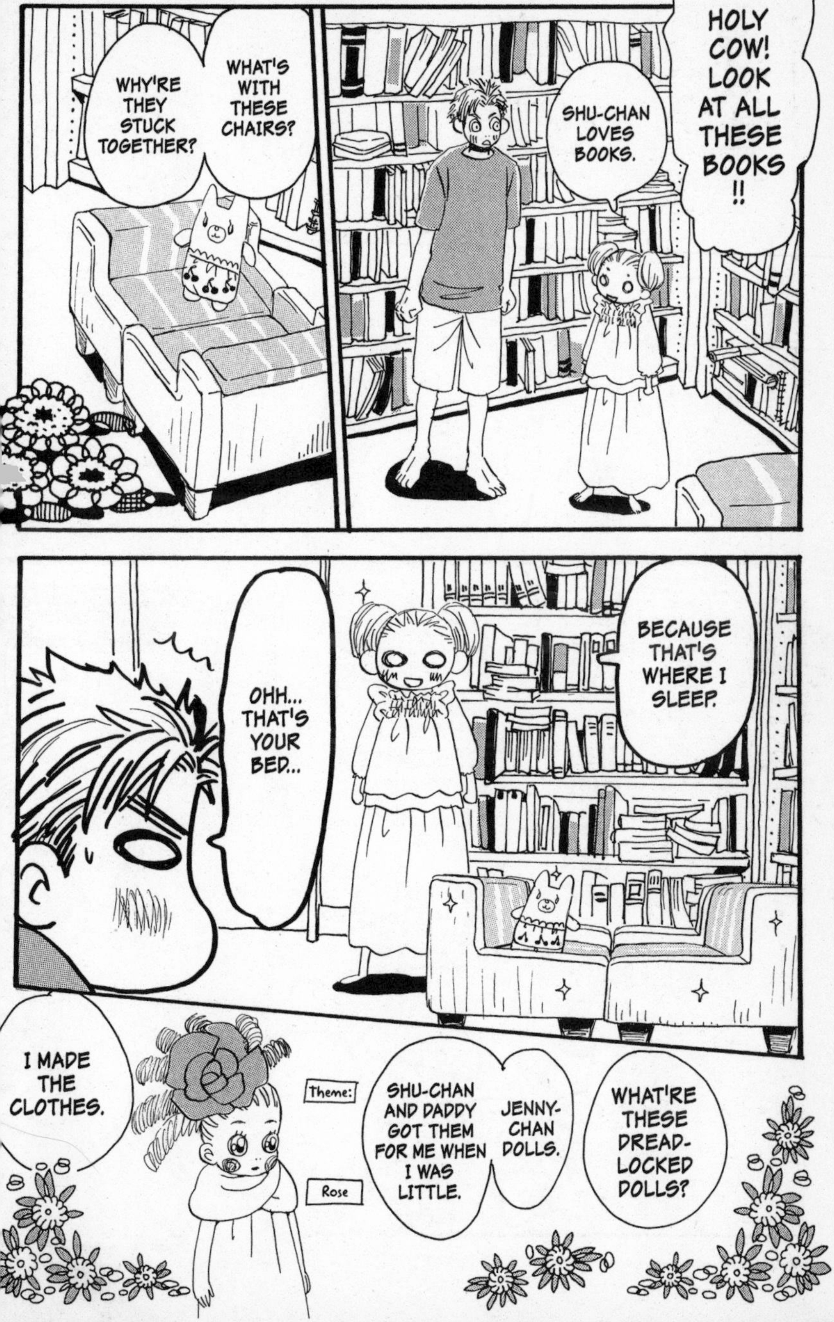
HOLY COW! LOOK AT ALL THESE BOOKS!!
SHU-CHAN LOVES BOOKS.
WHAT'S WITH THESE CHAIRS?
WHY'RE THEY STUCK TOGETHER?
BECAUSE THAT'S WHERE I SLEEP.
OHH... THAT'S YOUR BED...
WHAT'RE THESE DREAD-LOCKED DOLLS?
JENNY-CHAN DOLLS.
SHU-CHAN AND DADDY GOT THEM FOR ME WHEN I WAS LITTLE.
Theme:
Rose
I MADE THE CLOTHES.

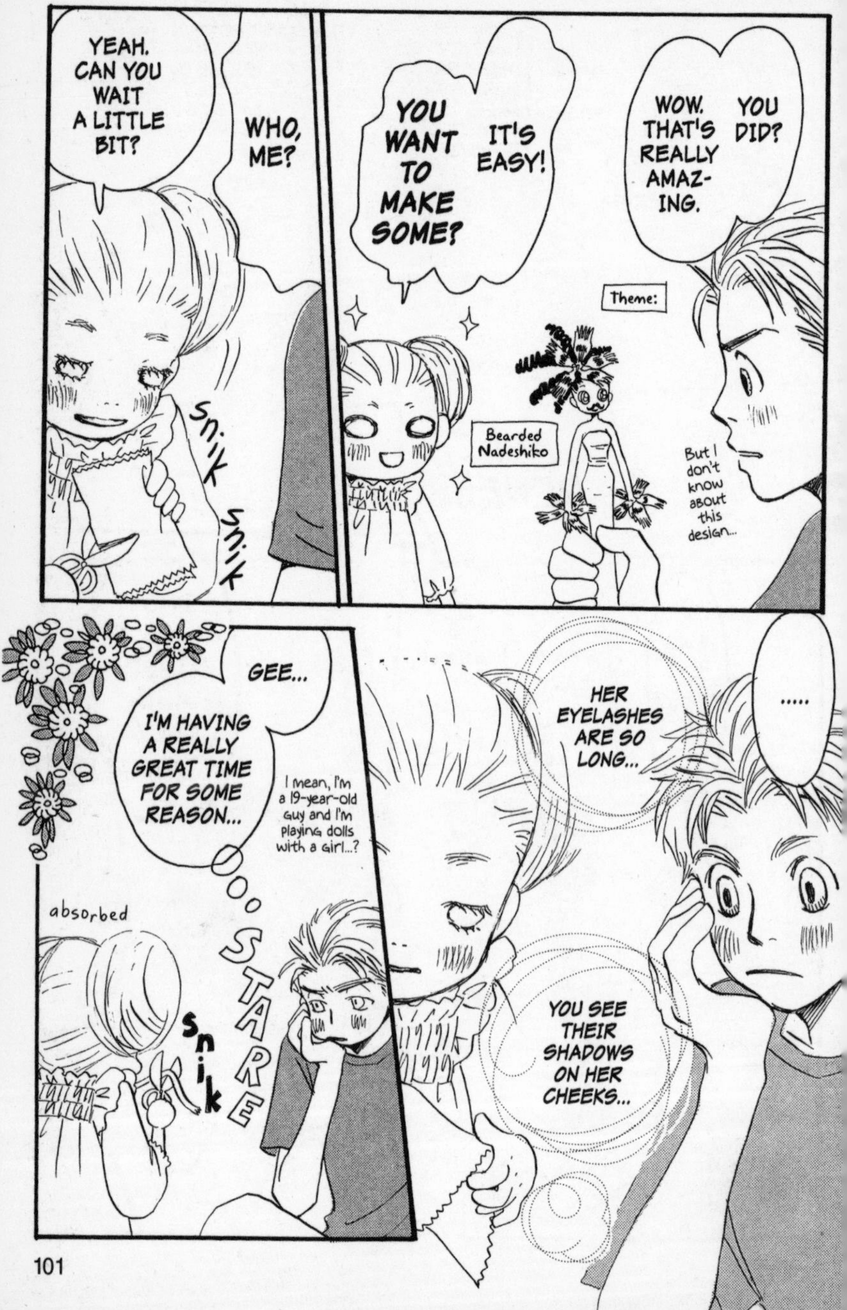
YOU DID?
WOW. THAT'S REALLY AMAZ-ING.
Theme:
Bearded Nadeshiko
But I don't know about this design...
IT'S EASY!
YOU WANT TO MAKE SOME?
WHO, ME?
YEAH. CAN YOU WAIT A LITTLE BIT?
snik
snik
.....
HER EYELASHES ARE SO LONG...
YOU SEE THEIR SHADOWS ON HER CHEEKS...
GEE...
I'M HAVING A REALLY GREAT TIME FOR SOME REASON...
I mean, I'm a 19-year-old guy and I'm playing dolls with a girl...?
STARE
snik
absorbed

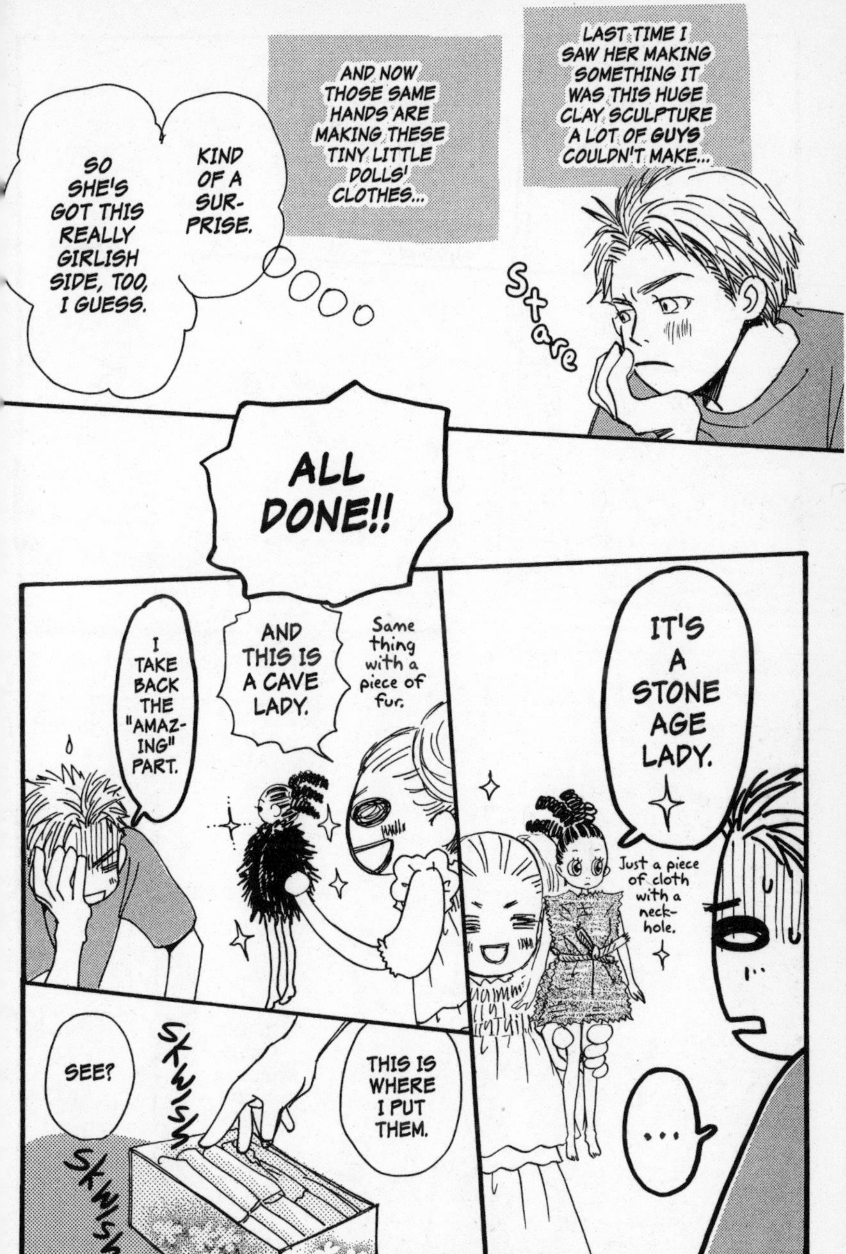
LAST TIME I SAW HER MAKING SOMETHING IT WAS THIS HUGE CLAY SCULPTURE A LOT OF GUYS COULDN'T MAKE...
AND NOW THOSE SAME HANDS ARE MAKING THESE TINY LITTLE DOLLS' CLOTHES...
Stare
KIND OF A SUR-PRISE.
SO SHE'S GOT THIS REALLY GIRLISH SIDE, TOO, I GUESS.
ALL DONE!!
IT'S A STONE AGE LADY.
Just a piece of cloth with a neck-hole.
...
AND THIS IS A CAVE LADY.
Same thing with a piece of fur.
I TAKE BACK THE "AMAZ-ING" PART.
THIS IS WHERE I PUT THEM.
SEE?
SKWISH
SKWISH

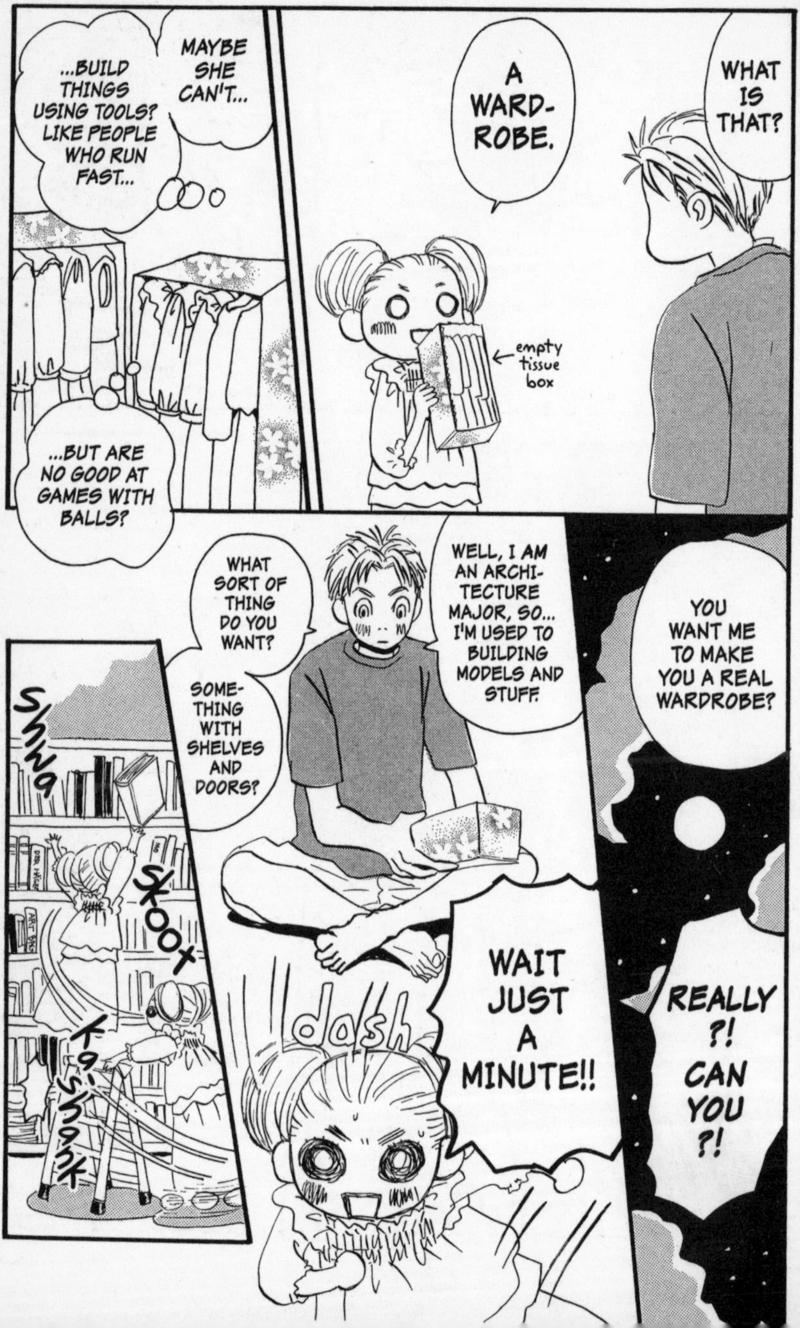
WHAT IS THAT?
A WARD-ROBE.
empty tissue box
MAYBE SHE CAN'T...
...BUILD THINGS USING TOOLS? LIKE PEOPLE WHO RUN FAST...
...BUT ARE NO GOOD AT GAMES WITH BALLS?
YOU WANT ME TO MAKE YOU A REAL WARDROBE?
REALLY ?! CAN YOU ?!
WELL, I AM AN ARCHI-TECTURE MAJOR, SO... I'M USED TO BUILDING MODELS AND STUFF.
WHAT SORT OF THING DO YOU WANT?
SOME-THING WITH SHELVES AND DOORS?
WAIT JUST A MINUTE!!
dash
shwa
skoot
ka-shank

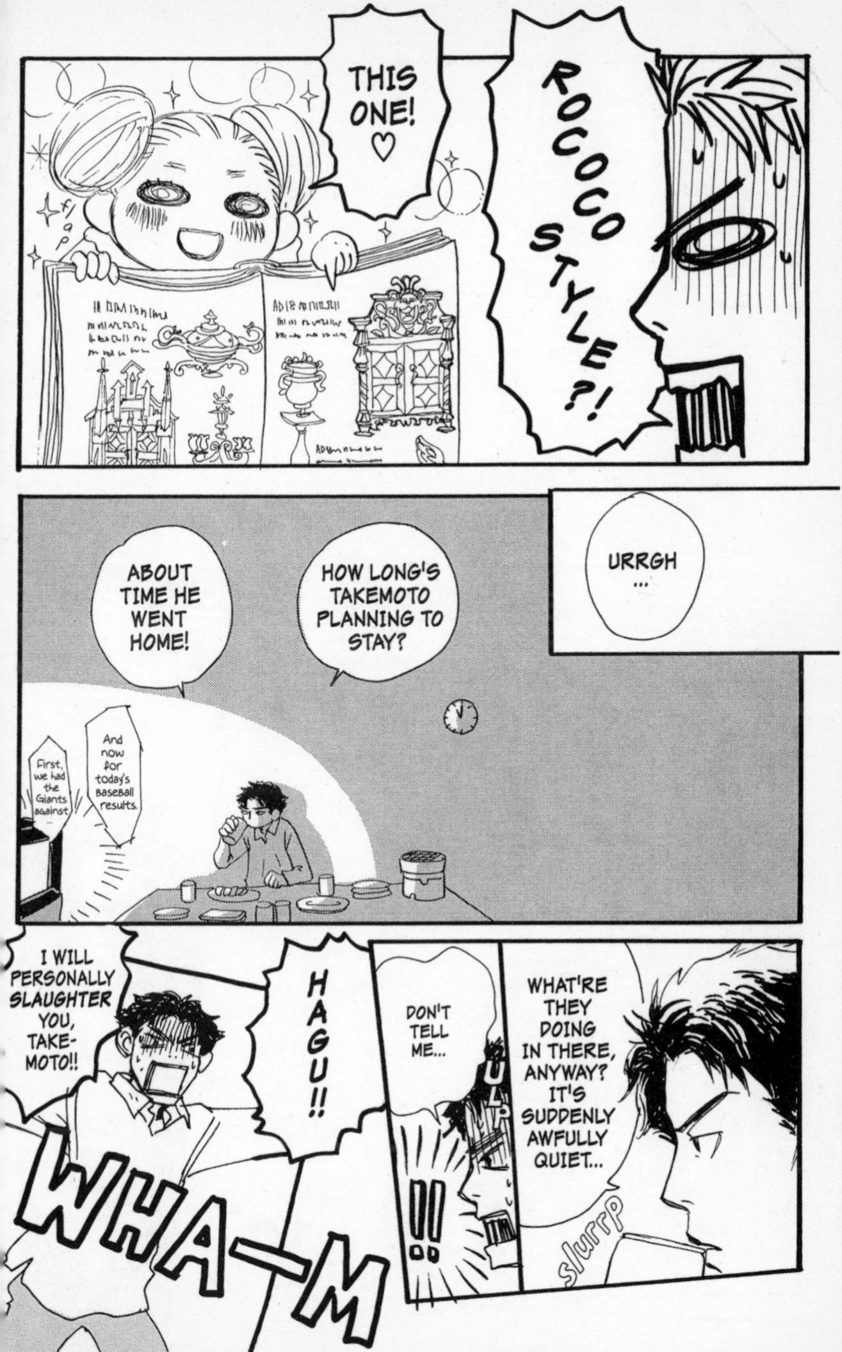
ROCOCO STYLE?!
THIS ONE! ♡
flap
URRGH ...
HOW LONG'S TAKEMOTO PLANNING TO STAY?
ABOUT TIME HE WENT HOME!
And now for today's Baseball results.
First, we had the Giants against ...
WHAT'RE THEY DOING IN THERE, ANYWAY? IT'S SUDDENLY AWFULLY QUIET...
slurrp
DON'T TELL ME...
GULP
!!
HAGU!!
I WILL PERSONALLY SLAUGHTER YOU, TAKE-MOTO!!
WHA-M

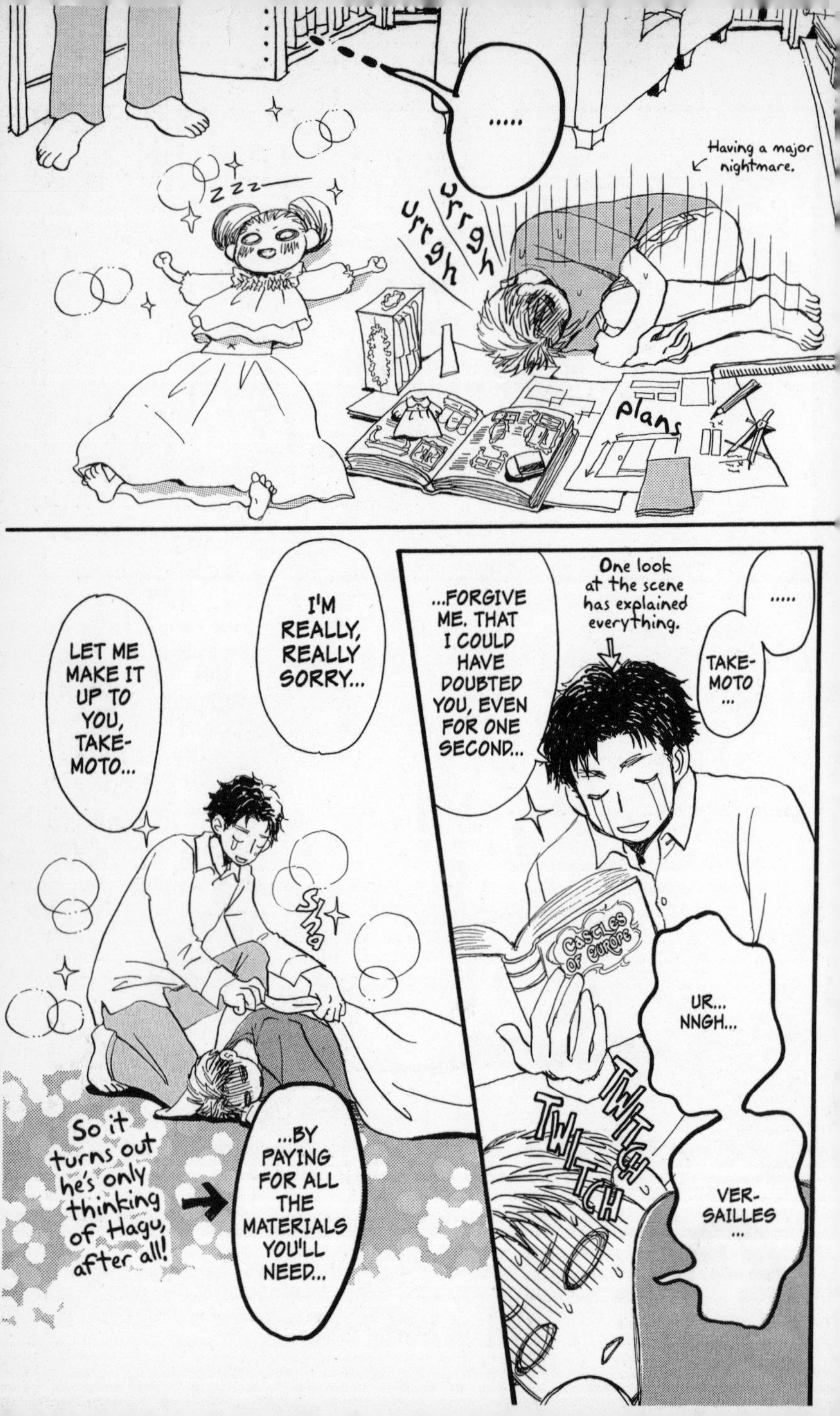

Having a major nightmare.
.....
urrgh
urrgh
plans
zzz
.....
TAKE-MOTO...
One look at the scene has explained everything.
...FORGIVE ME. THAT I COULD HAVE DOUBTED YOU, EVEN FOR ONE SECOND...
CASTLES OF EUROPE
UR... NNGH...
TWITCH
TWITCH
VER-SAILLES...
I'M REALLY, REALLY SORRY...
LET ME MAKE IT UP TO YOU, TAKE-MOTO...
Shu
...BY PAYING FOR ALL THE MATERIALS YOU'LL NEED...
So it turns out he's only thinking of Hagu, after all!

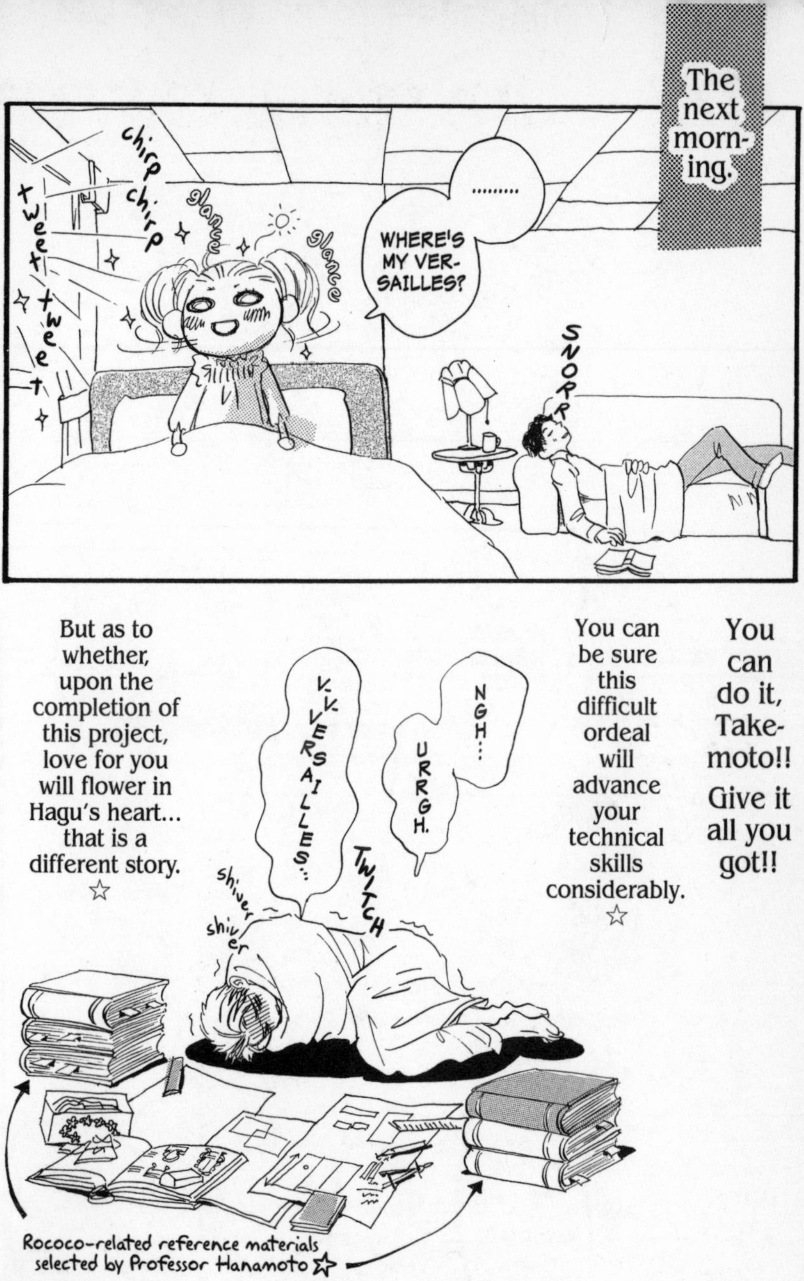
The next morning.
....
WHERE'S MY VERSAILLES?
SNORR
glance glance
chirp chirp
tweet tweet
You can do it, Takemoto!! Give it all you got!!
You can be sure this difficult ordeal will advance your technical skills considerably. ☆
NGH...
URRGH.
V-V-VERSAILLES...
TWITCH
shiver shiver
But as to whether, upon the completion of this project, love for you will flower in Hagu's heart... that is a different story. ☆
Rococo-related reference materials selected by Professor Hanamoto ☆

chapter 6—the end—

honey and clover

chapter 7

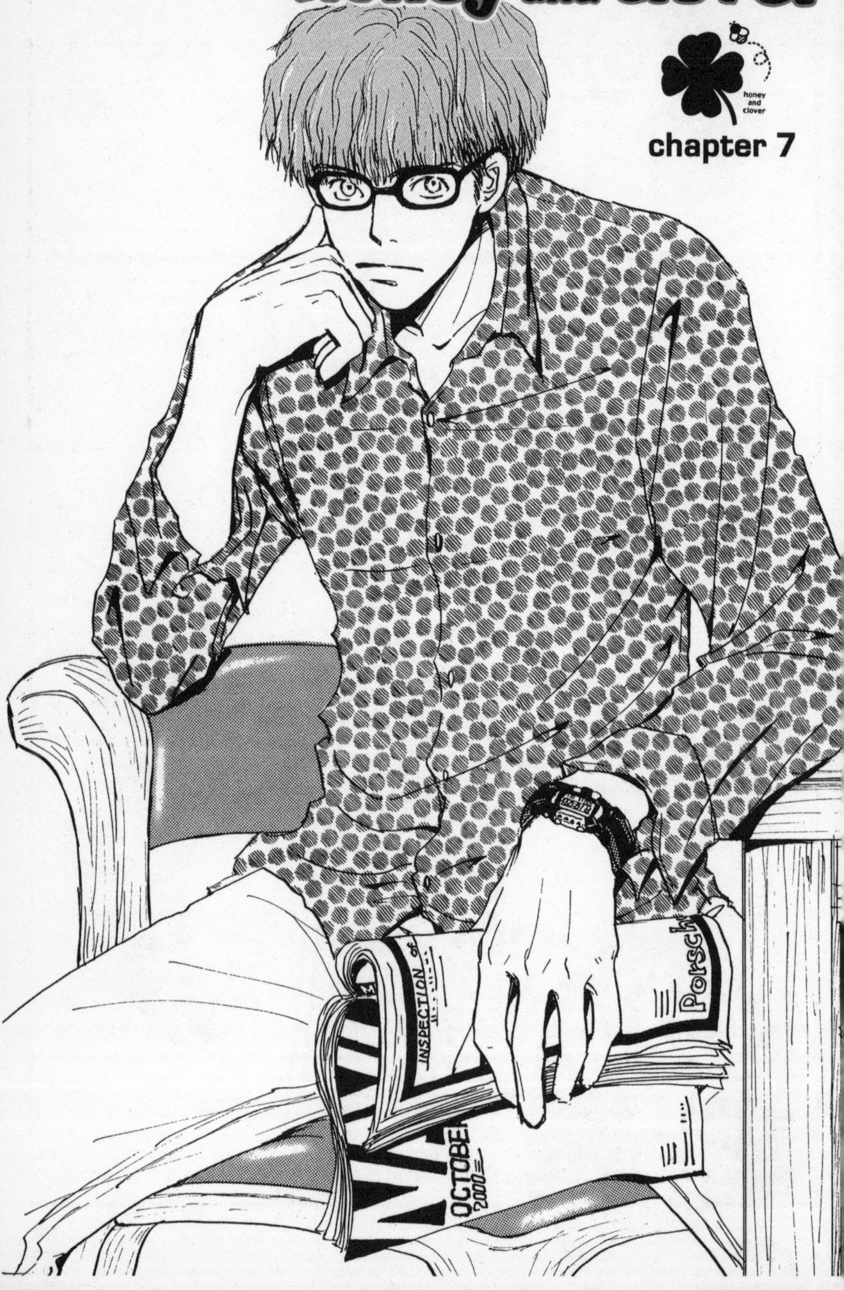

honey and clover
INSPECTION of
Porsch
OCTOBER
2000

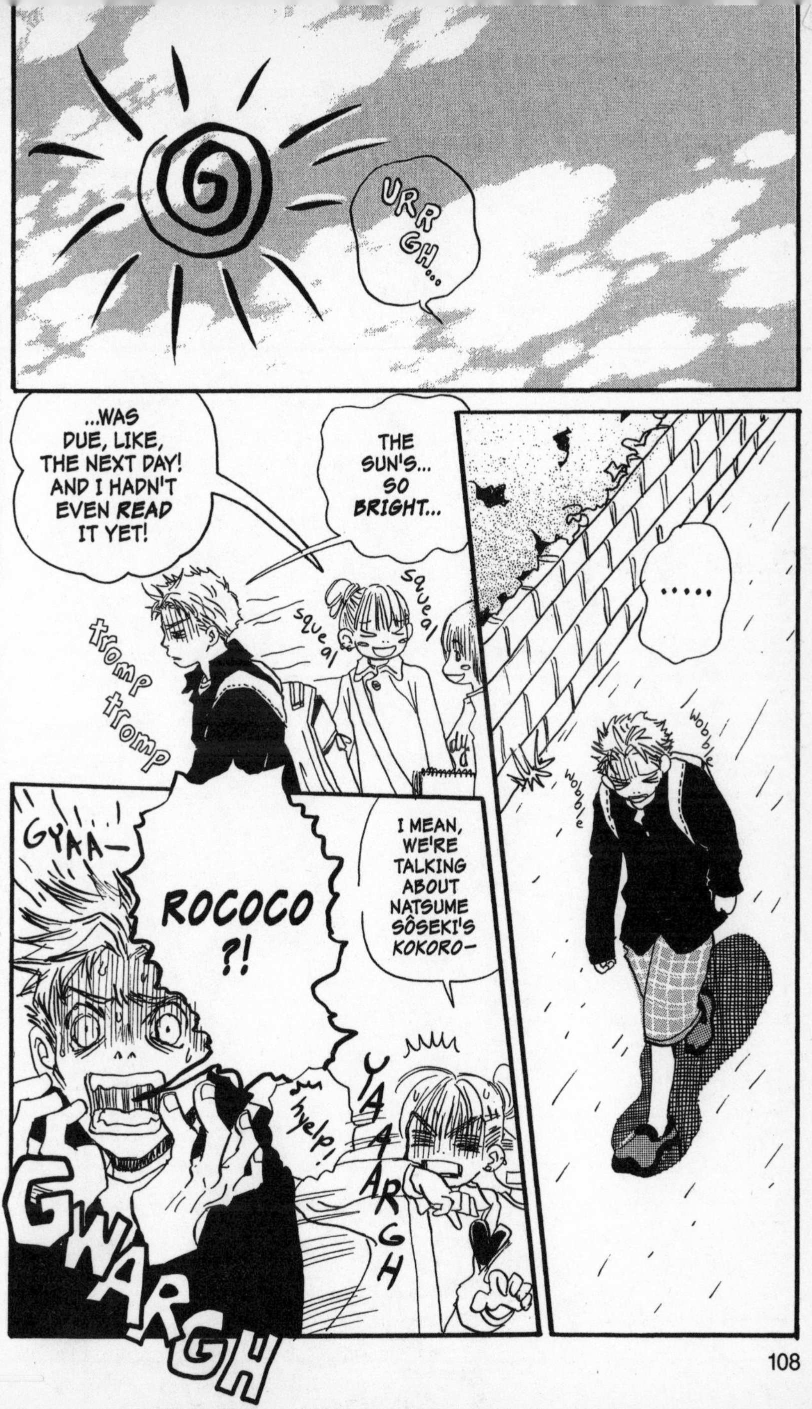
URRGH...
.....
wobble
wobble
THE SUN'S... SO BRIGHT...
...WAS DUE, LIKE, THE NEXT DAY! AND I HADN'T EVEN READ IT YET!
squeal
squeal
tromp tromp
I MEAN, WE'RE TALKING ABOUT NATSUME SÔSEKI'S KOKORO—
ROCOCO ?!
GYAA—
YAAAARGH
hyelp!
GWARGH

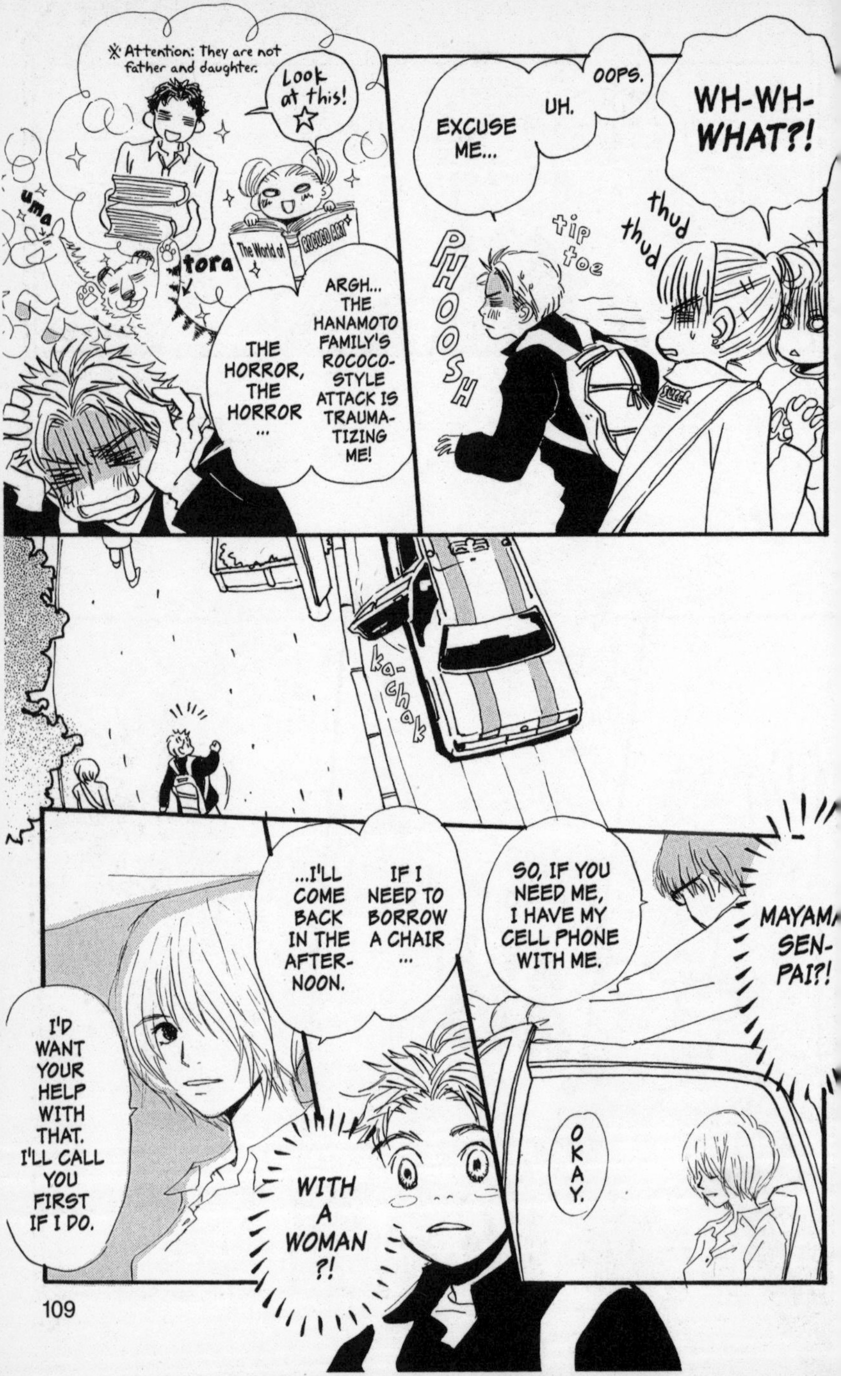

WH-WH-WHAT?!
OOPS.
UH.
EXCUSE ME...
thud thud
tip toe
PHOOOSH
※Attention: They are not father and daughter.
Look at this! ☆
uma
tora
The World of ROCOCO ART
ARGH... THE HANAMOTO FAMILY'S ROCOCO-STYLE ATTACK IS TRAUMATIZING ME!
THE HORROR, THE HORROR...
ka-chak
MAYAMA SEN-PAI?!
SO, IF YOU NEED ME, I HAVE MY CELL PHONE WITH ME.
IF I NEED TO BORROW A CHAIR...
...I'LL COME BACK IN THE AFTERNOON.
OKAY.
WITH A WOMAN?!
I'D WANT YOUR HELP WITH THAT. I'LL CALL YOU FIRST IF I DO.

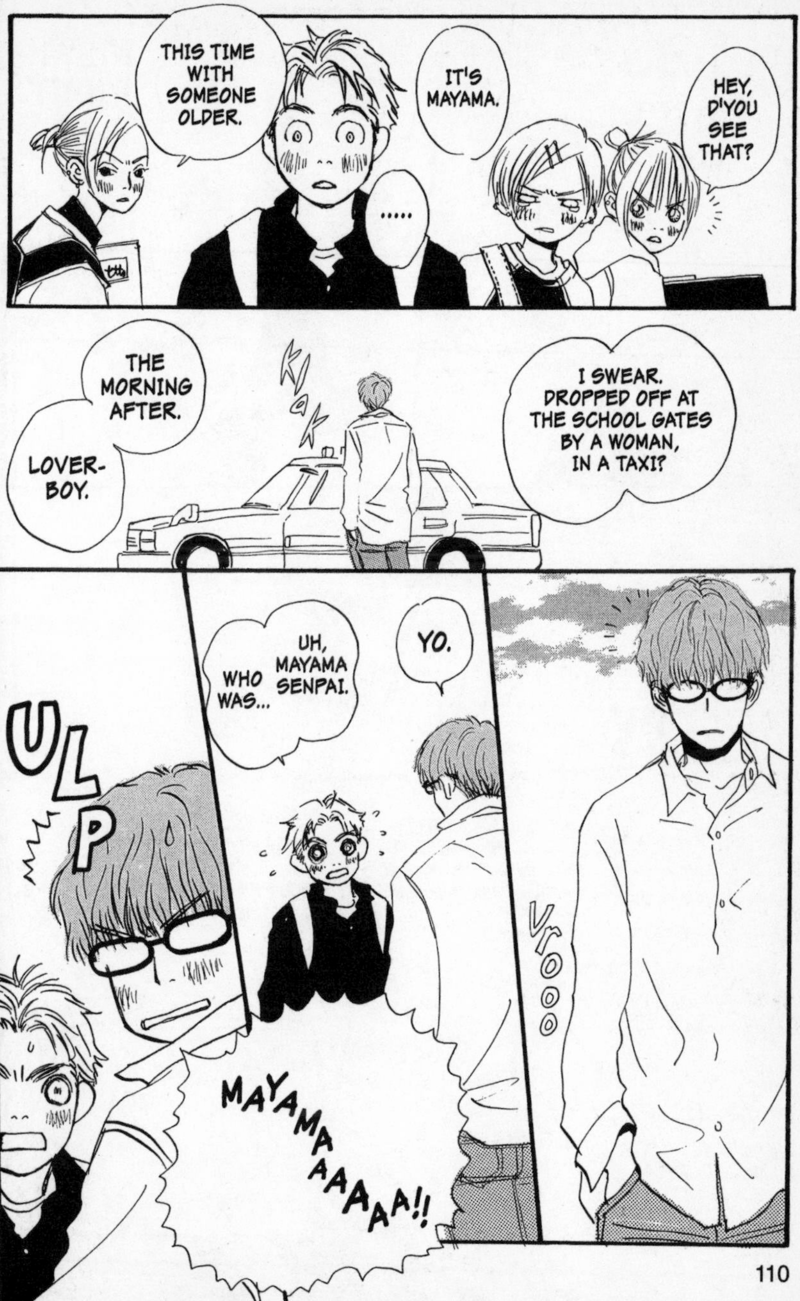
HEY, D'YOU SEE THAT?
IT'S MAYAMA.
.....
THIS TIME WITH SOMEONE OLDER.
I SWEAR. DROPPED OFF AT THE SCHOOL GATES BY A WOMAN, IN A TAXI?
KLAK
THE MORNING AFTER.
LOVER-BOY.
Vroooo
YO.
UH, MAYAMA SENPAI.
WHO WAS...
ULP
MAYAMAAAAAAA!!

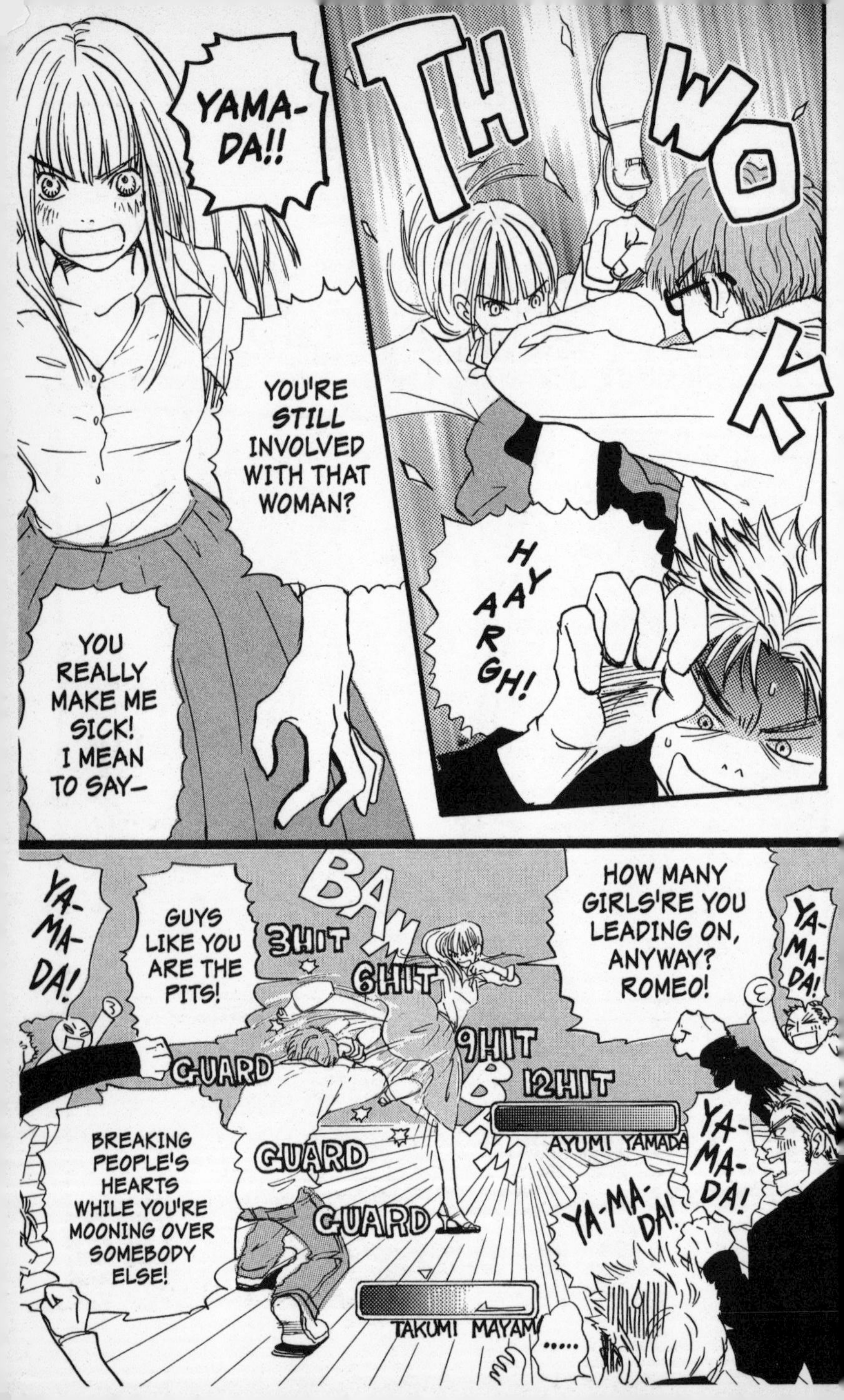
THWOK
HYAAARGH!
YAMA-DA!!
YOU'RE STILL INVOLVED WITH THAT WOMAN?
YOU REALLY MAKE ME SICK! I MEAN TO SAY—
YA-MA-DA!
HOW MANY GIRLS'RE YOU LEADING ON, ANYWAY? ROMEO!
BAM
GUYS LIKE YOU ARE THE PITS!
YA-MA-DA!
3HIT
6HIT
9HIT
12HIT
GUARD
BAM
AYUMI YAMADA
YA-MA-DA!
YA-MA-DA!
GUARD
GUARD
BREAKING PEOPLE'S HEARTS WHILE YOU'RE MOONING OVER SOMEBODY ELSE!
TAKUMI MAYAMA
.....

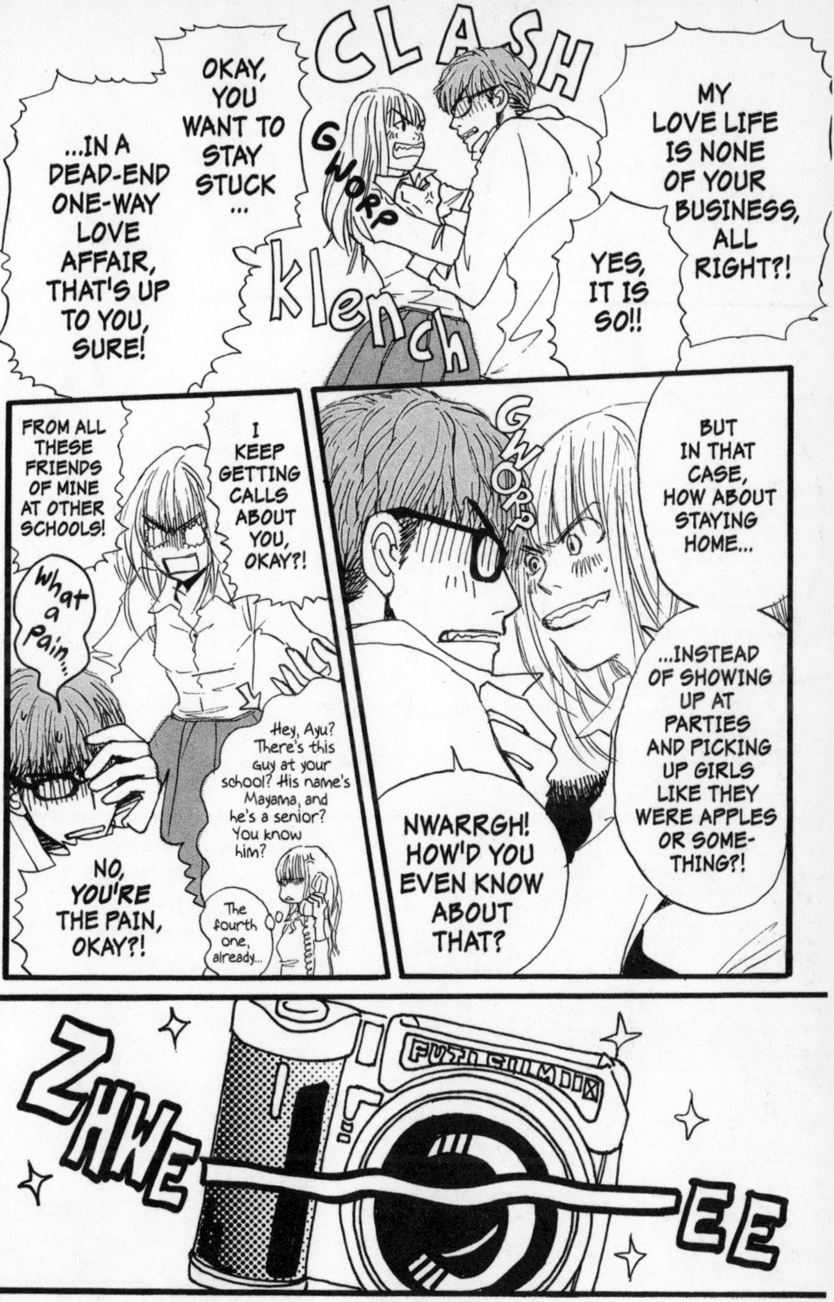
MY LOVE LIFE IS NONE OF YOUR BUSINESS, ALL RIGHT?!
YES, IT IS SO!!
CLASH
GWORP
klench
OKAY, YOU WANT TO STAY STUCK...
...IN A DEAD-END ONE-WAY LOVE AFFAIR, THAT'S UP TO YOU, SURE!
GWORP
BUT IN THAT CASE, HOW ABOUT STAYING HOME...
...INSTEAD OF SHOWING UP AT PARTIES AND PICKING UP GIRLS LIKE THEY WERE APPLES OR SOME-THING?!
NWARRGH! HOW'D YOU EVEN KNOW ABOUT THAT?
I KEEP GETTING CALLS ABOUT YOU, OKAY?!
FROM ALL THESE FRIENDS OF MINE AT OTHER SCHOOLS!
Hey, Ayu? There's this guy at your school? His name's Mayama, and he's a senior? You know him?
The fourth one, already...
What a pain...
NO, YOU'RE THE PAIN, OKAY?!
ZHWE—EE

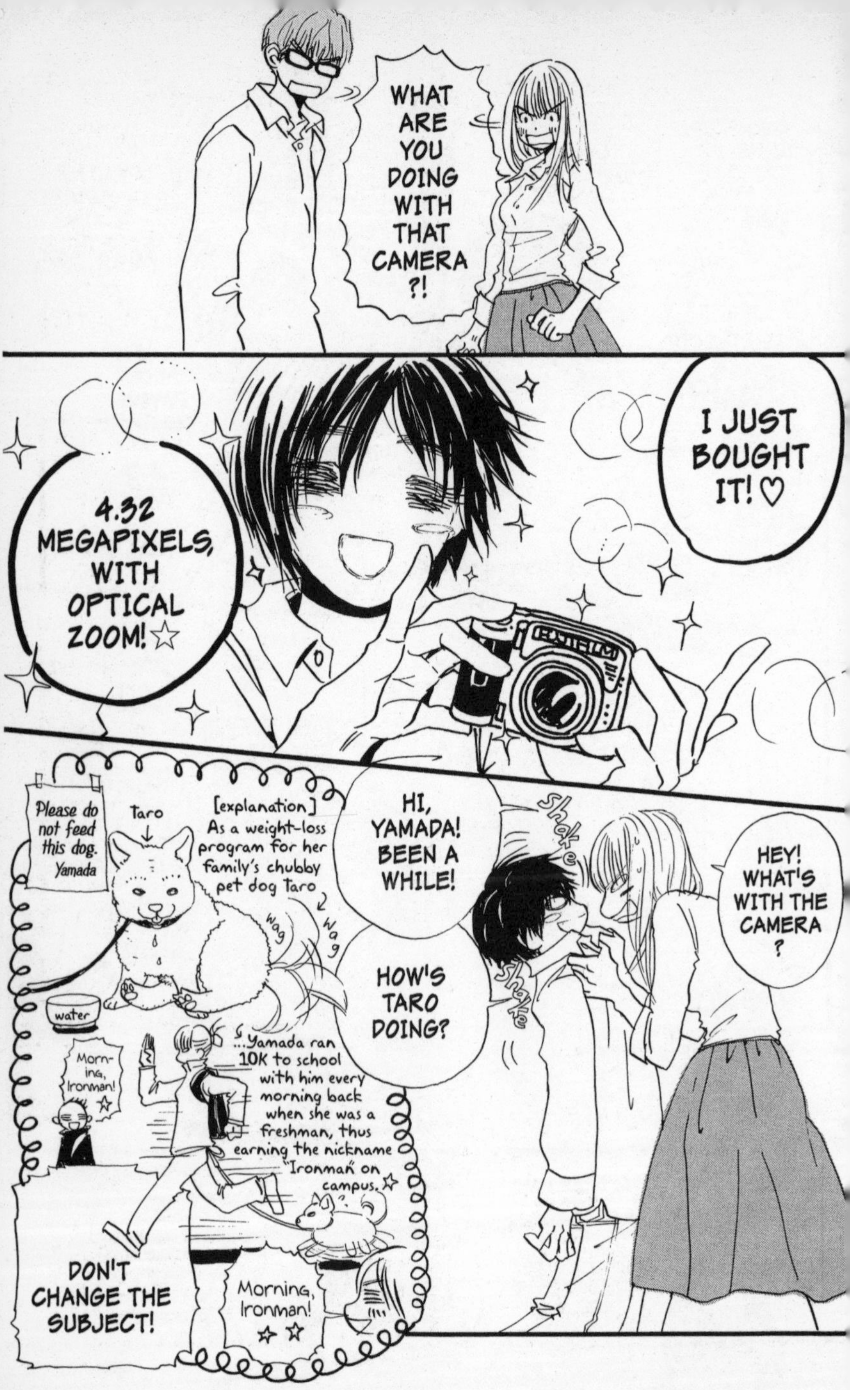
WHAT ARE YOU DOING WITH THAT CAMERA?!
I JUST BOUGHT IT! ♡
4.32 MEGAPIXELS, WITH OPTICAL ZOOM! ☆
HEY! WHAT'S WITH THE CAMERA?
Shake
Shake
HI, YAMADA! BEEN A WHILE!
HOW'S TARO DOING?
[explanation] As a weight-loss program for her family's chubby pet dog Taro
Taro
Please do not feed this dog. Yamada
wag wag
water
...Yamada ran 10K to school with him every morning back when she was a freshman, thus earning the nickname "Ironman" on campus. ☆
Morn-ing, Ironman! ☆
Morning, Ironman! ☆ ☆
DON'T CHANGE THE SUBJECT!

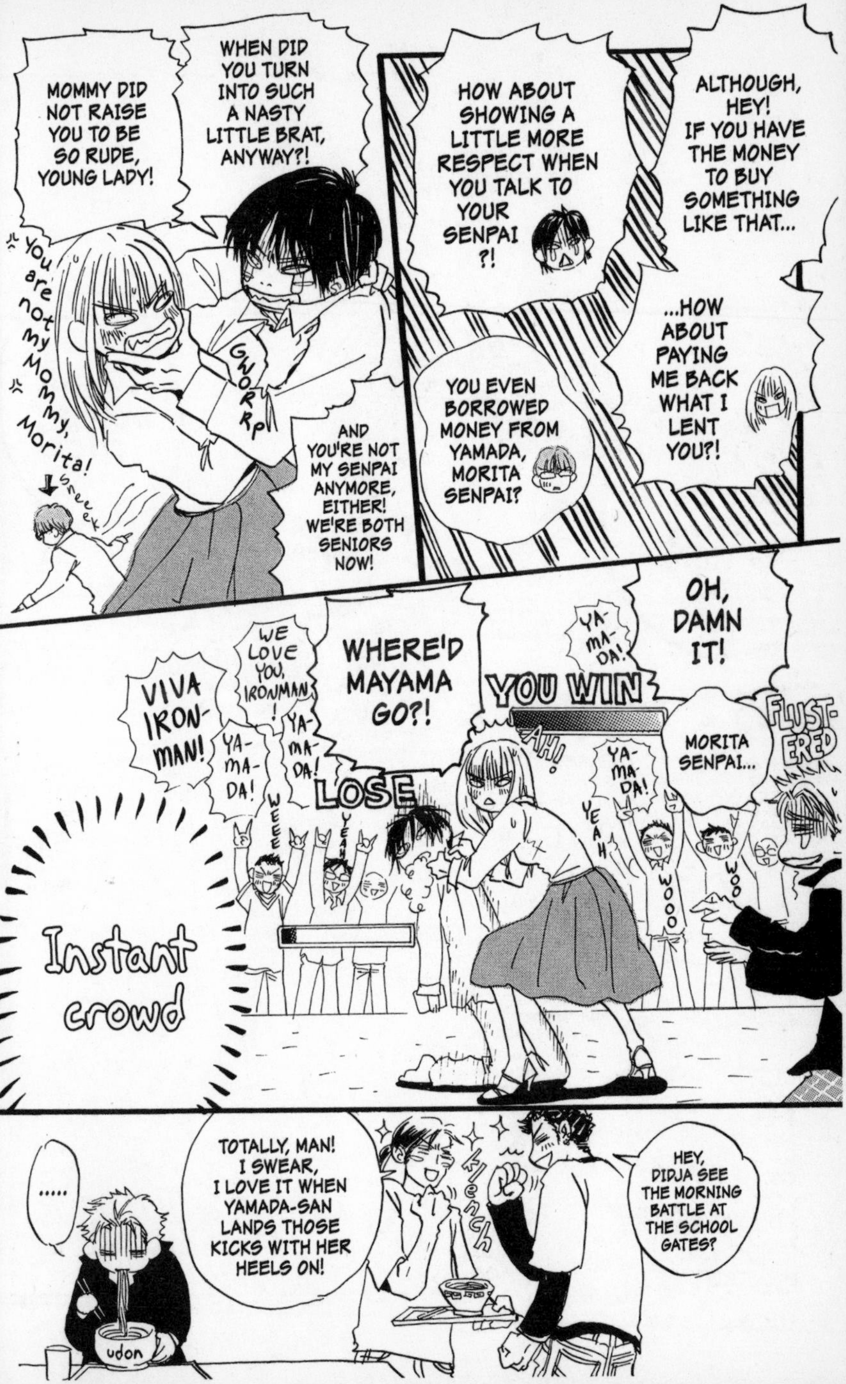
ALTHOUGH, HEY! IF YOU HAVE THE MONEY TO BUY SOMETHING LIKE THAT...
HOW ABOUT SHOWING A LITTLE MORE RESPECT WHEN YOU TALK TO YOUR SENPAI ?!
...HOW ABOUT PAYING ME BACK WHAT I LENT YOU?!
YOU EVEN BORROWED MONEY FROM YAMADA, MORITA SENPAI?
WHEN DID YOU TURN INTO SUCH A NASTY LITTLE BRAT, ANYWAY?!
MOMMY DID NOT RAISE YOU TO BE SO RUDE, YOUNG LADY!
GWORRP
You are not my Mommy, Morita!
AND YOU'RE NOT MY SENPAI ANYMORE, EITHER! WE'RE BOTH SENIORS NOW!
Sneeek
OH, DAMN IT!
YA-MA-DA!
YOU WIN
FLUST-ERED
MORITA SENPAI...
YA-MA-DA!
YEAH
WOOO
WOO
AH!
WHERE'D MAYAMA GO?!
WE LOVE YOU, IRONMAN!
YA-MA-DA!
VIVA IRON-MAN!
YA-MA-DA!
LOSE
WEEE
YEAH
Instant crowd
HEY, DIDJA SEE THE MORNING BATTLE AT THE SCHOOL GATES?
klench
TOTALLY, MAN! I SWEAR, I LOVE IT WHEN YAMADA-SAN LANDS THOSE KICKS WITH HER HEELS ON!
.....
udon

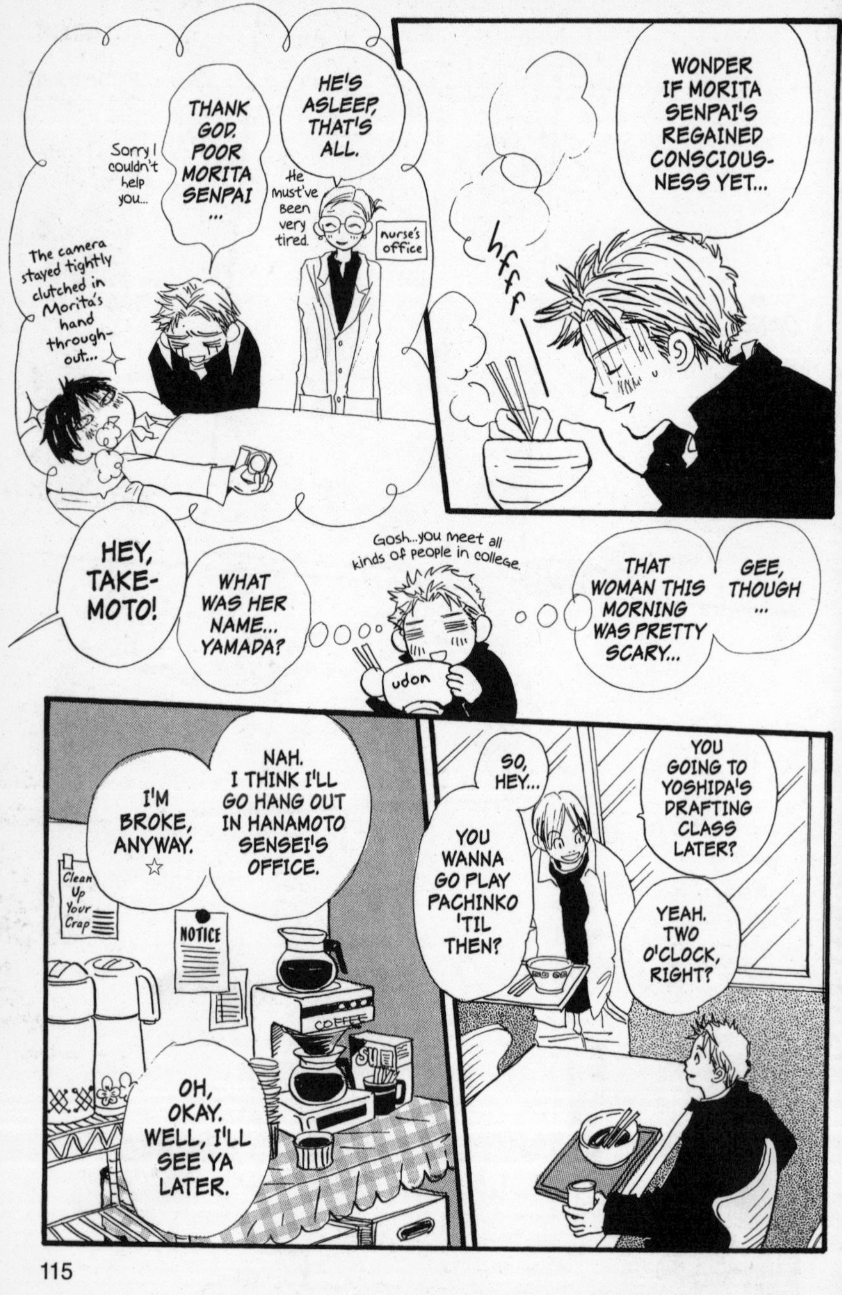
WONDER IF MORITA SENPAI'S REGAINED CONSCIOUS-NESS YET...
hfff
HE'S ASLEEP, THAT'S ALL.
He must've Been very tired.
nurse's office
THANK GOD. POOR MORITA SENPAI ...
Sorry I couldn't help you...
The camera stayed tightly clutched in Morita's hand through-out...
GEE, THOUGH ...
THAT WOMAN THIS MORNING WAS PRETTY SCARY...
Gosh...you meet all kinds of people in college.
udon
WHAT WAS HER NAME... YAMADA?
HEY, TAKE-MOTO!
YOU GOING TO YOSHIDA'S DRAFTING CLASS LATER?
SO, HEY...
YOU WANNA GO PLAY PACHINKO 'TIL THEN?
YEAH. TWO O'CLOCK, RIGHT?
NAH. I THINK I'LL GO HANG OUT IN HANAMOTO SENSEI'S OFFICE.
I'M BROKE, ANYWAY. ☆
Clean Up Your Crap
NOTICE
COFFEE
OH, OKAY. WELL, I'LL SEE YA LATER.

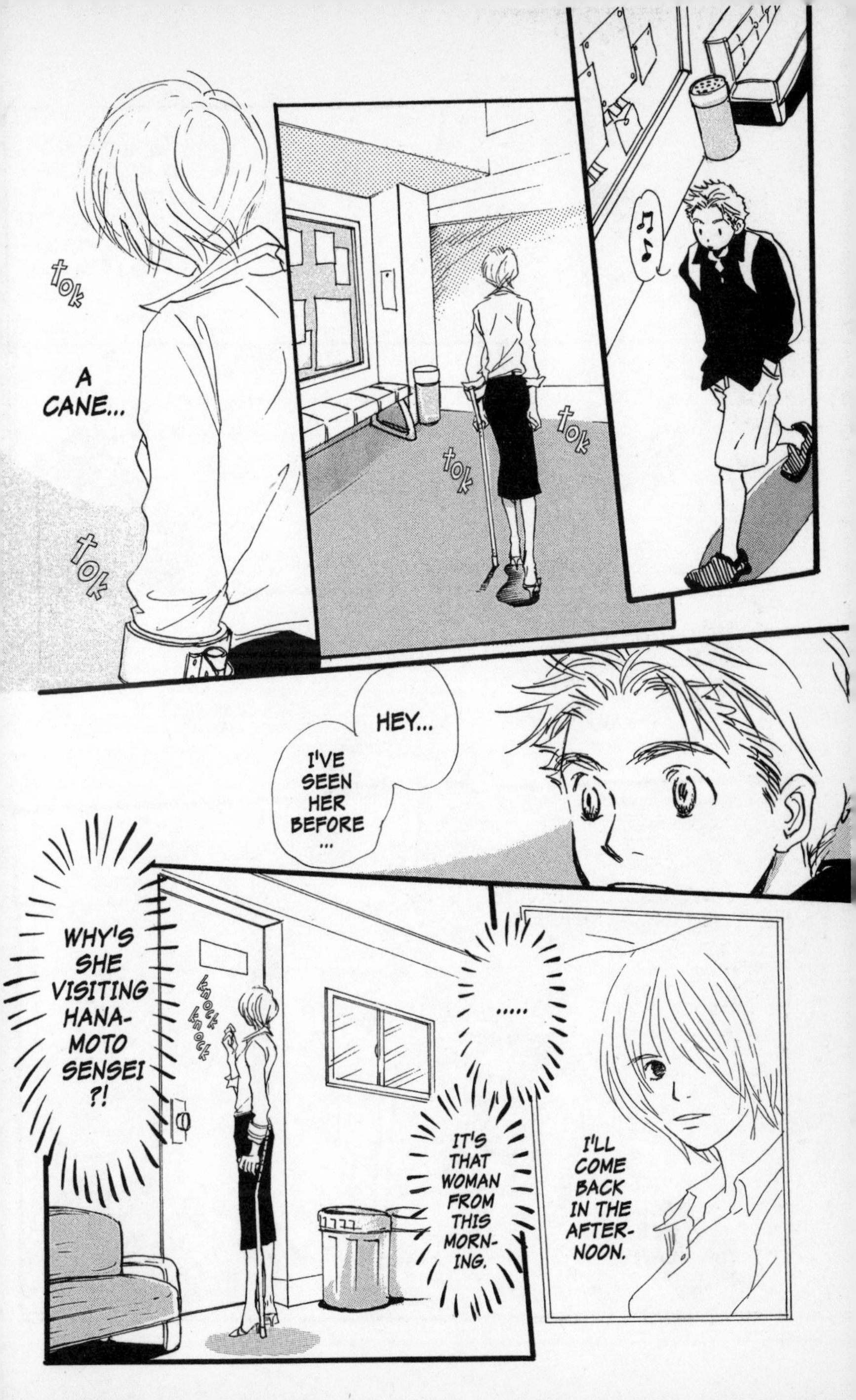
♪
tok
tok
A CANE...
tok
tok
HEY...
I'VE SEEN HER BEFORE ...
I'LL COME BACK IN THE AFTER-NOON.
.....
IT'S THAT WOMAN FROM THIS MORN-ING.
WHY'S SHE VISITING HANA-MOTO SENSEI ?!
knock knock

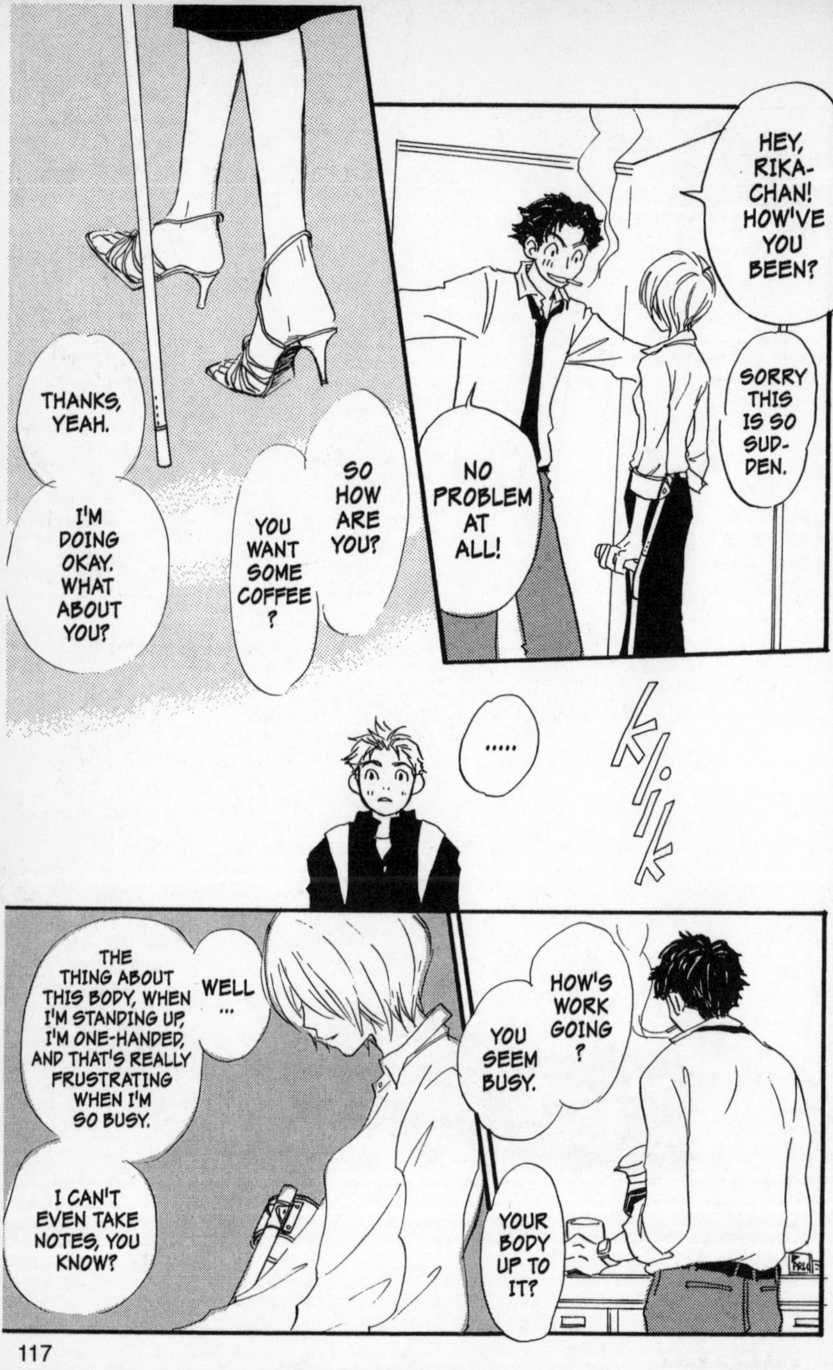
HEY, RIKA-CHAN! HOW'VE YOU BEEN?
SORRY THIS IS SO SUD-DEN.
NO PROBLEM AT ALL!
SO HOW ARE YOU?
YOU WANT SOME COFFEE?
THANKS, YEAH.
I'M DOING OKAY. WHAT ABOUT YOU?
klik
.....
HOW'S WORK GOING?
YOU SEEM BUSY.
YOUR BODY UP TO IT?
WELL ...
THE THING ABOUT THIS BODY, WHEN I'M STANDING UP, I'M ONE-HANDED, AND THAT'S REALLY FRUSTRATING WHEN I'M SO BUSY.
I CAN'T EVEN TAKE NOTES, YOU KNOW?

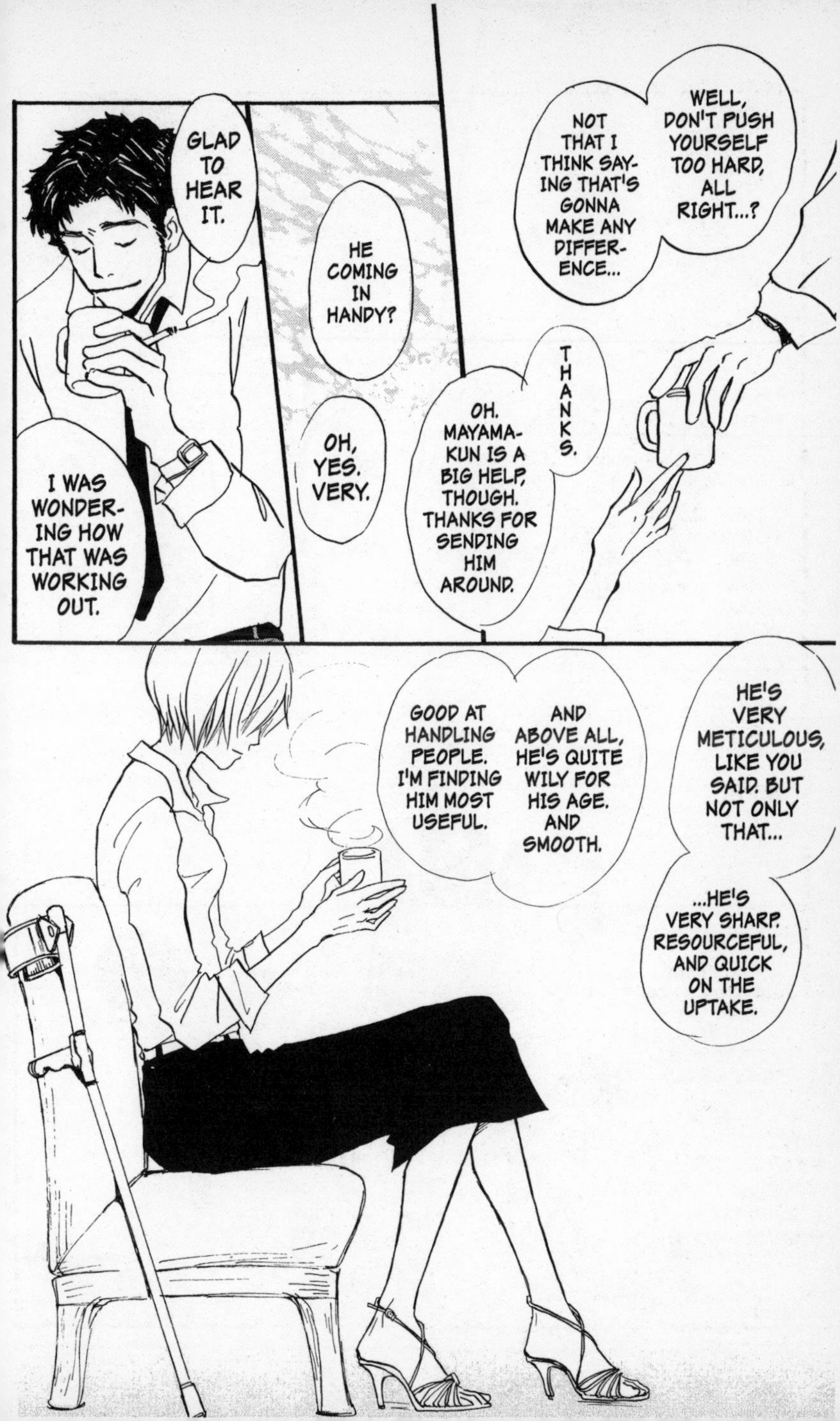
WELL, DON'T PUSH YOURSELF TOO HARD, ALL RIGHT...?
NOT THAT I THINK SAYING THAT'S GONNA MAKE ANY DIFFERENCE...
THANKS.
OH. MAYAMA-KUN IS A BIG HELP, THOUGH. THANKS FOR SENDING HIM AROUND.
HE COMING IN HANDY?
OH, YES. VERY.
GLAD TO HEAR IT.
I WAS WONDERING HOW THAT WAS WORKING OUT.
HE'S VERY METICULOUS, LIKE YOU SAID. BUT NOT ONLY THAT...
...HE'S VERY SHARP. RESOURCEFUL, AND QUICK ON THE UPTAKE.
AND ABOVE ALL, HE'S QUITE WILY FOR HIS AGE. AND SMOOTH.
GOOD AT HANDLING PEOPLE. I'M FINDING HIM MOST USEFUL.

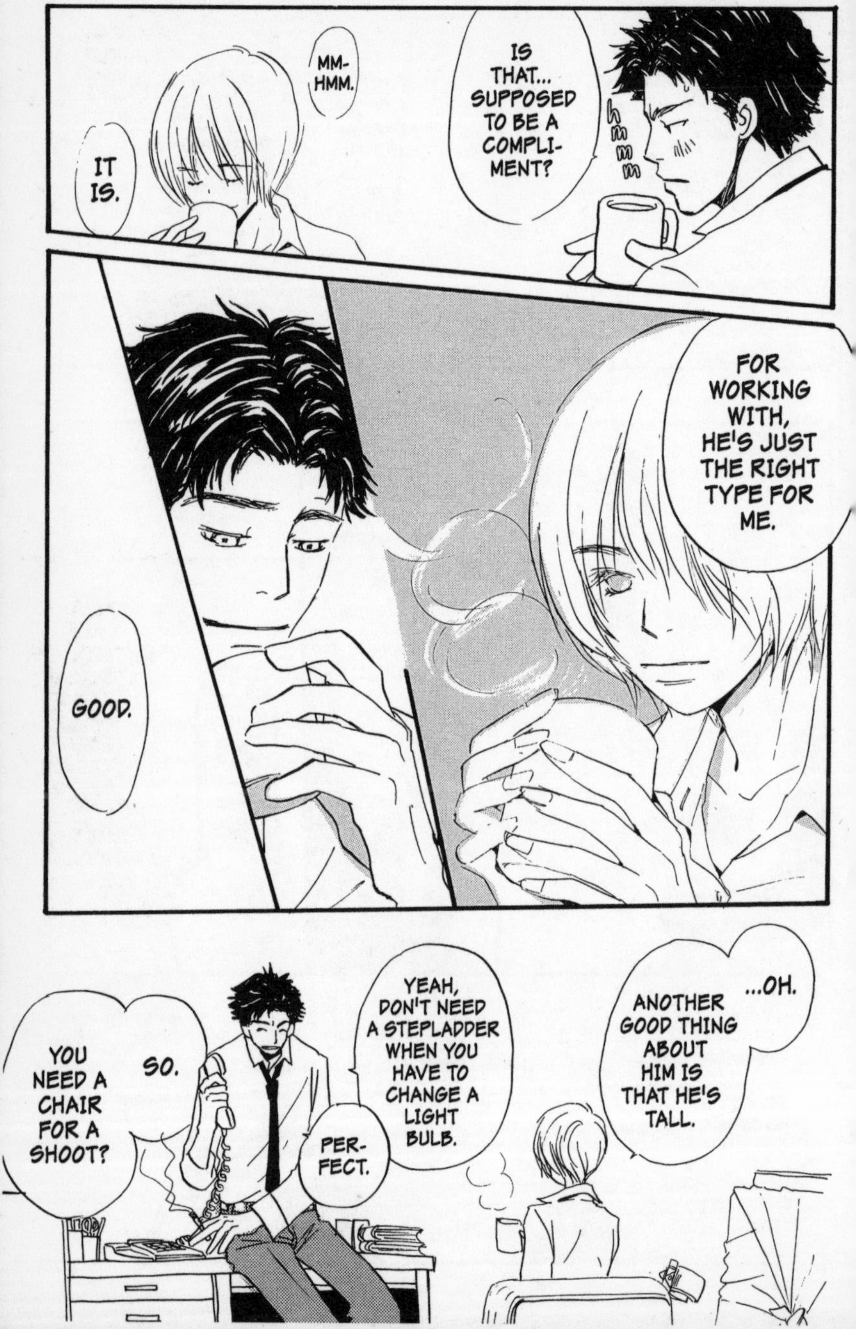
IS THAT... SUPPOSED TO BE A COMPLIMENT?
hmmm
MM-HMM.
IT IS.
FOR WORKING WITH, HE'S JUST THE RIGHT TYPE FOR ME.
GOOD.
...OH.
ANOTHER GOOD THING ABOUT HIM IS THAT HE'S TALL.
YEAH, DON'T NEED A STEPLADDER WHEN YOU HAVE TO CHANGE A LIGHT BULB.
PER-FECT.
SO.
YOU NEED A CHAIR FOR A SHOOT?

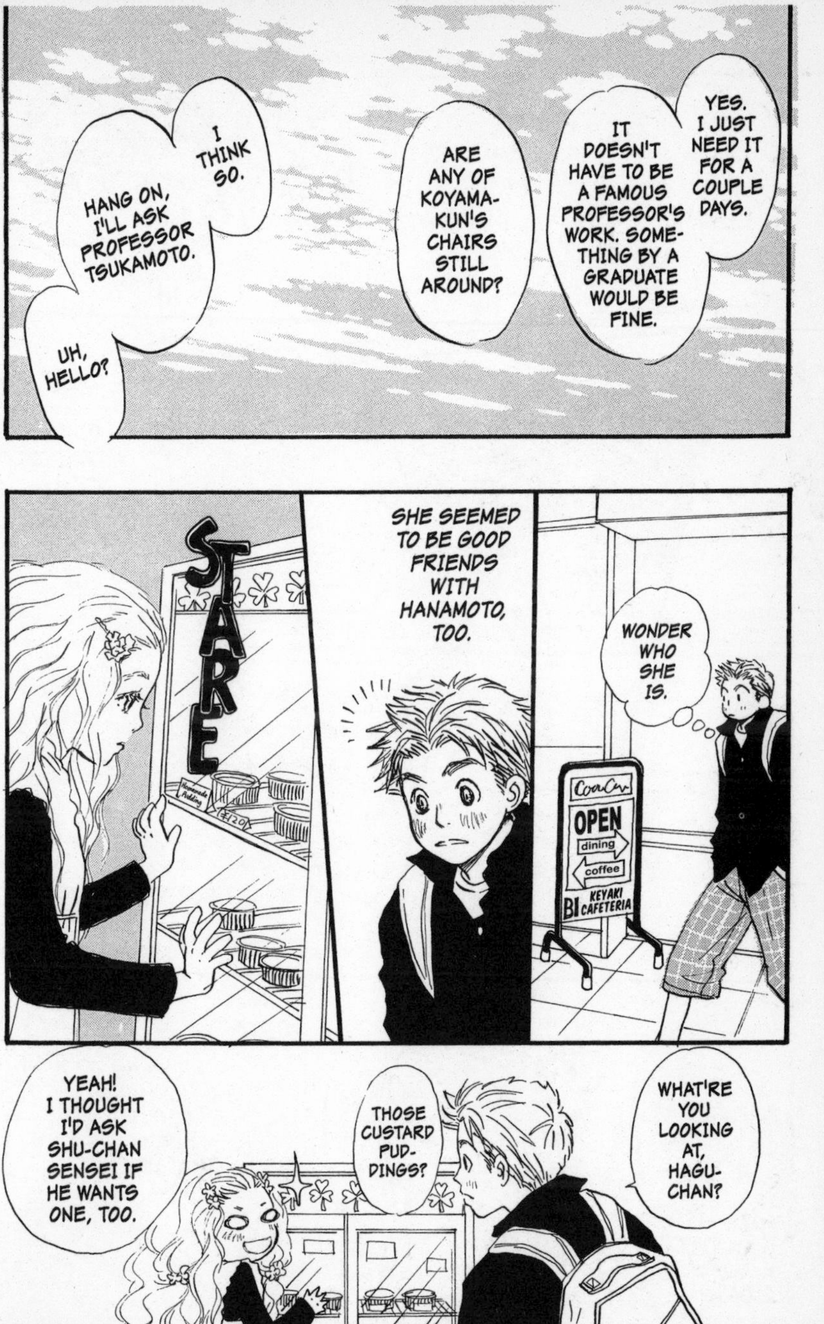
YES. I JUST NEED IT FOR A COUPLE DAYS.
IT DOESN'T HAVE TO BE A FAMOUS PROFESSOR'S WORK. SOMETHING BY A GRADUATE WOULD BE FINE.
ARE ANY OF KOYAMA-KUN'S CHAIRS STILL AROUND?
I THINK SO.
HANG ON, I'LL ASK PROFESSOR TSUKAMOTO.
UH, HELLO?
WONDER WHO SHE IS.
OPEN
dining
coffee
BI KEYAKI CAFETERIA
SHE SEEMED TO BE GOOD FRIENDS WITH HANAMOTO, TOO.
STARE
WHAT'RE YOU LOOKING AT, HAGU-CHAN?
THOSE CUSTARD PUD-DINGS?
YEAH! I THOUGHT I'D ASK SHU-CHAN SENSEI IF HE WANTS ONE, TOO.

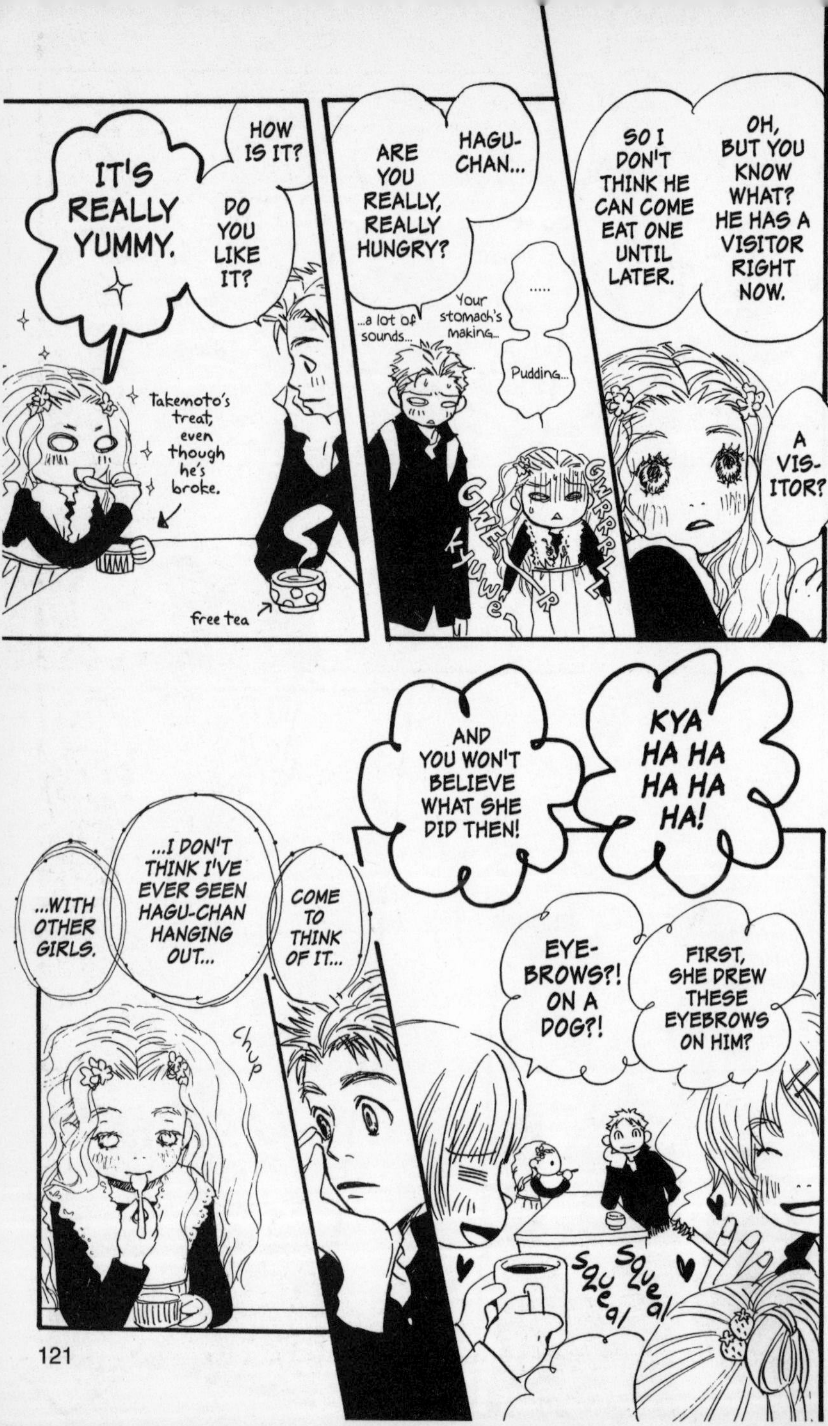
OH, BUT YOU KNOW WHAT? HE HAS A VISITOR RIGHT NOW.
SO I DON'T THINK HE CAN COME EAT ONE UNTIL LATER.
A VISITOR?
HAGU-CHAN...
ARE YOU REALLY, REALLY HUNGRY?
Your stomach's making...
...a lot of sounds...
.....
Pudding...
GWRRRL
HOW IS IT?
DO YOU LIKE IT?
IT'S REALLY YUMMY.
Takemoto's treat, even though he's broke.
free tea
KYA HA HA HA HA HA!
AND YOU WON'T BELIEVE WHAT SHE DID THEN!
FIRST, SHE DREW THESE EYEBROWS ON HIM?
EYE-BROWS?! ON A DOG?!
Squeal
squeal
COME TO THINK OF IT...
...I DON'T THINK I'VE EVER SEEN HAGU-CHAN HANGING OUT...
...WITH OTHER GIRLS.
chup

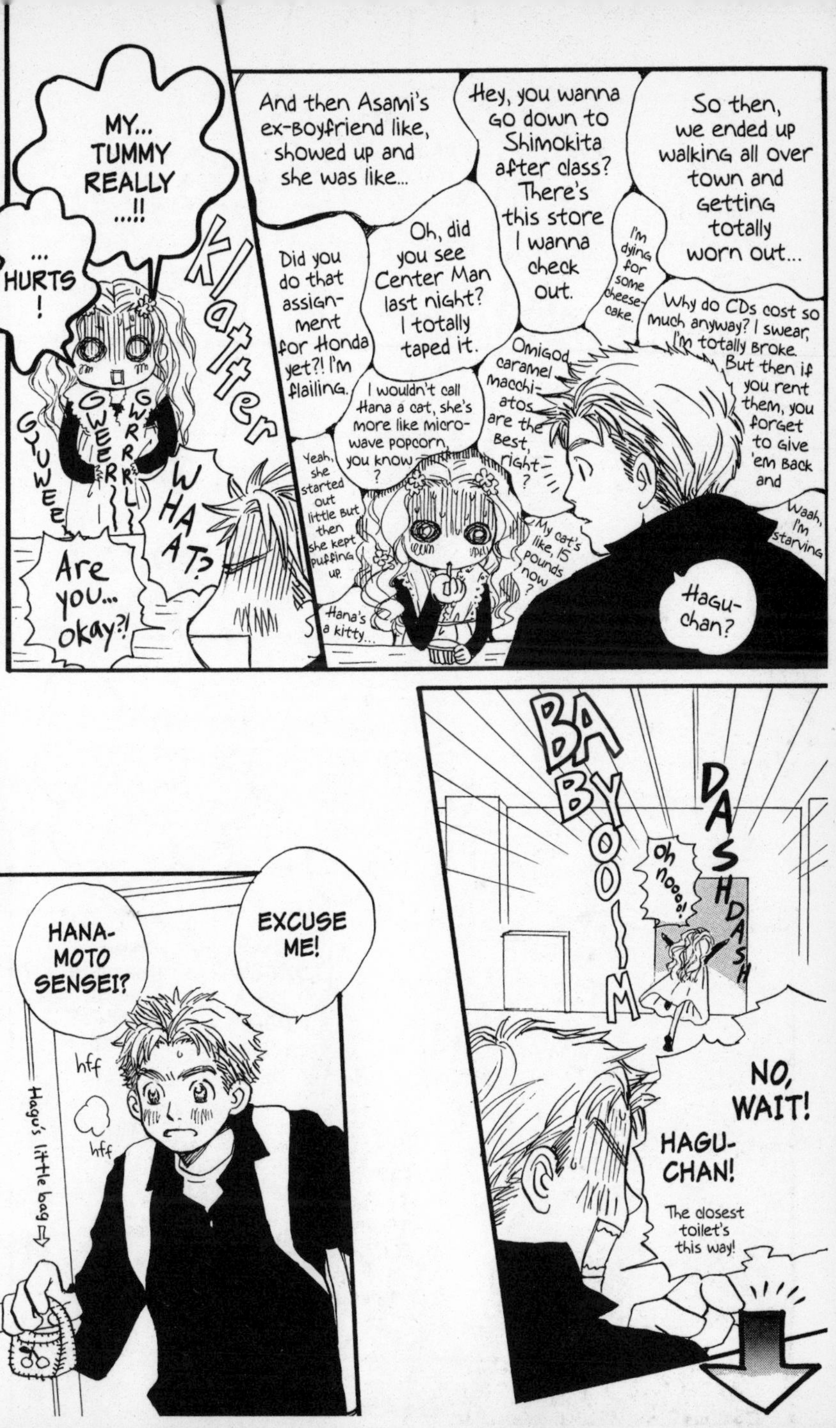
So then, we ended up walking all over town and getting totally worn out...
Hey, you wanna go down to Shimokita after class? There's this store I wanna check out.
And then Asami's ex-boyfriend like, showed up and she was like...
I'm dying for some cheese-cake.
Why do CDs cost so much anyway? I swear, I'm totally broke. But then if you rent them, you forget to give 'em back and
Oh, did you see Center Man last night? I totally taped it.
Did you do that assign-ment for Honda yet?! I'm flailing.
Omigod, caramel macchi-atos are the best, right?
I wouldn't call Hana a cat, she's more like micro-wave popcorn, you know?
Waah, I'm starving
My cat's like, 15 pounds now?
Yeah, she started out little but then she kept puffing up.
Hagu-chan?
Hana's a kitty...
Klatter
MY... TUMMY REALLY ...!!
... HURTS !
GWRRRL
GWEERR
GYUWEE
WHAAT?
Are you... okay?!
BABYOO—M
DASHDASH
Oh noooo!
NO, WAIT!
HAGU-CHAN!
The closest toilet's this way!
EXCUSE ME!
HANA-MOTO SENSEI?
hff
hff
Hagu's little bag ⇩

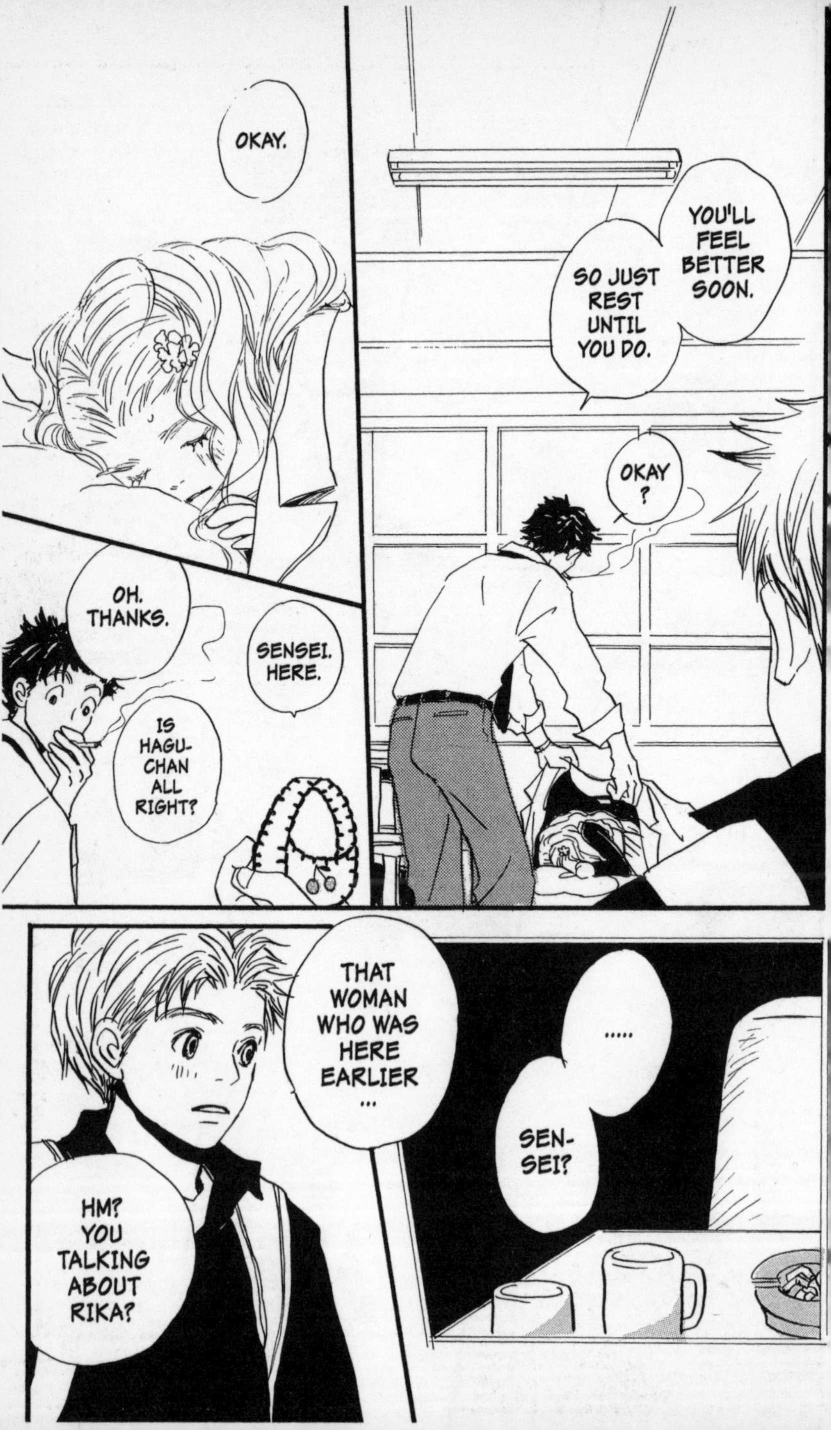
YOU'LL FEEL BETTER SOON.
SO JUST REST UNTIL YOU DO.
OKAY?
OKAY.
SENSEI. HERE.
OH. THANKS.
IS HAGU-CHAN ALL RIGHT?
.....
SEN-SEI?
THAT WOMAN WHO WAS HERE EARLIER ...
HM? YOU TALKING ABOUT RIKA?

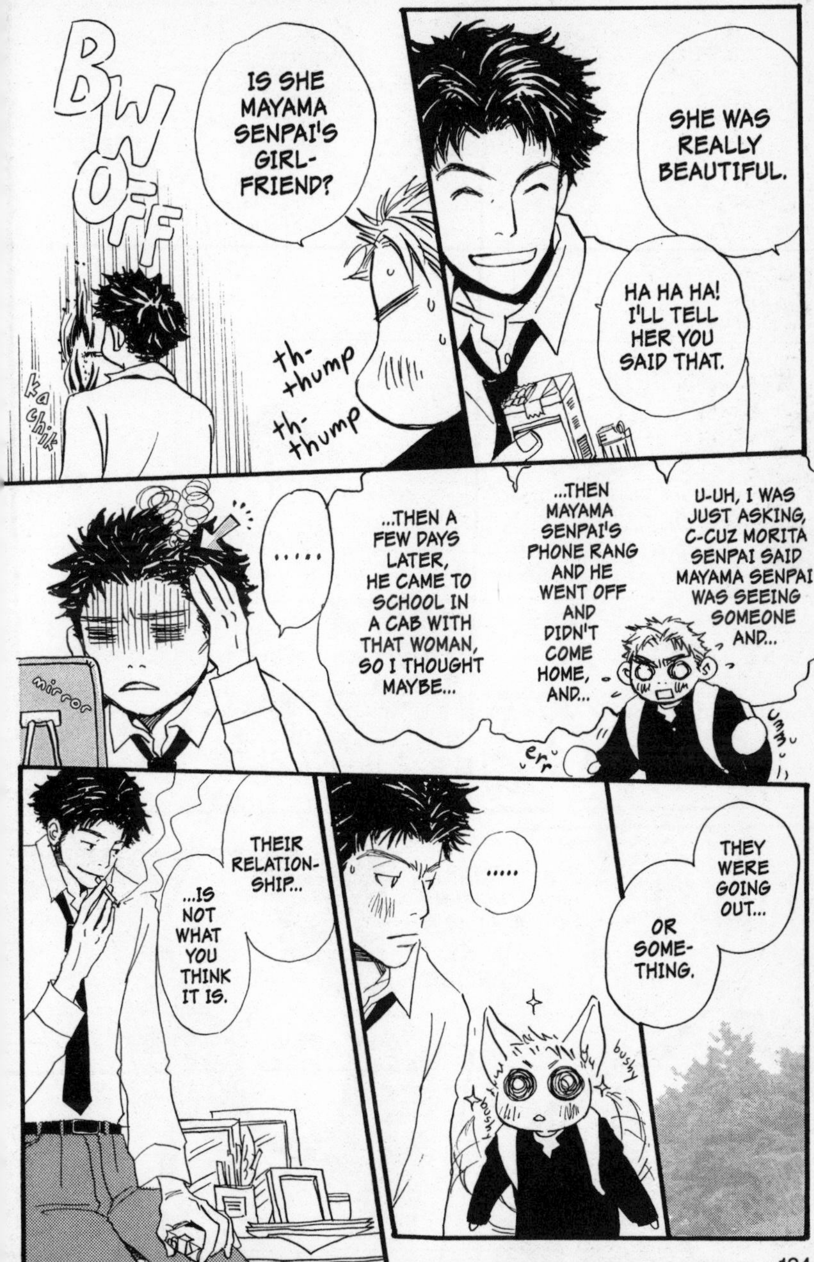
SHE WAS REALLY BEAUTIFUL.
HA HA HA! I'LL TELL HER YOU SAID THAT.
th-thump th-thump
IS SHE MAYAMA SENPAI'S GIRL-FRIEND?
BWOFF
ka chik
U-UH, I WAS JUST ASKING, C-CUZ MORITA SENPAI SAID MAYAMA SENPAI WAS SEEING SOMEONE AND...
...THEN MAYAMA SENPAI'S PHONE RANG AND HE WENT OFF AND DIDN'T COME HOME, AND...
...THEN A FEW DAYS LATER, HE CAME TO SCHOOL IN A CAB WITH THAT WOMAN, SO I THOUGHT MAYBE...
umm
err
.....
mirror
THEY WERE GOING OUT...
OR SOME-THING.
bushy
bushy
.....
THEIR RELATION-SHIP...
...IS NOT WHAT YOU THINK IT IS.

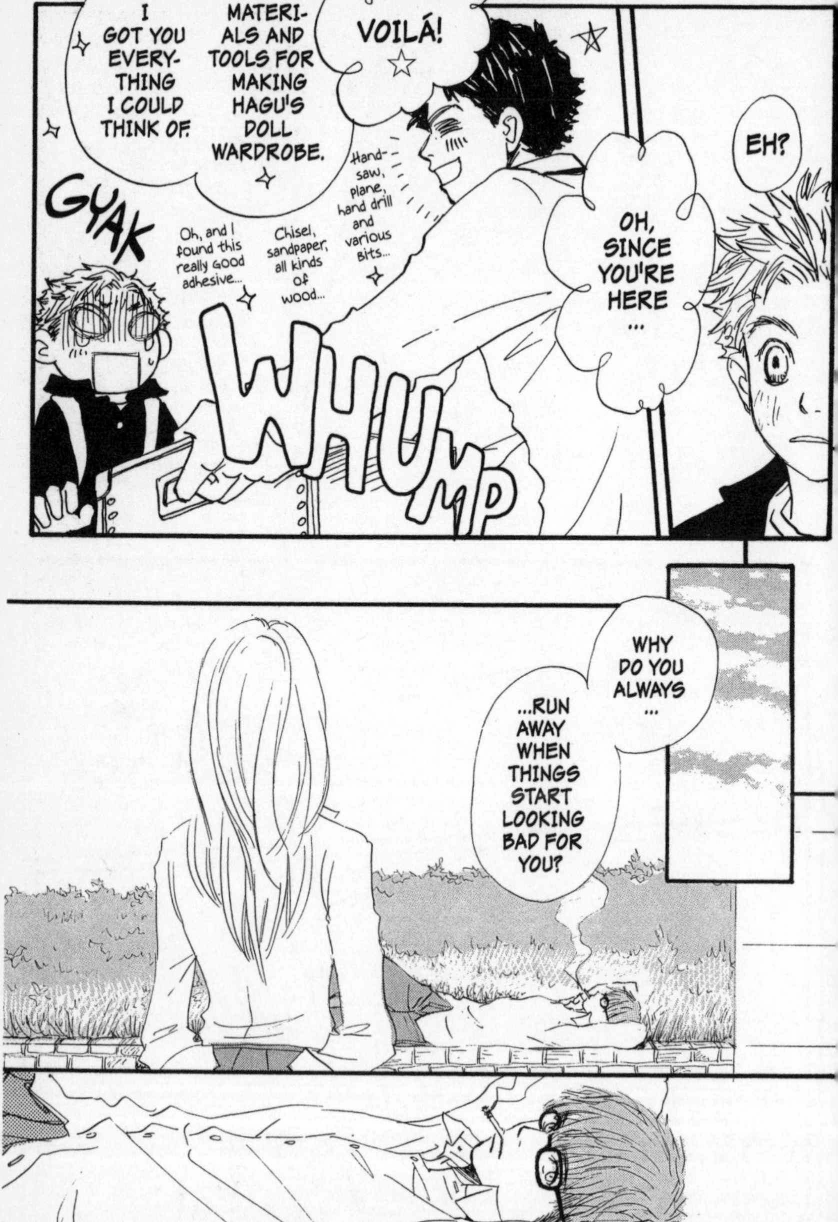
EH?
OH, SINCE YOU'RE HERE ...
VOILÁ!
MATERI-ALS AND TOOLS FOR MAKING HAGU'S DOLL WARDROBE.
I GOT YOU EVERY-THING I COULD THINK OF.
Hand-saw, plane, hand drill and various bits...
Chisel, sandpaper, all kinds of wood...
Oh, and I found this really good adhesive...
GYAK
WHUMP
WHY DO YOU ALWAYS ...
...RUN AWAY WHEN THINGS START LOOKING BAD FOR YOU?

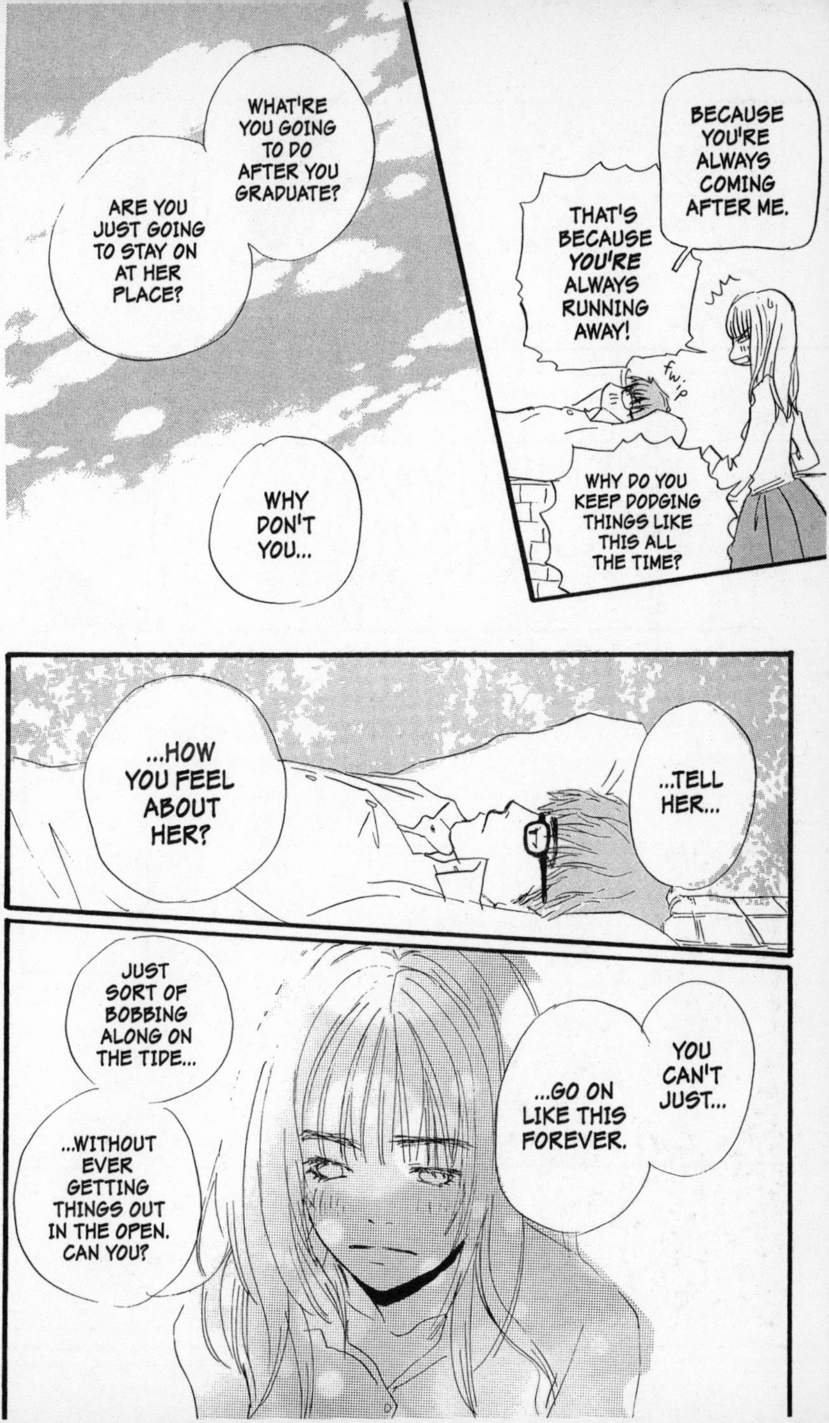
BECAUSE YOU'RE ALWAYS COMING AFTER ME.
THAT'S BECAUSE *YOU'RE* ALWAYS RUNNING AWAY!
fwip
WHY DO YOU KEEP DODGING THINGS LIKE THIS ALL THE TIME?
WHAT'RE YOU GOING TO DO AFTER YOU GRADUATE?
ARE YOU JUST GOING TO STAY ON AT HER PLACE?
WHY DON'T YOU...
...TELL HER...
...HOW YOU FEEL ABOUT HER?
YOU CAN'T JUST...
...GO ON LIKE THIS FOREVER.
JUST SORT OF BOBBING ALONG ON THE TIDE...
...WITHOUT EVER GETTING THINGS OUT IN THE OPEN. CAN YOU?

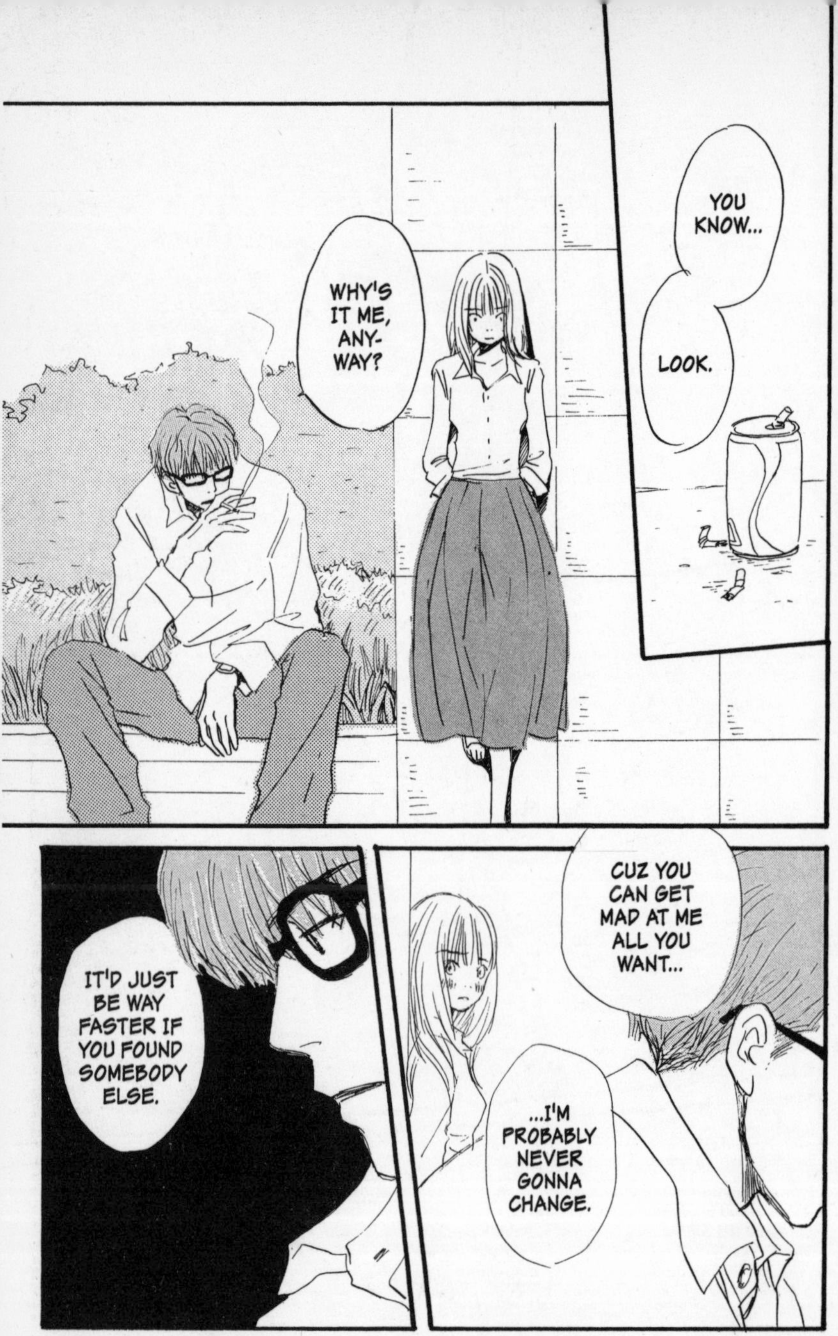
YOU KNOW...
LOOK.
WHY'S IT ME, ANY-WAY?
CUZ YOU CAN GET MAD AT ME ALL YOU WANT...
...I'M PROBABLY NEVER GONNA CHANGE.
IT'D JUST BE WAY FASTER IF YOU FOUND SOMEBODY ELSE.

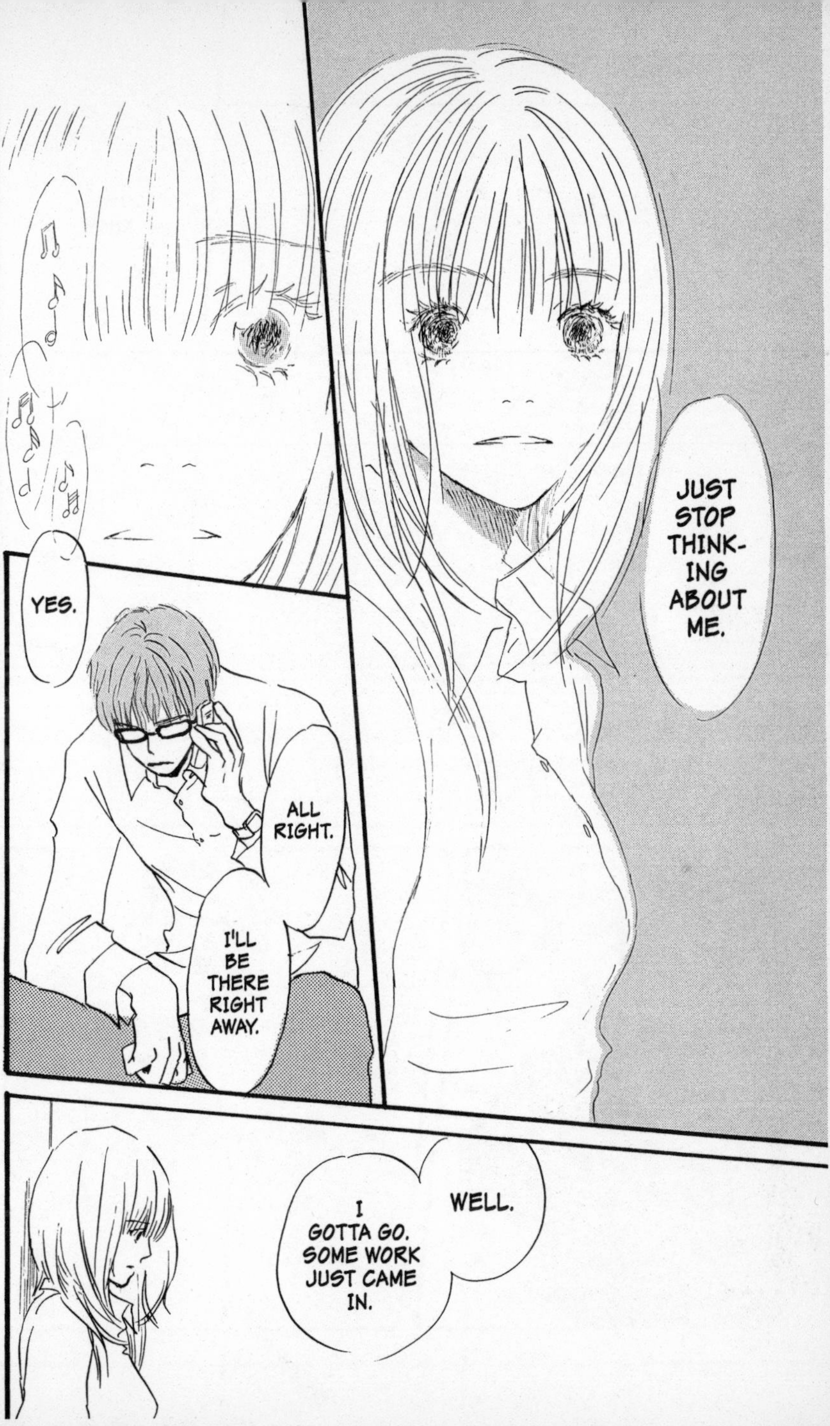
JUST STOP THINKING-ING ABOUT ME.
YES.
ALL RIGHT.
I'LL BE THERE RIGHT AWAY.
WELL.
I GOTTA GO. SOME WORK JUST CAME IN.

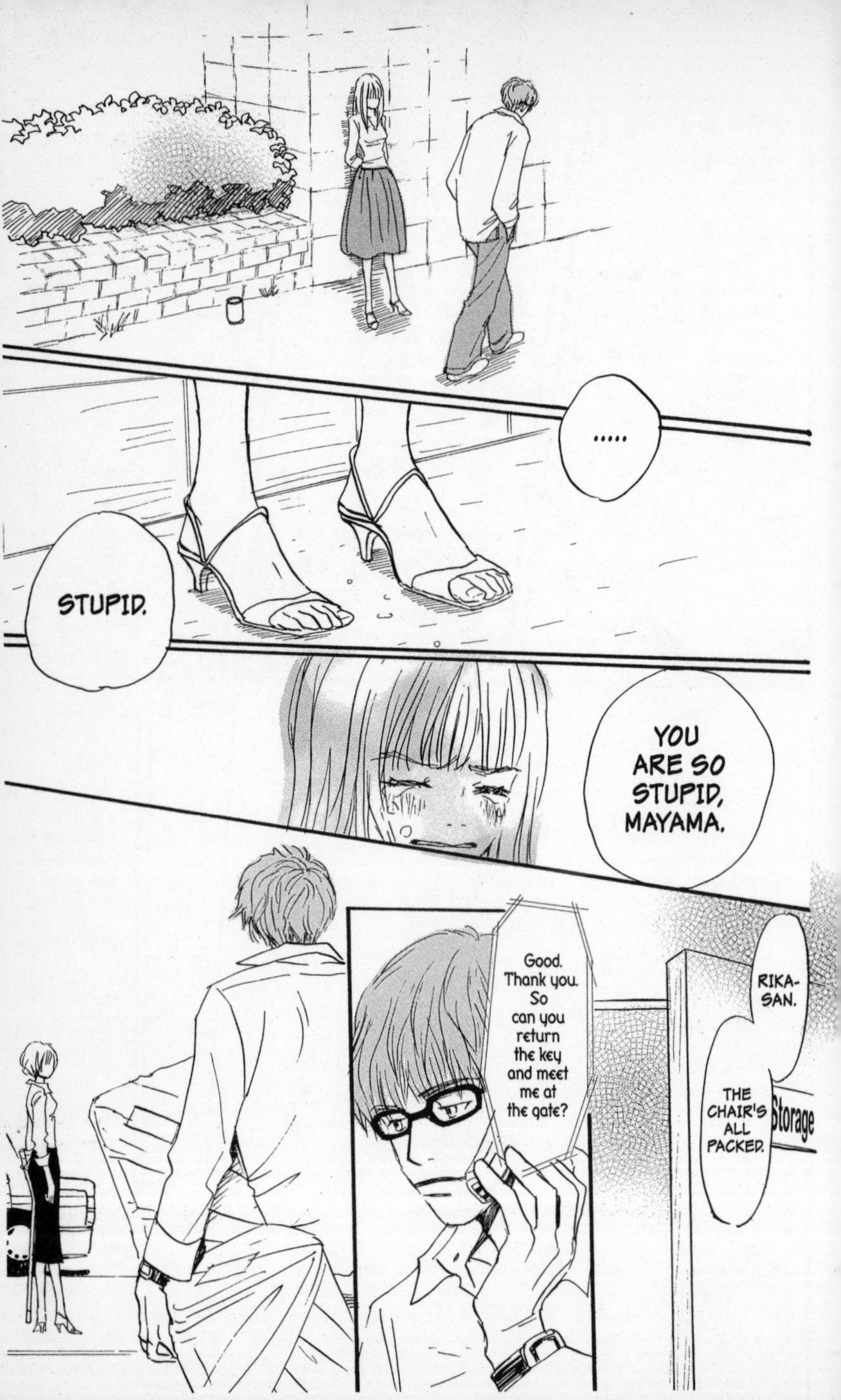
.....
STUPID.
YOU ARE SO STUPID, MAYAMA.
RIKA-SAN.
THE CHAIR'S ALL PACKED.
Storage
Good. Thank you. So can you return the key and meet me at the gate?

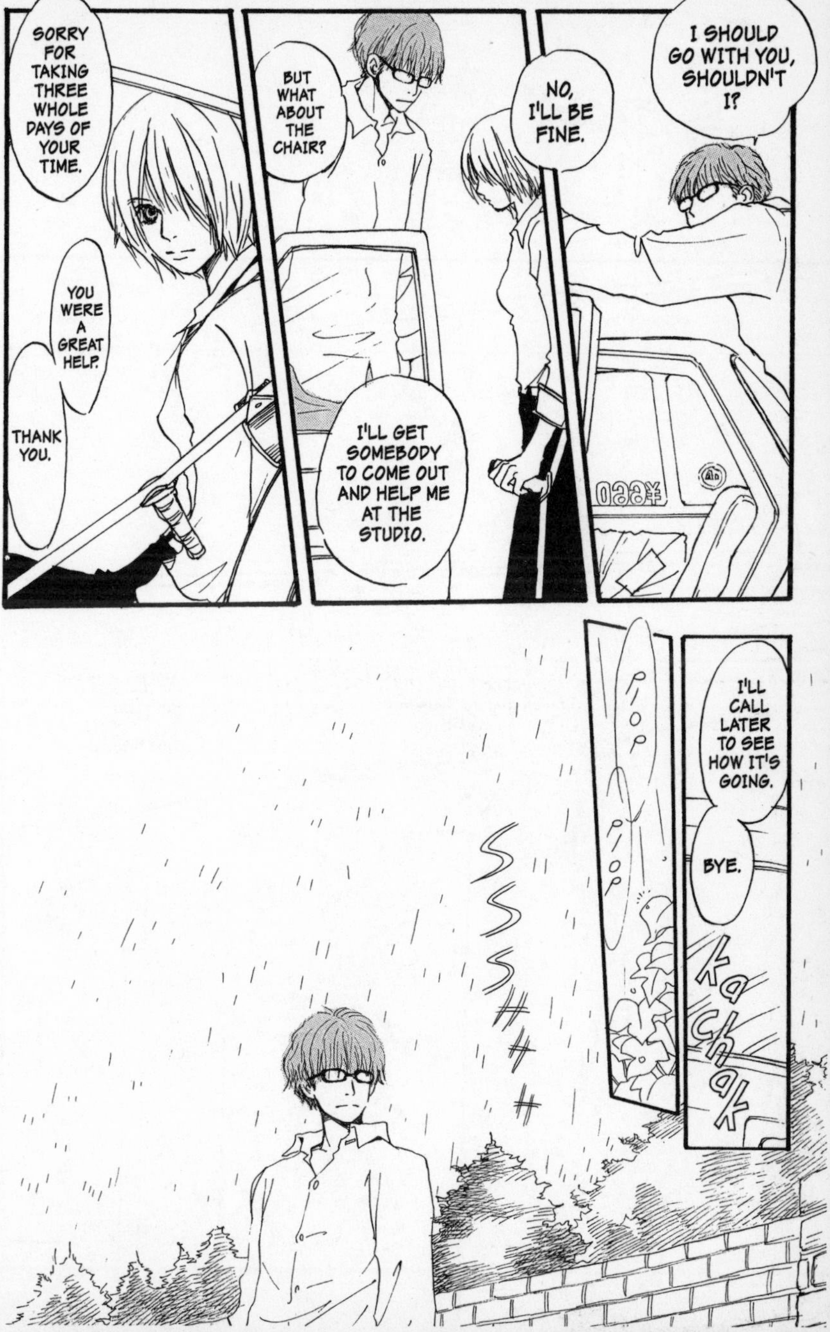
I SHOULD GO WITH YOU, SHOULDN'T I?
NO, I'LL BE FINE.
BUT WHAT ABOUT THE CHAIR?
I'LL GET SOMEBODY TO COME OUT AND HELP ME AT THE STUDIO.
SORRY FOR TAKING THREE WHOLE DAYS OF YOUR TIME.
YOU WERE A GREAT HELP.
THANK YOU.
I'LL CALL LATER TO SEE HOW IT'S GOING.
BYE.
kachak
plop
plop
SSSHHHH

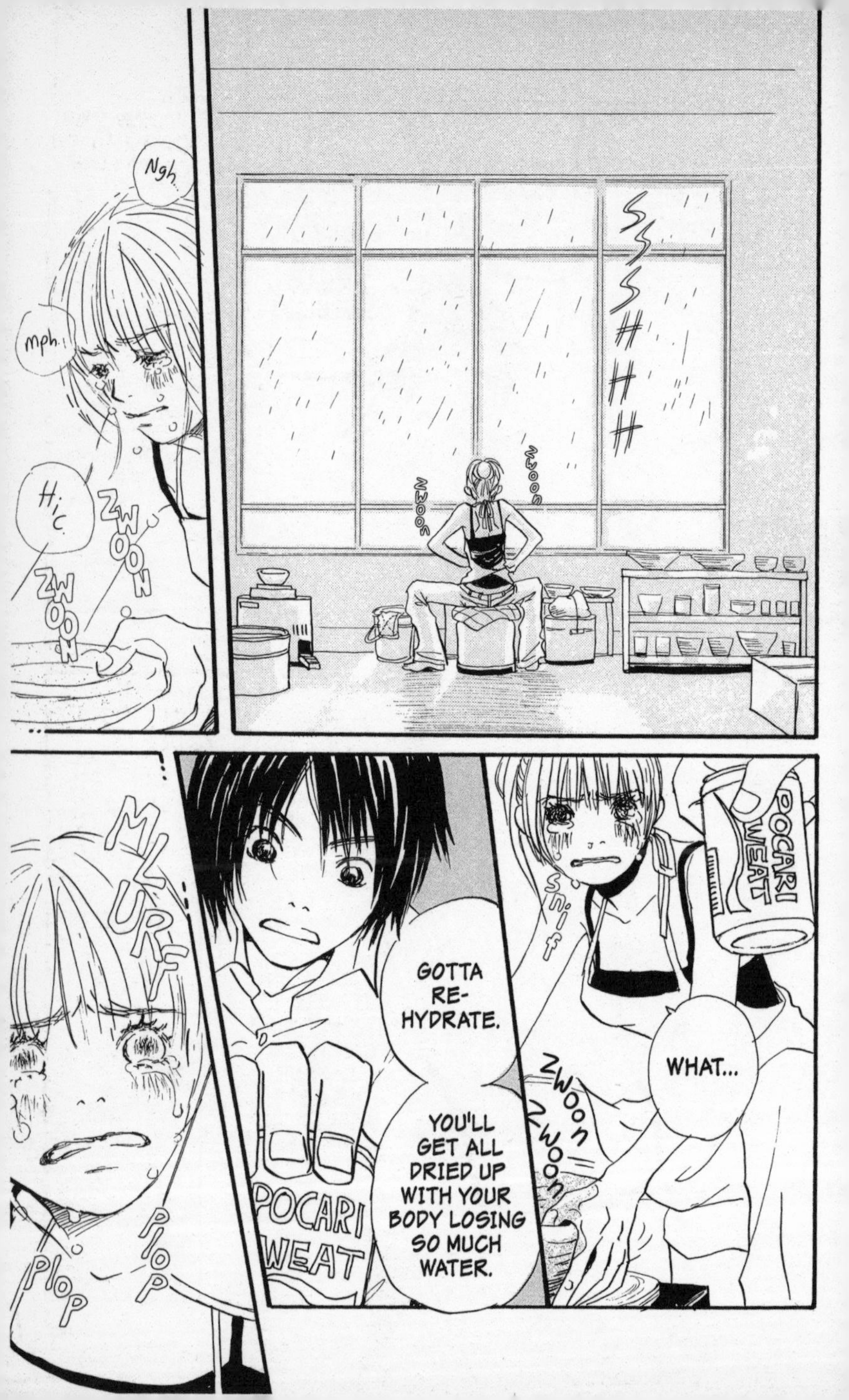
SSSHHHH
ZWOON
ZWOON
Ngh...
mph...
Hic.
ZWOON
ZWOON
POCARI WEAT
sniff
WHAT...
ZWOON
ZWOON
GOTTA RE-HYDRATE.
YOU'LL GET ALL DRIED UP WITH YOUR BODY LOSING SO MUCH WATER.
POCARI WEAT
MLURFF
PLOP
PLOP

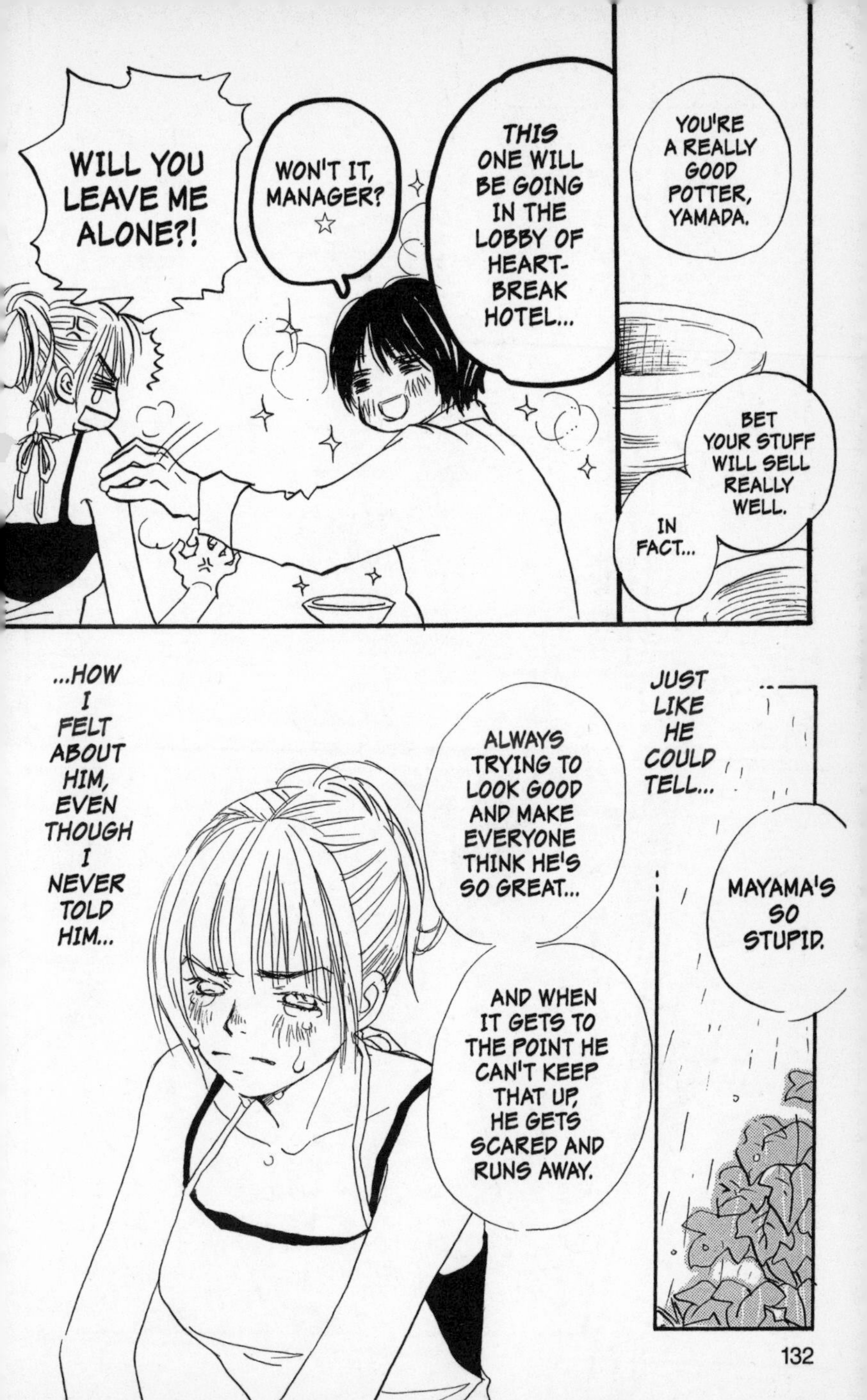
YOU'RE A REALLY GOOD POTTER, YAMADA.
BET YOUR STUFF WILL SELL REALLY WELL.
IN FACT...
THIS ONE WILL BE GOING IN THE LOBBY OF HEART-BREAK HOTEL...
WON'T IT, MANAGER?
WILL YOU LEAVE ME ALONE?!
MAYAMA'S SO STUPID.
ALWAYS TRYING TO LOOK GOOD AND MAKE EVERYONE THINK HE'S SO GREAT...
AND WHEN IT GETS TO THE POINT HE CAN'T KEEP THAT UP, HE GETS SCARED AND RUNS AWAY.
JUST LIKE HE COULD TELL...
...HOW I FELT ABOUT HIM, EVEN THOUGH I NEVER TOLD HIM...

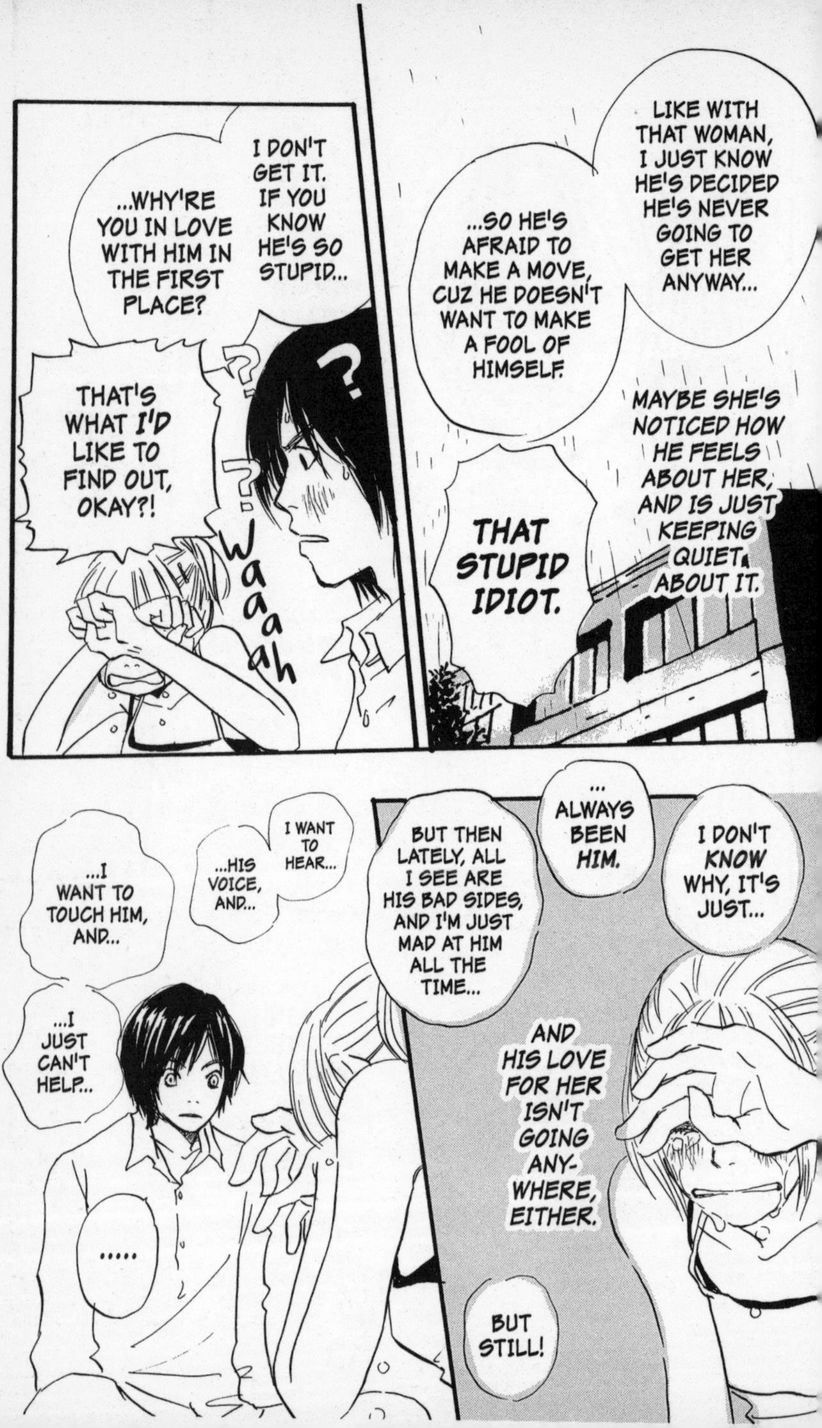
LIKE WITH THAT WOMAN, I JUST KNOW HE'S DECIDED HE'S NEVER GOING TO GET HER ANYWAY...
...SO HE'S AFRAID TO MAKE A MOVE, CUZ HE DOESN'T WANT TO MAKE A FOOL OF HIMSELF.
MAYBE SHE'S NOTICED HOW HE FEELS ABOUT HER, AND IS JUST KEEPING QUIET ABOUT IT.
THAT STUPID IDIOT.
I DON'T GET IT. IF YOU KNOW HE'S SO STUPID...
...WHY'RE YOU IN LOVE WITH HIM IN THE FIRST PLACE?
?
??
THAT'S WHAT I'D LIKE TO FIND OUT, OKAY?!
Waaaah
I DON'T KNOW WHY, IT'S JUST...
... ALWAYS BEEN HIM.
BUT THEN LATELY, ALL I SEE ARE HIS BAD SIDES, AND I'M JUST MAD AT HIM ALL THE TIME...
AND HIS LOVE FOR HER ISN'T GOING ANYWHERE, EITHER.
BUT STILL!
I WANT TO HEAR...
...HIS VOICE, AND...
...I WANT TO TOUCH HIM, AND...
...I JUST CAN'T HELP...
.....

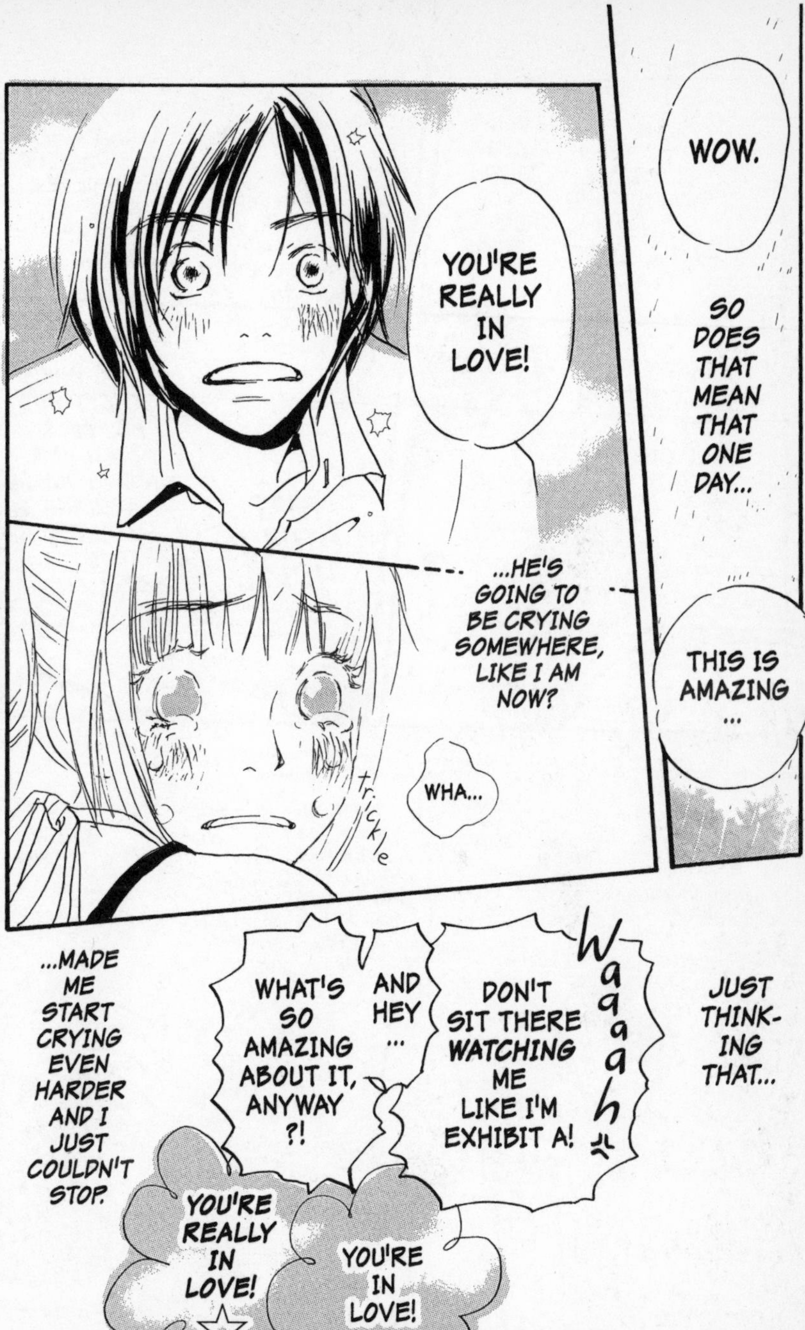
WOW.
SO DOES THAT MEAN THAT ONE DAY...
THIS IS AMAZING ...
YOU'RE REALLY IN LOVE!
...HE'S GOING TO BE CRYING SOMEWHERE, LIKE I AM NOW?
WHA...
trickle
JUST THINK-ING THAT...
Waaaah
DON'T SIT THERE WATCHING ME LIKE I'M EXHIBIT A!
AND HEY ...
WHAT'S SO AMAZING ABOUT IT, ANYWAY ?!
...MADE ME START CRYING EVEN HARDER AND I JUST COULDN'T STOP.
YOU'RE IN LOVE!
YOU'RE REALLY IN LOVE!

chapter 7—the end—

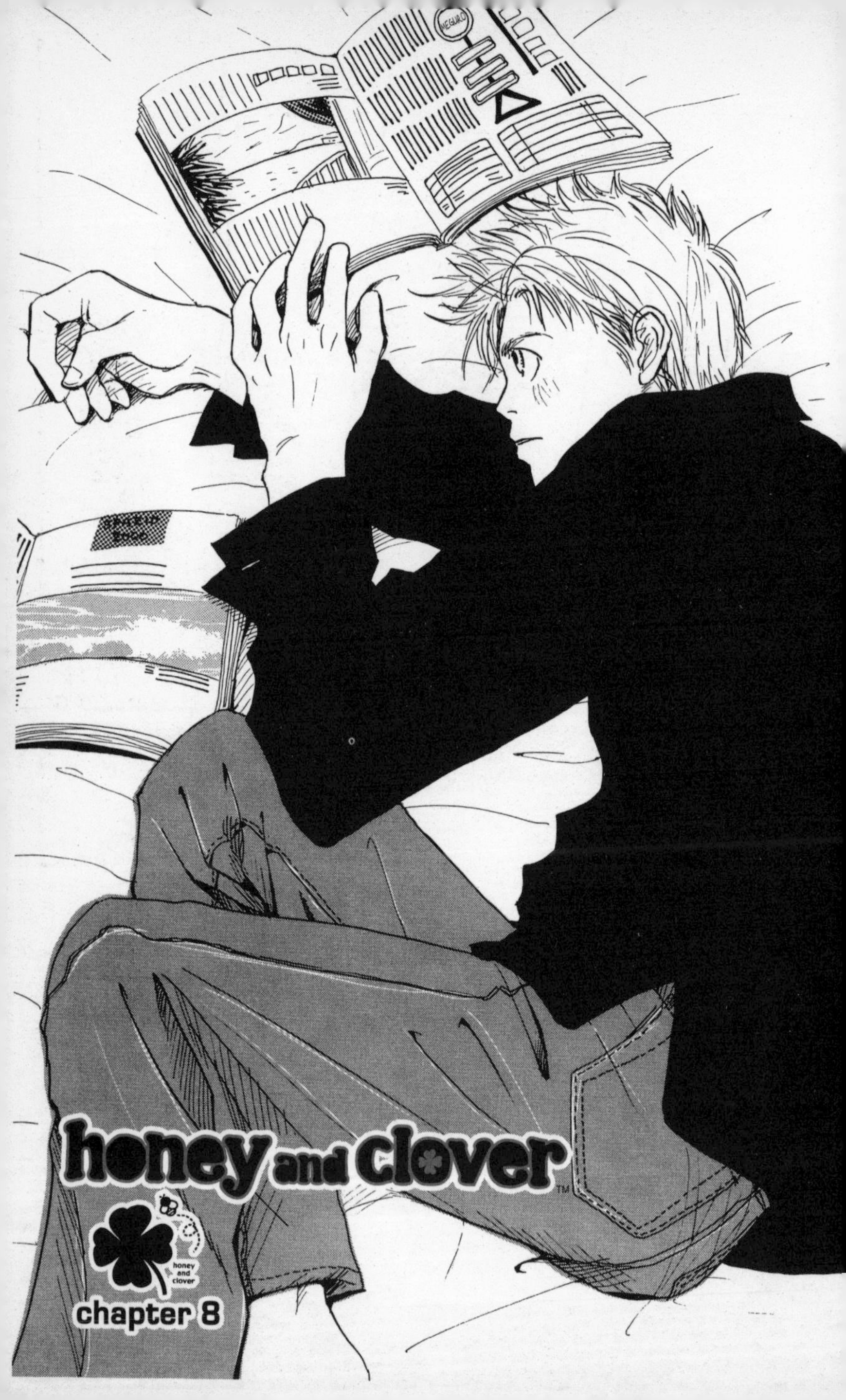
MEGURO
honey and clover™
honey and clover
chapter 8

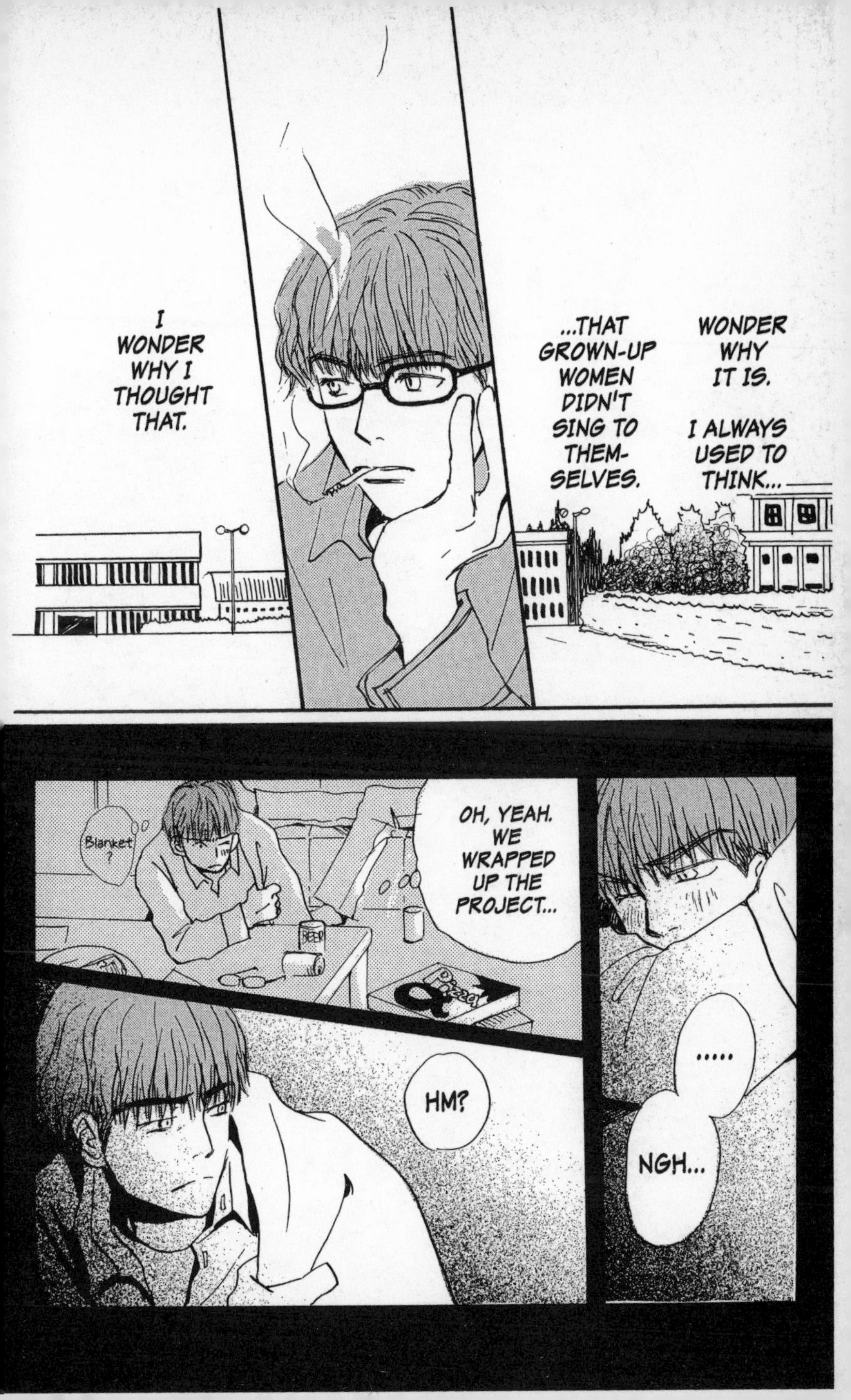
WONDER WHY IT IS.
I ALWAYS USED TO THINK...
...THAT GROWN-UP WOMEN DIDN'T SING TO THEMSELVES.
I WONDER WHY I THOUGHT THAT.
.....
NGH...
OH, YEAH. WE WRAPPED UP THE PROJECT...
Blanket?
BEER
Pizza
HM?

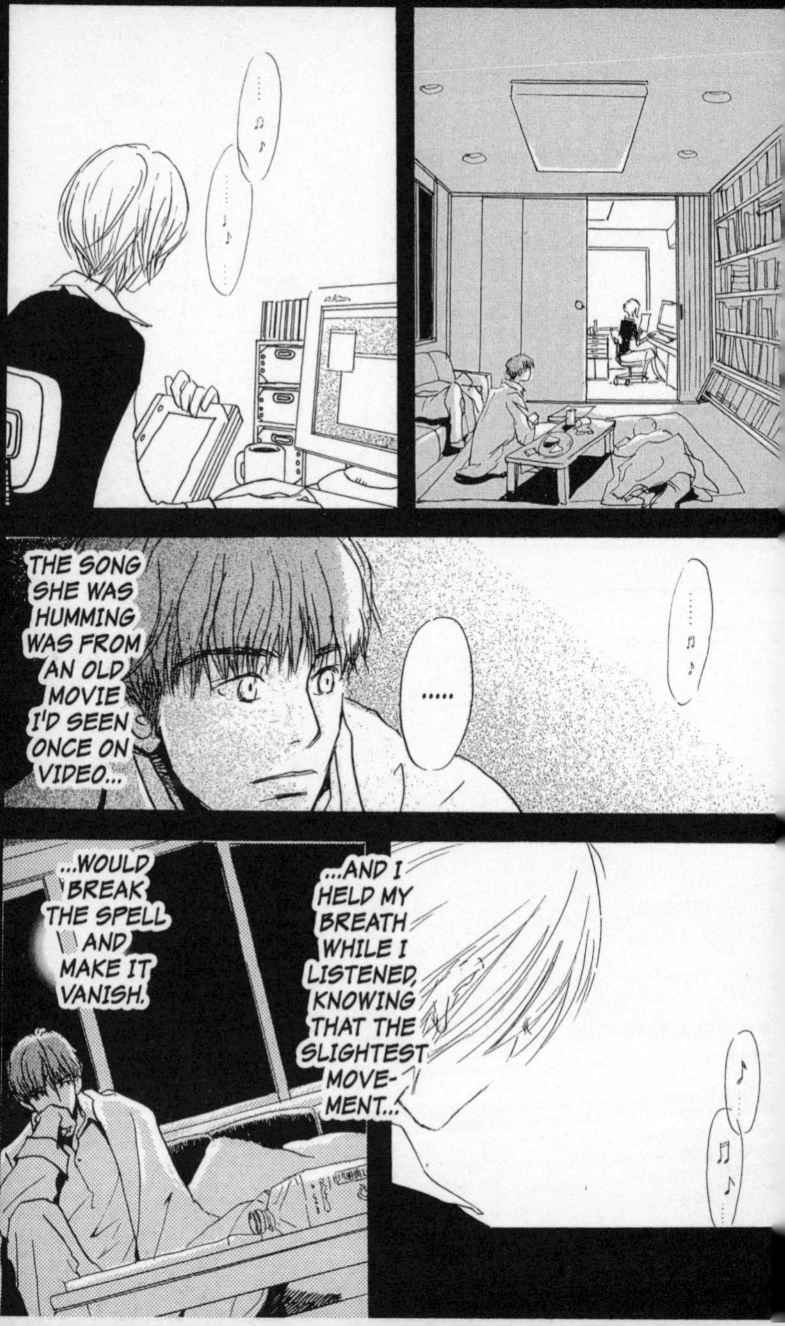

......♫ ♪
......♪ ♪ ......
......♫ ♪
.....
THE SONG SHE WAS HUMMING WAS FROM AN OLD MOVIE I'D SEEN ONCE ON VIDEO...
♪ ......
♫ ♪ ......
...AND I HELD MY BREATH WHILE I LISTENED, KNOWING THAT THE SLIGHTEST MOVEMENT...
...WOULD BREAK THE SPELL AND MAKE IT VANISH.

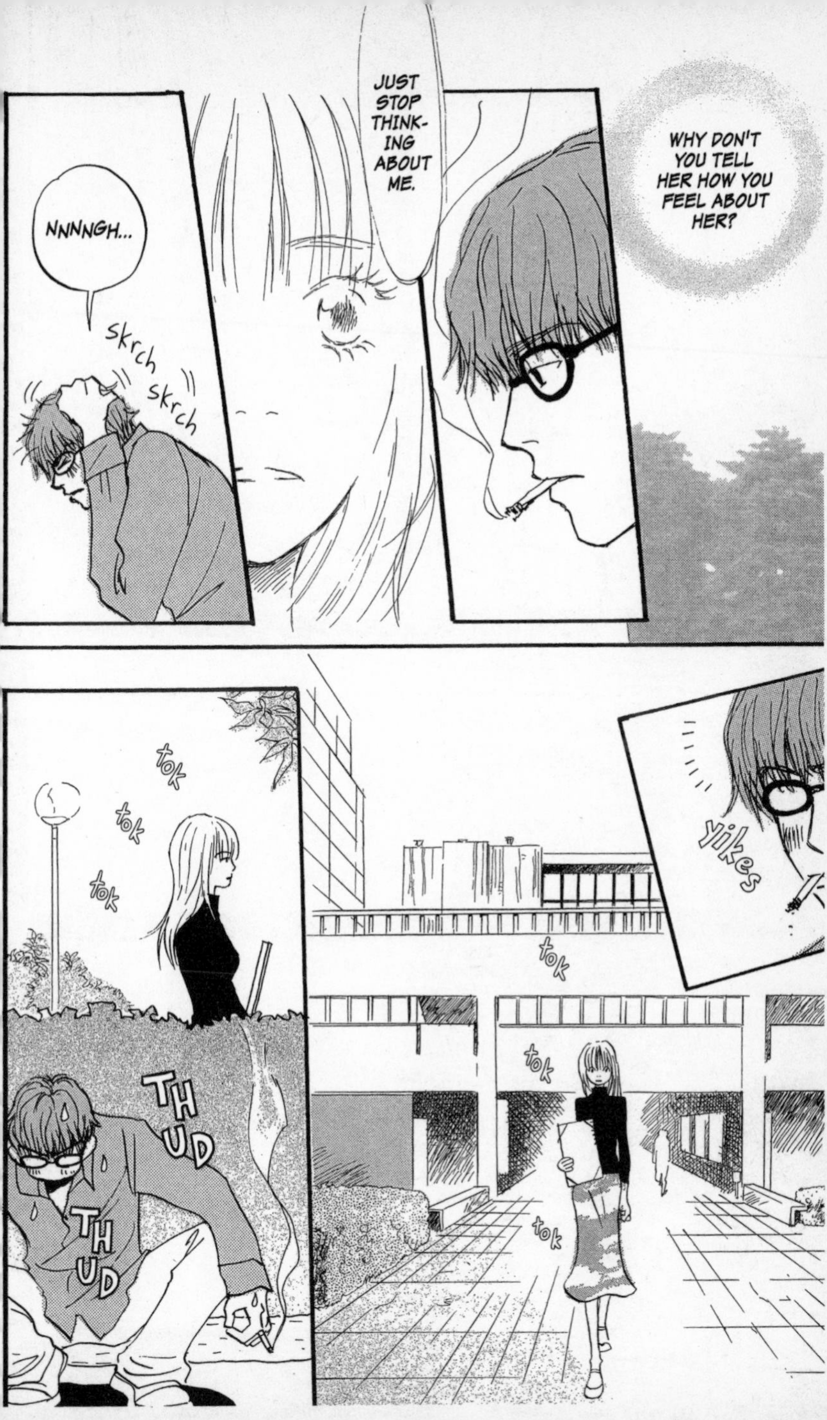
WHY DON'T YOU TELL HER HOW YOU FEEL ABOUT HER?
JUST STOP THINKING-ING ABOUT ME.
NNNNGH...
skrch skrch
Yikes
tok
tok
tok
tok
tok
tok
THUD
THUD

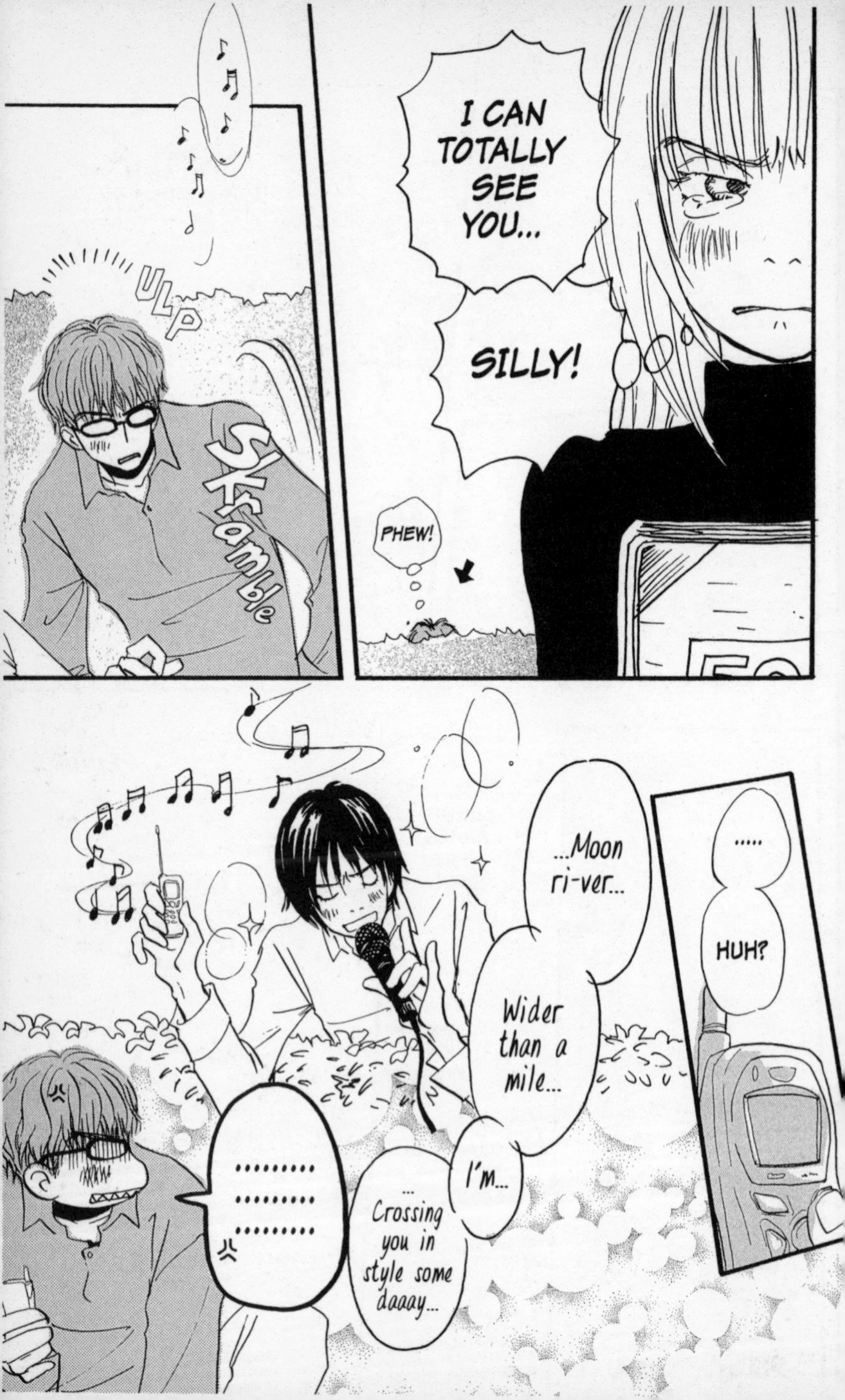
I CAN TOTALLY SEE YOU...
SILLY!
PHEW!
ULP
Skramble
.....
HUH?
...Moon ri-ver...
Wider than a mile...
I'm...
...Crossing you in style some daaay...
....
....
....

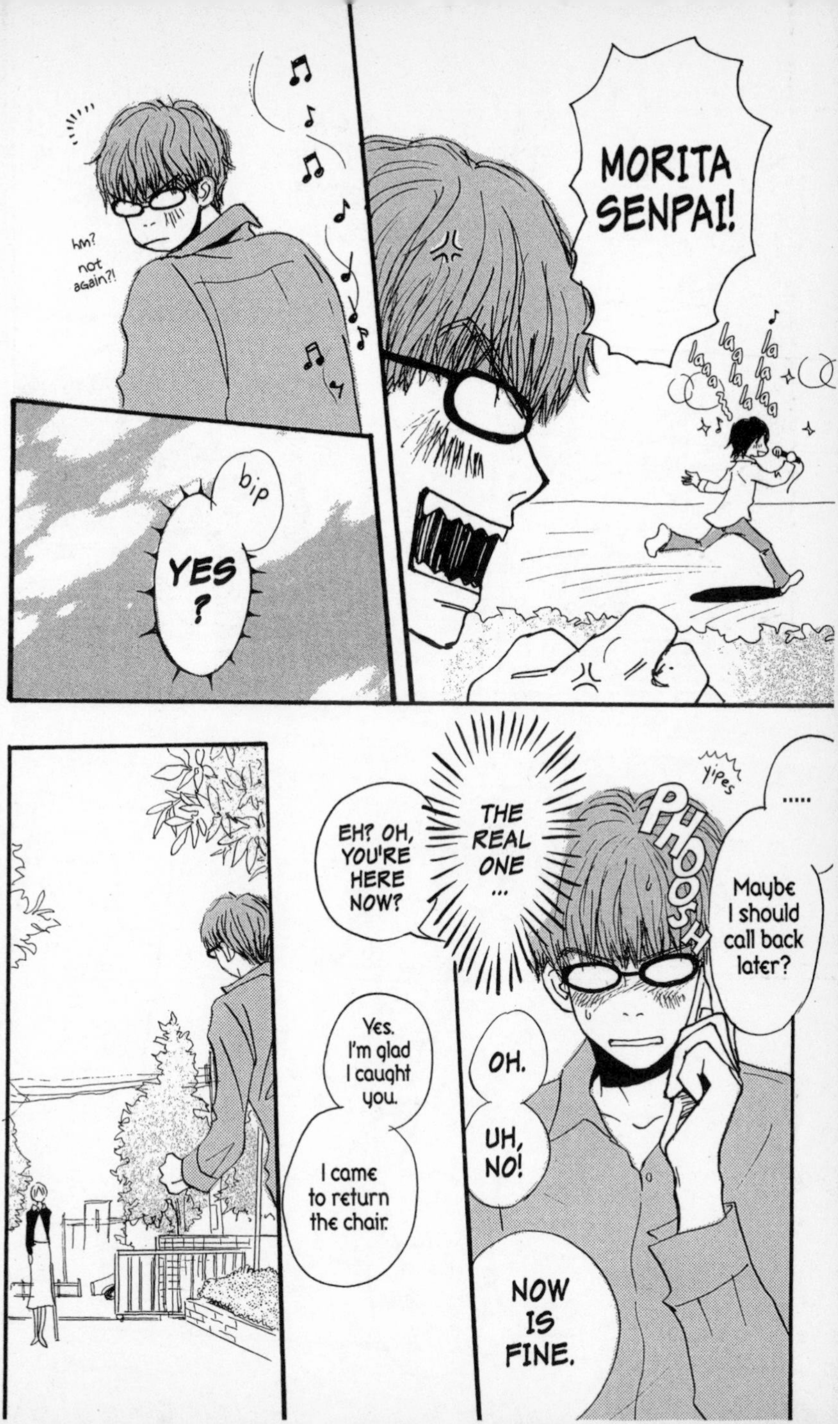
MORITA SENPAI!
laaa la la la laaa
la la
hm?
not again?!
bip
YES ?
.....
Maybe I should call back later?
yipes
PHOOSH
THE REAL ONE ...
EH? OH, YOU'RE HERE NOW?
OH.
UH, NO!
NOW IS FINE.
Yes. I'm glad I caught you.
I came to return the chair.

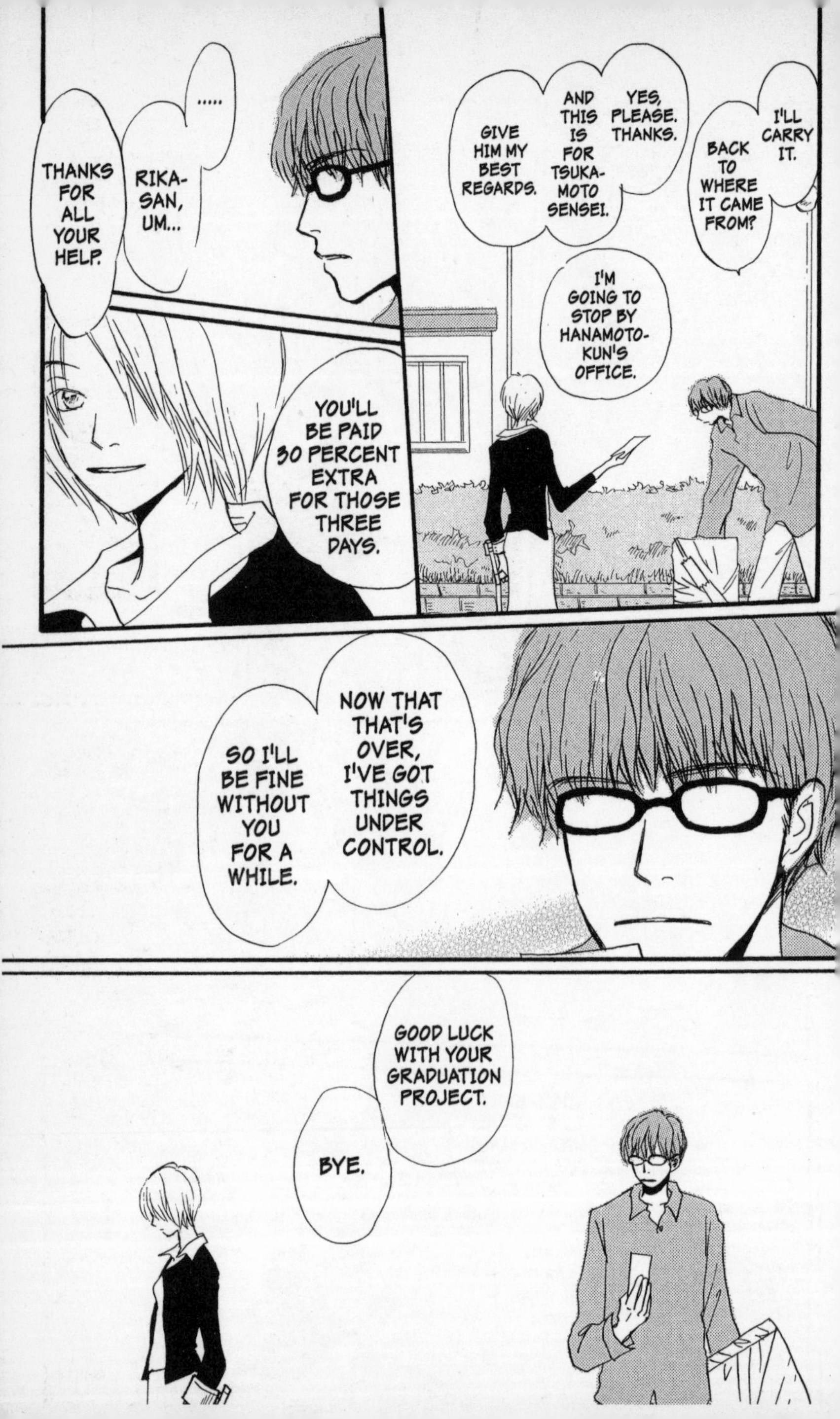
I'LL CARRY IT.
BACK TO WHERE IT CAME FROM?
YES, PLEASE. THANKS.
AND THIS IS FOR TSUKAMOTO SENSEI.
GIVE HIM MY BEST REGARDS.
I'M GOING TO STOP BY HANAMOTO-KUN'S OFFICE.
.....
RIKA-SAN, UM...
THANKS FOR ALL YOUR HELP.
YOU'LL BE PAID 30 PERCENT EXTRA FOR THOSE THREE DAYS.
NOW THAT THAT'S OVER, I'VE GOT THINGS UNDER CONTROL.
SO I'LL BE FINE WITHOUT YOU FOR A WHILE.
GOOD LUCK WITH YOUR GRADUATION PROJECT.
BYE.

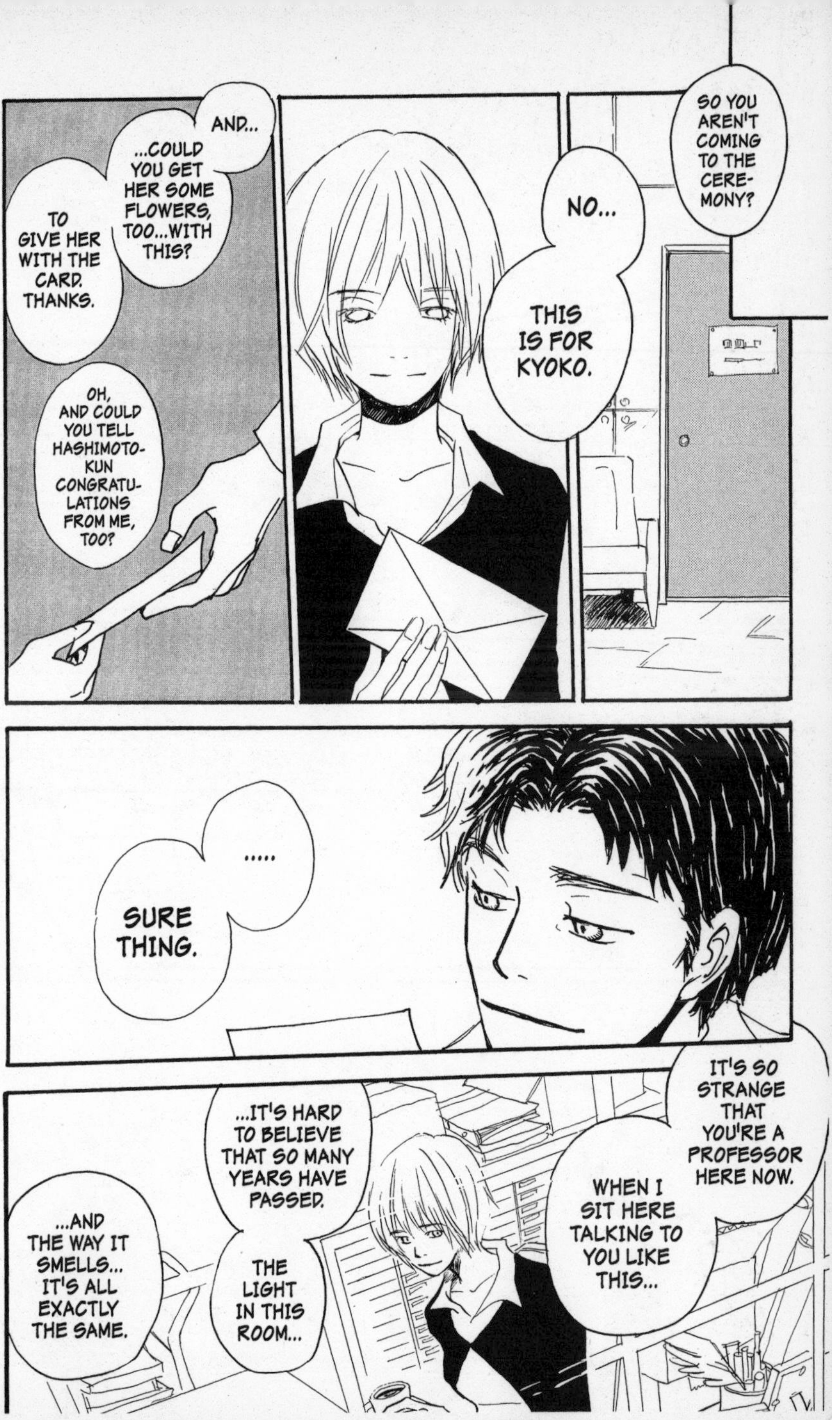
SO YOU AREN'T COMING TO THE CERE-MONY?
NO...
THIS IS FOR KYOKO.
AND...
...COULD YOU GET HER SOME FLOWERS, TOO...WITH THIS?
TO GIVE HER WITH THE CARD. THANKS.
OH, AND COULD YOU TELL HASHIMOTO-KUN CONGRATU-LATIONS FROM ME, TOO?
.....
SURE THING.
IT'S SO STRANGE THAT YOU'RE A PROFESSOR HERE NOW.
WHEN I SIT HERE TALKING TO YOU LIKE THIS...
...IT'S HARD TO BELIEVE THAT SO MANY YEARS HAVE PASSED.
THE LIGHT IN THIS ROOM...
...AND THE WAY IT SMELLS... IT'S ALL EXACTLY THE SAME.

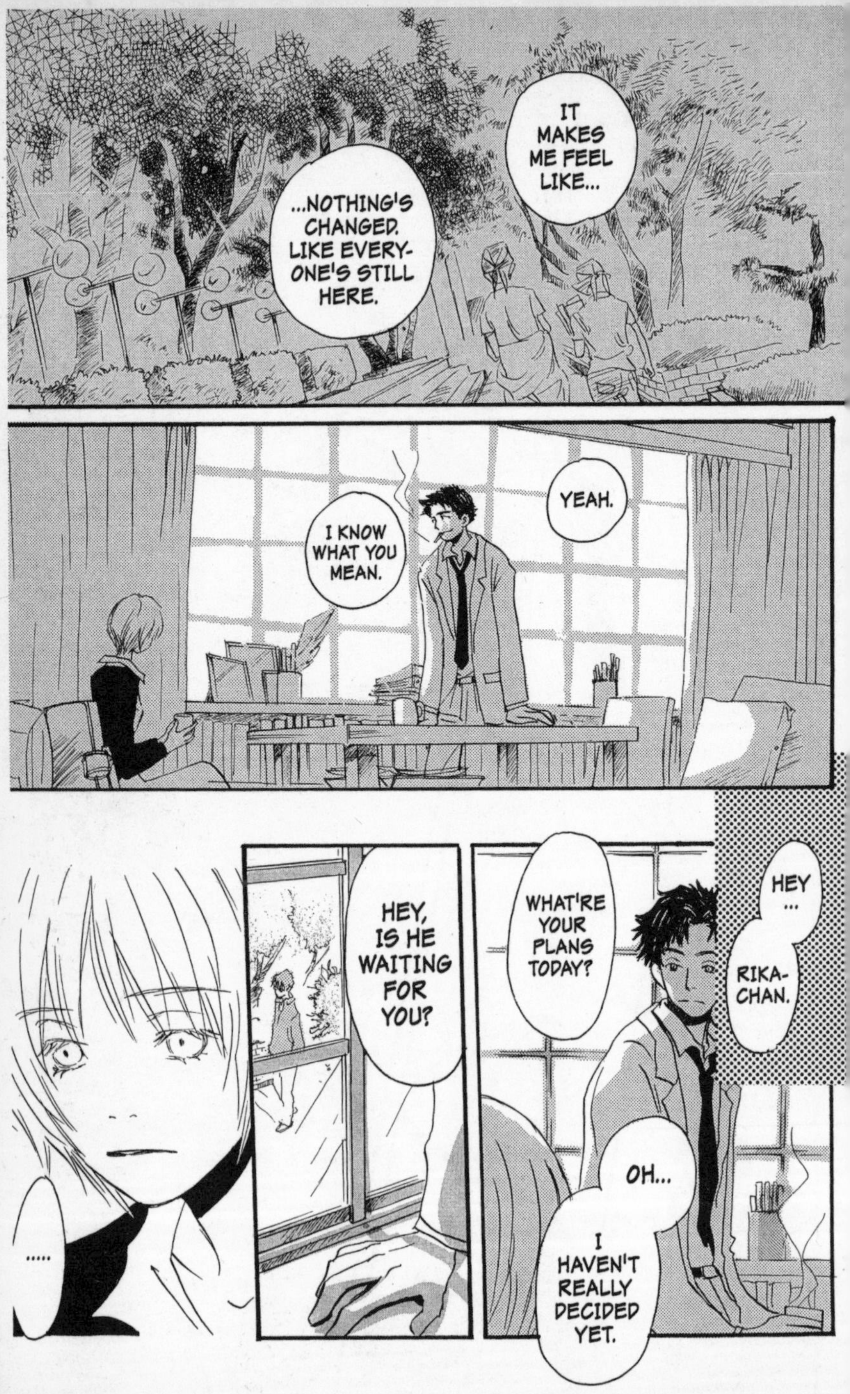
IT MAKES ME FEEL LIKE...
...NOTHING'S CHANGED. LIKE EVERY-ONE'S STILL HERE.
YEAH.
I KNOW WHAT YOU MEAN.
HEY ... RIKA-CHAN.
WHAT'RE YOUR PLANS TODAY?
OH...
I HAVEN'T REALLY DECIDED YET.
HEY, IS HE WAITING FOR YOU?
.....

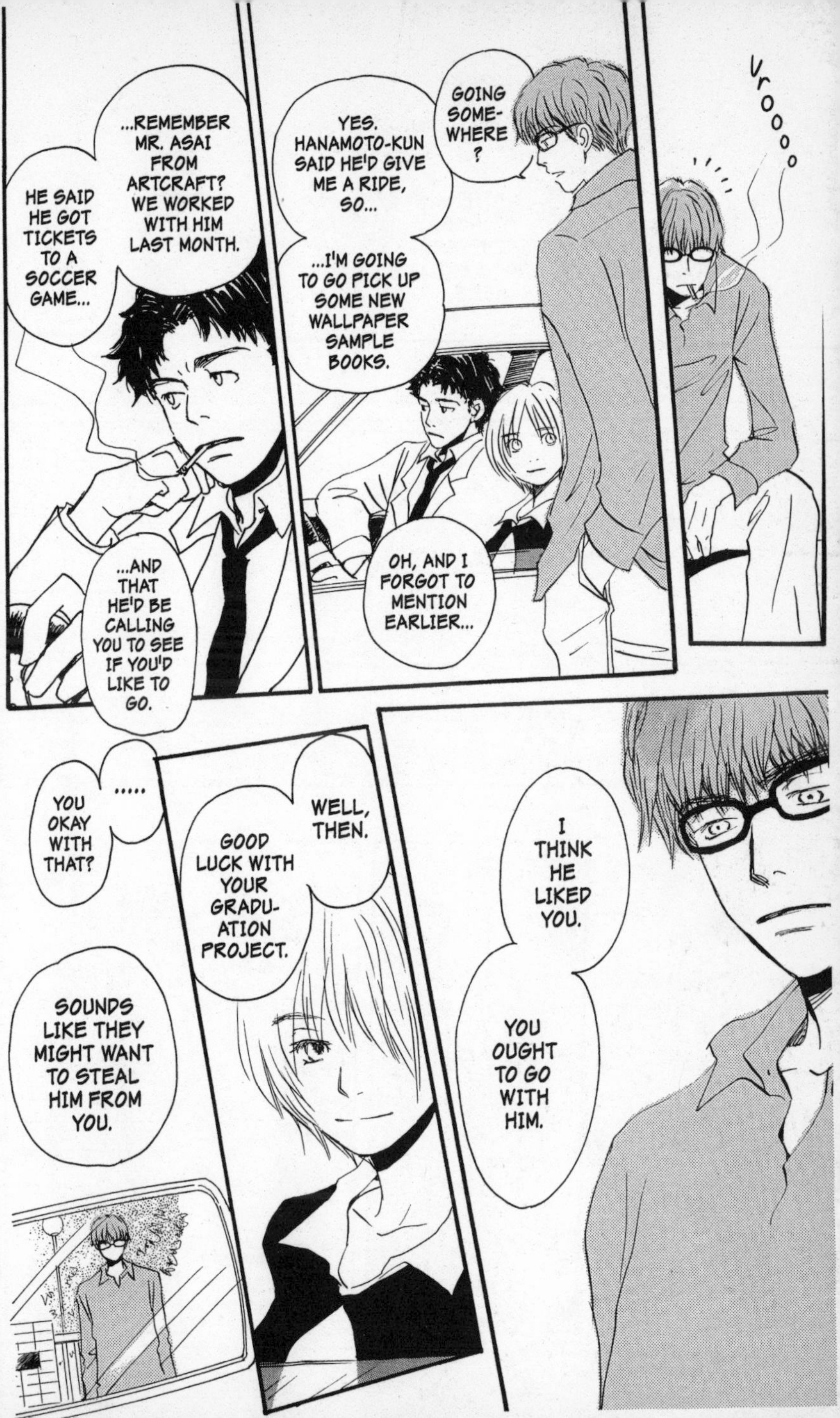
Vroooo
GOING SOMEWHERE?
YES. HANAMOTO-KUN SAID HE'D GIVE ME A RIDE, SO...
...I'M GOING TO GO PICK UP SOME NEW WALLPAPER SAMPLE BOOKS.
OH, AND I FORGOT TO MENTION EARLIER...
...REMEMBER MR. ASAI FROM ARTCRAFT? WE WORKED WITH HIM LAST MONTH.
HE SAID HE GOT TICKETS TO A SOCCER GAME...
...AND THAT HE'D BE CALLING YOU TO SEE IF YOU'D LIKE TO GO.
I THINK HE LIKED YOU.
YOU OUGHT TO GO WITH HIM.
WELL, THEN.
GOOD LUCK WITH YOUR GRADUATION PROJECT.
.....
YOU OKAY WITH THAT?
SOUNDS LIKE THEY MIGHT WANT TO STEAL HIM FROM YOU.

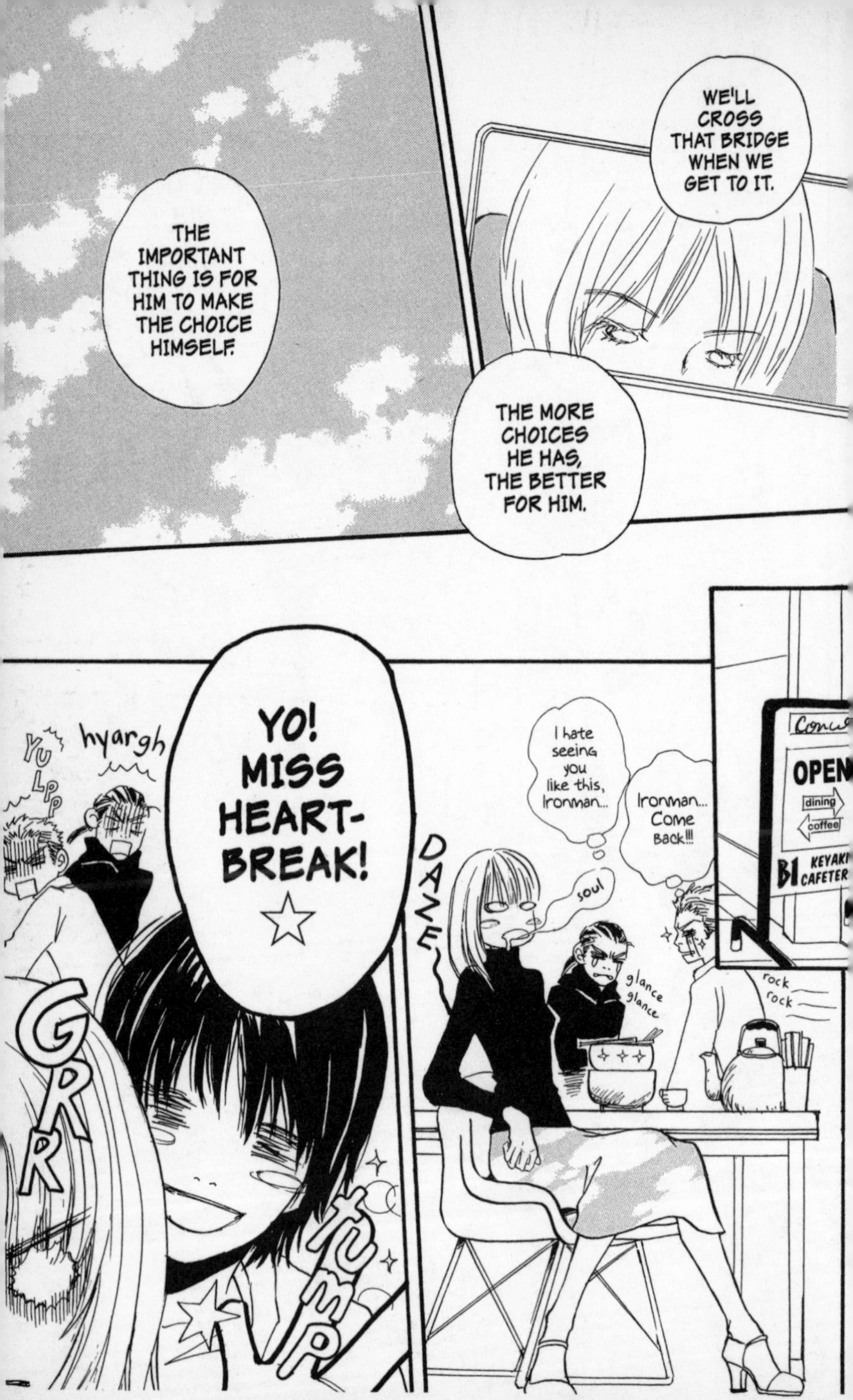
WE'LL CROSS THAT BRIDGE WHEN WE GET TO IT.
THE MORE CHOICES HE HAS, THE BETTER FOR HIM.
THE IMPORTANT THING IS FOR HIM TO MAKE THE CHOICE HIMSELF.
OPEN
dining
coffee
B1 KEYAKI CAFETER
Ironman... Come Back!!!
I hate seeing you like this, Ironman...
soul
rock rock
glance glance
DAZE
YO! MISS HEART-BREAK! ☆
hyargh
YULPP
GRR
tump

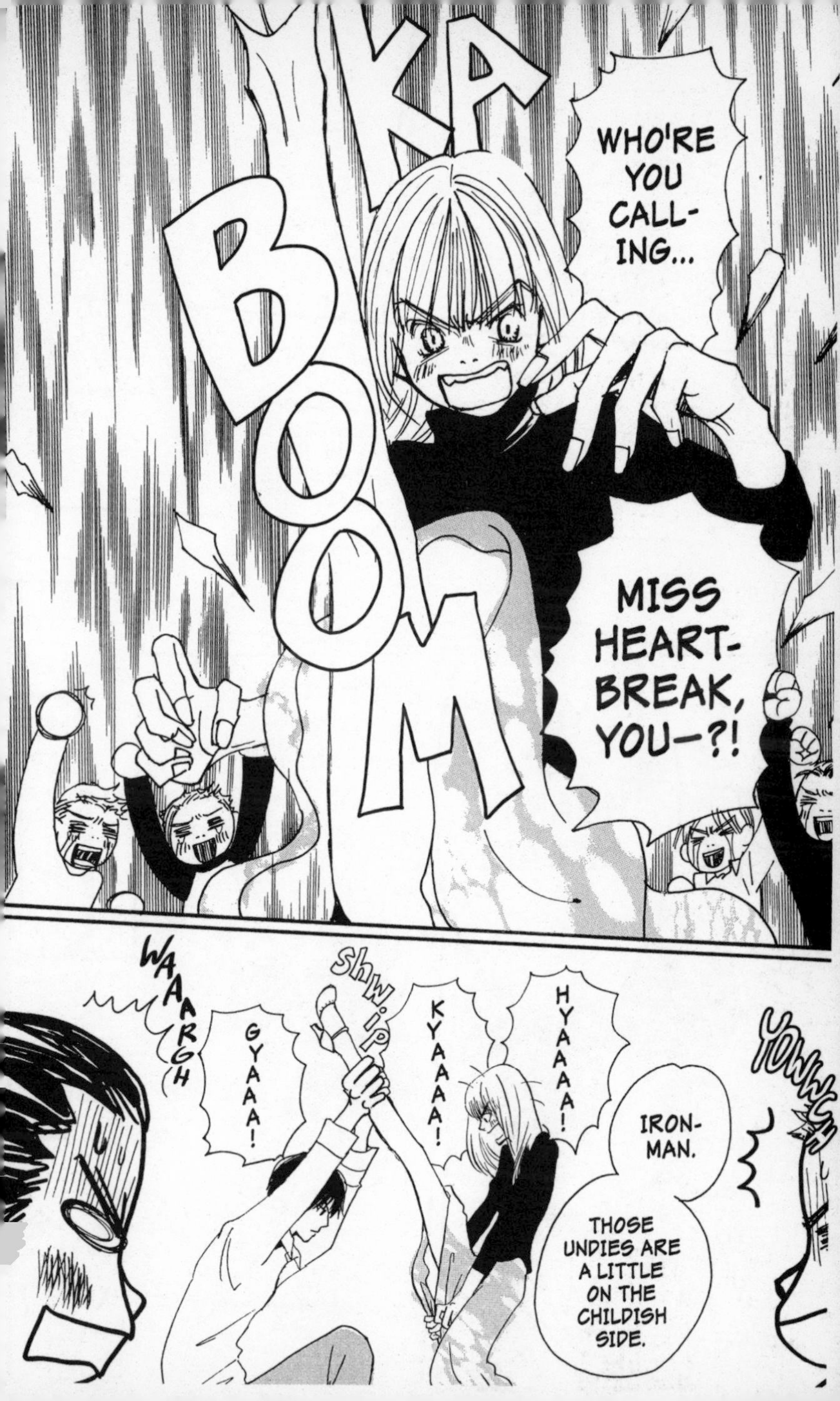
KA
BOOM
WHO'RE YOU CALLING... MISS HEART-BREAK, YOU—?!
YOWWCH
IRON-MAN.
THOSE UNDIES ARE A LITTLE ON THE CHILDISH SIDE.
HYAAAA!
KYAAAA!
Shwip
GYAAA!
WAAAARGH

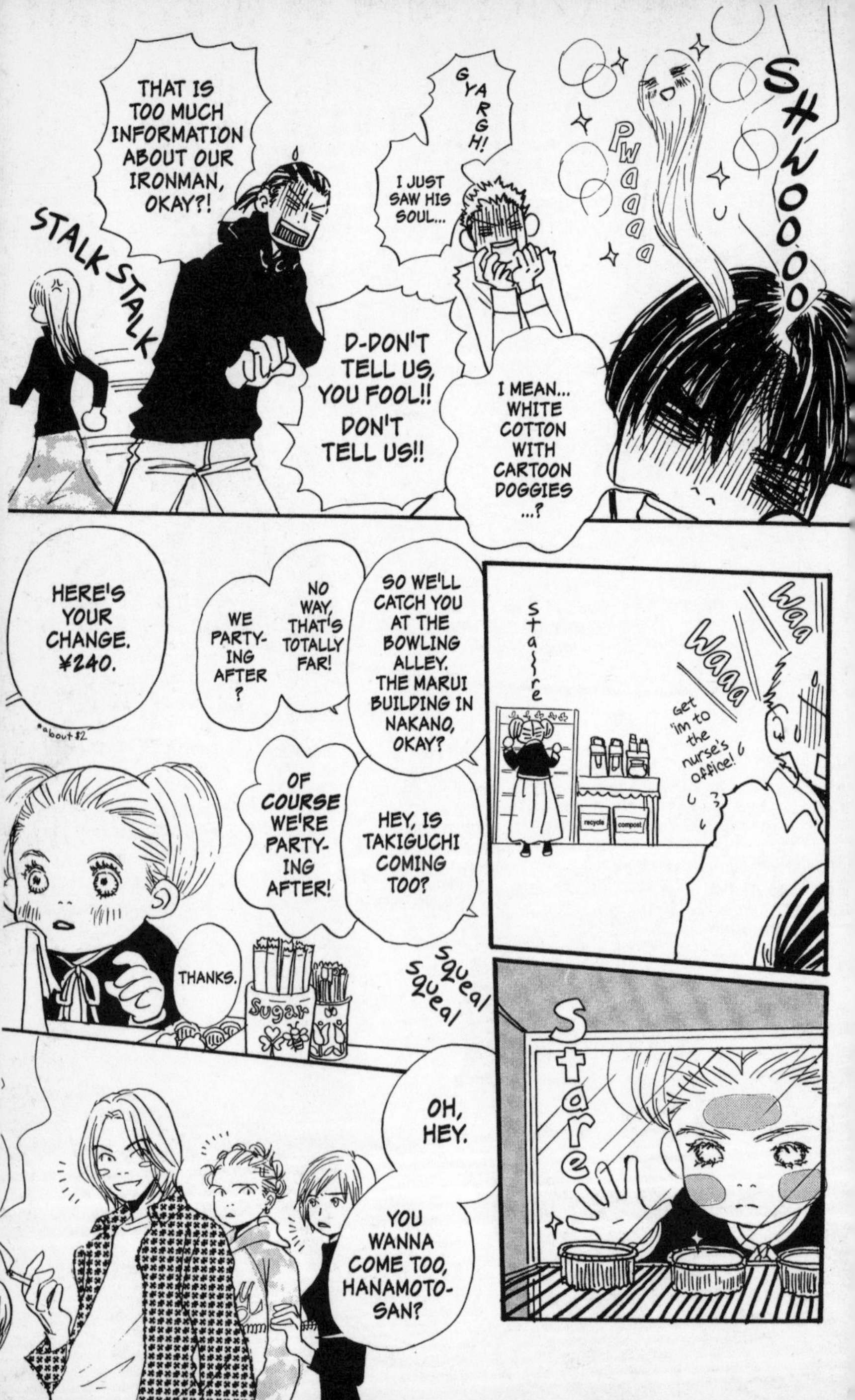
SHWOOOO
PWaaaa
GYARGH!
I JUST SAW HIS SOUL...
THAT IS TOO MUCH INFORMATION ABOUT OUR IRONMAN, OKAY?!
STALK STALK
I MEAN... WHITE COTTON WITH CARTOON DOGGIES ...?
D-DON'T TELL US, YOU FOOL!! DON'T TELL US!!
Waa Waaa
Get 'im to the nurse's office!
stare
recycle
compost
SO WE'LL CATCH YOU AT THE BOWLING ALLEY. THE MARUI BUILDING IN NAKANO, OKAY?
NO WAY, THAT'S TOTALLY FAR!
WE PARTY-ING AFTER?
HERE'S YOUR CHANGE. ¥240.
*about $2
HEY, IS TAKIGUCHI COMING TOO?
OF COURSE WE'RE PARTY-ING AFTER!
squeal squeal
Sugar
THANKS.
Stare
OH, HEY.
YOU WANNA COME TOO, HANAMOTO-SAN?

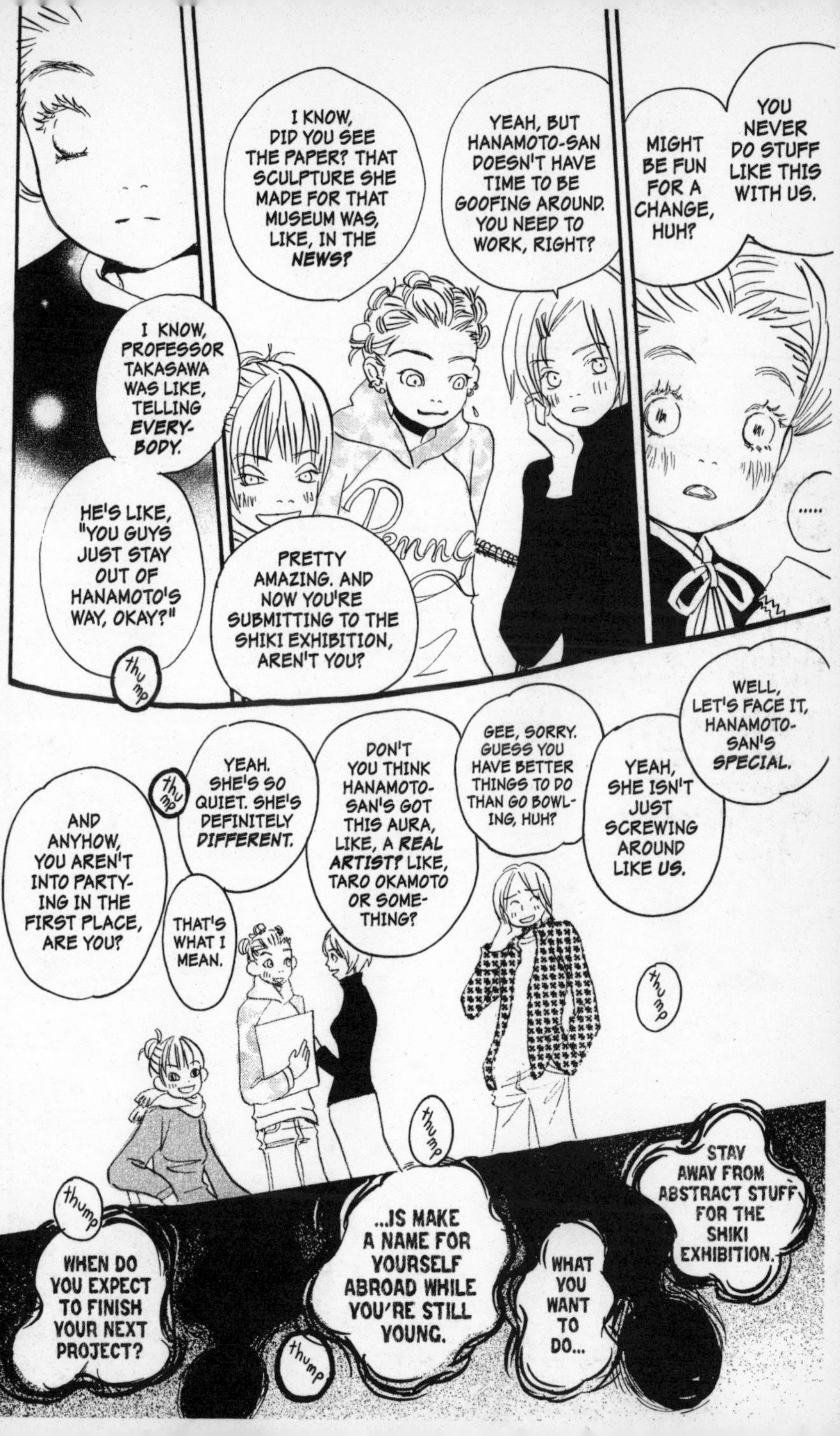
YOU NEVER DO STUFF LIKE THIS WITH US.
MIGHT BE FUN FOR A CHANGE, HUH?
.....
YEAH, BUT HANAMOTO-SAN DOESN'T HAVE TIME TO BE GOOFING AROUND. YOU NEED TO WORK, RIGHT?
I KNOW, DID YOU SEE THE PAPER? THAT SCULPTURE SHE MADE FOR THAT MUSEUM WAS, LIKE, IN THE NEWS?
PRETTY AMAZING. AND NOW YOU'RE SUBMITTING TO THE SHIKI EXHIBITION, AREN'T YOU?
I KNOW, PROFESSOR TAKASAWA WAS LIKE, TELLING EVERY-BODY.
HE'S LIKE, "YOU GUYS JUST STAY OUT OF HANAMOTO'S WAY, OKAY?"
thump
WELL, LET'S FACE IT, HANAMOTO-SAN'S SPECIAL.
YEAH, SHE ISN'T JUST SCREWING AROUND LIKE US.
GEE, SORRY. GUESS YOU HAVE BETTER THINGS TO DO THAN GO BOWL-ING, HUH?
thump
DON'T YOU THINK HANAMOTO-SAN'S GOT THIS AURA, LIKE, A REAL ARTIST? LIKE, TARO OKAMOTO OR SOME-THING?
thump
YEAH. SHE'S SO QUIET. SHE'S DEFINITELY DIFFERENT.
THAT'S WHAT I MEAN.
AND ANYHOW, YOU AREN'T INTO PARTY-ING IN THE FIRST PLACE, ARE YOU?
STAY AWAY FROM ABSTRACT STUFF FOR THE SHIKI EXHIBITION.
thump
WHAT YOU WANT TO DO...
...IS MAKE A NAME FOR YOURSELF ABROAD WHILE YOU'RE STILL YOUNG.
thump
thump
WHEN DO YOU EXPECT TO FINISH YOUR NEXT PROJECT?

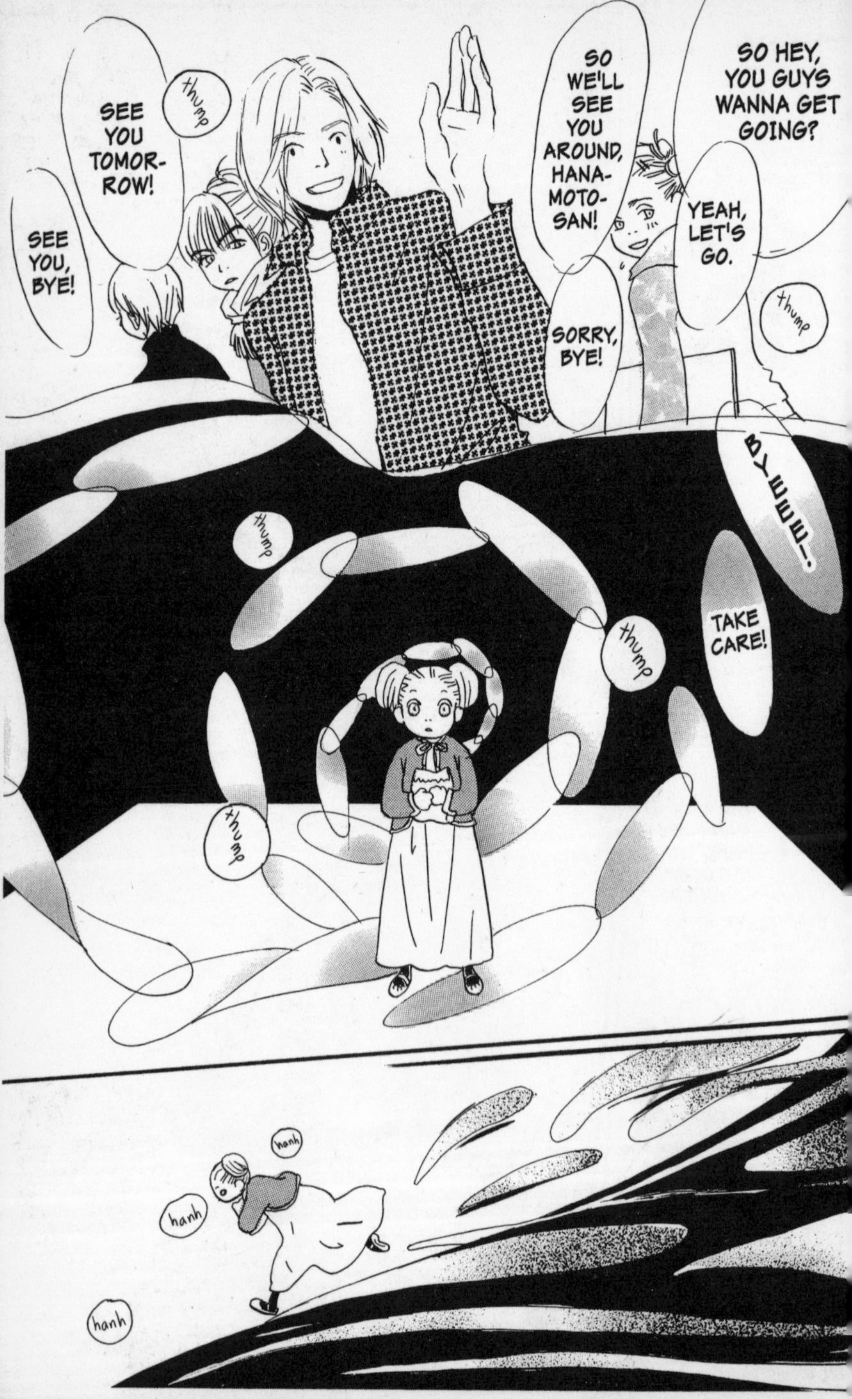
SO HEY, YOU GUYS WANNA GET GOING?
YEAH, LET'S GO.
thump
SO WE'LL SEE YOU AROUND, HANA-MOTO-SAN!
SORRY, BYE!
thump
SEE YOU TOMOR-ROW!
SEE YOU, BYE!
BYEEEE!
TAKE CARE!
thump
thump
thump
hanh
hanh
hanh

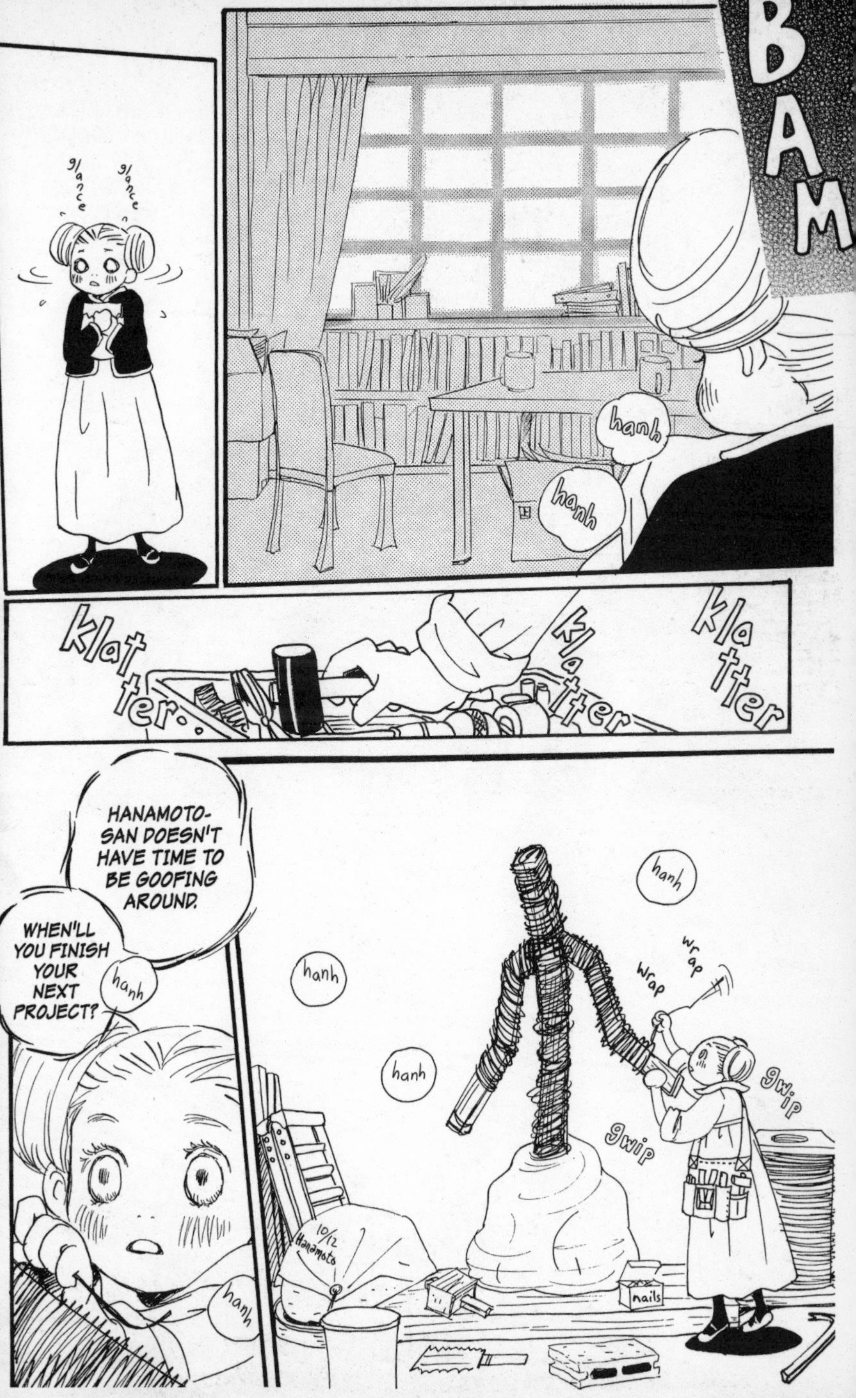

BAM
hanh
hanh
glance
glance
klatter
klatter
klatter
hanh
wrap
wrap
gwip
gwip
hanh
hanh
10/12 Hanamoto
nails
HANAMOTO-SAN DOESN'T HAVE TIME TO BE GOOFING AROUND.
WHEN'LL YOU FINISH YOUR NEXT PROJECT?
hanh
hanh

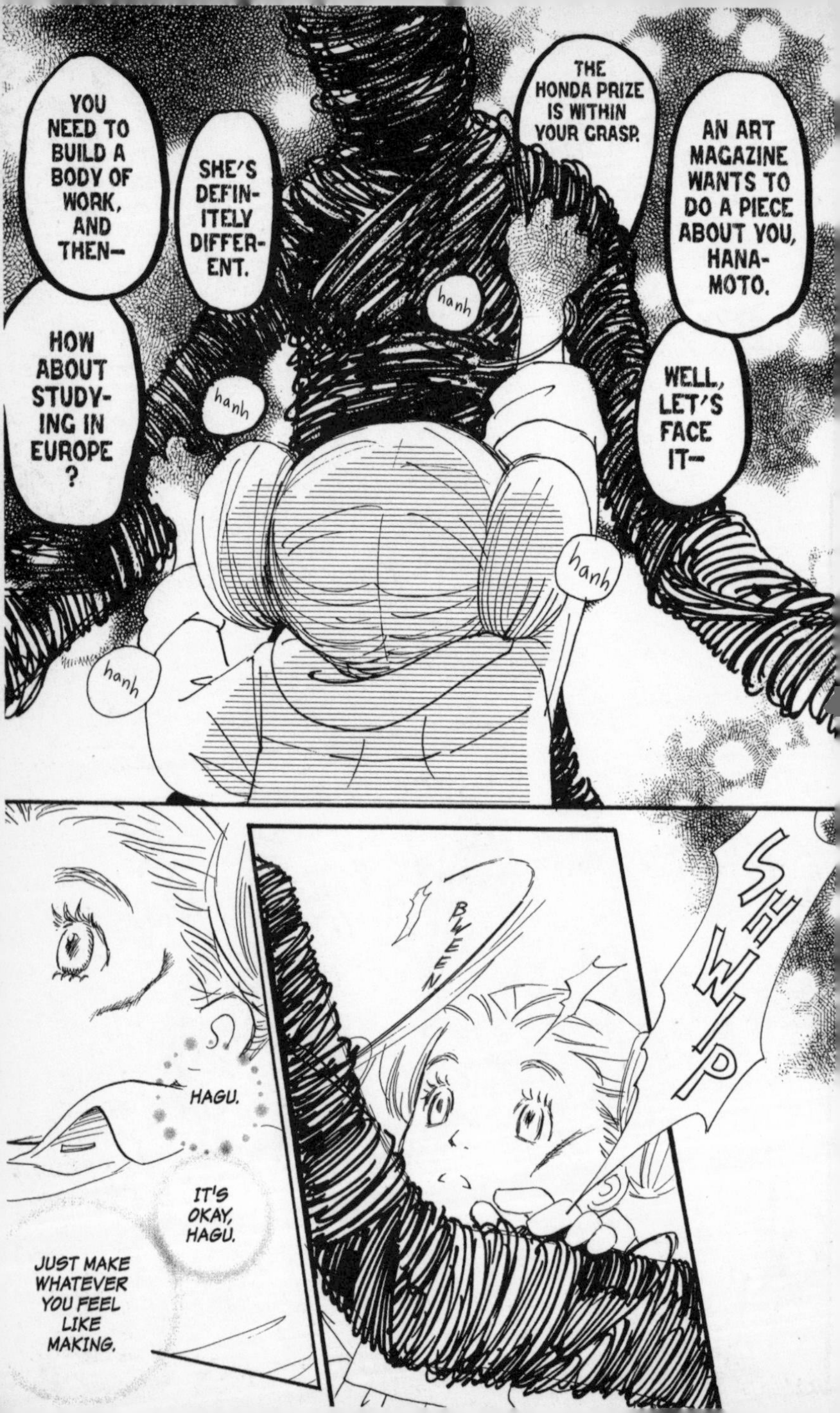
AN ART MAGAZINE WANTS TO DO A PIECE ABOUT YOU, HANAMOTO.
THE HONDA PRIZE IS WITHIN YOUR GRASP.
WELL, LET'S FACE IT—
SHE'S DEFINITELY DIFFERENT.
YOU NEED TO BUILD A BODY OF WORK, AND THEN—
hanh
hanh
HOW ABOUT STUDYING IN EUROPE?
hanh
hanh
SHWIP
BWEEN
HAGU.
IT'S OKAY, HAGU.
JUST MAKE WHATEVER YOU FEEL LIKE MAKING.

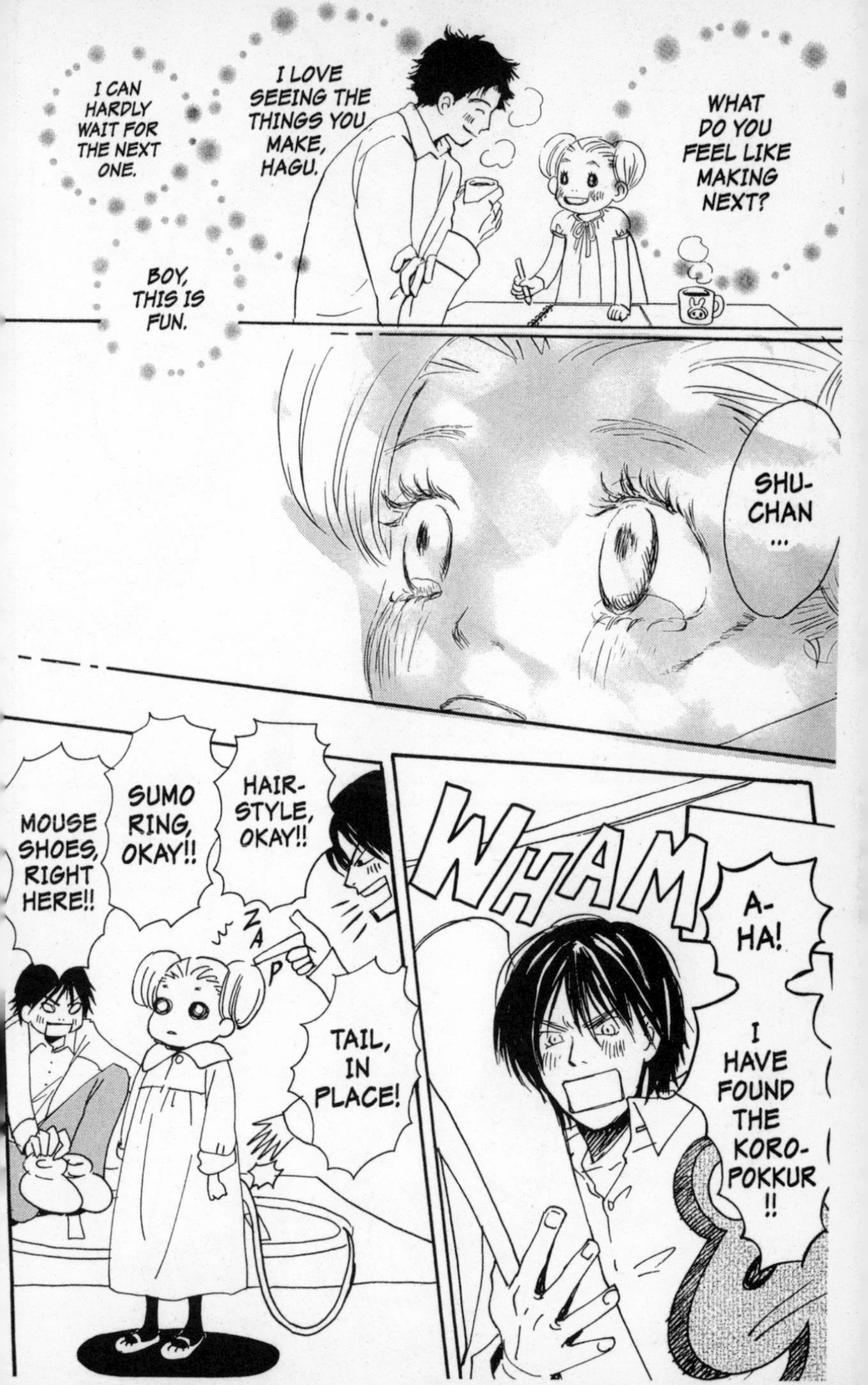
WHAT DO YOU FEEL LIKE MAKING NEXT?
I LOVE SEEING THE THINGS YOU MAKE, HAGU.
I CAN HARDLY WAIT FOR THE NEXT ONE.
BOY, THIS IS FUN.
SHU-CHAN...
WHAM
A-HA!
I HAVE FOUND THE KORO-POKKUR!!
HAIR-STYLE, OKAY!!
SUMO RING, OKAY!!
MOUSE SHOES, RIGHT HERE!!
ZAP
TAIL, IN PLACE!

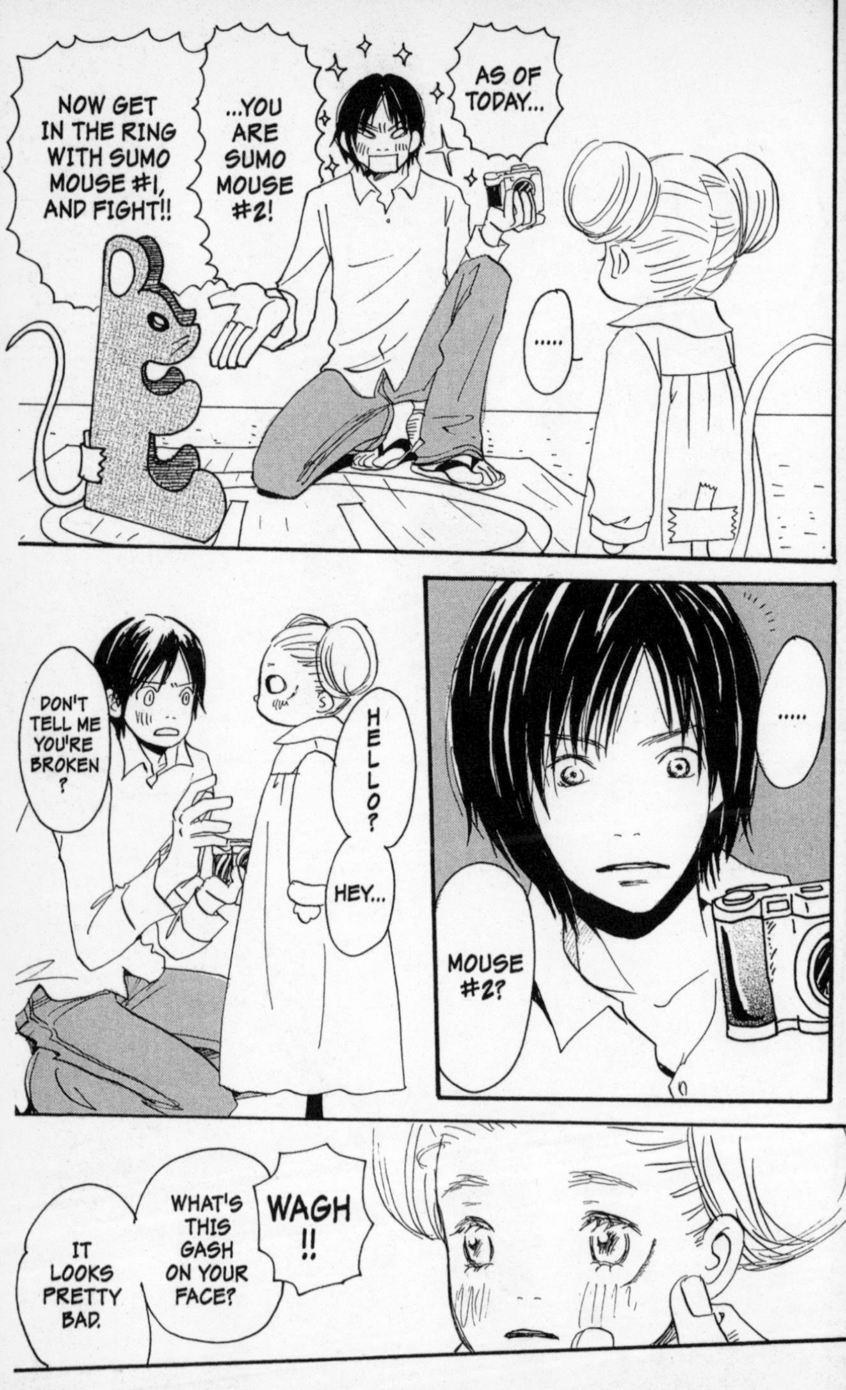
AS OF TODAY...
...YOU ARE SUMO MOUSE #2!
NOW GET IN THE RING WITH SUMO MOUSE #1, AND FIGHT!!
......
......
MOUSE #2?
HELLO?
HEY...
DON'T TELL ME YOU'RE BROKEN?
WAGH!!
WHAT'S THIS GASH ON YOUR FACE?
IT LOOKS PRETTY BAD.

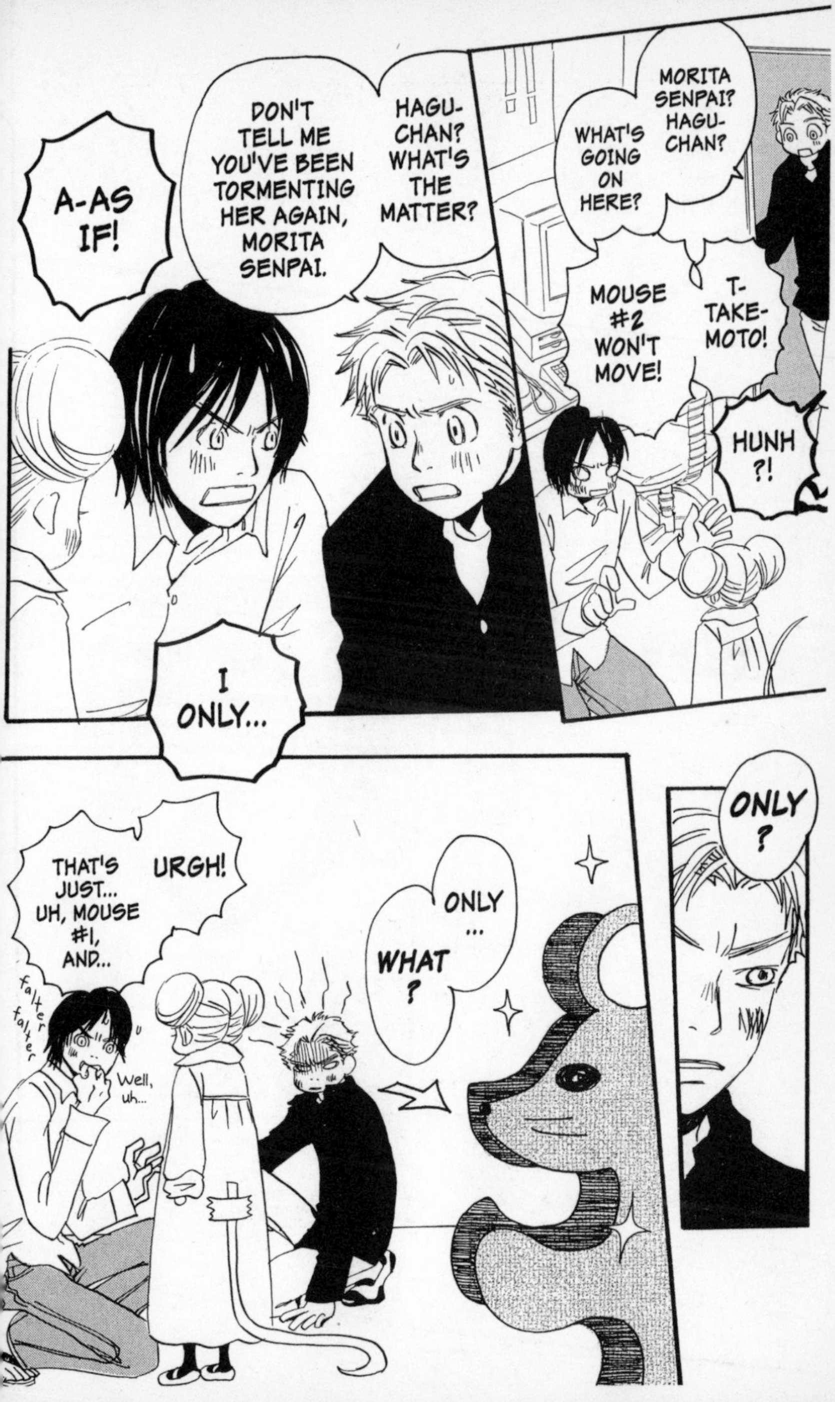
MORITA SENPAI? HAGU-CHAN?
WHAT'S GOING ON HERE?
T-TAKE-MOTO!
MOUSE #2 WON'T MOVE!
HUNH?!
HAGU-CHAN? WHAT'S THE MATTER?
DON'T TELL ME YOU'VE BEEN TORMENTING HER AGAIN, MORITA SENPAI.
A-AS IF!
I ONLY...
ONLY?
ONLY... WHAT?
URGH!
THAT'S JUST... UH, MOUSE #1, AND...
falter falter
Well, uh...

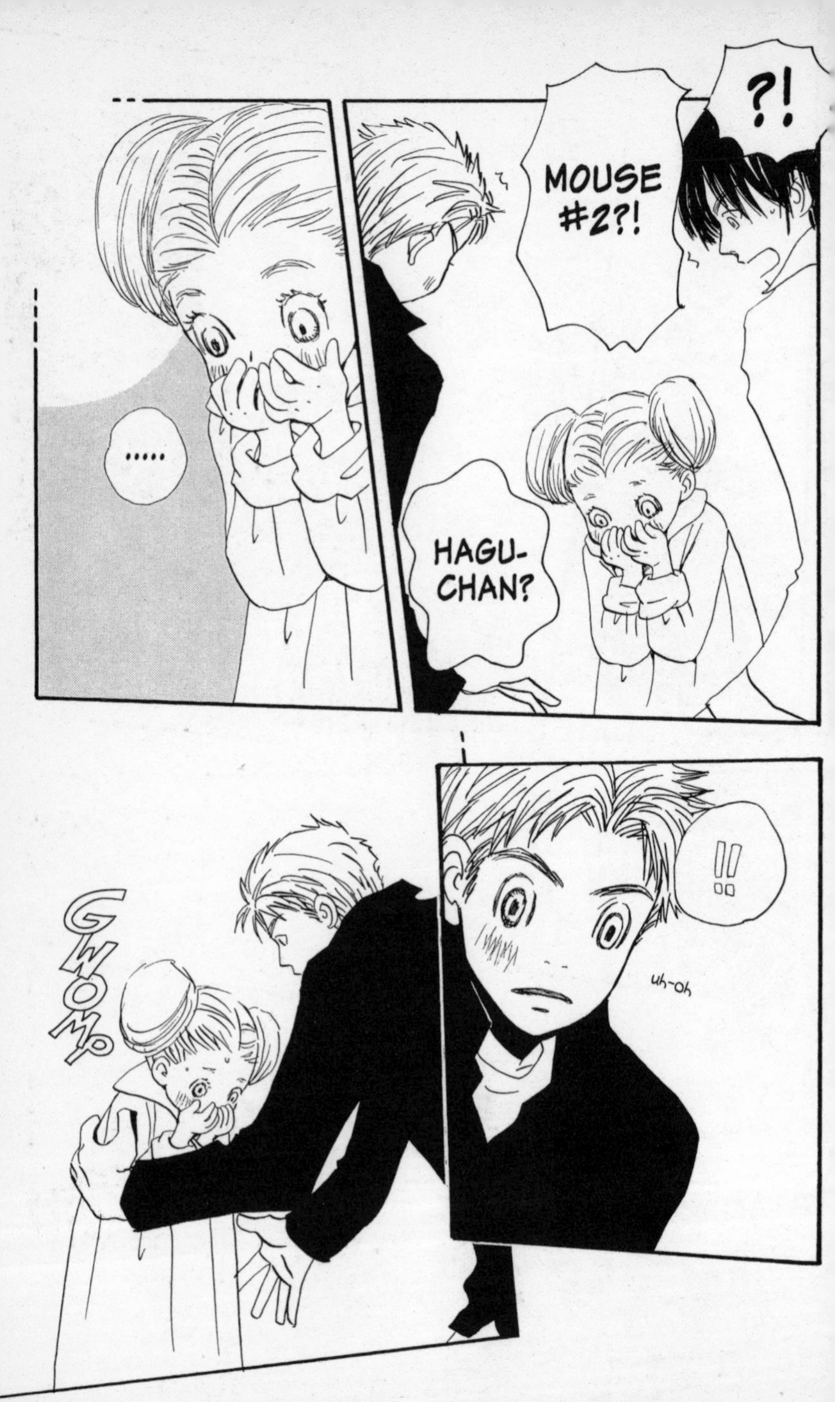
?!
MOUSE #2?!
HAGU-CHAN?
......
!!
uh-oh
GWOMP

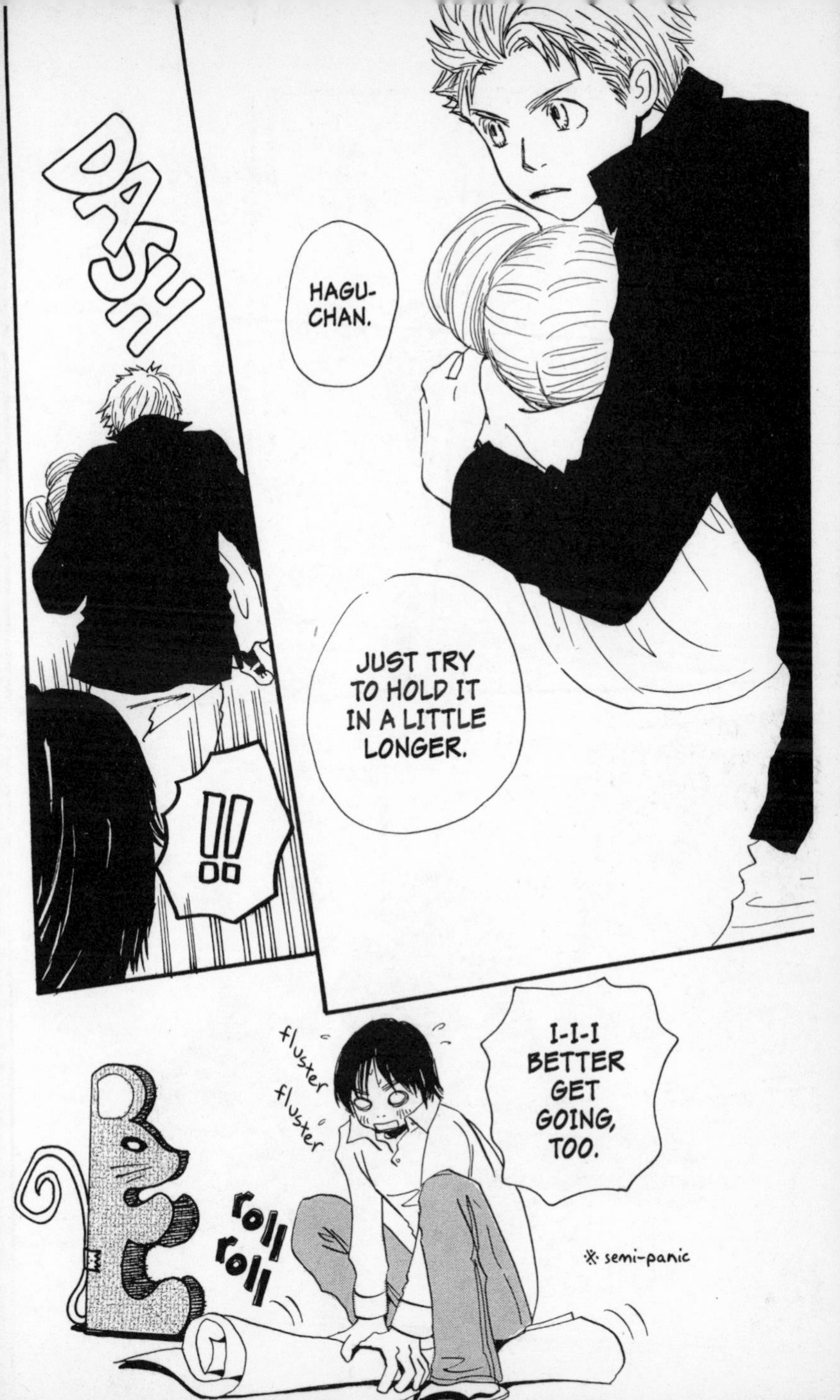
HAGU-CHAN.
JUST TRY TO HOLD IT IN A LITTLE LONGER.
DASH
!!
I-I-I BETTER GET GOING, TOO.
fluster fluster
roll roll
※ semi-panic

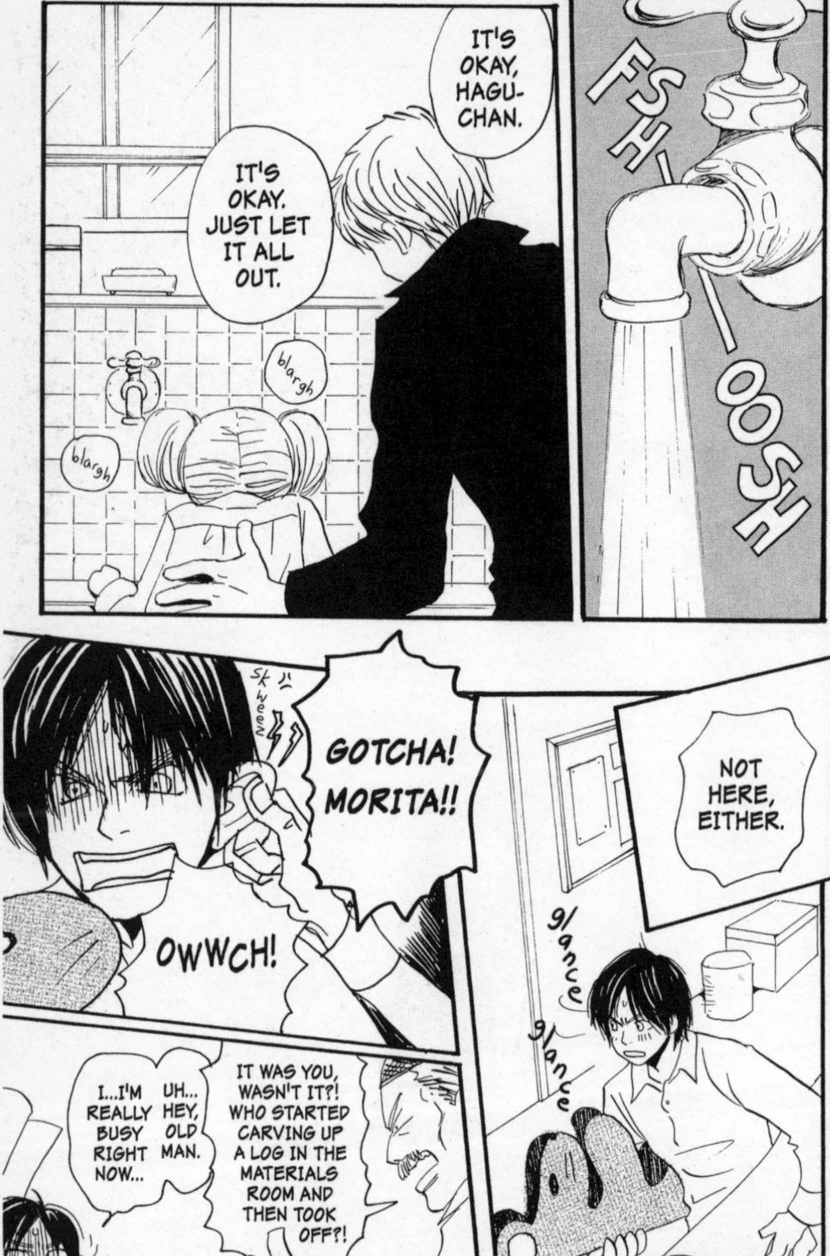
FSH-OOSH
IT'S OKAY, HAGU-CHAN.
IT'S OKAY. JUST LET IT ALL OUT.
blargh
blargh
NOT HERE, EITHER.
glance
glance
skweez
GOTCHA! MORITA!!
OWWCH!
IT WAS YOU, WASN'T IT?! WHO STARTED CARVING UP A LOG IN THE MATERIALS ROOM AND THEN TOOK OFF?!
UH... HEY, OLD MAN.
I...I'M REALLY BUSY RIGHT NOW...

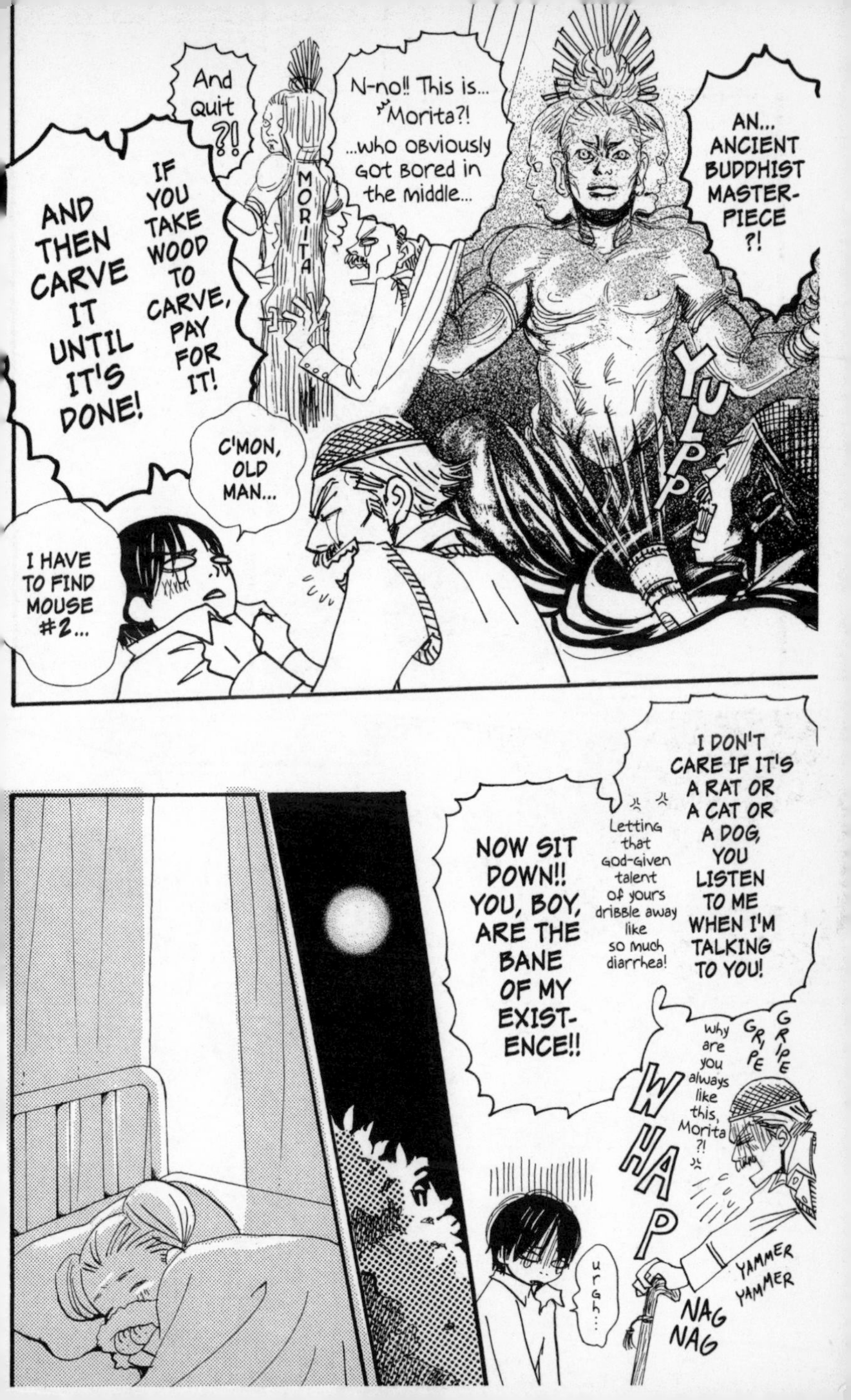
AN... ANCIENT BUDDHIST MASTER-PIECE?!
N-no!! This is... Morita?!
...who obviously got bored in the middle...
MORITA
And quit ?!
IF YOU TAKE WOOD TO CARVE, PAY FOR IT!
AND THEN CARVE IT UNTIL IT'S DONE!
YULPP
C'MON, OLD MAN...
I HAVE TO FIND MOUSE #2...
I DON'T CARE IF IT'S A RAT OR A CAT OR A DOG, YOU LISTEN TO ME WHEN I'M TALKING TO YOU!
Letting that God-given talent of yours dribble away like so much diarrhea!
NOW SIT DOWN!! YOU, BOY, ARE THE BANE OF MY EXISTENCE!!
GRIPE GRIPE
Why are you always like this, Morita?!
WHAP
YAMMER YAMMER
NAG NAG
urgh...

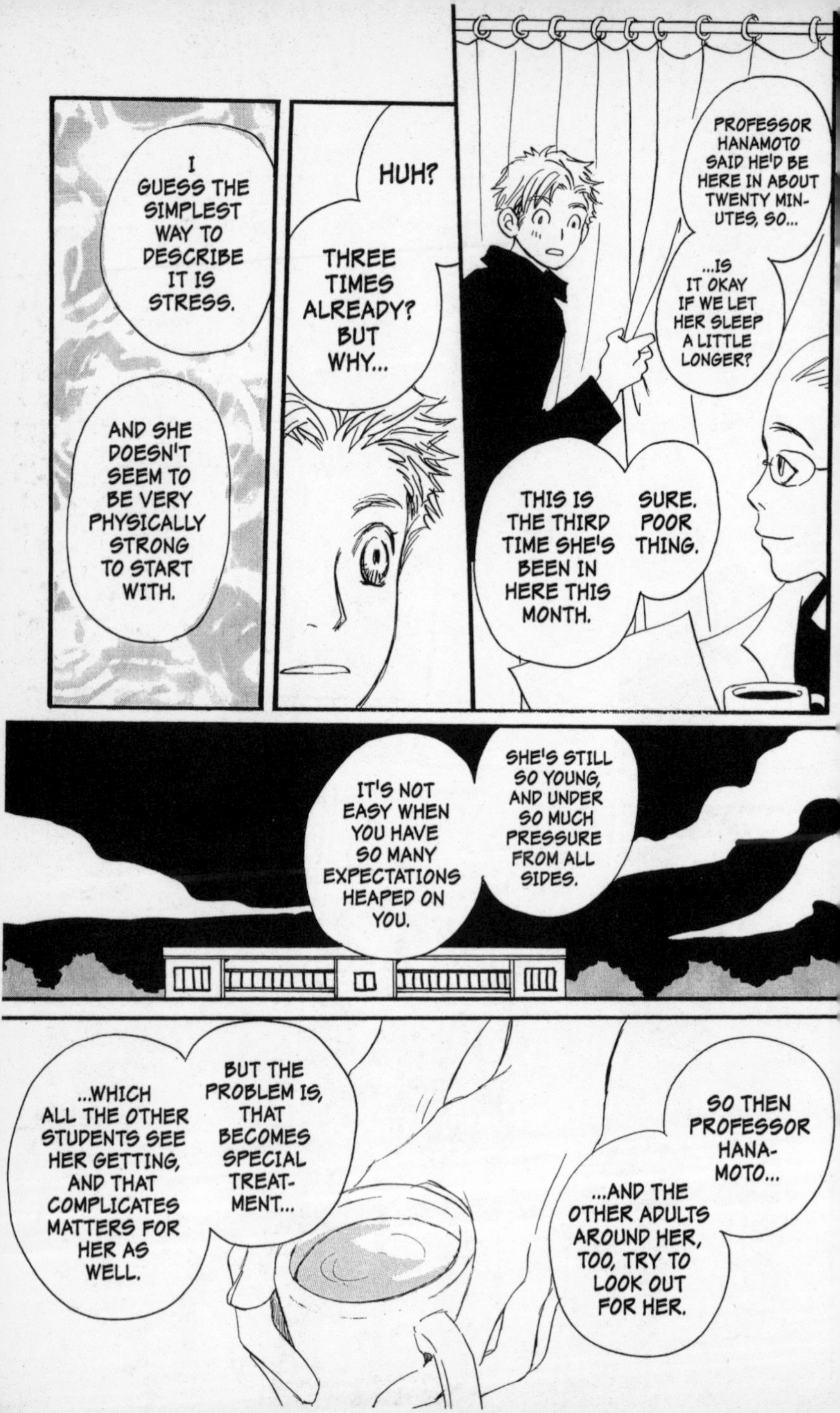
PROFESSOR HANAMOTO SAID HE'D BE HERE IN ABOUT TWENTY MIN-UTES, SO...
...IS IT OKAY IF WE LET HER SLEEP A LITTLE LONGER?
SURE. POOR THING.
THIS IS THE THIRD TIME SHE'S BEEN IN HERE THIS MONTH.
HUH?
THREE TIMES ALREADY? BUT WHY...
I GUESS THE SIMPLEST WAY TO DESCRIBE IT IS STRESS.
AND SHE DOESN'T SEEM TO BE VERY PHYSICALLY STRONG TO START WITH.
SHE'S STILL SO YOUNG, AND UNDER SO MUCH PRESSURE FROM ALL SIDES.
IT'S NOT EASY WHEN YOU HAVE SO MANY EXPECTATIONS HEAPED ON YOU.
SO THEN PROFESSOR HANA-MOTO...
...AND THE OTHER ADULTS AROUND HER, TOO, TRY TO LOOK OUT FOR HER.
BUT THE PROBLEM IS, THAT BECOMES SPECIAL TREAT-MENT...
...WHICH ALL THE OTHER STUDENTS SEE HER GETTING, AND THAT COMPLICATES MATTERS FOR HER AS WELL.

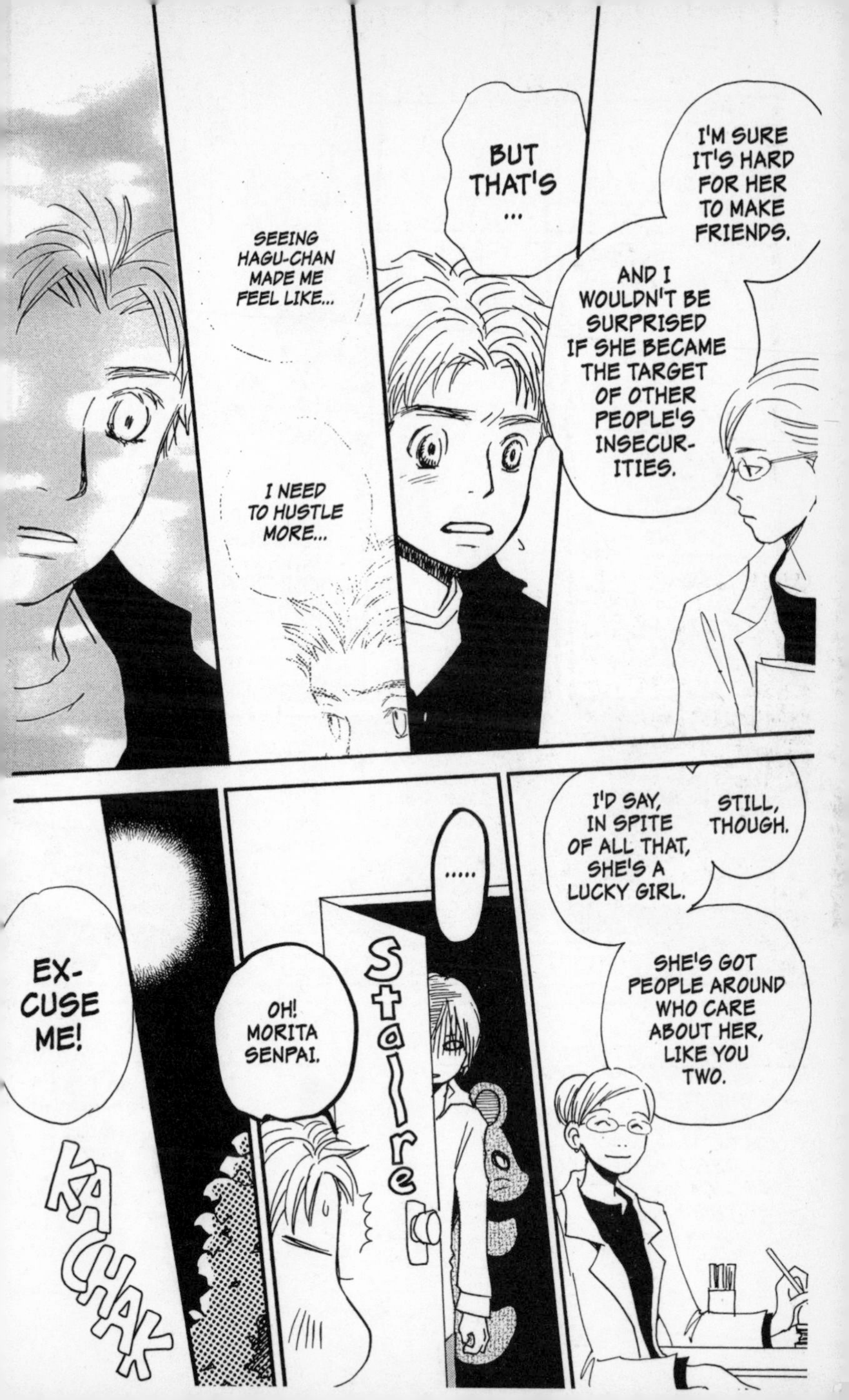

I'M SURE IT'S HARD FOR HER TO MAKE FRIENDS.
AND I WOULDN'T BE SURPRISED IF SHE BECAME THE TARGET OF OTHER PEOPLE'S INSECURITIES.
BUT THAT'S ...
SEEING HAGU-CHAN MADE ME FEEL LIKE...
I NEED TO HUSTLE MORE...
STILL, THOUGH.
I'D SAY, IN SPITE OF ALL THAT, SHE'S A LUCKY GIRL.
SHE'S GOT PEOPLE AROUND WHO CARE ABOUT HER, LIKE YOU TWO.
.....
Stare
OH! MORITA SENPAI.
EX-CUSE ME!
KACHAK

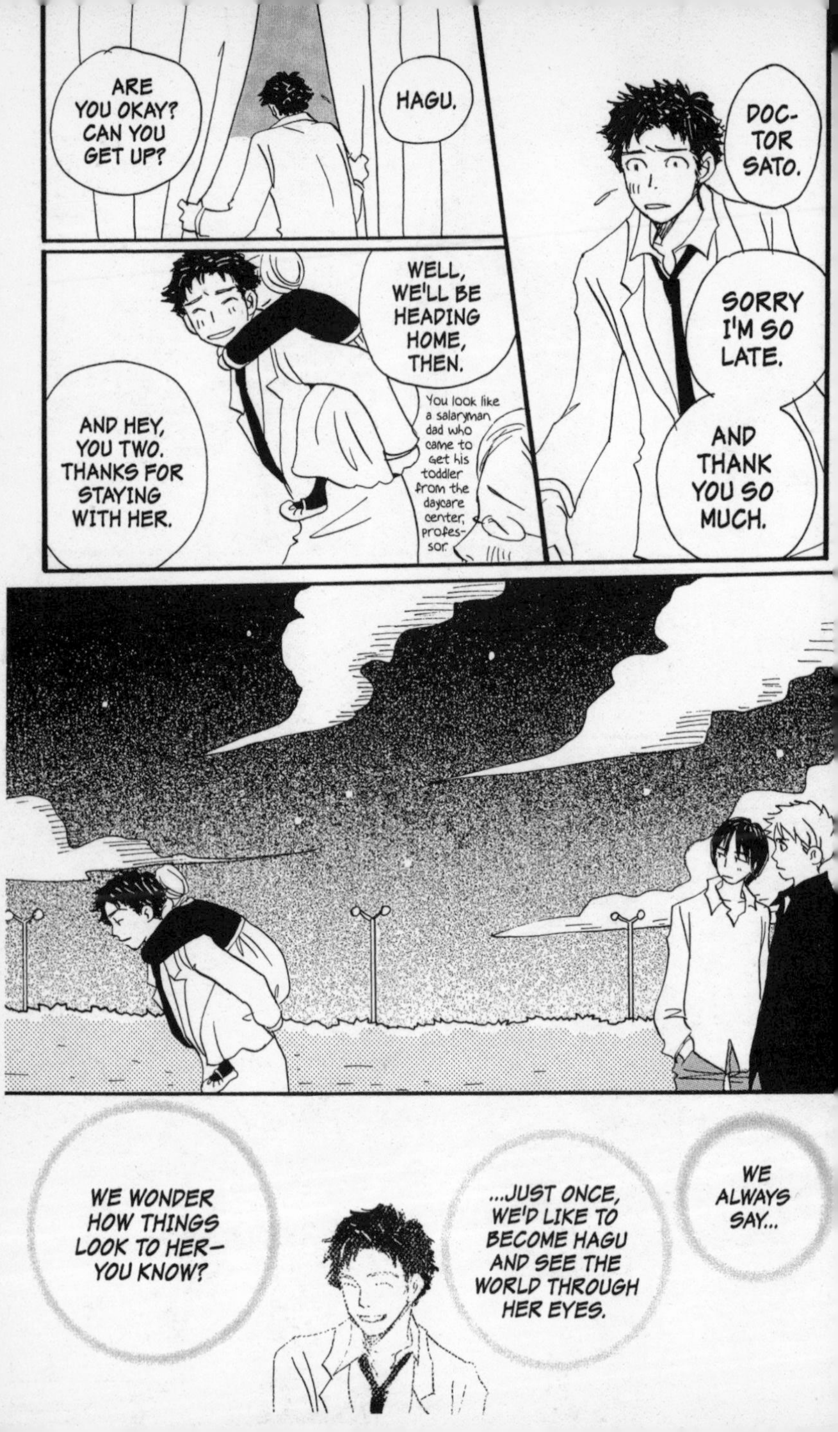
DOC-TOR SATO.
HAGU.
ARE YOU OKAY? CAN YOU GET UP?
SORRY I'M SO LATE.
AND THANK YOU SO MUCH.
WELL, WE'LL BE HEADING HOME, THEN.
You look like a salaryman dad who came to get his toddler from the daycare center, profes-sor.
AND HEY, YOU TWO. THANKS FOR STAYING WITH HER.
WE ALWAYS SAY...
...JUST ONCE, WE'D LIKE TO BECOME HAGU AND SEE THE WORLD THROUGH HER EYES.
WE WONDER HOW THINGS LOOK TO HER— YOU KNOW?

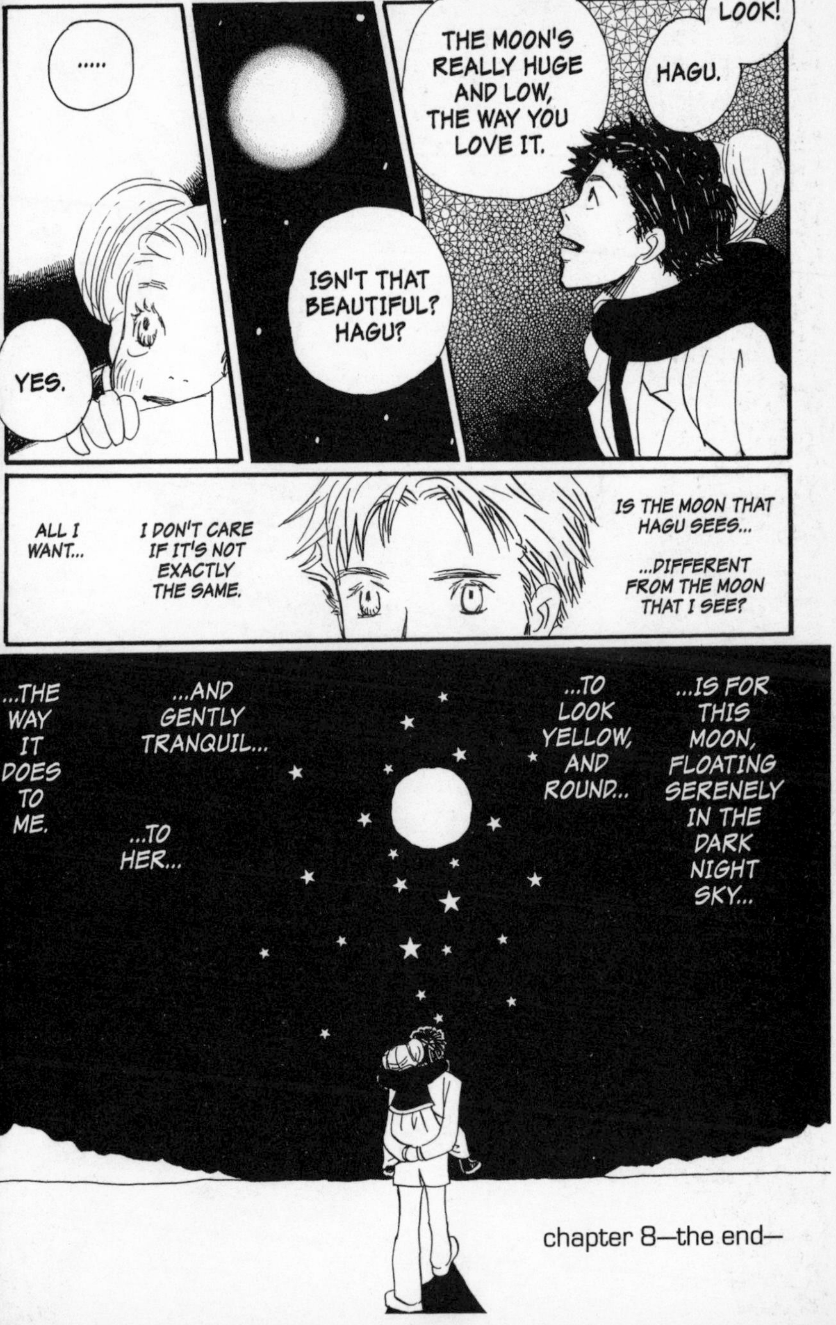
LOOK!
HAGU.
THE MOON'S REALLY HUGE AND LOW, THE WAY YOU LOVE IT.
ISN'T THAT BEAUTIFUL? HAGU?
.....
YES.
IS THE MOON THAT HAGU SEES...
...DIFFERENT FROM THE MOON THAT I SEE?
I DON'T CARE IF IT'S NOT EXACTLY THE SAME.
ALL I WANT...
...IS FOR THIS MOON, FLOATING SERENELY IN THE DARK NIGHT SKY...
...TO LOOK YELLOW, AND ROUND...
...AND GENTLY TRANQUIL...
...TO HER...
...THE WAY IT DOES TO ME.
chapter 8—the end—

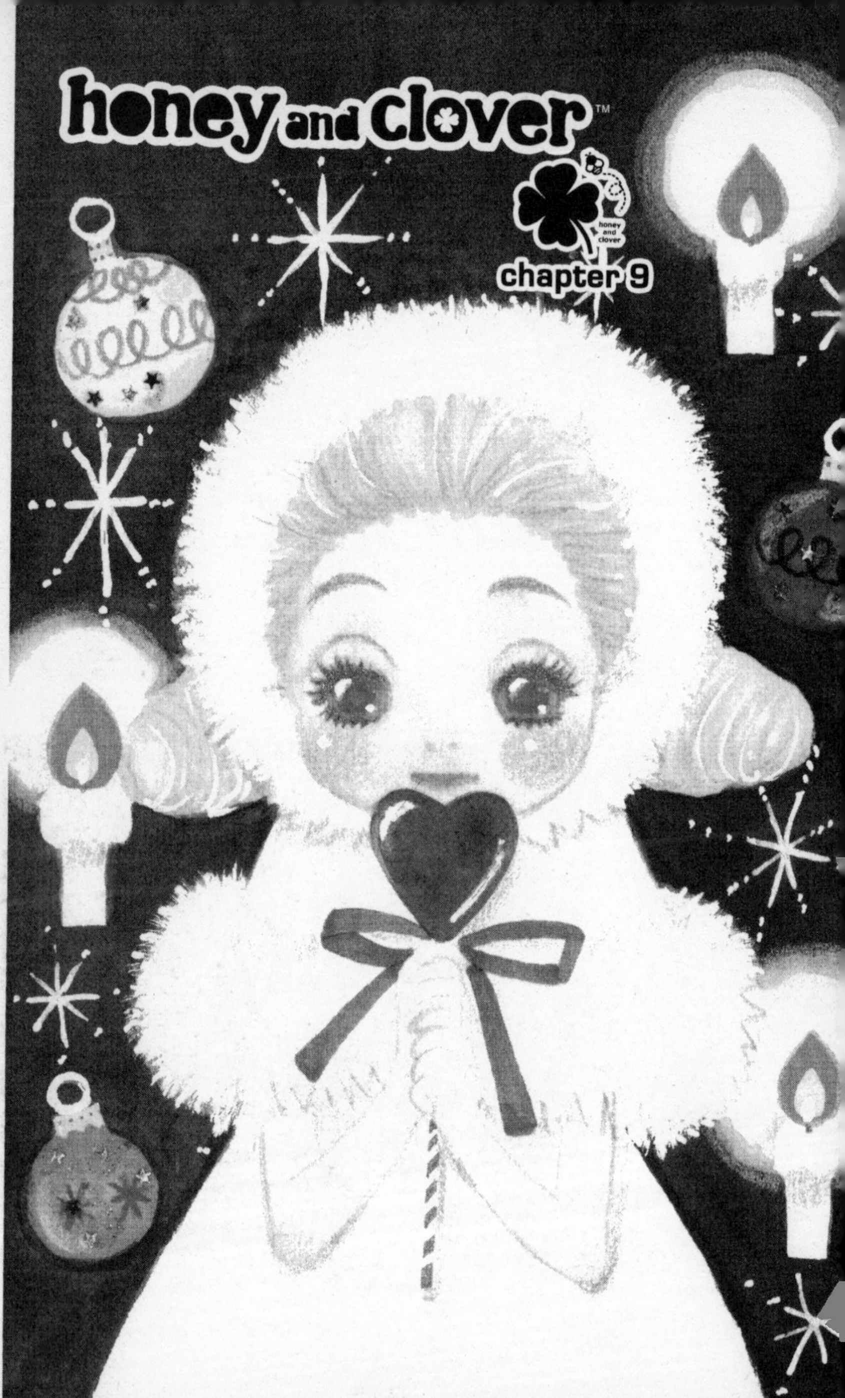
honey and clover™
honey and clover
chapter 9

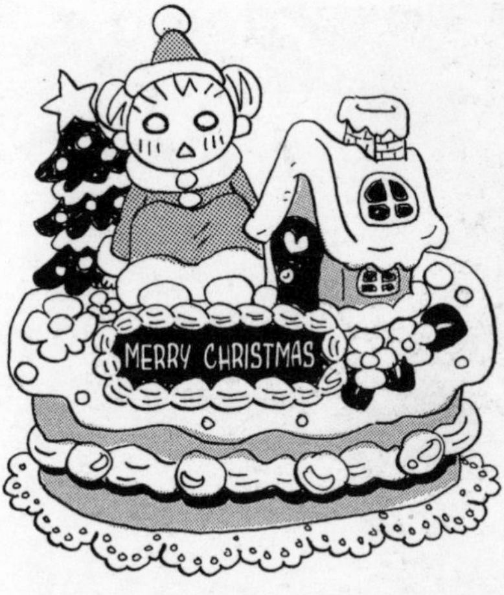
MERRY CHRISTMAS

made by Shinobu Morita

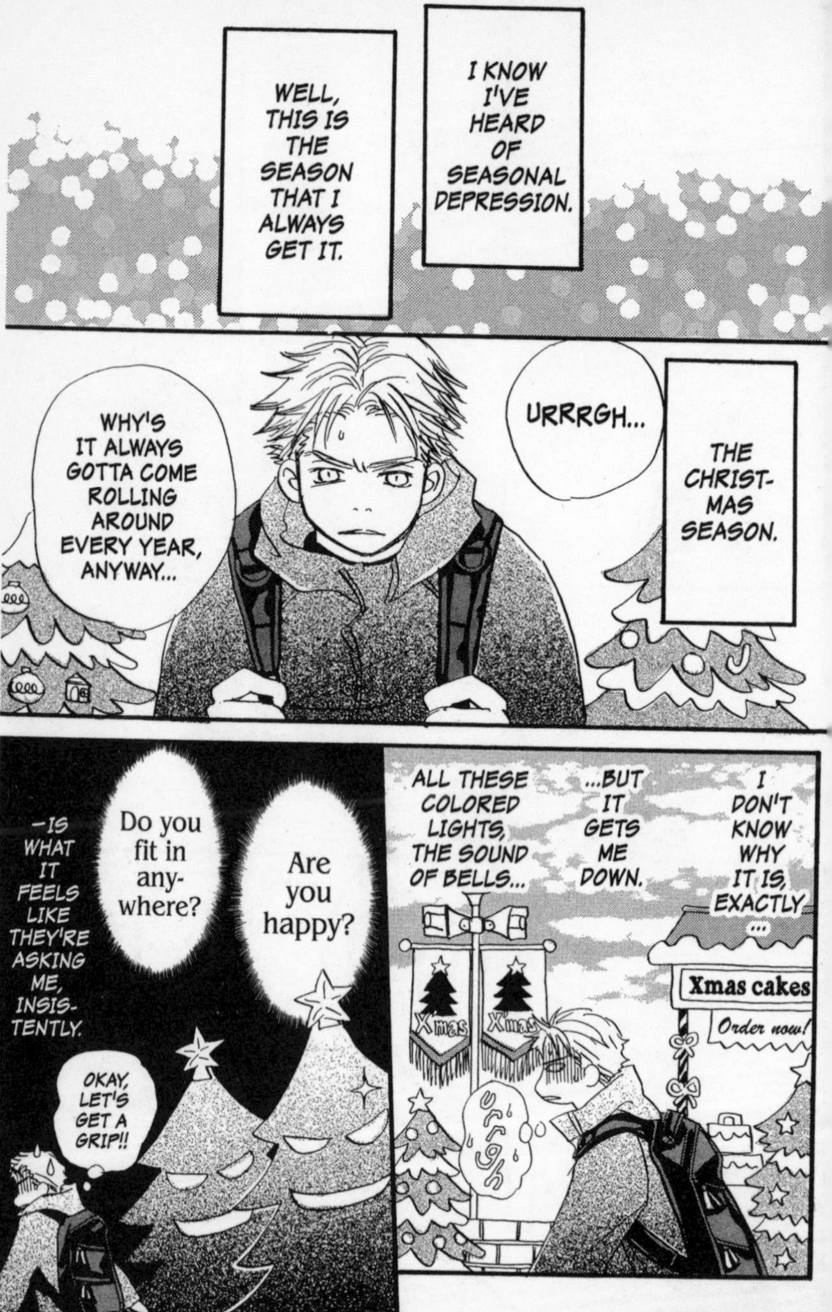
I KNOW I'VE HEARD OF SEASONAL DEPRESSION.
WELL, THIS IS THE SEASON THAT I ALWAYS GET IT.
THE CHRISTMAS SEASON.
URRRGH...
WHY'S IT ALWAYS GOTTA COME ROLLING AROUND EVERY YEAR, ANYWAY...
I DON'T KNOW WHY IT IS, EXACTLY...
...BUT IT GETS ME DOWN.
ALL THESE COLORED LIGHTS, THE SOUND OF BELLS...
Xmas cakes
Order now!
Xmas
X'mas
urrgh
Are you happy?
Do you fit in anywhere?
—IS WHAT IT FEELS LIKE THEY'RE ASKING ME, INSISTENTLY.
OKAY, LET'S GET A GRIP!!

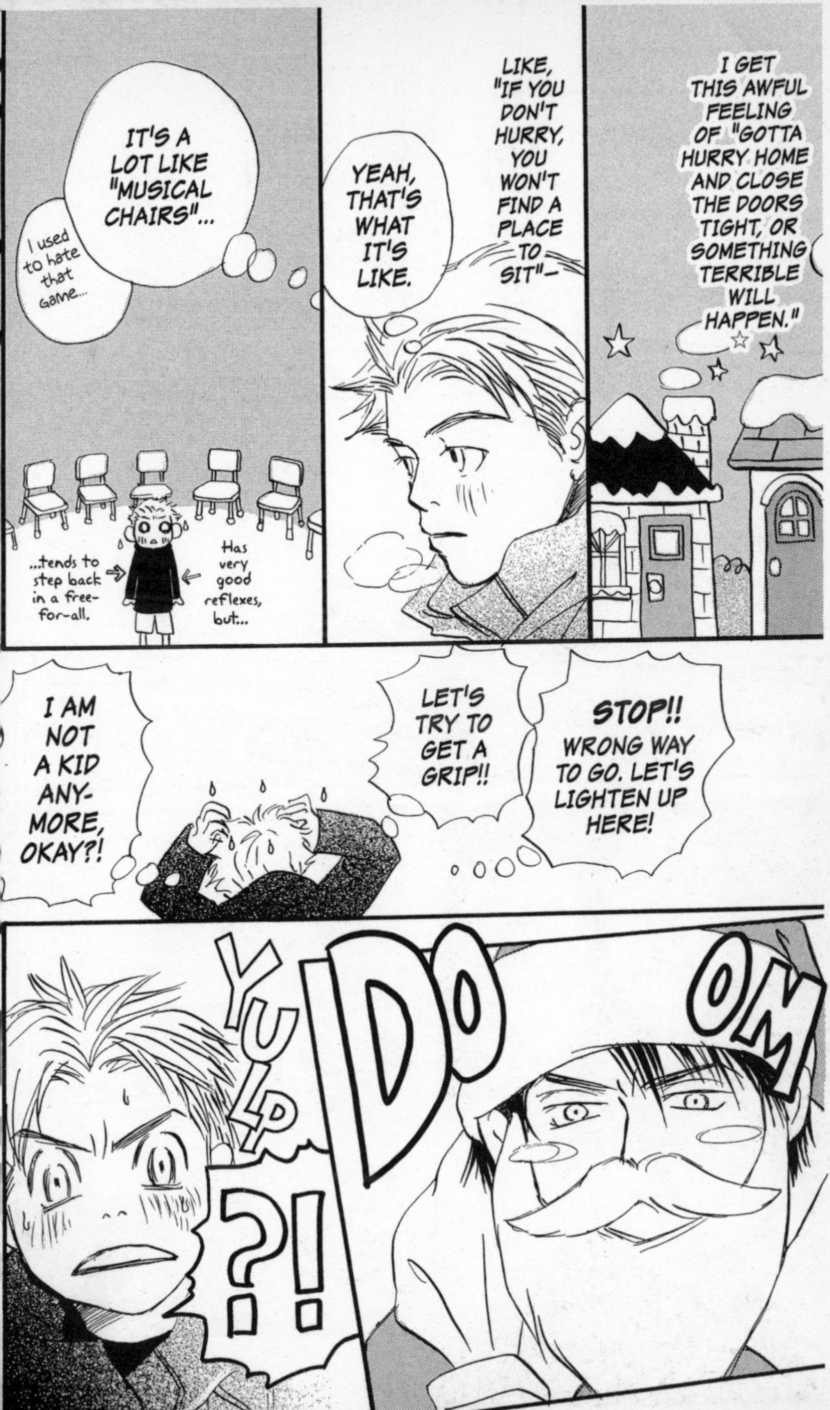
I GET THIS AWFUL FEELING OF "GOTTA HURRY HOME AND CLOSE THE DOORS TIGHT, OR SOMETHING TERRIBLE WILL HAPPEN."
LIKE, "IF YOU DON'T HURRY, YOU WON'T FIND A PLACE TO SIT"—
YEAH, THAT'S WHAT IT'S LIKE.
IT'S A LOT LIKE "MUSICAL CHAIRS"...
I used to hate that game...
Has very good reflexes, but...
...tends to step back in a free-for-all.
STOP!! WRONG WAY TO GO. LET'S LIGHTEN UP HERE!
LET'S TRY TO GET A GRIP!!
I AM NOT A KID ANY-MORE, OKAY?!
DOOM
YULP
?!

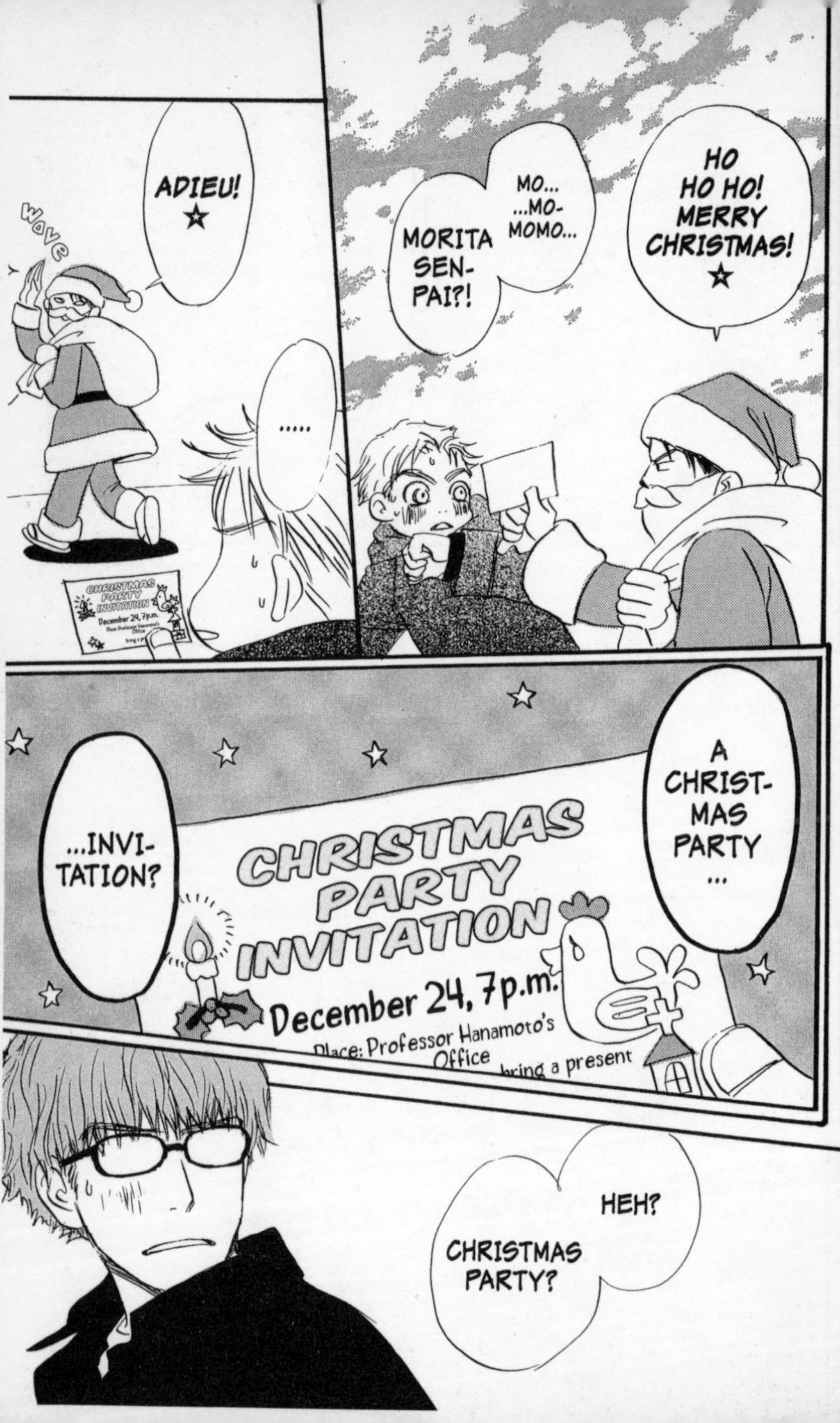
HO HO HO! MERRY CHRISTMAS! ☆
MO... ...MO-MOMO...
MORITA SENPAI?!
ADIEU! ☆
wave
.....
CHRISTMAS PARTY INVITATION
A CHRIST-MAS PARTY ...
...INVI-TATION?
CHRISTMAS PARTY INVITATION
December 24, 7 p.m.
Place: Professor Hanamoto's Office
bring a present
HEH?
CHRISTMAS PARTY?

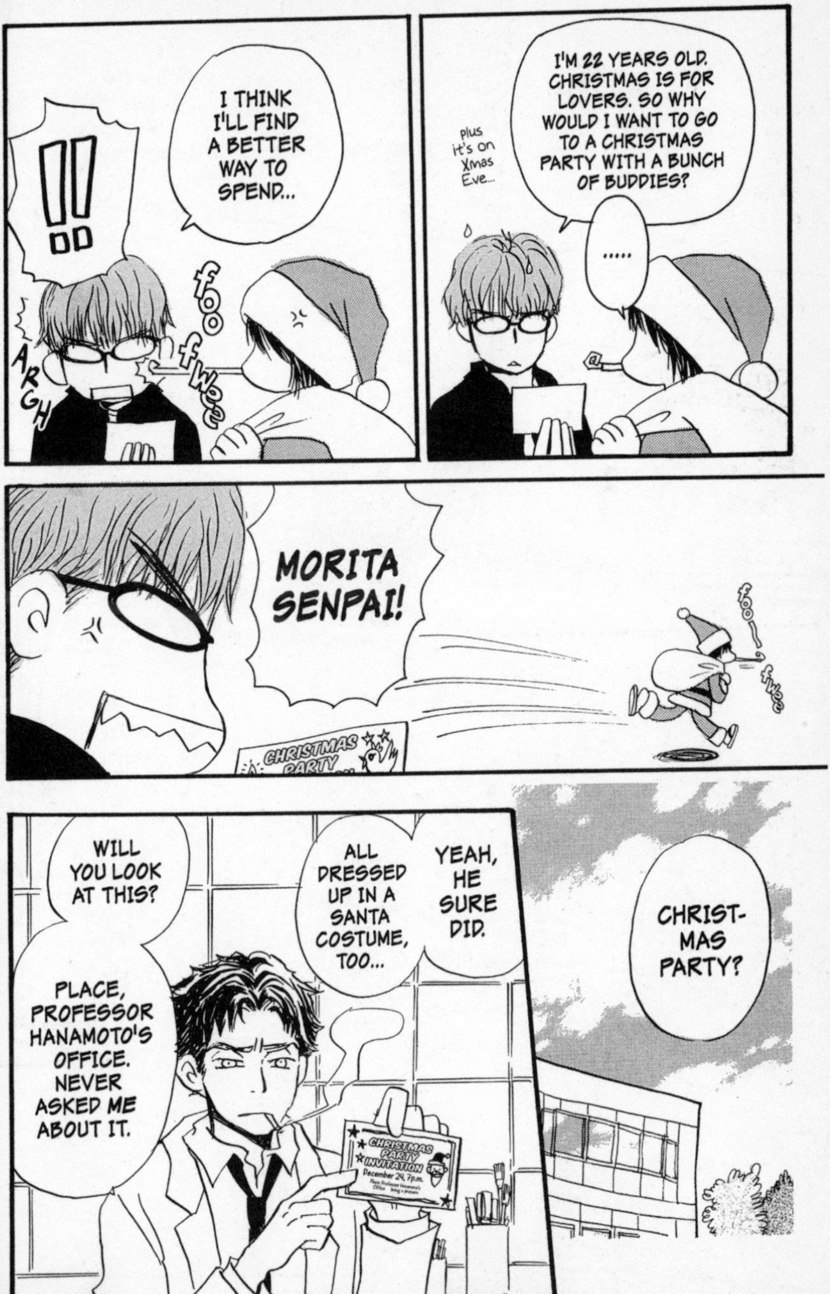
I'M 22 YEARS OLD. CHRISTMAS IS FOR LOVERS. SO WHY WOULD I WANT TO GO TO A CHRISTMAS PARTY WITH A BUNCH OF BUDDIES?
plus it's on Xmas Eve...
.....
I THINK I'LL FIND A BETTER WAY TO SPEND...
!!
foo fwee
ARGH
MORITA SENPAI!
foo— fwee
CHRISTMAS PARTY
CHRIST-MAS PARTY?
YEAH, HE SURE DID.
ALL DRESSED UP IN A SANTA COSTUME, TOO...
WILL YOU LOOK AT THIS?
PLACE, PROFESSOR HANAMOTO'S OFFICE. NEVER ASKED ME ABOUT IT.
CHRISTMAS PARTY INVITATION
December 24, 7p.m.

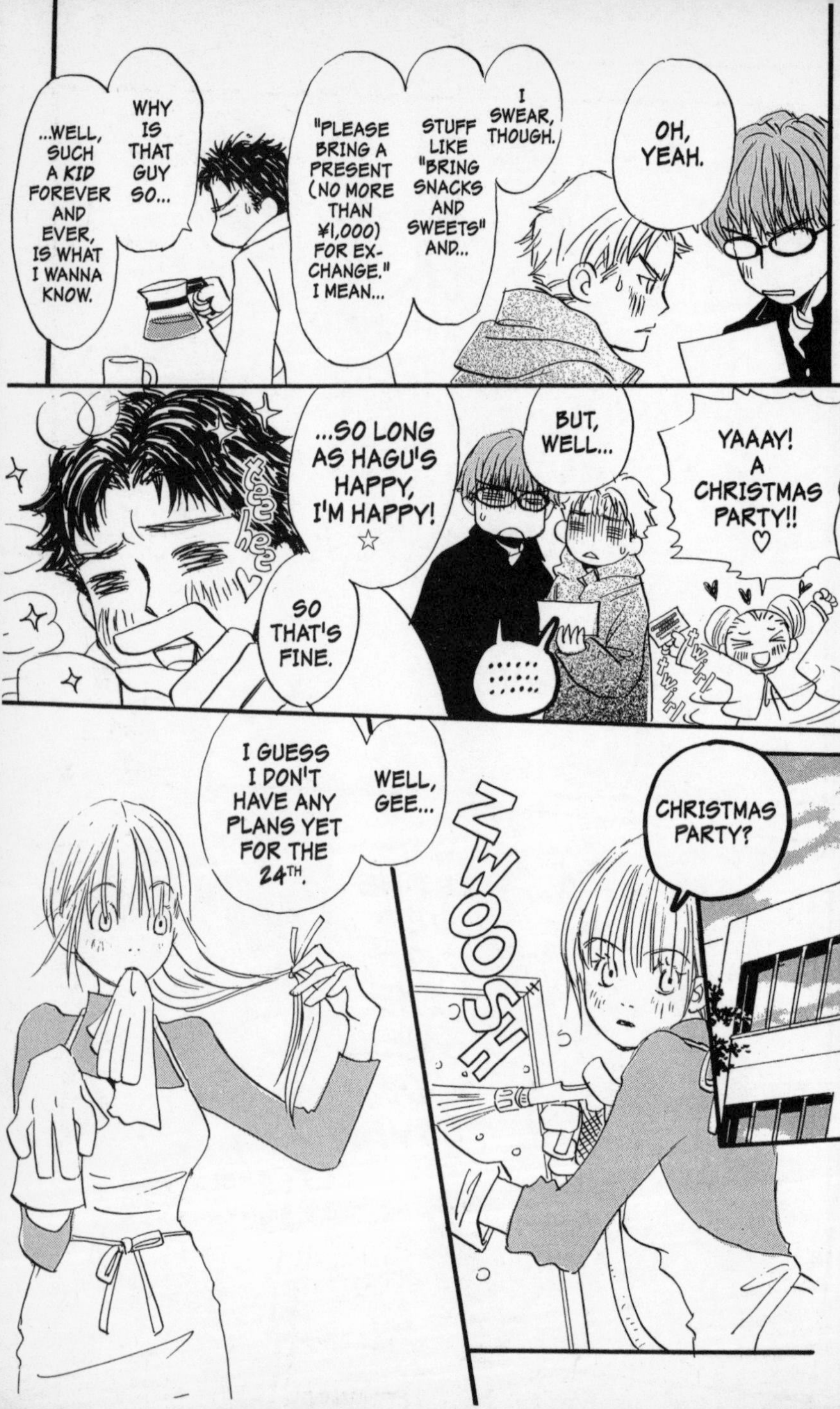
OH, YEAH.
I SWEAR, THOUGH.
STUFF LIKE "BRING SNACKS AND SWEETS" AND...
"PLEASE BRING A PRESENT (NO MORE THAN ¥1,000) FOR EXCHANGE." I MEAN...
WHY IS THAT GUY SO...
...WELL, SUCH A KID FOREVER AND EVER, IS WHAT I WANNA KNOW.
YAAAY! A CHRISTMAS PARTY!! ♡
twirl twirl
BUT, WELL...
......
...SO LONG AS HAGU'S HAPPY, I'M HAPPY! ☆
teehee
SO THAT'S FINE.
CHRISTMAS PARTY?
WHOOSH
WELL, GEE...
I GUESS I DON'T HAVE ANY PLANS YET FOR THE 24TH.

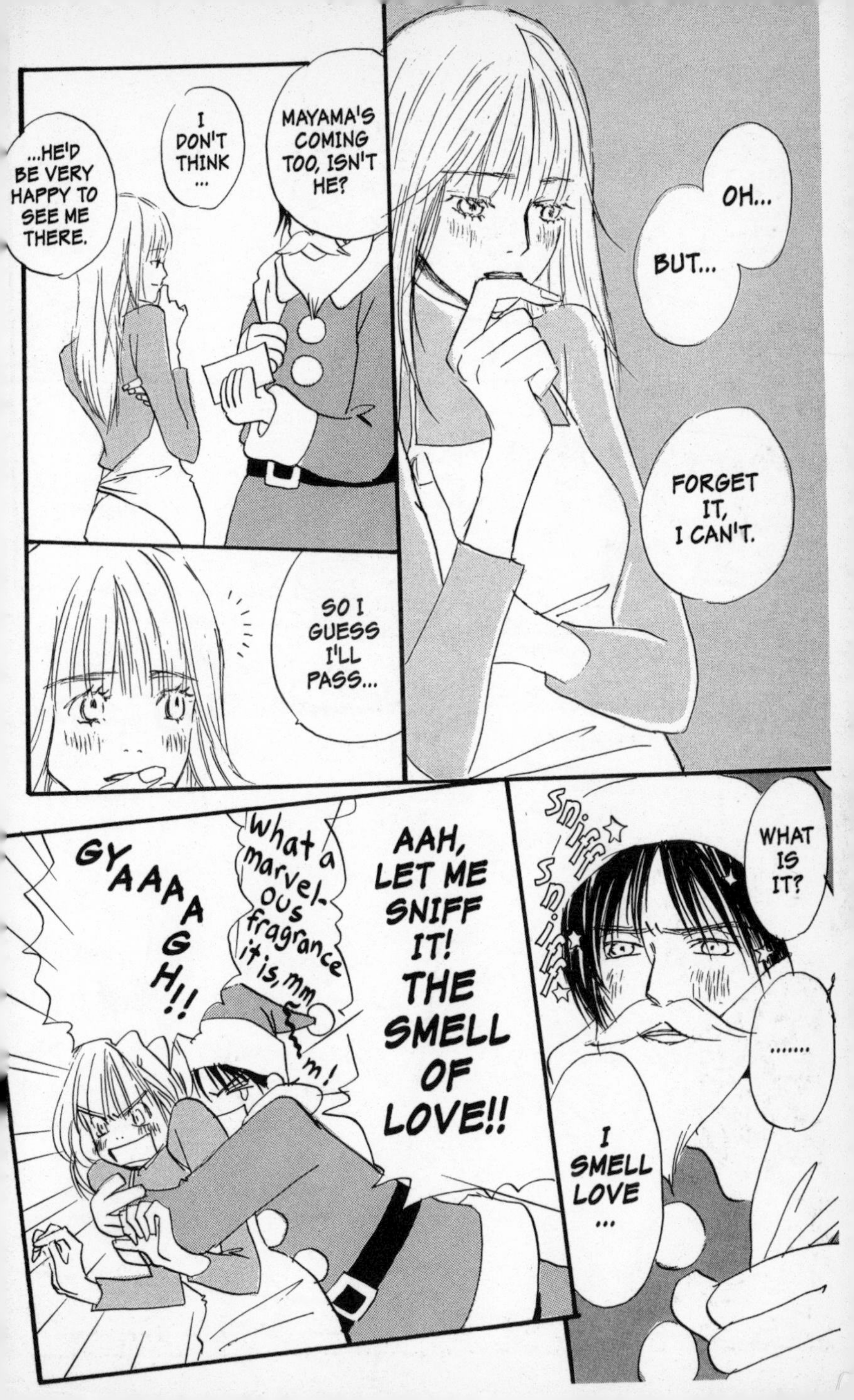
OH...
BUT...
FORGET IT, I CAN'T.
MAYAMA'S COMING TOO, ISN'T HE?
I DON'T THINK ...
...HE'D BE VERY HAPPY TO SEE ME THERE.
SO I GUESS I'LL PASS...
WHAT IS IT?
Sniff Sniff
....
I SMELL LOVE ...
AAH, LET ME SNIFF IT! THE SMELL OF LOVE!!
what a marvel-ous fragrance it is, mmm!
GYAAAAGH!!

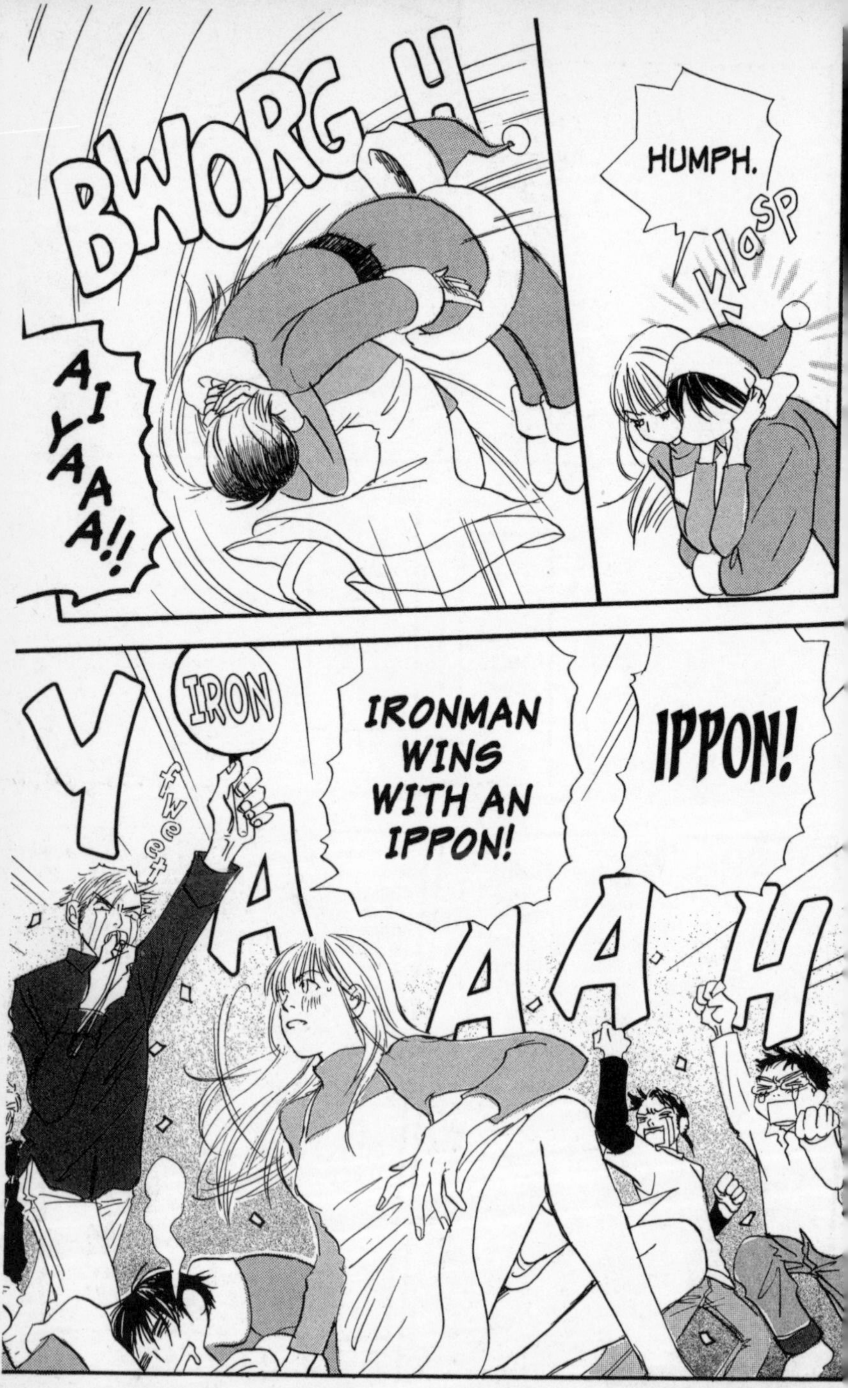
HUMPH.
klasp
BWORGH
AIYAAA!!
IPPON!
IRONMAN WINS WITH AN IPPON!
IRON
fweet
YAAAAH

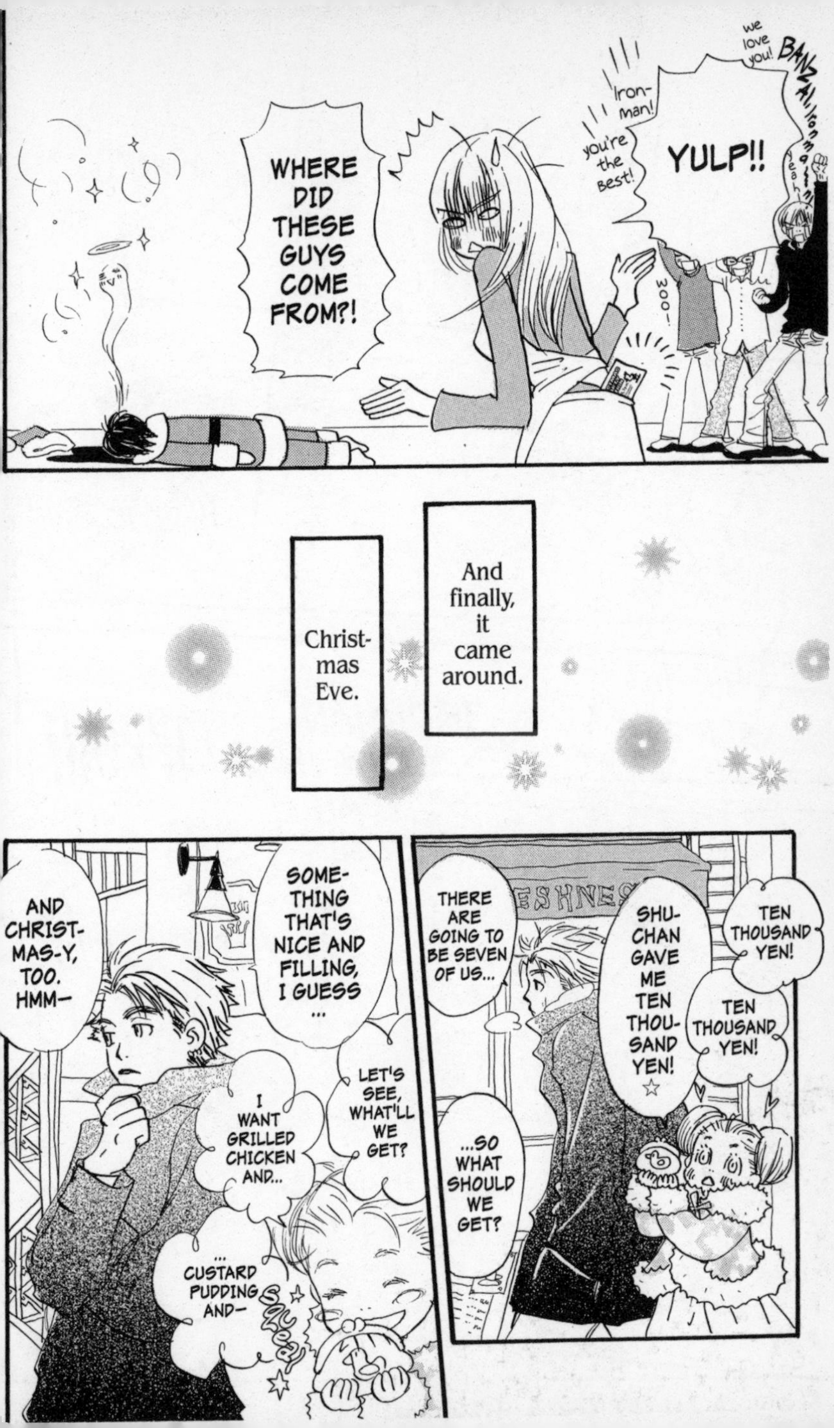
we love you!
BANZAI! Iron man! yeah!
YULP!!
Iron-man!
you're the Best!
WOO!
WHERE DID THESE GUYS COME FROM?!
And finally, it came around.
Christmas Eve.
TEN THOUSAND YEN!
TEN THOUSAND YEN!
SHU-CHAN GAVE ME TEN THOUSAND YEN! ☆
THERE ARE GOING TO BE SEVEN OF US...
...SO WHAT SHOULD WE GET?
SOMETHING THAT'S NICE AND FILLING, I GUESS ...
AND CHRISTMAS-Y, TOO. HMM—
LET'S SEE, WHAT'LL WE GET?
I WANT GRILLED CHICKEN AND...
... CUSTARD PUDDING AND—
Squeal

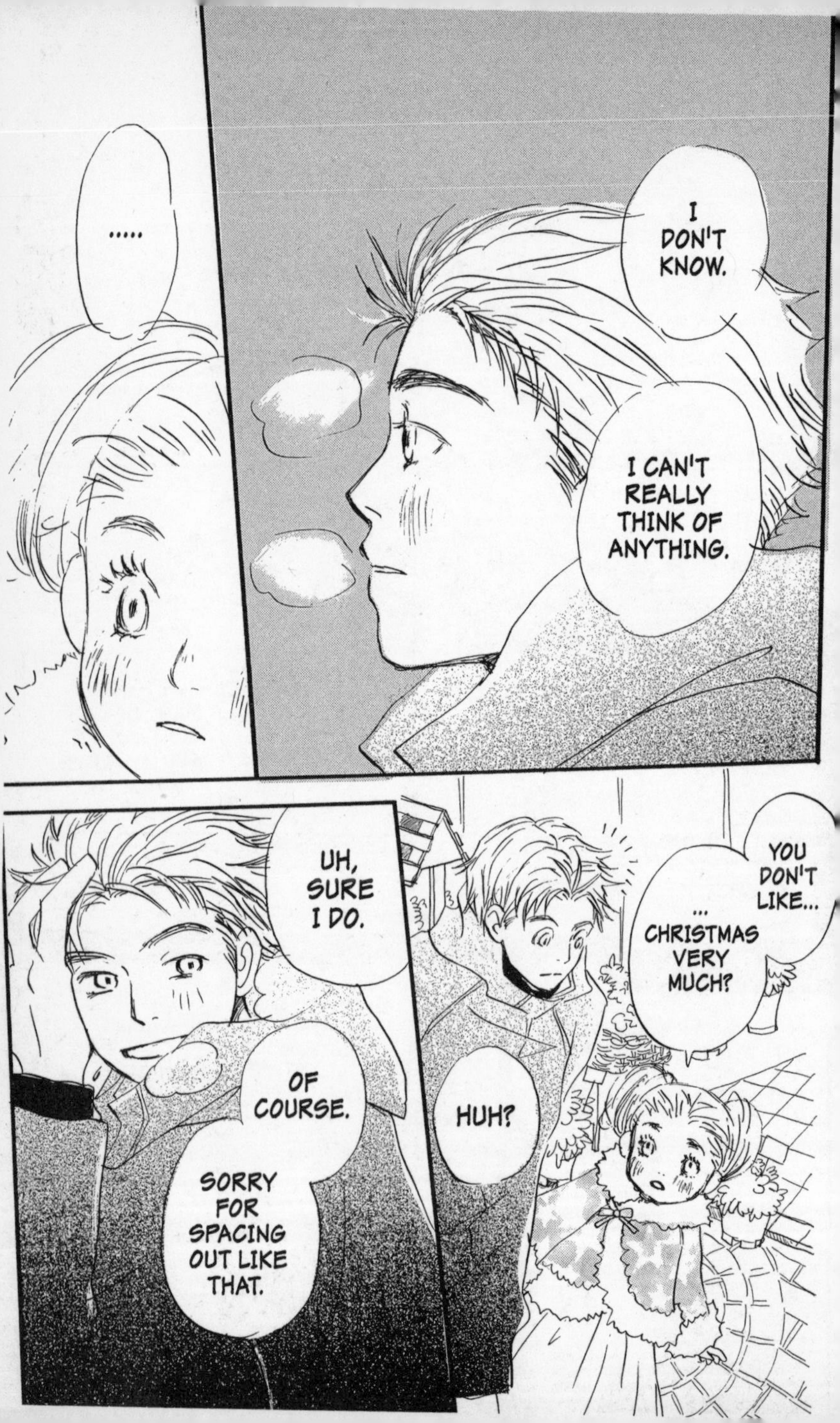
I DON'T KNOW.
I CAN'T REALLY THINK OF ANYTHING.
.....
YOU DON'T LIKE...
... CHRISTMAS VERY MUCH?
HUH?
UH, SURE I DO.
OF COURSE.
SORRY FOR SPACING OUT LIKE THAT.

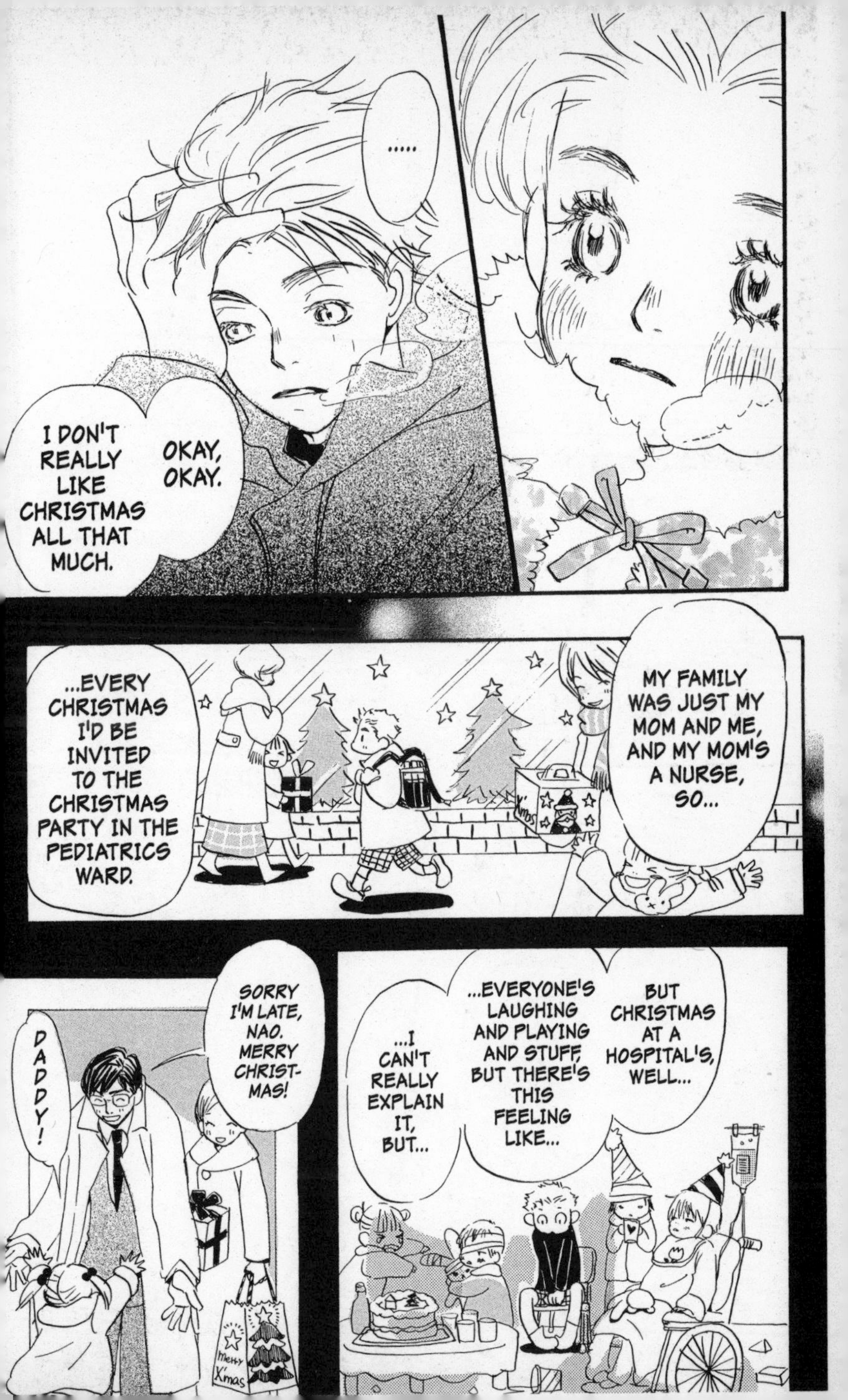
.....
OKAY, OKAY.
I DON'T REALLY LIKE CHRISTMAS ALL THAT MUCH.
MY FAMILY WAS JUST MY MOM AND ME, AND MY MOM'S A NURSE, SO...
X'mas
...EVERY CHRISTMAS I'D BE INVITED TO THE CHRISTMAS PARTY IN THE PEDIATRICS WARD.
BUT CHRISTMAS AT A HOSPITAL'S, WELL...
...EVERYONE'S LAUGHING AND PLAYING AND STUFF, BUT THERE'S THIS FEELING LIKE...
...I CAN'T REALLY EXPLAIN IT, BUT...
SORRY I'M LATE, NAO. MERRY CHRIST-MAS!
DADDY!
Merry X'mas

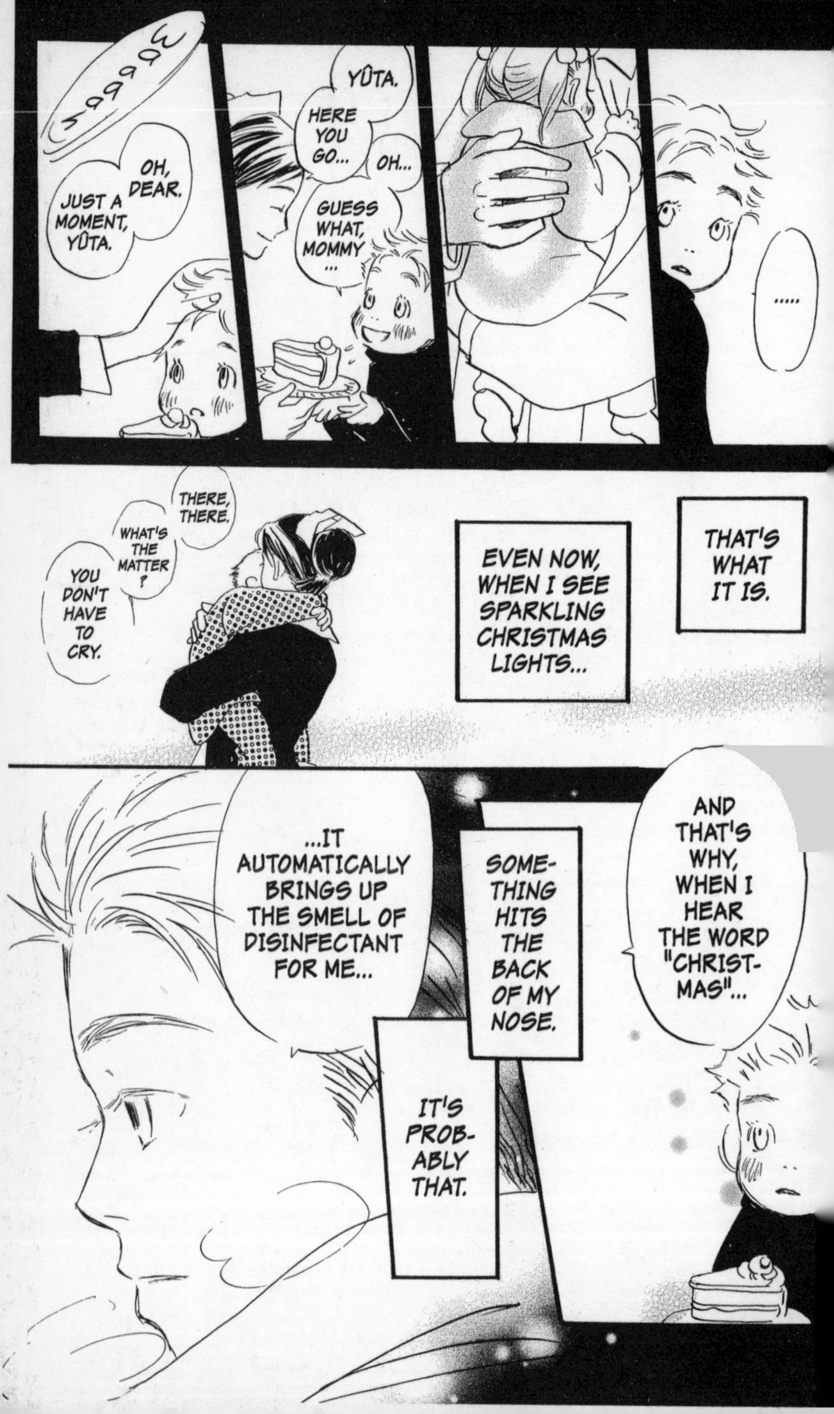

.....
YÛTA.
HERE YOU GO...
OH...
GUESS WHAT, MOMMY ...
Waaaah
OH, DEAR.
JUST A MOMENT, YÛTA.
THAT'S WHAT IT IS.
EVEN NOW, WHEN I SEE SPARKLING CHRISTMAS LIGHTS...
THERE, THERE.
WHAT'S THE MATTER?
YOU DON'T HAVE TO CRY.
AND THAT'S WHY, WHEN I HEAR THE WORD "CHRIST-MAS"...
SOME-THING HITS THE BACK OF MY NOSE.
...IT AUTOMATICALLY BRINGS UP THE SMELL OF DISINFECTANT FOR ME...
IT'S PROBABLY THAT.

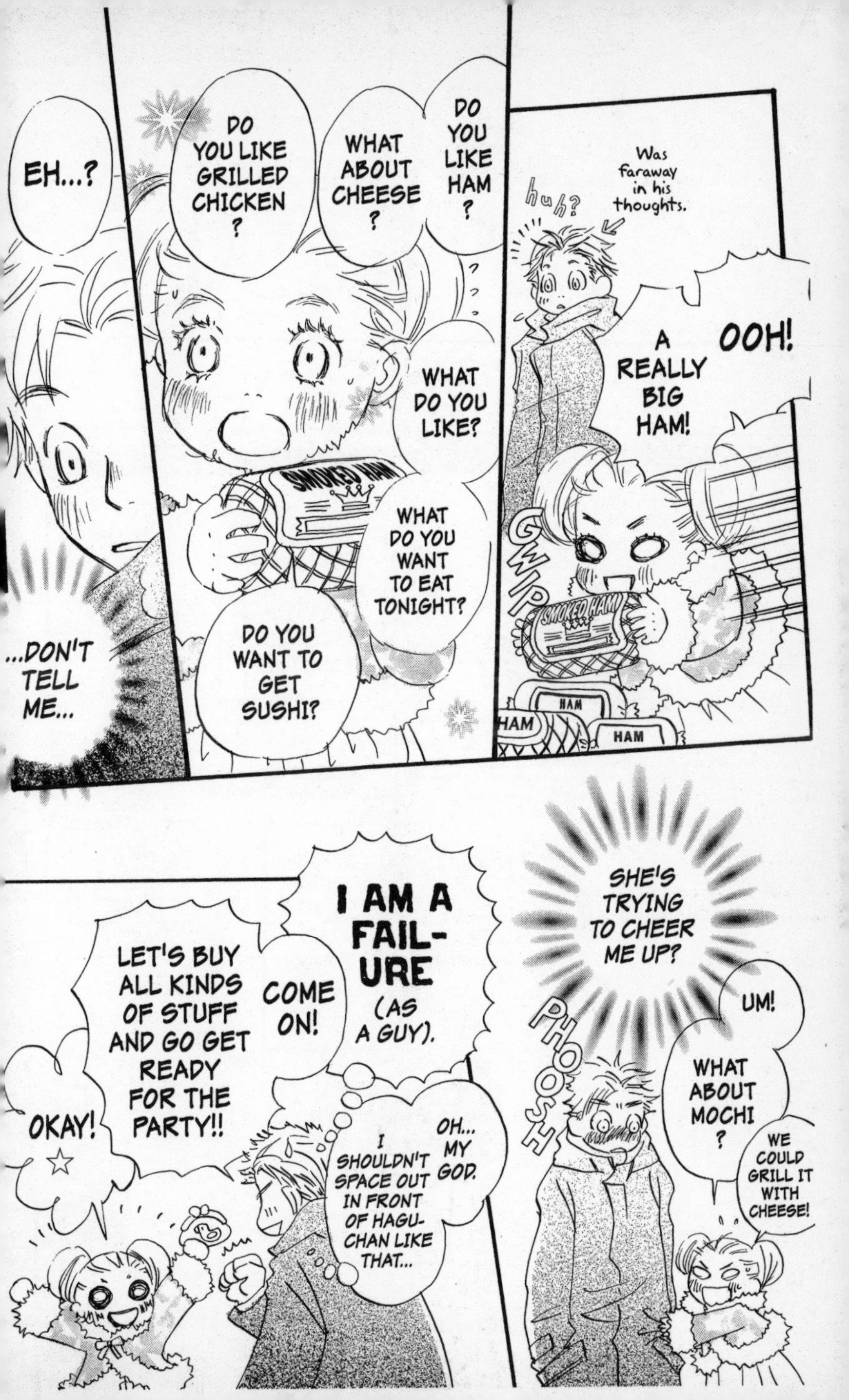
Was faraway in his thoughts.
huh?
OOH!
A REALLY BIG HAM!
GWIP
SMOKED HAM
HAM
HAM
HAM
DO YOU LIKE HAM?
WHAT ABOUT CHEESE?
DO YOU LIKE GRILLED CHICKEN?
SMOKED HAM
WHAT DO YOU LIKE?
WHAT DO YOU WANT TO EAT TONIGHT?
DO YOU WANT TO GET SUSHI?
EH...?
...DON'T TELL ME...
SHE'S TRYING TO CHEER ME UP?
UM!
WHAT ABOUT MOCHI?
WE COULD GRILL IT WITH CHEESE!
PHOOSH
I AM A FAIL-URE (AS A GUY).
OH... MY GOD.
I SHOULDN'T SPACE OUT IN FRONT OF HAGU-CHAN LIKE THAT...
COME ON!
LET'S BUY ALL KINDS OF STUFF AND GO GET READY FOR THE PARTY!!
OKAY! ☆

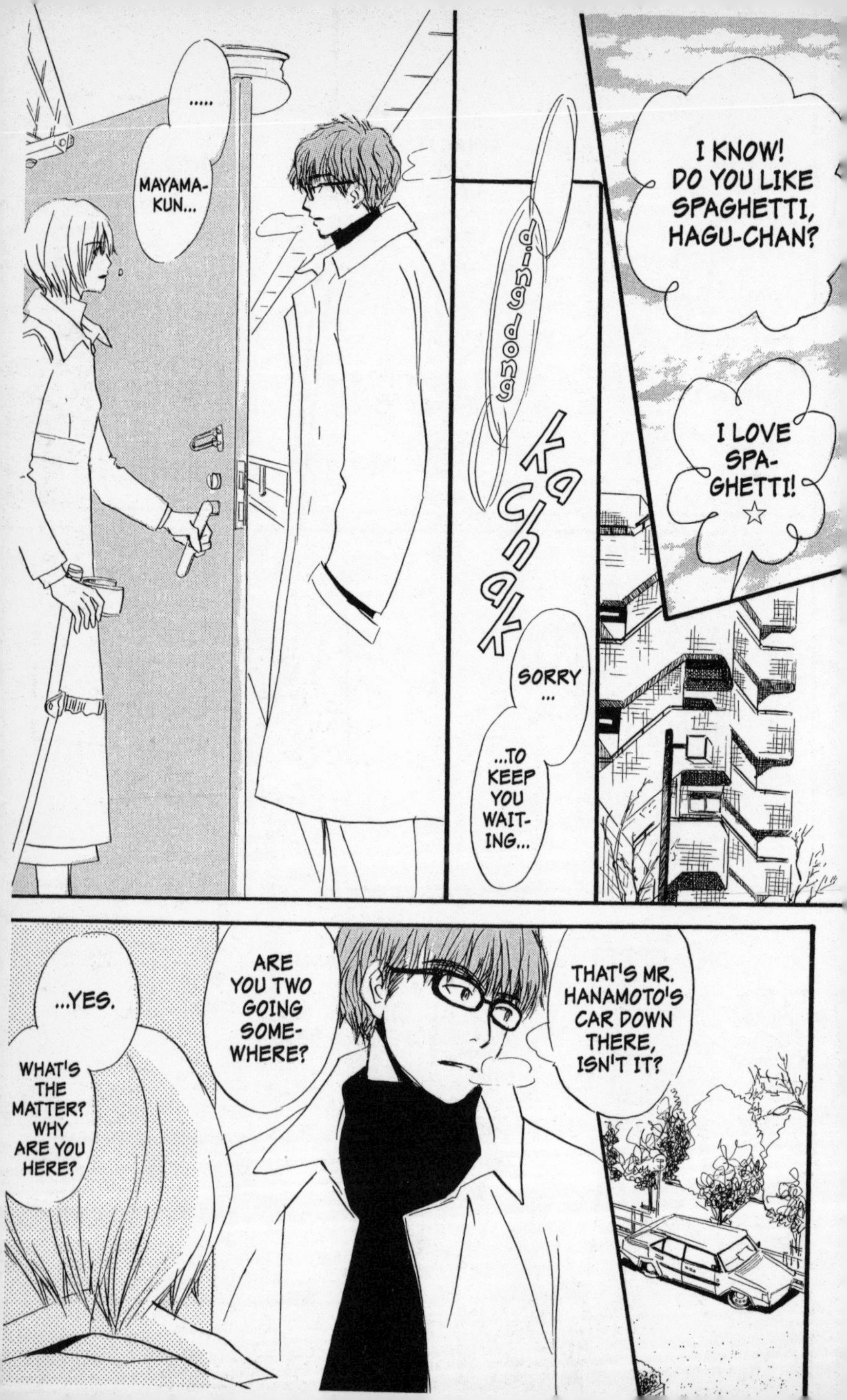
I KNOW! DO YOU LIKE SPAGHETTI, HAGU-CHAN?
I LOVE SPA-GHETTI! ☆
ding dong
ka chak
SORRY ...
...TO KEEP YOU WAIT-ING...
.....
MAYAMA-KUN...
THAT'S MR. HANAMOTO'S CAR DOWN THERE, ISN'T IT?
ARE YOU TWO GOING SOME-WHERE?
...YES.
WHAT'S THE MATTER? WHY ARE YOU HERE?

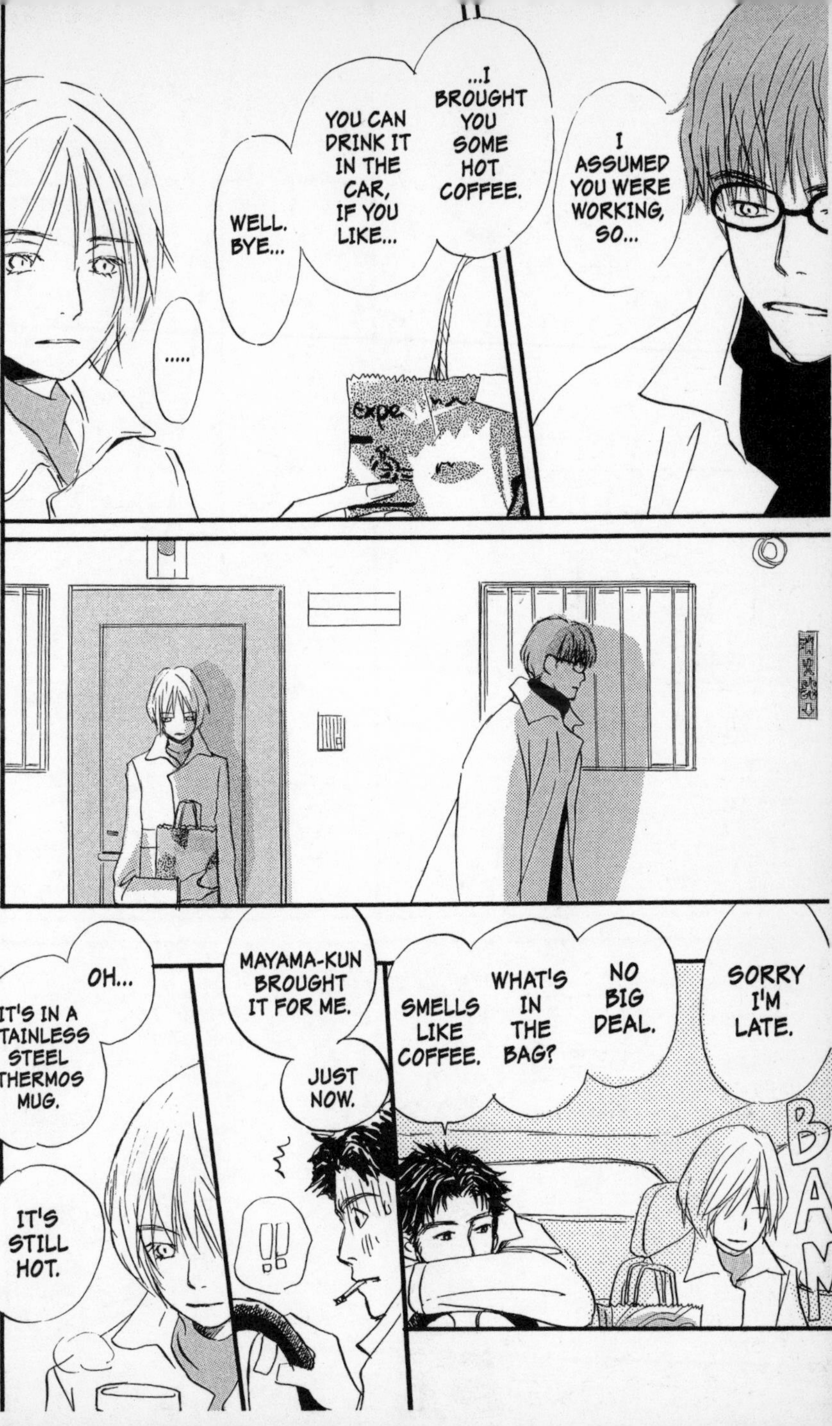
I ASSUMED YOU WERE WORKING, SO...
...I BROUGHT YOU SOME HOT COFFEE.
YOU CAN DRINK IT IN THE CAR, IF YOU LIKE...
WELL. BYE...
.....
SORRY I'M LATE.
BAM
NO BIG DEAL.
WHAT'S IN THE BAG?
SMELLS LIKE COFFEE.
MAYAMA-KUN BROUGHT IT FOR ME.
JUST NOW.
!!
OH...
IT'S IN A STAINLESS STEEL THERMOS MUG.
IT'S STILL HOT.

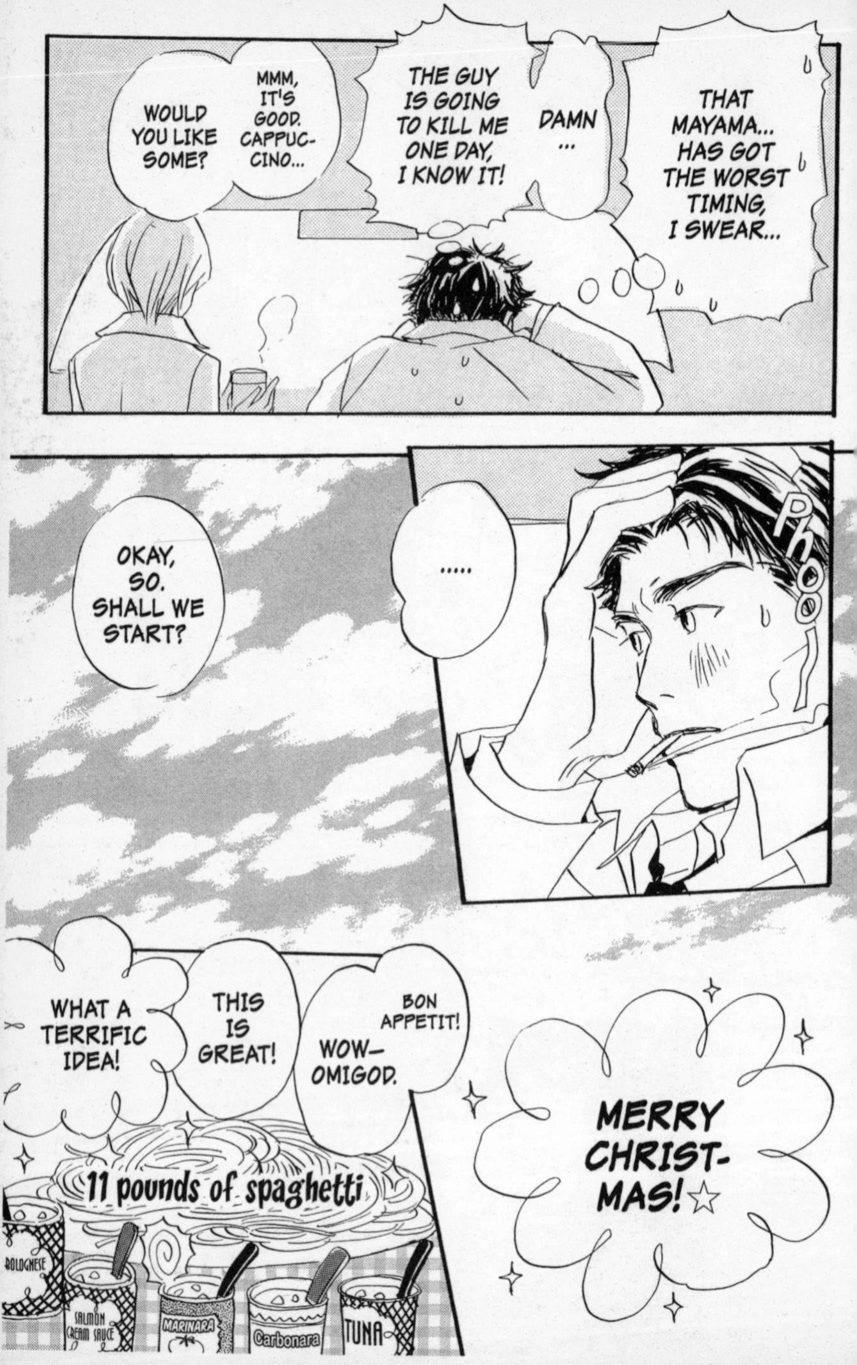
THAT MAYAMA... HAS GOT THE WORST TIMING, I SWEAR...
DAMN ...
THE GUY IS GOING TO KILL ME ONE DAY, I KNOW IT!
MMM, IT'S GOOD. CAPPUCCINO...
WOULD YOU LIKE SOME?
Phooo
.....
OKAY, SO. SHALL WE START?
MERRY CHRISTMAS!☆
BON APPETIT!
WOW—OMIGOD.
THIS IS GREAT!
WHAT A TERRIFIC IDEA!
11 pounds of spaghetti
TUNA
Carbonara
MARINARA
SALMON CREAM SAUCE
BOLOGNESE

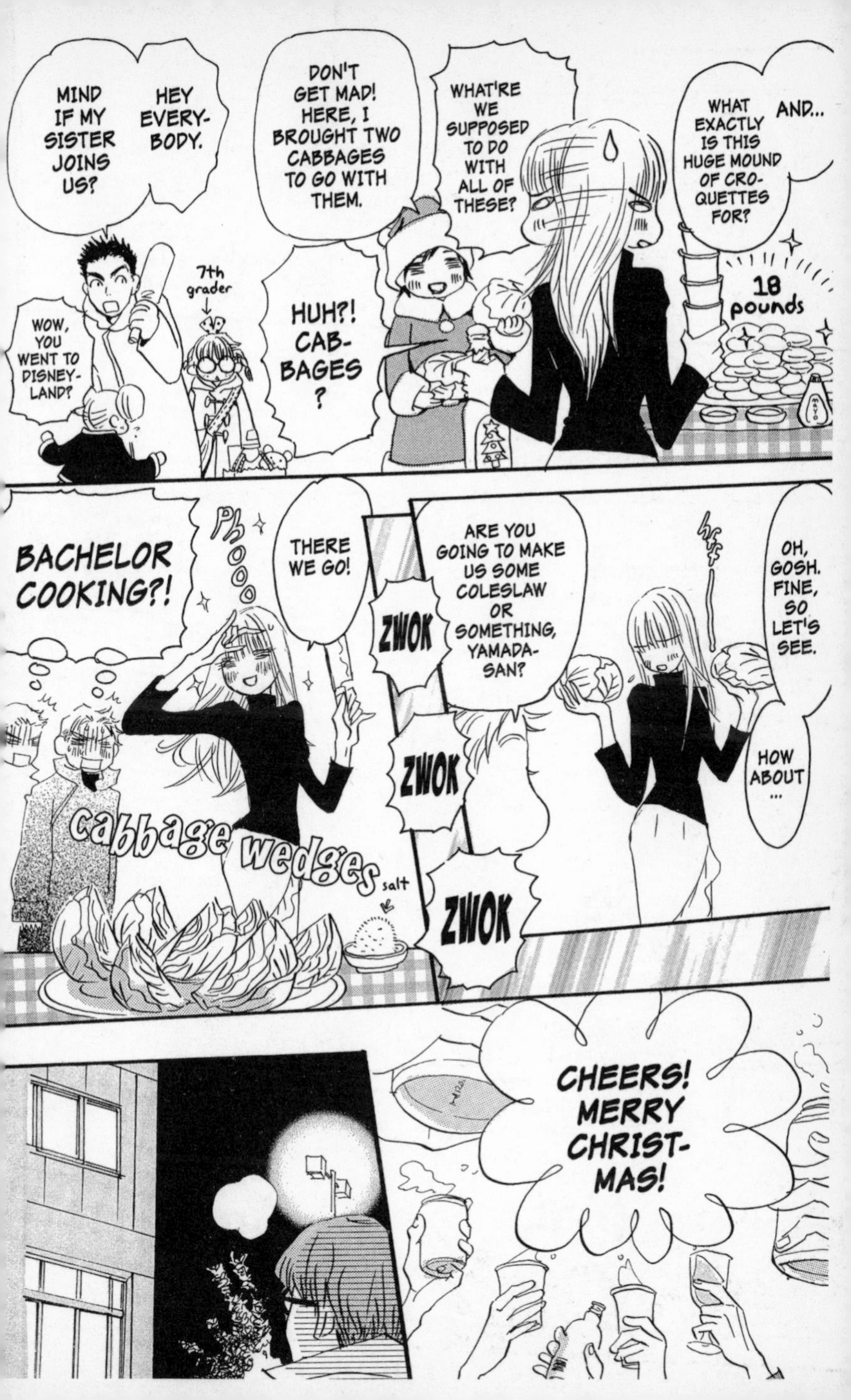
AND...
WHAT EXACTLY IS THIS HUGE MOUND OF CRO-QUETTES FOR?
18 pounds
MAYO
WHAT'RE WE SUPPOSED TO DO WITH ALL OF THESE?
DON'T GET MAD! HERE, I BROUGHT TWO CABBAGES TO GO WITH THEM.
HUH?! CAB-BAGES ?
HEY EVERY-BODY.
MIND IF MY SISTER JOINS US?
7th grader
WOW, YOU WENT TO DISNEY-LAND?
OH, GOSH. FINE, SO LET'S SEE.
HOW ABOUT ...
ARE YOU GOING TO MAKE US SOME COLESLAW OR SOMETHING, YAMADA-SAN?
ZWOK
ZWOK
ZWOK
THERE WE GO!
Phoooo
BACHELOR COOKING?!
cabbage wedges
salt
CHEERS! MERRY CHRIST-MAS!

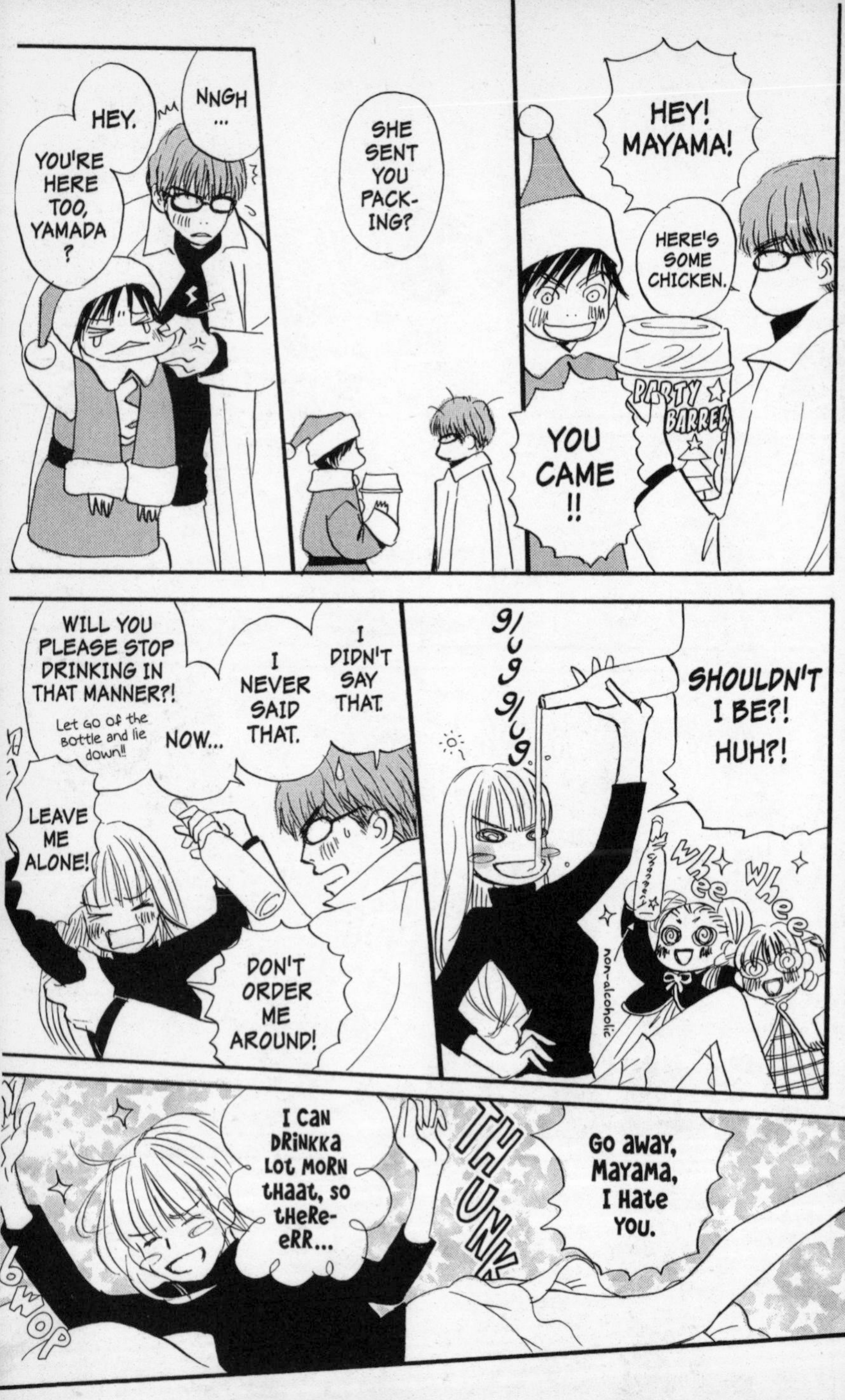
HEY! MAYAMA!
HERE'S SOME CHICKEN.
PARTY ★ BARREL
YOU CAME!!
SHE SENT YOU PACK-ING?
NNGH ...
HEY.
YOU'RE HERE TOO, YAMADA?
SHOULDN'T I BE?! HUH?!
glug glug
whee whee
non-alcoholic
I DIDN'T SAY THAT.
I NEVER SAID THAT.
WILL YOU PLEASE STOP DRINKING IN THAT MANNER?!
Let go of the bottle and lie down!!
NOW...
LEAVE ME ALONE!
DON'T ORDER ME AROUND!
Go away, Mayama, I hate you.
THUNK
I can drinkka lot morn thaat, so there-eRR...
bwop

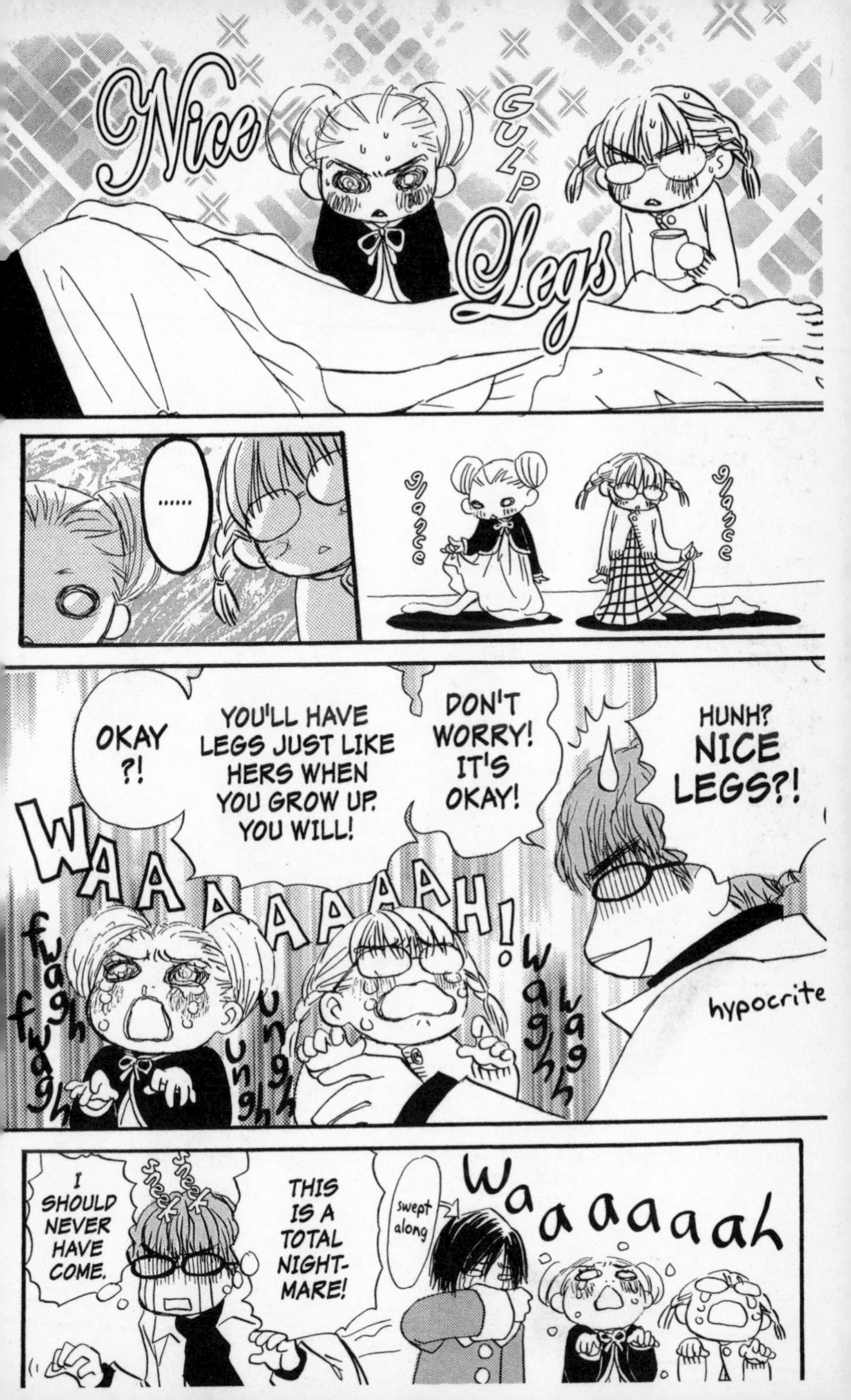
GULP
Nice Legs
glance
glance
......
HUNH? NICE LEGS?!
DON'T WORRY! IT'S OKAY!
YOU'LL HAVE LEGS JUST LIKE HERS WHEN YOU GROW UP. YOU WILL!
OKAY ?!
WAAAAAAAH!
hypocrite
wagh wagh
ungh ungh
fwagh fwagh
Waaaaaah
swept along
THIS IS A TOTAL NIGHT-MARE!
I SHOULD NEVER HAVE COME.
sneak sneak

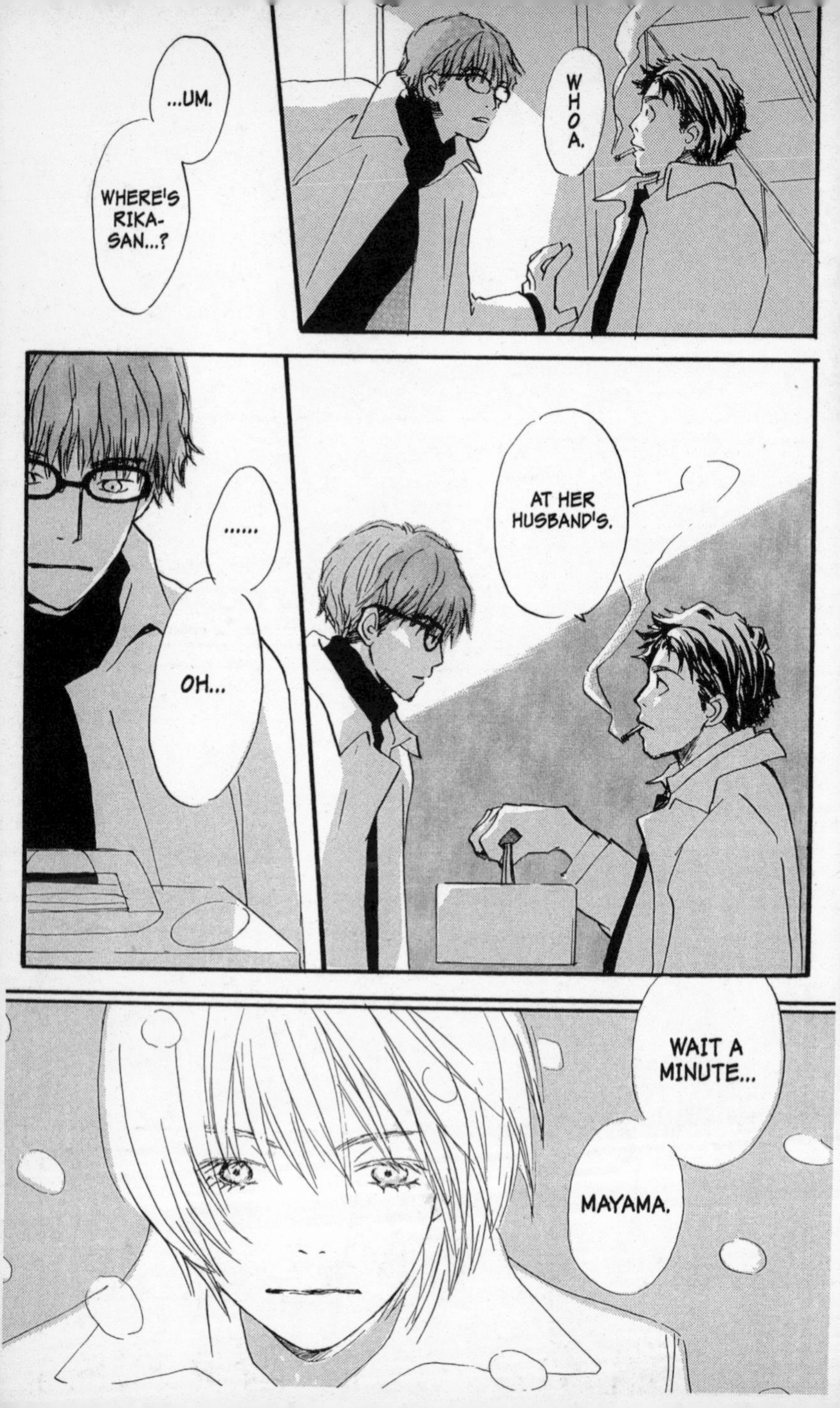
WHOA.
...UM.
WHERE'S RIKA-SAN...?
AT HER HUSBAND'S.
......
OH...
WAIT A MINUTE...
MAYAMA.

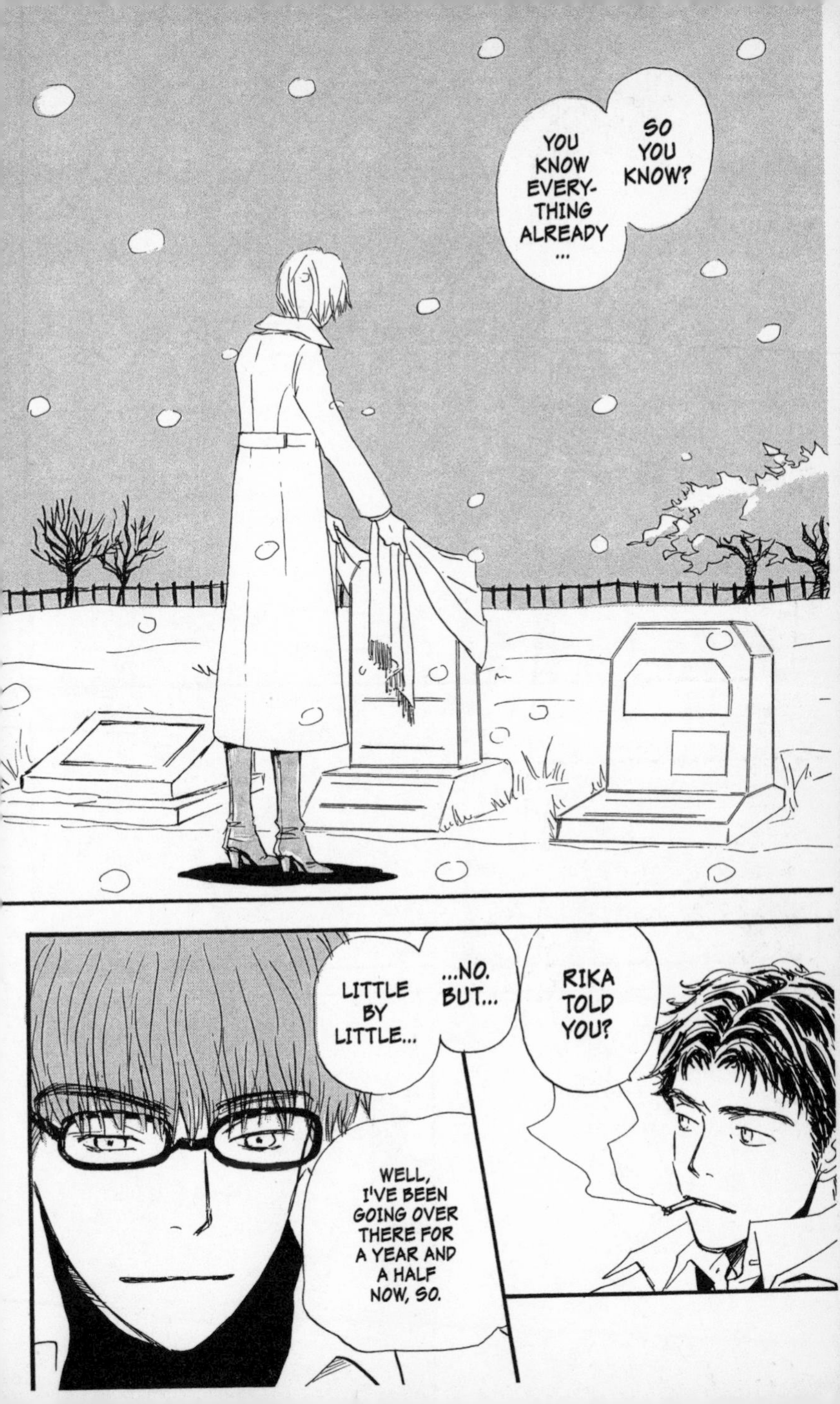
SO YOU KNOW?
YOU KNOW EVERYTHING ALREADY ...
RIKA TOLD YOU?
...NO. BUT...
LITTLE BY LITTLE...
WELL, I'VE BEEN GOING OVER THERE FOR A YEAR AND A HALF NOW, SO.

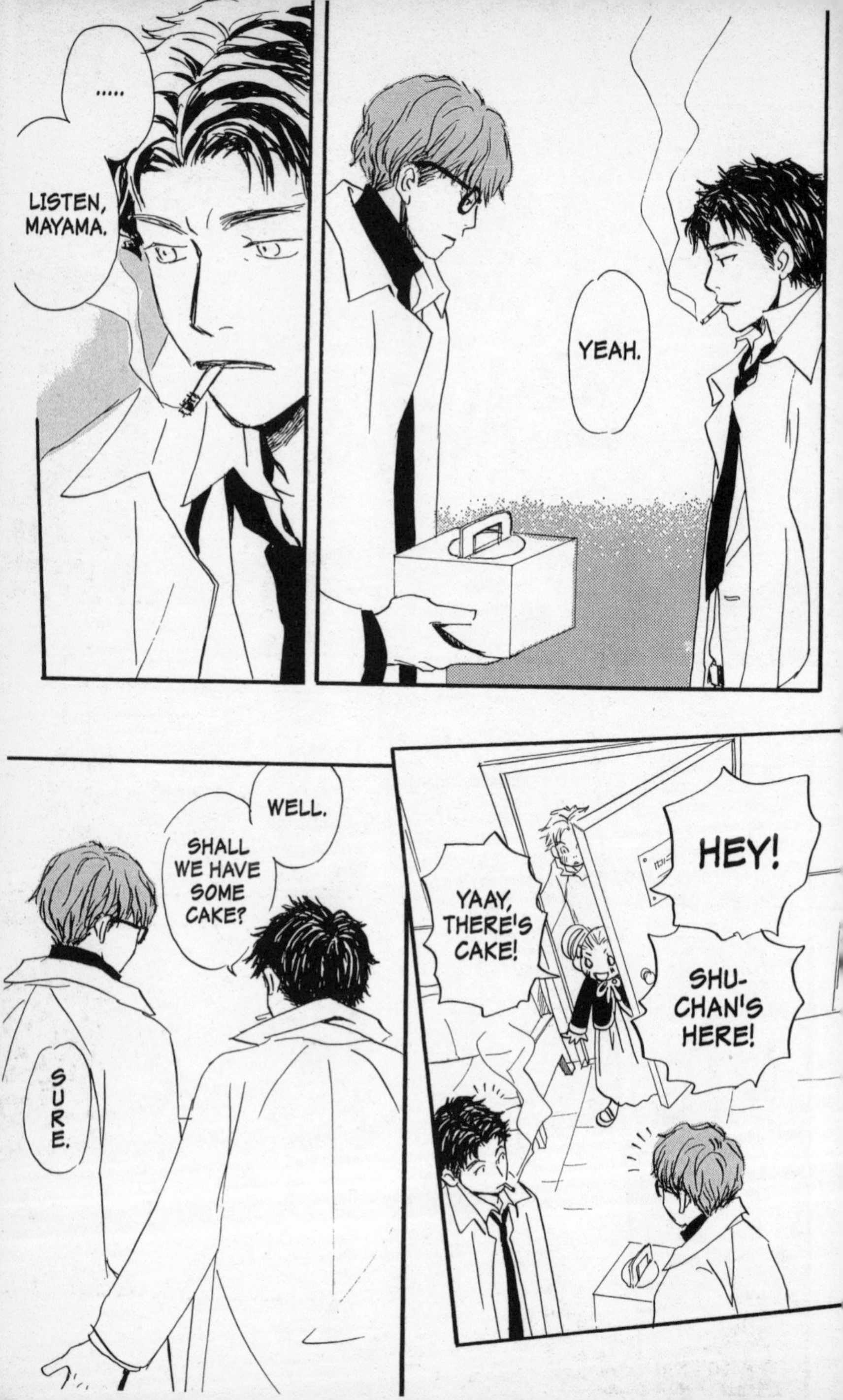
YEAH.
.....
LISTEN, MAYAMA.
HEY!
SHU-CHAN'S HERE!
YAAY, THERE'S CAKE!
WELL.
SHALL WE HAVE SOME CAKE?
SURE.

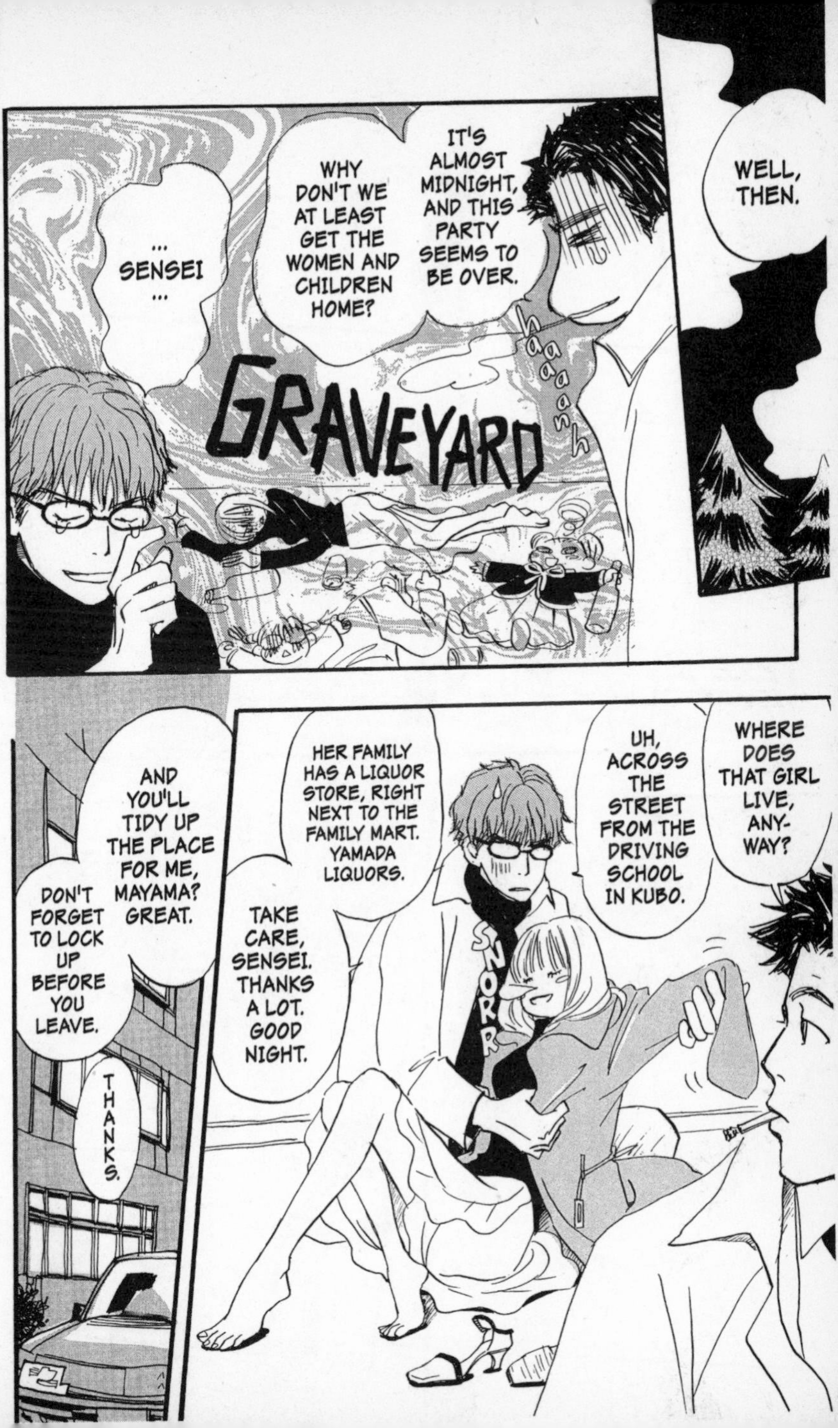
WELL, THEN.
IT'S ALMOST MIDNIGHT, AND THIS PARTY SEEMS TO BE OVER.
WHY DON'T WE AT LEAST GET THE WOMEN AND CHILDREN HOME?
haaaaanh
GRAVEYARD
... SENSEI ...
WHERE DOES THAT GIRL LIVE, ANY-WAY?
UH, ACROSS THE STREET FROM THE DRIVING SCHOOL IN KUBO.
HER FAMILY HAS A LIQUOR STORE, RIGHT NEXT TO THE FAMILY MART. YAMADA LIQUORS.
SNORR
TAKE CARE, SENSEI. THANKS A LOT. GOOD NIGHT.
AND YOU'LL TIDY UP THE PLACE FOR ME, MAYAMA? GREAT.
DON'T FORGET TO LOCK UP BEFORE YOU LEAVE.
THANKS.

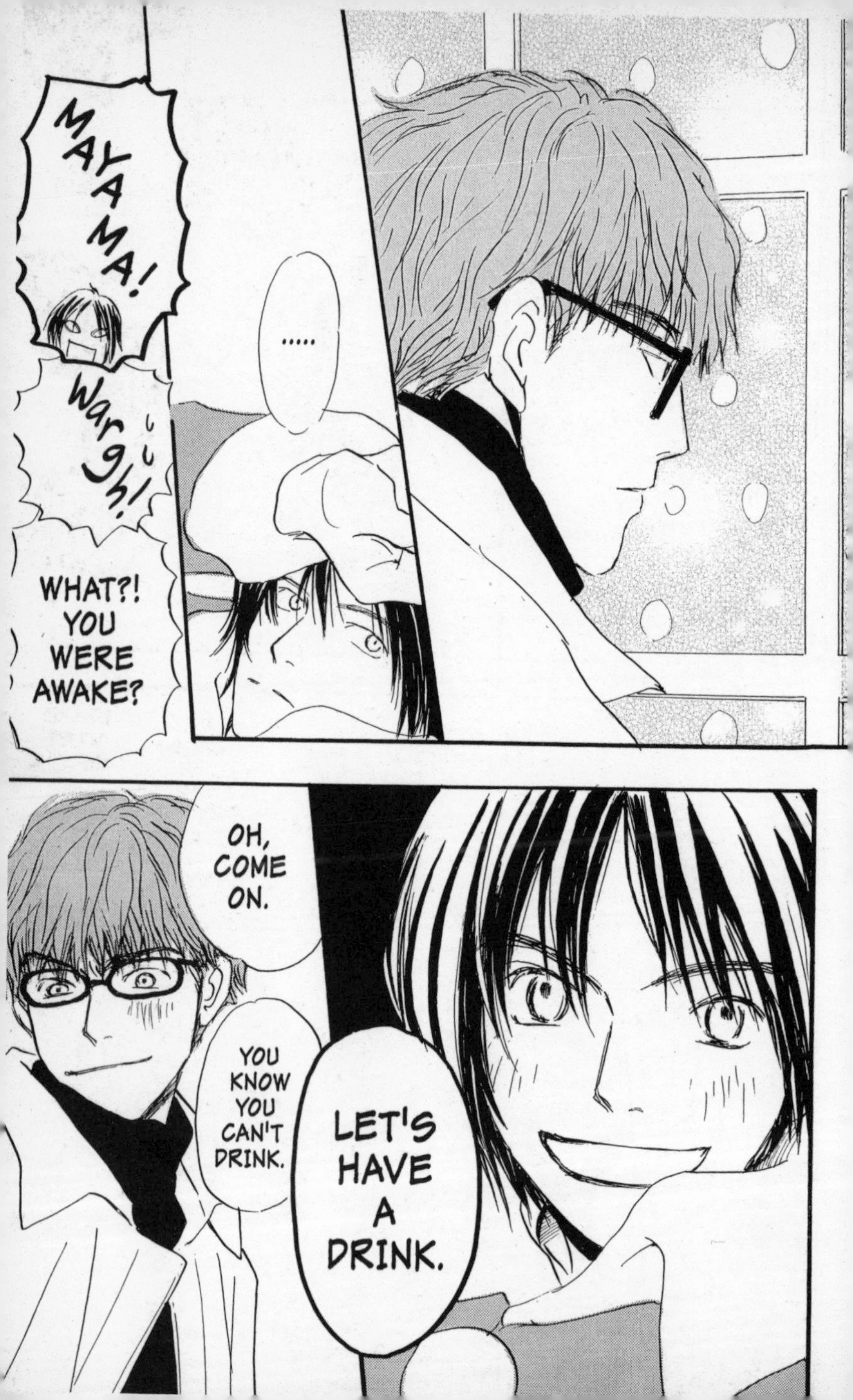
.....
MAYAMA!
Wargh!
WHAT?! YOU WERE AWAKE?
LET'S HAVE A DRINK.
OH, COME ON.
YOU KNOW YOU CAN'T DRINK.

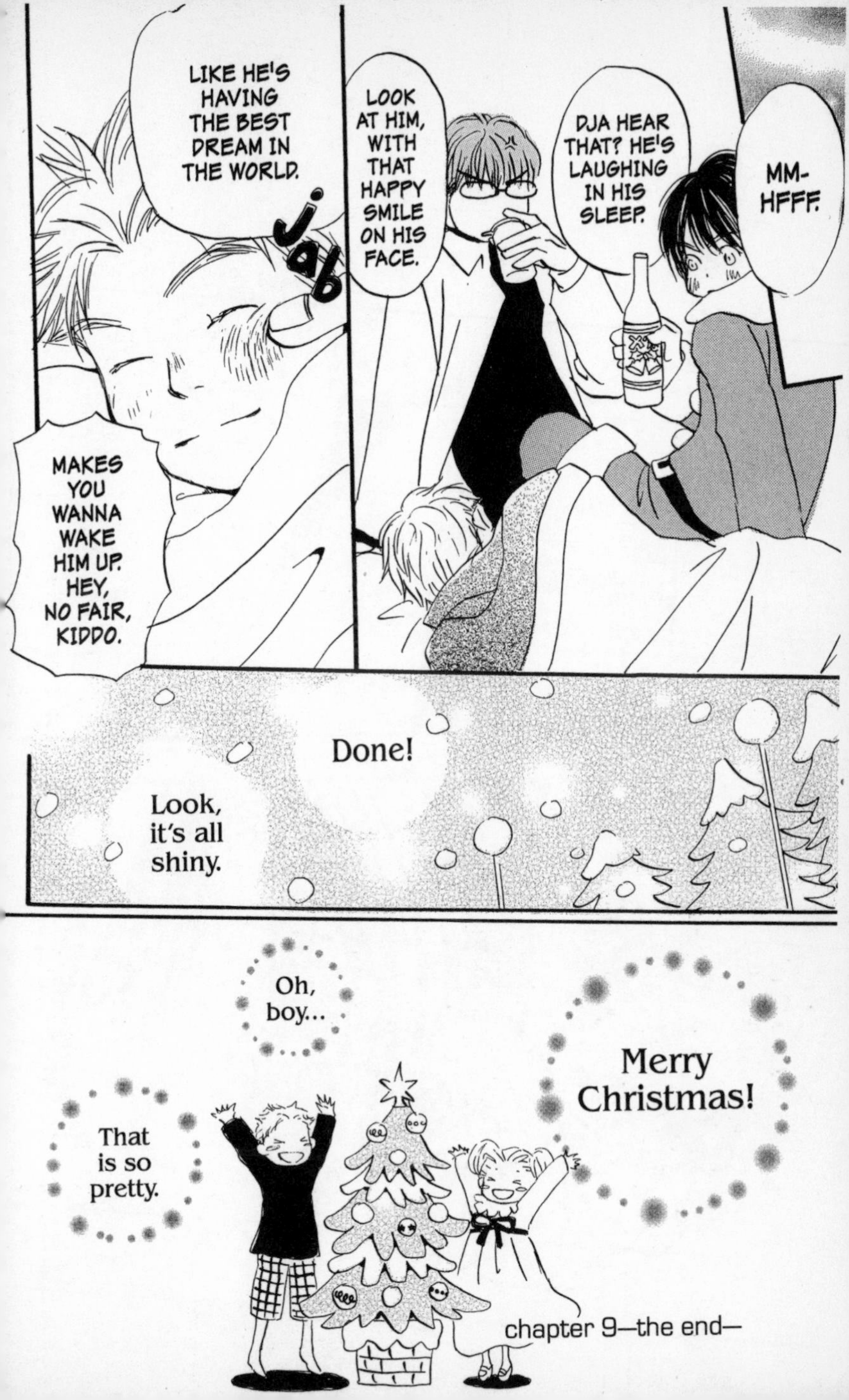
MM-HFFF.
DJA HEAR THAT? HE'S LAUGHING IN HIS SLEEP.
LOOK AT HIM, WITH THAT HAPPY SMILE ON HIS FACE.
LIKE HE'S HAVING THE BEST DREAM IN THE WORLD.
Jab
MAKES YOU WANNA WAKE HIM UP. HEY, NO FAIR, KIDDO.
Done!
Look, it's all shiny.
Merry Christmas!
Oh, boy...
That is so pretty.
chapter 9—the end—

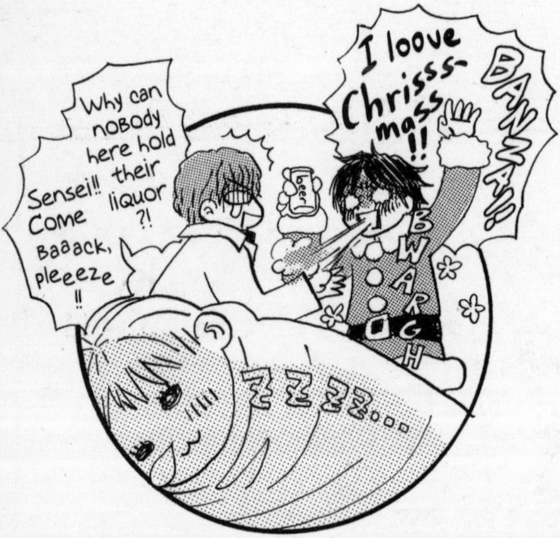
I loove Chrisss-mass !!
BANZAI!!
Why can nobody here hold their liquor ?!
Sensei!! Come Baaack, pleeeze !!
BWAROGH
ZZZZ...

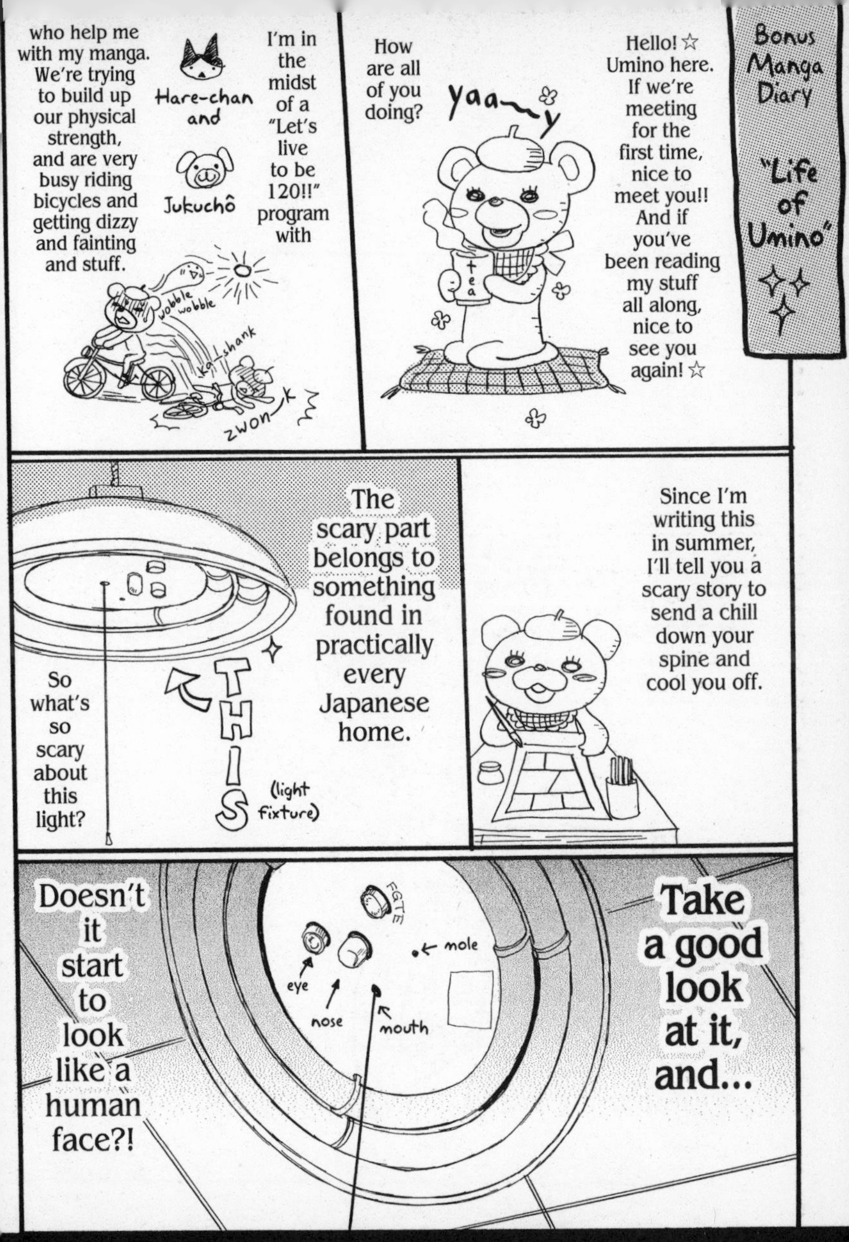
Bonus Manga Diary
"Life of Umino"
Hello! ☆ Umino here. If we're meeting for the first time, nice to meet you!! And if you've been reading my stuff all along, nice to see you again! ☆
yaa~y
How are all of you doing?
tea
I'm in the midst of a "Let's live to be 120!!" program with
Hare-chan and
Jukuchô
who help me with my manga. We're trying to build up our physical strength, and are very busy riding bicycles and getting dizzy and fainting and stuff.
wobble wobble
ka-shank
zwon—k
Since I'm writing this in summer, I'll tell you a scary story to send a chill down your spine and cool you off.
The scary part belongs to something found in practically every Japanese home.
THIS
(light fixture)
So what's so scary about this light?
Take a good look at it, and...
FGTE
mole
eye
nose
mouth
Doesn't it start to look like a human face?!

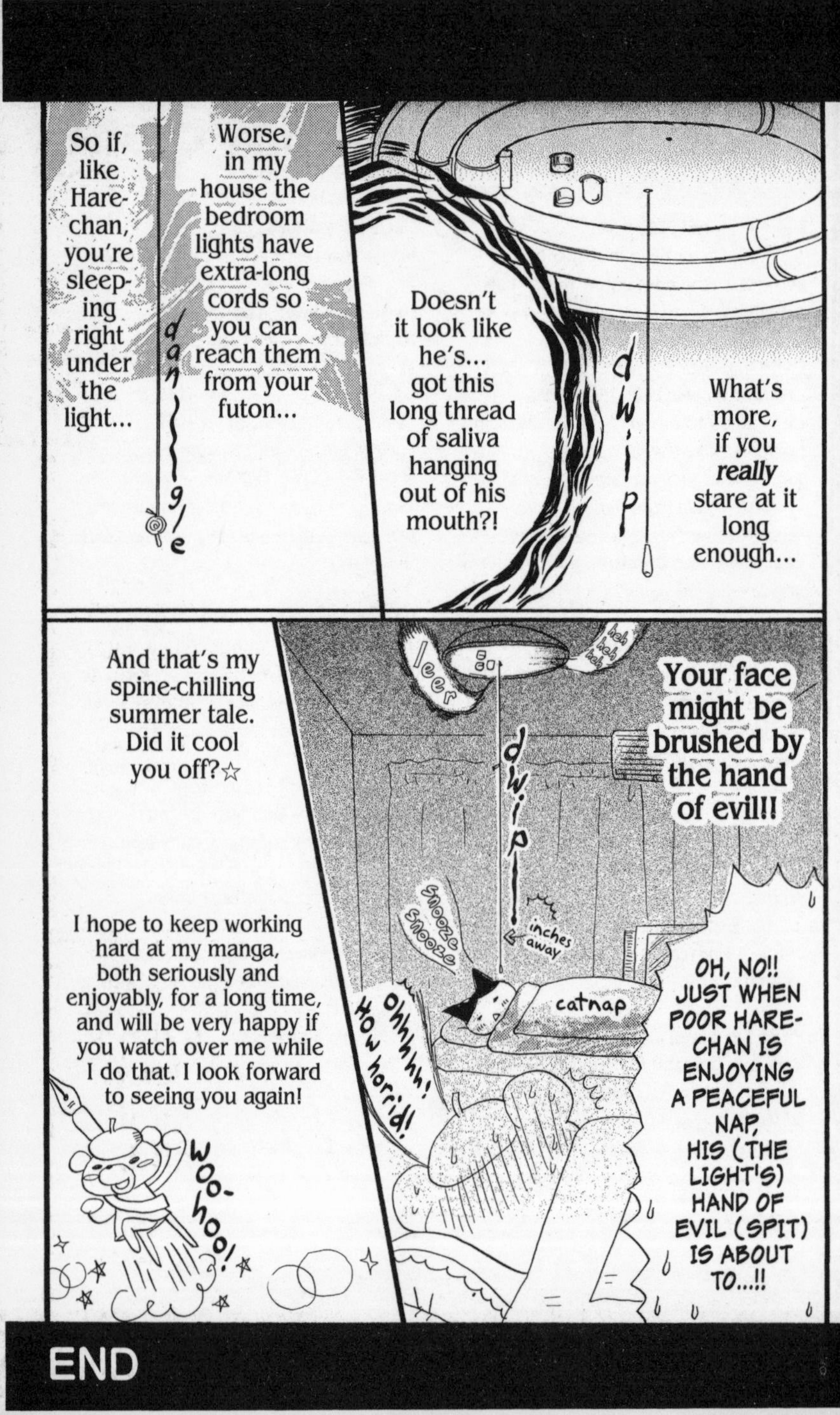
What's more, if you *really* stare at it long enough...
dwip
Doesn't it look like he's... got this long thread of saliva hanging out of his mouth?!
Worse, in my house the bedroom lights have extra-long cords so you can reach them from your futon...
dangle
So if, like Hare-chan, you're sleeping right under the light...
Your face might be brushed by the hand of evil!!
heh heh heh
leer
dwip
OH, NO!! JUST WHEN POOR HARE-CHAN IS ENJOYING A PEACEFUL NAP, HIS (THE LIGHT'S) HAND OF EVIL (SPIT) IS ABOUT TO...!!
inches away
snooze snooze
catnap
Ohhhhh! How horrid!
And that's my spine-chilling summer tale. Did it cool you off?☆
I hope to keep working hard at my manga, both seriously and enjoyably, for a long time, and will be very happy if you watch over me while I do that. I look forward to seeing you again!
Woo-hoo!
END

Honey and Clover Study Guide

Page 4, panel 2: Senpai
An honorific or term of respect for someone who has senior status in an organization, such as school or a club.

Page 4, panel 2: Croquettes
Croquettes, also called *korokke*, were introduced to Japan in the 1900s from France. Unlike the French version, Japanese croquettes are patty-shaped. They are made from a mash of various ingredients such as meat, seafood, vegetables and potatoes, then breaded and deep-fried.

Page 21, panel 5: Koropokkur
Also spelled *korobokkur*, these creatures from Ainu mythology are somewhat similar to leprechauns or fairies. The word means "little people who live under giant butterbur leaves."

Page 31, panel 3: Teppanyaki
Teppanyaki is a type of Japanese cuisine where meat, seafood, and vegetables are cooked on an iron griddle. The word comes from teppan (iron plate) and yaki (grilled).

Page 58, panel 4: Somen noodles
Very thin wheat flour noodles, usually served cold with a broth-like dipping sauce.

Page 59, panel 2: Kalbi
Korean barbequed ribs. Also called *galbi*.

Page 59, panel 5: Lohmeyer
August Lohmeyer was a German sausage maker who came to Japan as a POW in 1914, and started a ham and sausage factory in Tokyo in 1921. The style of ham production he introduced is still called the "Lohmeyer method" in Japan. Lohmeyer senpai is named after the style of ham he brings, rather than the brand.

Page 60, panel 5: JA Shonai
JA stands for Japan Agriculture and Shonai is a region in Yamagata prefecture on Honshu island, where Lohmeyer senpai's family farm is located.

Page 79, panel 1: Suzumushi
Also known as bell bugs because of their ringing, bell-like chirp. Suzumushi are usually heard in the fall, while the cicada song is heard in high summer.

Page 80, panel 3: Nozawa-na
A type of turnip green grown in northern Japan. It is good in stir-fries or steamed and is often pickled.

Page 85, panel 1: Yen Shop Takefuji's TV commercial
Takefuji is a consumer credit and loan company known for its commercials of dancing girls.

Page 85, panel 1: Arashi's "A-RA-SHI"
Arashi (Storm) is a five-member boy band founded by Johnny's Entertainment. "A-RA-SHI" was their first single.

Page 85, panel 1: Mago
Mago (Grandchild) is an enka song written by Itsuro Oizumi about his grandchildren. When it hit the Japanese mainstream in 1999, Mago was touted as an enka revival.

Page 93, panel 4: System 6 Mac
System 6 was the operating system for Macs from 1989 to 1991. It was designed to work on machines with as little as 1MB of memory and no hard drive, and could be stored on a floppy disk. Because computers running System 6 had so little memory, they processed data very slowly.

Page 101, panel 1: Bearded nadeshiko
A member of the *dianthus* family, most likely *d. plumarius*. Called pinks or fringed pinks in English, these wild flowers are a delicate pink color with frilled edges.

Page 102, panel 3: Stone Age
The Japanese Stone Age is called the Jomon Period, a prehistoric era from 10,000 BCE to 300 BCE. *Jomon* means "marking" and refers to the marks the Jomon people made in clay using cords wrapped around sticks.

Page 108, panel 4: Natsume Sôseki's Kokoro
Natsume Sôseki (1867-1916). Considered to be the Charles Dickens of Japan, his novel *Kokoro* (heart or spirit) explores the nuances of personal relationships and feelings of loneliness.

Page 109, panel 2: Tora and Uma
The words *tora* (tiger) and *uma* (horse) said together sound like the Japanese pronunciation of "trauma."

Page 122, panel 1: Shimokita
Also called Shimokitazawa, an arty, bohemian neighborhood in Tokyo.

Page 148, panel 4: Taro Okamoto
A Japanese abstract and avant-garde artist (1911-1996).

Page 171, panel 3: Ippon
A martial arts term that means "one full point," the highest score a fighter can achieve. Yamada's ippon is awarded because her throw ended with Morita on his back.

Thinking I ought to be more fit, even though it's kind of far, I rode to Nishi-Ogikubo by bicycle! Going was easy—I did it in 36 minutes. But on the way back I got dizzy and it took two and a half hours...
-Chica Umino

Chica Umino was born in Tokyo and started out as a product designer and illustrator. Her beloved manga *Honey and Clover* debuted in 2000 and received the Kodansha Manga Award in 2003. *Honey and Clover* was also nominated for the Tezuka Culture Prize and an award from the Japan Media Arts Festival.

HONEY AND CLOVER
VOL. 1
The Shojo Beat Manga Edition

This manga volume contains material that was originally published in English in *Shojo Beat* magazine, September 2007-January 2008. Artwork in the magazine may have been slightly altered from that presented here.

STORY AND ART BY CHICA UMINO

English Translation & Adaptation/Akemi Wegmuller
Touch-up Art & Lettering/Sabrina Heep
Design/Yukiko Whitley
Editor/Pancha Diaz

Editor in Chief, Books/Alvin Lu
Editor in Chief, Magazines/Marc Weidenbaum
VP of Publishing Licensing/Rika Inouye
VP of Sales/Gonzalo Ferreyra
Sr. VP of Marketing/Liza Coppola
Publisher/Hyoe Narita

Moon River
from Paramount Picture BREAKFAST AT TIFFANY'S
Words by Johnny Mercer
Music by Henry Mancini
Copyright ©1961 (Renewed 1989) by Famous Music LLC
International Copyright Secured. All Rights Reserved

store.viz.com

Printed in Canada

Published by VIZ Media, LLC
P.O. Box 77010
San Francisco, CA 94107

Shojo Beat Manga Edition
10 9 8 7 6 5 4 3 2 1
First printing, March 2008

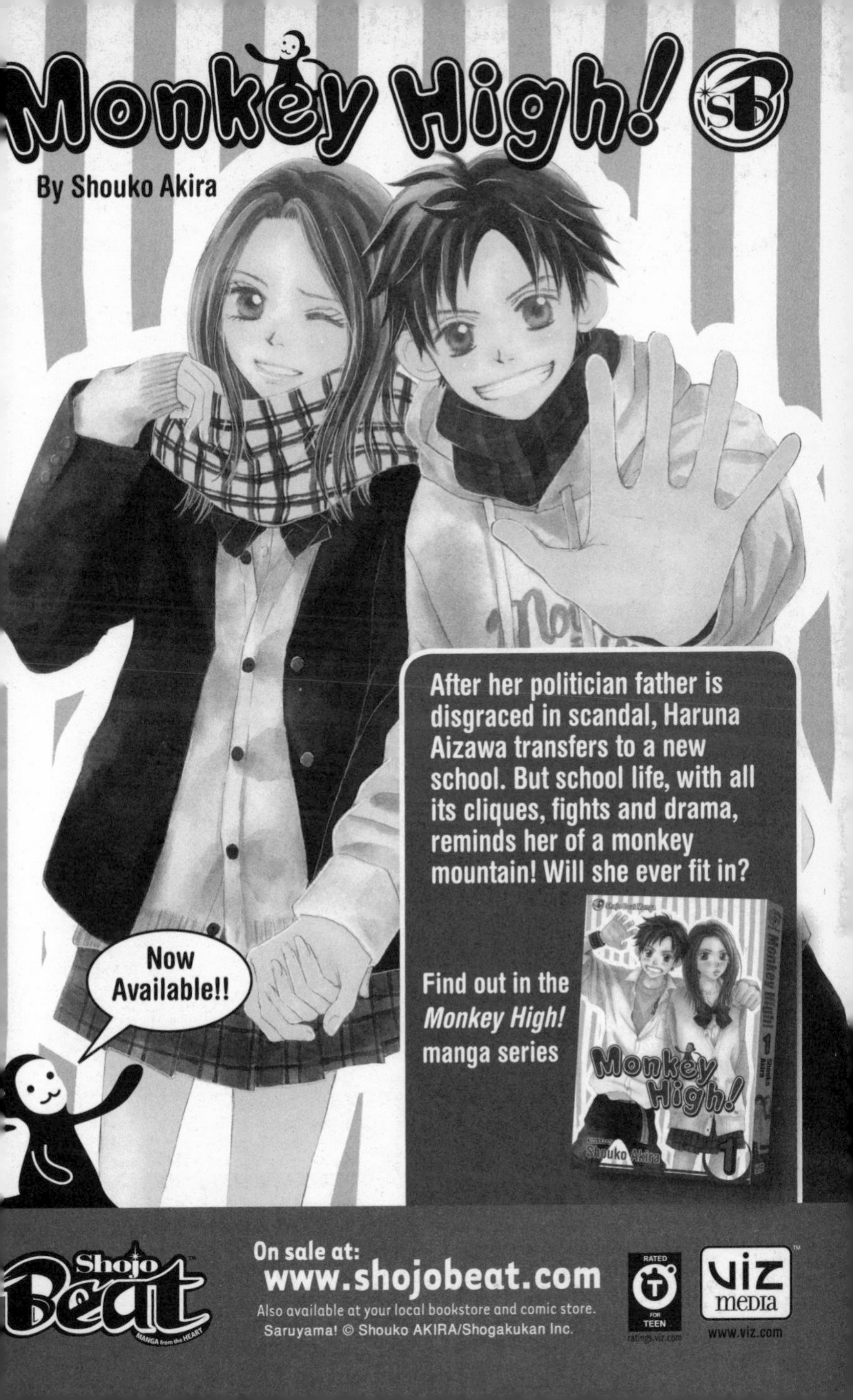

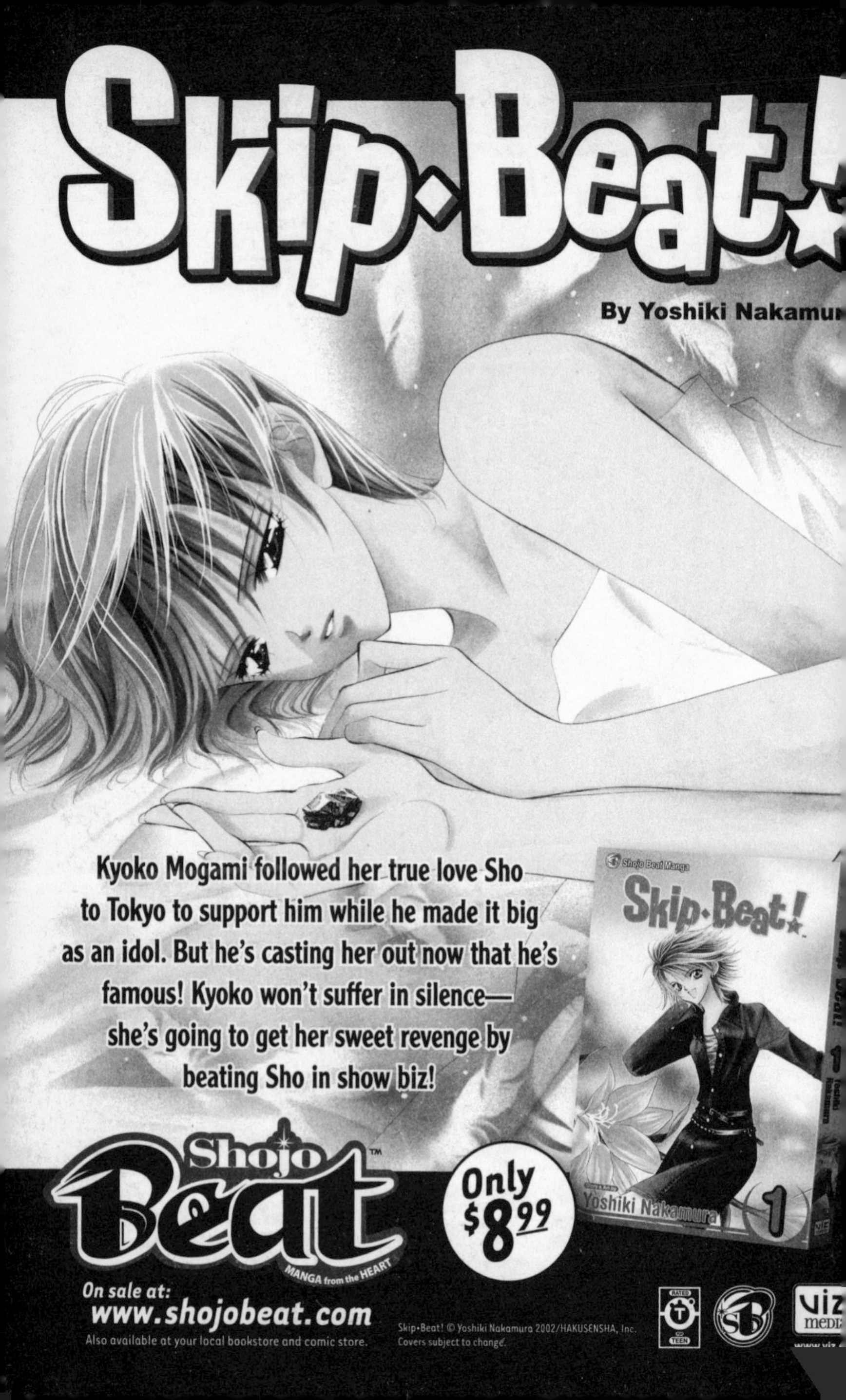
Skip·Beat!
By Yoshiki Nakamur
Kyoko Mogami followed her true love Sho to Tokyo to support him while he made it big as an idol. But he's casting her out now that he's famous! Kyoko won't suffer in silence—she's going to get her sweet revenge by beating Sho in show biz!
Shojo Beat Manga
Skip·Beat!
Yoshiki Nakamura
1
Shojo Beat™
MANGA from the HEART
Only $8.99
On sale at:
www.shojobeat.com
Also available at your local bookstore and comic store.
Skip•Beat! © Yoshiki Nakamura 2002/HAKUSENSHA, Inc.
Covers subject to change.
RATED T TEEN
VIZ MEDIA

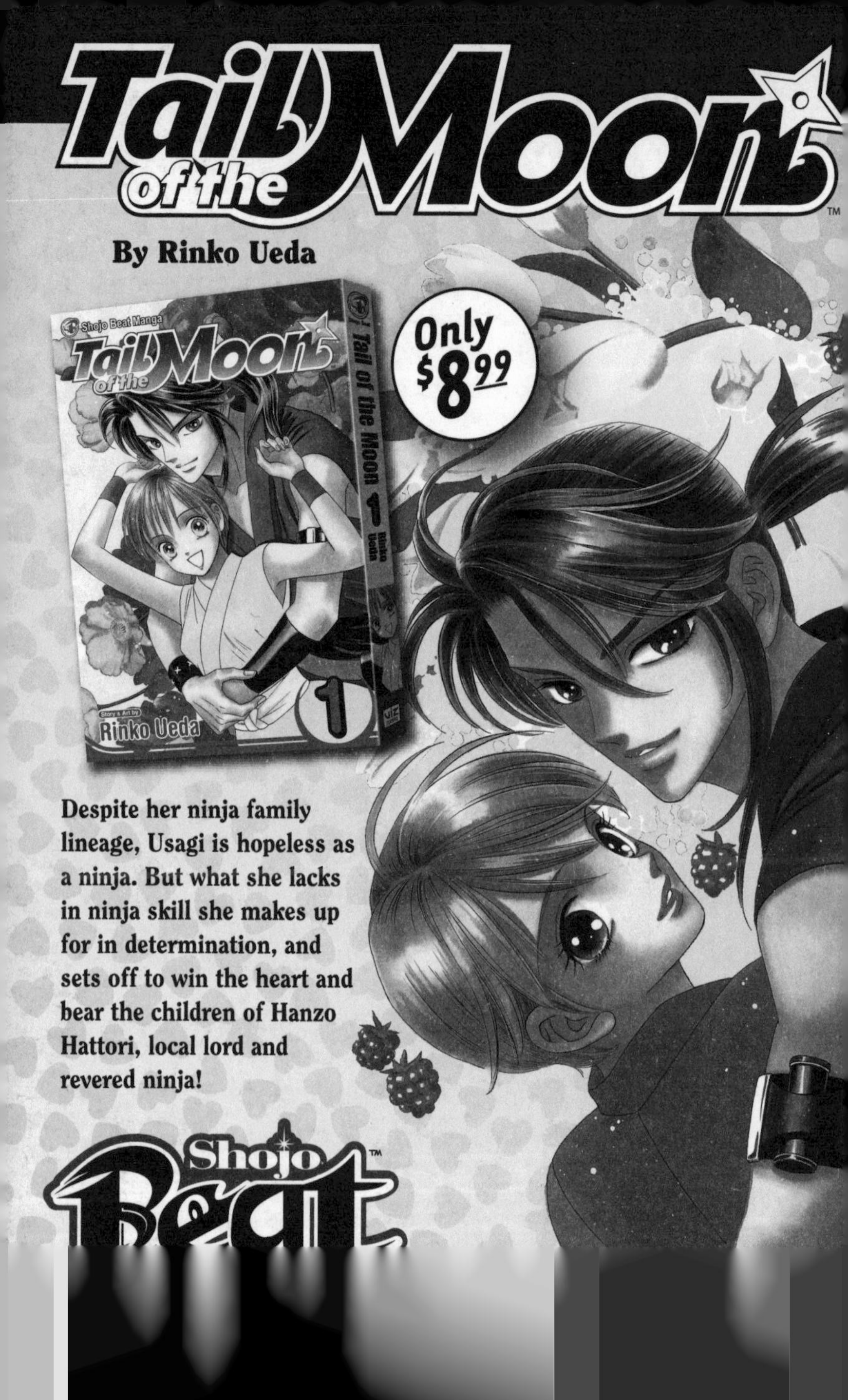
Tail of the Moon™
By Rinko Ueda
Shojo Beat Manga
Tail of the Moon
Story & Art by
Rinko Ueda
1
Tail of the Moon 1 Rinko Ueda
Only $8.99
Despite her ninja family lineage, Usagi is hopeless as a ninja. But what she lacks in ninja skill she makes up for in determination, and sets off to win the heart and bear the children of Hanzo Hattori, local lord and revered ninja!
Shojo Beat™
[redacted]

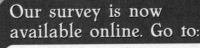

Find the Beat online!
Check us out at

www.shojobeat.com!

Shojo Beat

honey and clove

Vol. **8**

Story & Art by
Chica Umino

honey and clover

Volume 8
CONTENTS

honey and clover

chapter 47

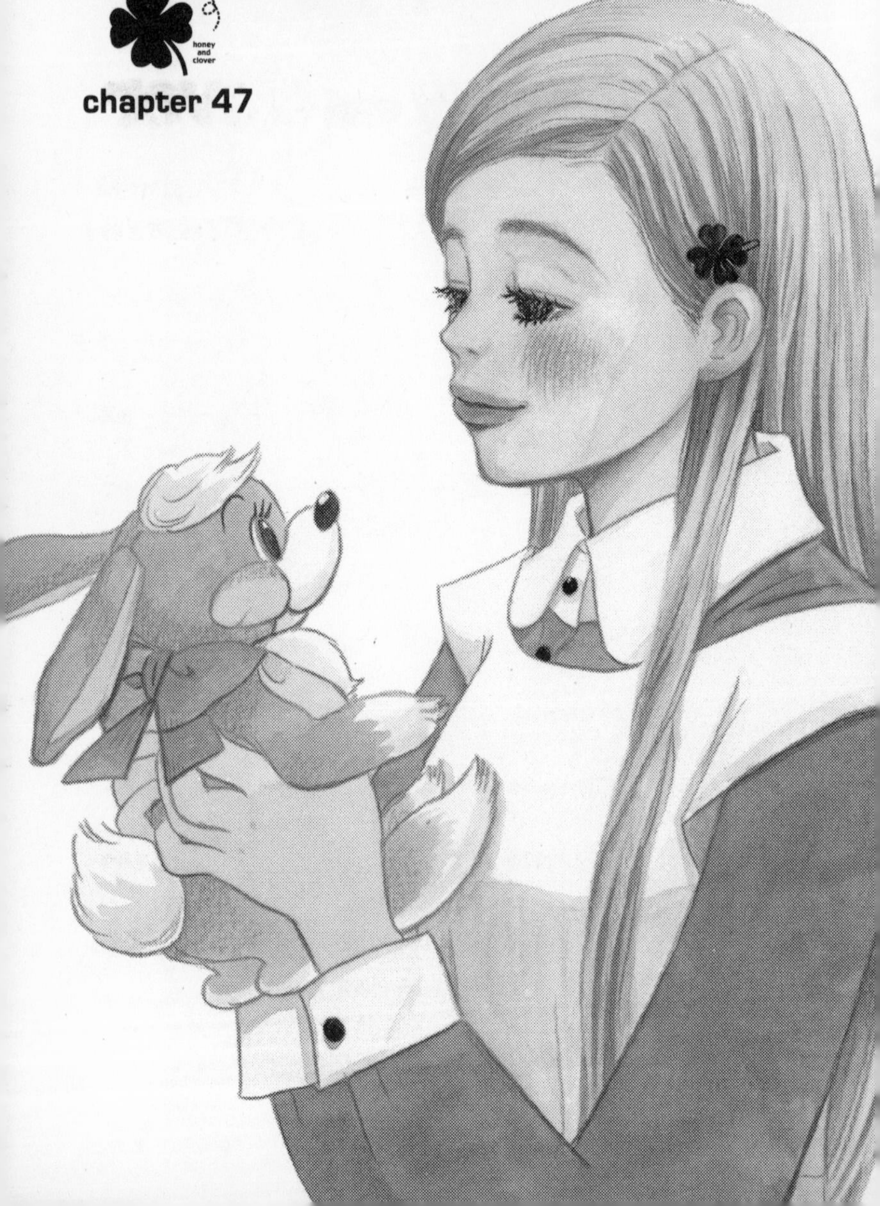

✧ Capsule ★ Honey ✦ Clover ❀

♥ Hagu ⇨ In charge of magic stick ✧ ✦

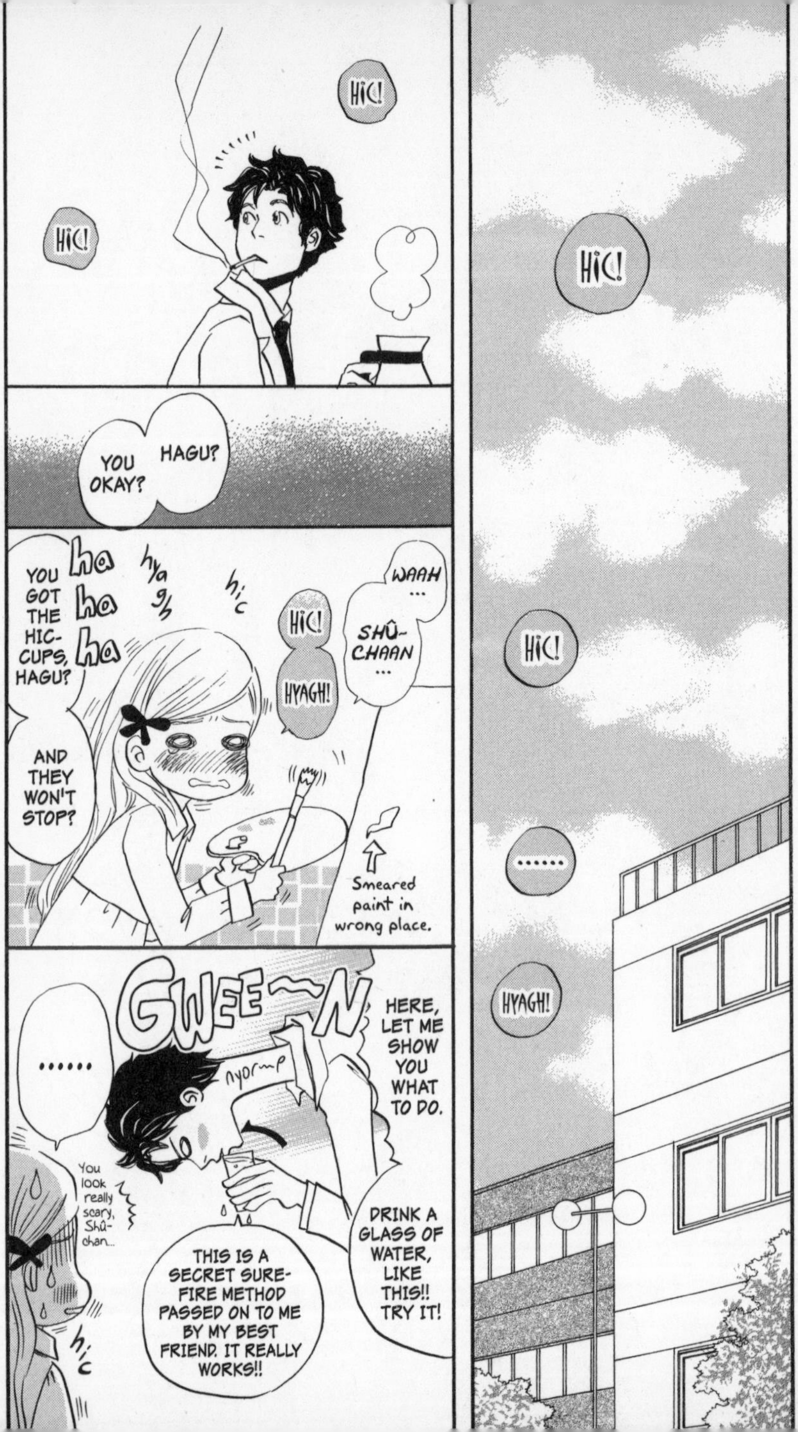
HIC!
HIC!
......
HYAGH!
HIC!
HIC!
HAGU?
YOU OKAY?
WAAH... SHÛ-CHAAN...
HIC!
HYAGH!
hic
hyagh
ha ha ha
YOU GOT THE HIC-CUPS, HAGU?
AND THEY WON'T STOP?
Smeared paint in wrong place.
HERE, LET ME SHOW YOU WHAT TO DO.
GWEE~N
nyormp
......
DRINK A GLASS OF WATER, LIKE THIS!! TRY IT!
THIS IS A SECRET SURE-FIRE METHOD PASSED ON TO ME BY MY BEST FRIEND. IT REALLY WORKS!!
You look really scary, Shû-chan...
hic

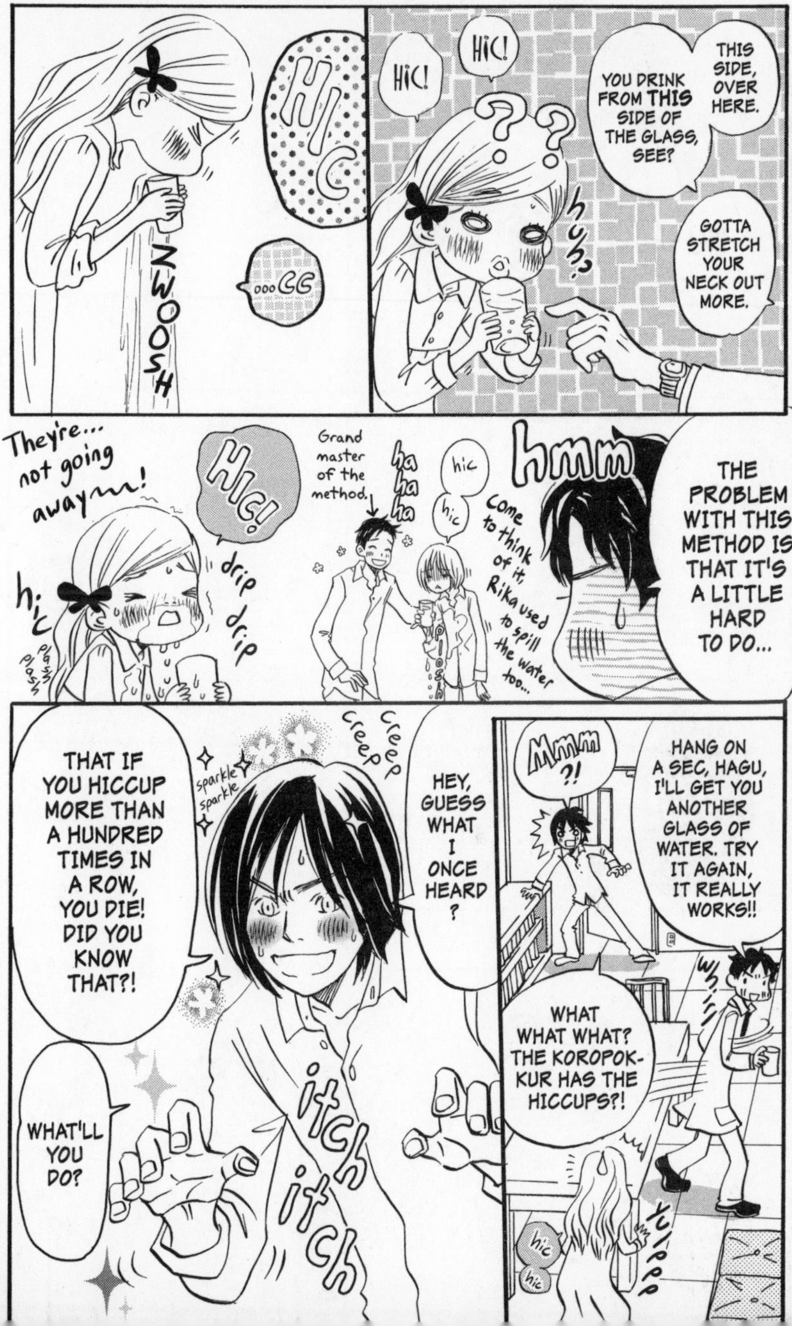
THIS SIDE, OVER HERE.
YOU DRINK FROM THIS SIDE OF THE GLASS, SEE?
HIC!
HIC!
huh?
GOTTA STRETCH YOUR NECK OUT MORE.
HIC
...CC
ZWOOSH
hmm
THE PROBLEM WITH THIS METHOD IS THAT IT'S A LITTLE HARD TO DO...
Come to think of it, Rika used to spill the water too...
hic
hic
ha ha ha
Grand master of the method.
splosh
They're... not going awayyy!
HIC!
drip drip
hic
plash plash
HANG ON A SEC, HAGU, I'LL GET YOU ANOTHER GLASS OF WATER. TRY IT AGAIN, IT REALLY WORKS!!
Mmm ?!
WHAT WHAT WHAT? THE KOROPOKKUR HAS THE HICCUPS?!
hic
hic
creep creep
HEY, GUESS WHAT I ONCE HEARD?
THAT IF YOU HICCUP MORE THAN A HUNDRED TIMES IN A ROW, YOU DIE! DID YOU KNOW THAT?!
sparkle sparkle
WHAT'LL YOU DO?
itch itch

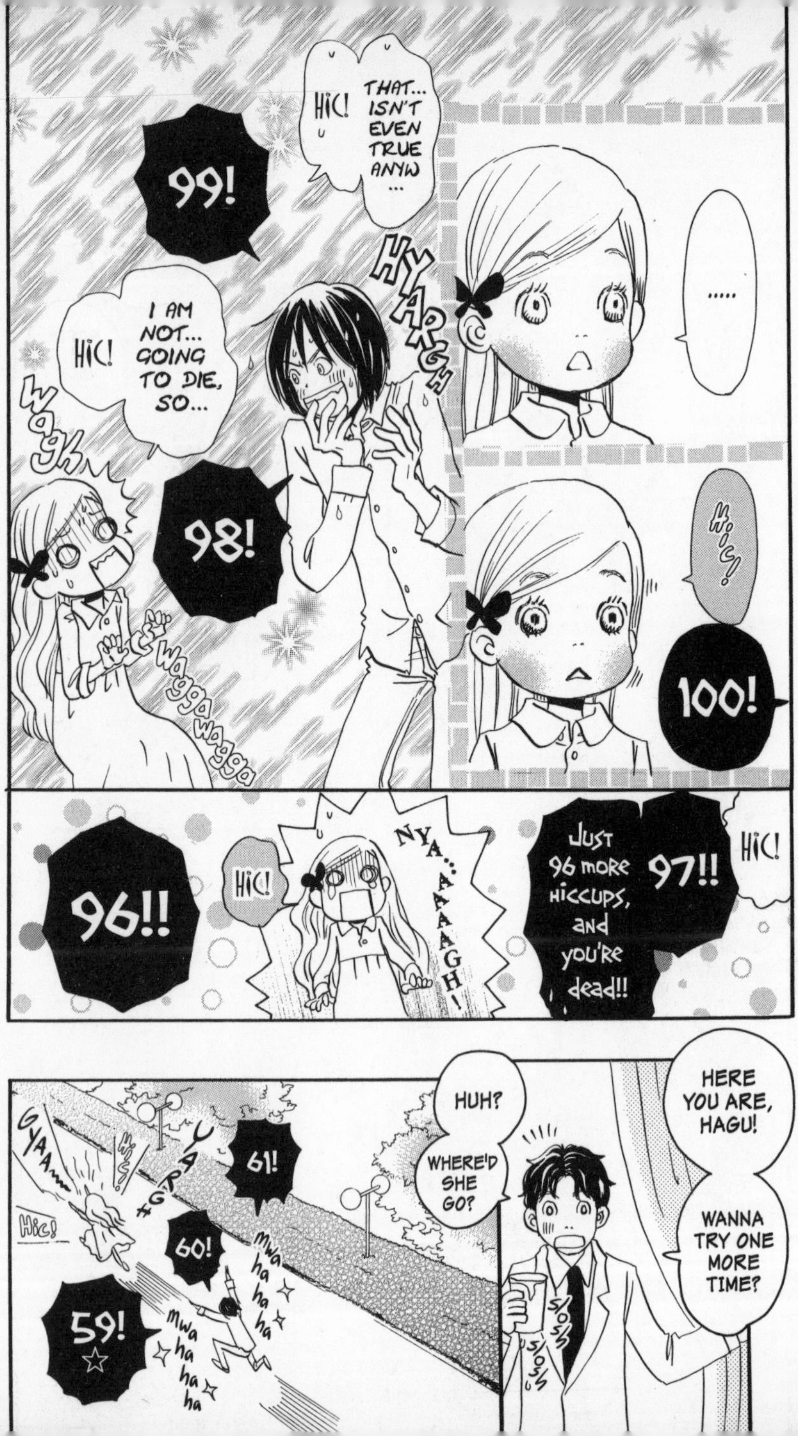
.....
Hic!
100!
HiC!
THAT... ISN'T EVEN TRUE ANYW...
99!
HYARGH
HiC!
I AM NOT... GOING TO DIE, SO...
98!
Waagh
Wagga wagga
HiC!
97!!
Just 96 more hiccups, and you're dead!!
NYA... AAAAGH!
HiC!
96!!
HERE YOU ARE, HAGU!
WANNA TRY ONE MORE TIME?
HUH?
WHERE'D SHE GO?
slosh slosh
61!
YAARGH
Hic!
GYAA
Hic!
60!
mwa ha ha ha ha
59!
mwa ha ha ha ha

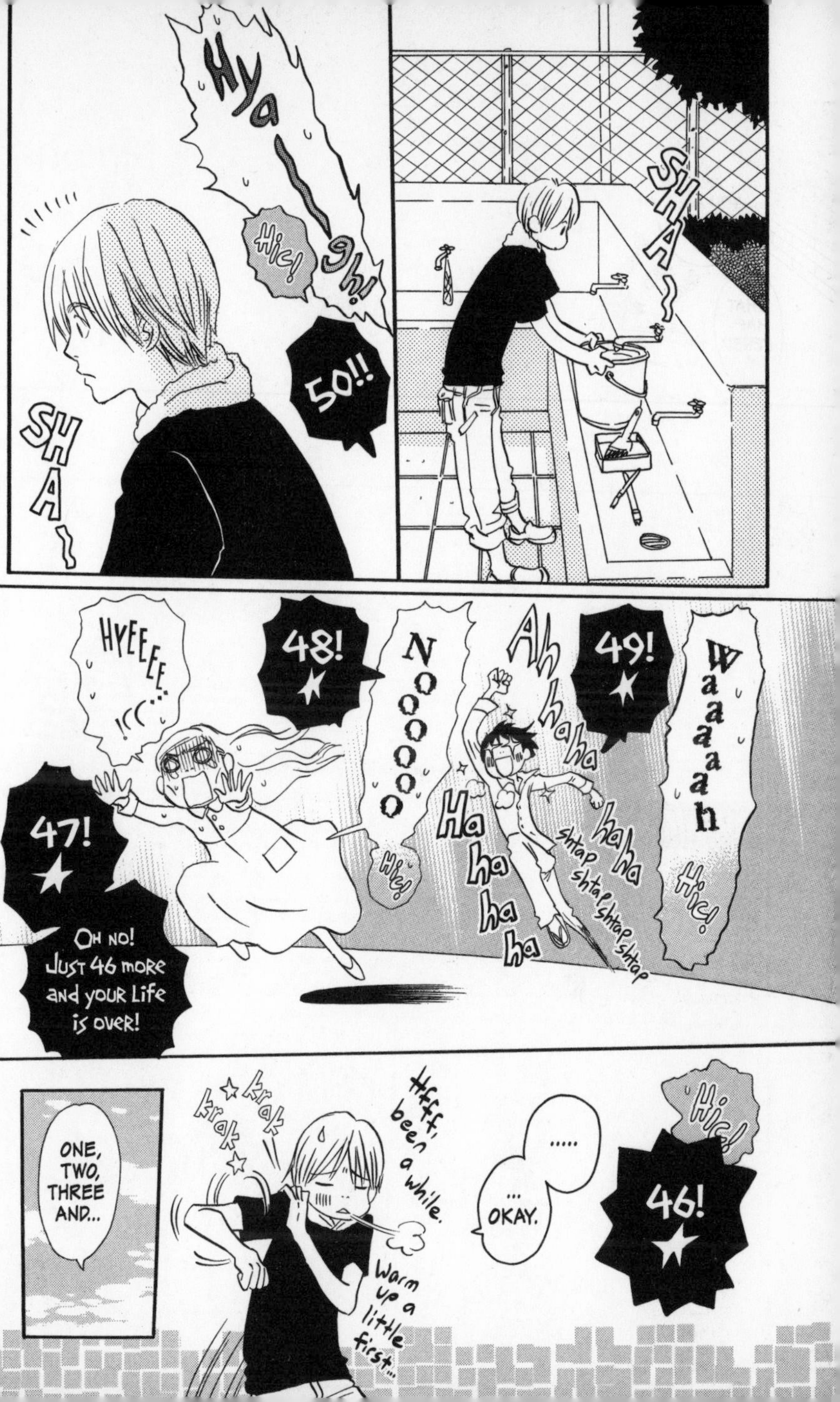
SHA~
Hya——gh!
Hic!
50!!
SHA~
Waaaaaah
Hic!
49!
Ah haha hahaha
shtap shtap shtap shtap
Ha ha ha ha ha
Nooooooo
Hic!
48!
HYEEEE...!((
47!
Oh no! Just 46 more and your life is over!
Hic!
46!
.....
... OKAY.
Hfff, been a while.
Warm up a little first...
krak krak
ONE, TWO, THREE AND...

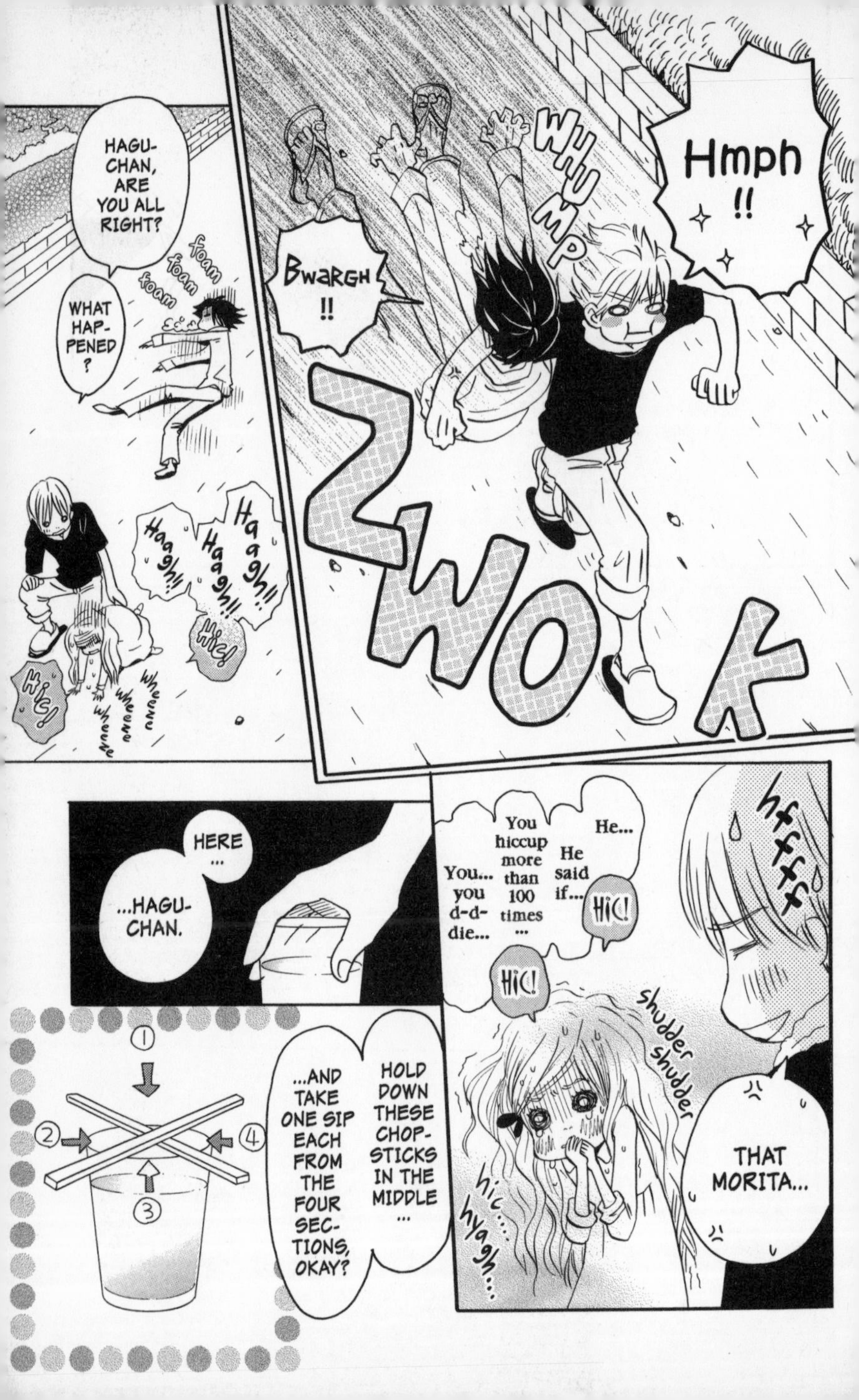
Hmph!!
WHUMP
Bwargh!!
ZWOK
HAGU-CHAN, ARE YOU ALL RIGHT?
foam foam foam
WHAT HAPPENED?
Haagh!! Haagh!! Haagh!!
Hic!
wheeze wheeze wheeze
Hic!
hffff
He...
He said if...
Hic!
You hiccup more than 100 times...
You... you d-d-die...
Hic!
shudder shudder
hic... hyagh...
THAT MORITA...
HERE...
...HAGU-CHAN.
HOLD DOWN THESE CHOPSTICKS IN THE MIDDLE...
...AND TAKE ONE SIP EACH FROM THE FOUR SECTIONS, OKAY?
①
②
③
④

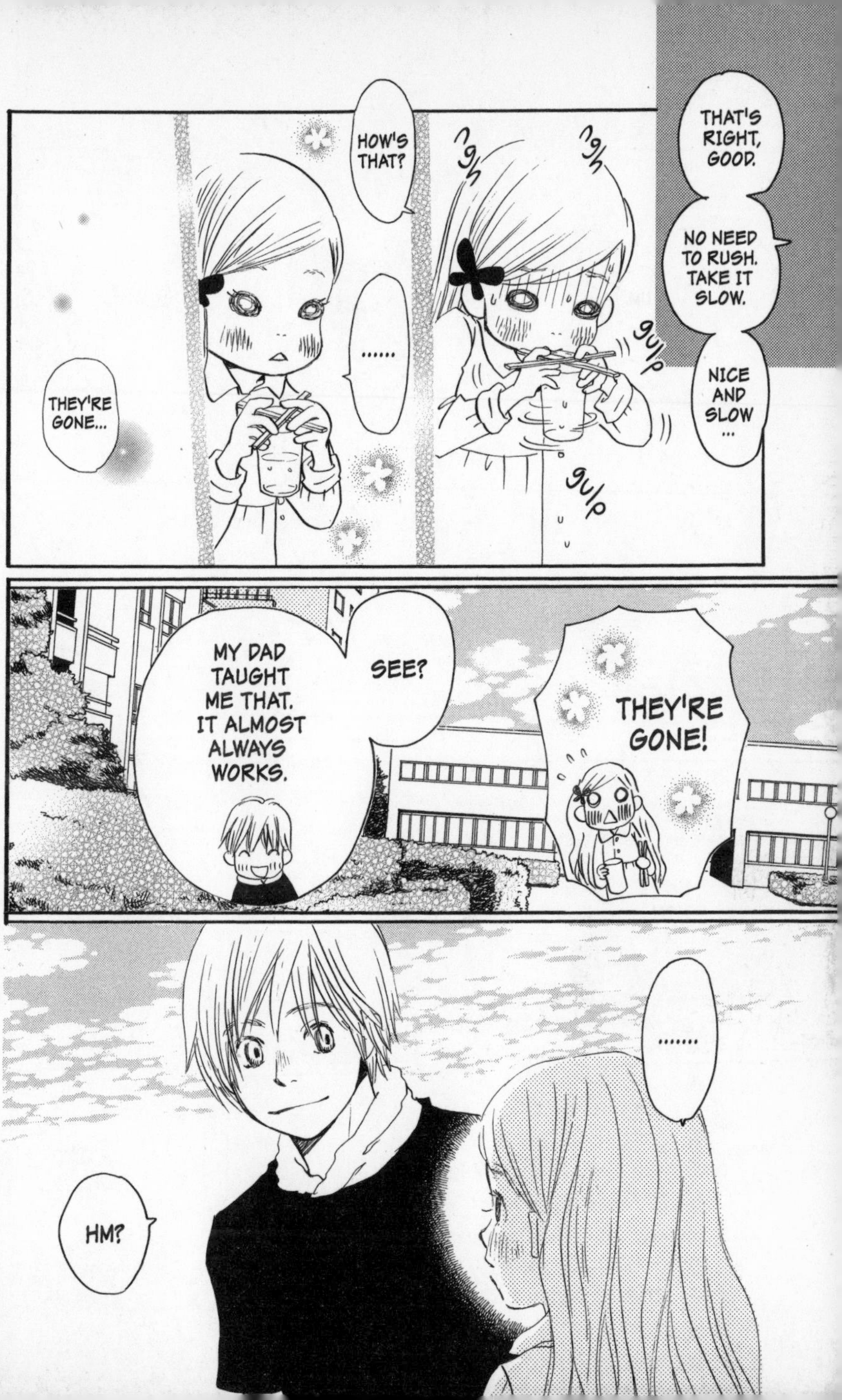
THAT'S RIGHT, GOOD.
NO NEED TO RUSH. TAKE IT SLOW.
NICE AND SLOW...
ugh
ugh
gulp
gulp
HOW'S THAT?
......
THEY'RE GONE...
THEY'RE GONE!
SEE?
MY DAD TAUGHT ME THAT. IT ALMOST ALWAYS WORKS.
......
HM?

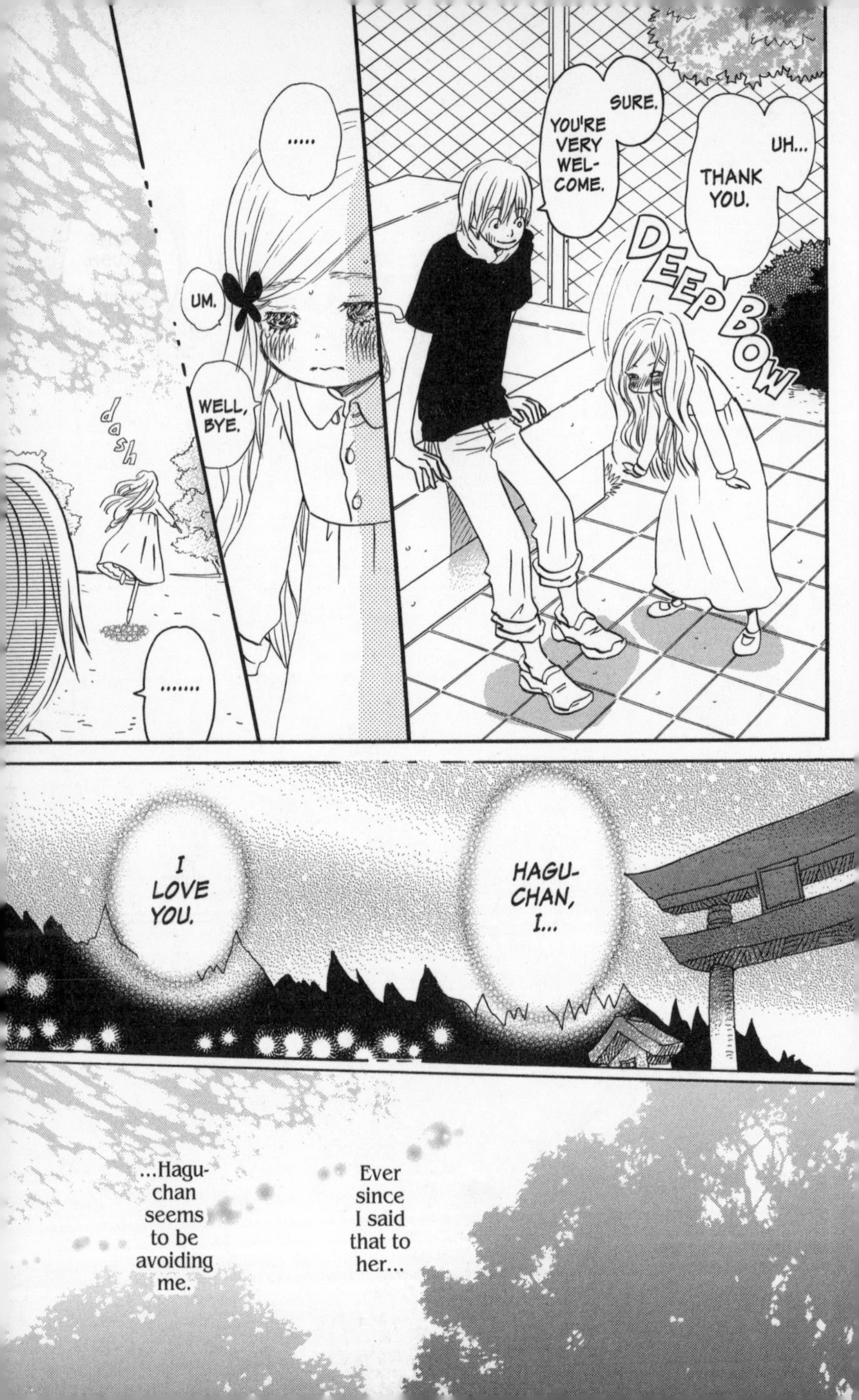
UH... THANK YOU.
DEEP BOW
SURE. YOU'RE VERY WEL-COME.
.....
UM.
WELL, BYE.
dash
....
HAGU-CHAN, I...
I LOVE YOU.
Ever since I said that to her...
...Hagu-chan seems to be avoiding me.

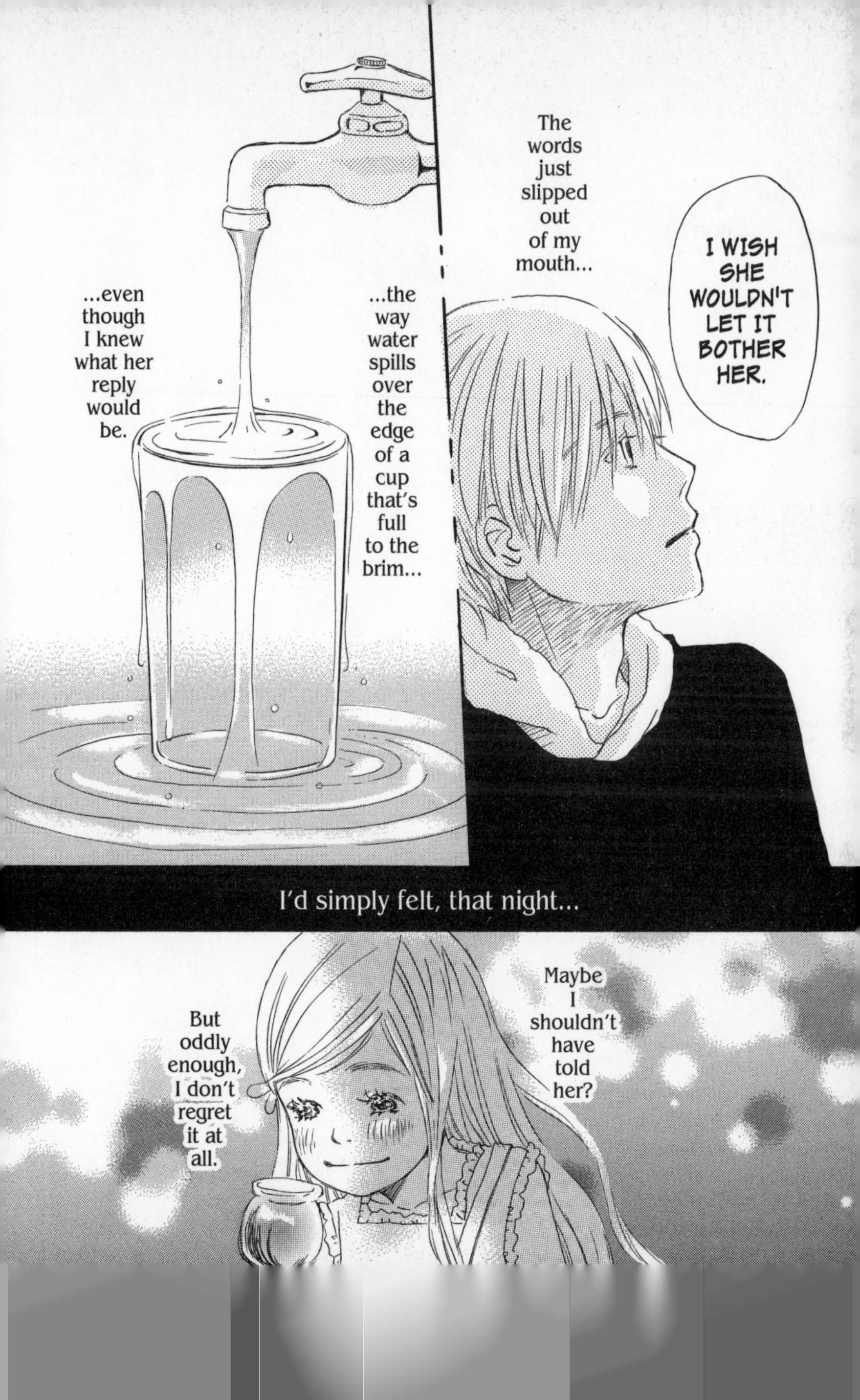
I WISH SHE WOULDN'T LET IT BOTHER HER.
The words just slipped out of my mouth...
...the way water spills over the edge of a cup that's full to the brim...
...even though I knew what her reply would be.
I'd simply felt, that night...
Maybe I shouldn't have told her?
But oddly enough, I don't regret it at all.

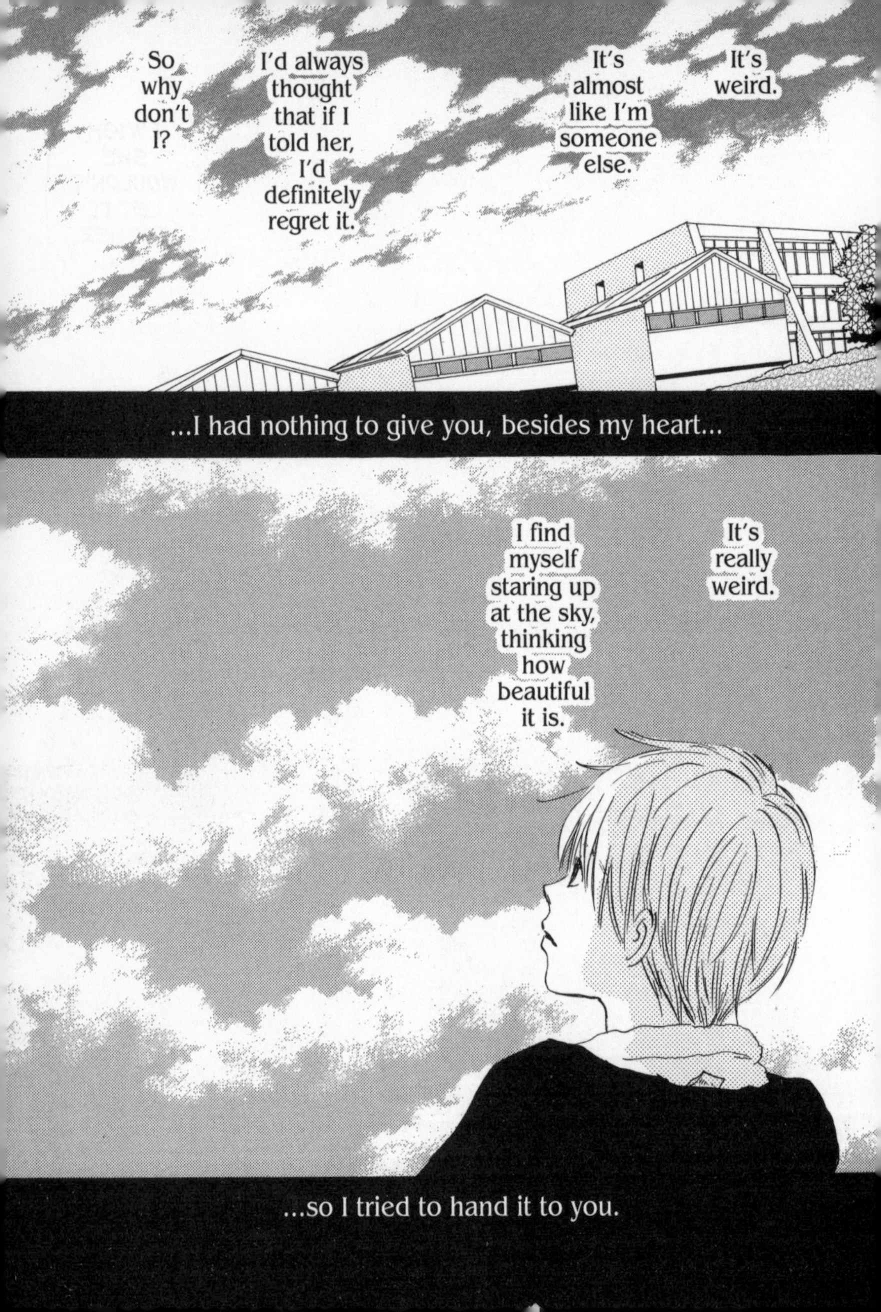
It's weird.
It's almost like I'm someone else.
I'd always thought that if I told her, I'd definitely regret it.
So why don't I?
...I had nothing to give you, besides my heart...
It's really weird.
I find myself staring up at the sky, thinking how beautiful it is.
...so I tried to hand it to you.

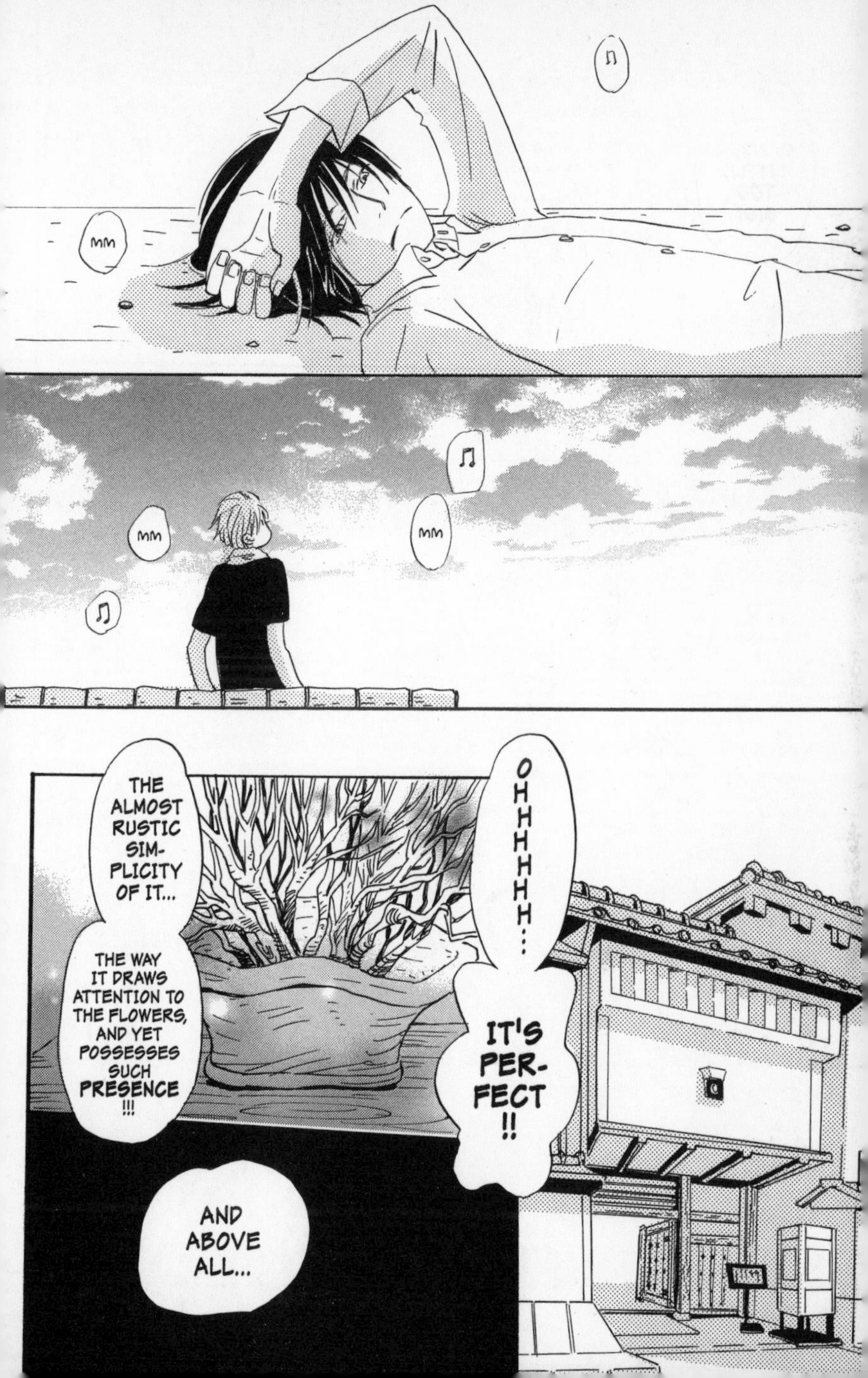
♫
MM
♫
MM
MM
♫
OHHHHHH...
IT'S PER-FECT!!
THE ALMOST RUSTIC SIM-PLICITY OF IT...
THE WAY IT DRAWS ATTENTION TO THE FLOWERS, AND YET POSSESSES SUCH PRESENCE!!!
AND ABOVE ALL...

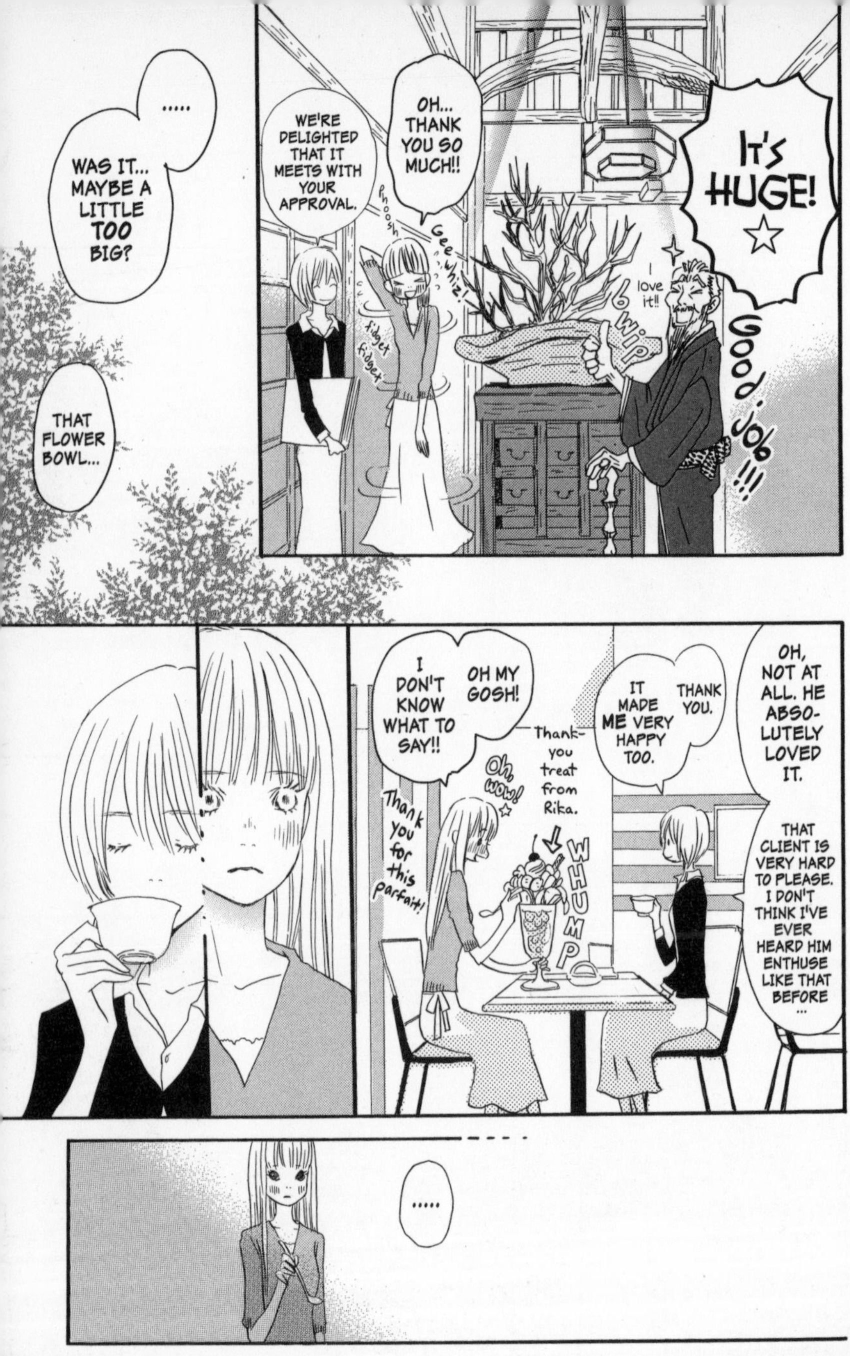
It's HUGE! ☆
Good job!!!
I love it!!
bwip
OH... THANK YOU SO MUCH!!
Gee whiz!
Phoosh
fidget fidget
WE'RE DELIGHTED THAT IT MEETS WITH YOUR APPROVAL.
.....
WAS IT... MAYBE A LITTLE TOO BIG?
THAT FLOWER BOWL...
OH, NOT AT ALL. HE ABSOLUTELY LOVED IT.
THAT CLIENT IS VERY HARD TO PLEASE. I DON'T THINK I'VE EVER HEARD HIM ENTHUSE LIKE THAT BEFORE...
THANK YOU.
IT MADE ME VERY HAPPY TOO.
Thank-you treat from Rika.
OH MY GOSH!
I DON'T KNOW WHAT TO SAY!!
Oh, wow! ☆
WHUMP
Thank you for this parfait!
.....

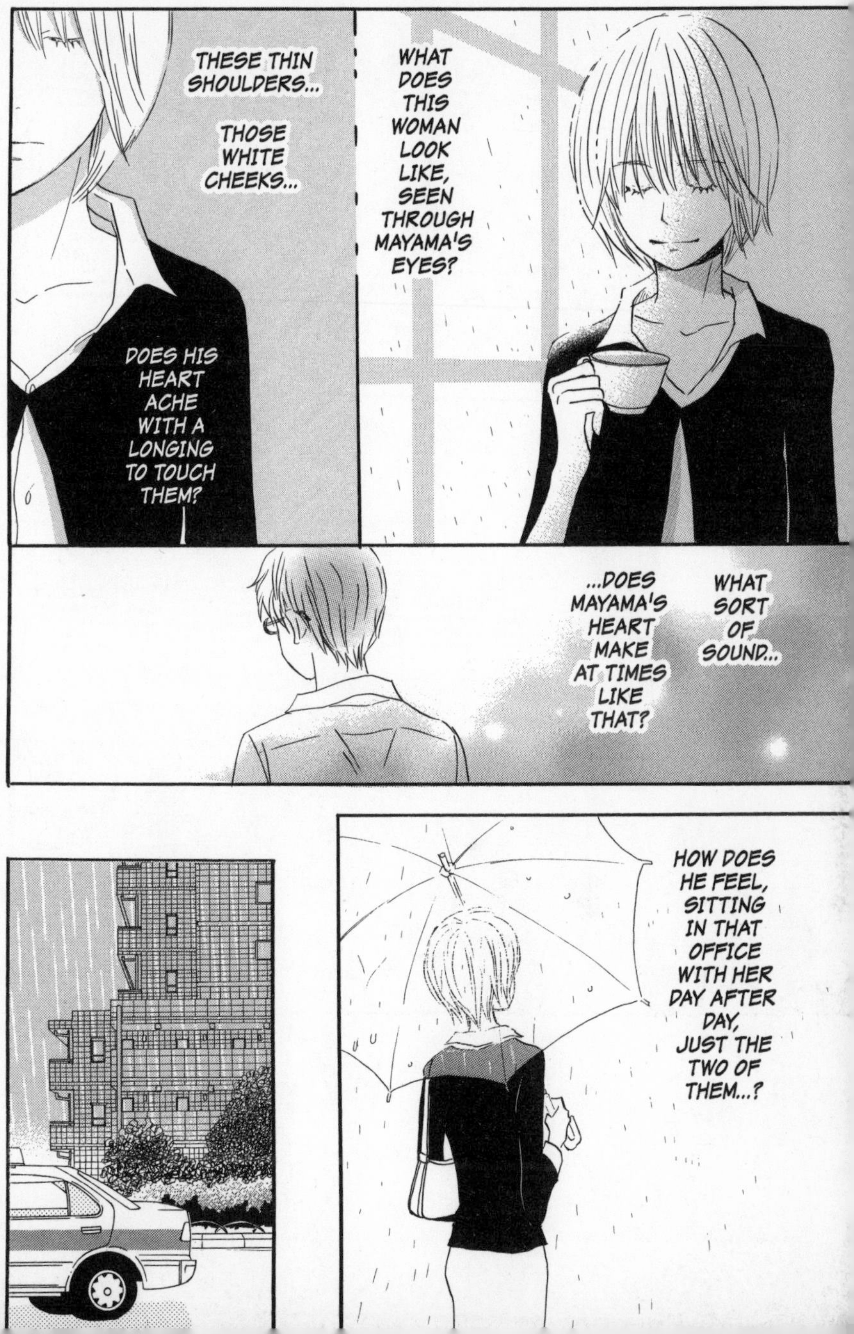
WHAT DOES THIS WOMAN LOOK LIKE, SEEN THROUGH MAYAMA'S EYES?
THESE THIN SHOULDERS...
THOSE WHITE CHEEKS...
DOES HIS HEART ACHE WITH A LONGING TO TOUCH THEM?
WHAT SORT OF SOUND...
...DOES MAYAMA'S HEART MAKE AT TIMES LIKE THAT?
HOW DOES HE FEEL, SITTING IN THAT OFFICE WITH HER DAY AFTER DAY, JUST THE TWO OF THEM...?

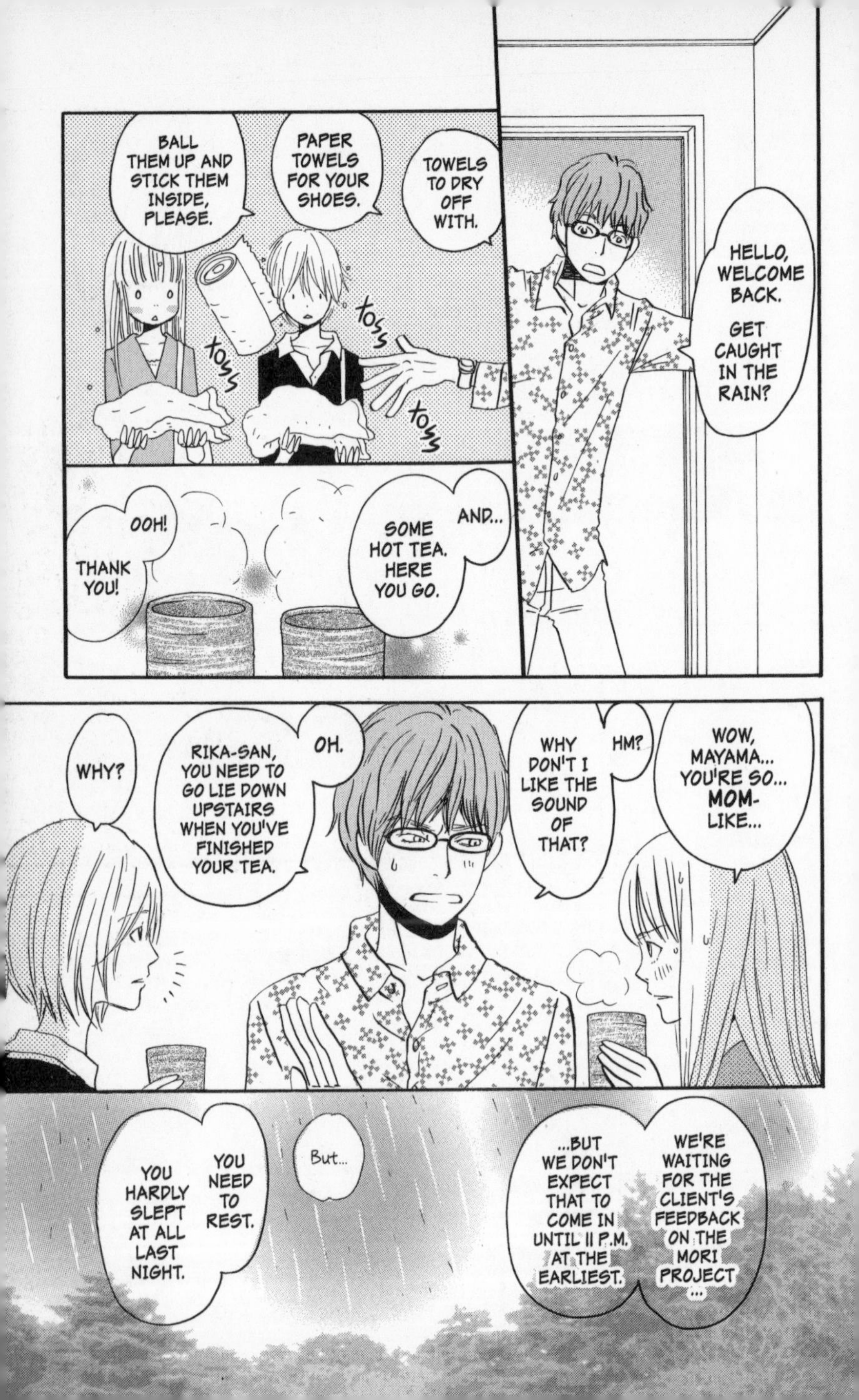
HELLO, WELCOME BACK.
GET CAUGHT IN THE RAIN?
TOWELS TO DRY OFF WITH.
XOSS
PAPER TOWELS FOR YOUR SHOES.
XOSS
BALL THEM UP AND STICK THEM INSIDE, PLEASE.
XOSS
AND...
SOME HOT TEA. HERE YOU GO.
OOH!
THANK YOU!
WOW, MAYAMA... YOU'RE SO... MOM-LIKE...
HM?
WHY DON'T I LIKE THE SOUND OF THAT?
OH.
RIKA-SAN, YOU NEED TO GO LIE DOWN UPSTAIRS WHEN YOU'VE FINISHED YOUR TEA.
WHY?
WE'RE WAITING FOR THE CLIENT'S FEEDBACK ON THE MORI PROJECT...
...BUT WE DON'T EXPECT THAT TO COME IN UNTIL 11 P.M. AT THE EARLIEST.
But...
YOU NEED TO REST.
YOU HARDLY SLEPT AT ALL LAST NIGHT.

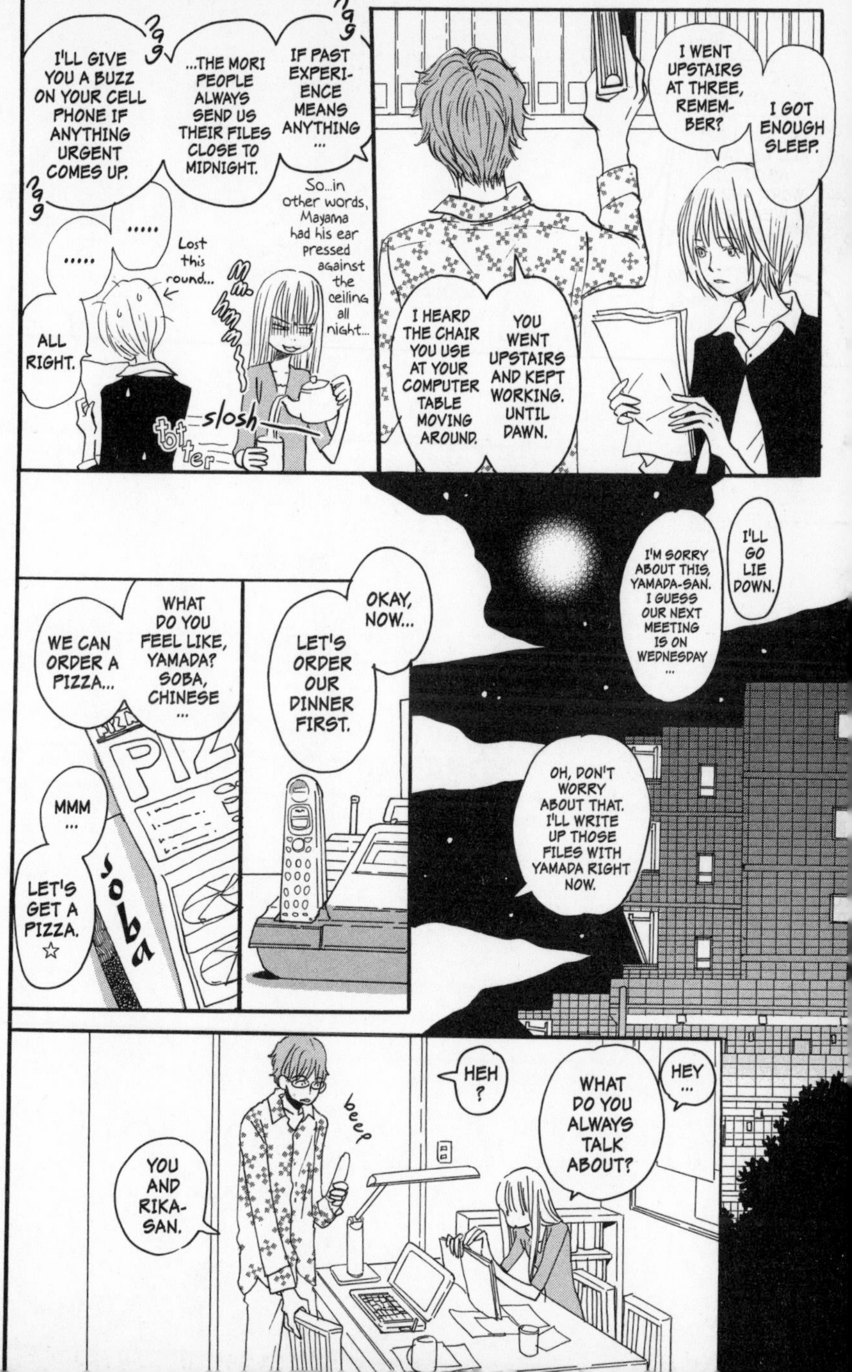
I WENT UPSTAIRS AT THREE, REMEMBER?
I GOT ENOUGH SLEEP.
YOU WENT UPSTAIRS AND KEPT WORKING. UNTIL DAWN.
I HEARD THE CHAIR YOU USE AT YOUR COMPUTER TABLE MOVING AROUND.
nag
IF PAST EXPERIENCE MEANS ANYTHING...
nag
...THE MORI PEOPLE ALWAYS SEND US THEIR FILES CLOSE TO MIDNIGHT.
I'LL GIVE YOU A BUZZ ON YOUR CELL PHONE IF ANYTHING URGENT COMES UP.
nag
So...in other words, Mayama had his ear pressed against the ceiling all night...
Mmhmm
.....
.....
Lost this round...
ALL RIGHT.
slosh
totter
I'LL GO LIE DOWN.
I'M SORRY ABOUT THIS, YAMADA-SAN. I GUESS OUR NEXT MEETING IS ON WEDNESDAY...
OH, DON'T WORRY ABOUT THAT. I'LL WRITE UP THOSE FILES WITH YAMADA RIGHT NOW.
OKAY, NOW...
LET'S ORDER OUR DINNER FIRST.
WHAT DO YOU FEEL LIKE, YAMADA? SOBA, CHINESE...
WE CAN ORDER A PIZZA...
PIZ
soba
MMM...
LET'S GET A PIZZA. ☆
HEY...
WHAT DO YOU ALWAYS TALK ABOUT?
HEH?
beep
YOU AND RIKA-SAN.

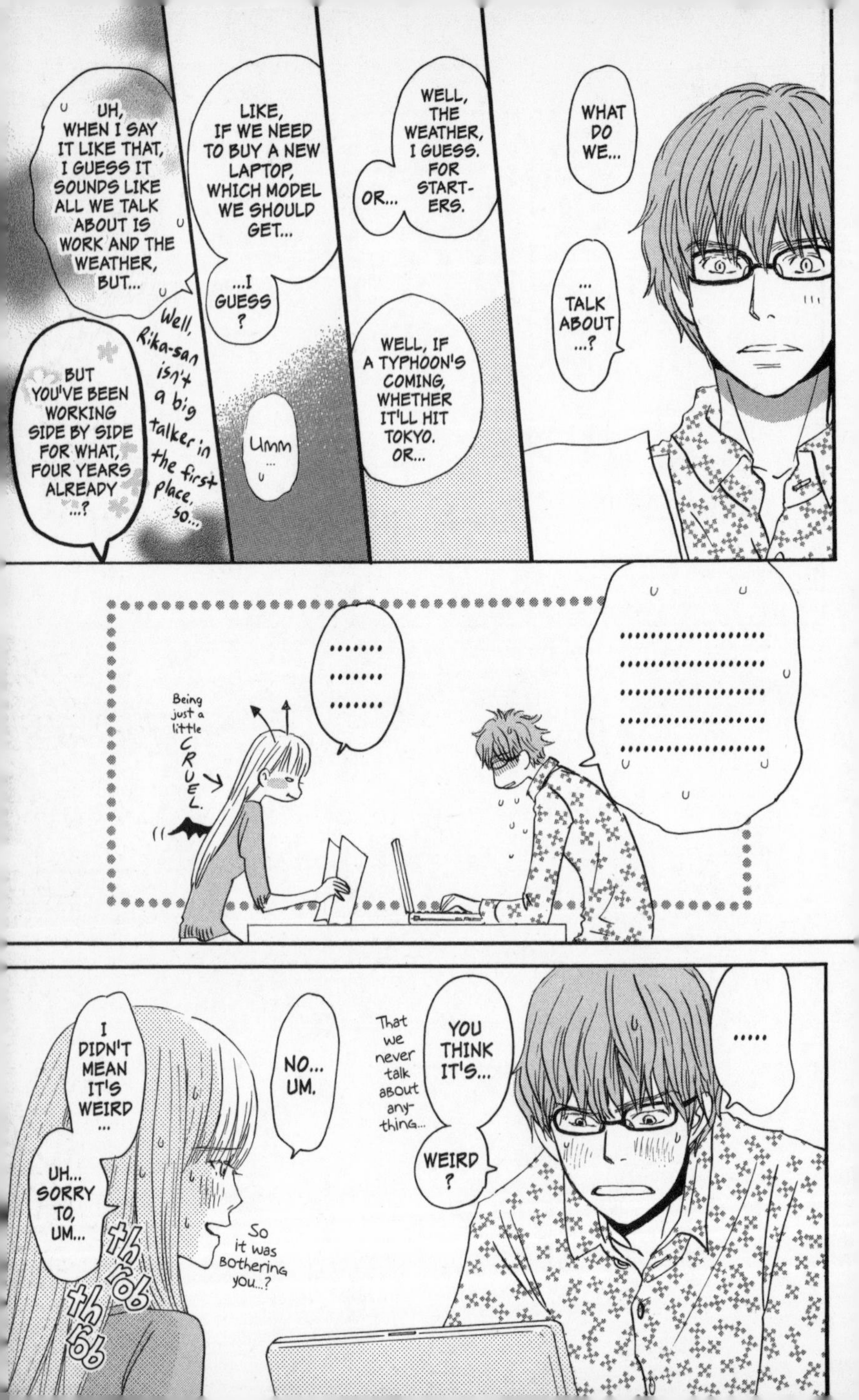
WHAT DO WE...
...TALK ABOUT...?
WELL, THE WEATHER, I GUESS. FOR STARTERS.
OR...
WELL, IF A TYPHOON'S COMING, WHETHER IT'LL HIT TOKYO. OR...
LIKE, IF WE NEED TO BUY A NEW LAPTOP, WHICH MODEL WE SHOULD GET...
...I GUESS?
Umm...
UH, WHEN I SAY IT LIKE THAT, I GUESS IT SOUNDS LIKE ALL WE TALK ABOUT IS WORK AND THE WEATHER, BUT...
Well, Rika-san isn't a big talker in the first place, so...
BUT YOU'VE BEEN WORKING SIDE BY SIDE FOR WHAT, FOUR YEARS ALREADY...?
....
....
Being just a little CRUEL.
.....
YOU THINK IT'S...
WEIRD?
That we never talk about anything...
NO... UM.
I DIDN'T MEAN IT'S WEIRD...
So it was bothering you...?
UH... SORRY TO, UM...
throb throb

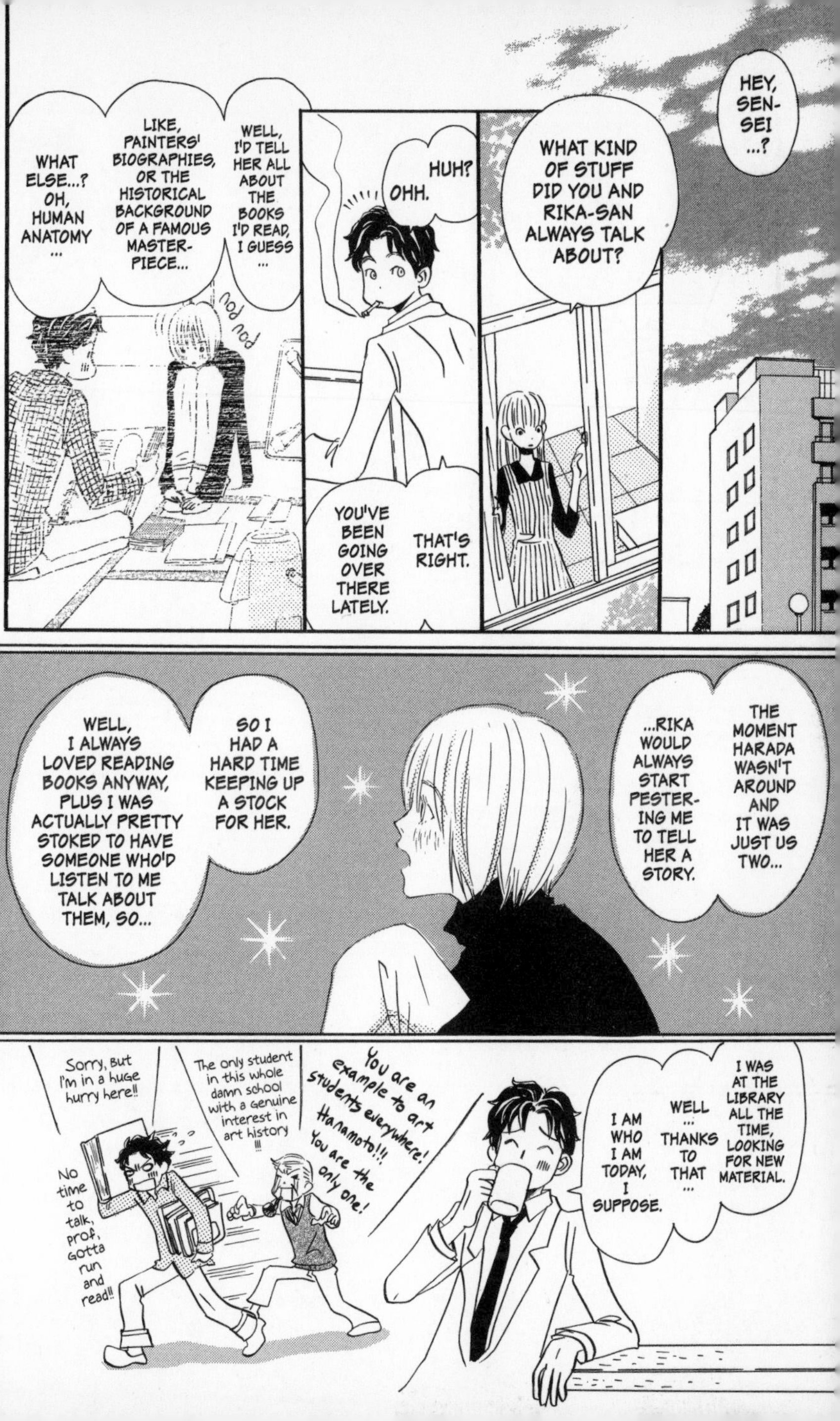
HEY, SENSEI...?
WHAT KIND OF STUFF DID YOU AND RIKA-SAN ALWAYS TALK ABOUT?
HUH?
OHH.
THAT'S RIGHT.
YOU'VE BEEN GOING OVER THERE LATELY.
WELL, I'D TELL HER ALL ABOUT THE BOOKS I'D READ, I GUESS...
LIKE, PAINTERS' BIOGRAPHIES, OR THE HISTORICAL BACKGROUND OF A FAMOUS MASTERPIECE...
WHAT ELSE...? OH, HUMAN ANATOMY...
nod nod
THE MOMENT HARADA WASN'T AROUND AND IT WAS JUST US TWO...
...RIKA WOULD ALWAYS START PESTERING ME TO TELL HER A STORY.
SO I HAD A HARD TIME KEEPING UP A STOCK FOR HER.
WELL, I ALWAYS LOVED READING BOOKS ANYWAY, PLUS I WAS ACTUALLY PRETTY STOKED TO HAVE SOMEONE WHO'D LISTEN TO ME TALK ABOUT THEM, SO...
I WAS AT THE LIBRARY ALL THE TIME, LOOKING FOR NEW MATERIAL.
WELL... THANKS TO THAT...
I AM WHO I AM TODAY, I SUPPOSE.
You are an example to art students everywhere! Hanamoto!!! You are the only one!
The only student in this whole damn school with a genuine interest in art history!!!
Sorry, But I'm in a huge hurry here!!
No time to talk, prof, Gotta run and read!!

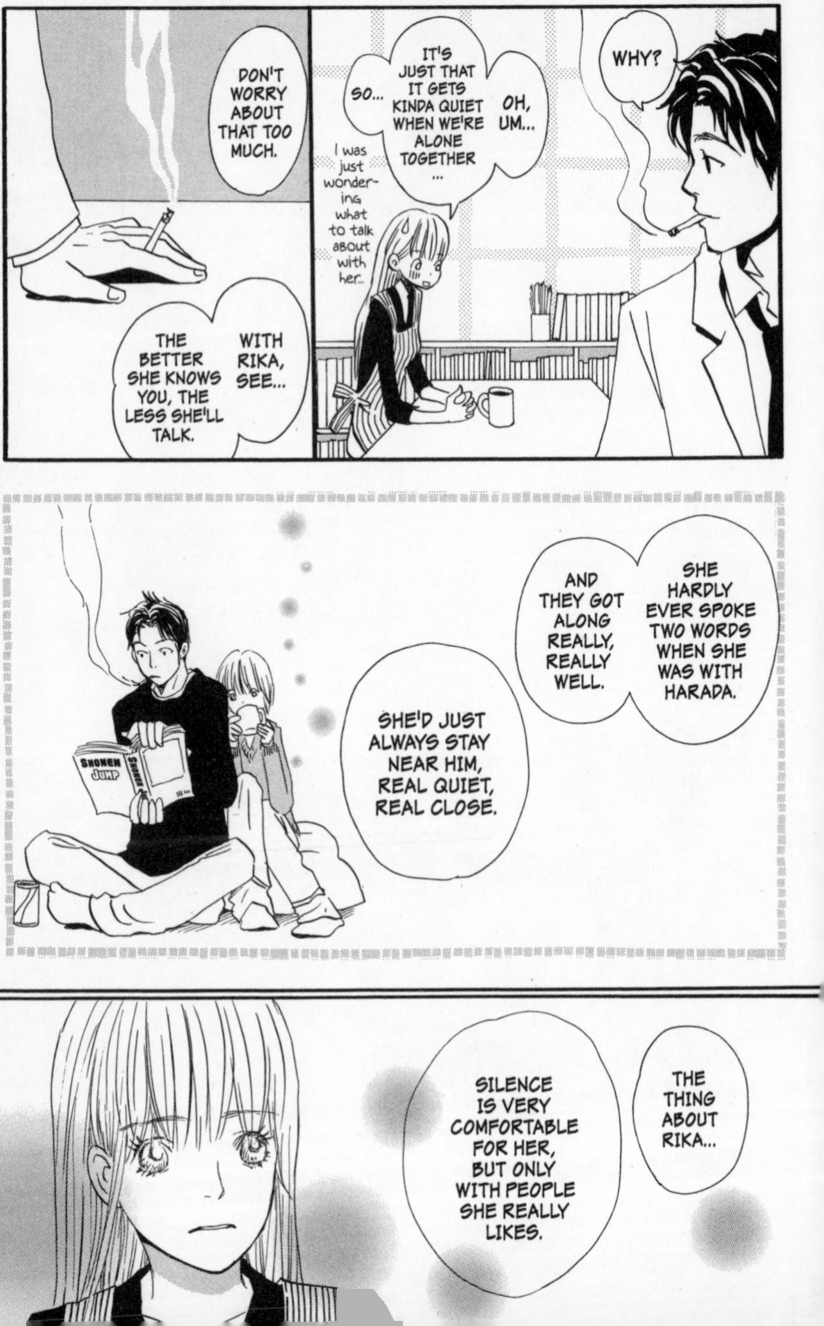
WHY?
OH, UM...
IT'S JUST THAT IT GETS KINDA QUIET WHEN WE'RE ALONE TOGETHER...
SO...
I was just wondering what to talk about with her...
DON'T WORRY ABOUT THAT TOO MUCH.
WITH RIKA, SEE...
THE BETTER SHE KNOWS YOU, THE LESS SHE'LL TALK.
SHE HARDLY EVER SPOKE TWO WORDS WHEN SHE WAS WITH HARADA.
AND THEY GOT ALONG REALLY, REALLY WELL.
SHE'D JUST ALWAYS STAY NEAR HIM, REAL QUIET, REAL CLOSE.
SHONEN JUMP
THE THING ABOUT RIKA...
SILENCE IS VERY COMFORTABLE FOR HER, BUT ONLY WITH PEOPLE SHE REALLY LIKES.

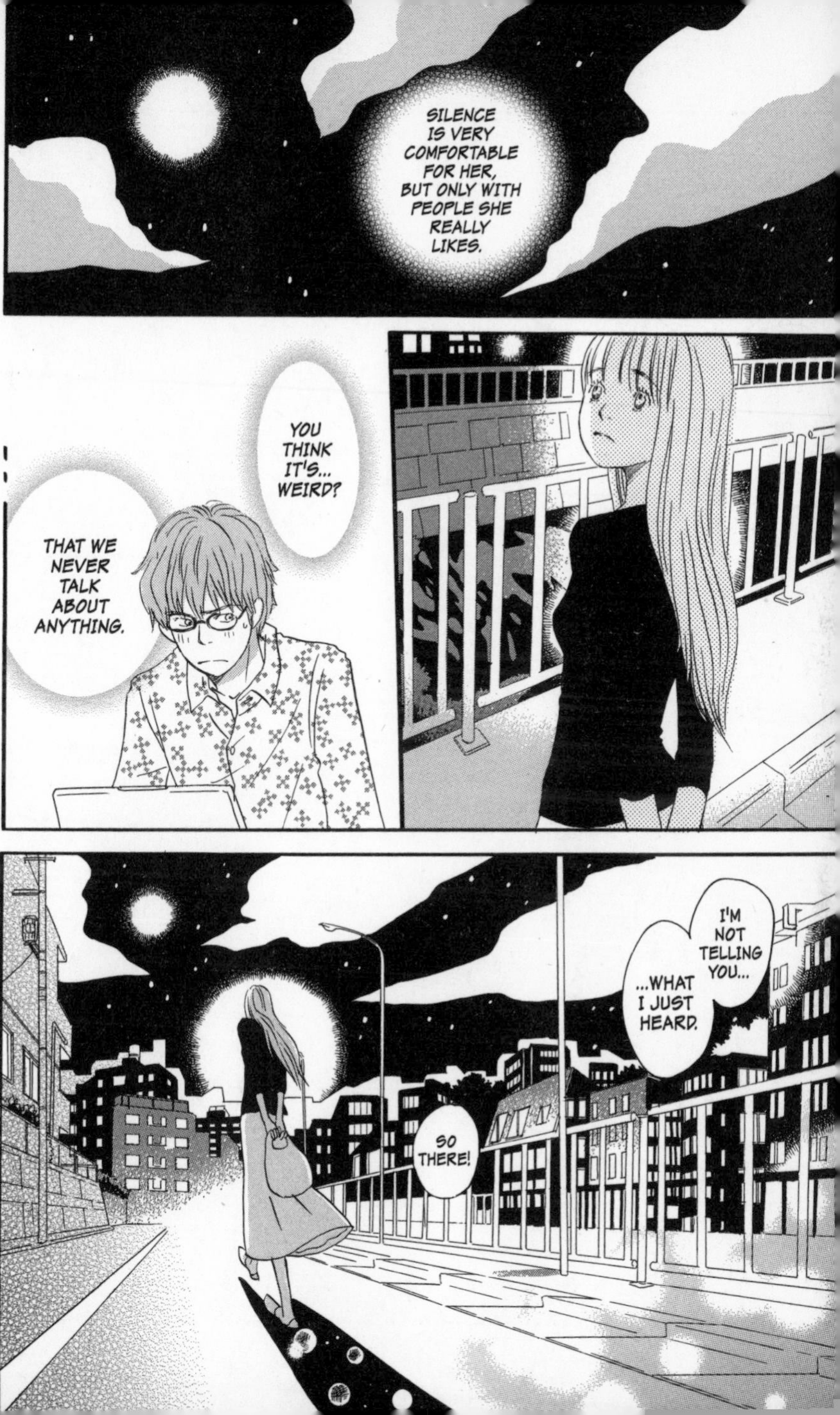
SILENCE IS VERY COMFORTABLE FOR HER, BUT ONLY WITH PEOPLE SHE REALLY LIKES.
YOU THINK IT'S... WEIRD?
THAT WE NEVER TALK ABOUT ANYTHING.
I'M NOT TELLING YOU...
...WHAT I JUST HEARD.
SO THERE!

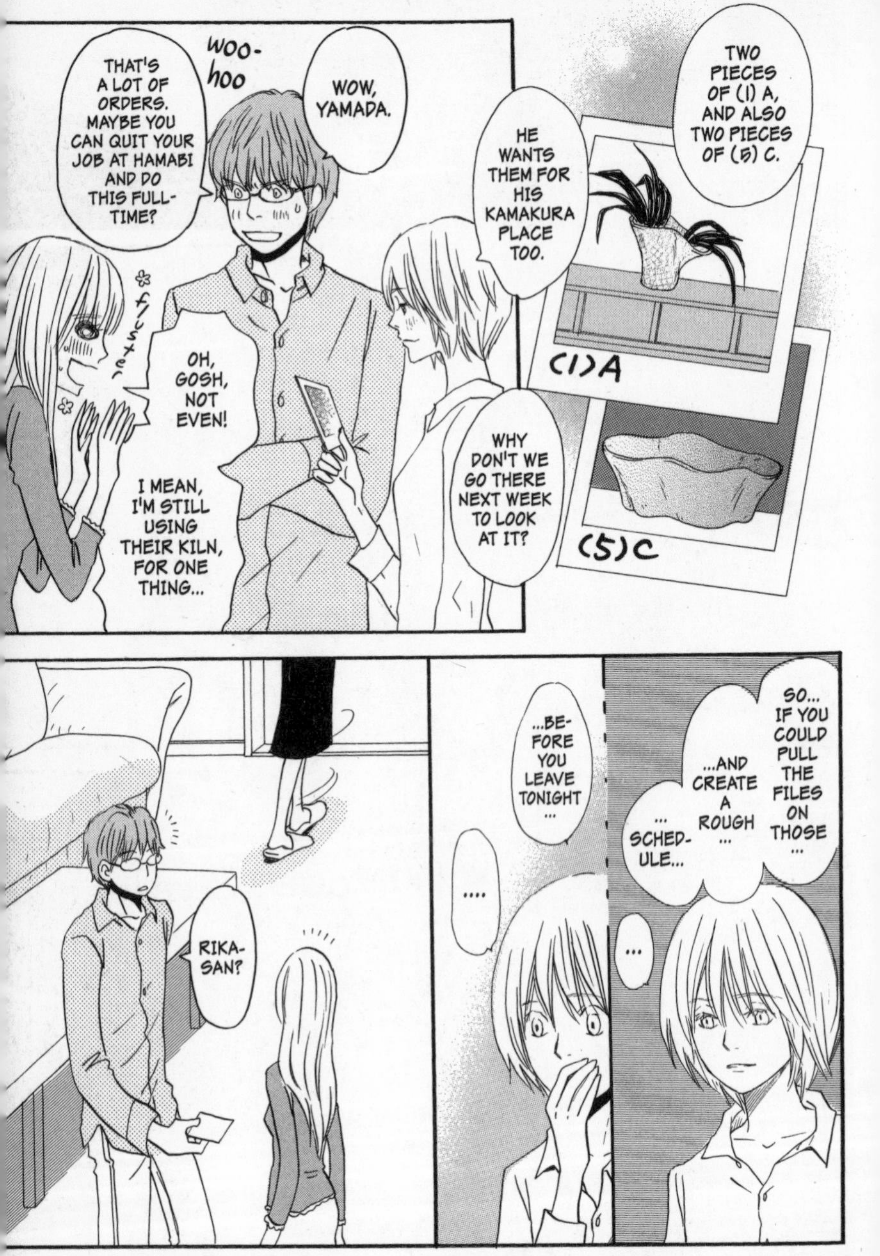
TWO PIECES OF (1) A, AND ALSO TWO PIECES OF (5) C.
HE WANTS THEM FOR HIS KAMAKURA PLACE TOO.
(1)A
(5)C
WHY DON'T WE GO THERE NEXT WEEK TO LOOK AT IT?
WOW, YAMADA.
woo-hoo
THAT'S A LOT OF ORDERS. MAYBE YOU CAN QUIT YOUR JOB AT HAMABI AND DO THIS FULL-TIME?
fluster
OH, GOSH, NOT EVEN!
I MEAN, I'M STILL USING THEIR KILN, FOR ONE THING...
SO... IF YOU COULD PULL THE FILES ON THOSE...
...AND CREATE A ROUGH...
...SCHED-ULE...
...
...BE-FORE YOU LEAVE TONIGHT...
....
RIKA-SAN?

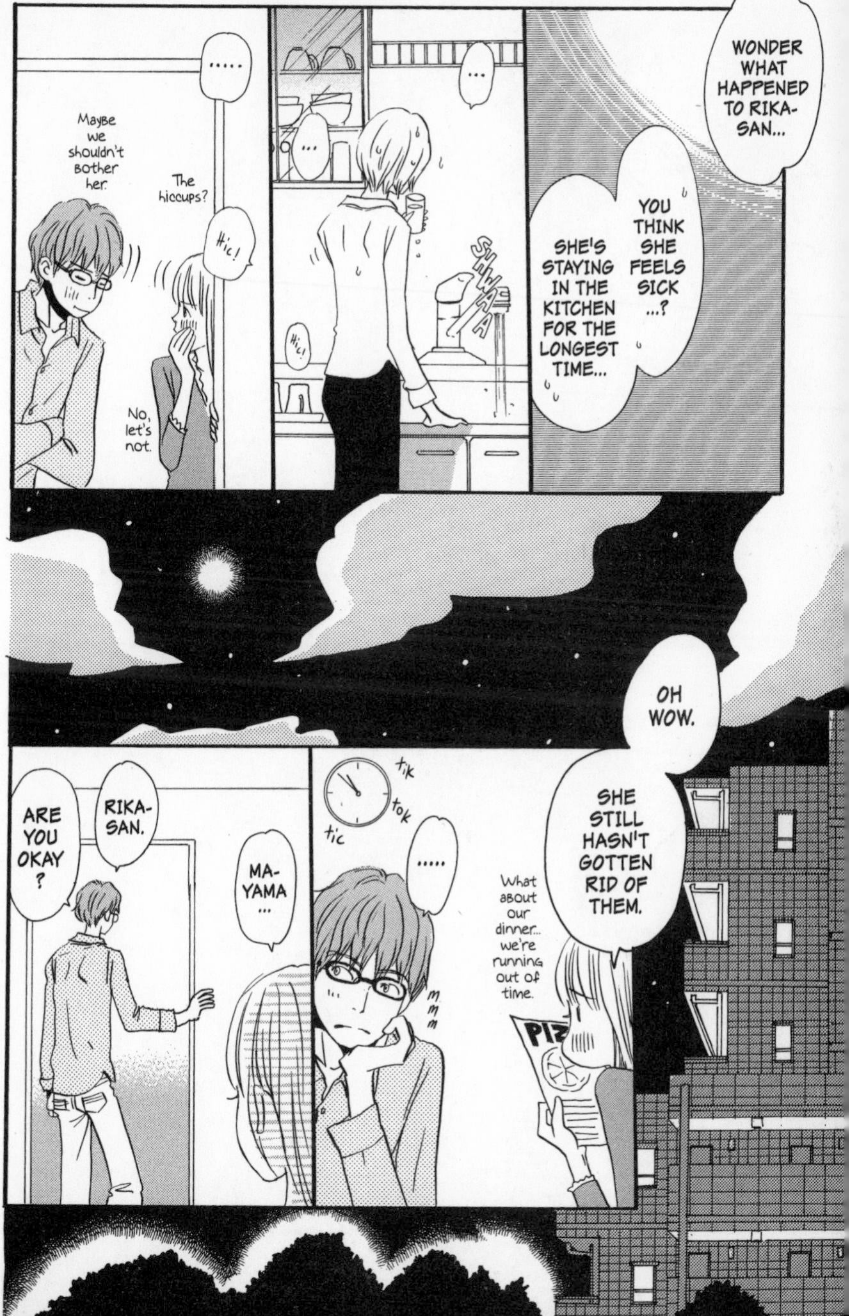
WONDER WHAT HAPPENED TO RIKA-SAN...
YOU THINK SHE FEELS SICK ...?
SHE'S STAYING IN THE KITCHEN FOR THE LONGEST TIME...
...
SHWAA
...
Hic!
.....
Hic!
The hiccups?
Maybe we shouldn't bother her.
No, let's not.
OH WOW.
SHE STILL HASN'T GOTTEN RID OF THEM.
What about our dinner... we're running out of time.
PIZ
tik
tok
tic
.....
mmm
MA-YAMA...
RIKA-SAN.
ARE YOU OKAY?

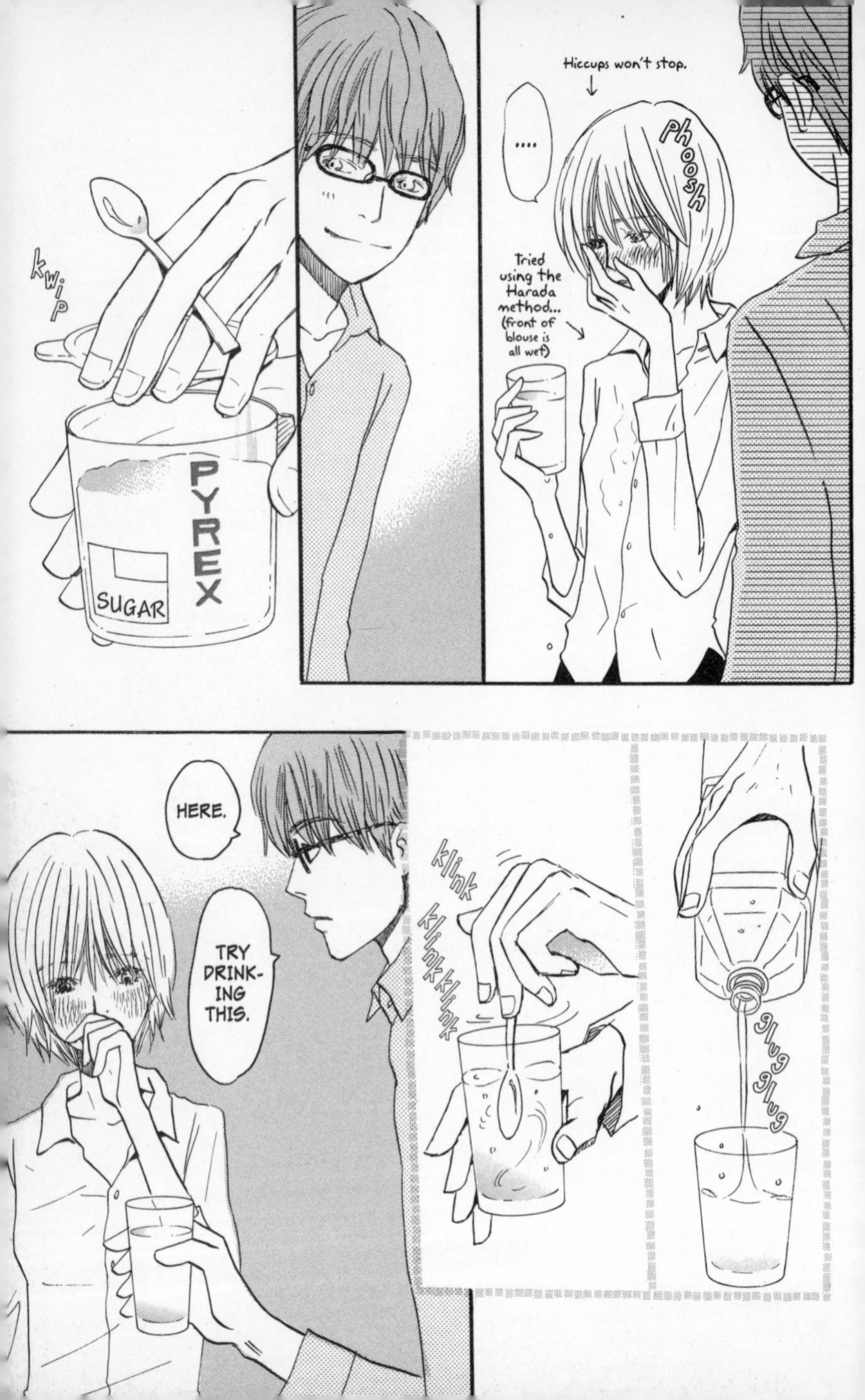
Hiccups won't stop.
....
Phoosh
Tried using the Harada method... (front of blouse is all wet)
kwip
PYREX
SUGAR
glug glug
klink klinkklink
HERE.
TRY DRINK-ING THIS.

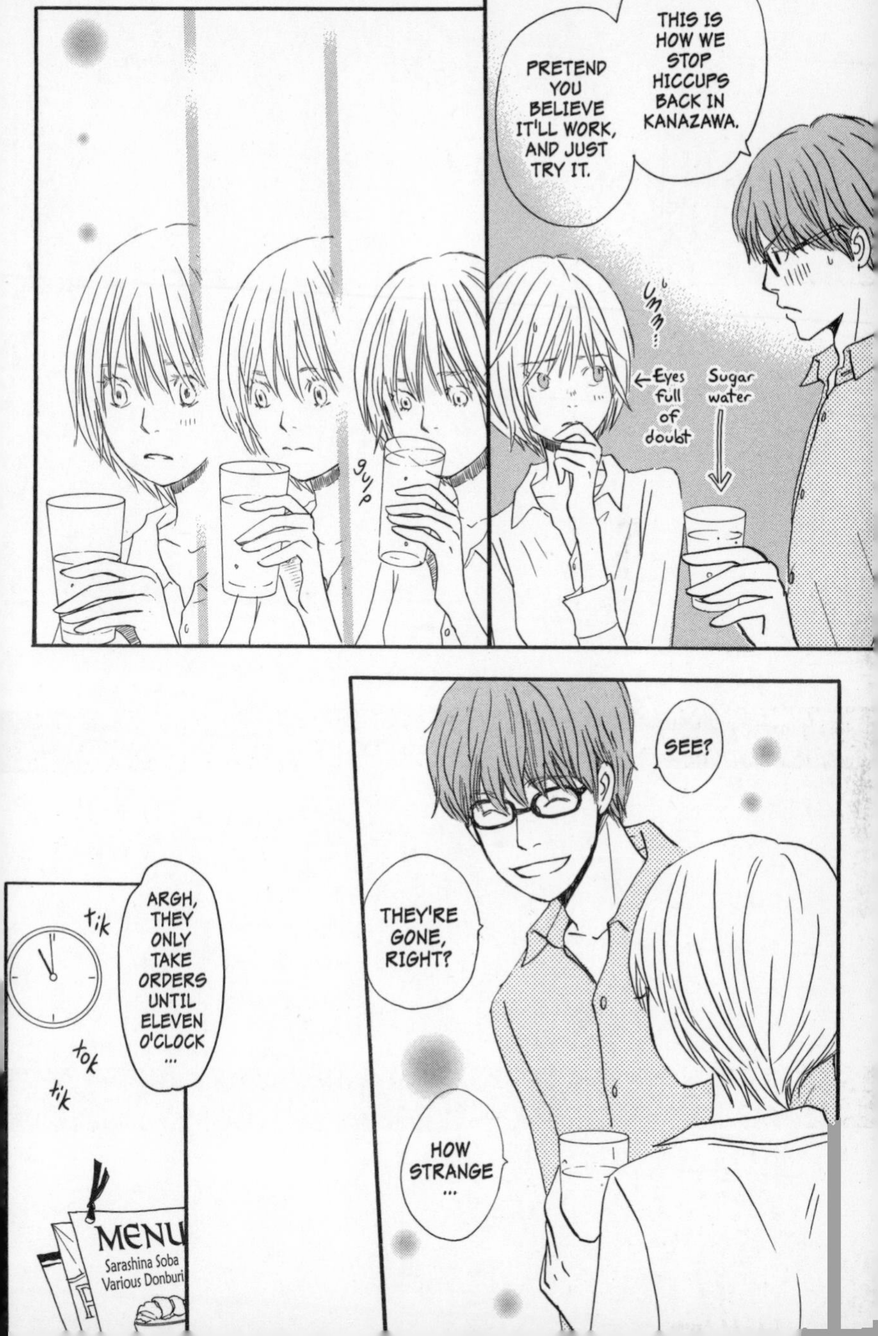
THIS IS HOW WE STOP HICCUPS BACK IN KANAZAWA.
PRETEND YOU BELIEVE IT'LL WORK, AND JUST TRY IT.
Umm...
Sugar water
Eyes full of doubt
gulp
SEE?
THEY'RE GONE, RIGHT?
HOW STRANGE...
tik
tok
tik
ARGH, THEY ONLY TAKE ORDERS UNTIL ELEVEN O'CLOCK...
MENU
Sarashina Soba
Various Donburi

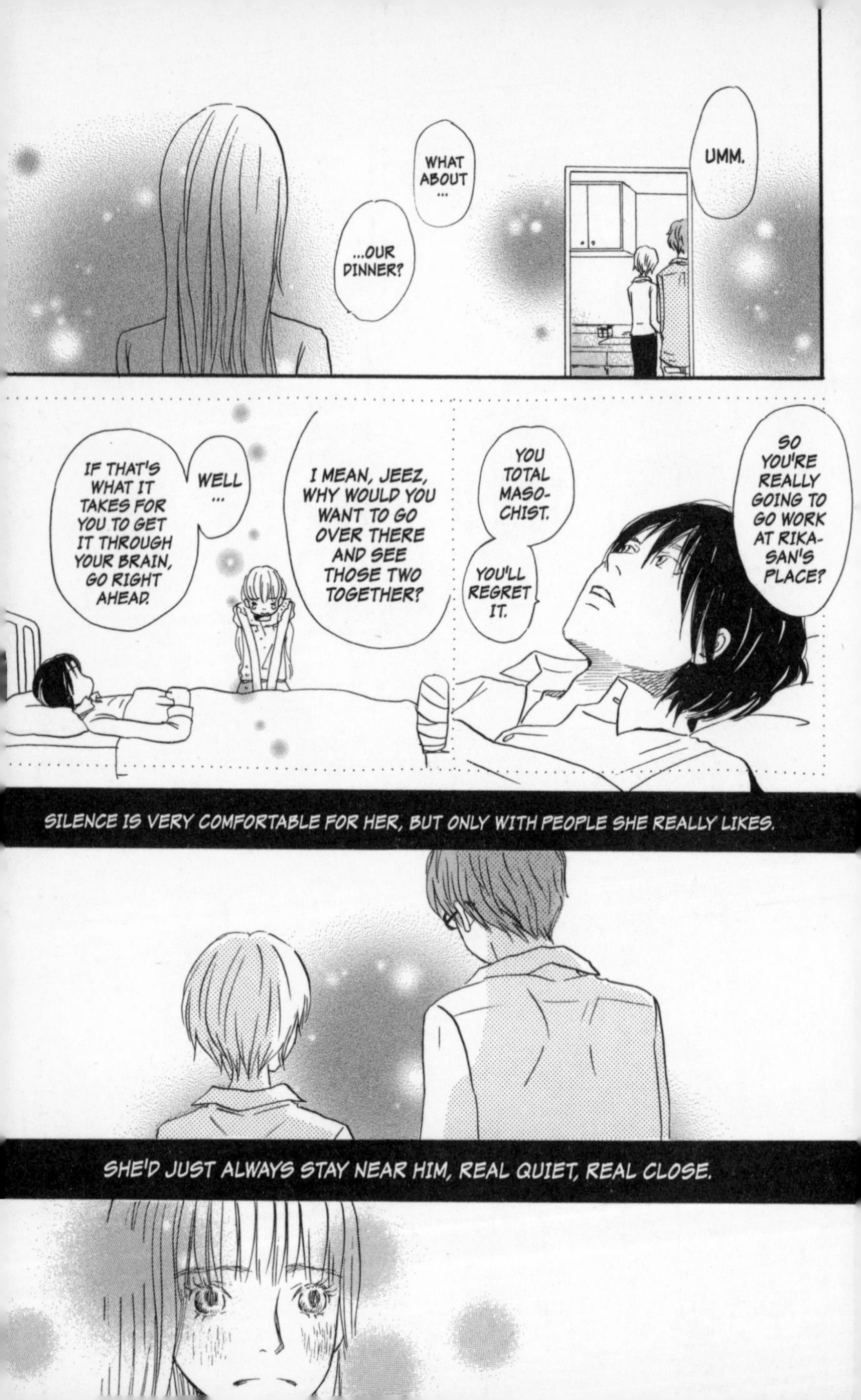
UMM.
WHAT ABOUT ...
...OUR DINNER?
SO YOU'RE REALLY GOING TO GO WORK AT RIKA-SAN'S PLACE?
YOU TOTAL MASO-CHIST.
YOU'LL REGRET IT.
I MEAN, JEEZ, WHY WOULD YOU WANT TO GO OVER THERE AND SEE THOSE TWO TOGETHER?
WELL ...
IF THAT'S WHAT IT TAKES FOR YOU TO GET IT THROUGH YOUR BRAIN, GO RIGHT AHEAD.
SILENCE IS VERY COMFORTABLE FOR HER, BUT ONLY WITH PEOPLE SHE REALLY LIKES.
SHE'D JUST ALWAYS STAY NEAR HIM, REAL QUIET, REAL CLOSE.

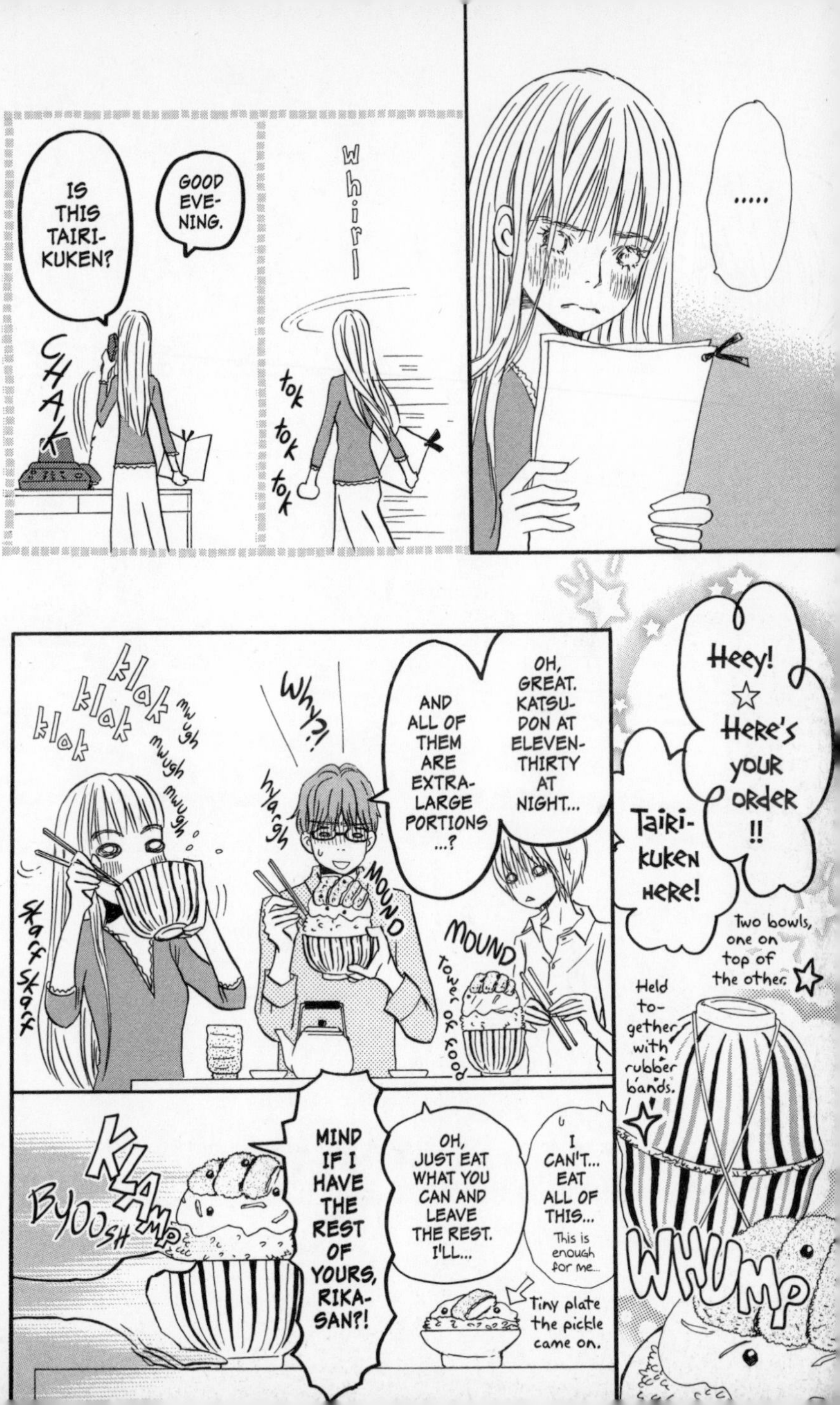
.....
whirl
tok tok tok
GOOD EVENING.
IS THIS TAIRIKUKEN?
CHAK
Heey! ☆ Here's your order!!
Tairikuken here!
Two bowls, one on top of the other. ☆
Held together with rubber bands.
WHUMP
OH, GREAT. KATSUDON AT ELEVEN-THIRTY AT NIGHT...
AND ALL OF THEM ARE EXTRA-LARGE PORTIONS...?
Why?!
hyagh
MOUND
MOUND
tower of food
klak klak klak
mwugh mwugh mwugh
skarf skarf
I CAN'T... EAT ALL OF THIS...
This is enough for me...
Tiny plate the pickle came on.
OH, JUST EAT WHAT YOU CAN AND LEAVE THE REST. I'LL...
MIND IF I HAVE THE REST OF YOURS, RIKA-SAN?!
KLAMP
BYOOSH

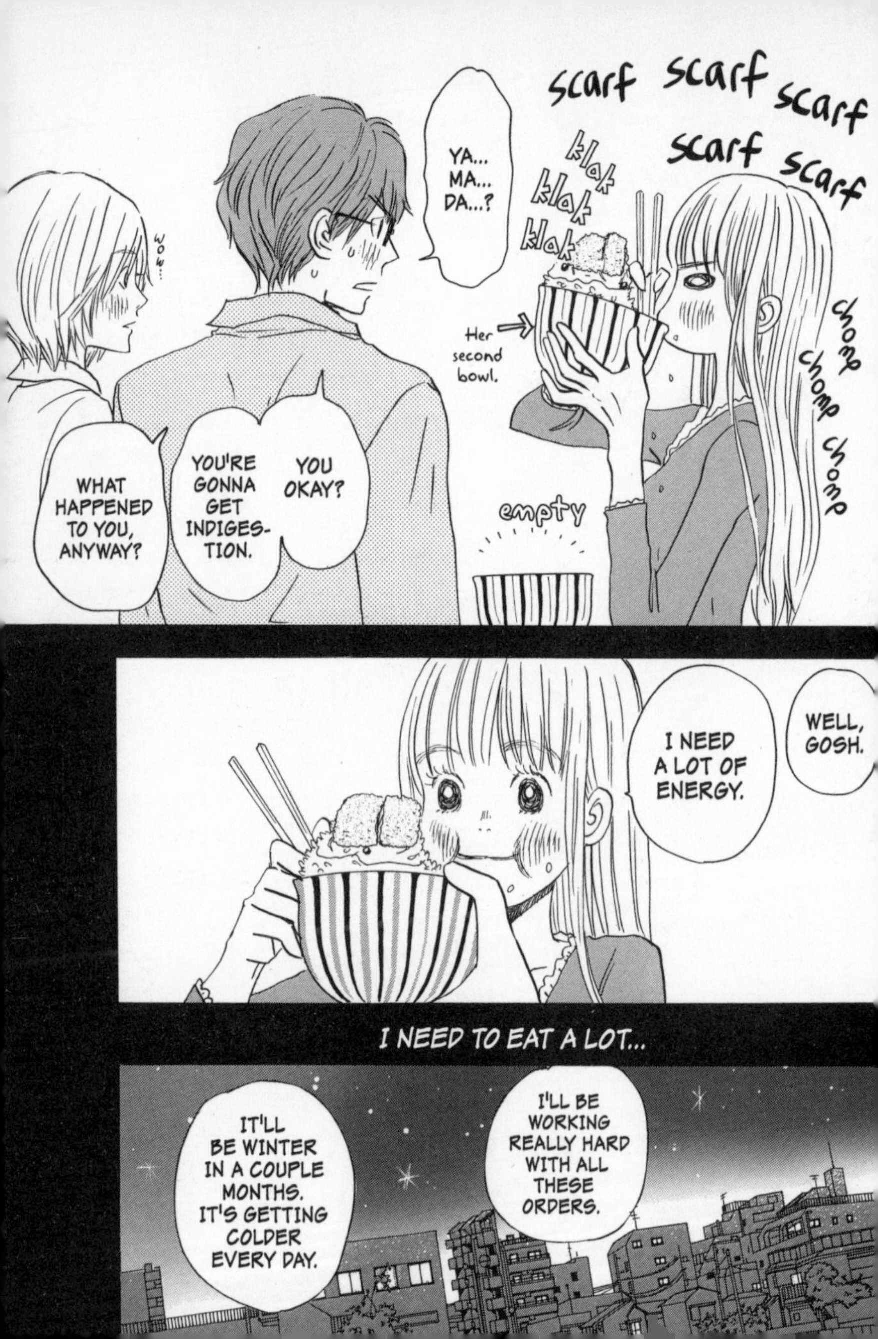
scarf scarf scarf
scarf scarf
chomp chomp chomp
klak klak klak
YA... MA... DA...?
Her second bowl.
wow...
empty
YOU OKAY?
YOU'RE GONNA GET INDIGES-TION.
WHAT HAPPENED TO YOU, ANYWAY?
WELL, GOSH.
I NEED A LOT OF ENERGY.
I NEED TO EAT A LOT...
I'LL BE WORKING REALLY HARD WITH ALL THESE ORDERS.
IT'LL BE WINTER IN A COUPLE MONTHS. IT'S GETTING COLDER EVERY DAY.

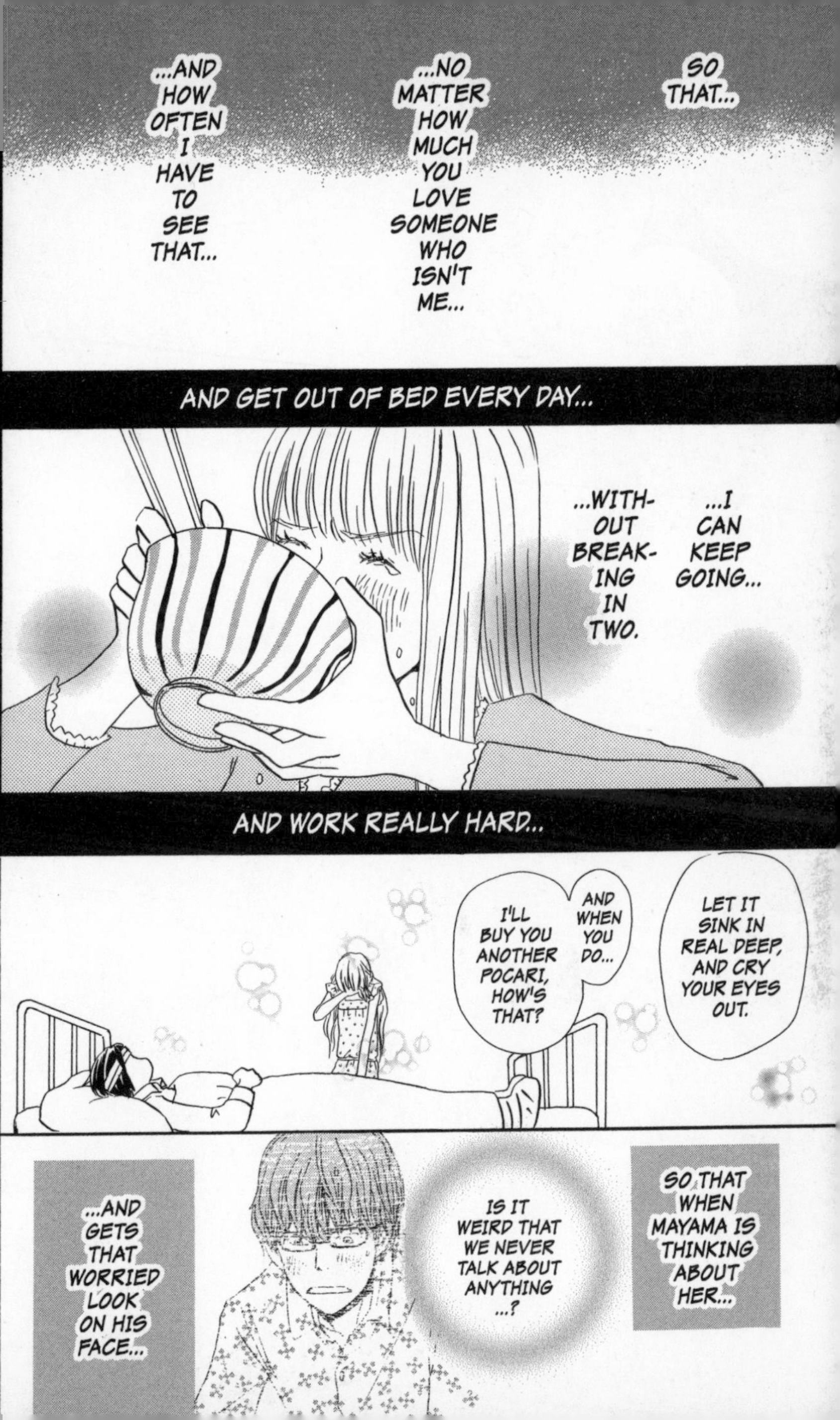
SO THAT...
...NO MATTER HOW MUCH YOU LOVE SOMEONE WHO ISN'T ME...
...AND HOW OFTEN I HAVE TO SEE THAT...
AND GET OUT OF BED EVERY DAY...
...I CAN KEEP GOING...
...WITH-OUT BREAK-ING IN TWO.
AND WORK REALLY HARD...
LET IT SINK IN REAL DEEP, AND CRY YOUR EYES OUT.
AND WHEN YOU DO...
I'LL BUY YOU ANOTHER POCARI, HOW'S THAT?
SO THAT WHEN MAYAMA IS THINKING ABOUT HER...
IS IT WEIRD THAT WE NEVER TALK ABOUT ANYTHING ...?
...AND GETS THAT WORRIED LOOK ON HIS FACE...

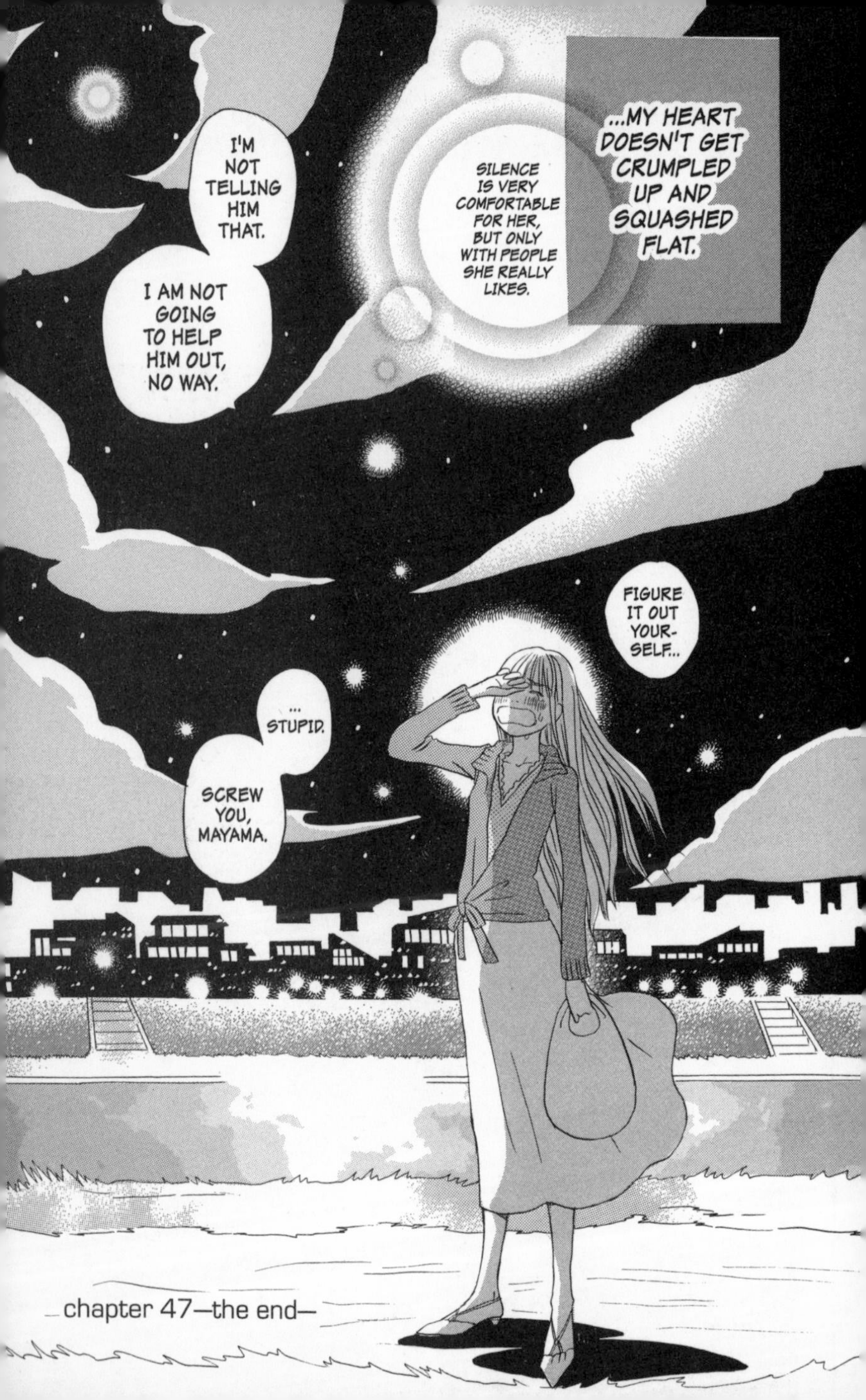
...MY HEART DOESN'T GET CRUMPLED UP AND SQUASHED FLAT.
SILENCE IS VERY COMFORTABLE FOR HER, BUT ONLY WITH PEOPLE SHE REALLY LIKES.
I'M NOT TELLING HIM THAT.
I AM NOT GOING TO HELP HIM OUT, NO WAY.
FIGURE IT OUT YOUR-SELF...
... STUPID.
SCREW YOU, MAYAMA.
chapter 47—the end—

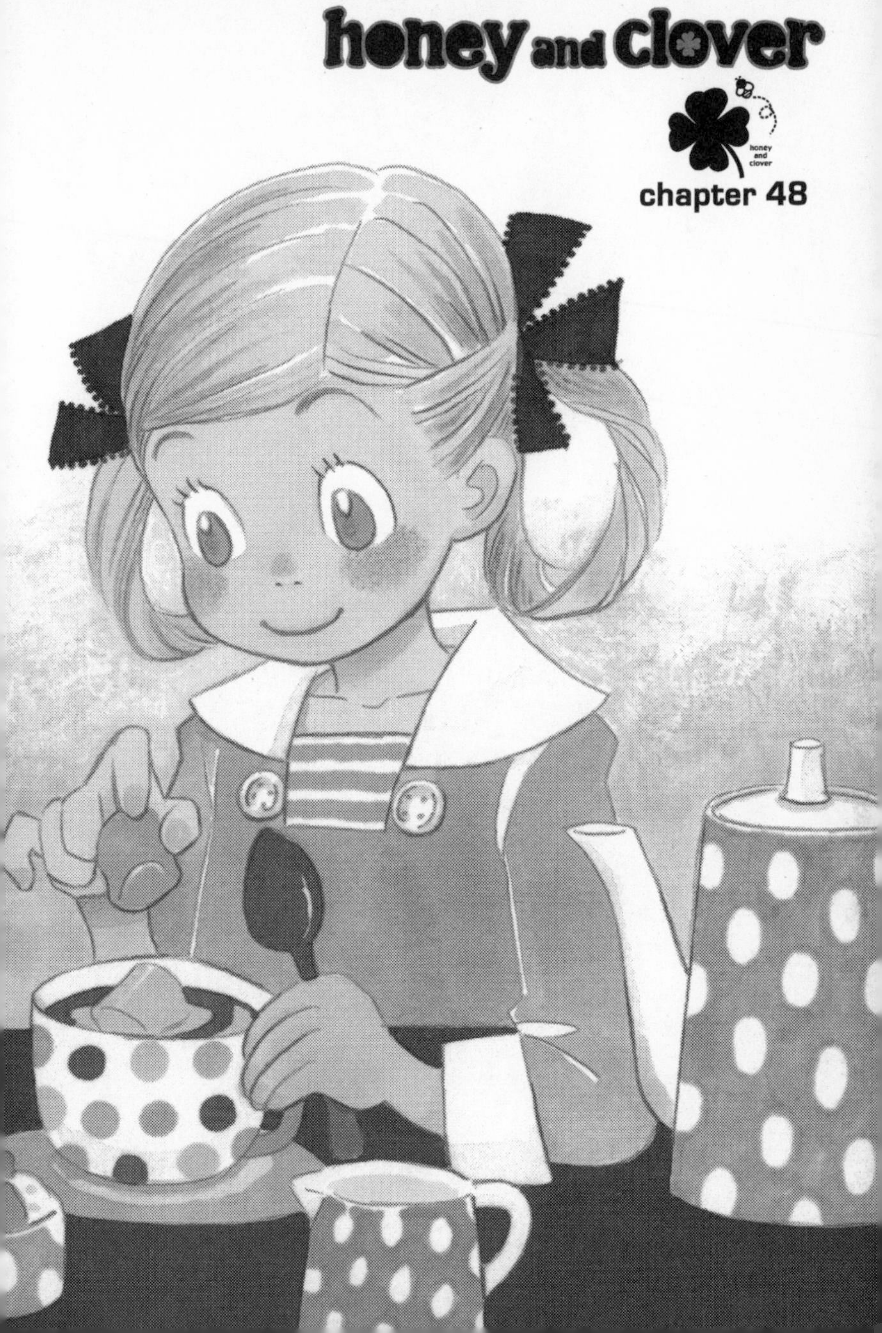
honey and clover
honey and clover
chapter 48

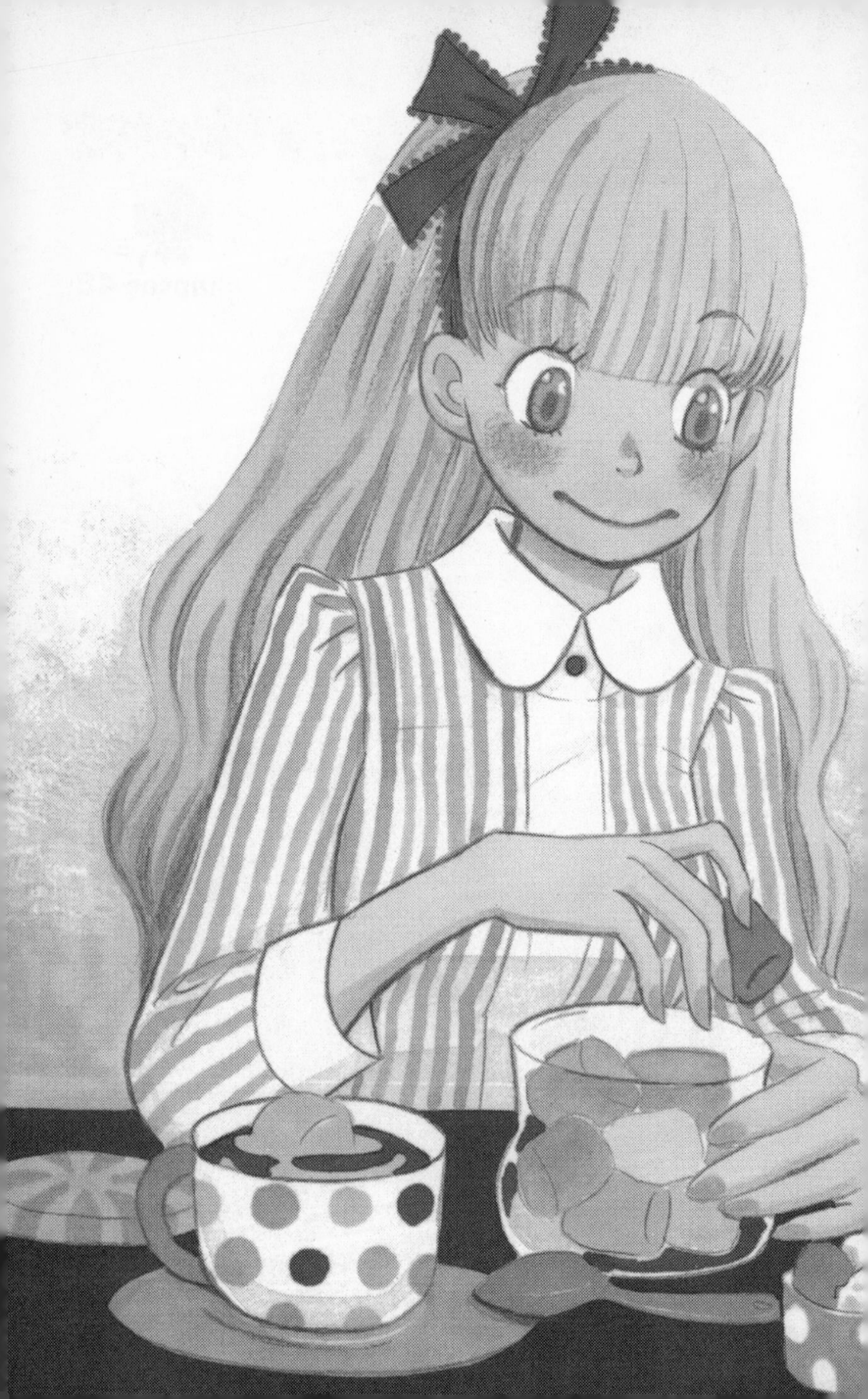

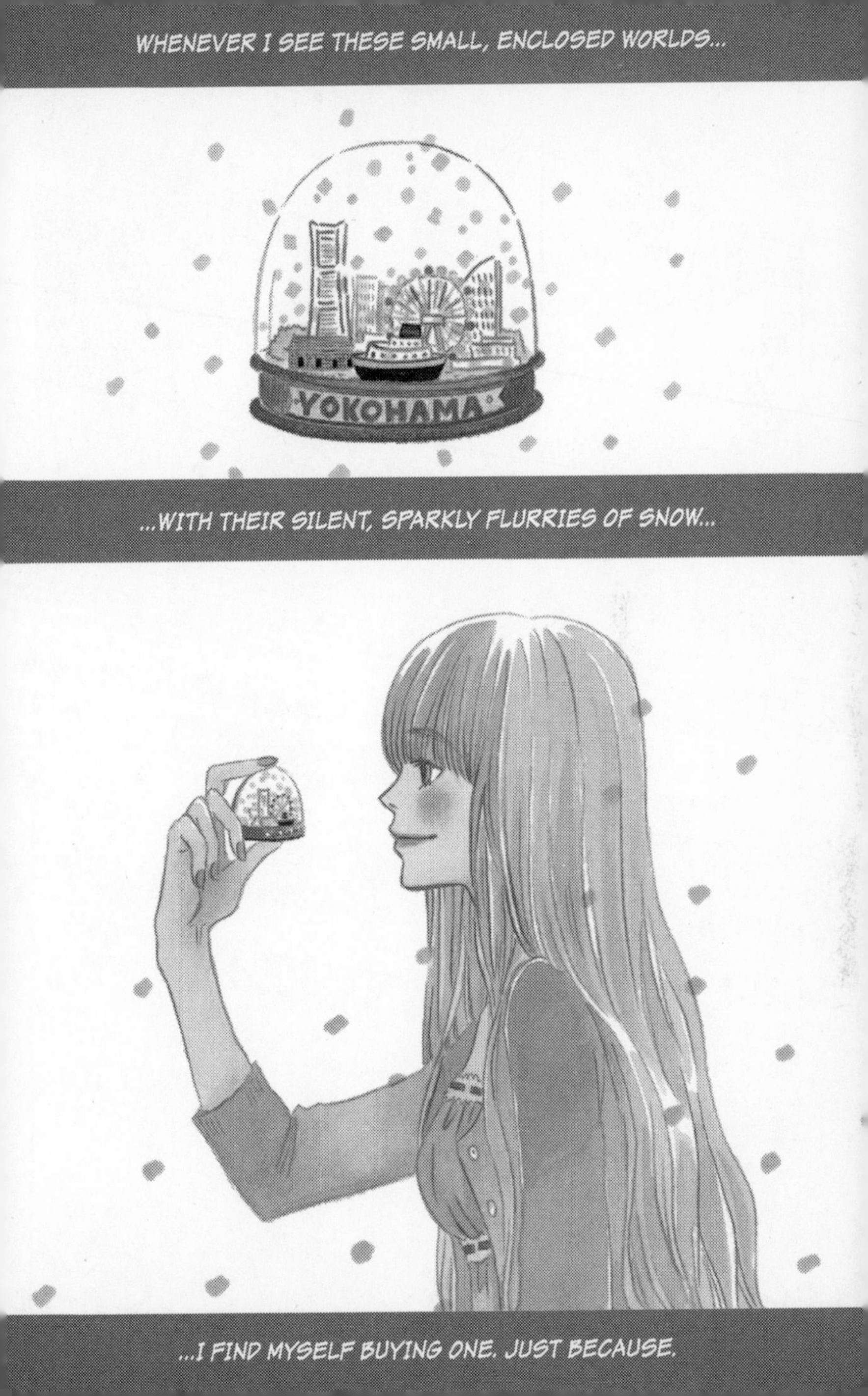
WHENEVER I SEE THESE SMALL, ENCLOSED WORLDS...
YOKOHAMA
...WITH THEIR SILENT, SPARKLY FLURRIES OF SNOW...
...I FIND MYSELF BUYING ONE. JUST BECAUSE.

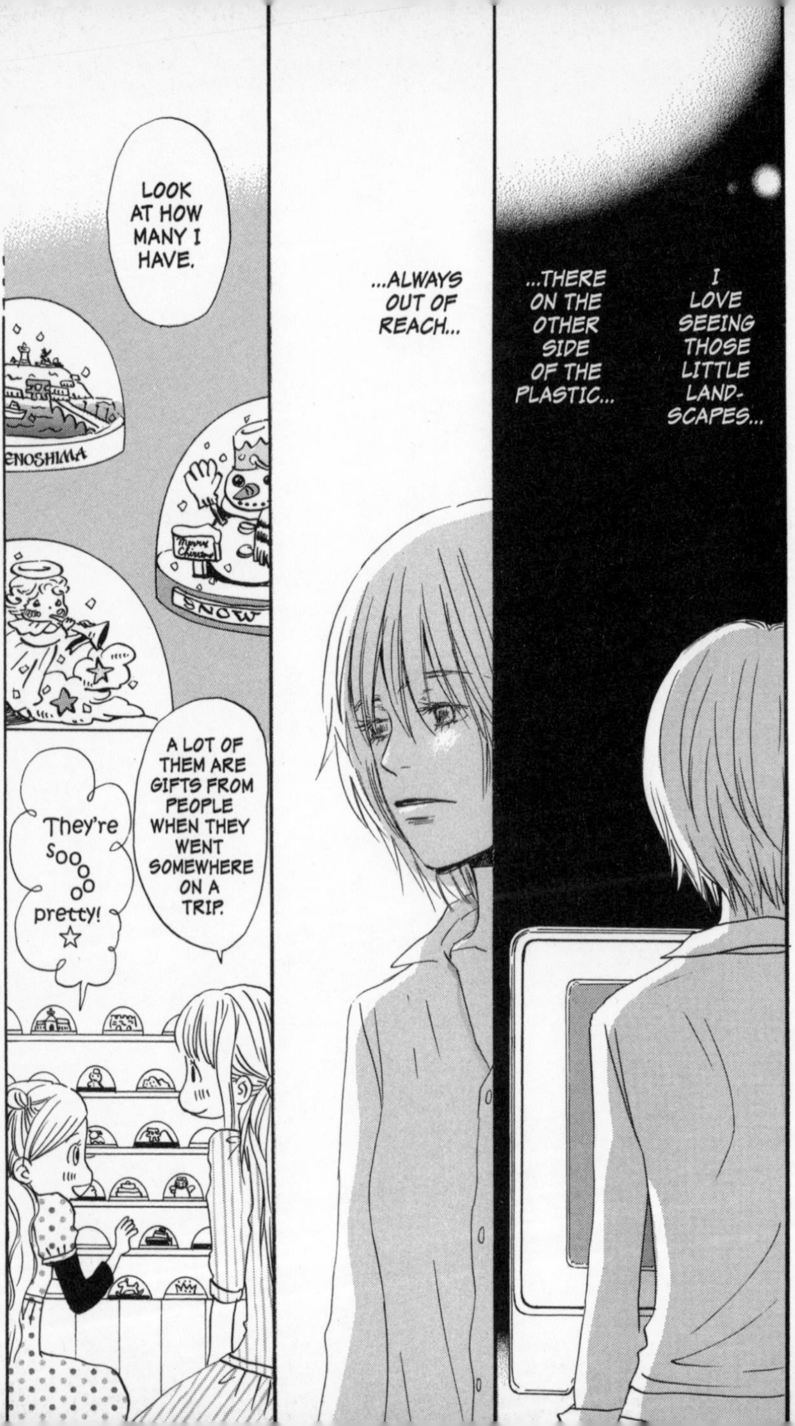
I LOVE SEEING THOSE LITTLE LANDSCAPES...
...THERE ON THE OTHER SIDE OF THE PLASTIC...
...ALWAYS OUT OF REACH...
LOOK AT HOW MANY I HAVE.
ENOSHIMA
SNOW
A LOT OF THEM ARE GIFTS FROM PEOPLE WHEN THEY WENT SOMEWHERE ON A TRIP.
They're soooooo pretty! ☆

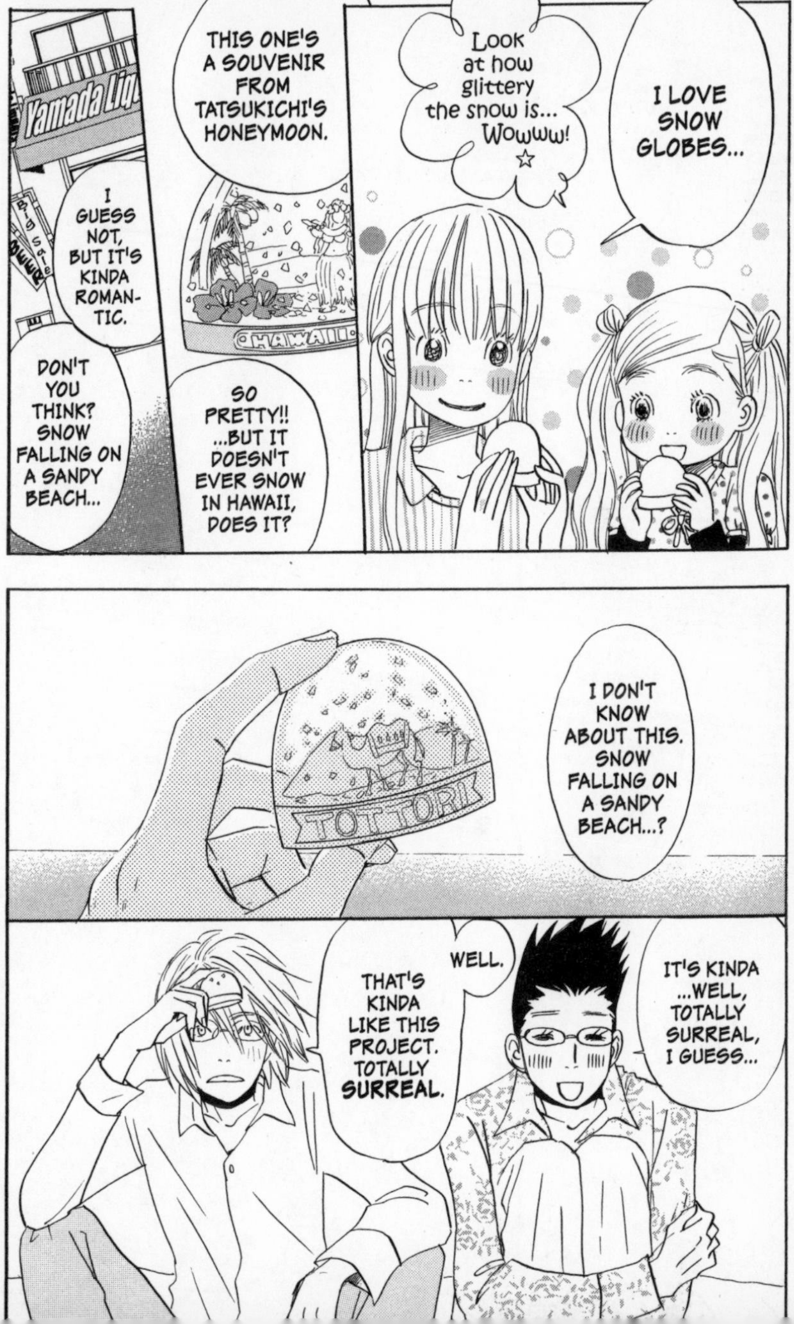
I LOVE SNOW GLOBES...
Look at how glittery the snow is... Wowww! ☆
THIS ONE'S A SOUVENIR FROM TATSUKICHI'S HONEYMOON.
HAWAII
SO PRETTY!! ...BUT IT DOESN'T EVER SNOW IN HAWAII, DOES IT?
Yamada Liq
Big Sale
I GUESS NOT, BUT IT'S KINDA ROMANTIC.
DON'T YOU THINK? SNOW FALLING ON A SANDY BEACH...
I DON'T KNOW ABOUT THIS. SNOW FALLING ON A SANDY BEACH...?
TOTTORI
IT'S KINDA ...WELL, TOTALLY SURREAL, I GUESS...
WELL.
THAT'S KINDA LIKE THIS PROJECT. TOTALLY SURREAL.

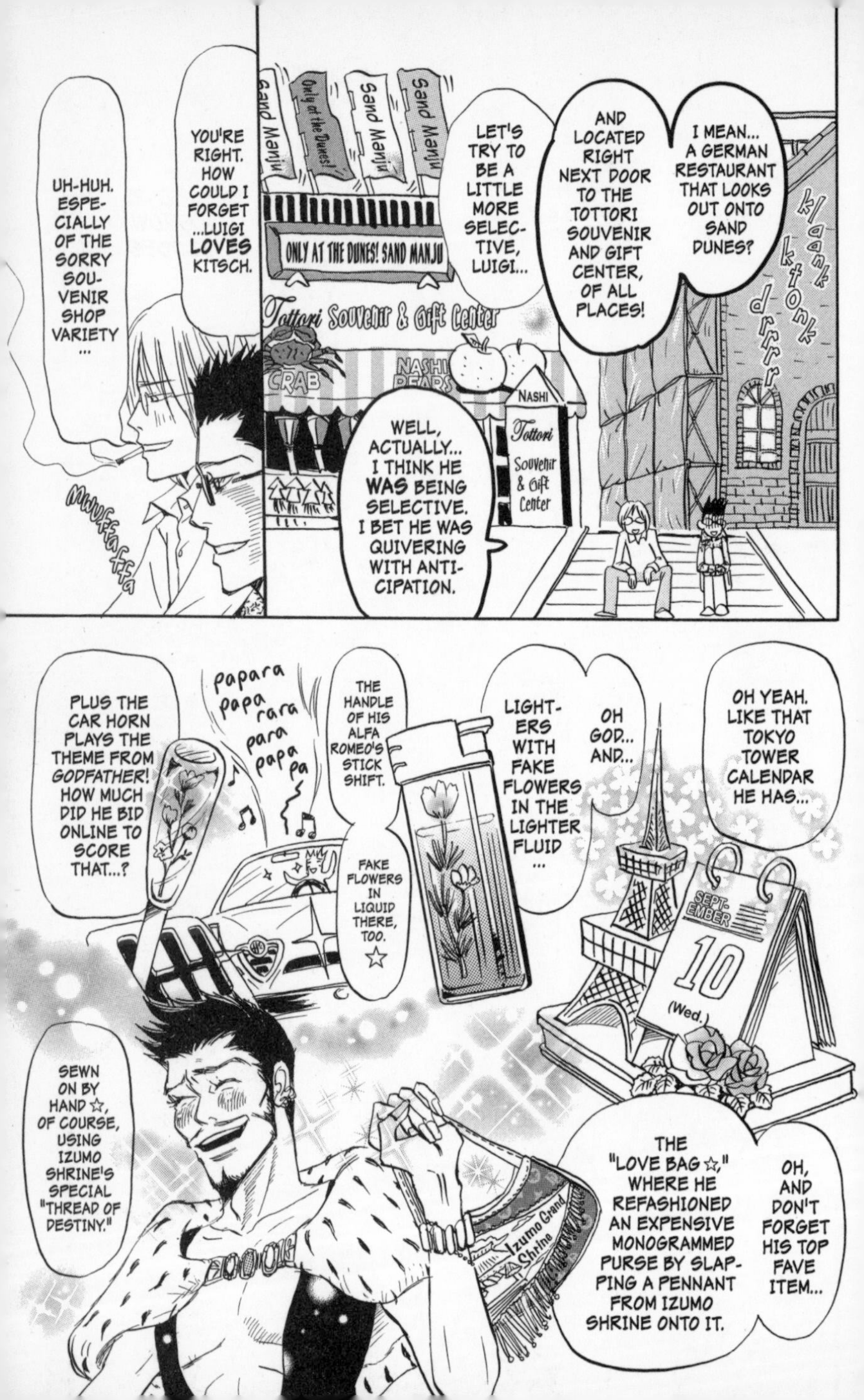
I MEAN... A GERMAN RESTAURANT THAT LOOKS OUT ONTO SAND DUNES?
AND LOCATED RIGHT NEXT DOOR TO THE TOTTORI SOUVENIR AND GIFT CENTER, OF ALL PLACES!
klaank ktonk drrrr
Sand Manju
Sand Manju
Only at the Dunes!
Sand Manju
LET'S TRY TO BE A LITTLE MORE SELECTIVE, LUIGI...
ONLY AT THE DUNES! SAND MANJU
Tottori Souvenir & Gift Center
CRAB
NASHI PEARS
NASHI Tottori Souvenir & Gift Center
WELL, ACTUALLY... I THINK HE WAS BEING SELECTIVE. I BET HE WAS QUIVERING WITH ANTICIPATION.
YOU'RE RIGHT. HOW COULD I FORGET ...LUIGI LOVES KITSCH.
UH-HUH. ESPECIALLY OF THE SORRY SOUVENIR SHOP VARIETY...
mwuffaffa
OH YEAH. LIKE THAT TOKYO TOWER CALENDAR HE HAS...
OH GOD... AND...
LIGHTERS WITH FAKE FLOWERS IN THE LIGHTER FLUID...
THE HANDLE OF HIS ALFA ROMEO'S STICK SHIFT.
FAKE FLOWERS IN LIQUID THERE, TOO. ☆
papara papa rara para papa pa
PLUS THE CAR HORN PLAYS THE THEME FROM GODFATHER! HOW MUCH DID HE BID ONLINE TO SCORE THAT...?
SEPT-EMBER 10 (Wed.)
OH, AND DON'T FORGET HIS TOP FAVE ITEM...
THE "LOVE BAG☆," WHERE HE REFASHIONED AN EXPENSIVE MONOGRAMMED PURSE BY SLAPPING A PENNANT FROM IZUMO SHRINE ONTO IT.
Izumo Grand Shrine
SEWN ON BY HAND☆, OF COURSE, USING IZUMO SHRINE'S SPECIAL "THREAD OF DESTINY."

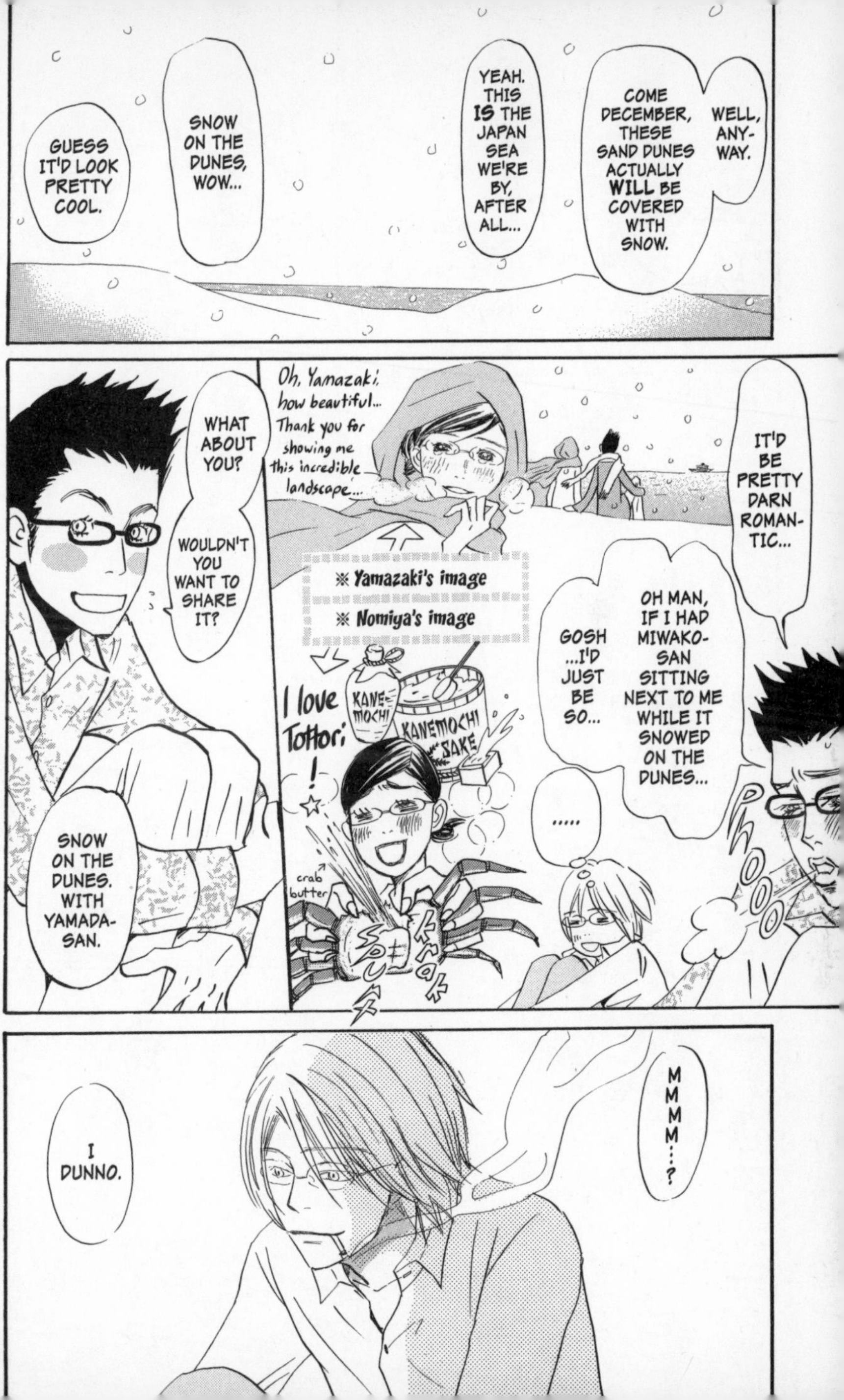
WELL, ANYWAY.
COME DECEMBER, THESE SAND DUNES ACTUALLY WILL BE COVERED WITH SNOW.
YEAH. THIS IS THE JAPAN SEA WE'RE BY, AFTER ALL...
SNOW ON THE DUNES, WOW...
GUESS IT'D LOOK PRETTY COOL.
IT'D BE PRETTY DARN ROMANTIC...
OH MAN, IF I HAD MIWAKO-SAN SITTING NEXT TO ME WHILE IT SNOWED ON THE DUNES...
GOSH ...I'D JUST BE SO...
PHOOO
.....
Oh, Yamazaki, how beautiful... Thank you for showing me this incredible landscape...
※ Yamazaki's image
※ Nomiya's image
KANEMOCHI
KANEMOCHI SAKE
I love Tottori!
crab butter
krak
SPLUX
WHAT ABOUT YOU?
WOULDN'T YOU WANT TO SHARE IT?
SNOW ON THE DUNES. WITH YAMADA-SAN.
MMMM...?
I DUNNO.

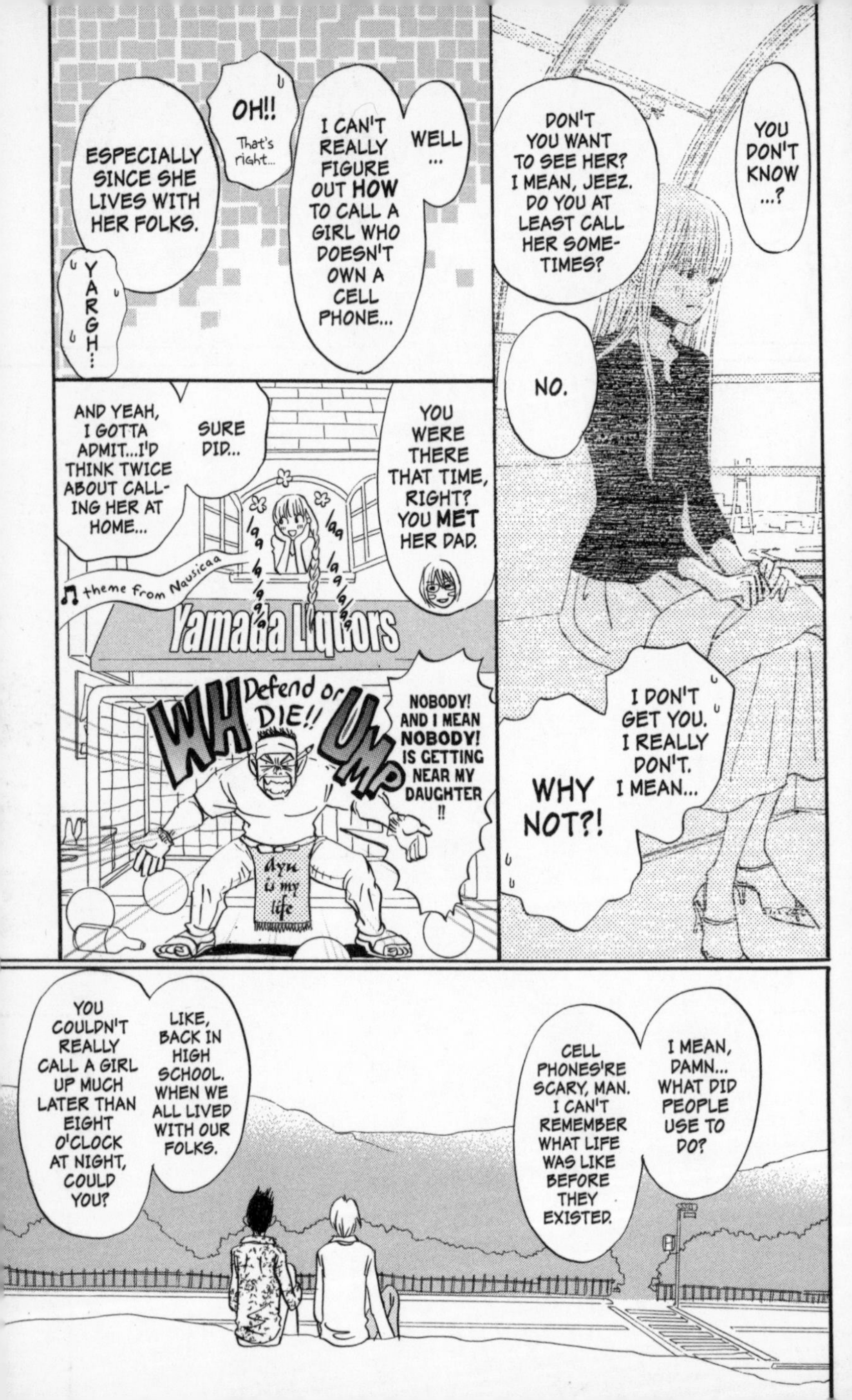
YOU DON'T KNOW ...?
DON'T YOU WANT TO SEE HER? I MEAN, JEEZ. DO YOU AT LEAST CALL HER SOME-TIMES?
NO.
I DON'T GET YOU. I REALLY DON'T. I MEAN...
WHY NOT?!
WELL ...
I CAN'T REALLY FIGURE OUT HOW TO CALL A GIRL WHO DOESN'T OWN A CELL PHONE...
OH!! That's right...
ESPECIALLY SINCE SHE LIVES WITH HER FOLKS.
YARGH...
YOU WERE THERE THAT TIME, RIGHT? YOU MET HER DAD.
SURE DID...
AND YEAH, I GOTTA ADMIT...I'D THINK TWICE ABOUT CALLING HER AT HOME...
♫ theme from Nausicaa
la la la la la la la la la la la la
Yamada Liquors
WHUMP
Defend or DIE!!
NOBODY! AND I MEAN NOBODY! IS GETTING NEAR MY DAUGHTER!!
Ayu is my life
I MEAN, DAMN... WHAT DID PEOPLE USE TO DO?
CELL PHONES'RE SCARY, MAN. I CAN'T REMEMBER WHAT LIFE WAS LIKE BEFORE THEY EXISTED.
LIKE, BACK IN HIGH SCHOOL. WHEN WE ALL LIVED WITH OUR FOLKS.
YOU COULDN'T REALLY CALL A GIRL UP MUCH LATER THAN EIGHT O'CLOCK AT NIGHT, COULD YOU?

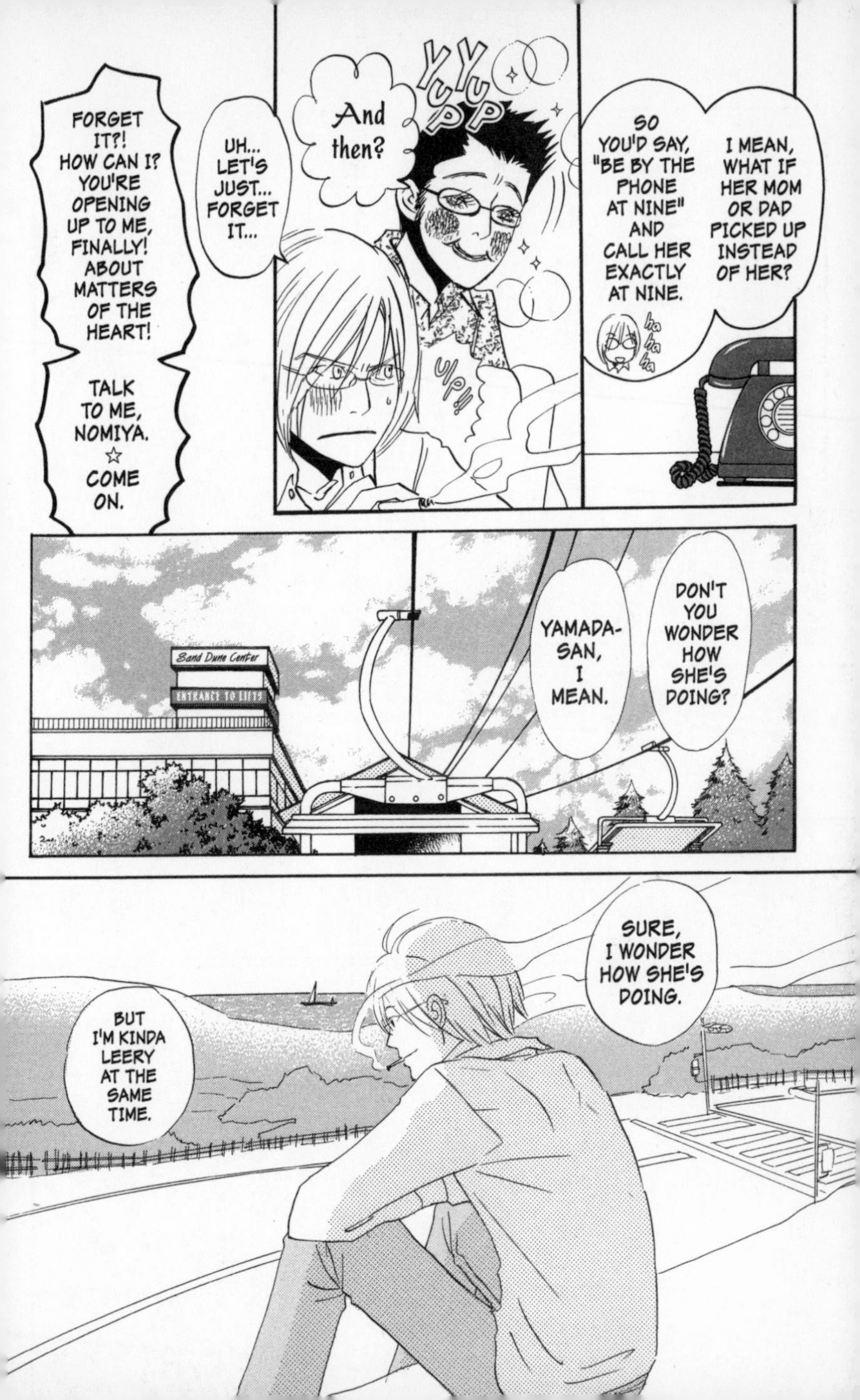
I MEAN, WHAT IF HER MOM OR DAD PICKED UP INSTEAD OF HER?
SO YOU'D SAY, "BE BY THE PHONE AT NINE" AND CALL HER EXACTLY AT NINE.
ha ha ha
YUP YUP
And then?
UP!!
UH... LET'S JUST... FORGET IT...
FORGET IT?! HOW CAN I? YOU'RE OPENING UP TO ME, FINALLY! ABOUT MATTERS OF THE HEART!
TALK TO ME, NOMIYA. ☆ COME ON.
DON'T YOU WONDER HOW SHE'S DOING?
YAMADA-SAN, I MEAN.
Sand Dune Center
ENTRANCE TO LIFTS
SURE, I WONDER HOW SHE'S DOING.
BUT I'M KINDA LEERY AT THE SAME TIME.

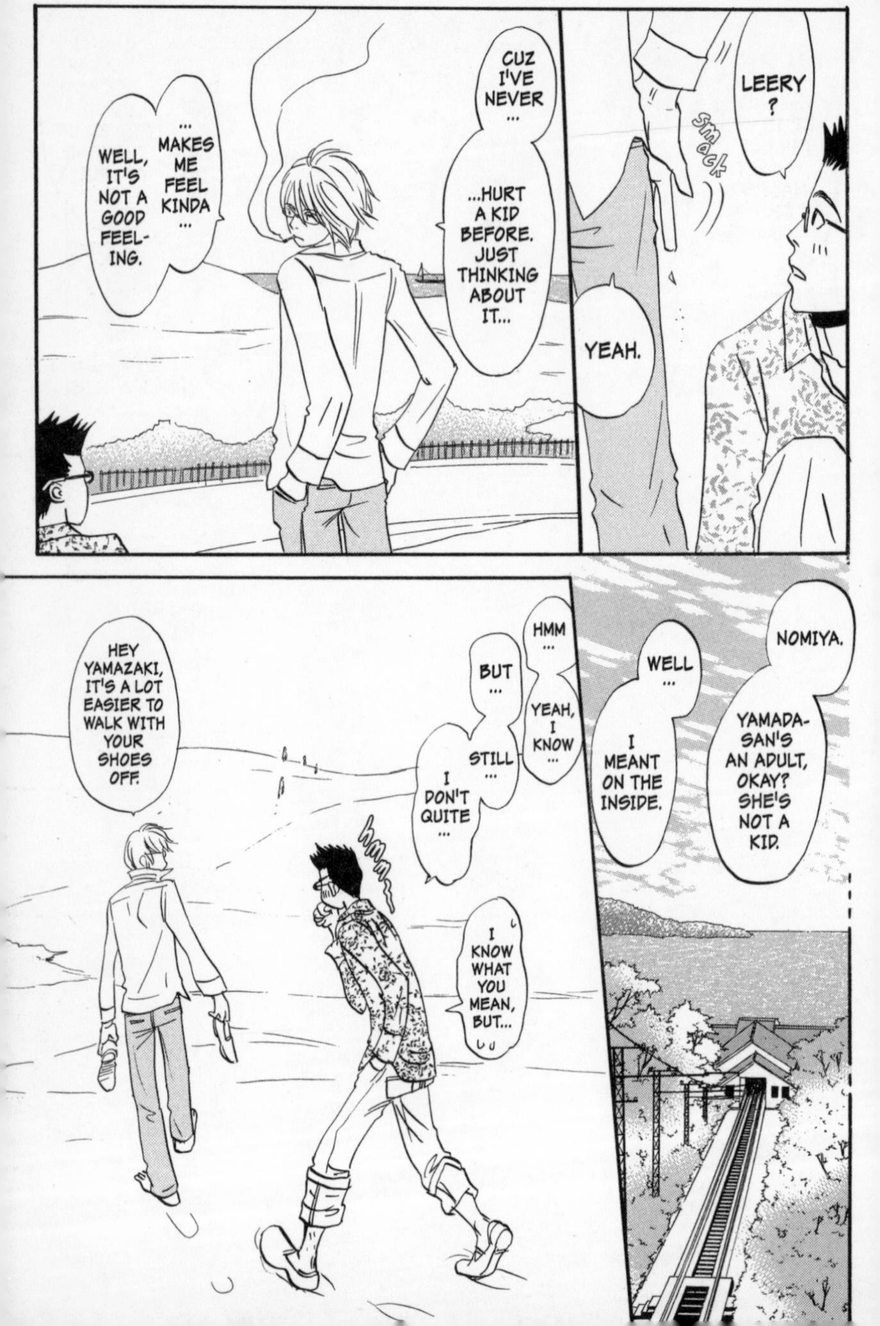
LEERY ?
Smack
YEAH.
CUZ I'VE NEVER ...
...HURT A KID BEFORE. JUST THINKING ABOUT IT...
... MAKES ME FEEL KINDA ...
WELL, IT'S NOT A GOOD FEEL-ING.
NOMIYA.
YAMADA-SAN'S AN ADULT, OKAY? SHE'S NOT A KID.
WELL ...
I MEANT ON THE INSIDE.
HMM ...
YEAH, I KNOW ...
BUT ...
STILL ...
I DON'T QUITE ...
hmm
I KNOW WHAT YOU MEAN, BUT...
HEY YAMAZAKI, IT'S A LOT EASIER TO WALK WITH YOUR SHOES OFF.

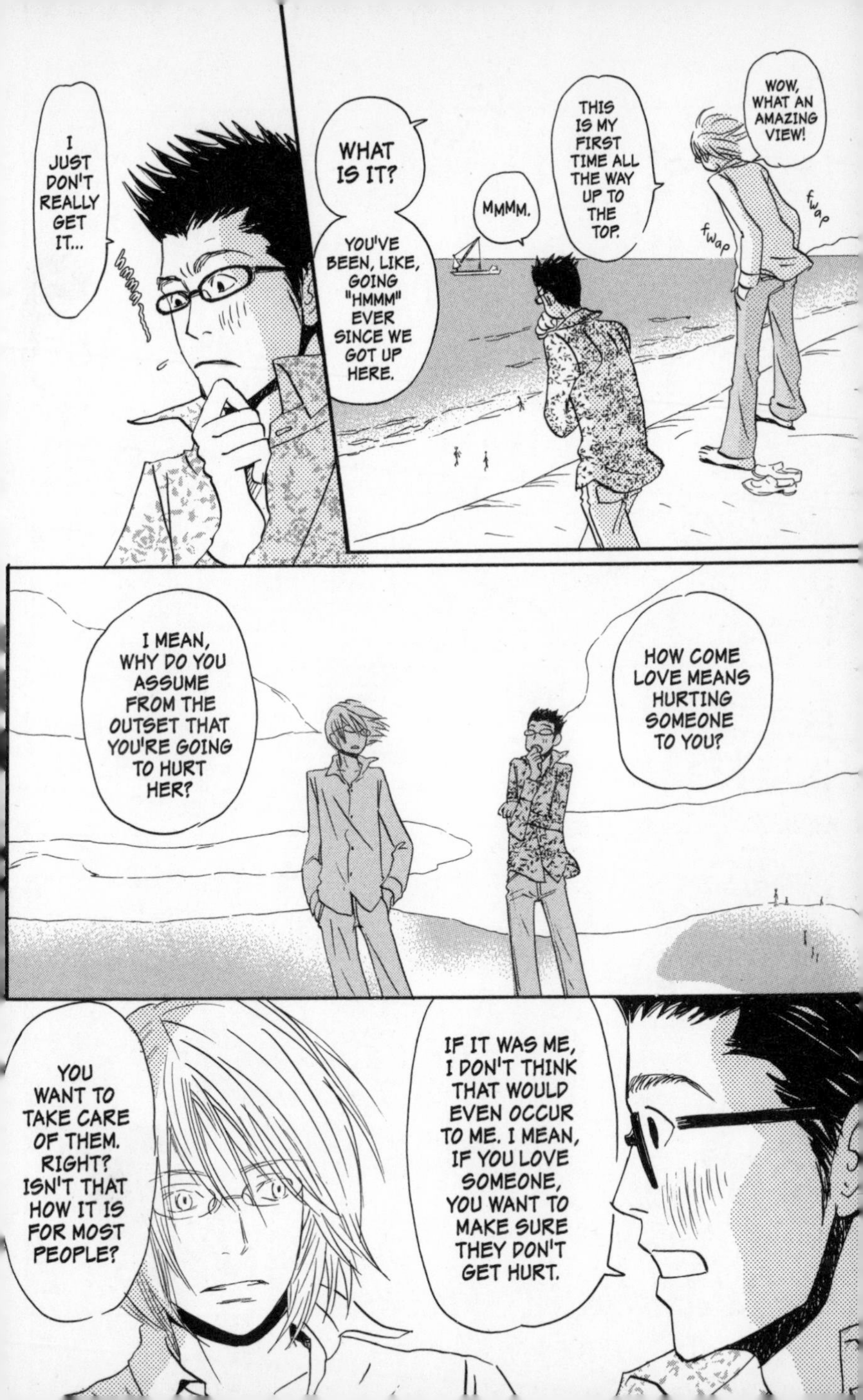
WOW, WHAT AN AMAZING VIEW!
fwap
fwap
THIS IS MY FIRST TIME ALL THE WAY UP TO THE TOP.
MMMM.
WHAT IS IT?
YOU'VE BEEN, LIKE, GOING "HMMM" EVER SINCE WE GOT UP HERE.
I JUST DON'T REALLY GET IT...
hmmm
HOW COME LOVE MEANS HURTING SOMEONE TO YOU?
I MEAN, WHY DO YOU ASSUME FROM THE OUTSET THAT YOU'RE GOING TO HURT HER?
IF IT WAS ME, I DON'T THINK THAT WOULD EVEN OCCUR TO ME. I MEAN, IF YOU LOVE SOMEONE, YOU WANT TO MAKE SURE THEY DON'T GET HURT.
YOU WANT TO TAKE CARE OF THEM. RIGHT? ISN'T THAT HOW IT IS FOR MOST PEOPLE?

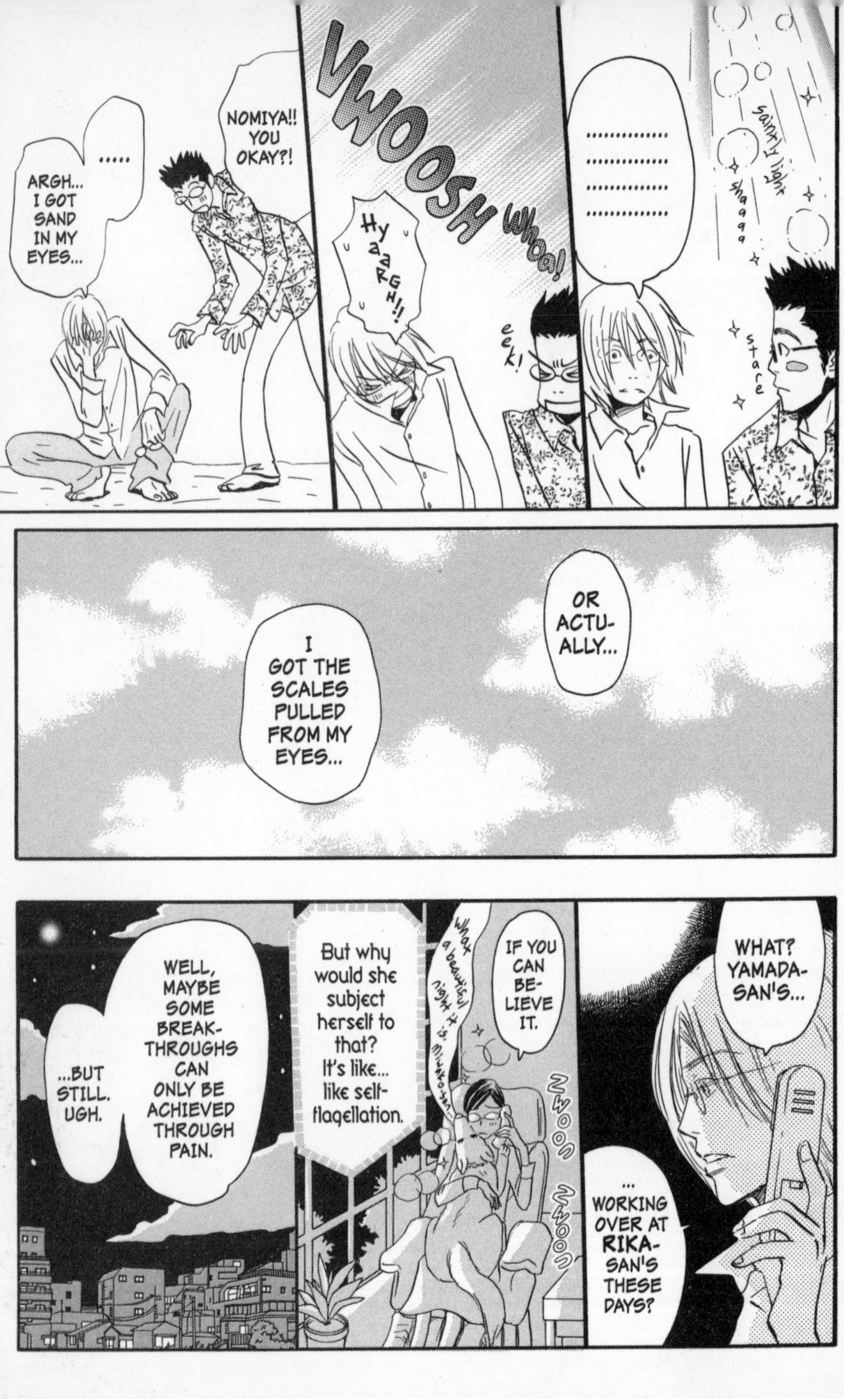
saintly light
shaaaa
stare
....
....
....
....
VWOOSH
Whoa!
eek!
Hyaargh!!
NOMIYA!! YOU OKAY?!
.....
ARGH... I GOT SAND IN MY EYES...
OR ACTUALLY...
I GOT THE SCALES PULLED FROM MY EYES...
WHAT? YAMADA-SAN'S...
...WORKING OVER AT RIKA-SAN'S THESE DAYS?
IF YOU CAN BELIEVE IT.
What a beautiful night it is, Miyamoto-san...
ZWOON
ZWOON
But why would she subject herself to that? It's like... like self-flagellation.
WELL, MAYBE SOME BREAKTHROUGHS CAN ONLY BE ACHIEVED THROUGH PAIN.
...BUT STILL. UGH.

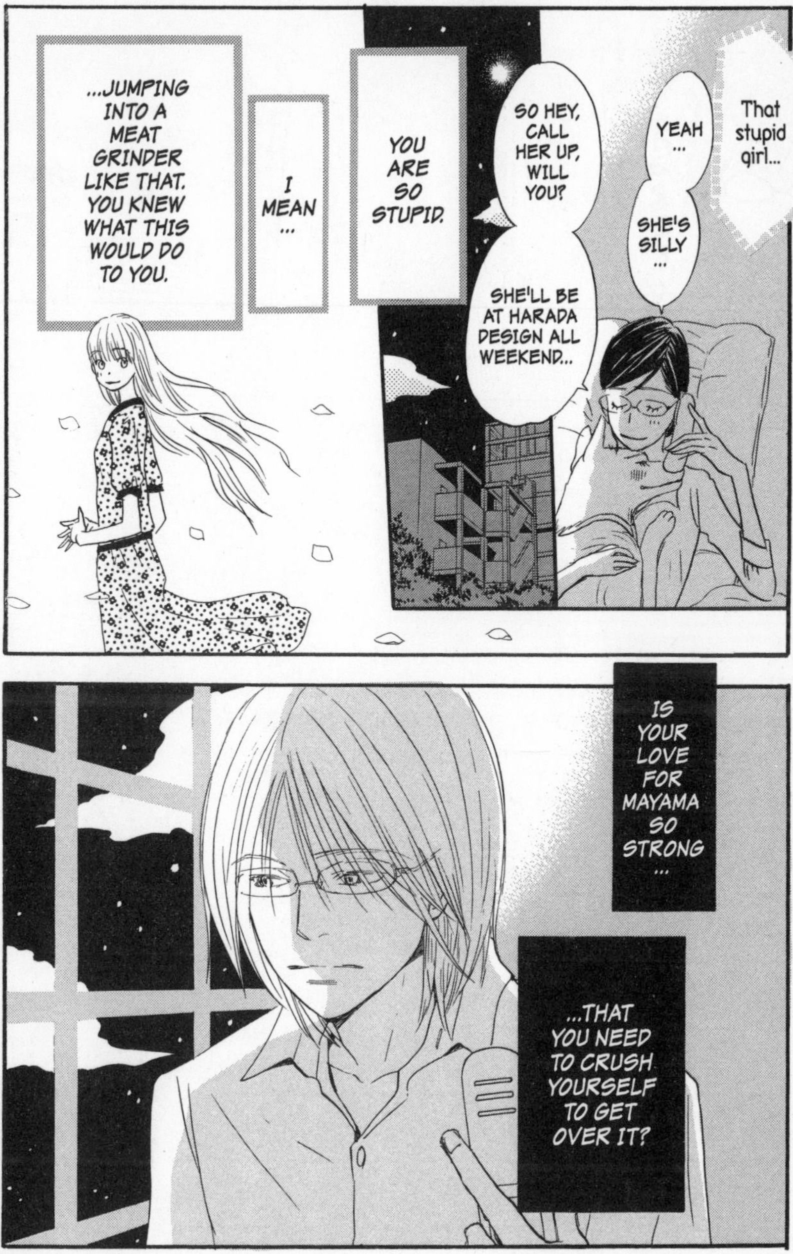
That stupid girl...
YEAH...
SHE'S SILLY...
SO HEY, CALL HER UP, WILL YOU?
SHE'LL BE AT HARADA DESIGN ALL WEEKEND...
YOU ARE SO STUPID.
I MEAN...
...JUMPING INTO A MEAT GRINDER LIKE THAT. YOU KNEW WHAT THIS WOULD DO TO YOU.
IS YOUR LOVE FOR MAYAMA SO STRONG...
...THAT YOU NEED TO CRUSH YOURSELF TO GET OVER IT?

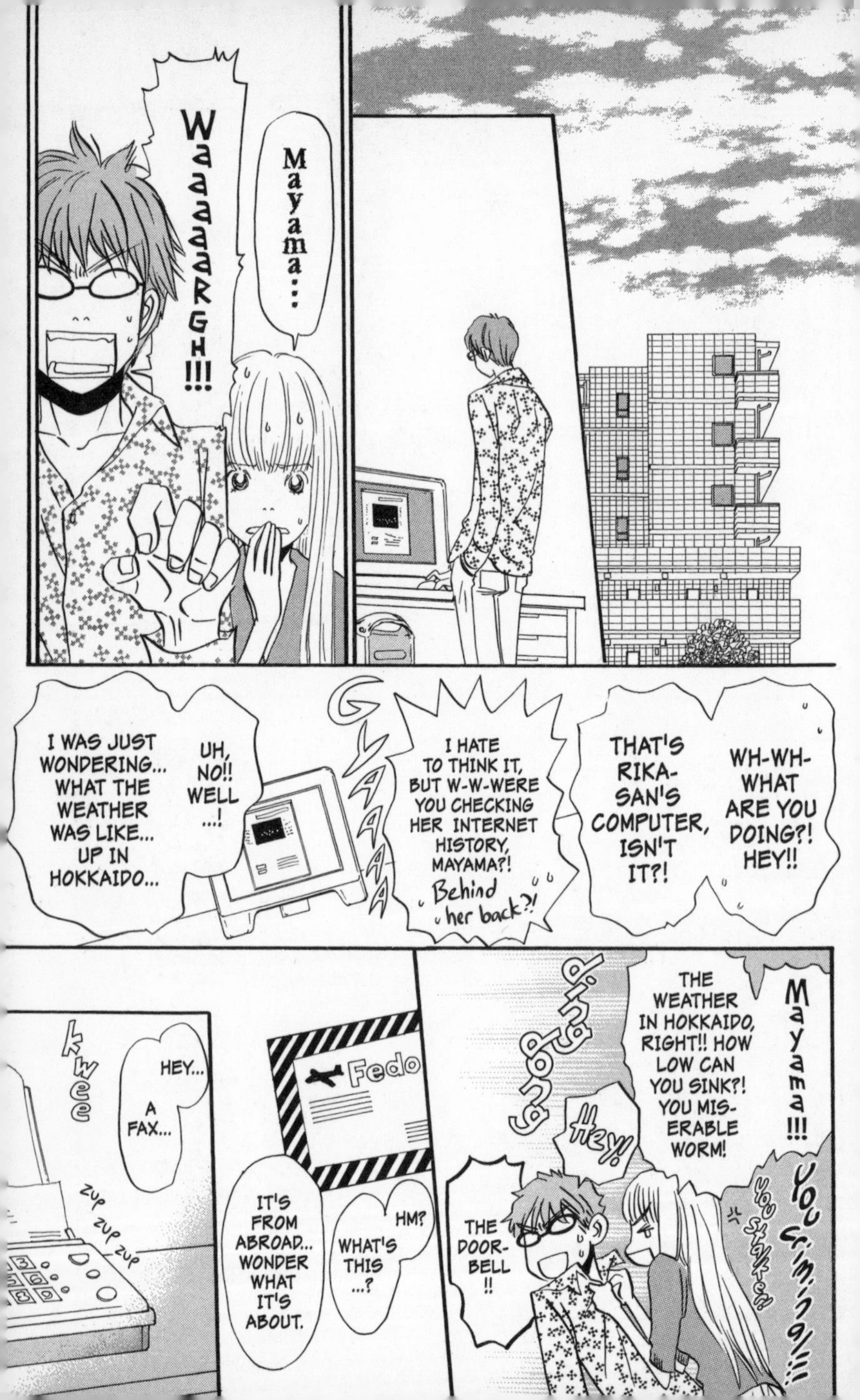
Mayama...
Waaaaargh!!!
WH-WH-WHAT ARE YOU DOING?! HEY!!
THAT'S RIKA-SAN'S COMPUTER, ISN'T IT?!
GYAAAAA
I HATE TO THINK IT, BUT W-W-WERE YOU CHECKING HER INTERNET HISTORY, MAYAMA?!
Behind her back?!
UH, NO!! WELL...!
I WAS JUST WONDERING... WHAT THE WEATHER WAS LIKE... UP IN HOKKAIDO...
Mayama!!!
THE WEATHER IN HOKKAIDO, RIGHT!! HOW LOW CAN YOU SINK?! YOU MIS-ERABLE WORM!
ding dong
Hey!
You criminal!!!
You stalker!
THE DOOR-BELL!!
Fedo
HM? WHAT'S THIS ...?
IT'S FROM ABROAD... WONDER WHAT IT'S ABOUT.
HEY... A FAX...
kwee
zup zup zup

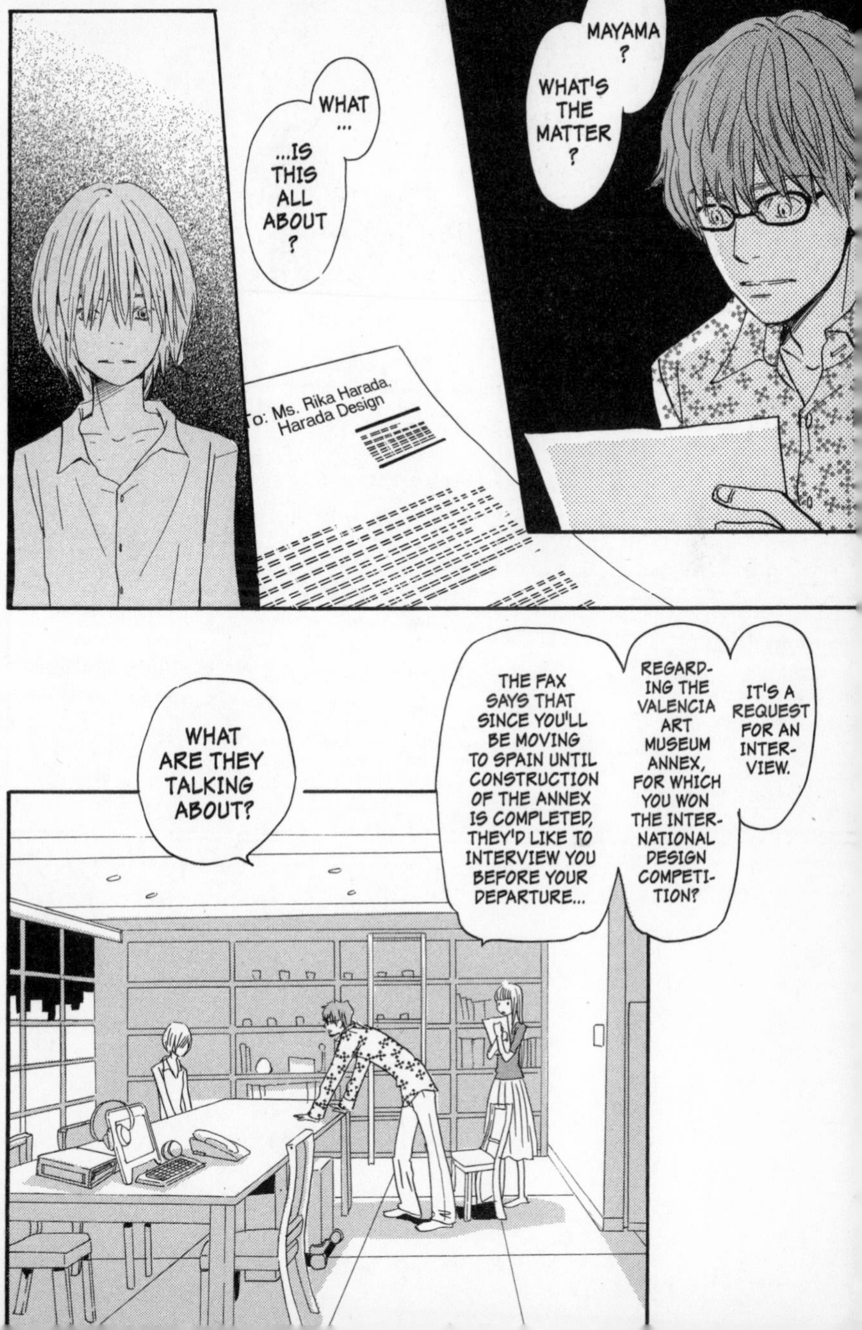
MAYAMA?
WHAT'S THE MATTER?
WHAT...
...IS THIS ALL ABOUT?
To: Ms. Rika Harada, Harada Design
IT'S A REQUEST FOR AN INTERVIEW.
REGARDING THE VALENCIA ART MUSEUM ANNEX, FOR WHICH YOU WON THE INTERNATIONAL DESIGN COMPETITION?
THE FAX SAYS THAT SINCE YOU'LL BE MOVING TO SPAIN UNTIL CONSTRUCTION OF THE ANNEX IS COMPLETED, THEY'D LIKE TO INTERVIEW YOU BEFORE YOUR DEPARTURE...
WHAT ARE THEY TALKING ABOUT?

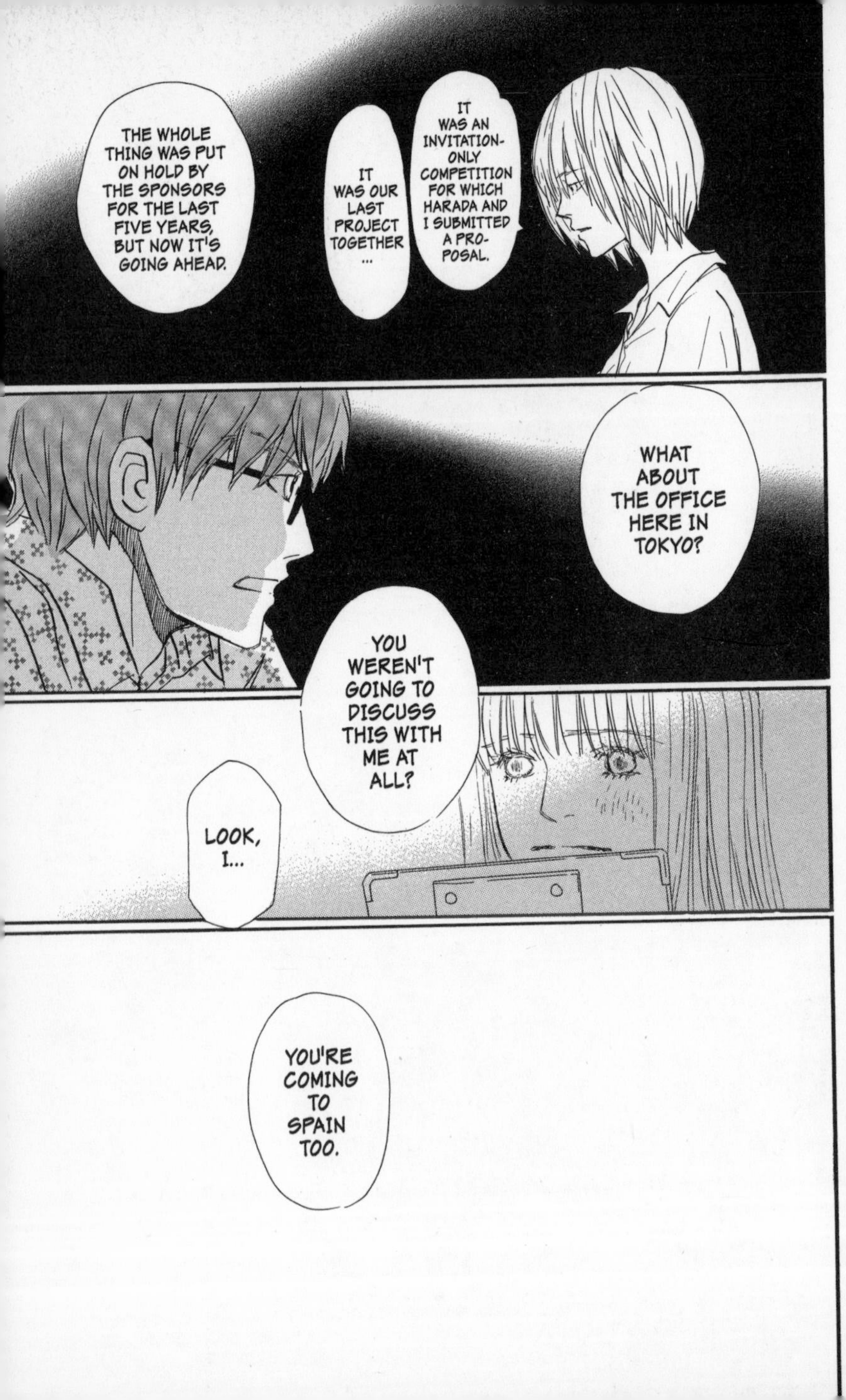
IT WAS AN INVITATION-ONLY COMPETITION FOR WHICH HARADA AND I SUBMITTED A PROPOSAL.
IT WAS OUR LAST PROJECT TOGETHER ...
THE WHOLE THING WAS PUT ON HOLD BY THE SPONSORS FOR THE LAST FIVE YEARS, BUT NOW IT'S GOING AHEAD.
WHAT ABOUT THE OFFICE HERE IN TOKYO?
YOU WEREN'T GOING TO DISCUSS THIS WITH ME AT ALL?
LOOK, I...
YOU'RE COMING TO SPAIN TOO.

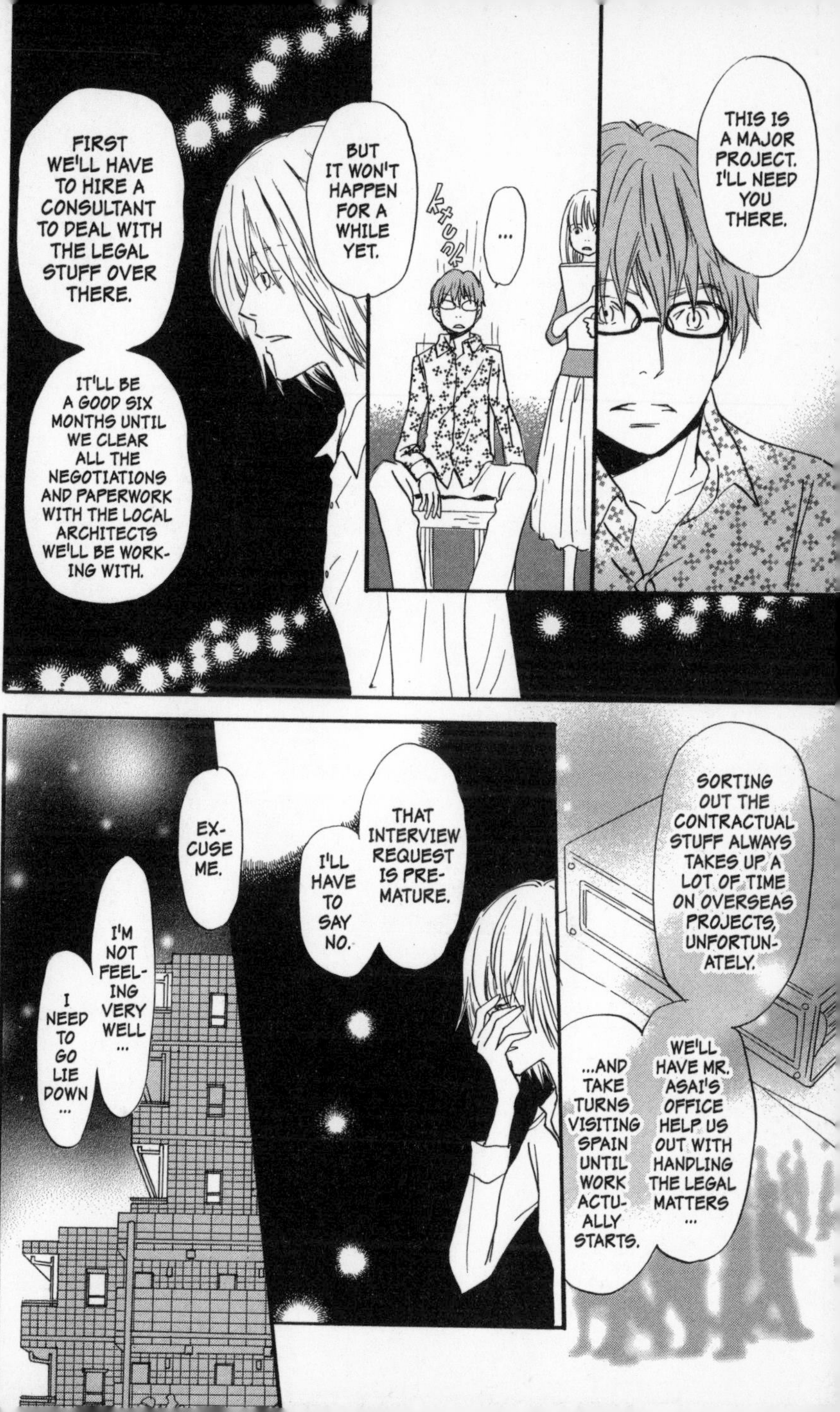
THIS IS A MAJOR PROJECT. I'LL NEED YOU THERE.
...
BUT IT WON'T HAPPEN FOR A WHILE YET.
FIRST WE'LL HAVE TO HIRE A CONSULTANT TO DEAL WITH THE LEGAL STUFF OVER THERE.
IT'LL BE A GOOD SIX MONTHS UNTIL WE CLEAR ALL THE NEGOTIATIONS AND PAPERWORK WITH THE LOCAL ARCHITECTS WE'LL BE WORKING WITH.
SORTING OUT THE CONTRACTUAL STUFF ALWAYS TAKES UP A LOT OF TIME ON OVERSEAS PROJECTS, UNFORTUNATELY.
WE'LL HAVE MR. ASAI'S OFFICE HELP US OUT WITH HANDLING THE LEGAL MATTERS ...
...AND TAKE TURNS VISITING SPAIN UNTIL WORK ACTUALLY STARTS.
THAT INTERVIEW REQUEST IS PREMATURE.
I'LL HAVE TO SAY NO.
EXCUSE ME.
I'M NOT FEELING VERY WELL ...
I NEED TO GO LIE DOWN ...

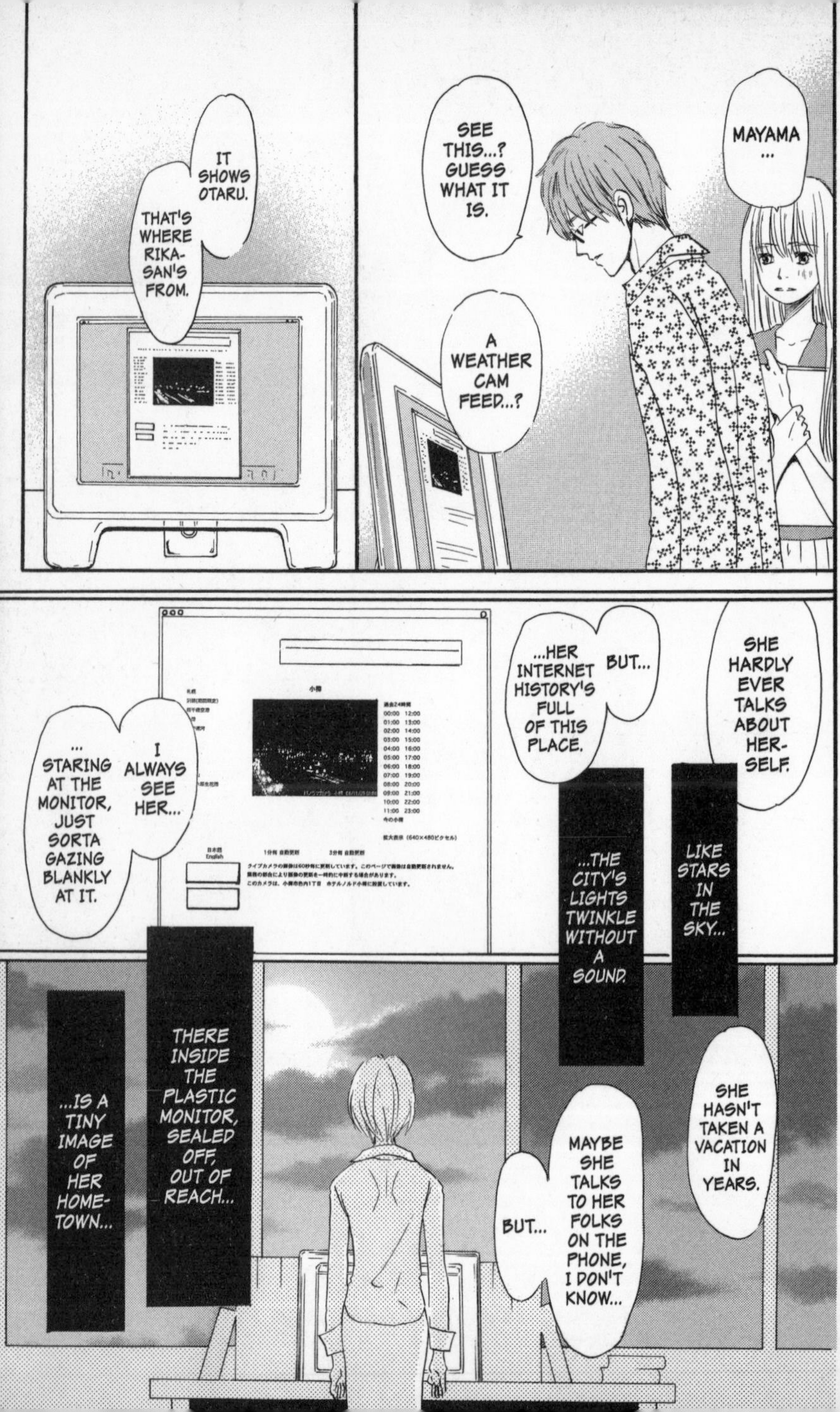
MAYAMA ...
SEE THIS...? GUESS WHAT IT IS.
A WEATHER CAM FEED...?
IT SHOWS OTARU.
THAT'S WHERE RIKA-SAN'S FROM.
SHE HARDLY EVER TALKS ABOUT HER-SELF.
BUT...
...HER INTERNET HISTORY'S FULL OF THIS PLACE.
I ALWAYS SEE HER...
... STARING AT THE MONITOR, JUST SORTA GAZING BLANKLY AT IT.
LIKE STARS IN THE SKY...
...THE CITY'S LIGHTS TWINKLE WITHOUT A SOUND.
SHE HASN'T TAKEN A VACATION IN YEARS.
MAYBE SHE TALKS TO HER FOLKS ON THE PHONE, I DON'T KNOW...
BUT...
THERE INSIDE THE PLASTIC MONITOR, SEALED OFF, OUT OF REACH...
...IS A TINY IMAGE OF HER HOME-TOWN...

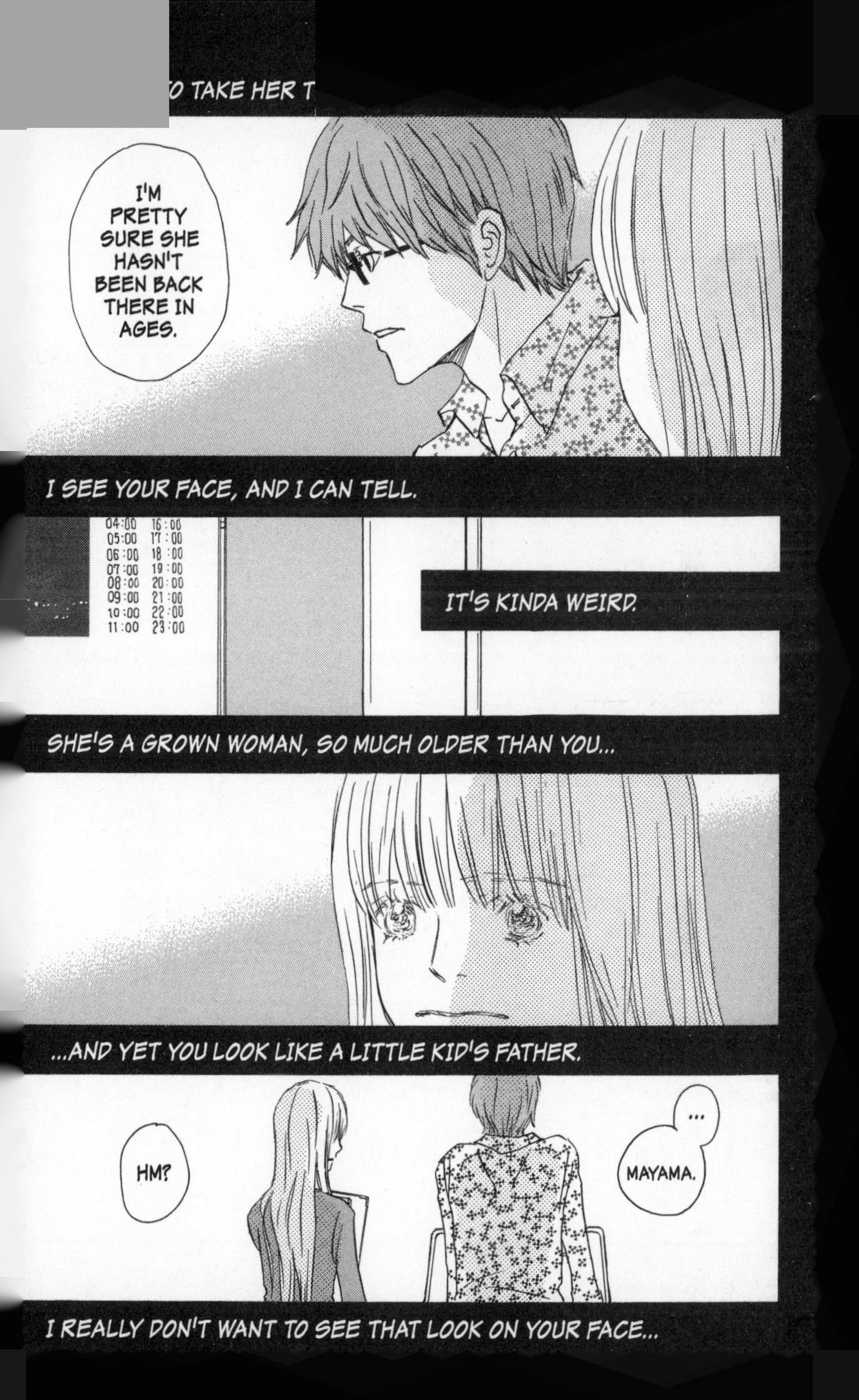
O TAKE HER T
I'M PRETTY SURE SHE HASN'T BEEN BACK THERE IN AGES.
I SEE YOUR FACE, AND I CAN TELL.
04:00 16:00
05:00 17:00
06:00 18:00
07:00 19:00
08:00 20:00
09:00 21:00
10:00 22:00
11:00 23:00
IT'S KINDA WEIRD.
SHE'S A GROWN WOMAN, SO MUCH OLDER THAN YOU...
...AND YET YOU LOOK LIKE A LITTLE KID'S FATHER.
...
MAYAMA.
HM?
I REALLY DON'T WANT TO SEE THAT LOOK ON YOUR FACE...

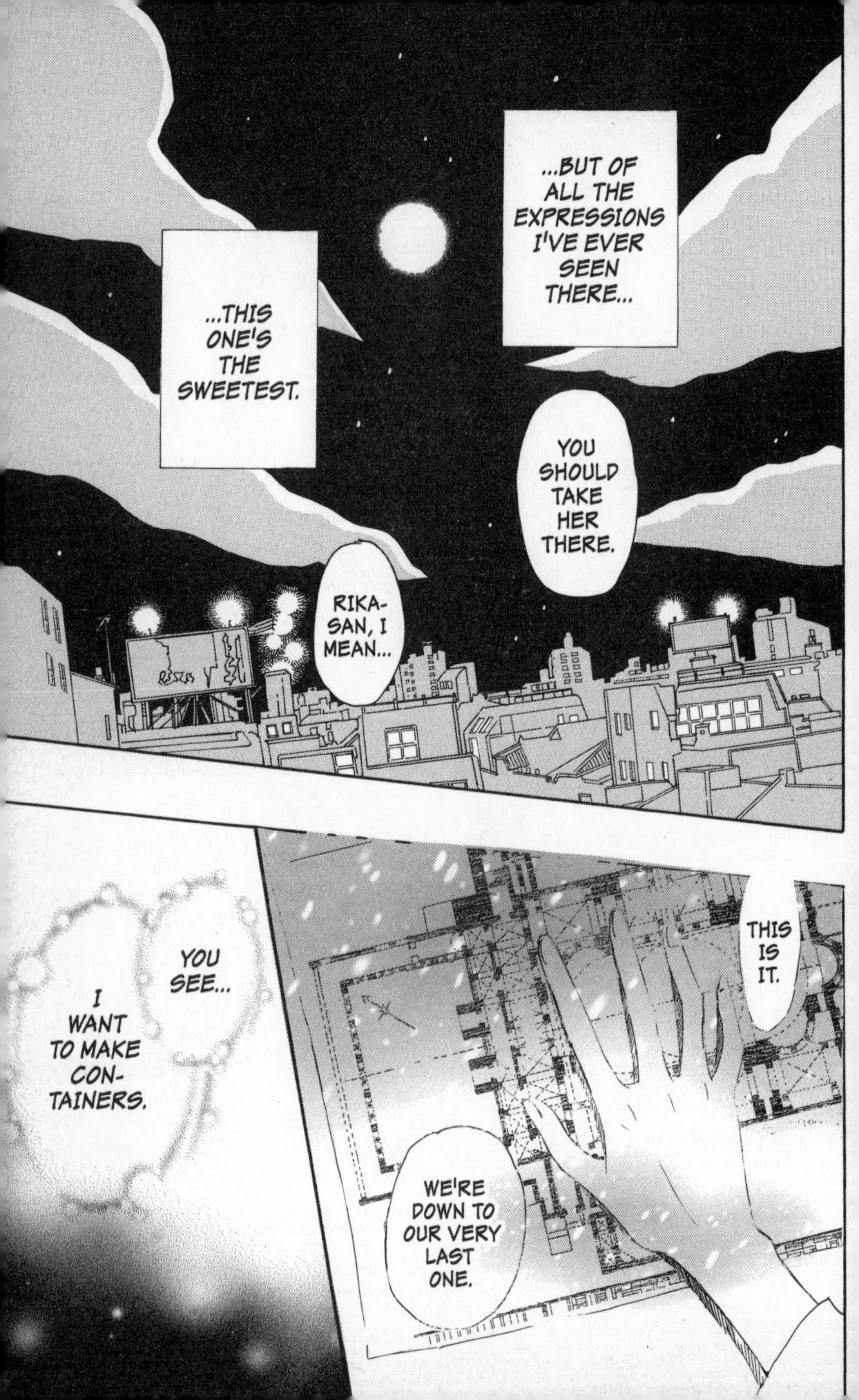
...BUT OF ALL THE EXPRESSIONS I'VE EVER SEEN THERE...
...THIS ONE'S THE SWEETEST.
YOU SHOULD TAKE HER THERE.
RIKA-SAN, I MEAN...
THIS IS IT.
WE'RE DOWN TO OUR VERY LAST ONE.
YOU SEE...
I WANT TO MAKE CON-TAINERS.

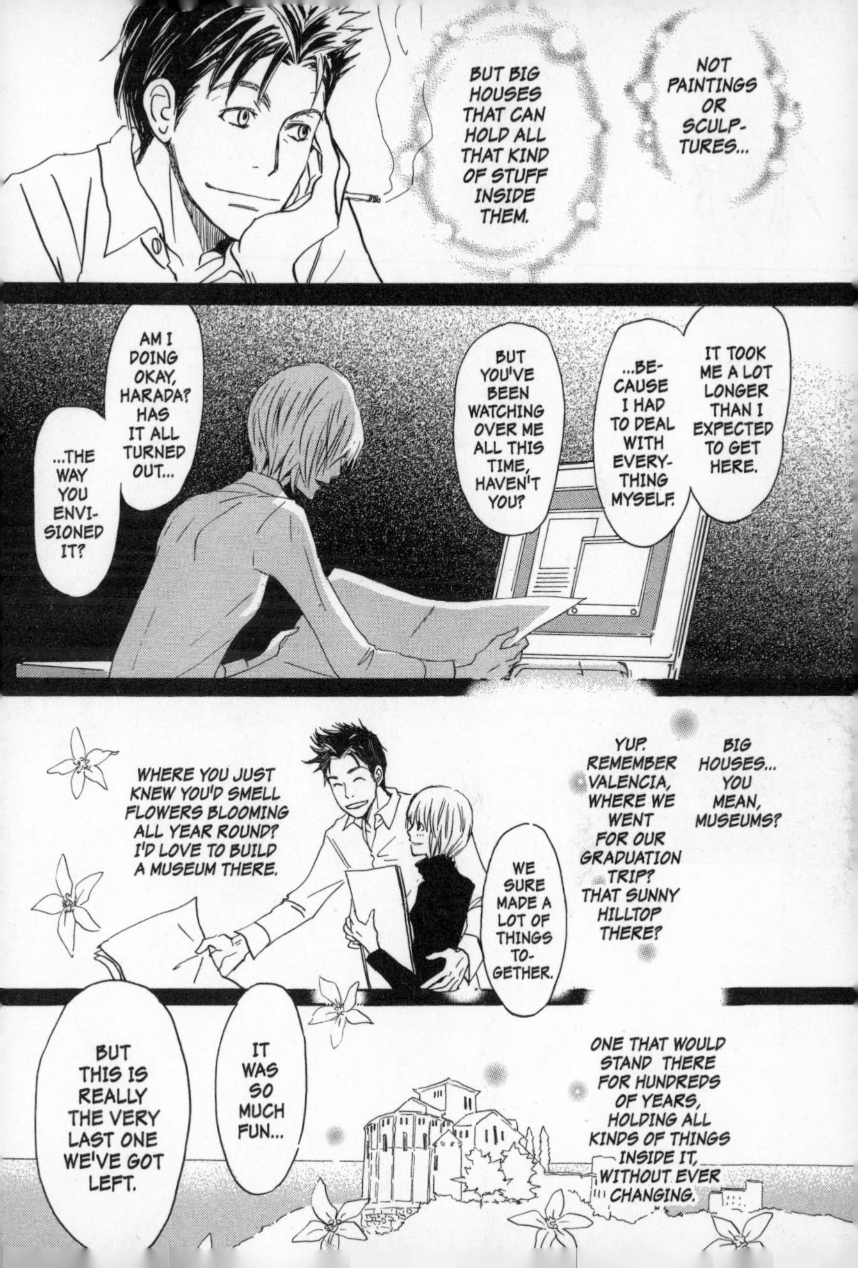
NOT PAINTINGS OR SCULPTURES...
BUT BIG HOUSES THAT CAN HOLD ALL THAT KIND OF STUFF INSIDE THEM.
IT TOOK ME A LOT LONGER THAN I EXPECTED TO GET HERE.
...BECAUSE I HAD TO DEAL WITH EVERYTHING MYSELF.
BUT YOU'VE BEEN WATCHING OVER ME ALL THIS TIME, HAVEN'T YOU?
AM I DOING OKAY, HARADA? HAS IT ALL TURNED OUT...
...THE WAY YOU ENVISIONED IT?
BIG HOUSES... YOU MEAN, MUSEUMS?
YUP. REMEMBER VALENCIA, WHERE WE WENT FOR OUR GRADUATION TRIP? THAT SUNNY HILLTOP THERE?
WHERE YOU JUST KNEW YOU'D SMELL FLOWERS BLOOMING ALL YEAR ROUND? I'D LOVE TO BUILD A MUSEUM THERE.
ONE THAT WOULD STAND THERE FOR HUNDREDS OF YEARS, HOLDING ALL KINDS OF THINGS INSIDE IT, WITHOUT EVER CHANGING.
WE SURE MADE A LOT OF THINGS TOGETHER.
IT WAS SO MUCH FUN...
BUT THIS IS REALLY THE VERY LAST ONE WE'VE GOT LEFT.

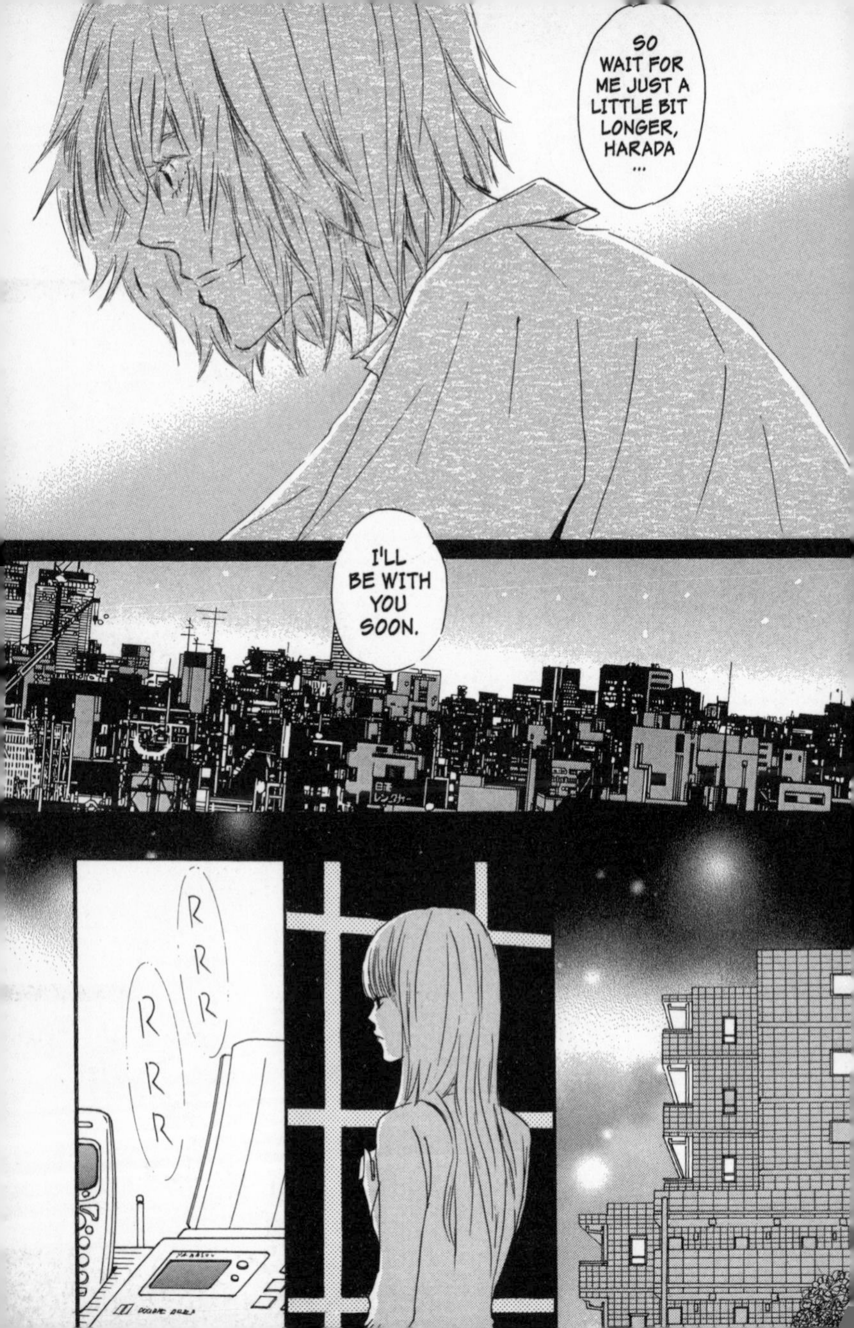
SO WAIT FOR ME JUST A LITTLE BIT LONGER, HARADA ...
I'LL BE WITH YOU SOON.
RRR
RRR

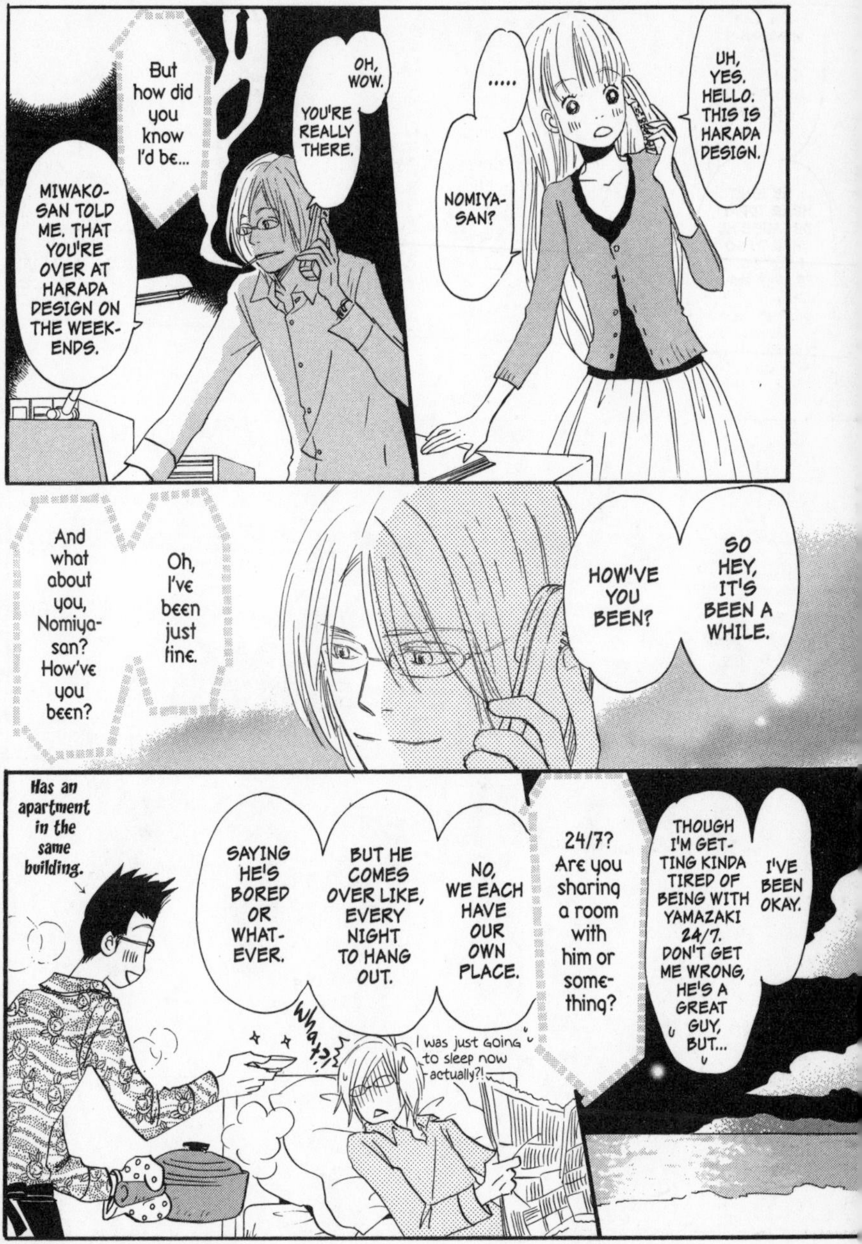
UH, YES. HELLO. THIS IS HARADA DESIGN.
.....
NOMIYA-SAN?
OH, WOW. YOU'RE REALLY THERE.
But how did you know I'd be...
MIWAKO-SAN TOLD ME. THAT YOU'RE OVER AT HARADA DESIGN ON THE WEEK-ENDS.
SO HEY, IT'S BEEN A WHILE.
HOW'VE YOU BEEN?
Oh, I've been just fine.
And what about you, Nomiya-san? How've you been?
I'VE BEEN OKAY.
THOUGH I'M GET-TING KINDA TIRED OF BEING WITH YAMAZAKI 24/7. DON'T GET ME WRONG, HE'S A GREAT GUY, BUT...
24/7? Are you sharing a room with him or some-thing?
NO, WE EACH HAVE OUR OWN PLACE.
BUT HE COMES OVER LIKE, EVERY NIGHT TO HANG OUT.
SAYING HE'S BORED OR WHAT-EVER.
What?!
I was just going to sleep now actually?!
Has an apartment in the same building.

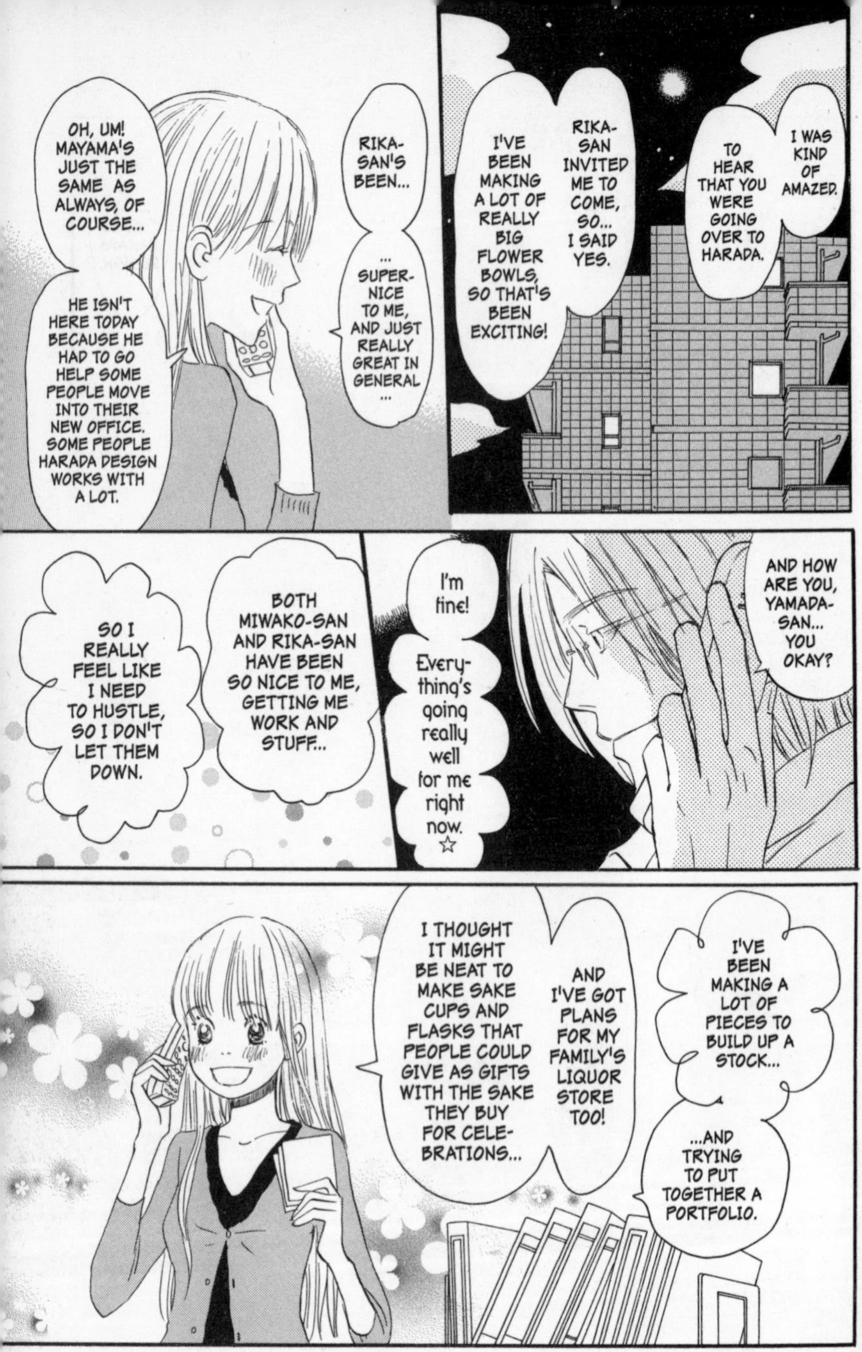
I WAS KIND OF AMAZED.
TO HEAR THAT YOU WERE GOING OVER TO HARADA.
RIKA-SAN INVITED ME TO COME, SO... I SAID YES.
I'VE BEEN MAKING A LOT OF REALLY BIG FLOWER BOWLS, SO THAT'S BEEN EXCITING!
RIKA-SAN'S BEEN...
... SUPER-NICE TO ME, AND JUST REALLY GREAT IN GENERAL ...
OH, UM! MAYAMA'S JUST THE SAME AS ALWAYS, OF COURSE...
HE ISN'T HERE TODAY BECAUSE HE HAD TO GO HELP SOME PEOPLE MOVE INTO THEIR NEW OFFICE. SOME PEOPLE HARADA DESIGN WORKS WITH A LOT.
AND HOW ARE YOU, YAMADA-SAN... YOU OKAY?
I'm fine!
Everything's going really well for me right now. ☆
BOTH MIWAKO-SAN AND RIKA-SAN HAVE BEEN SO NICE TO ME, GETTING ME WORK AND STUFF...
SO I REALLY FEEL LIKE I NEED TO HUSTLE, SO I DON'T LET THEM DOWN.
I'VE BEEN MAKING A LOT OF PIECES TO BUILD UP A STOCK...
...AND TRYING TO PUT TOGETHER A PORTFOLIO.
AND I'VE GOT PLANS FOR MY FAMILY'S LIQUOR STORE TOO!
I THOUGHT IT MIGHT BE NEAT TO MAKE SAKE CUPS AND FLASKS THAT PEOPLE COULD GIVE AS GIFTS WITH THE SAKE THEY BUY FOR CELEBRATIONS...

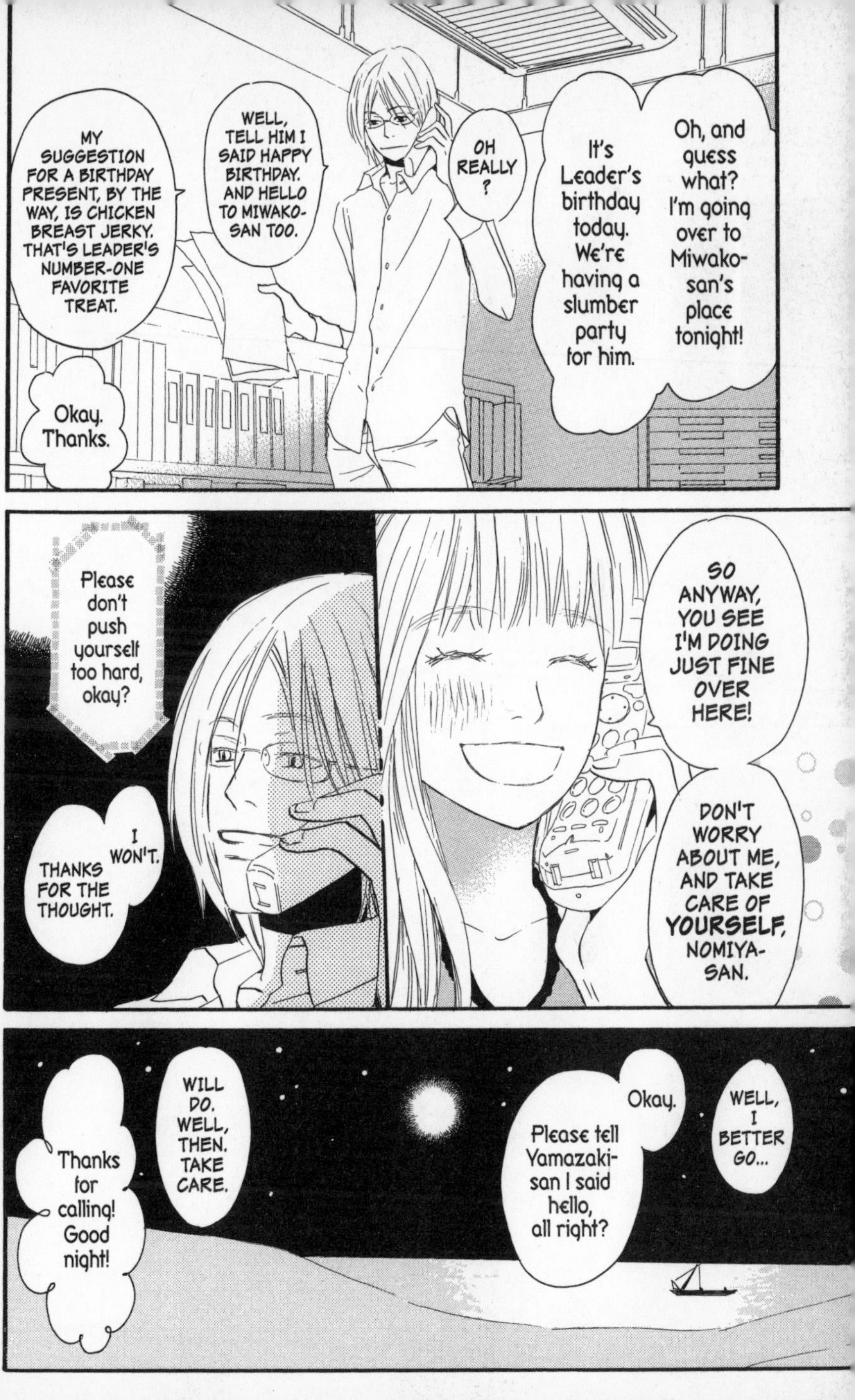
Oh, and guess what? I'm going over to Miwako-san's place tonight!
It's Leader's birthday today. We're having a slumber party for him.
OH REALLY?
WELL, TELL HIM I SAID HAPPY BIRTHDAY. AND HELLO TO MIWAKO-SAN TOO.
MY SUGGESTION FOR A BIRTHDAY PRESENT, BY THE WAY, IS CHICKEN BREAST JERKY. THAT'S LEADER'S NUMBER-ONE FAVORITE TREAT.
Okay. Thanks.
SO ANYWAY, YOU SEE I'M DOING JUST FINE OVER HERE!
DON'T WORRY ABOUT ME, AND TAKE CARE OF YOURSELF, NOMIYA-SAN.
Please don't push yourself too hard, okay?
I WON'T.
THANKS FOR THE THOUGHT.
WELL, I BETTER GO...
Okay.
Please tell Yamazaki-san I said hello, all right?
WILL DO. WELL, THEN. TAKE CARE.
Thanks for calling! Good night!

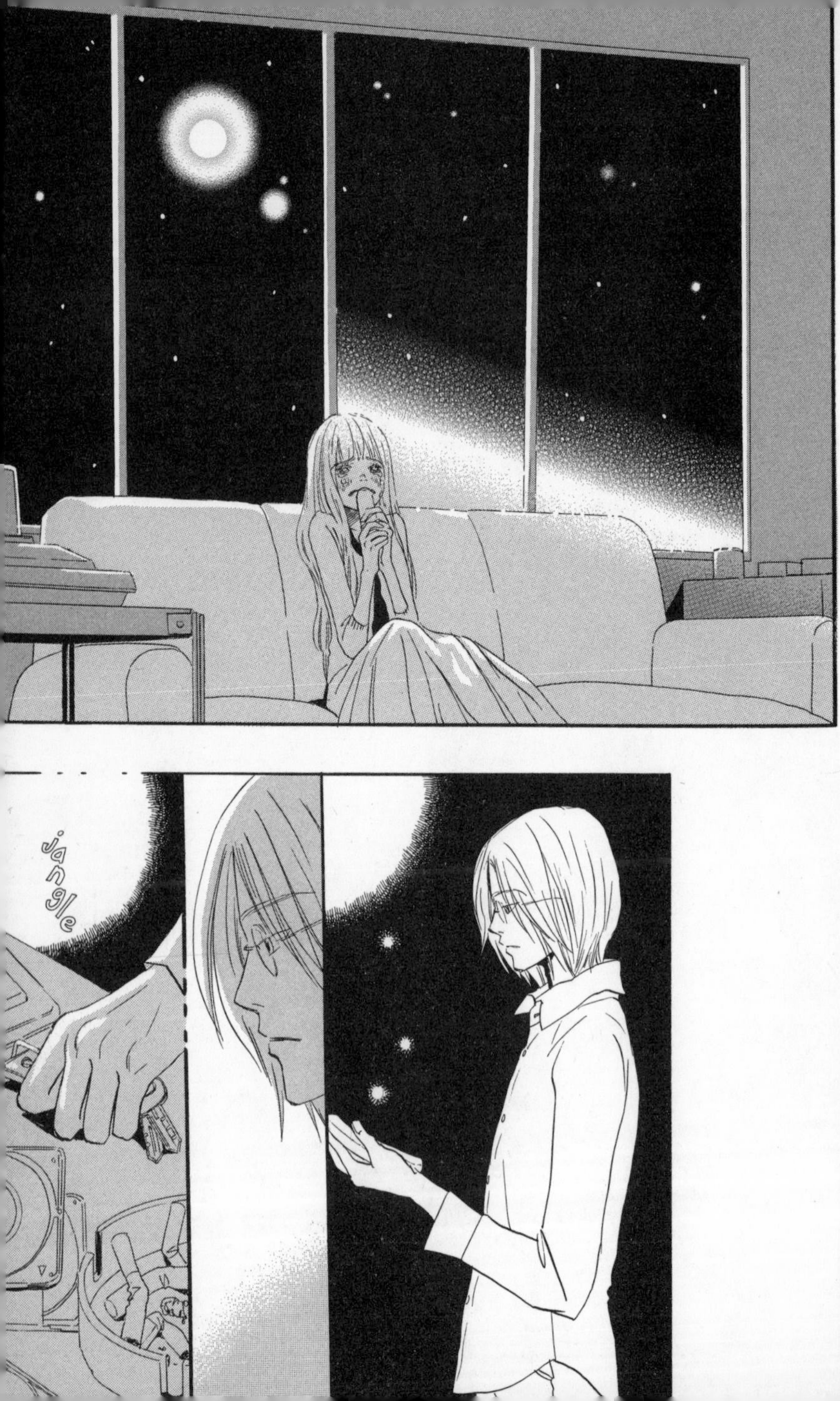
jangle

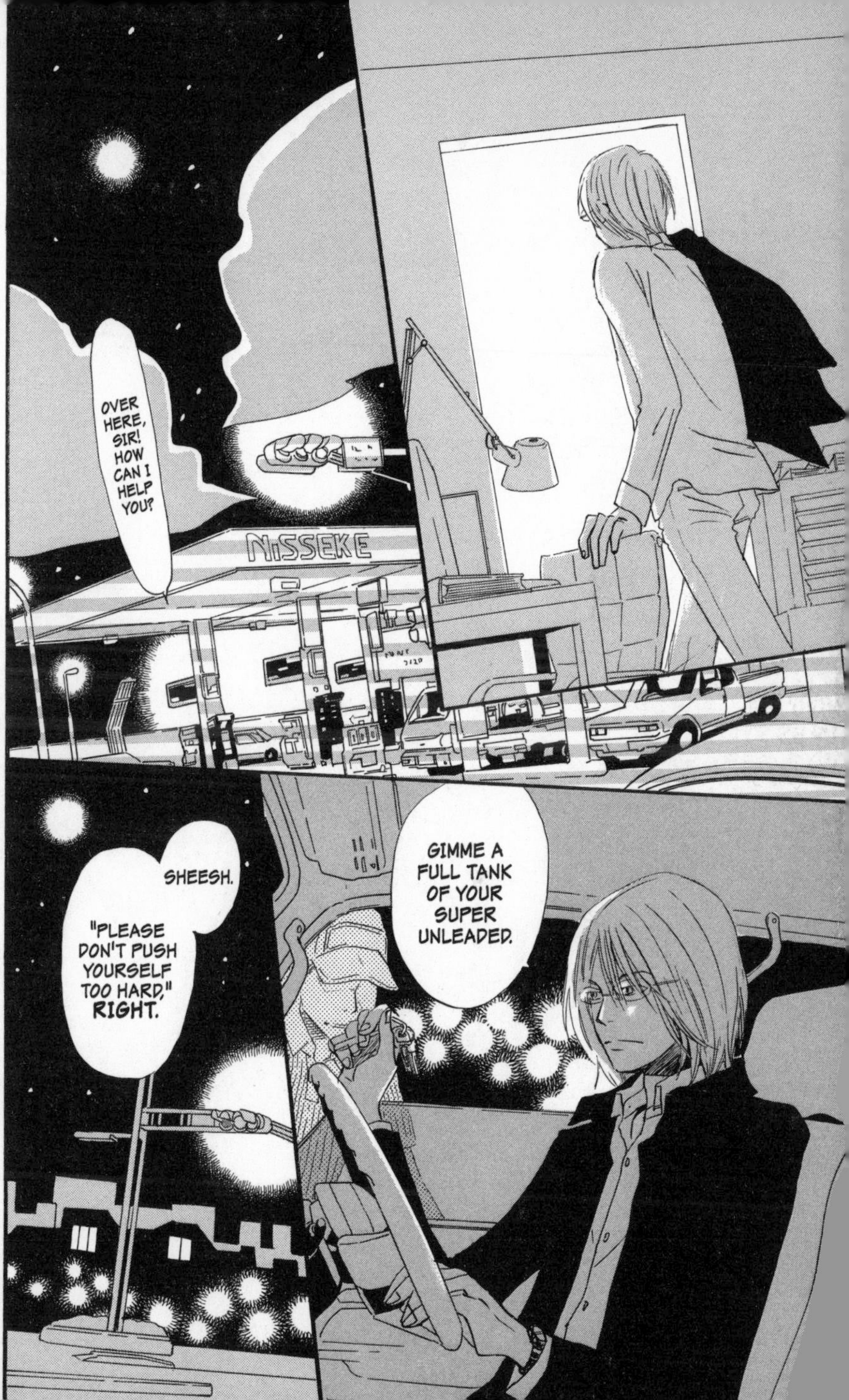
OVER HERE, SIR! HOW CAN I HELP YOU?
NiSSEKE
GIMME A FULL TANK OF YOUR SUPER UNLEADED.
SHEESH.
"PLEASE DON'T PUSH YOURSELF TOO HARD," RIGHT.

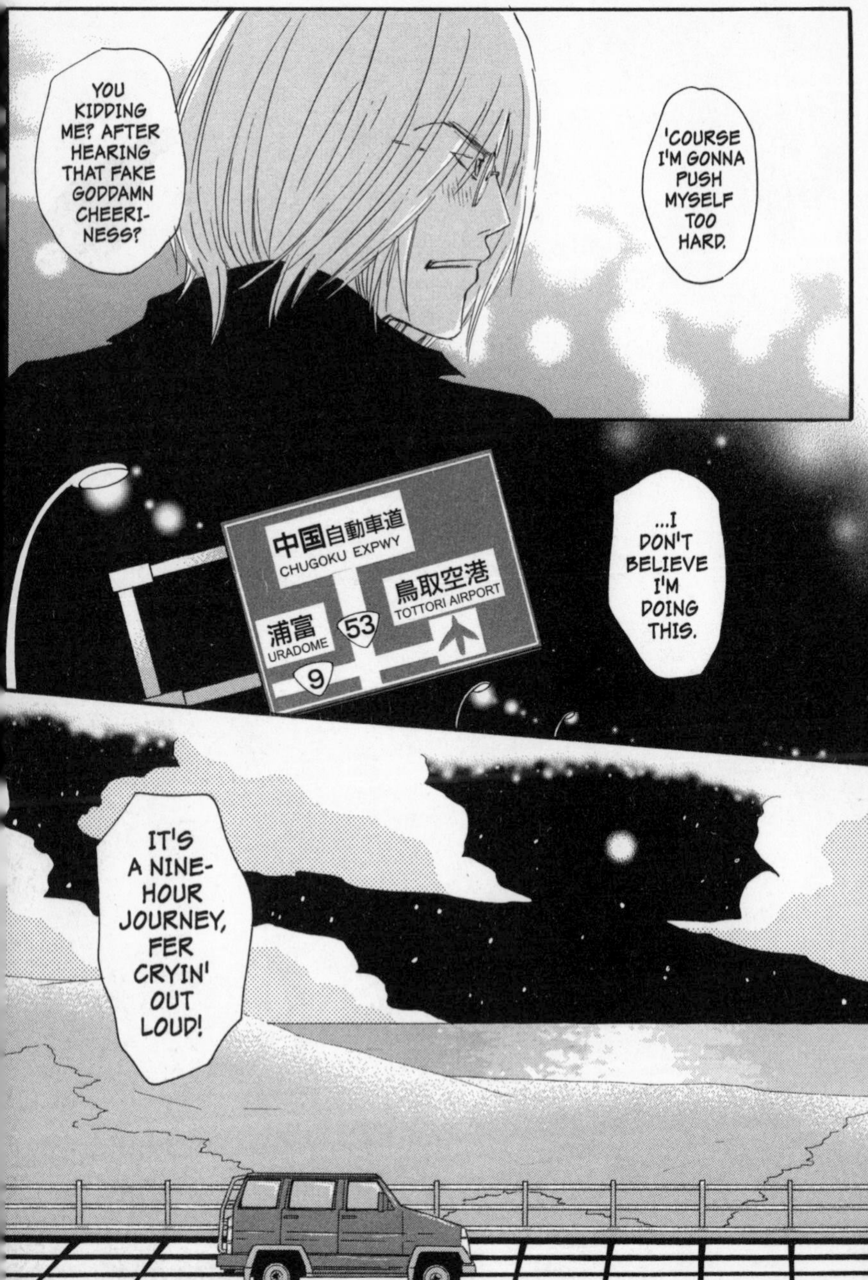
'COURSE I'M GONNA PUSH MYSELF TOO HARD.
YOU KIDDING ME? AFTER HEARING THAT FAKE GODDAMN CHEERI-NESS?
...I DON'T BELIEVE I'M DOING THIS.
中国自動車道
CHUGOKU EXPWY
鳥取空港
TOTTORI AIRPORT
53
浦富
URADOME
9
IT'S A NINE-HOUR JOURNEY, FER CRYIN' OUT LOUD!

chapter 48—the end—

Giant monster type

Silly Cosplay Action Figures

Hard-boiled type

Classic movie type

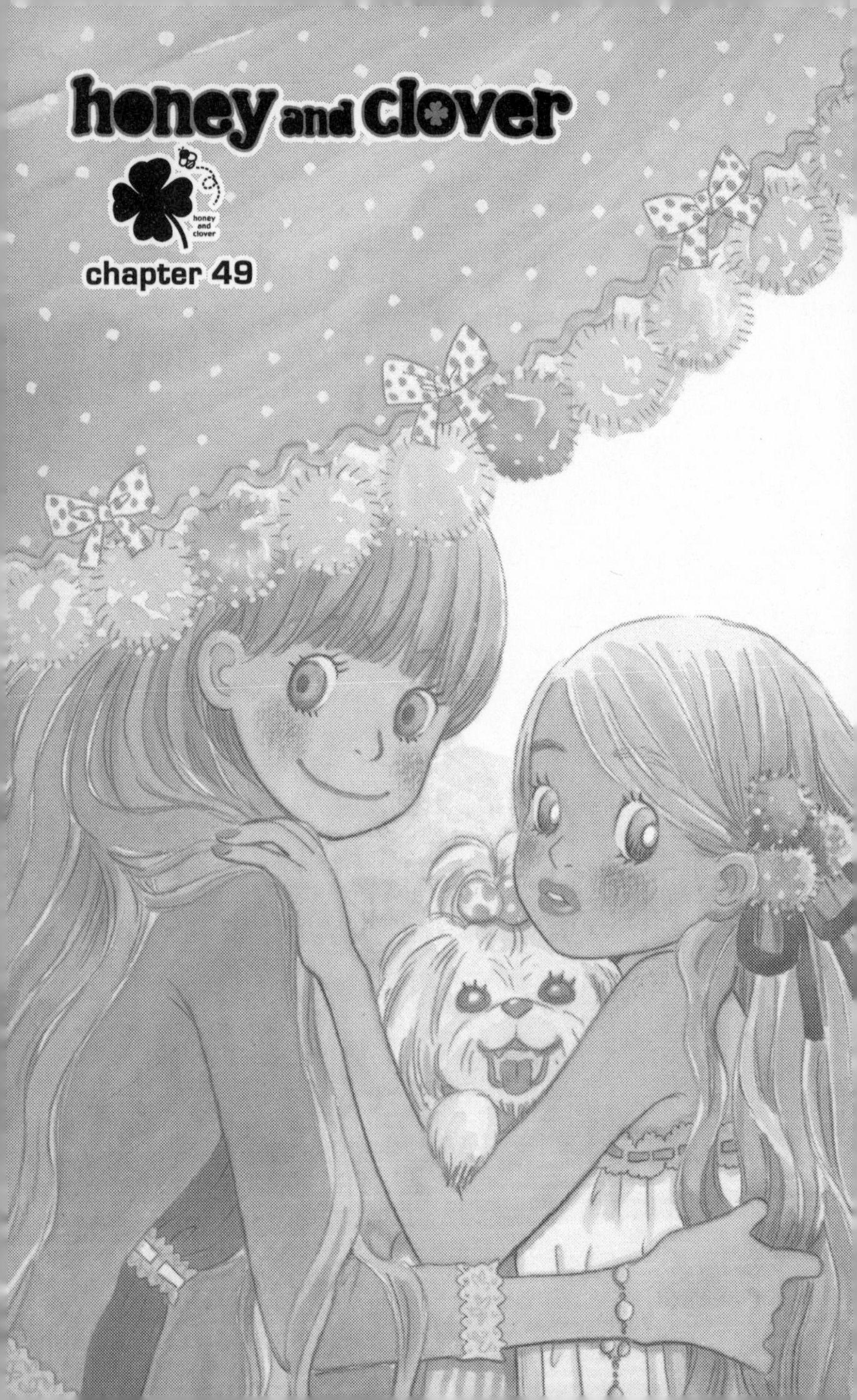
honey and clover
honey and clover
chapter 49

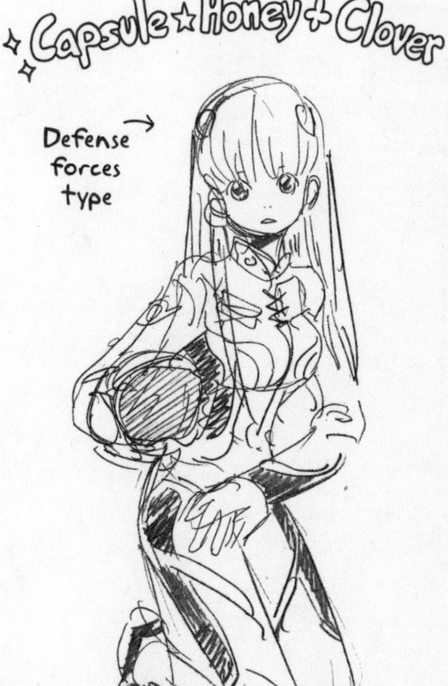Capsule★Honey★Clover
Defense forces type

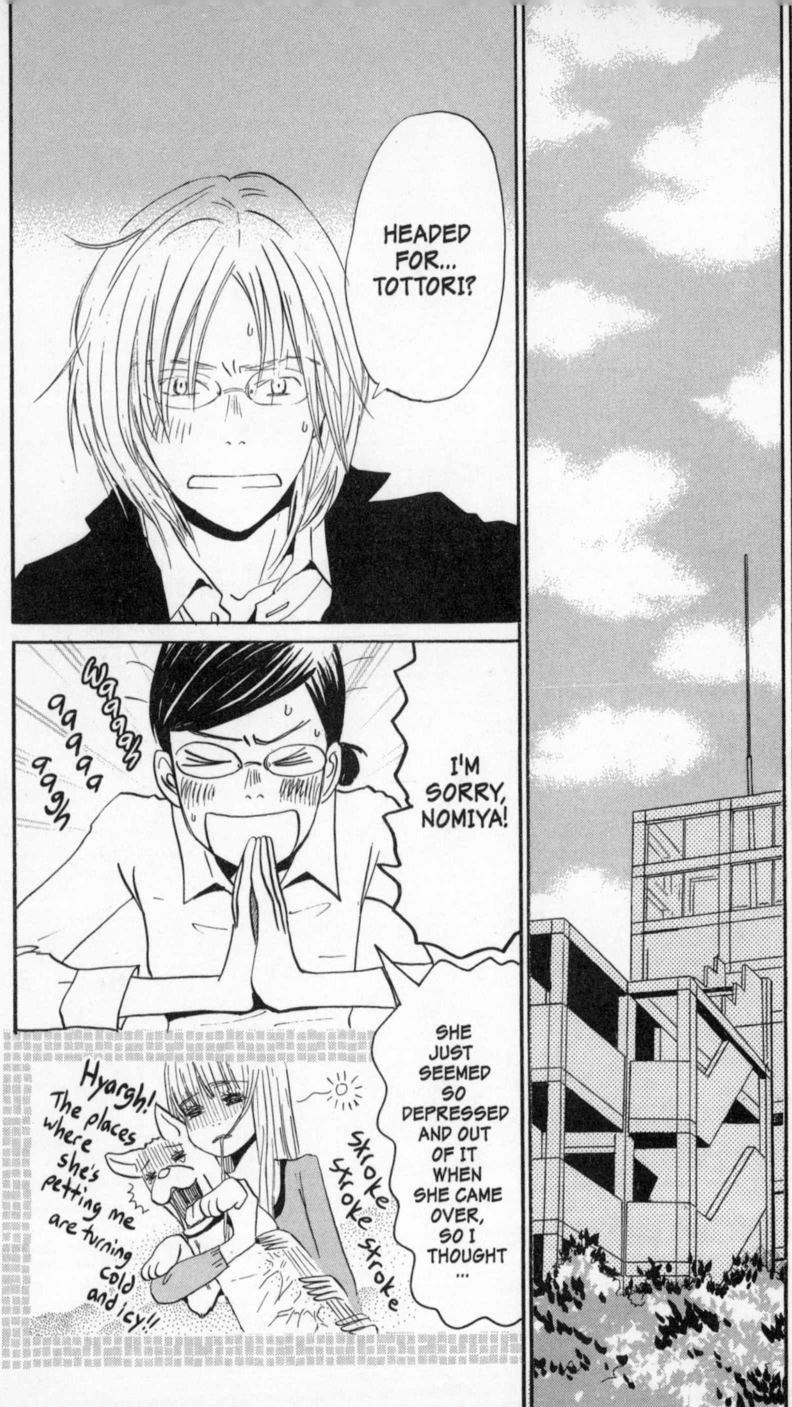
HEADED FOR... TOTTORI?
I'M SORRY, NOMIYA!
Waaaah aaaaa aagh
SHE JUST SEEMED SO DEPRESSED AND OUT OF IT WHEN SHE CAME OVER, SO I THOUGHT ...
stroke stroke stroke
Hyargh! The places where she's petting me are turning cold and icy!!

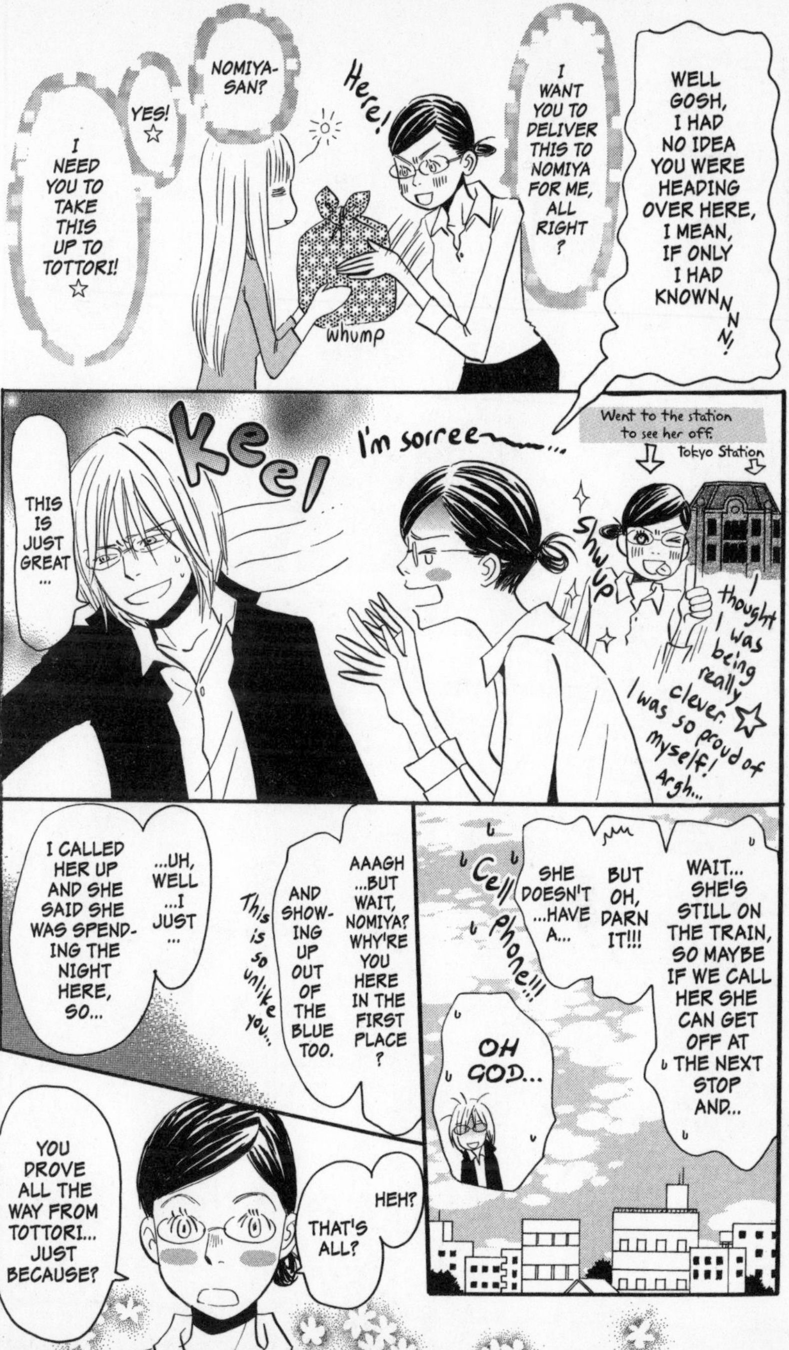
WELL GOSH, I HAD NO IDEA YOU WERE HEADING OVER HERE, I MEAN, IF ONLY I HAD KNOWNNNN!
I WANT YOU TO DELIVER THIS TO NOMIYA FOR ME, ALL RIGHT?
Here!
NOMIYA-SAN?
YES! ☆
I NEED YOU TO TAKE THIS UP TO TOTTORI! ☆
whump
Went to the station to see her off.
Tokyo Station
I thought I was being really clever. ☆
I was so proud of myself! Argh...
Shwup
I'm sorree—...
Keel
THIS IS JUST GREAT ...
WAIT... SHE'S STILL ON THE TRAIN, SO MAYBE IF WE CALL HER SHE CAN GET OFF AT THE NEXT STOP AND...
BUT OH, DARN IT!!!
SHE DOESN'T ...HAVE A...
Cell phone!!!
OH GOD...
AAAGH ...BUT WAIT, NOMIYA? WHY'RE YOU HERE IN THE FIRST PLACE?
AND SHOWING UP OUT OF THE BLUE TOO.
This is so unlike you...
...UH, WELL ...I JUST ...
I CALLED HER UP AND SHE SAID SHE WAS SPENDING THE NIGHT HERE, SO...
HEH?
THAT'S ALL?
YOU DROVE ALL THE WAY FROM TOTTORI... JUST BECAUSE?

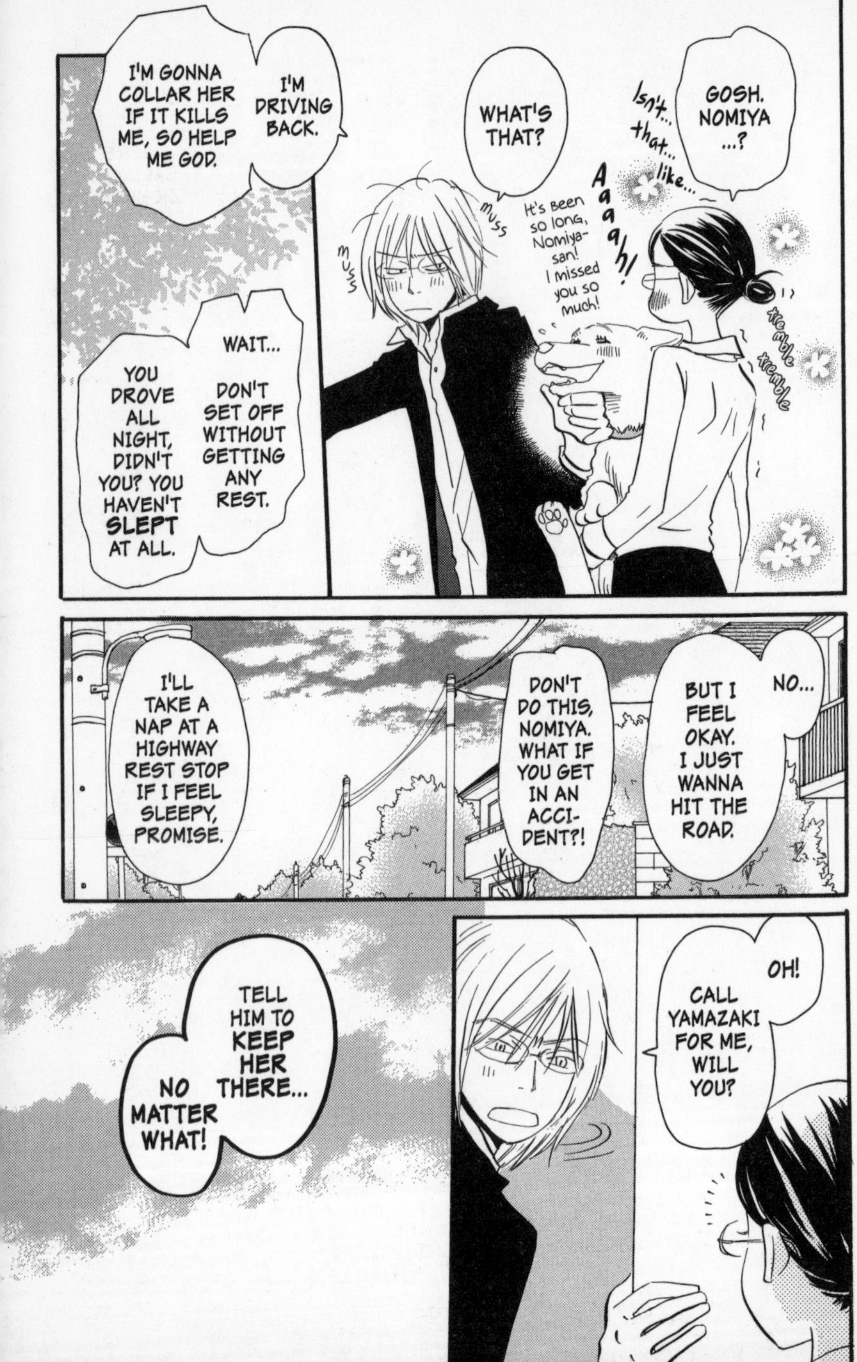
GOSH. NOMIYA ...?
Isn't... that... like...
WHAT'S THAT?
MUSS
MUSS
Aaaah!
It's been so long, Nomiya-san! I missed you so much!
tremble tremble
I'M DRIVING BACK.
I'M GONNA COLLAR HER IF IT KILLS ME, SO HELP ME GOD.
WAIT... DON'T SET OFF WITHOUT GETTING ANY REST.
YOU DROVE ALL NIGHT, DIDN'T YOU? YOU HAVEN'T **SLEPT** AT ALL.
NO... BUT I FEEL OKAY. I JUST WANNA HIT THE ROAD.
DON'T DO THIS, NOMIYA. WHAT IF YOU GET IN AN ACCI-DENT?!
I'LL TAKE A NAP AT A HIGHWAY REST STOP IF I FEEL SLEEPY, PROMISE.
OH! CALL YAMAZAKI FOR ME, WILL YOU?
TELL HIM TO **KEEP HER** THERE... NO MATTER WHAT!

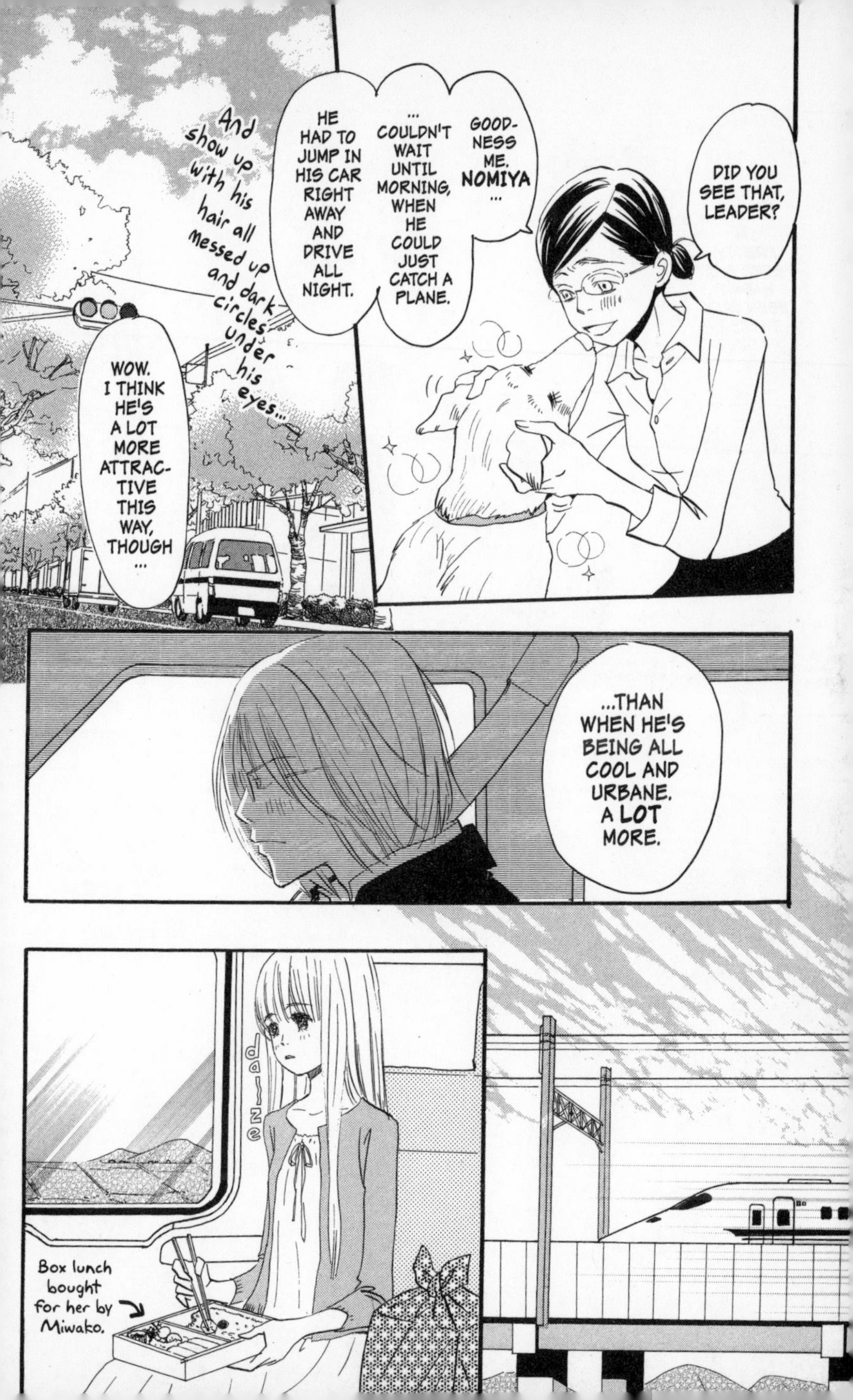
DID YOU SEE THAT, LEADER?
GOODNESS ME. NOMIYA...
...COULDN'T WAIT UNTIL MORNING, WHEN HE COULD JUST CATCH A PLANE.
HE HAD TO JUMP IN HIS CAR RIGHT AWAY AND DRIVE ALL NIGHT.
And show up with his hair all messed up and dark circles under his eyes...
WOW. I THINK HE'S A LOT MORE ATTRACTIVE THIS WAY, THOUGH...
...THAN WHEN HE'S BEING ALL COOL AND URBANE. A LOT MORE.
da~ze
Box lunch bought for her by Miwako.

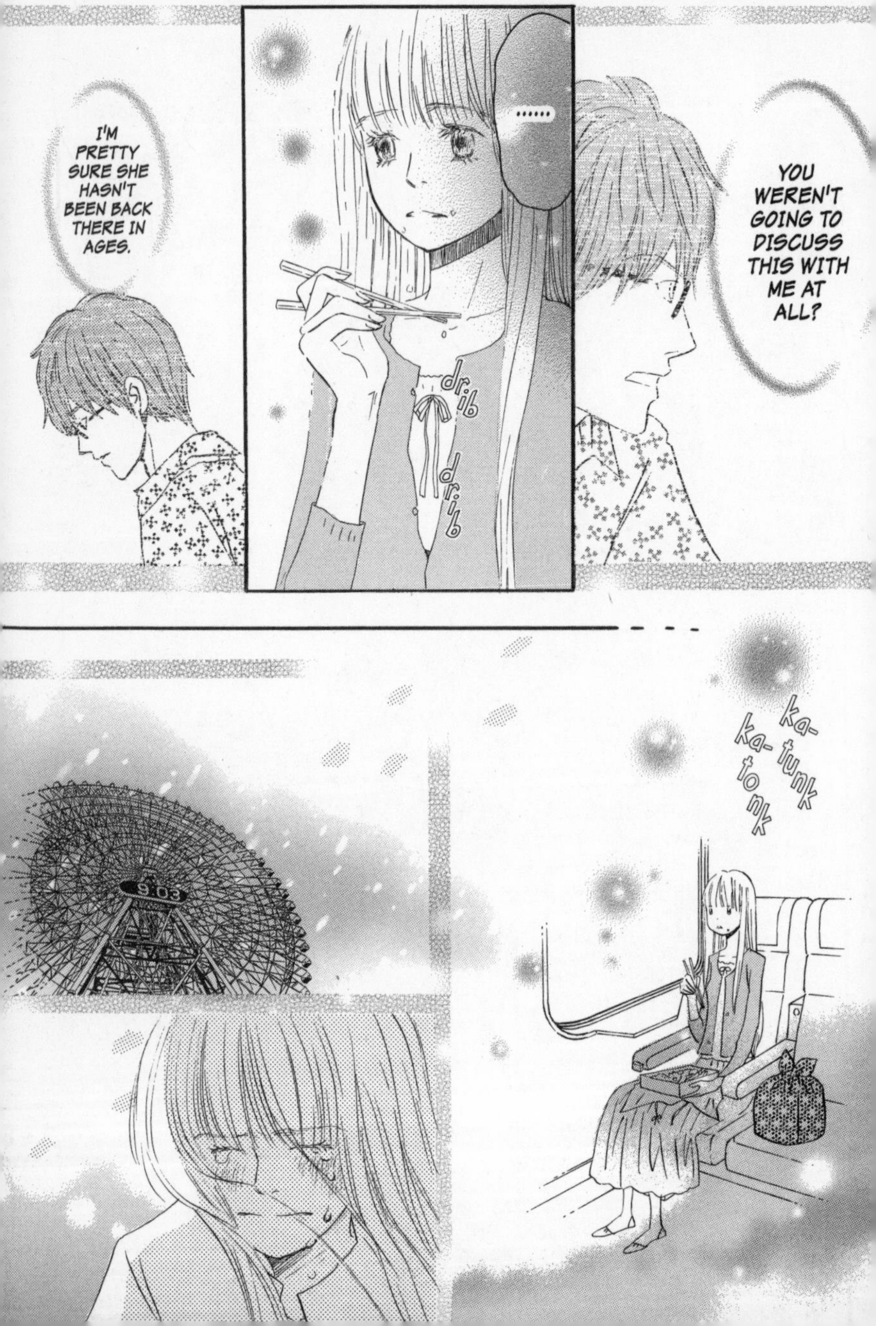
YOU WEREN'T GOING TO DISCUSS THIS WITH ME AT ALL?
......
drib drib
I'M PRETTY SURE SHE HASN'T BEEN BACK THERE IN AGES.
ka-tunk ka-tonk
9:03

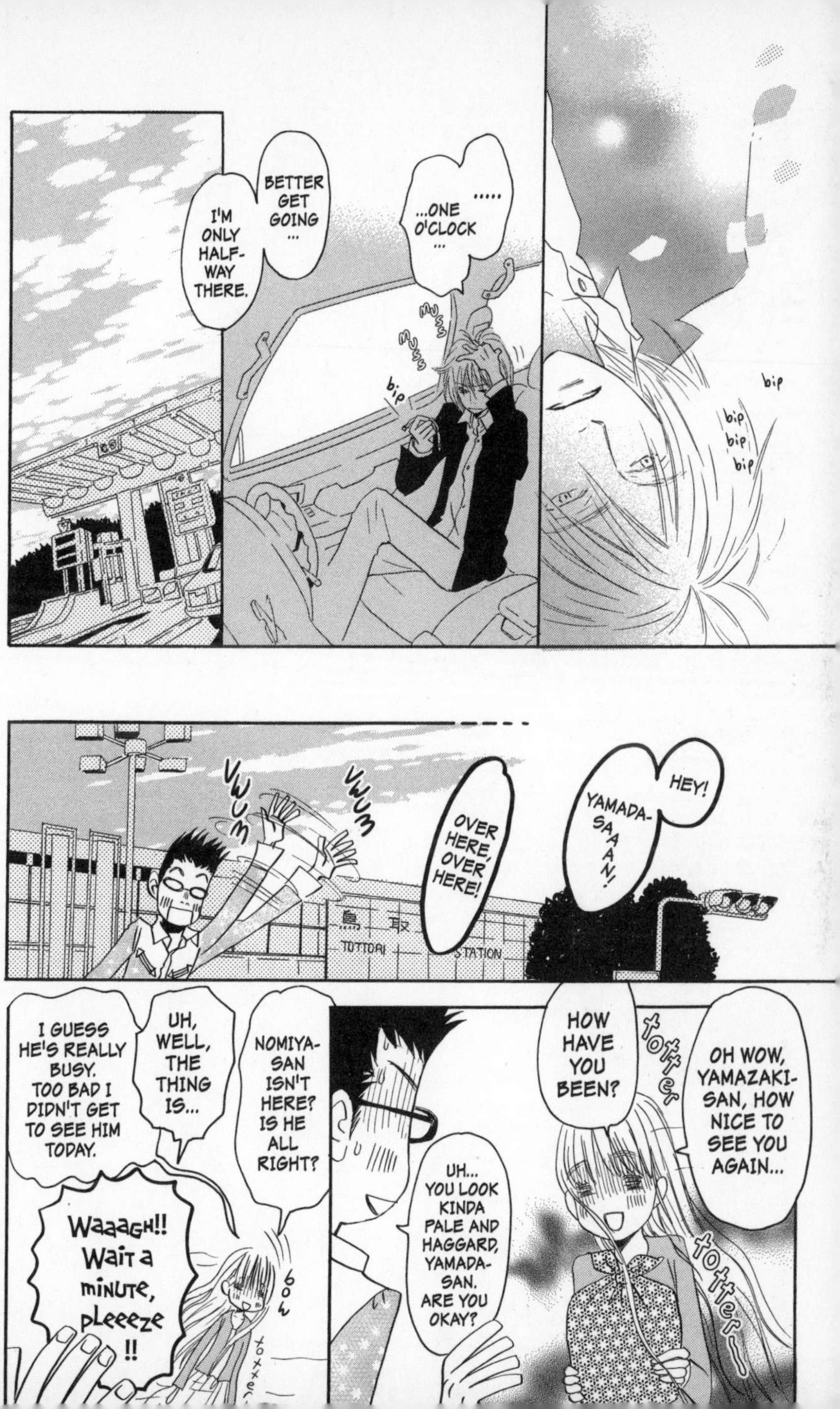
bip
bip
bip
bip
.....
...ONE O'CLOCK ...
MUSS MUSS
bip
BETTER GET GOING ...
I'M ONLY HALF-WAY THERE.
HEY!
YAMADA-SAAAAN!
OVER HERE, OVER HERE!
VWUM
VWUM
TOTTORI STATION
OH WOW, YAMAZAKI-SAN, HOW NICE TO SEE YOU AGAIN...
totter
HOW HAVE YOU BEEN?
totter
UH... YOU LOOK KINDA PALE AND HAGGARD, YAMADA-SAN. ARE YOU OKAY?
NOMIYA-SAN ISN'T HERE? IS HE ALL RIGHT?
UH, WELL, THE THING IS...
I GUESS HE'S REALLY BUSY. TOO BAD I DIDN'T GET TO SEE HIM TODAY.
bow
Waaagh!! Wait a minute, pleeeze !!
totter

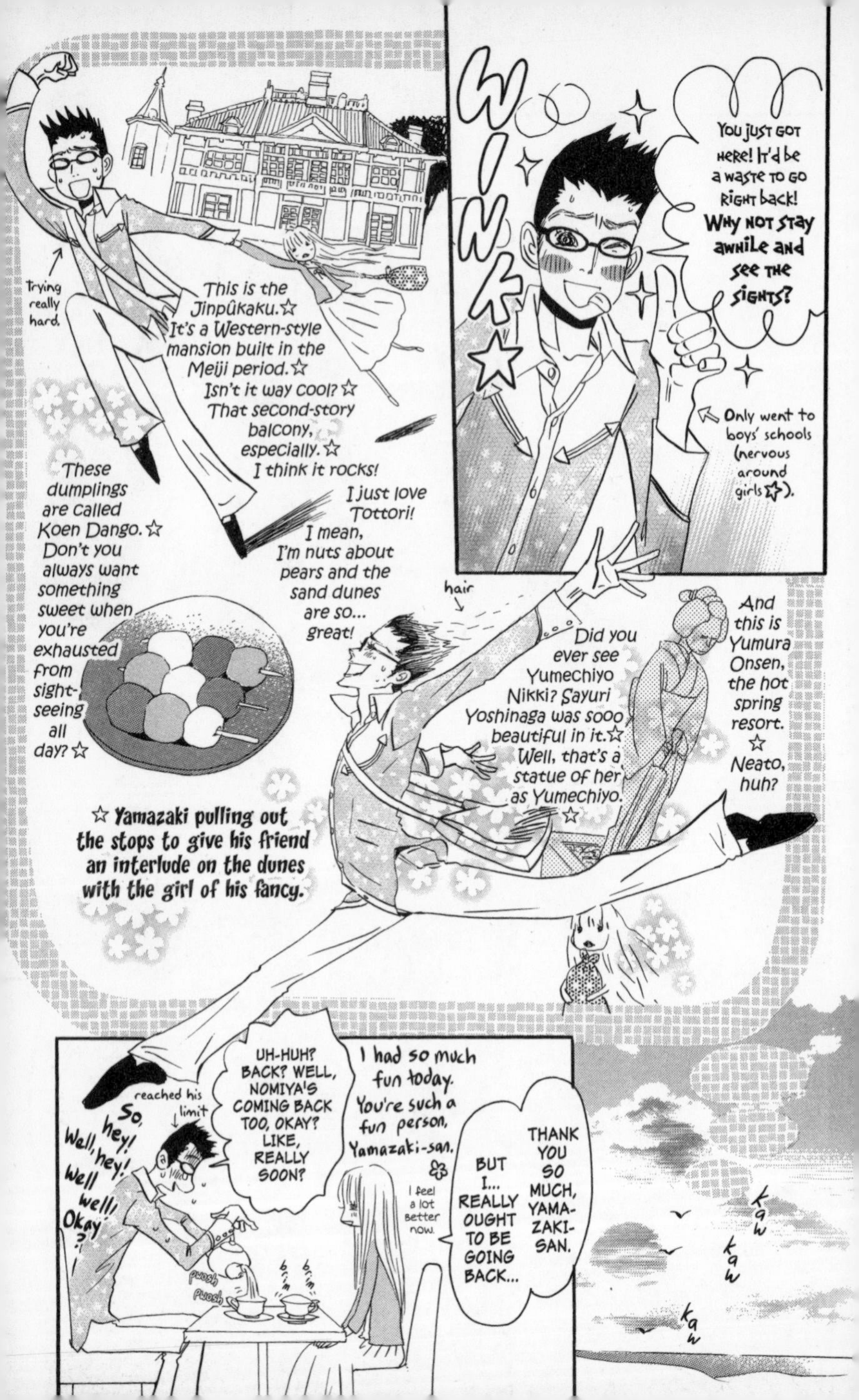
WINK
You just got here! It'd be a waste to go right back! Why not stay awhile and see the sights?
Only went to boys' schools (nervous around girls☆).
This is the Jinpûkaku.☆ It's a Western-style mansion built in the Meiji period.☆ Isn't it way cool?☆ That second-story balcony, especially.☆ I think it rocks!
Trying really hard.
I just love Tottori! I mean, I'm nuts about pears and the sand dunes are so... great!
These dumplings are called Koen Dango.☆ Don't you always want something sweet when you're exhausted from sight-seeing all day?☆
hair
And this is Yumura Onsen, the hot spring resort.☆ Neato, huh?
Did you ever see Yumechiyo Nikki? Sayuri Yoshinaga was sooo beautiful in it.☆ Well, that's a statue of her as Yumechiyo.☆
☆ Yamazaki pulling out the stops to give his friend an interlude on the dunes with the girl of his fancy.
kaw kaw
kaw
THANK YOU SO MUCH, YAMA-ZAKI-SAN.
BUT I... REALLY OUGHT TO BE GOING BACK...
I had so much fun today. You're such a fun person, Yamazaki-san.
I feel a lot better now.
UH-HUH? BACK? WELL, NOMIYA'S COMING BACK TOO, OKAY? LIKE, REALLY SOON?
So, hey! Well, hey! Well well, Okay?!
reached his limit
brim brim
pwosh pwosh

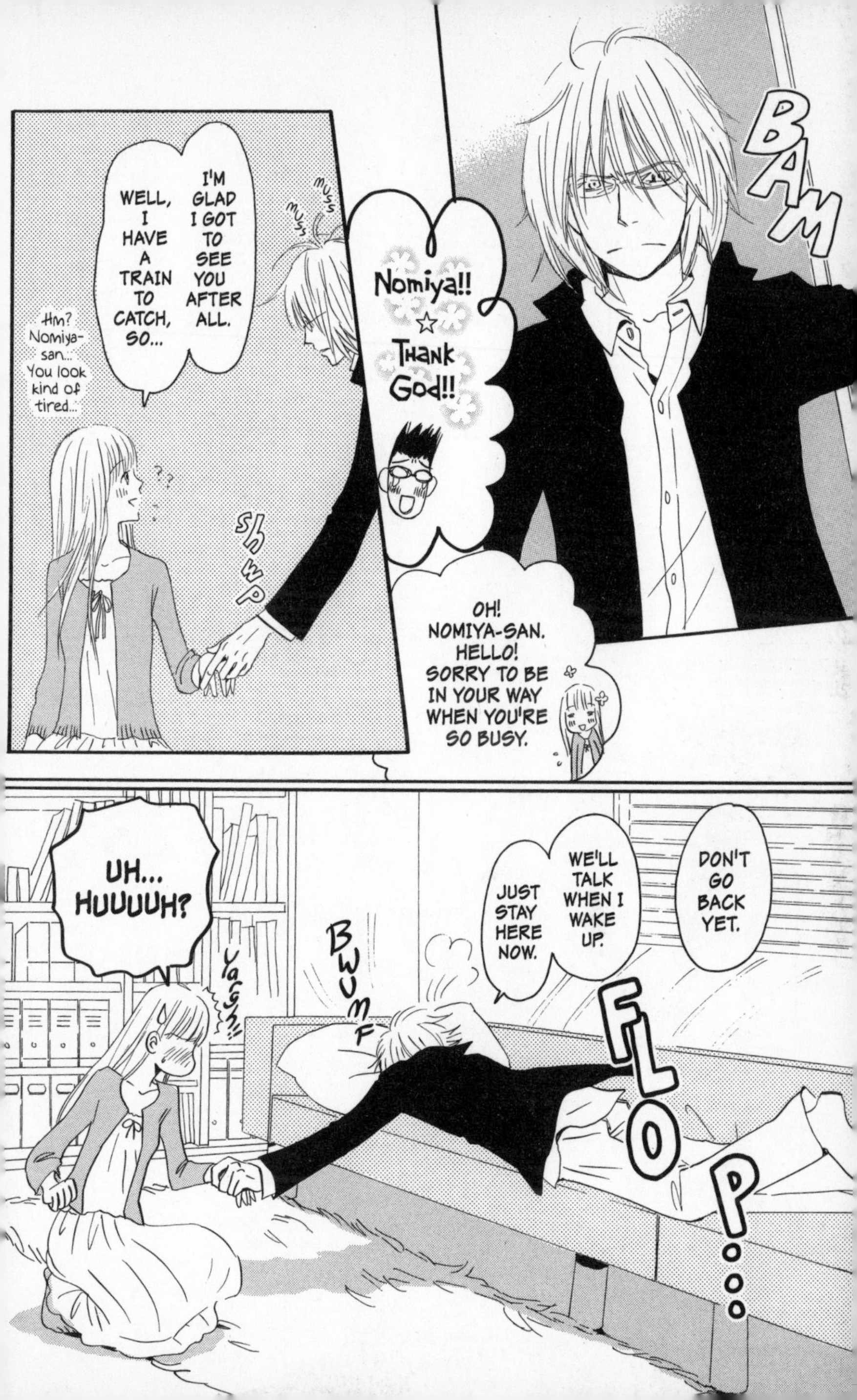
BAM
Nomiya!! ☆ Thank God!!
OH! NOMIYA-SAN. HELLO! SORRY TO BE IN YOUR WAY WHEN YOU'RE SO BUSY.
I'M GLAD I GOT TO SEE YOU AFTER ALL.
WELL, I HAVE A TRAIN TO CATCH, SO...
muss muss
Hm? Nomiya-san... You look kind of tired...
shwp
DON'T GO BACK YET.
WE'LL TALK WHEN I WAKE UP.
JUST STAY HERE NOW.
FLOP...
BWUMF
Yaagh!!
UH... HUUUUH?

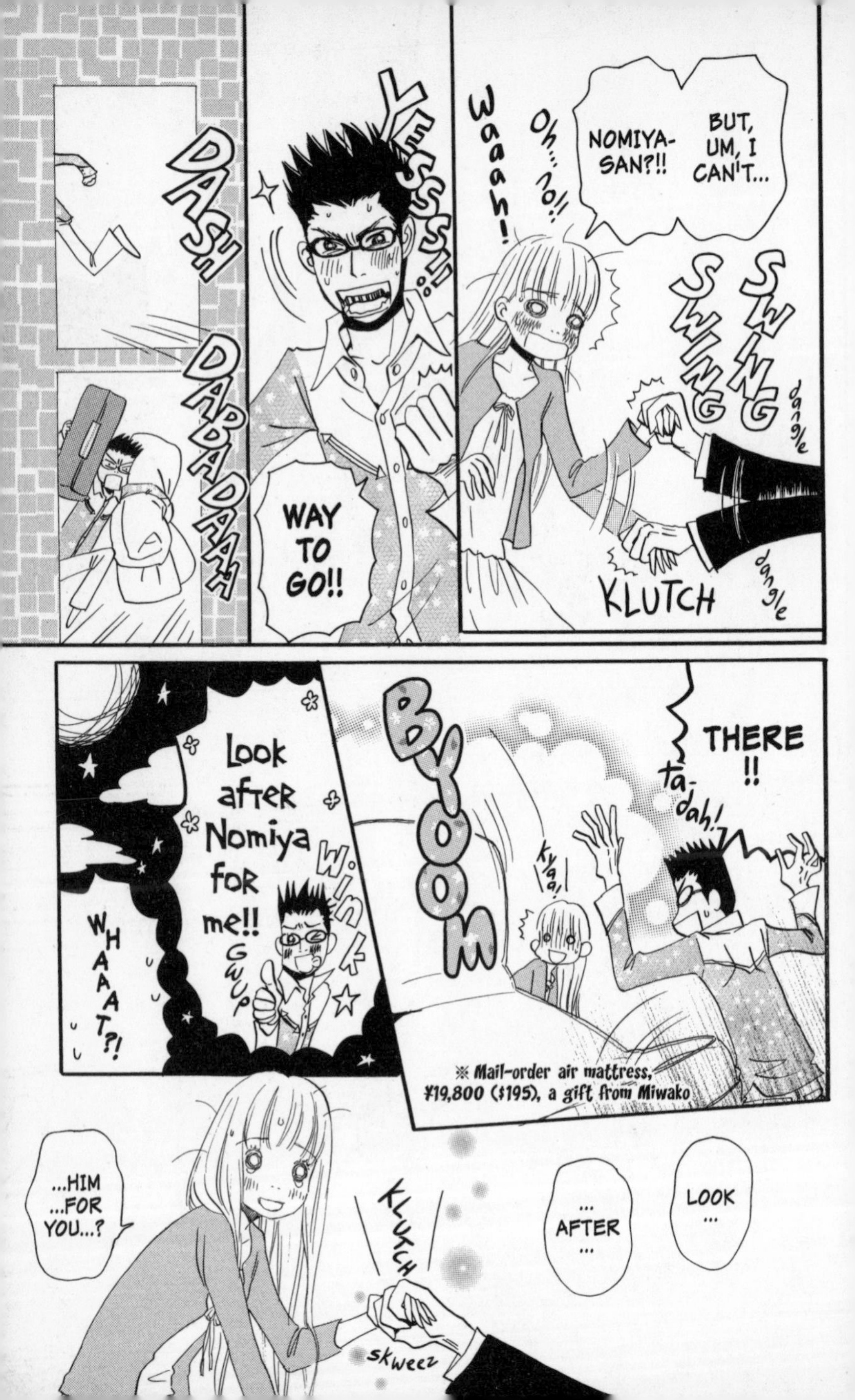
NOMIYA-SAN?!! BUT, UM, I CAN'T...
Oh... no!!
Waaah!
SWING SWING
dangle dangle
KLUTCH
YESSS!!
WAY TO GO!!
DASH
DADADAAAH
THERE!!
ta-dah!
BYOOOM
kya!
※ Mail-order air mattress, ¥19,800 ($195), a gift from Miwako
Look after Nomiya for me!!
wink
GWUP
WHAAAAT?!
LOOK...
...AFTER...
KLUTCH
skweez
...HIM ...FOR YOU...?

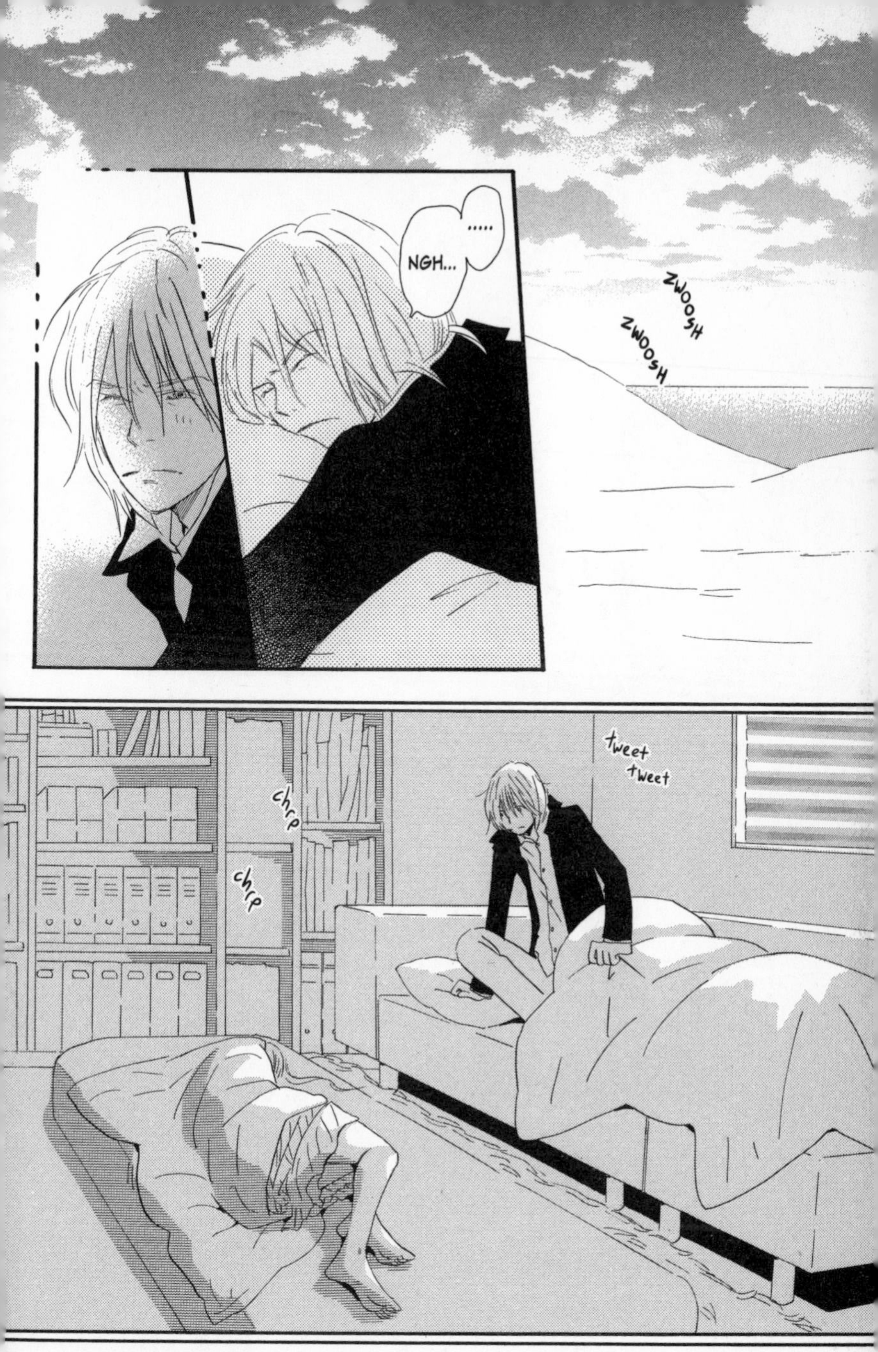
ZWOOSH
ZWOOSH
.....
NGH...
tweet tweet
chrp
chrp

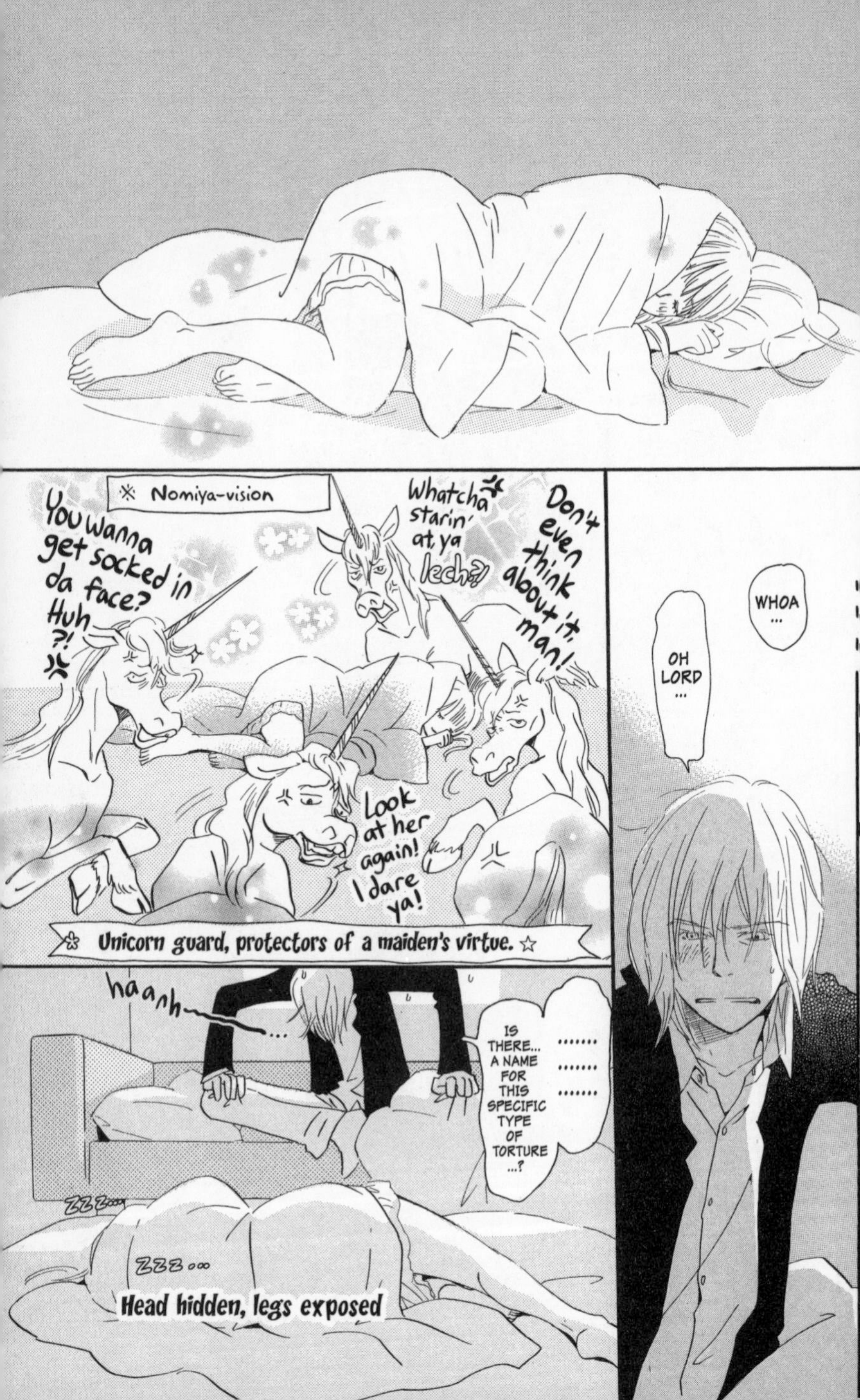
WHOA...
OH LORD...
Don't even think about it, man!
Whatcha starin' at ya lech?!
※ Nomiya-vision
You wanna get socked in da face? Huh?!
Look at her again! I dare ya!
✿ Unicorn guard, protectors of a maiden's virtue. ☆
IS THERE... A NAME FOR THIS SPECIFIC TYPE OF TORTURE ...?
....
....
....
haanh—...
zzz...
zzz...
Head hidden, legs exposed

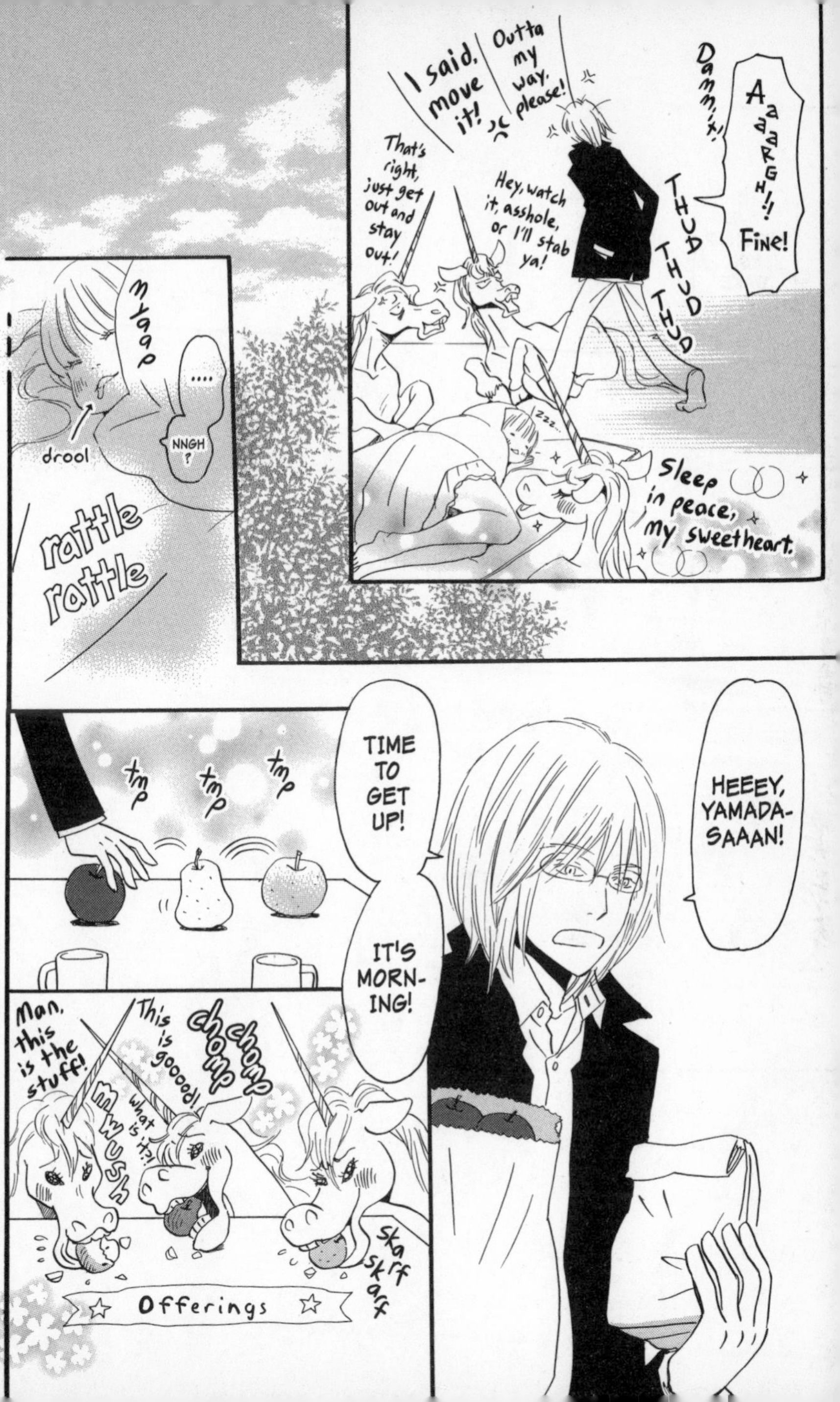
Aaaargh!!
Fine!
Dammit!
THUD
THUD
THUD
Outta my way, please!
I said, move it!
Hey, watch it, asshole, or I'll stab ya!
That's right, just get out and stay out!
zzz...
Sleep in peace, my sweetheart.
Myaaap
....
NNGH?
drool
rattle rattle
HEEEY, YAMADA-SAAAN!
TIME TO GET UP!
IT'S MORNING!
tmp
tmp
tmp
skarf skarf
chomp chomp
This is gooood!
what is it?!
mush
Man, this is the stuff!
☆ Offerings ☆

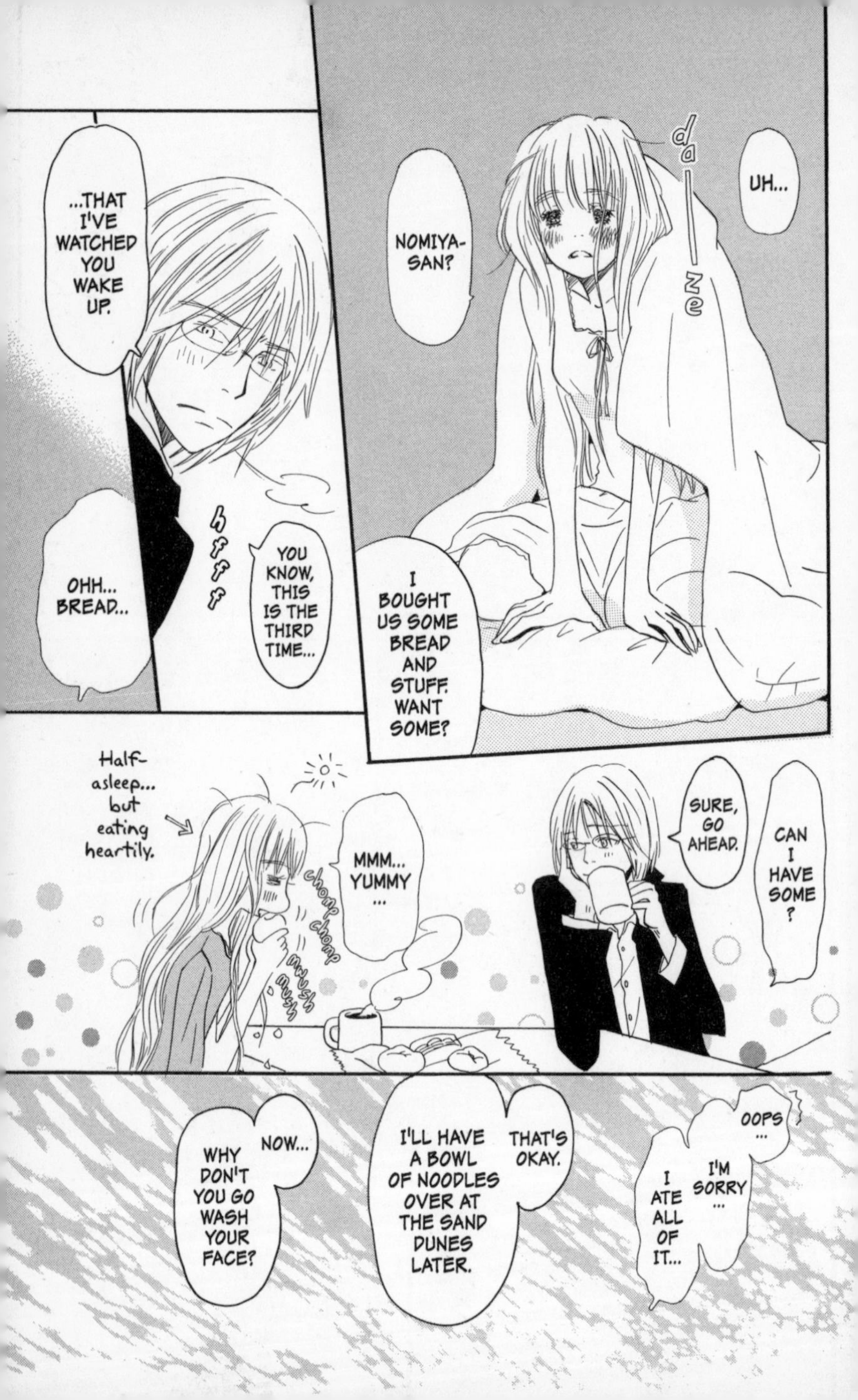
UH...
da—ze
NOMIYA-SAN?
I BOUGHT US SOME BREAD AND STUFF. WANT SOME?
OHH... BREAD...
hfff
YOU KNOW, THIS IS THE THIRD TIME...
...THAT I'VE WATCHED YOU WAKE UP.
CAN I HAVE SOME?
SURE, GO AHEAD.
MMM... YUMMY...
chomp chomp
mush mush
Half-asleep... but eating heartily.
OOPS...
I'M SORRY...
I ATE ALL OF IT...
THAT'S OKAY.
I'LL HAVE A BOWL OF NOODLES OVER AT THE SAND DUNES LATER.
NOW...
WHY DON'T YOU GO WASH YOUR FACE?

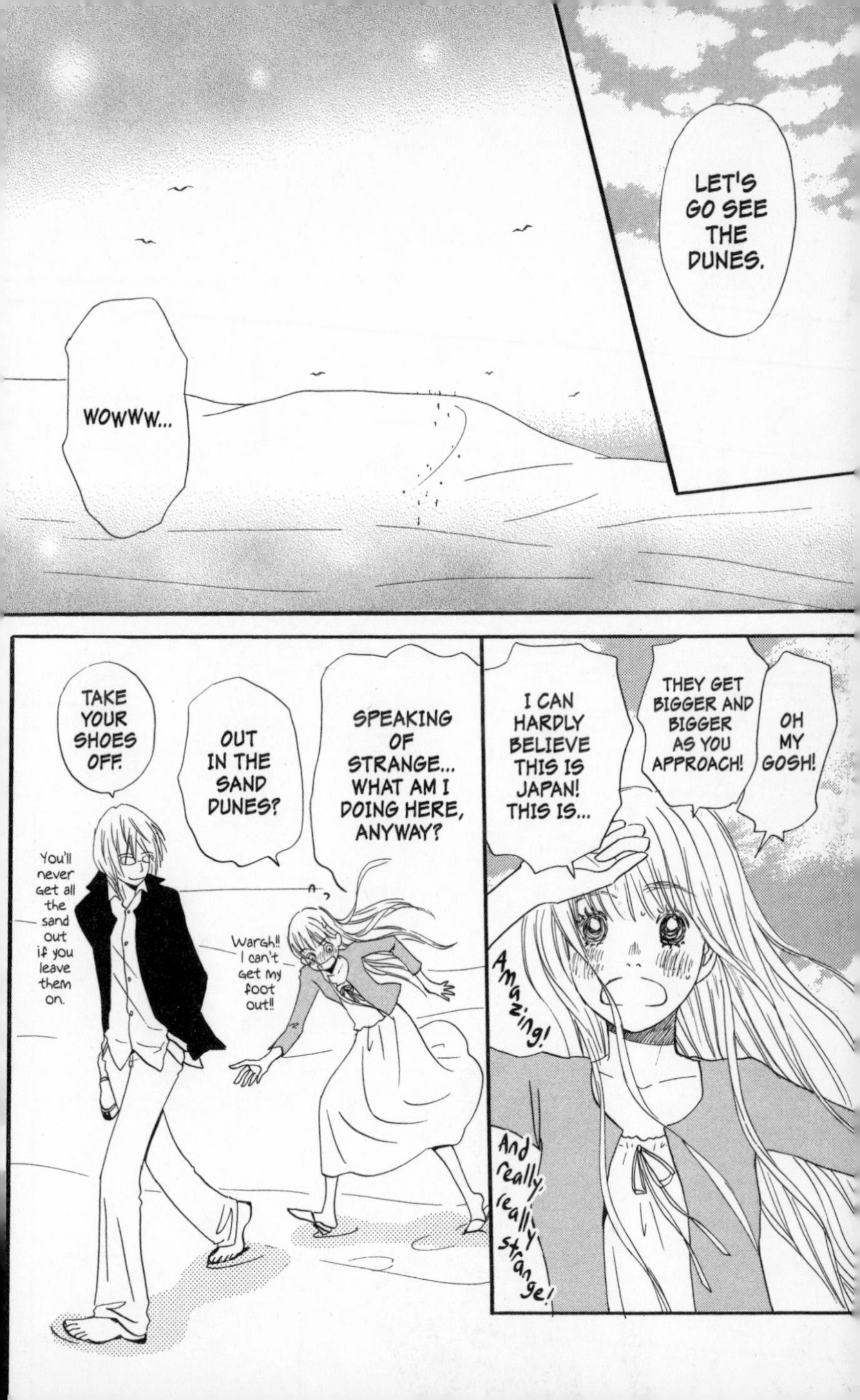
LET'S GO SEE THE DUNES.
WOWWW...
OH MY GOSH!
THEY GET BIGGER AND BIGGER AS YOU APPROACH!
I CAN HARDLY BELIEVE THIS IS JAPAN! THIS IS...
Amazing!
And really, really strange!
SPEAKING OF STRANGE... WHAT AM I DOING HERE, ANYWAY?
OUT IN THE SAND DUNES?
TAKE YOUR SHOES OFF.
Wargh!! I can't get my foot out!!
You'll never get all the sand out if you leave them on.

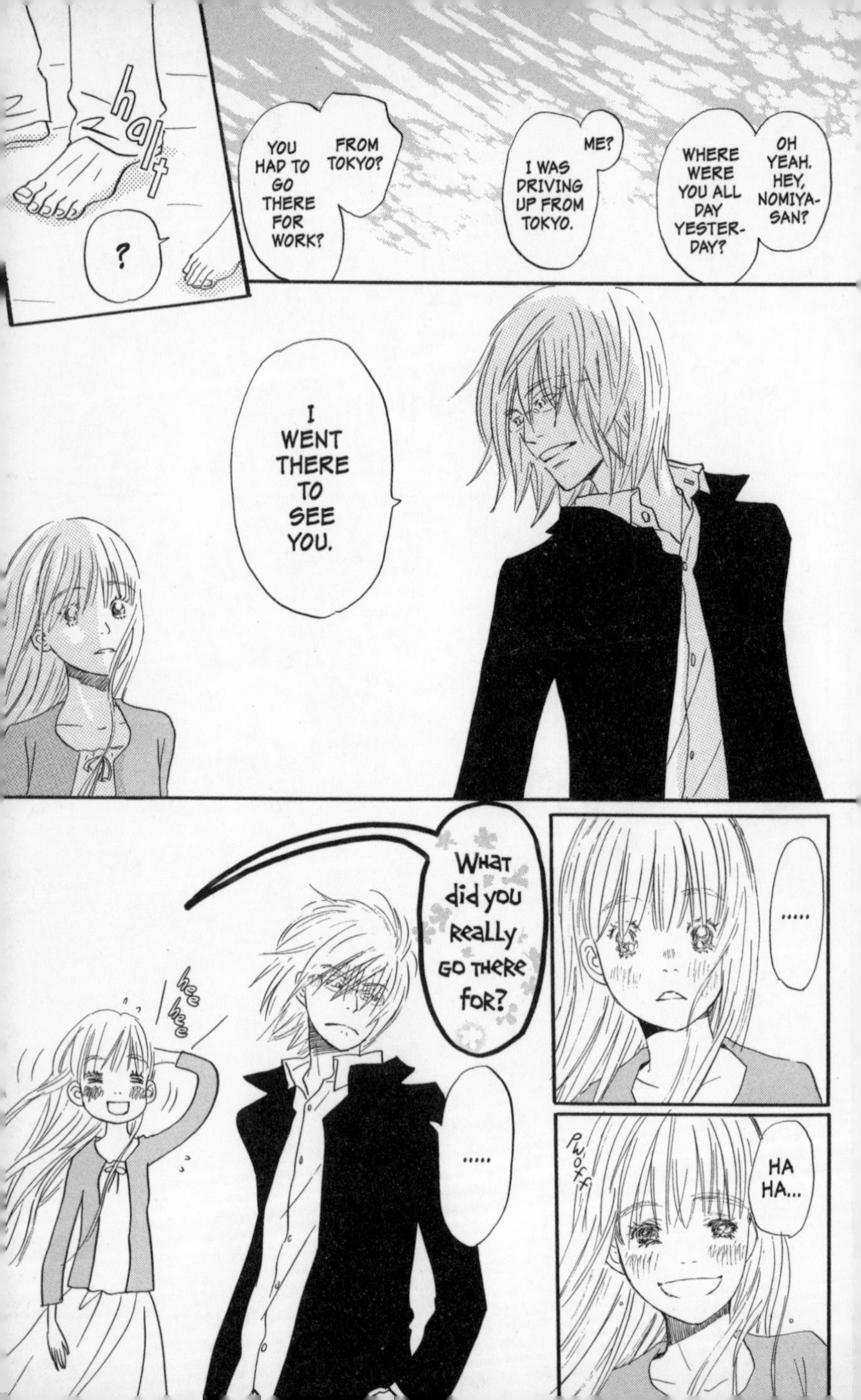
OH YEAH. HEY, NOMIYA-SAN?
WHERE WERE YOU ALL DAY YESTER-DAY?
ME?
I WAS DRIVING UP FROM TOKYO.
FROM TOKYO?
YOU HAD TO GO THERE FOR WORK?
halt
?
I WENT THERE TO SEE YOU.
.....
HA HA...
Pwoff
What did you really go there for?
.....
hee hee

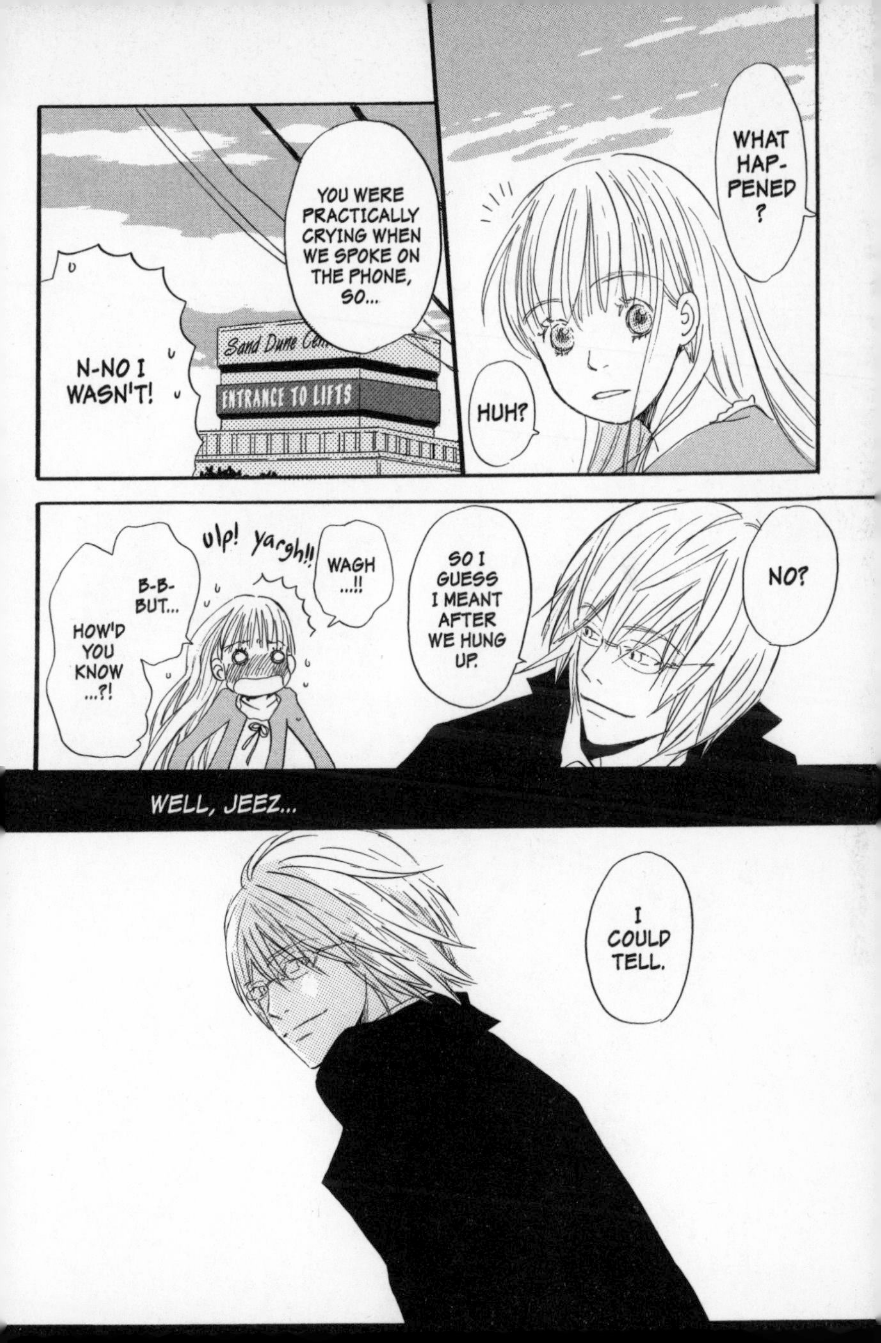
WHAT HAP-PENED?
HUH?
YOU WERE PRACTICALLY CRYING WHEN WE SPOKE ON THE PHONE, SO...
ENTRANCE TO LIFTS
N-NO I WASN'T!
NO?
SO I GUESS I MEANT AFTER WE HUNG UP.
WAGH ...!!
ulp! yargh!!
B-B-BUT...
HOW'D YOU KNOW ...?!
WELL, JEEZ...
I COULD TELL.

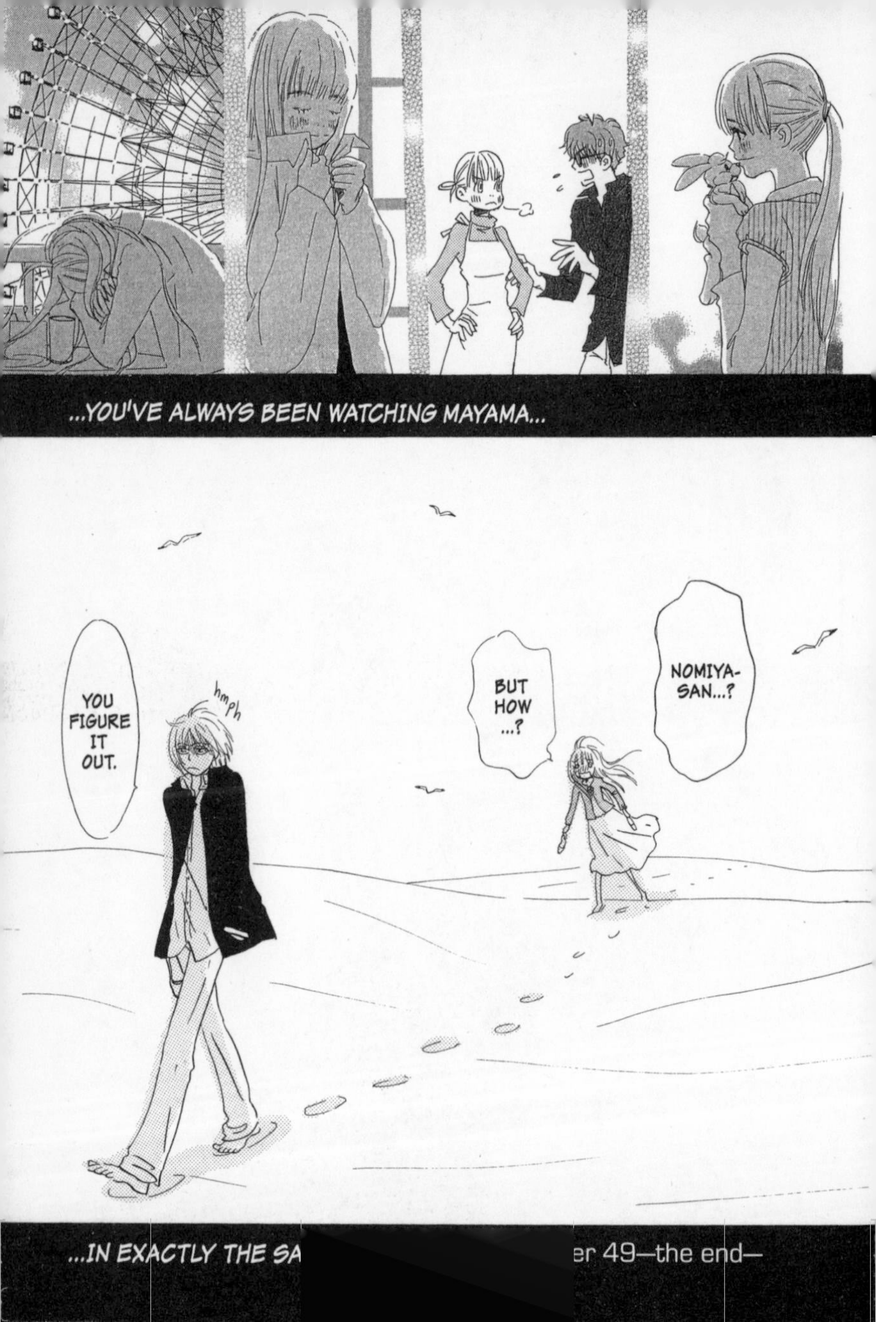
...YOU'VE ALWAYS BEEN WATCHING MAYAMA...
NOMIYA-SAN...?
BUT HOW ...?
hmph
YOU FIGURE IT OUT.
...IN EXACTLY THE SA[redacted]er 49—the end—

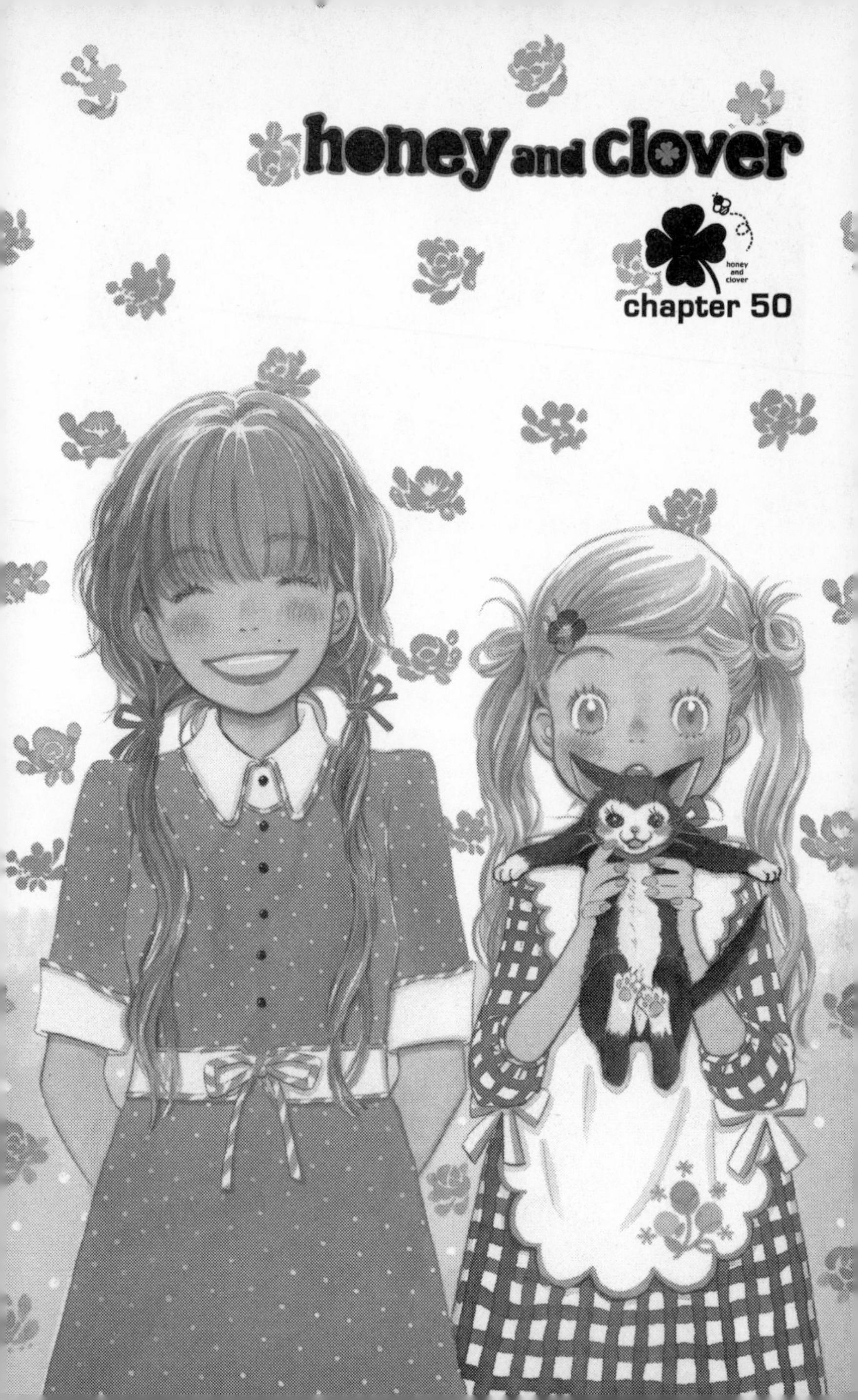
honey and clover
honey and clover
chapter 50

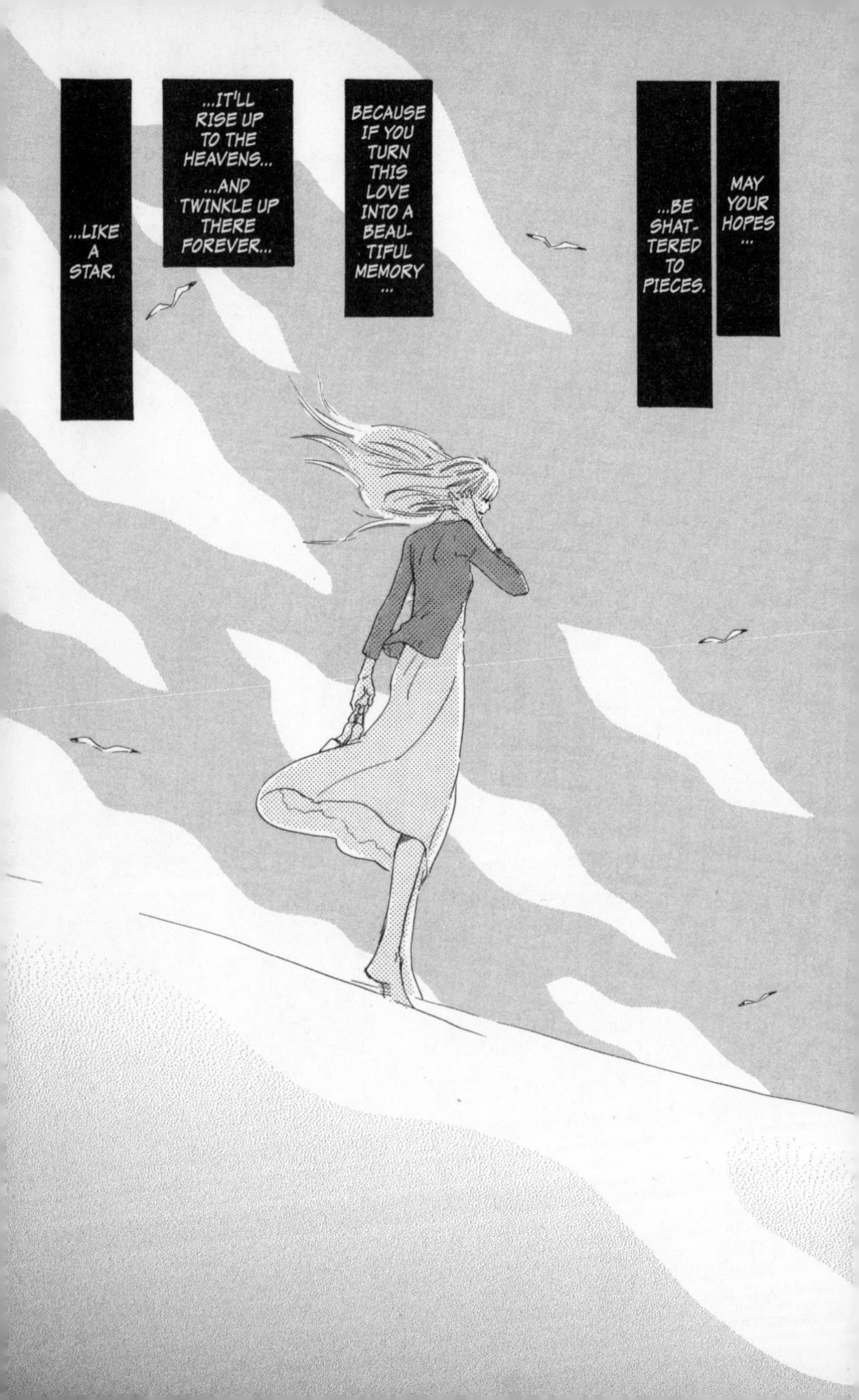
MAY YOUR HOPES ...
...BE SHATTERED TO PIECES.
BECAUSE IF YOU TURN THIS LOVE INTO A BEAUTIFUL MEMORY ...
...IT'LL RISE UP TO THE HEAVENS...
...AND TWINKLE UP THERE FOREVER...
...LIKE A STAR.

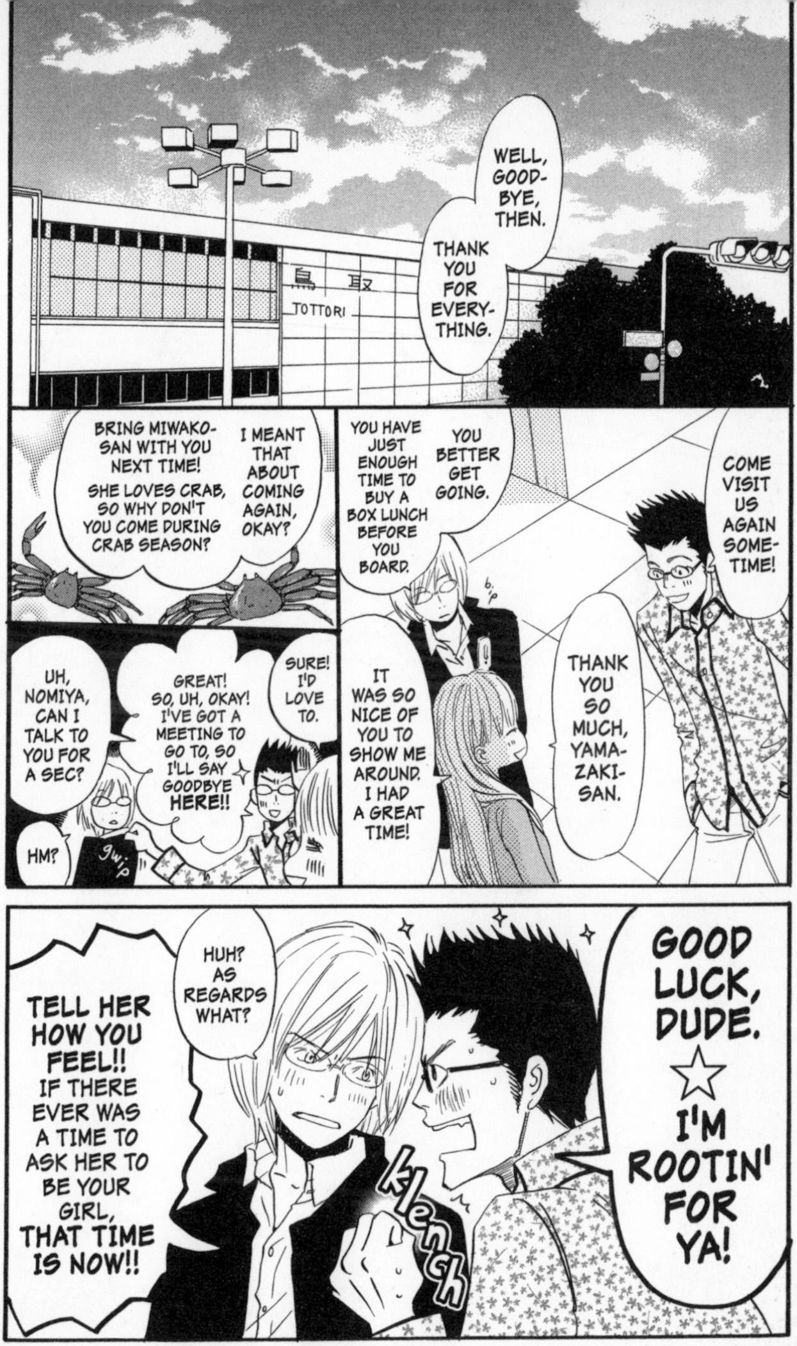
WELL, GOODBYE, THEN.
THANK YOU FOR EVERYTHING.
鳥取
TOTTORI
COME VISIT US AGAIN SOMETIME!
YOU BETTER GET GOING.
YOU HAVE JUST ENOUGH TIME TO BUY A BOX LUNCH BEFORE YOU BOARD.
bip
THANK YOU SO MUCH, YAMAZAKI-SAN.
IT WAS SO NICE OF YOU TO SHOW ME AROUND. I HAD A GREAT TIME!
I MEANT THAT ABOUT COMING AGAIN, OKAY?
BRING MIWAKO-SAN WITH YOU NEXT TIME!
SHE LOVES CRAB, SO WHY DON'T YOU COME DURING CRAB SEASON?
SURE! I'D LOVE TO.
GREAT! SO, UH, OKAY! I'VE GOT A MEETING TO GO TO, SO I'LL SAY GOODBYE HERE!!
UH, NOMIYA, CAN I TALK TO YOU FOR A SEC?
HM?
gwip
GOOD LUCK, DUDE. ☆ I'M ROOTIN' FOR YA!
HUH? AS REGARDS WHAT?
TELL HER HOW YOU FEEL!! IF THERE EVER WAS A TIME TO ASK HER TO BE YOUR GIRL, THAT TIME IS NOW!!
klench

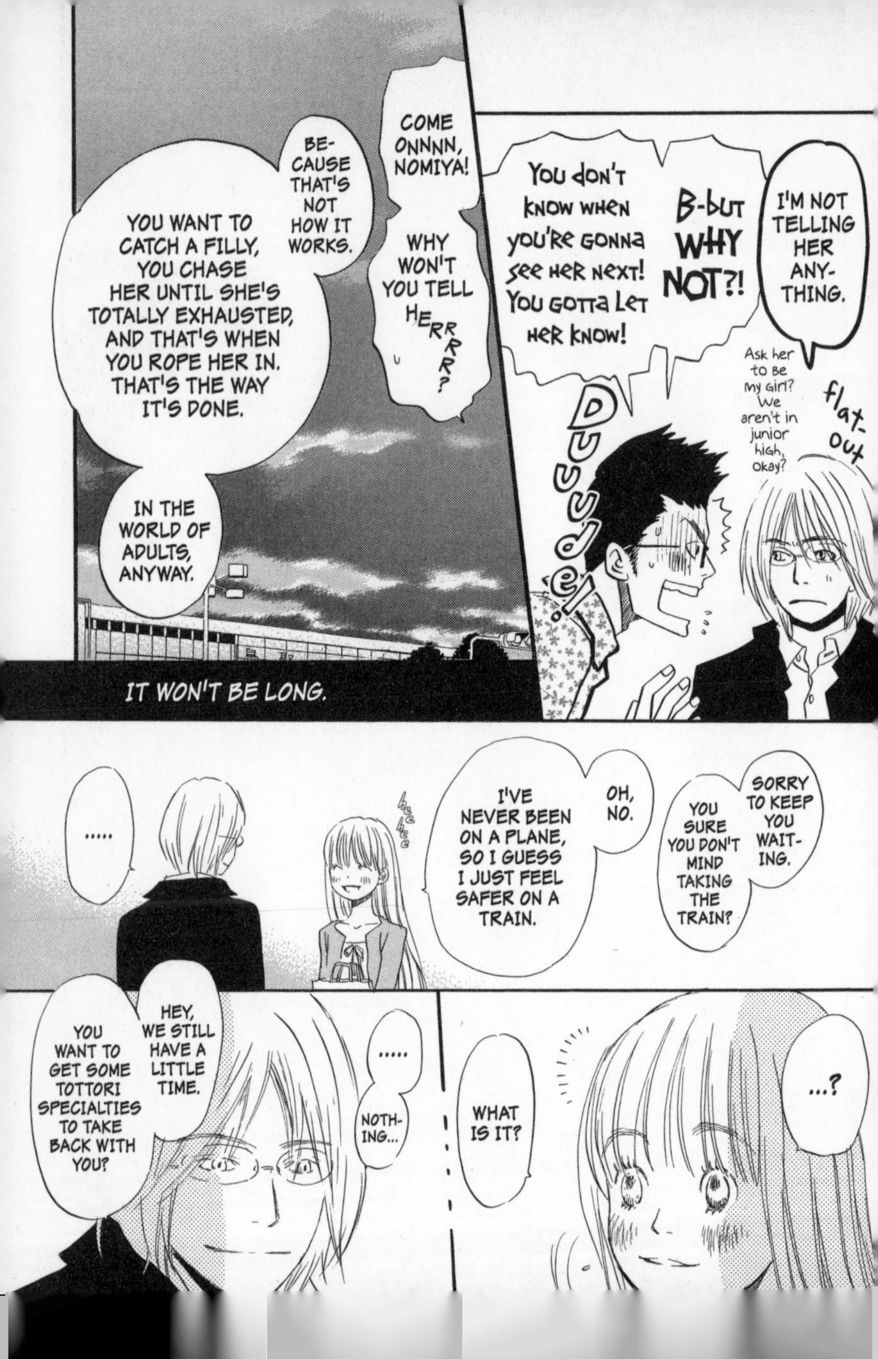
I'M NOT TELLING HER ANYTHING.
flat-out
Ask her to be my girl? We aren't in junior high, okay?
B-but WHY NOT?!
You don't know when you're gonna see her next! You gotta let her know!
Duuude!
COME ONNNN, NOMIYA!
WHY WON'T YOU TELL HERRRR?
BE-CAUSE THAT'S NOT HOW IT WORKS.
YOU WANT TO CATCH A FILLY, YOU CHASE HER UNTIL SHE'S TOTALLY EXHAUSTED, AND THAT'S WHEN YOU ROPE HER IN. THAT'S THE WAY IT'S DONE.
IN THE WORLD OF ADULTS, ANYWAY.
IT WON'T BE LONG.
SORRY TO KEEP YOU WAIT-ING.
YOU SURE YOU DON'T MIND TAKING THE TRAIN?
OH, NO.
I'VE NEVER BEEN ON A PLANE, SO I GUESS I JUST FEEL SAFER ON A TRAIN.
hee hee
.....
...?
WHAT IS IT?
.....
NOTH-ING...
HEY, WE STILL HAVE A LITTLE TIME.
YOU WANT TO GET SOME TOTTORI SPECIALTIES TO TAKE BACK WITH YOU?

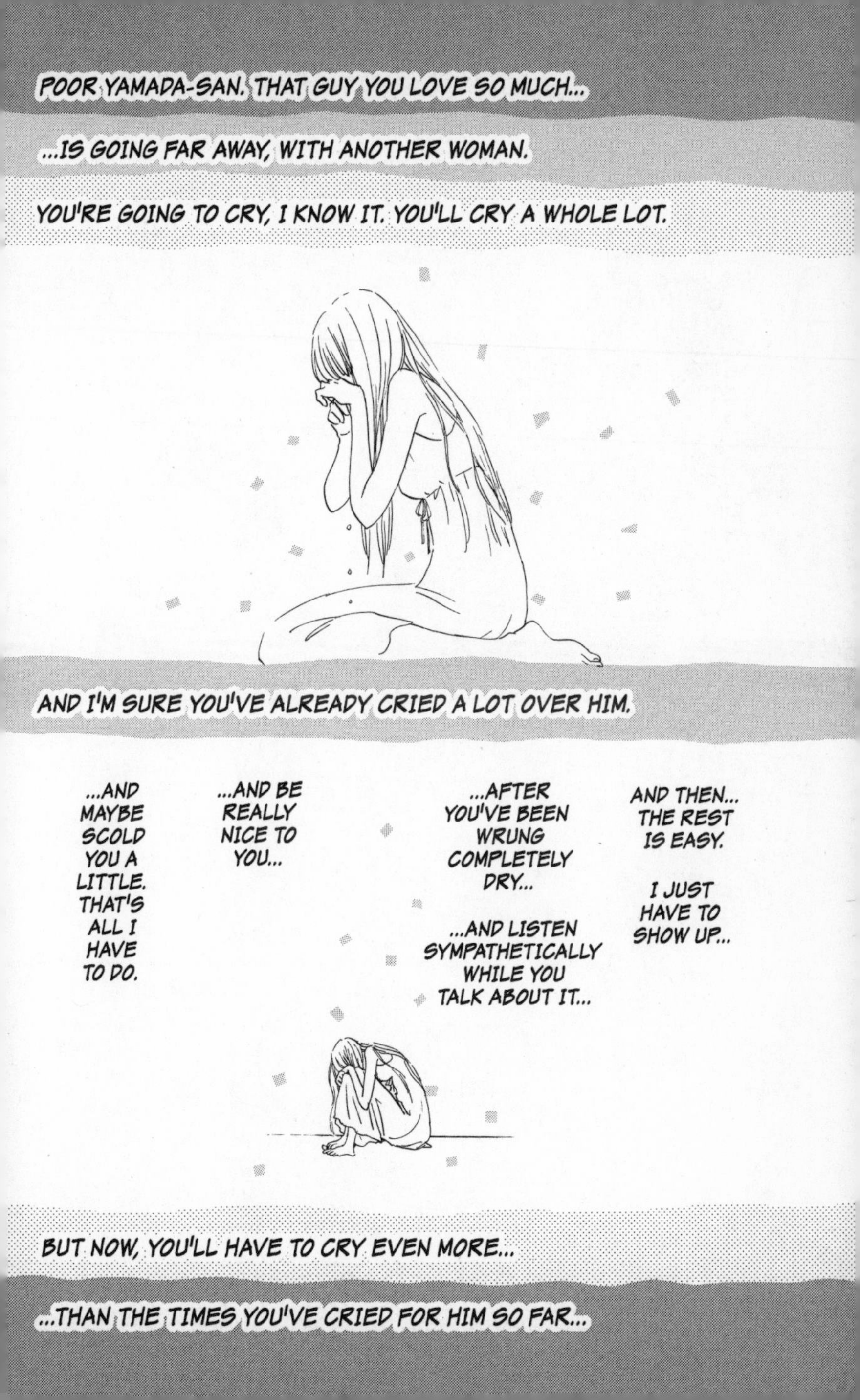
POOR YAMADA-SAN. THAT GUY YOU LOVE SO MUCH...
...IS GOING FAR AWAY, WITH ANOTHER WOMAN.
YOU'RE GOING TO CRY, I KNOW IT. YOU'LL CRY A WHOLE LOT.
AND I'M SURE YOU'VE ALREADY CRIED A LOT OVER HIM.
AND THEN... THE REST IS EASY.
I JUST HAVE TO SHOW UP...
...AFTER YOU'VE BEEN WRUNG COMPLETELY DRY...
...AND LISTEN SYMPATHETICALLY WHILE YOU TALK ABOUT IT...
...AND BE REALLY NICE TO YOU...
...AND MAYBE SCOLD YOU A LITTLE. THAT'S ALL I HAVE TO DO.
BUT NOW, YOU'LL HAVE TO CRY EVEN MORE...
...THAN THE TIMES YOU'VE CRIED FOR HIM SO FAR...

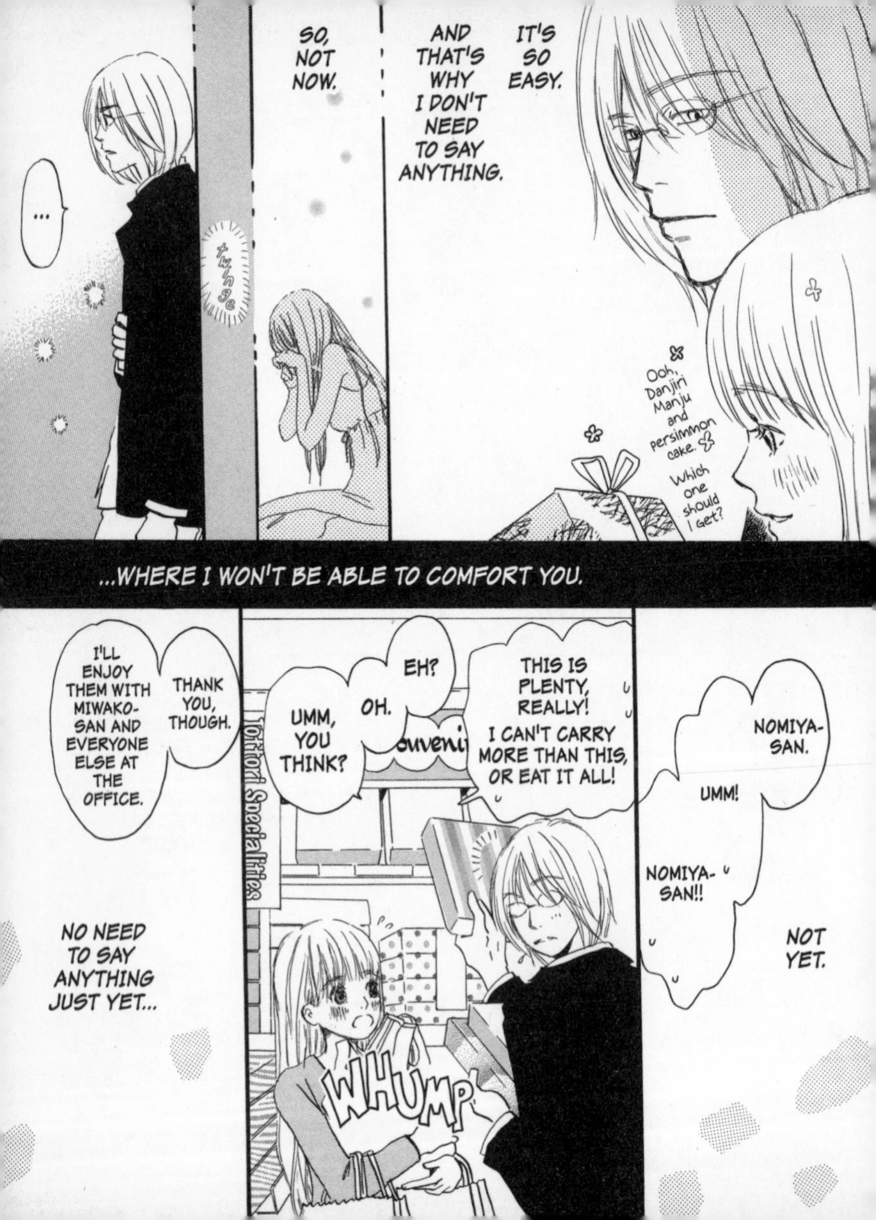
IT'S SO EASY.
Ooh, Danjiri Manju and persimmon cake.
Which one should I get?
AND THAT'S WHY I DON'T NEED TO SAY ANYTHING.
SO, NOT NOW.
twinge
...
...WHERE I WON'T BE ABLE TO COMFORT YOU.
NOMIYA-SAN.
UMM!
NOMIYA-SAN!!
NOT YET.
THIS IS PLENTY, REALLY!
I CAN'T CARRY MORE THAN THIS, OR EAT IT ALL!
EH?
OH.
UMM, YOU THINK?
Tottori Specialities
WHUMP
THANK YOU, THOUGH.
I'LL ENJOY THEM WITH MIWAKO-SAN AND EVERYONE ELSE AT THE OFFICE.
NO NEED TO SAY ANYTHING JUST YET...

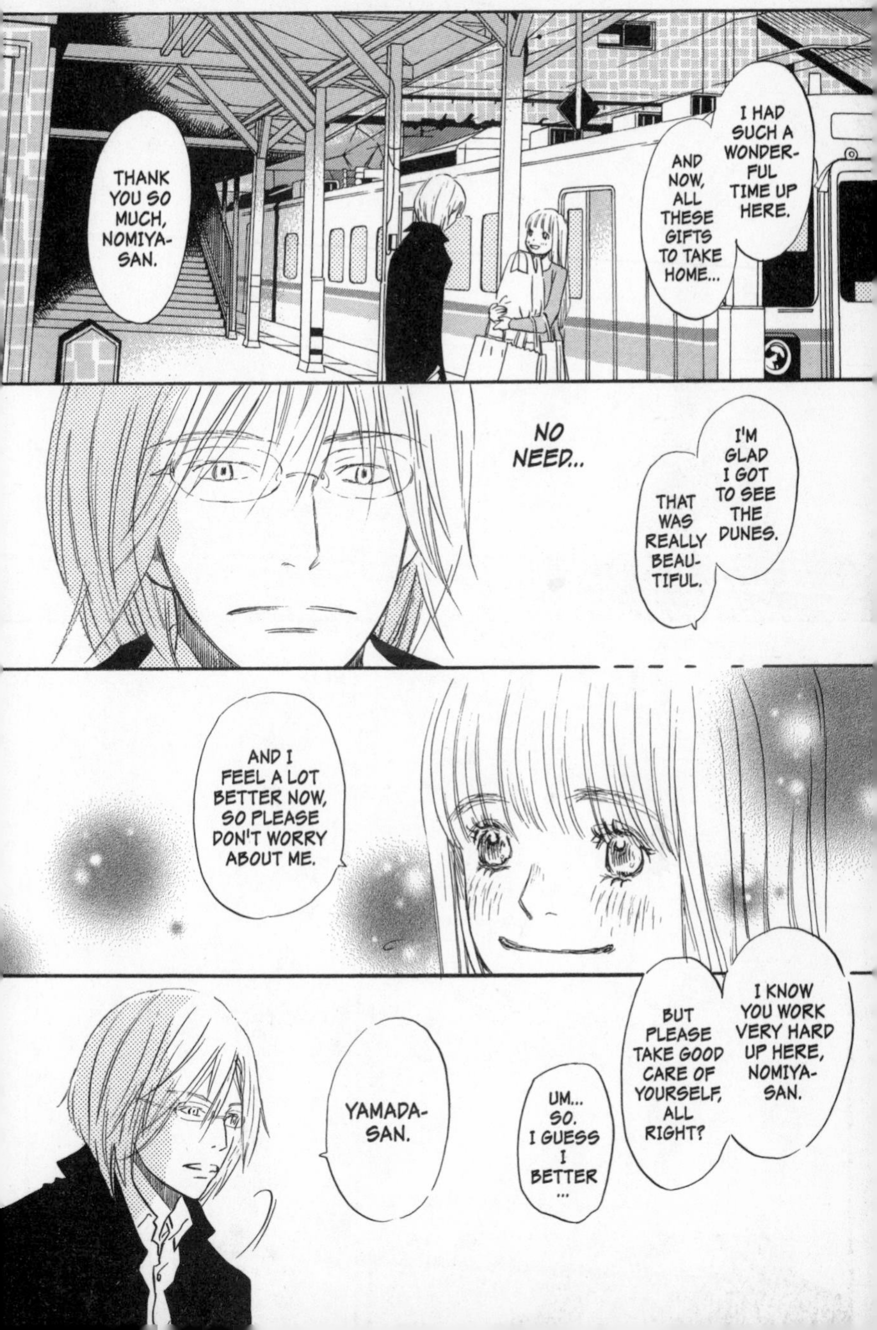

I HAD SUCH A WONDER-FUL TIME UP HERE.
AND NOW, ALL THESE GIFTS TO TAKE HOME...
THANK YOU SO MUCH, NOMIYA-SAN.
I'M GLAD I GOT TO SEE THE DUNES.
THAT WAS REALLY BEAU-TIFUL.
NO NEED...
AND I FEEL A LOT BETTER NOW, SO PLEASE DON'T WORRY ABOUT ME.
I KNOW YOU WORK VERY HARD UP HERE, NOMIYA-SAN.
BUT PLEASE TAKE GOOD CARE OF YOURSELF, ALL RIGHT?
UM... SO. I GUESS I BETTER ...
YAMADA-SAN.

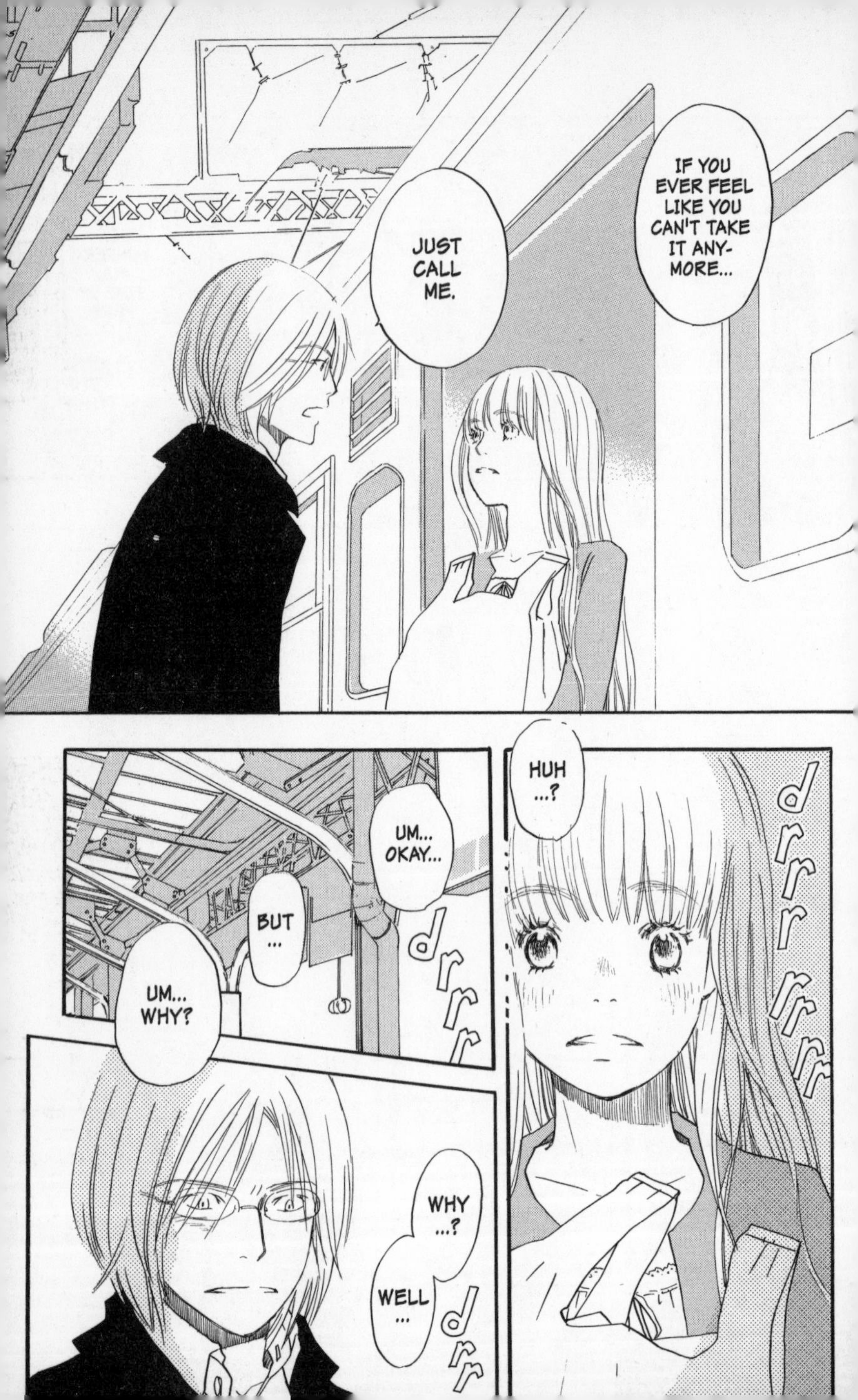
IF YOU EVER FEEL LIKE YOU CAN'T TAKE IT ANY- MORE...
JUST CALL ME.
HUH ...?
drrrrrr
UM... OKAY...
BUT ...
UM... WHY?
drrr
WHY ...?
WELL ...
drr

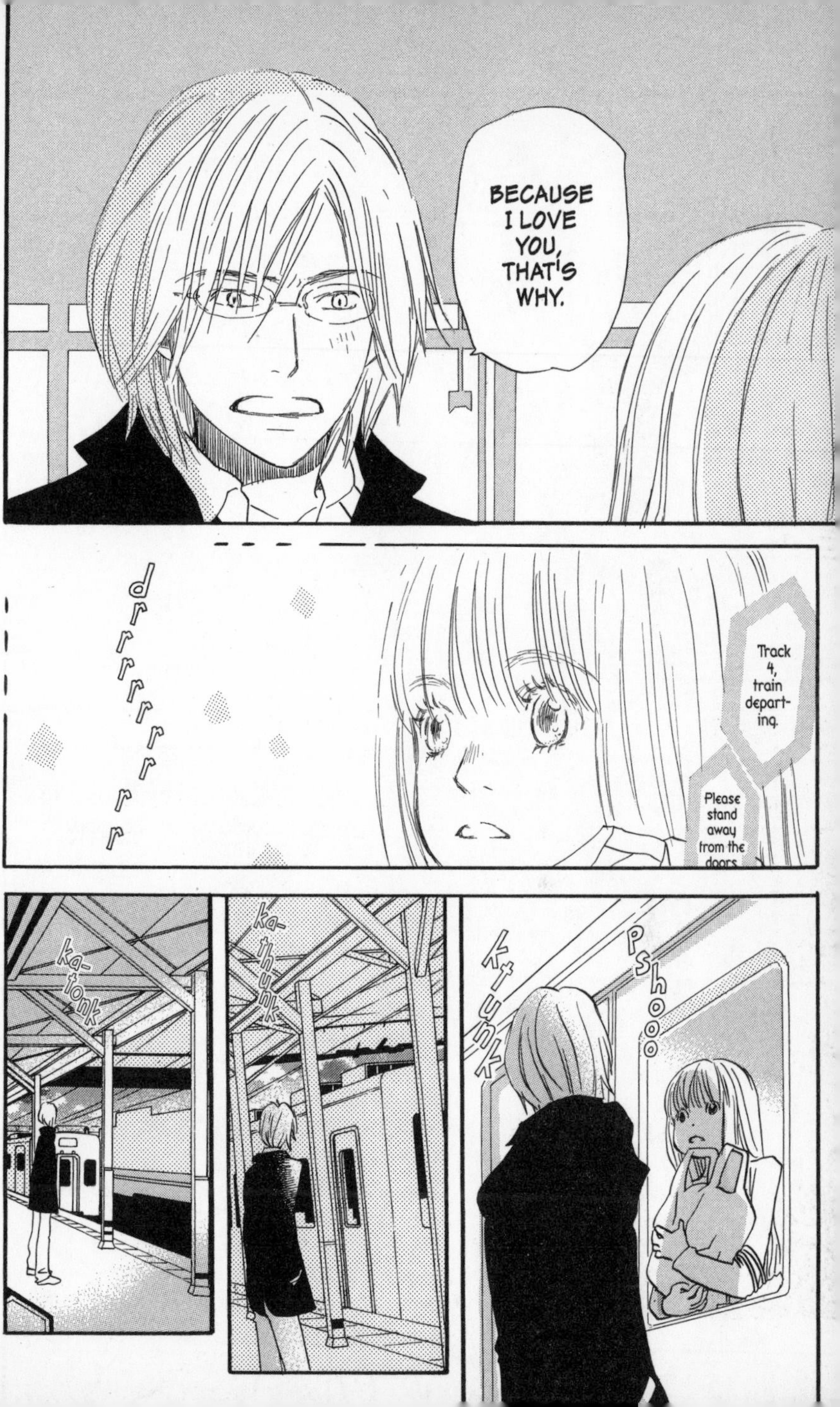
BECAUSE I LOVE YOU, THAT'S WHY.
Track 4, train depart-ing.
Please stand away from the doors.
drrrrrrrrr
Pshooo
ktunk
ka-thunk
ka-tonk

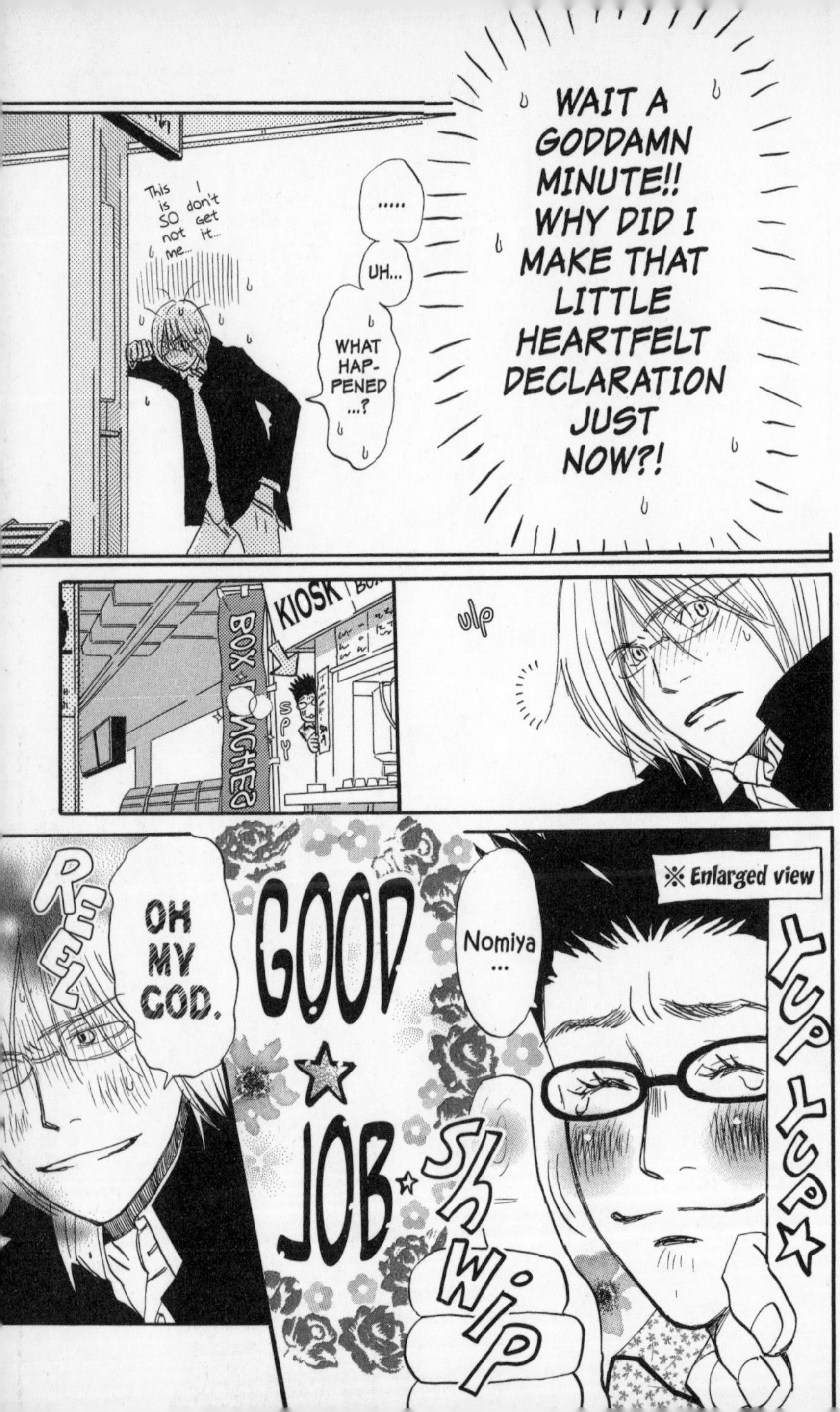

WAIT A GODDAMN MINUTE!! WHY DID I MAKE THAT LITTLE HEARTFELT DECLARATION JUST NOW?!
.....
UH...
WHAT HAP-PENED ...?
I don't get it...
This is SO not me...
ulp
KIOSK
BOX LUNCHES
SPY
※ Enlarged view
YUP YUP☆
Nomiya ...
SHWIP
GOOD☆JOB☆
OH MY GOD.
REEL

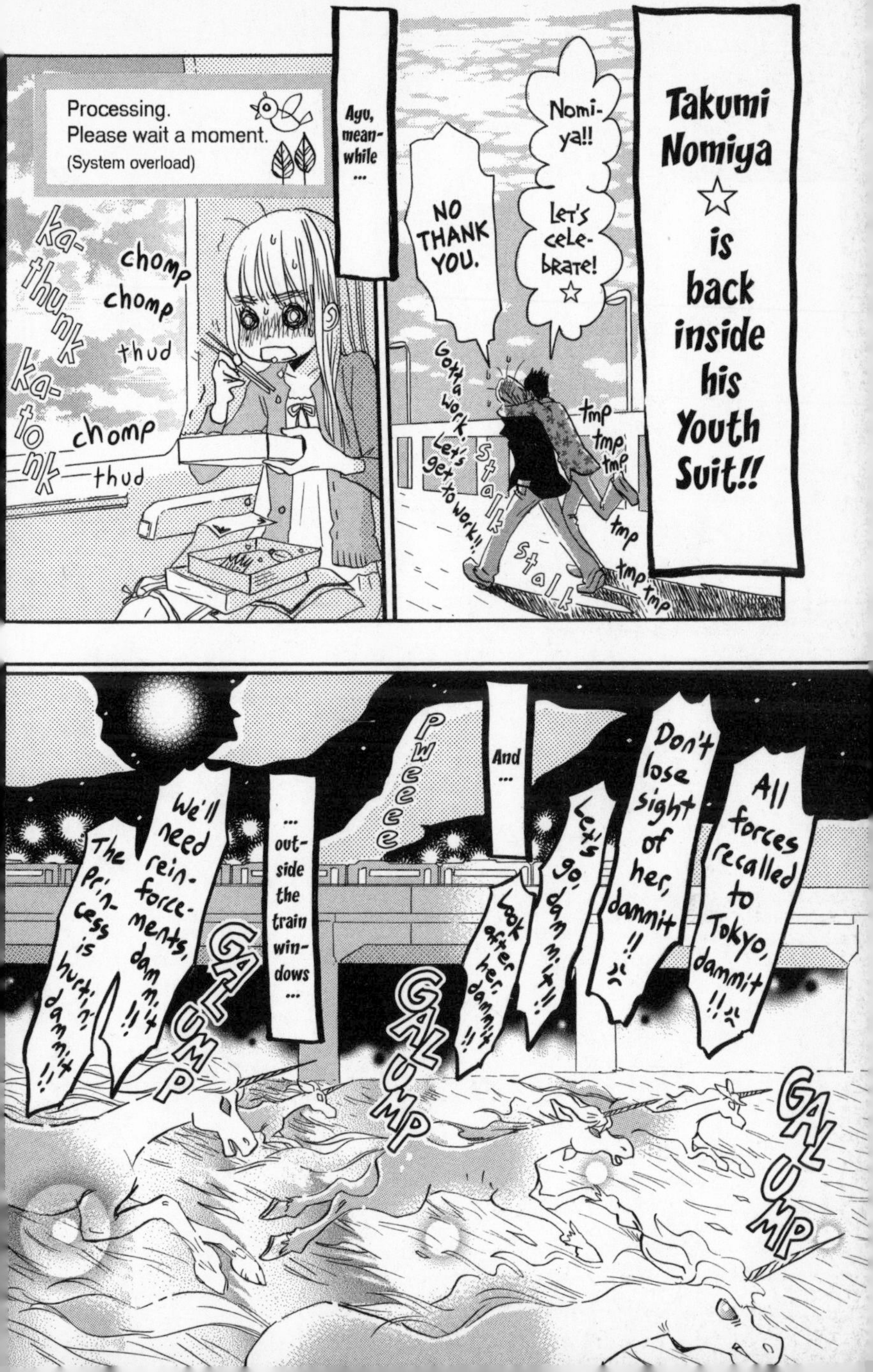
Takumi Nomiya ☆ is back inside his Youth Suit!!
Nomi-ya!!
Let's cele-brate! ☆
NO THANK YOU.
Gotta work. Let's get to work!!
stalk
stalk
tmp tmp tmp
tmp
tmp tmp tmp
Ayu, meanwhile ...
Processing.
Please wait a moment.
(System overload)
chomp
chomp
thud
chomp
thud
ka-thunk
ka-tonk
All forces recalled to Tokyo, dammit!!
Don't lose sight of her, dammit!!
And ...
Let's go, dammit!!
Look after her, dammit!!
Pweeee
... outside the train windows ...
We'll need reinforcements, dammit!!
The Princess is hurt, dammit!!
GALUMP
GALUMP
GALUMP

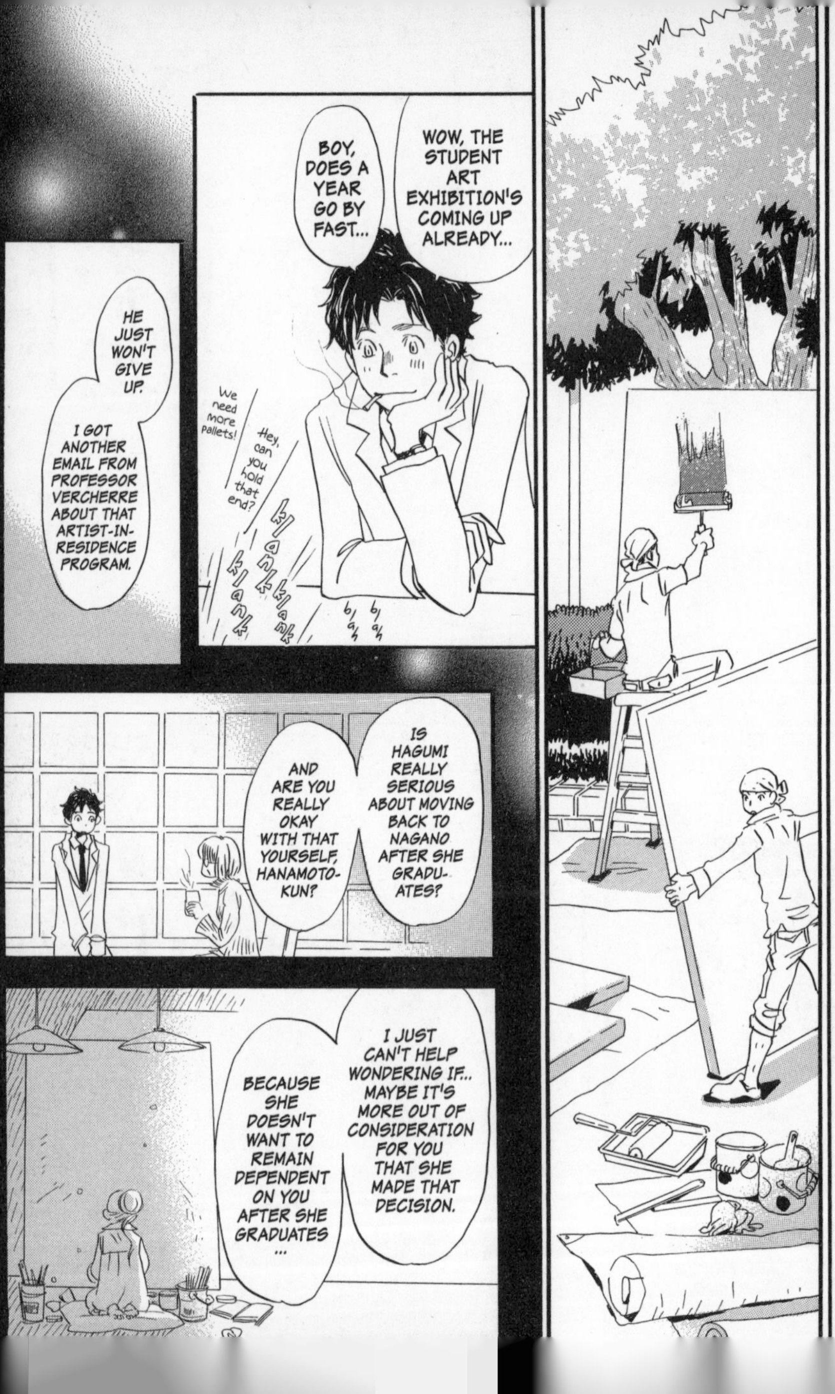
WOW, THE STUDENT ART EXHIBITION'S COMING UP ALREADY...
BOY, DOES A YEAR GO BY FAST...
Hey, can you hold that end?
We need more pallets!
klank klank klank klank
blah blah
HE JUST WON'T GIVE UP.
I GOT ANOTHER EMAIL FROM PROFESSOR VERCHERRE ABOUT THAT ARTIST-IN-RESIDENCE PROGRAM.
IS HAGUMI REALLY SERIOUS ABOUT MOVING BACK TO NAGANO AFTER SHE GRADUATES?
AND ARE YOU REALLY OKAY WITH THAT YOURSELF, HANAMOTO-KUN?
I JUST CAN'T HELP WONDERING IF... MAYBE IT'S MORE OUT OF CONSIDERATION FOR YOU THAT SHE MADE THAT DECISION.
BECAUSE SHE DOESN'T WANT TO REMAIN DEPENDENT ON YOU AFTER SHE GRADUATES...

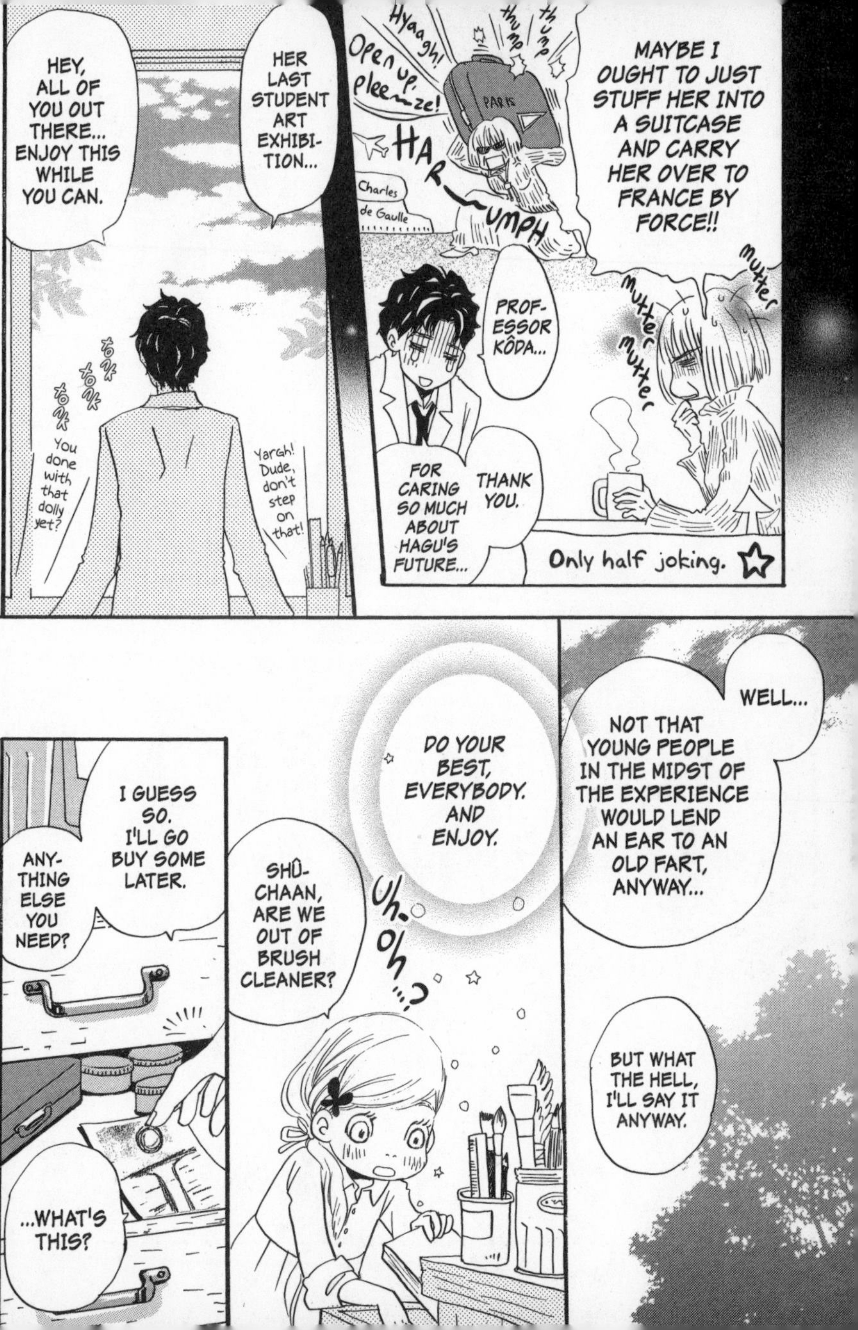

MAYBE I OUGHT TO JUST STUFF HER INTO A SUITCASE AND CARRY HER OVER TO FRANCE BY FORCE!!
thump thump
Hyaaagh!
Open up, pleeeze!
PARIS
HAR-UMPH
Charles de Gaulle
mutter mutter mutter
PROFESSOR KÔDA...
THANK YOU.
FOR CARING SO MUCH ABOUT HAGU'S FUTURE...
Only half joking.
HER LAST STUDENT ART EXHIBITION...
HEY, ALL OF YOU OUT THERE... ENJOY THIS WHILE YOU CAN.
tonk tonk tonk
Yargh! Dude, don't step on that!
You done with that dolly yet?
WELL...
NOT THAT YOUNG PEOPLE IN THE MIDST OF THE EXPERIENCE WOULD LEND AN EAR TO AN OLD FART, ANYWAY...
BUT WHAT THE HELL, I'LL SAY IT ANYWAY.
DO YOUR BEST, EVERYBODY. AND ENJOY.
SHÛ-CHAAN, ARE WE OUT OF BRUSH CLEANER?
Uh-oh...?
I GUESS SO. I'LL GO BUY SOME LATER.
ANYTHING ELSE YOU NEED?
...WHAT'S THIS?

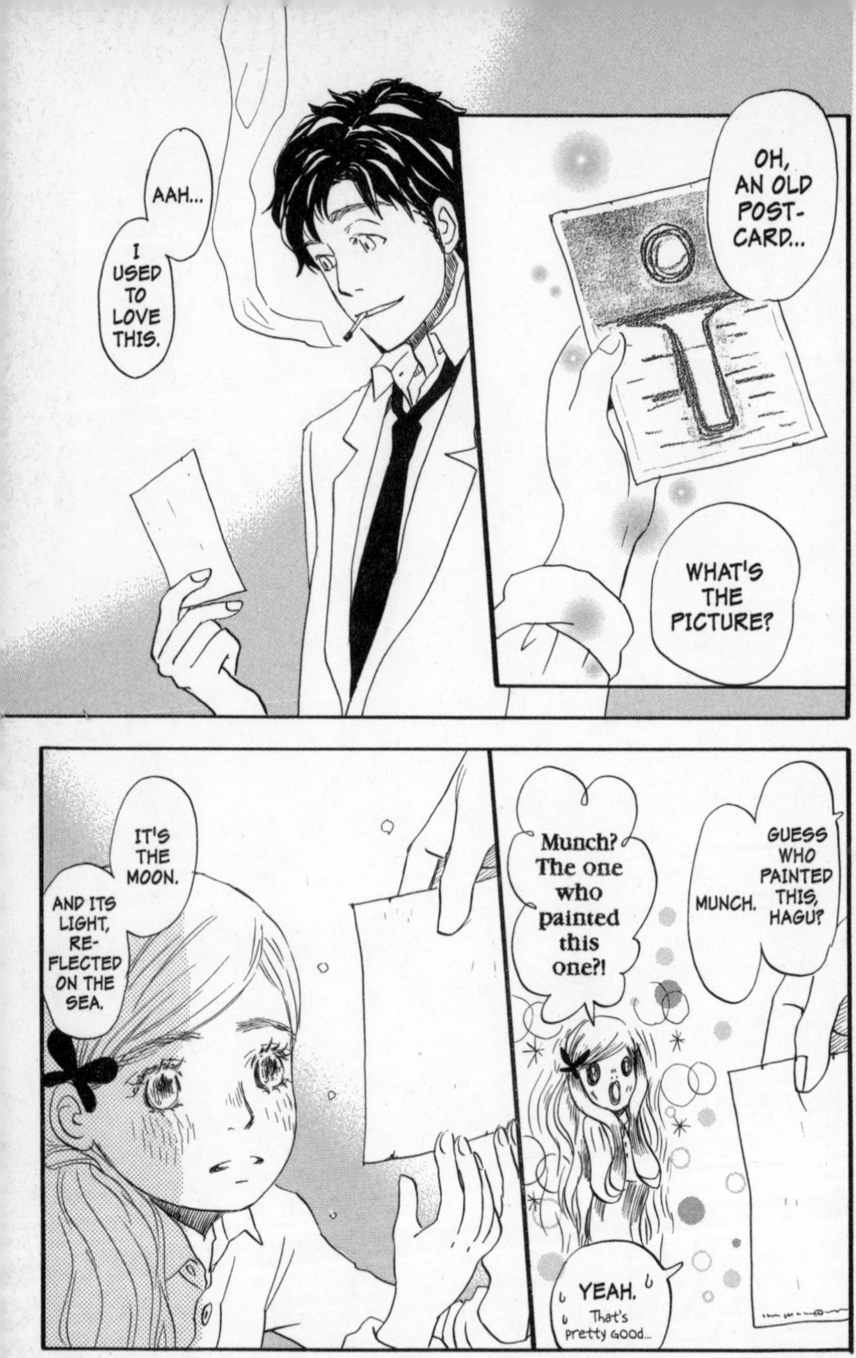
OH, AN OLD POST-CARD...
WHAT'S THE PICTURE?
AAH...
I USED TO LOVE THIS.
GUESS WHO PAINTED THIS, HAGU?
MUNCH.
Munch? The one who painted this one?!
YEAH.
That's pretty good...
IT'S THE MOON.
AND ITS LIGHT, RE-FLECTED ON THE SEA.

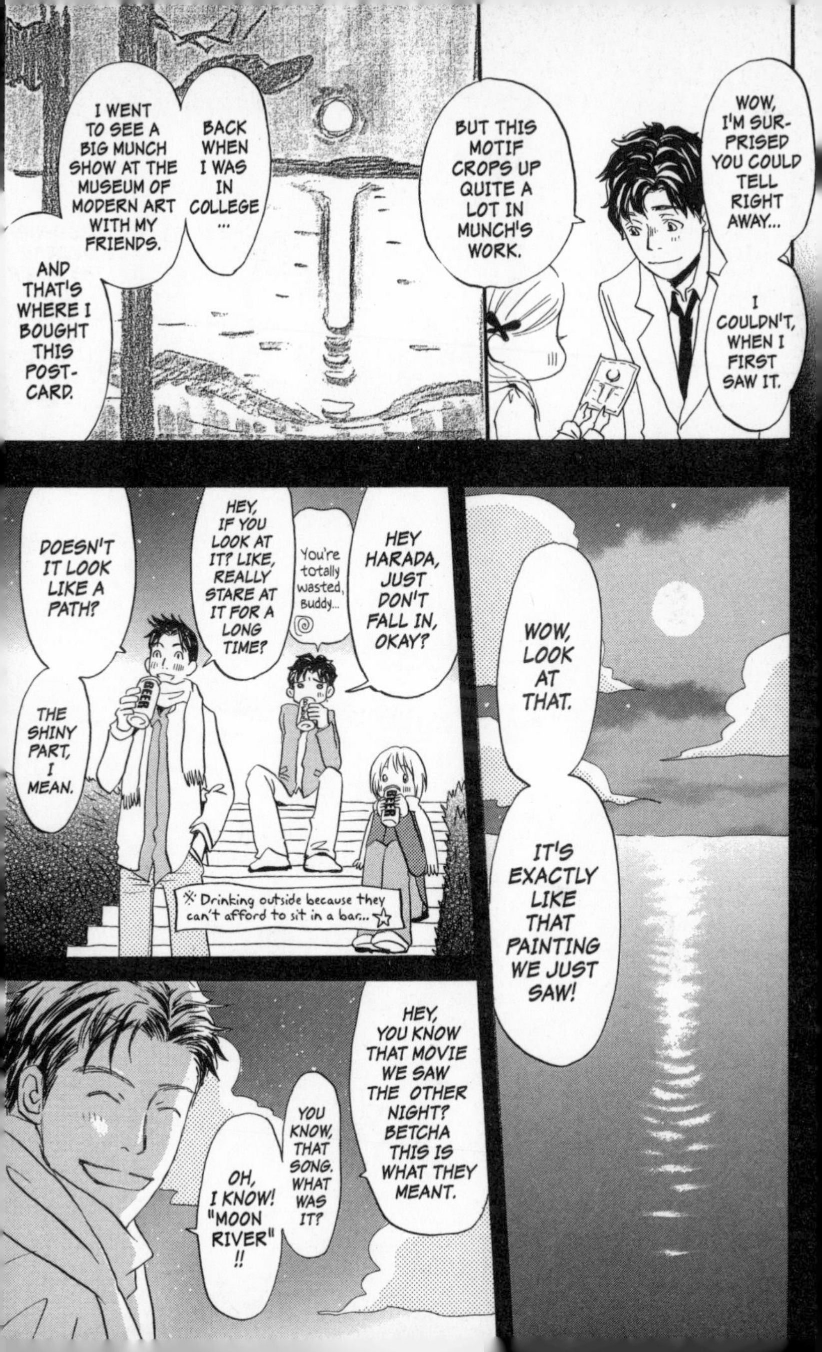
WOW, I'M SURPRISED YOU COULD TELL RIGHT AWAY...
I COULDN'T, WHEN I FIRST SAW IT.
BUT THIS MOTIF CROPS UP QUITE A LOT IN MUNCH'S WORK.
BACK WHEN I WAS IN COLLEGE...
I WENT TO SEE A BIG MUNCH SHOW AT THE MUSEUM OF MODERN ART WITH MY FRIENDS.
AND THAT'S WHERE I BOUGHT THIS POSTCARD.
WOW, LOOK AT THAT.
IT'S EXACTLY LIKE THAT PAINTING WE JUST SAW!
HEY HARADA, JUST DON'T FALL IN, OKAY?
You're totally wasted, buddy...
HEY, IF YOU LOOK AT IT? LIKE, REALLY STARE AT IT FOR A LONG TIME?
DOESN'T IT LOOK LIKE A PATH?
THE SHINY PART, I MEAN.
BEER
BEER
BEER
※ Drinking outside because they can't afford to sit in a bar... ☆
HEY, YOU KNOW THAT MOVIE WE SAW THE OTHER NIGHT? BETCHA THIS IS WHAT THEY MEANT.
YOU KNOW, THAT SONG. WHAT WAS IT?
OH, I KNOW! "MOON RIVER" !!

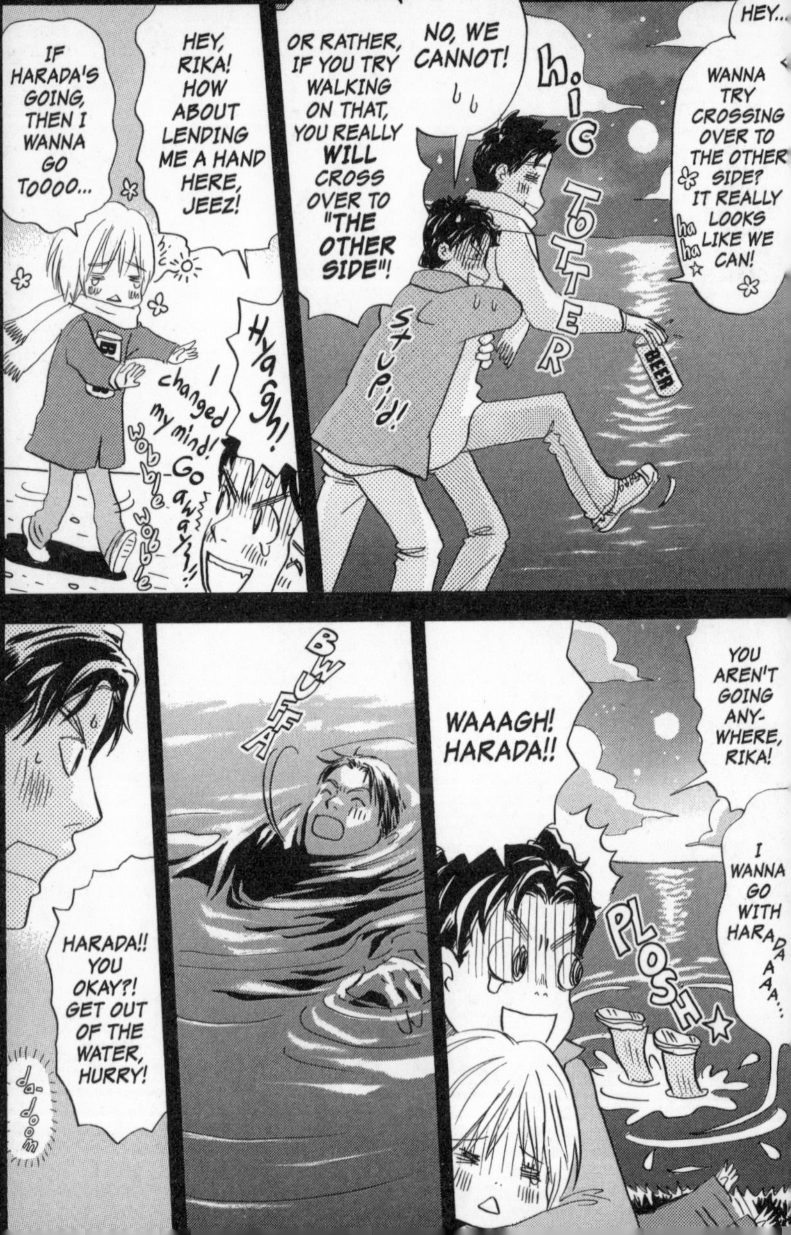
HEY...
WANNA TRY CROSSING OVER TO THE OTHER SIDE? IT REALLY LOOKS LIKE WE CAN!
ha ha ☆
hic
TOTTER
NO, WE CANNOT!
STUPID!
OR RATHER, IF YOU TRY WALKING ON THAT, YOU REALLY WILL CROSS OVER TO "THE OTHER SIDE"!
HEY, RIKA! HOW ABOUT LENDING ME A HAND HERE, JEEZ!
IF HARADA'S GOING, THEN I WANNA GO TOOOO...
Hyaagh!
I changed my mind! Go away!!
wobble wobble
YOU AREN'T GOING ANY-WHERE, RIKA!
I WANNA GO WITH HARADAAAA...
WAAAGH! HARADA!!
PLOSH☆
BWUFFA
HARADA!! YOU OKAY?! GET OUT OF THE WATER, HURRY!
da-doom

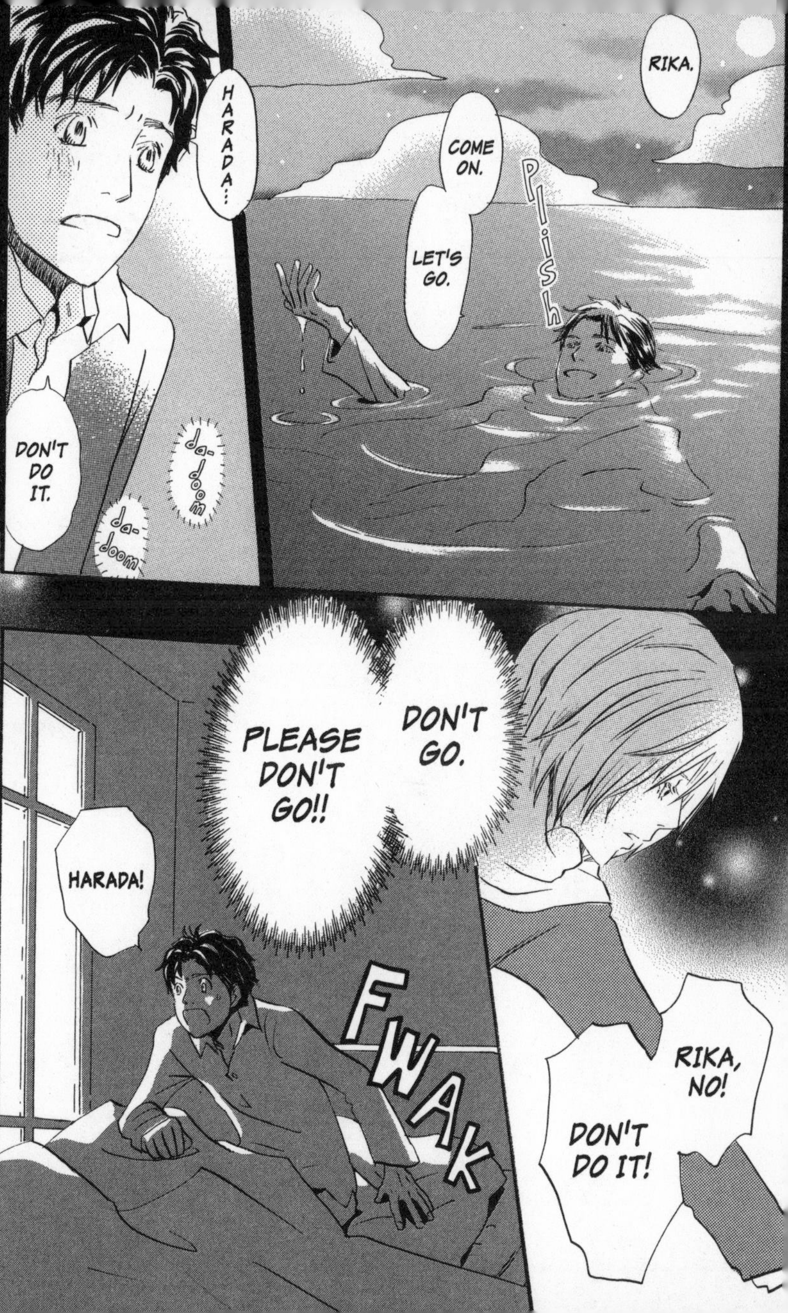
RIKA.
COME ON.
LET'S GO.
Plish
HARADA...
DON'T DO IT.
da-doom
da-doom
DON'T GO.
PLEASE DON'T GO!!
RIKA, NO!
DON'T DO IT!
HARADA!
FWAK

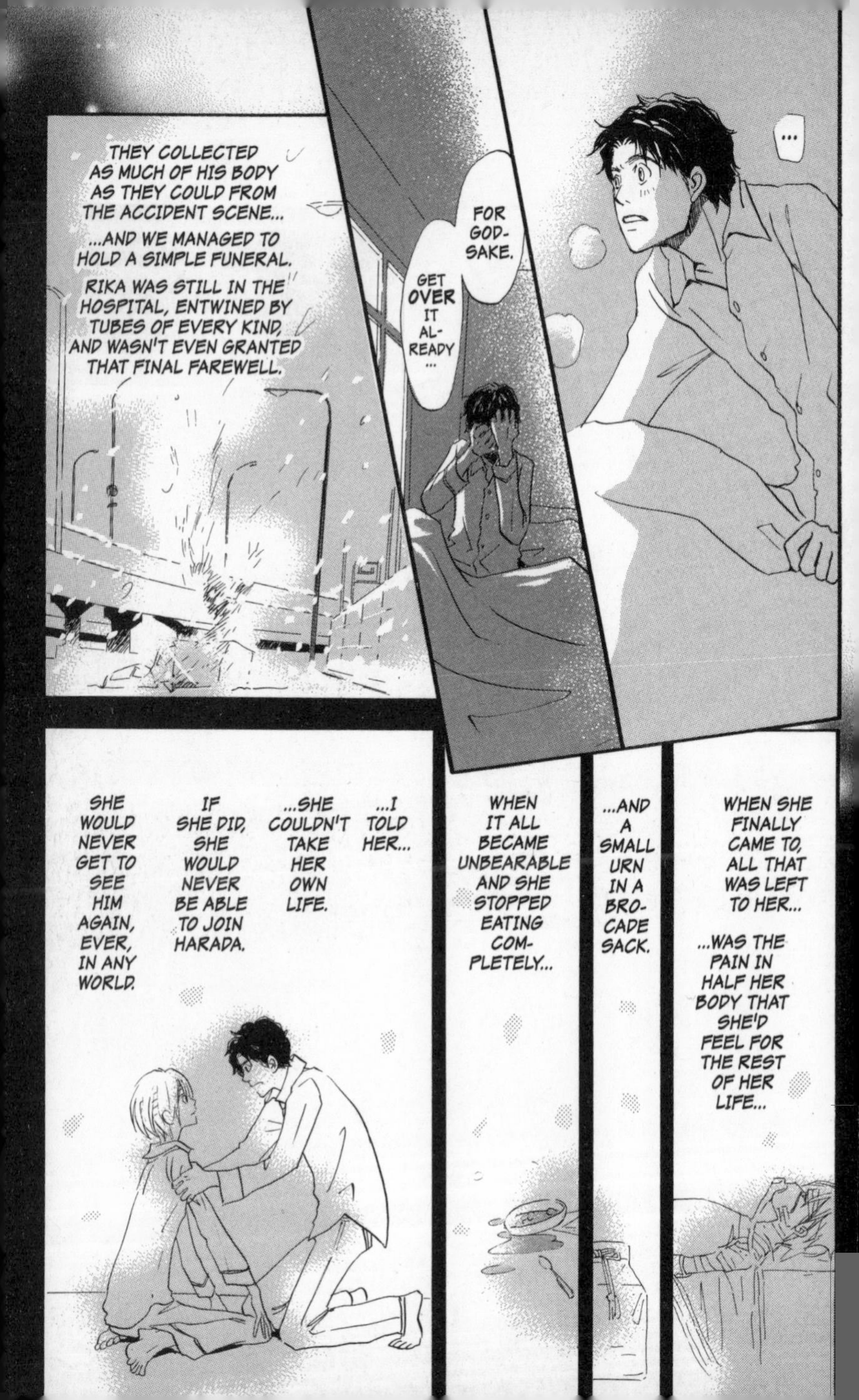
...
FOR GODSAKE.
GET **OVER** IT ALREADY...
THEY COLLECTED AS MUCH OF HIS BODY AS THEY COULD FROM THE ACCIDENT SCENE...
...AND WE MANAGED TO HOLD A SIMPLE FUNERAL.
RIKA WAS STILL IN THE HOSPITAL, ENTWINED BY TUBES OF EVERY KIND, AND WASN'T EVEN GRANTED THAT FINAL FAREWELL.
WHEN SHE FINALLY CAME TO, ALL THAT WAS LEFT TO HER...
...WAS THE PAIN IN HALF HER BODY THAT SHE'D FEEL FOR THE REST OF HER LIFE...
...AND A SMALL URN IN A BROCADE SACK.
WHEN IT ALL BECAME UNBEARABLE AND SHE STOPPED EATING COMPLETELY...
...I TOLD HER...
...SHE COULDN'T TAKE HER OWN LIFE.
IF SHE DID, SHE WOULD NEVER BE ABLE TO JOIN HARADA.
SHE WOULD NEVER GET TO SEE HIM AGAIN, EVER, IN ANY WORLD.

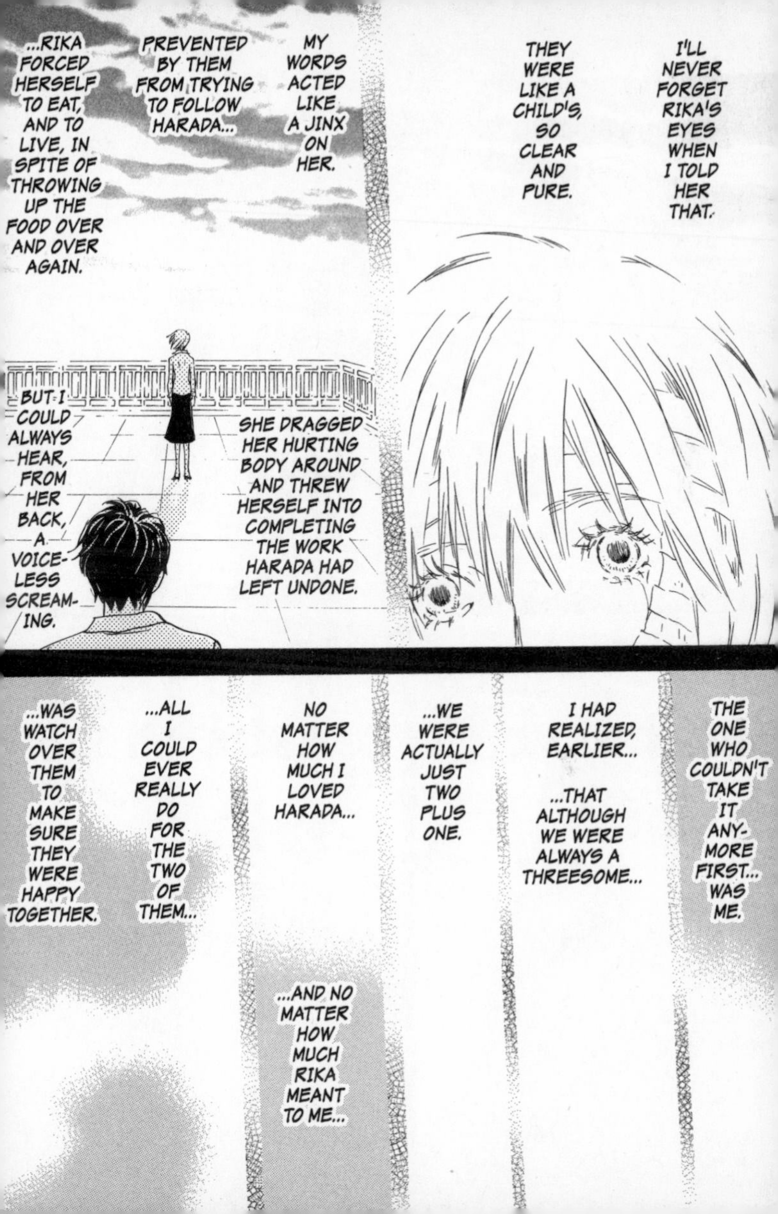
I'LL NEVER FORGET RIKA'S EYES WHEN I TOLD HER THAT.
THEY WERE LIKE A CHILD'S, SO CLEAR AND PURE.
MY WORDS ACTED LIKE A JINX ON HER.
PREVENTED BY THEM FROM TRYING TO FOLLOW HARADA...
...RIKA FORCED HERSELF TO EAT, AND TO LIVE, IN SPITE OF THROWING UP THE FOOD OVER AND OVER AGAIN.
SHE DRAGGED HER HURTING BODY AROUND AND THREW HERSELF INTO COMPLETING THE WORK HARADA HAD LEFT UNDONE.
BUT I COULD ALWAYS HEAR, FROM HER BACK, A VOICELESS SCREAMING.
THE ONE WHO COULDN'T TAKE IT ANYMORE FIRST... WAS ME.
I HAD REALIZED, EARLIER...
...THAT ALTHOUGH WE WERE ALWAYS A THREESOME...
...WE WERE ACTUALLY JUST TWO PLUS ONE.
NO MATTER HOW MUCH I LOVED HARADA...
...AND NO MATTER HOW MUCH RIKA MEANT TO ME...
...ALL I COULD EVER REALLY DO FOR THE TWO OF THEM...
...WAS WATCH OVER THEM TO MAKE SURE THEY WERE HAPPY TOGETHER.

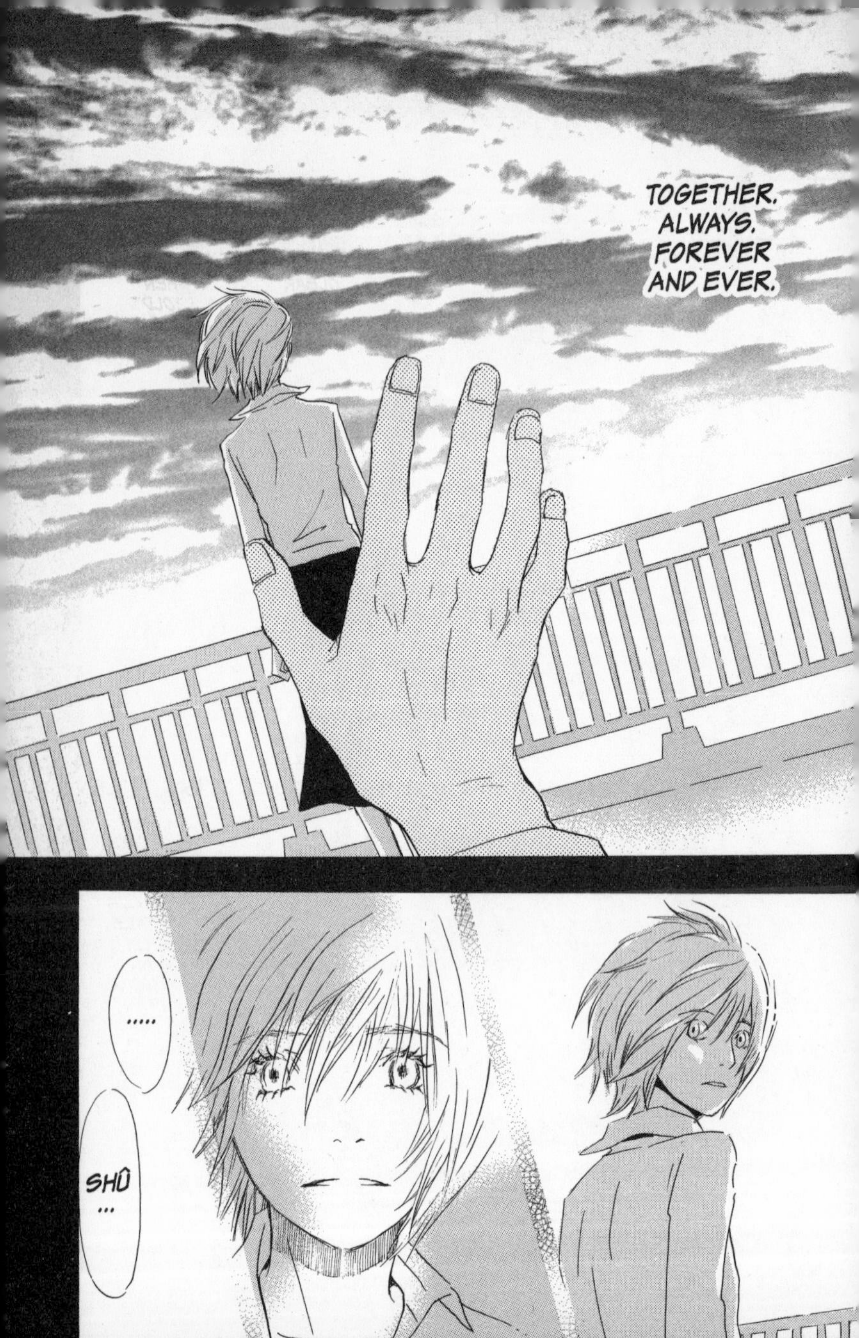
TOGETHER. ALWAYS. FOREVER AND EVER.
.....
SHÛ ...

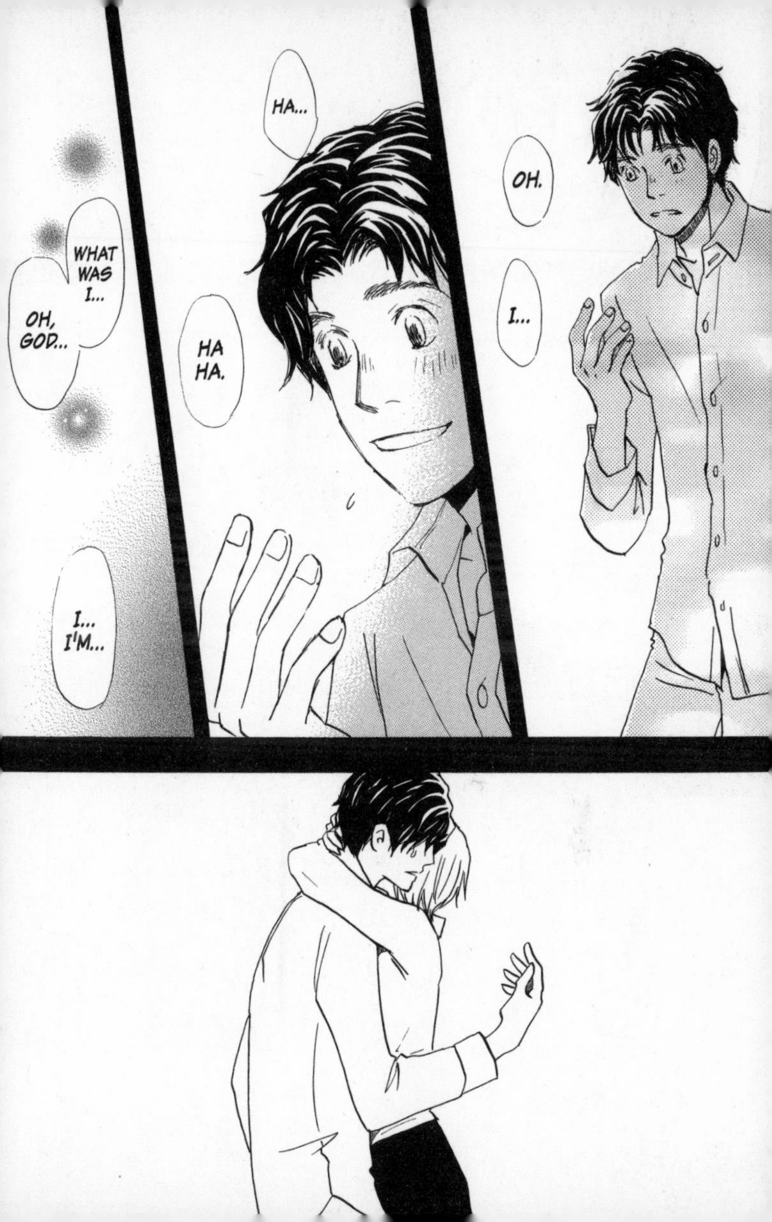
OH.
I...
HA...
HA HA.
WHAT WAS I...
OH, GOD...
I... I'M...

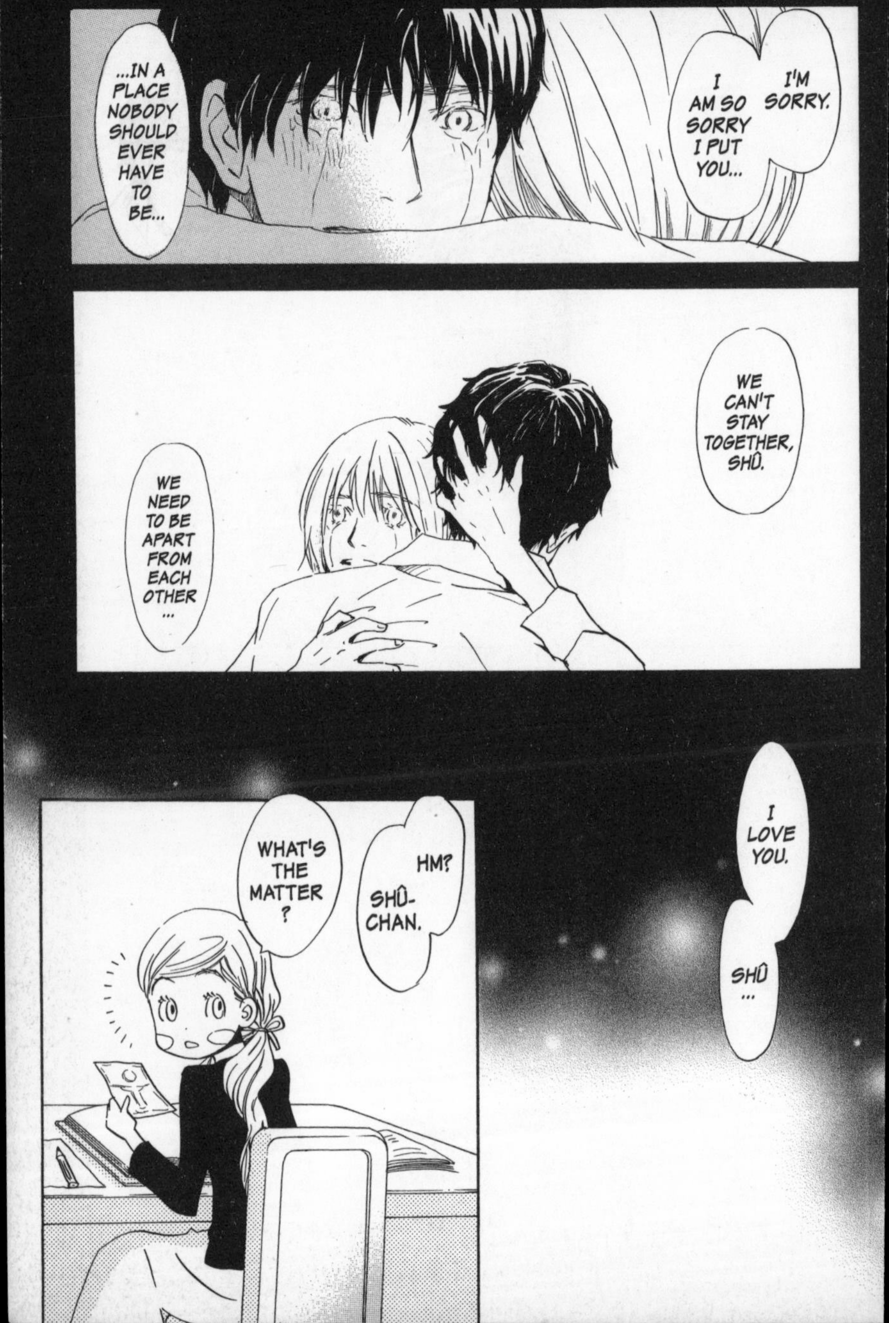
I'M SORRY.
I AM SO SORRY I PUT YOU...
...IN A PLACE NOBODY SHOULD EVER HAVE TO BE...
WE CAN'T STAY TOGETHER, SHÛ.
WE NEED TO BE APART FROM EACH OTHER...
I LOVE YOU.
SHÛ...
HM?
SHÛ-CHAN.
WHAT'S THE MATTER?

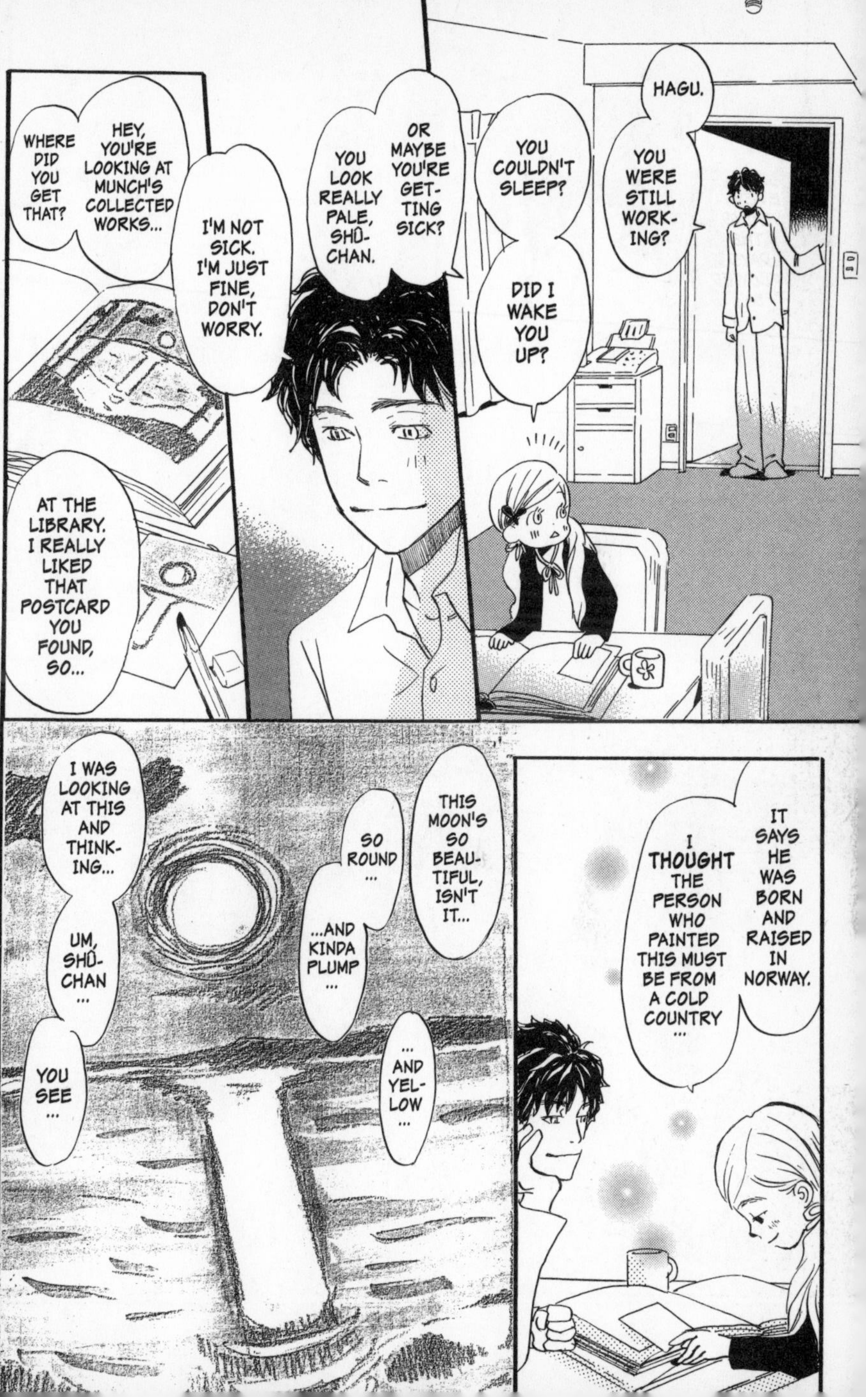
HAGU.
YOU WERE STILL WORKING?
YOU COULDN'T SLEEP?
DID I WAKE YOU UP?
OR MAYBE YOU'RE GET-TING SICK?
YOU LOOK REALLY PALE, SHŪ-CHAN.
I'M NOT SICK. I'M JUST FINE, DON'T WORRY.
HEY, YOU'RE LOOKING AT MUNCH'S COLLECTED WORKS...
WHERE DID YOU GET THAT?
AT THE LIBRARY. I REALLY LIKED THAT POSTCARD YOU FOUND, SO...
IT SAYS HE WAS BORN AND RAISED IN NORWAY.
I THOUGHT THE PERSON WHO PAINTED THIS MUST BE FROM A COLD COUNTRY...
THIS MOON'S SO BEAU-TIFUL, ISN'T IT...
SO ROUND...
...AND KINDA PLUMP...
...AND YEL-LOW...
I WAS LOOKING AT THIS AND THINK-ING...
UM, SHŪ-CHAN...
YOU SEE...

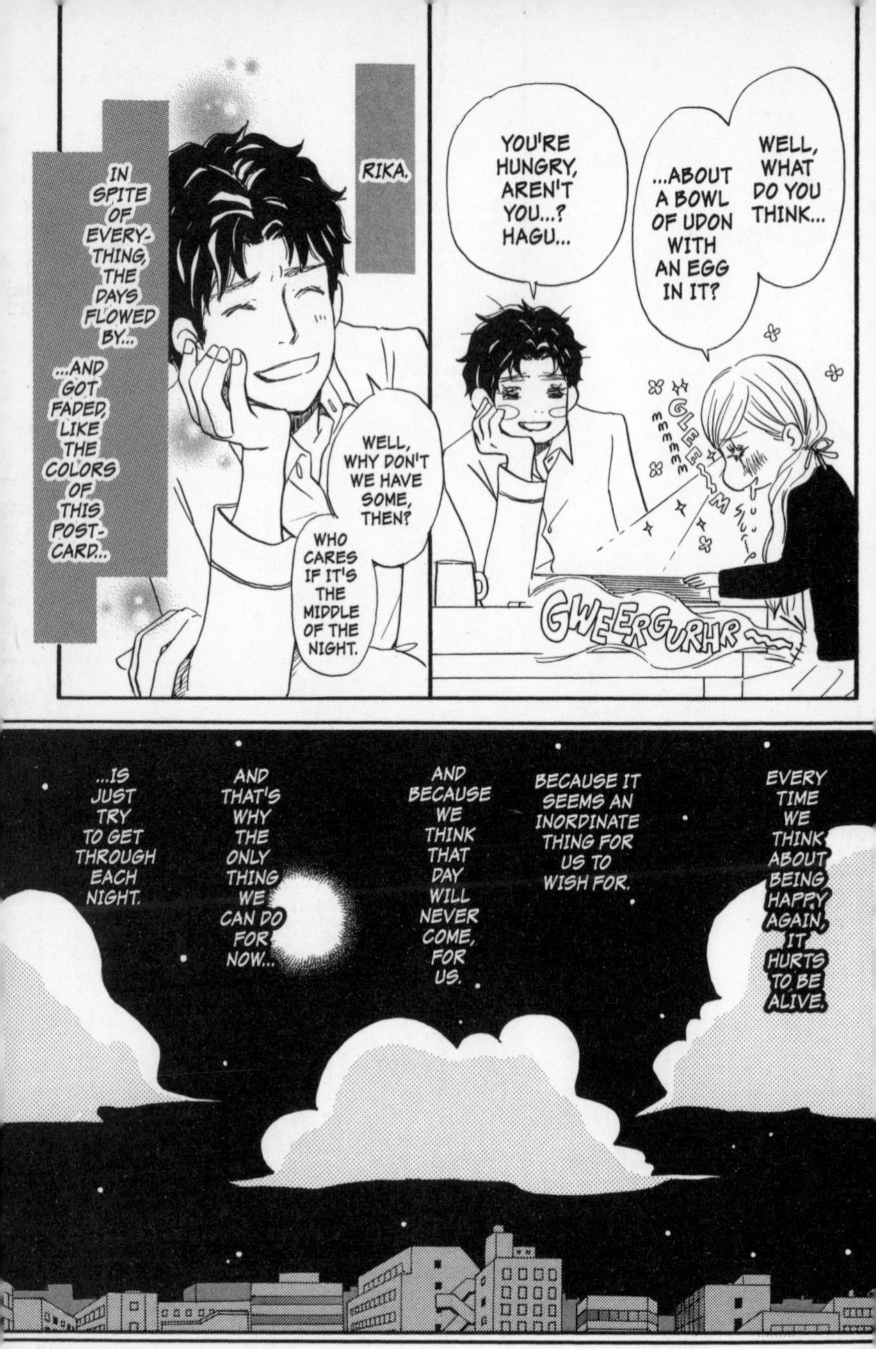
WELL, WHAT DO YOU THINK...
...ABOUT A BOWL OF UDON WITH AN EGG IN IT?
YOU'RE HUNGRY, AREN'T YOU...? HAGU...
GLEEM
GWEERGURHR
RIKA.
WELL, WHY DON'T WE HAVE SOME, THEN?
WHO CARES IF IT'S THE MIDDLE OF THE NIGHT.
IN SPITE OF EVERYTHING, THE DAYS FLOWED BY...
...AND GOT FADED, LIKE THE COLORS OF THIS POSTCARD...
EVERY TIME WE THINK ABOUT BEING HAPPY AGAIN, IT HURTS TO BE ALIVE.
BECAUSE IT SEEMS AN INORDINATE THING FOR US TO WISH FOR.
AND BECAUSE WE THINK THAT DAY WILL NEVER COME, FOR US.
AND THAT'S WHY THE ONLY THING WE CAN DO FOR NOW...
...IS JUST TRY TO GET THROUGH EACH NIGHT.

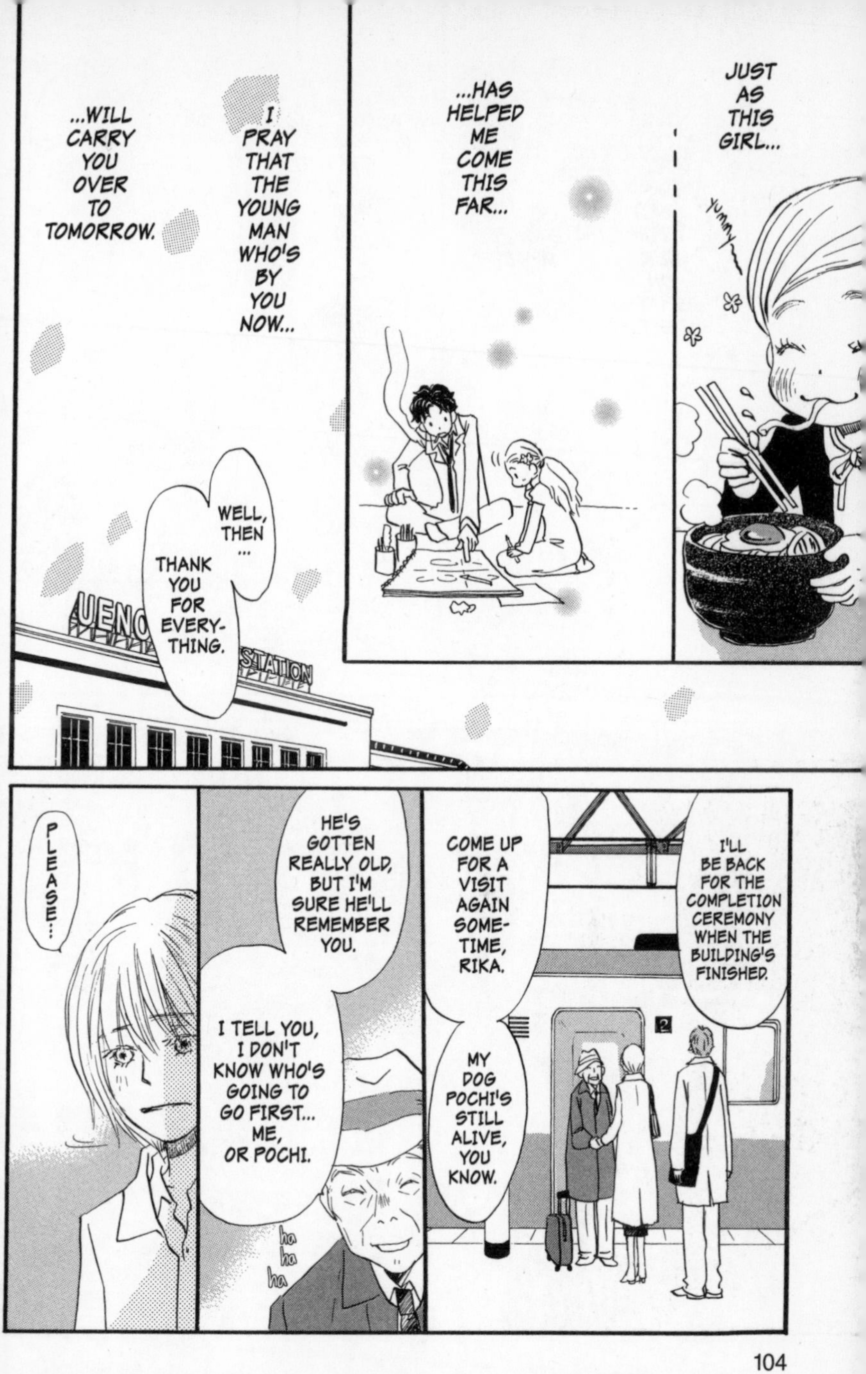
JUST AS THIS GIRL...
yummy
...HAS HELPED ME COME THIS FAR...
I PRAY THAT THE YOUNG MAN WHO'S BY YOU NOW...
...WILL CARRY YOU OVER TO TOMORROW.
WELL, THEN ...
THANK YOU FOR EVERY-THING.
UENO STATION
I'LL BE BACK FOR THE COMPLETION CEREMONY WHEN THE BUILDING'S FINISHED.
COME UP FOR A VISIT AGAIN SOME-TIME, RIKA.
MY DOG POCHI'S STILL ALIVE, YOU KNOW.
HE'S GOTTEN REALLY OLD, BUT I'M SURE HE'LL REMEMBER YOU.
I TELL YOU, I DON'T KNOW WHO'S GOING TO GO FIRST... ME, OR POCHI.
ha ha ha
PLEASE...

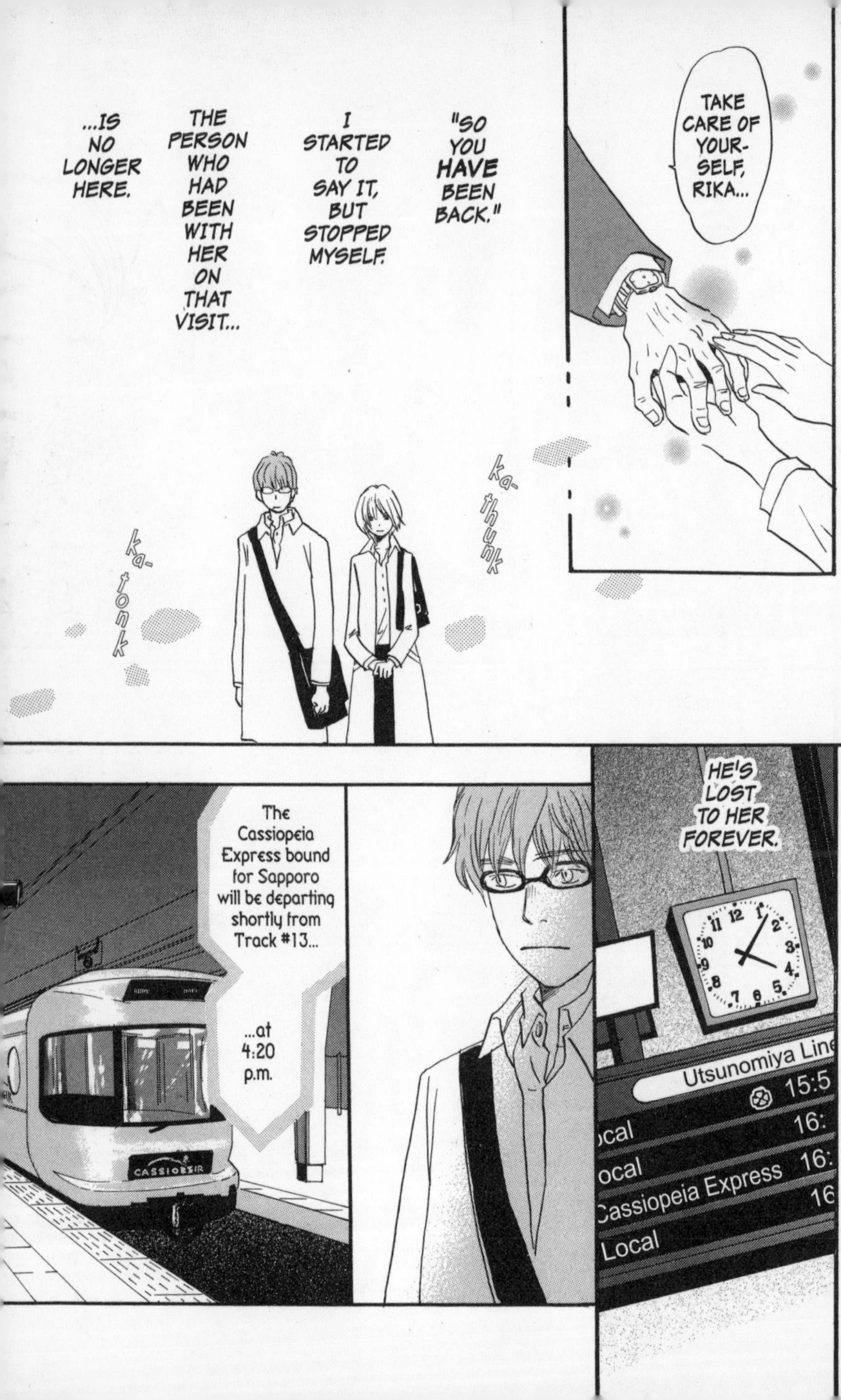
TAKE CARE OF YOUR-SELF, RIKA...
"SO YOU HAVE BEEN BACK."
I STARTED TO SAY IT, BUT STOPPED MYSELF.
THE PERSON WHO HAD BEEN WITH HER ON THAT VISIT...
...IS NO LONGER HERE.
ka-thunk
ka-tonk
HE'S LOST TO HER FOREVER.
Utsunomiya Line
15:5
ocal 16:
ocal 16:
Cassiopeia Express 16:
16
Local
The Cassiopeia Express bound for Sapporo will be departing shortly from Track #13...
...at 4:20 p.m.

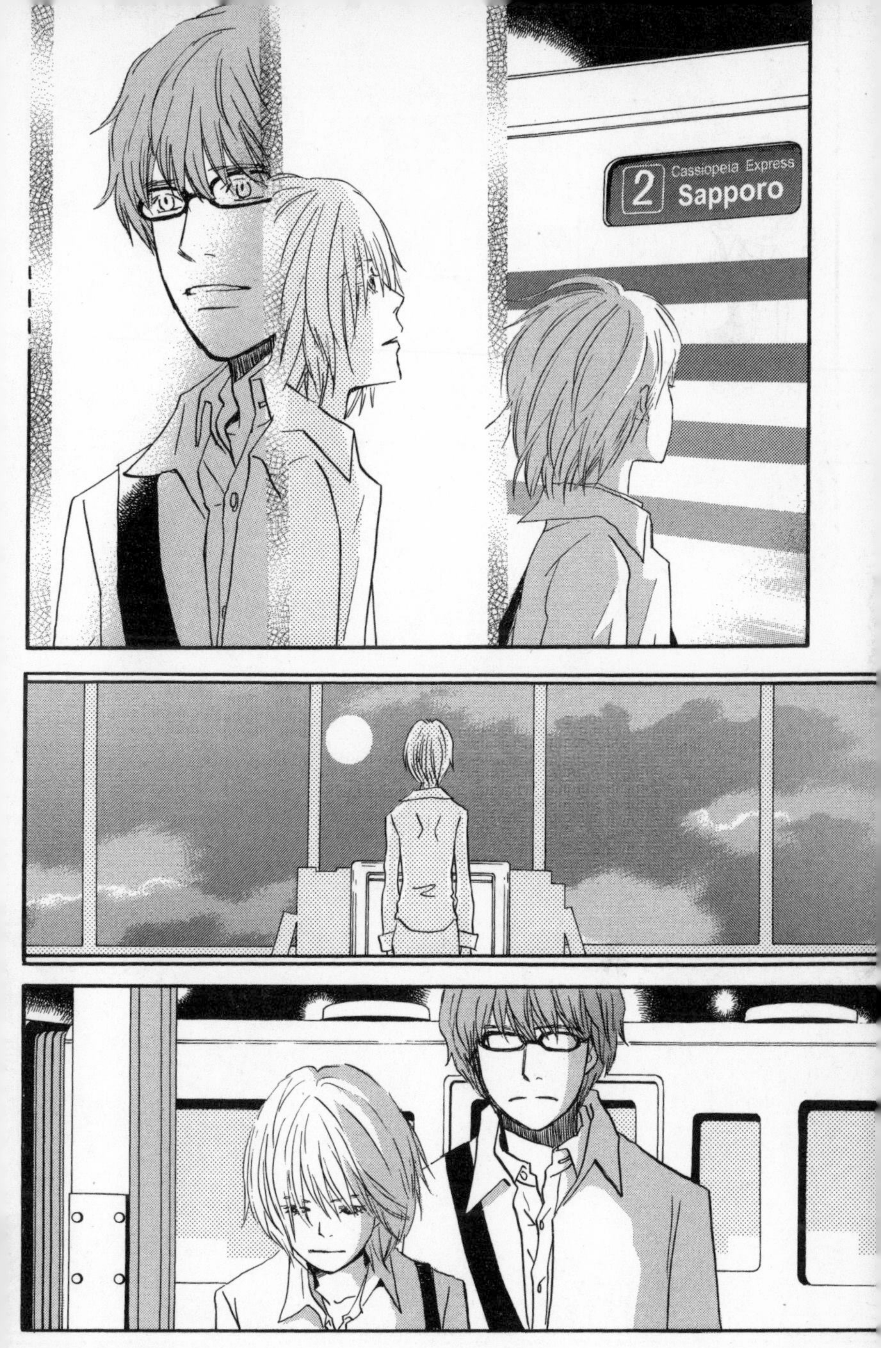
2 Cassiopeia Express
Sapporo

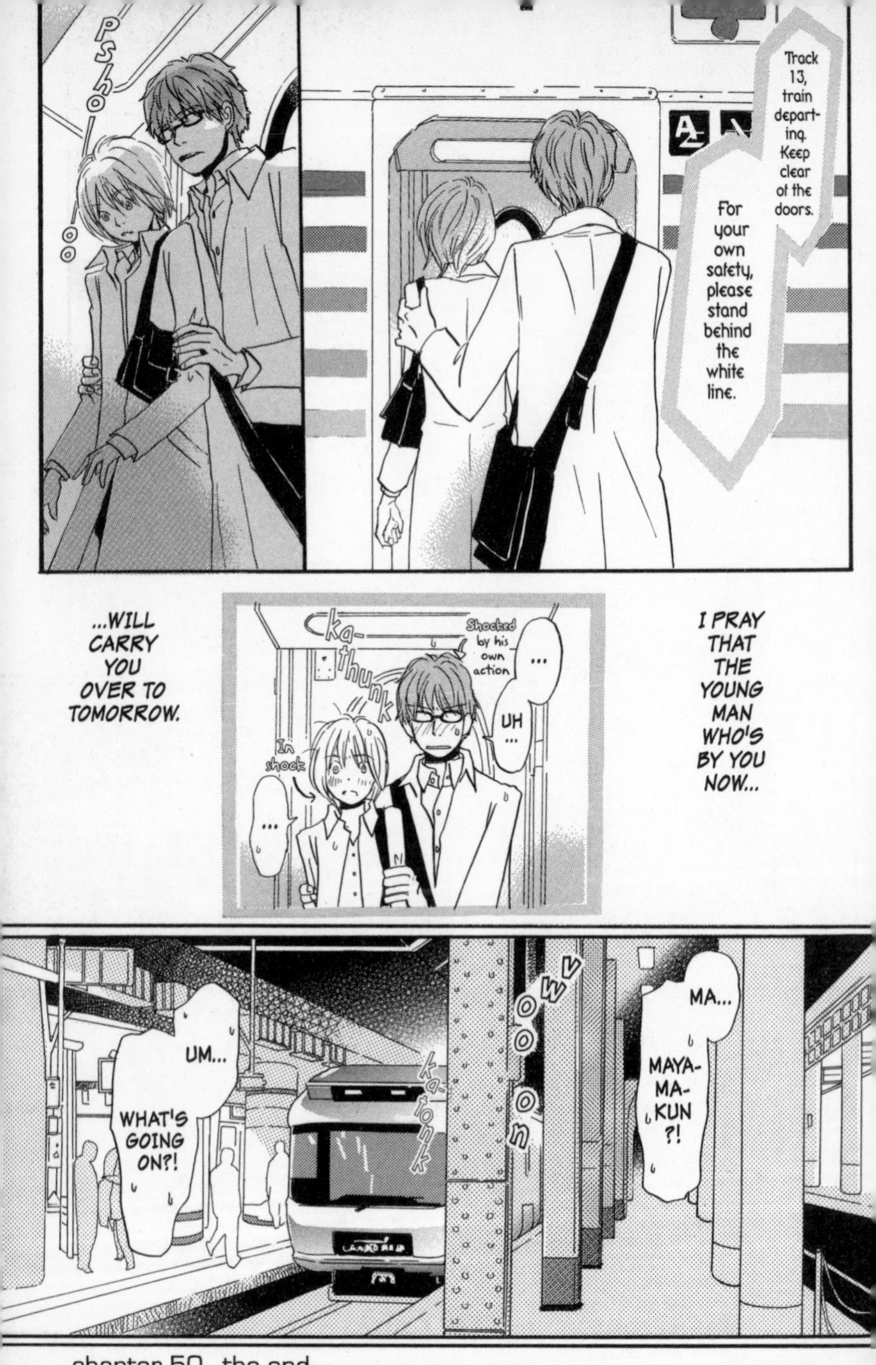
Track 13, train departing. Keep clear of the doors.
For your own safety, please stand behind the white line.
psholoo
I PRAY THAT THE YOUNG MAN WHO'S BY YOU NOW...
ka-thunk
Shocked by his own action
...
UH ...
In shock
...
...WILL CARRY YOU OVER TO TOMORROW.
MA...
MAYA-MA-KUN?!
vooooon
ka-tonk
UM...
WHAT'S GOING ON?!

chapter 50—the end—

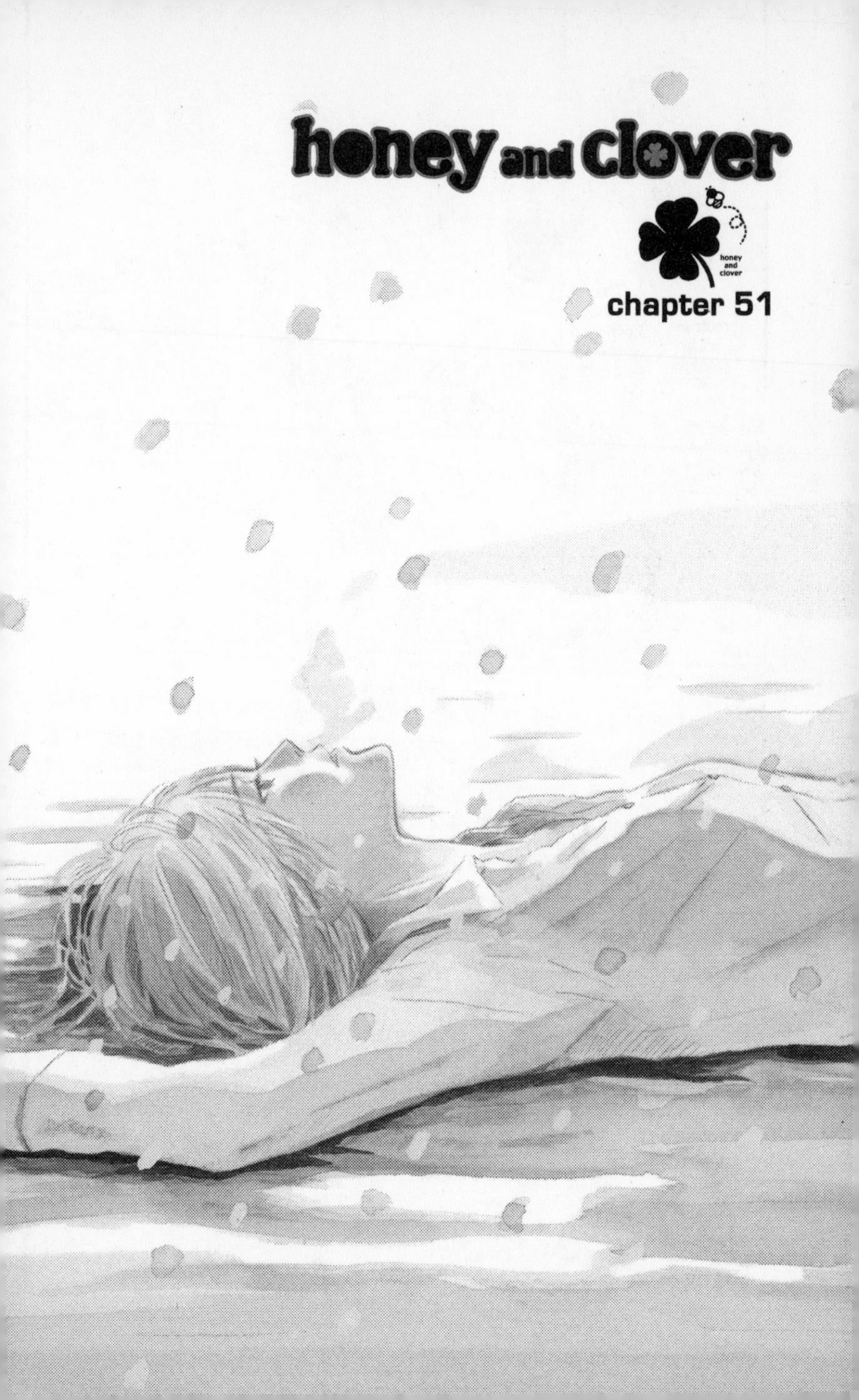
honey and clover
honey and clover
chapter 51

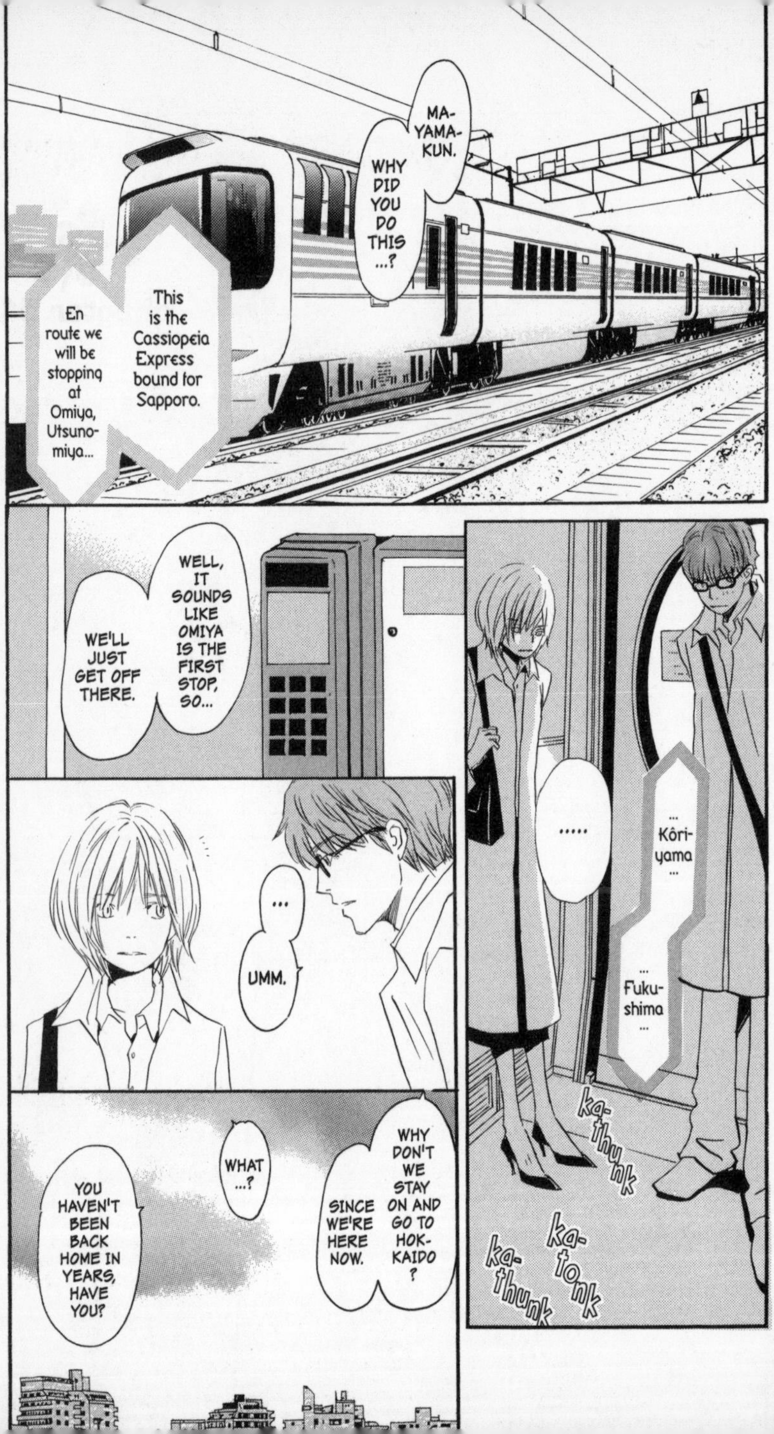
MA-YAMA-KUN.
WHY DID YOU DO THIS ...?
This is the Cassiopeia Express bound for Sapporo.
En route we will be stopping at Omiya, Utsunomiya...
... Kôri-yama ...
......
... Fuku-shima ...
ka-thunk
ka-tonk
ka-thunk
WELL, IT SOUNDS LIKE OMIYA IS THE FIRST STOP, SO...
WE'LL JUST GET OFF THERE.
...
UMM.
WHY DON'T WE STAY ON AND GO TO HOK-KAIDO ?
SINCE WE'RE HERE NOW.
WHAT ...?
YOU HAVEN'T BEEN BACK HOME IN YEARS, HAVE YOU?

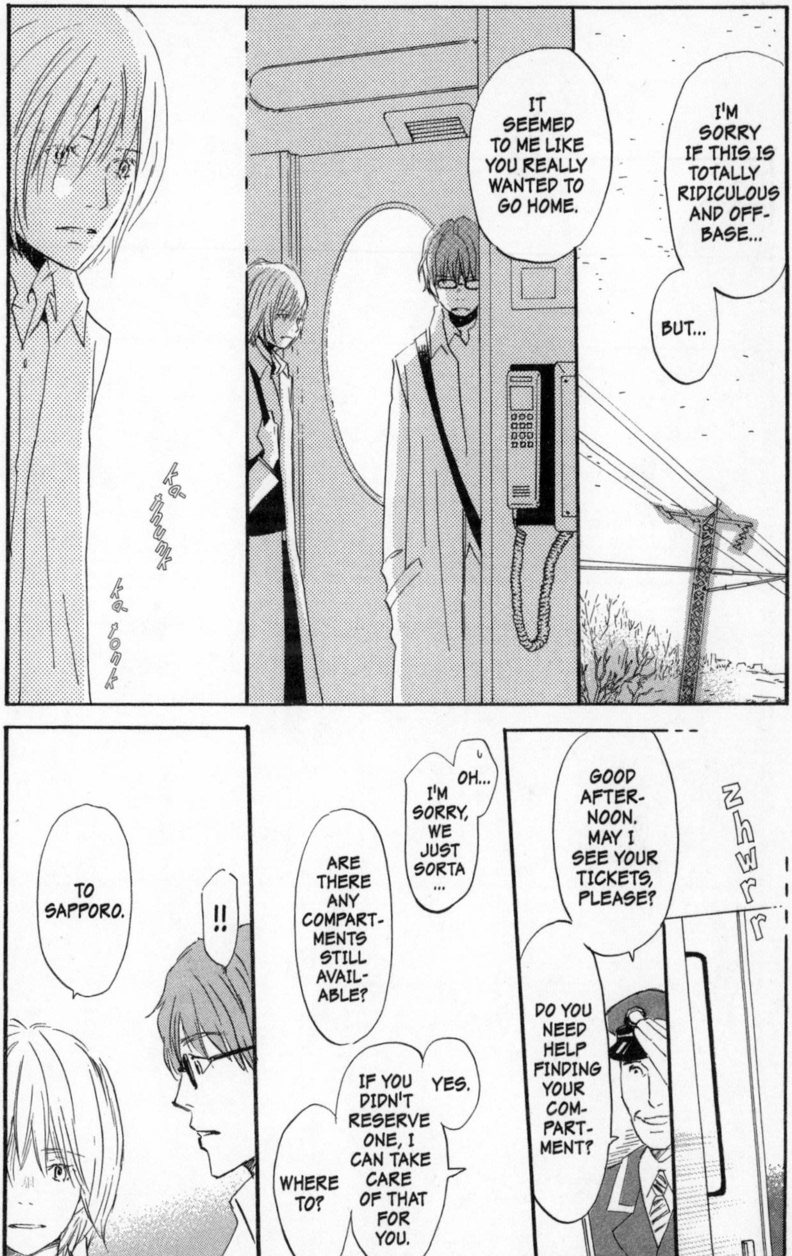
I'M SORRY IF THIS IS TOTALLY RIDICULOUS AND OFF-BASE...
BUT...
IT SEEMED TO ME LIKE YOU REALLY WANTED TO GO HOME.
ka-thunk
ka-tonk
zhwrr
GOOD AFTERNOON. MAY I SEE YOUR TICKETS, PLEASE?
DO YOU NEED HELP FINDING YOUR COMPARTMENT?
OH... I'M SORRY, WE JUST SORTA ...
ARE THERE ANY COMPARTMENTS STILL AVAILABLE?
YES.
IF YOU DIDN'T RESERVE ONE, I CAN TAKE CARE OF THAT FOR YOU.
WHERE TO?
!!
TO SAPPORO.

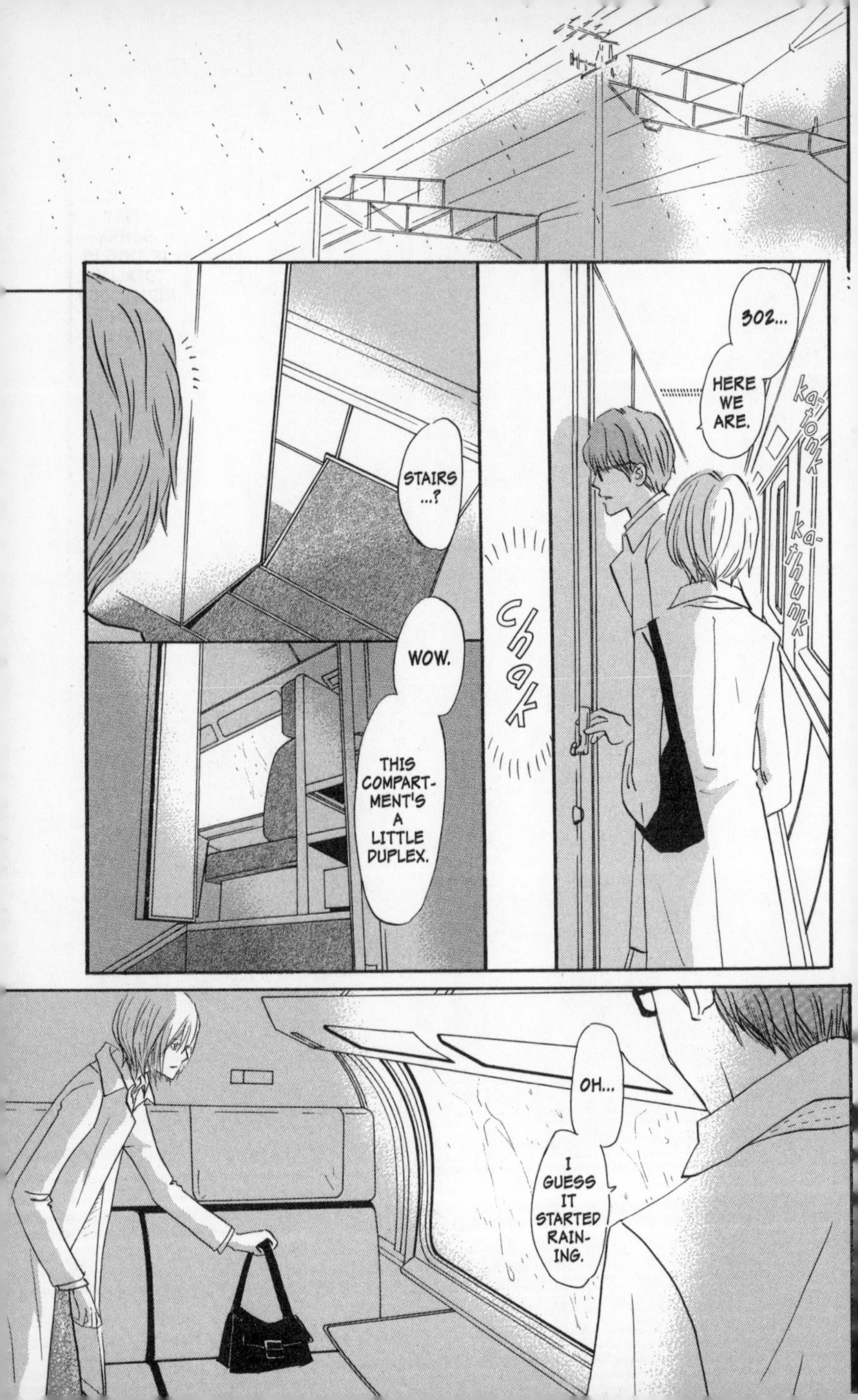
302...
HERE WE ARE.
ka-tonk
ka-thunk
chak
STAIRS ...?
WOW.
THIS COMPARTMENT'S A LITTLE DUPLEX.
OH...
I GUESS IT STARTED RAINING.

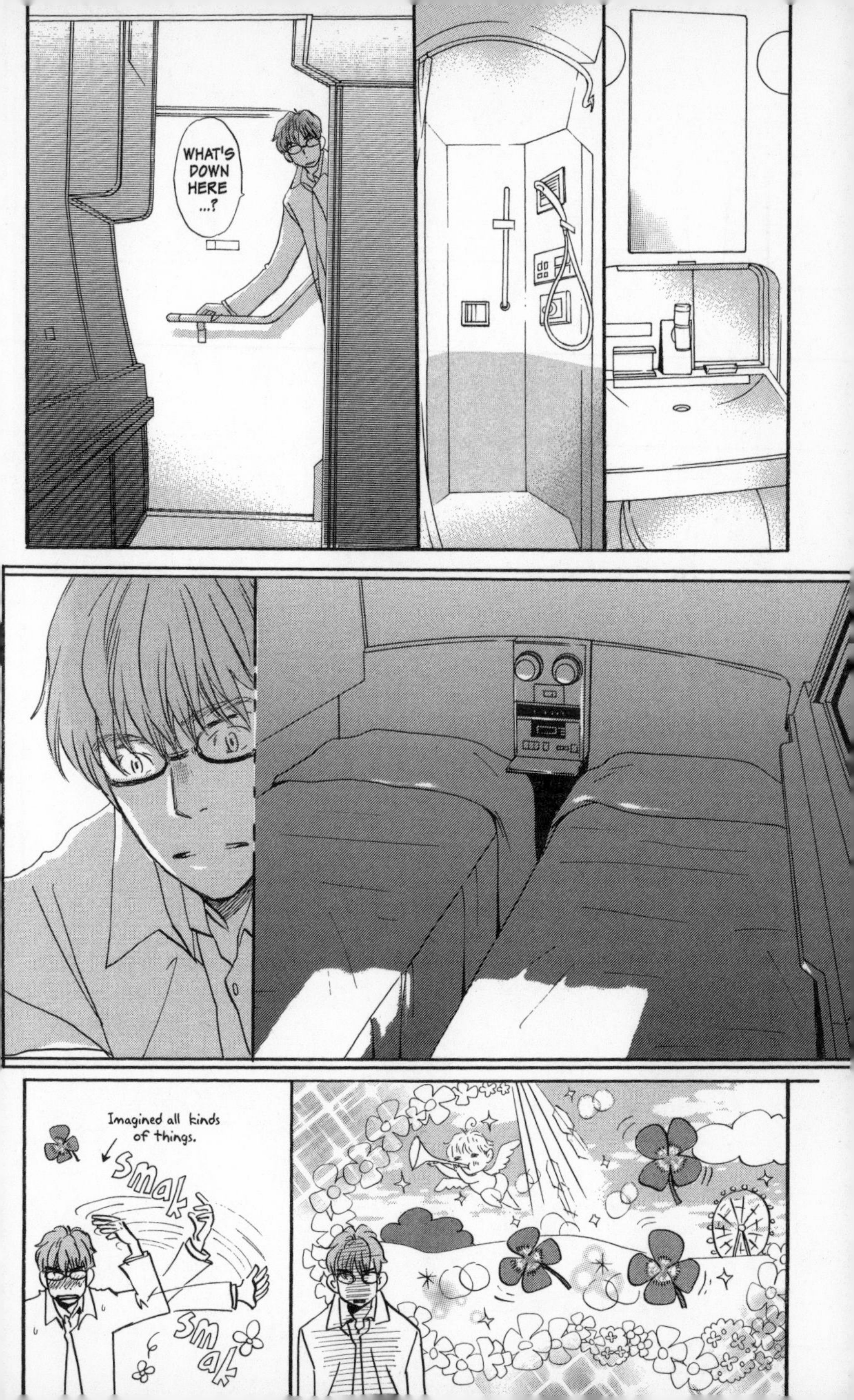
WHAT'S DOWN HERE ...?
Imagined all kinds of things.
Smak
Smak

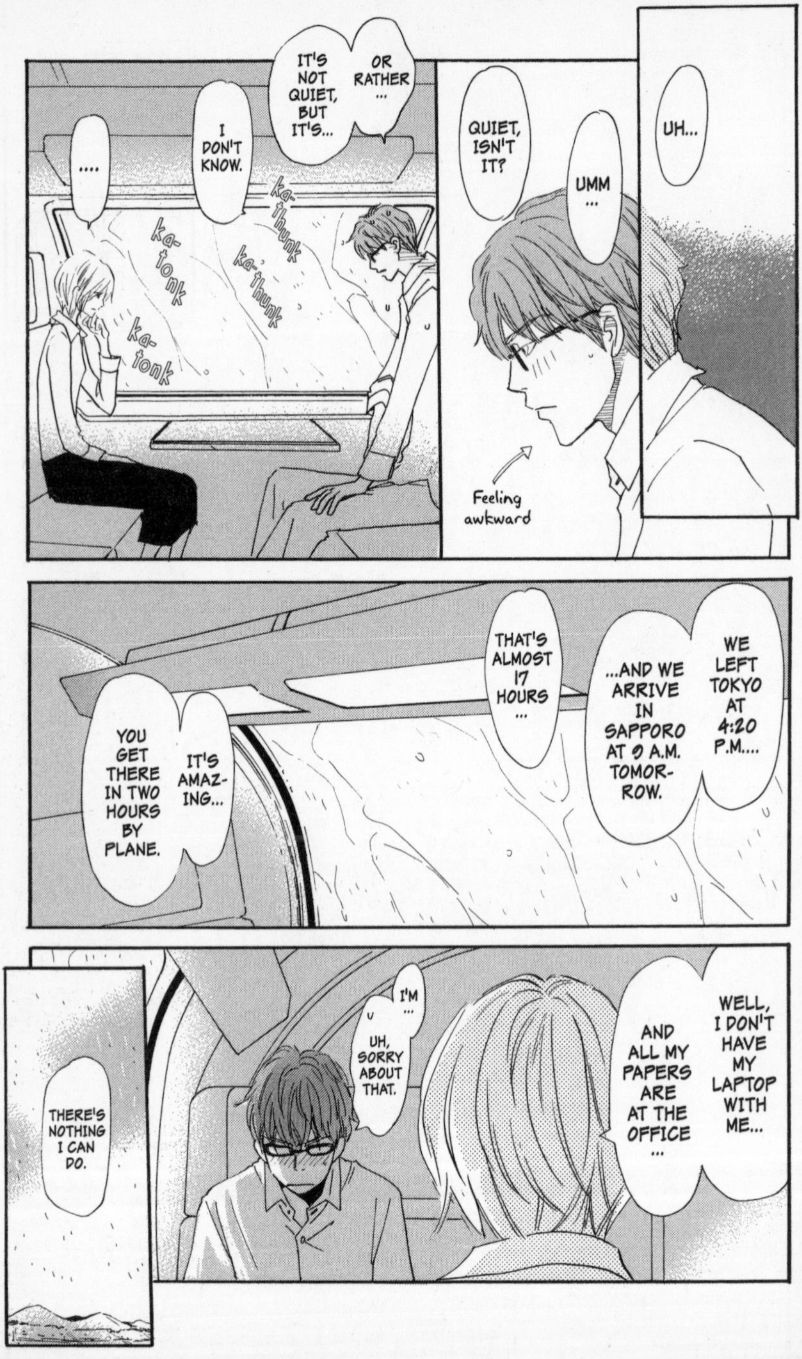
UH...
UMM ...
QUIET, ISN'T IT?
Feeling awkward
OR RATHER ...
IT'S NOT QUIET, BUT IT'S...
I DON'T KNOW.
....
ka-thunk ka-thunk
ka-tonk ka-tonk
WE LEFT TOKYO AT 4:20 P.M....
...AND WE ARRIVE IN SAPPORO AT 9 A.M. TOMORROW.
THAT'S ALMOST 17 HOURS ...
IT'S AMAZING...
YOU GET THERE IN TWO HOURS BY PLANE.
WELL, I DON'T HAVE MY LAPTOP WITH ME...
AND ALL MY PAPERS ARE AT THE OFFICE ...
I'M ...
UH, SORRY ABOUT THAT.
THERE'S NOTHING I CAN DO.

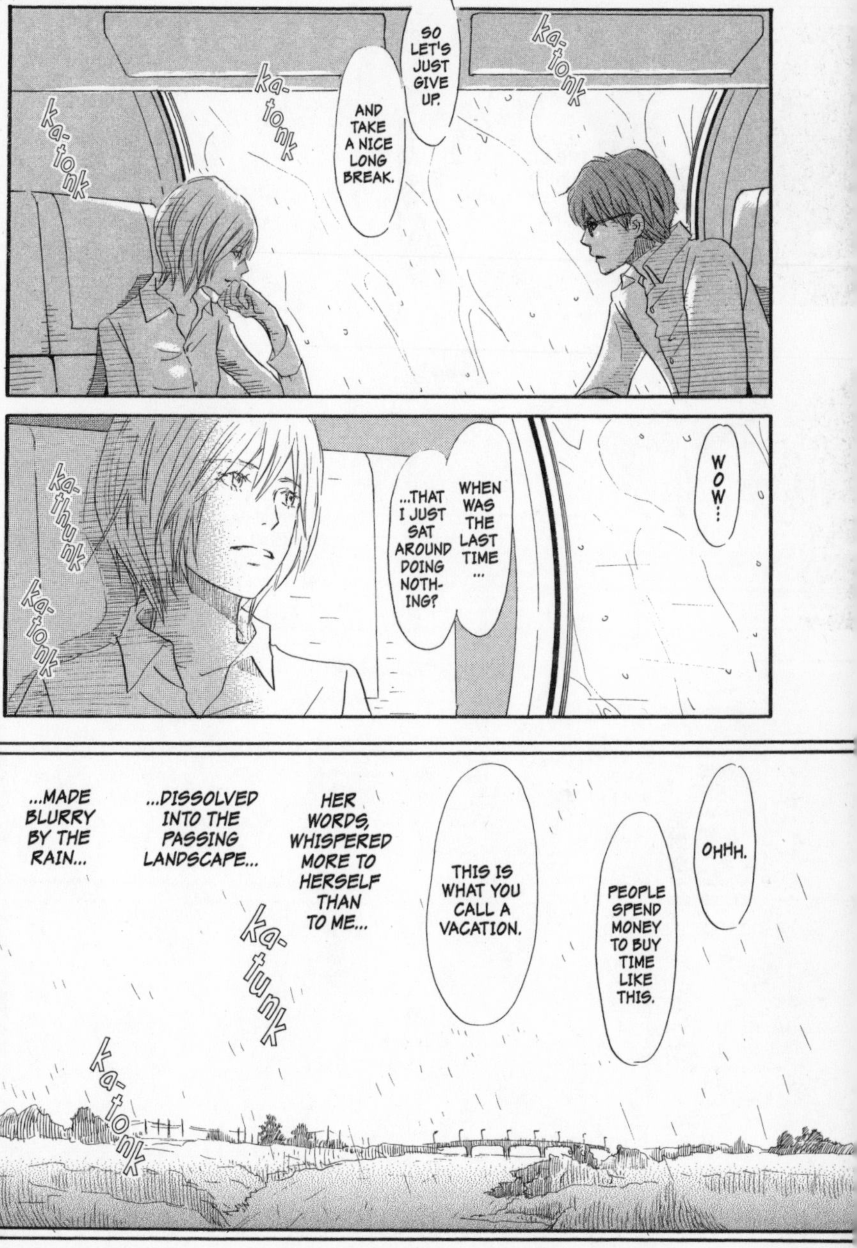
ka-tonk
SO LET'S JUST GIVE UP.
AND TAKE A NICE LONG BREAK.
ka-tonk
ka-tonk
WOW...
WHEN WAS THE LAST TIME...
...THAT I JUST SAT AROUND DOING NOTH-ING?
ka-thunk
ka-tonk
OHHH.
PEOPLE SPEND MONEY TO BUY TIME LIKE THIS.
THIS IS WHAT YOU CALL A VACATION.
HER WORDS, WHISPERED MORE TO HERSELF THAN TO ME...
ka-tunk
...DISSOLVED INTO THE PASSING LANDSCAPE...
...MADE BLURRY BY THE RAIN...
ka-tonk

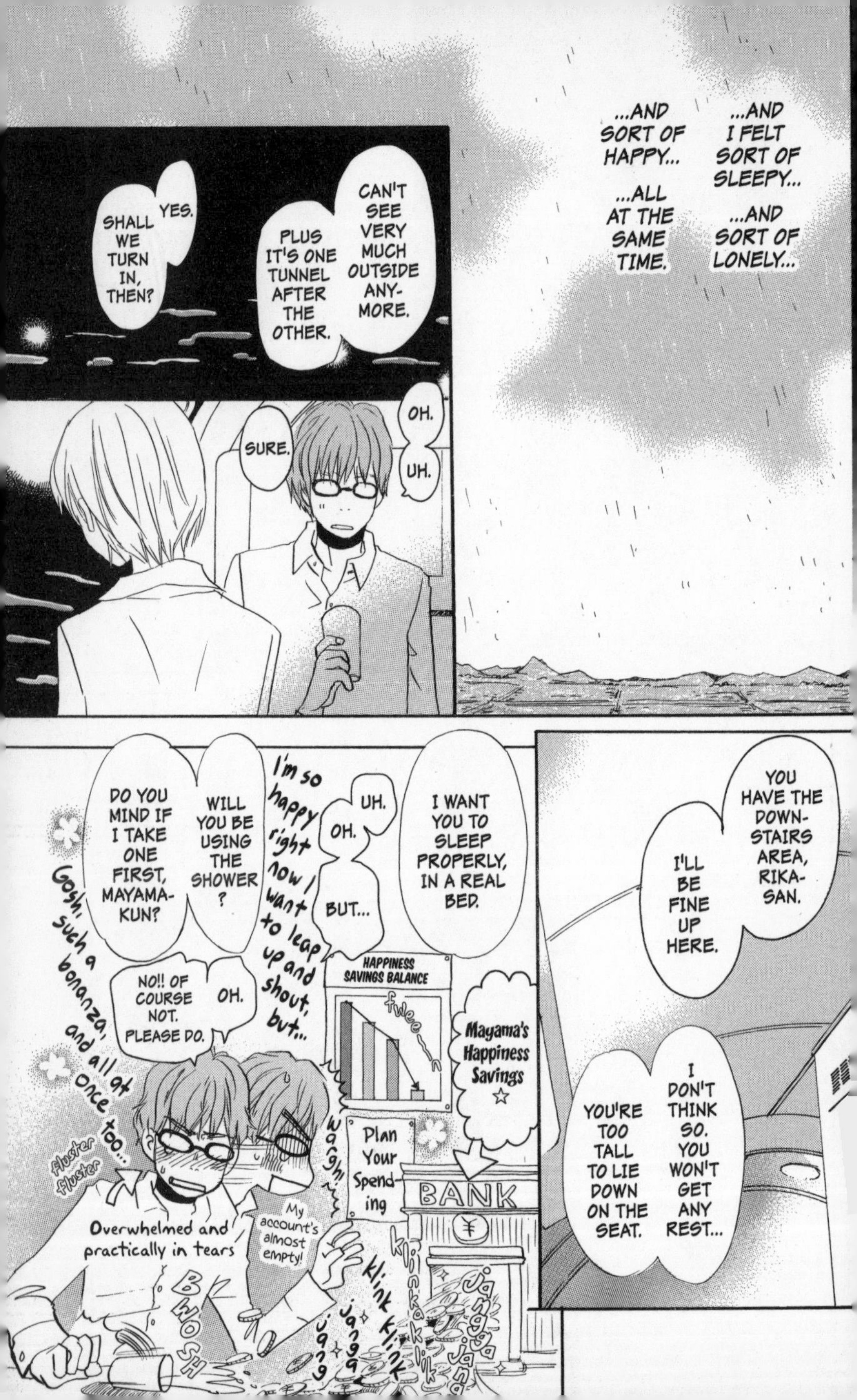
...AND I FELT SORT OF SLEEPY...
...AND SORT OF LONELY...
...AND SORT OF HAPPY...
...ALL AT THE SAME TIME.
CAN'T SEE VERY MUCH OUTSIDE ANYMORE.
PLUS IT'S ONE TUNNEL AFTER THE OTHER.
YES.
SHALL WE TURN IN, THEN?
OH.
UH.
SURE.
YOU HAVE THE DOWNSTAIRS AREA, RIKA-SAN.
I'LL BE FINE UP HERE.
I DON'T THINK SO. YOU WON'T GET ANY REST...
YOU'RE TOO TALL TO LIE DOWN ON THE SEAT.
I WANT YOU TO SLEEP PROPERLY, IN A REAL BED.
UH.
OH.
BUT...
I'm so happy right now I want to leap up and shout, but...
WILL YOU BE USING THE SHOWER?
DO YOU MIND IF I TAKE ONE FIRST, MAYAMA-KUN?
OH.
NO!! OF COURSE NOT. PLEASE DO.
Gosh, such a bonanza, and all at once too...
HAPPINESS SAVINGS BALANCE
fwee~n
Mayama's Happiness Savings ☆
Plan Your Spending
BANK
Wargh!
fluster fluster
Overwhelmed and practically in tears
My account's almost empty!
BWOSH
klink klink klink
janga janga
janga janga

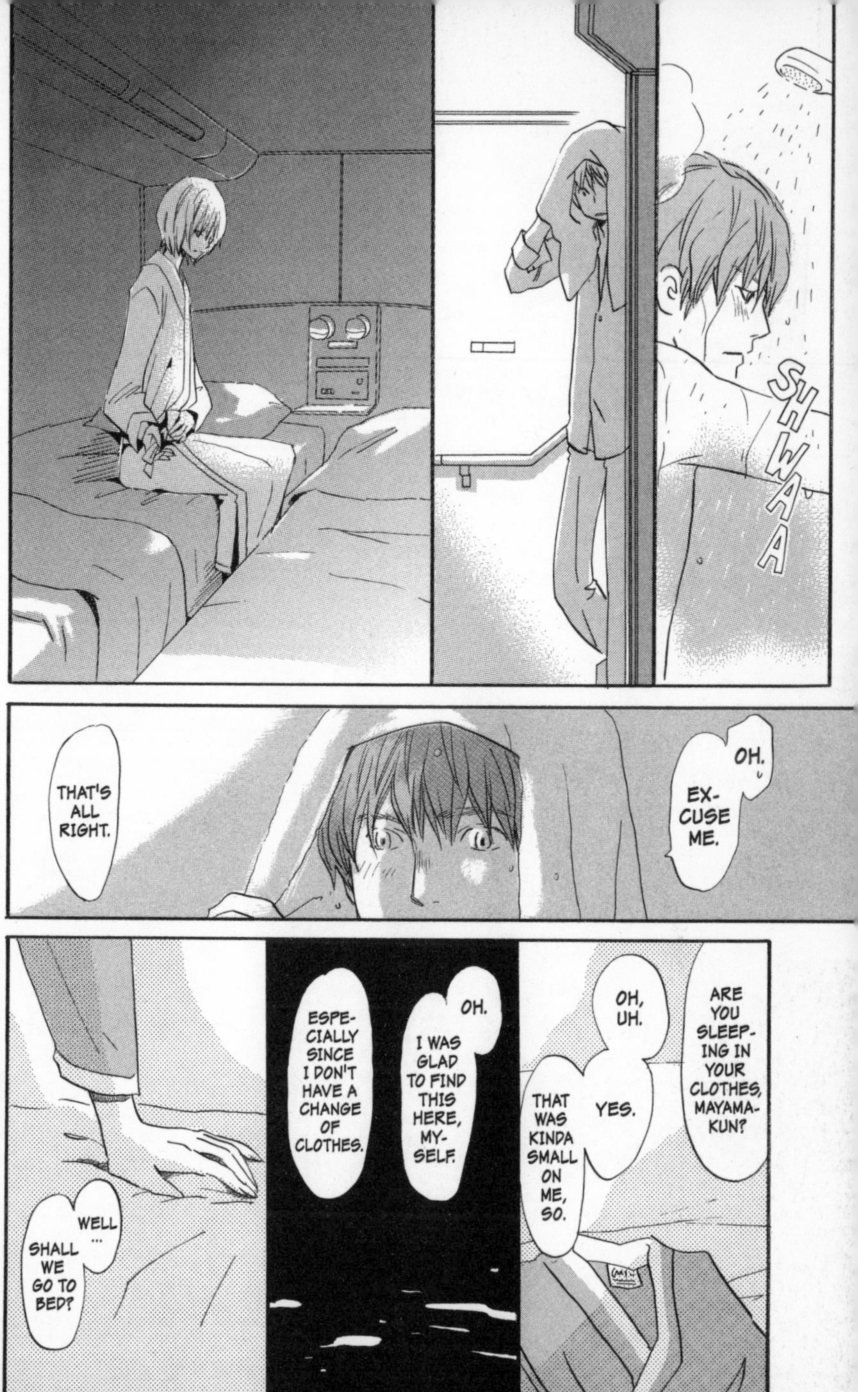
SHWAA
OH.
EXCUSE ME.
THAT'S ALL RIGHT.
ARE YOU SLEEPING IN YOUR CLOTHES, MAYAMA-KUN?
OH, UH.
YES.
THAT WAS KINDA SMALL ON ME, SO.
OH.
I WAS GLAD TO FIND THIS HERE, MYSELF.
ESPECIALLY SINCE I DON'T HAVE A CHANGE OF CLOTHES.
WELL ...
SHALL WE GO TO BED?

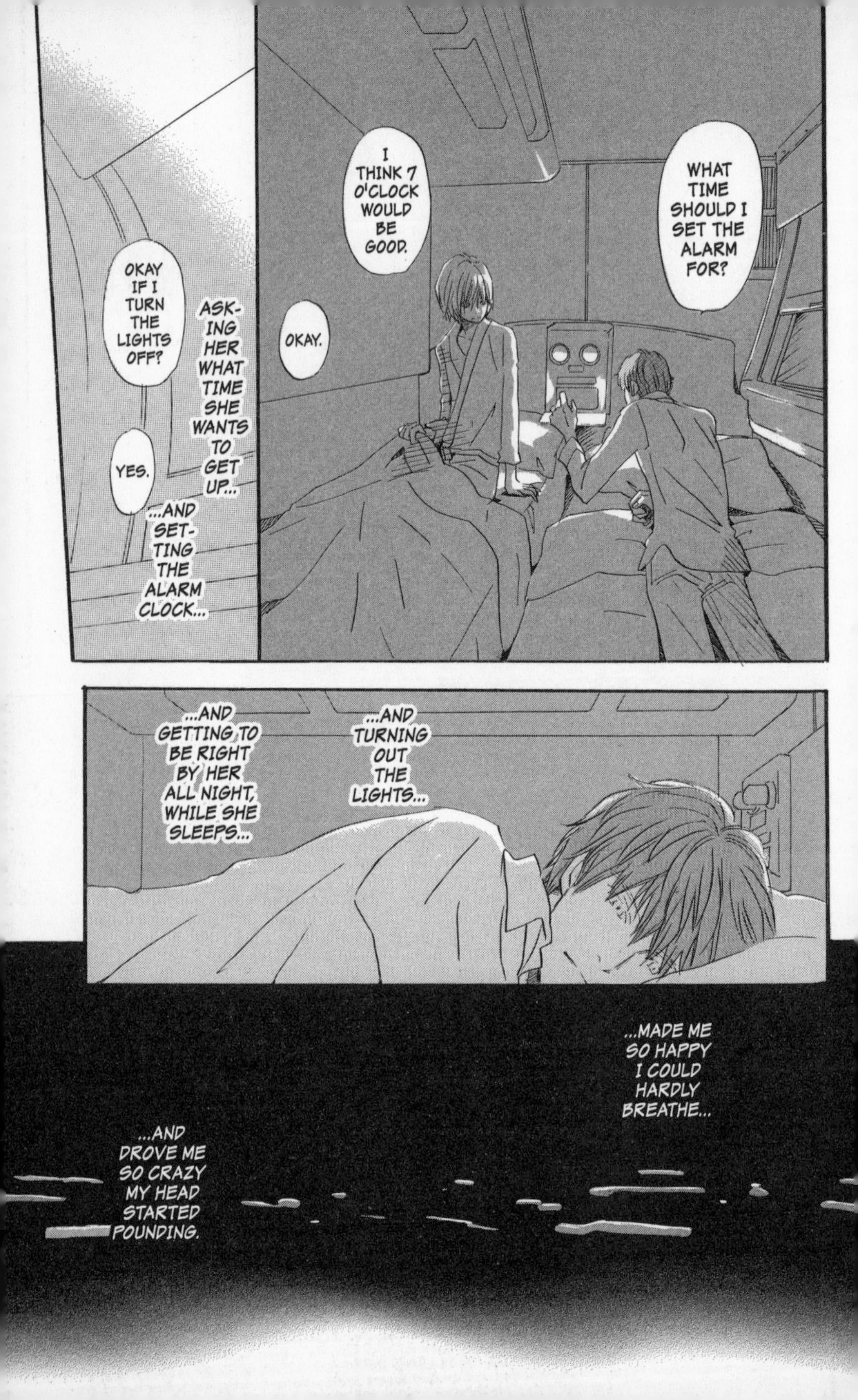
WHAT TIME SHOULD I SET THE ALARM FOR?
I THINK 7 O'CLOCK WOULD BE GOOD.
OKAY.
ASK-ING HER WHAT TIME SHE WANTS TO GET UP...
OKAY IF I TURN THE LIGHTS OFF?
YES.
...AND SET-TING THE ALARM CLOCK...
...AND TURNING OUT THE LIGHTS...
...AND GETTING TO BE RIGHT BY HER ALL NIGHT, WHILE SHE SLEEPS...
...MADE ME SO HAPPY I COULD HARDLY BREATHE...
...AND DROVE ME SO CRAZY MY HEAD STARTED POUNDING.

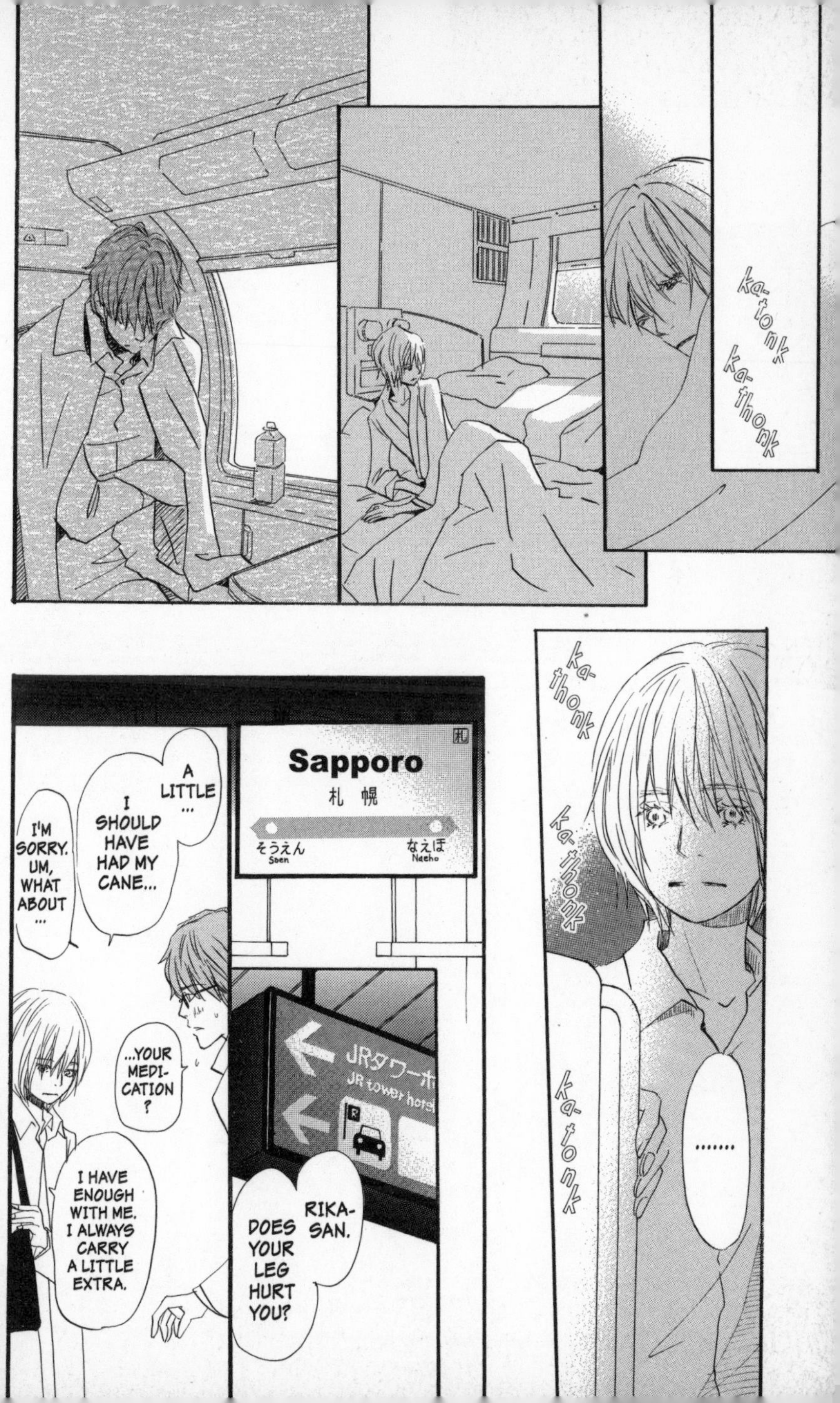
ka-tonk
ka-thonk
ka-thonk
ka-thonk
ka-tonk
....
Sapporo
札幌
そうえん
Soen
なえぼ
Naeho
JRタワーホ
JR tower hote
RIKA-SAN.
DOES YOUR LEG HURT YOU?
A LITTLE...
I SHOULD HAVE HAD MY CANE...
I'M SORRY. UM, WHAT ABOUT...
...YOUR MEDICATION?
I HAVE ENOUGH WITH ME. I ALWAYS CARRY A LITTLE EXTRA.

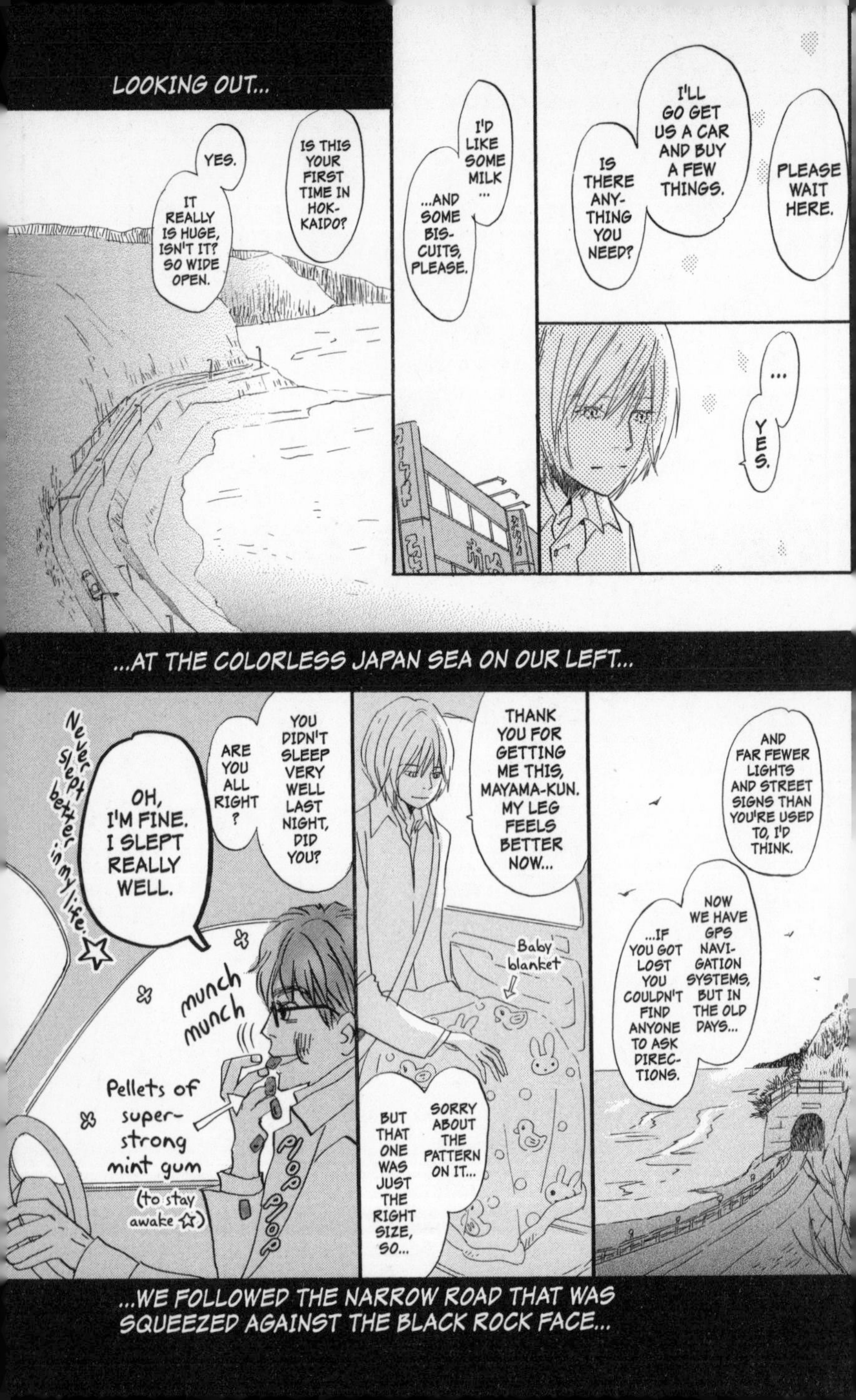
PLEASE WAIT HERE.
I'LL GO GET US A CAR AND BUY A FEW THINGS.
IS THERE ANYTHING YOU NEED?
... YES.
I'D LIKE SOME MILK...
...AND SOME BISCUITS, PLEASE.
LOOKING OUT...
IS THIS YOUR FIRST TIME IN HOKKAIDO?
YES.
IT REALLY IS HUGE, ISN'T IT? SO WIDE OPEN.
...AT THE COLORLESS JAPAN SEA ON OUR LEFT...
AND FAR FEWER LIGHTS AND STREET SIGNS THAN YOU'RE USED TO, I'D THINK.
NOW WE HAVE GPS NAVIGATION SYSTEMS, BUT IN THE OLD DAYS...
...IF YOU GOT LOST YOU COULDN'T FIND ANYONE TO ASK DIRECTIONS.
THANK YOU FOR GETTING ME THIS, MAYAMA-KUN. MY LEG FEELS BETTER NOW...
Baby blanket
SORRY ABOUT THE PATTERN ON IT...
BUT THAT ONE WAS JUST THE RIGHT SIZE, SO...
YOU DIDN'T SLEEP VERY WELL LAST NIGHT, DID YOU?
ARE YOU ALL RIGHT?
OH, I'M FINE. I SLEPT REALLY WELL.
Never slept better in my life.
munch munch
Pellets of super-strong mint gum
(to stay awake)
plop plop
...WE FOLLOWED THE NARROW ROAD THAT WAS SQUEEZED AGAINST THE BLACK ROCK FACE...

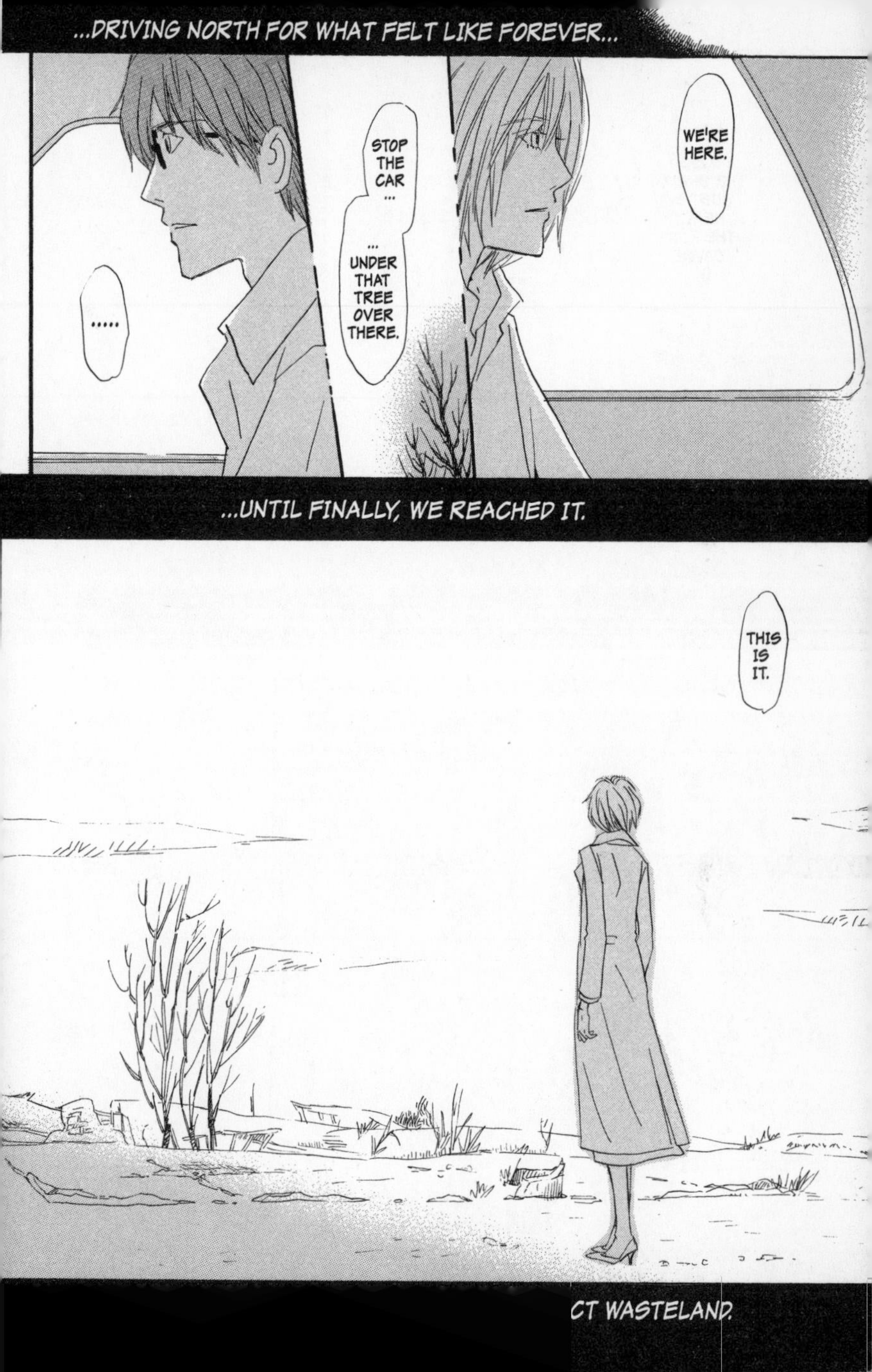
...DRIVING NORTH FOR WHAT FELT LIKE FOREVER...
WE'RE HERE.
STOP THE CAR...
...UNDER THAT TREE OVER THERE.
......
...UNTIL FINALLY, WE REACHED IT.
THIS IS IT.
CT WASTELAND.

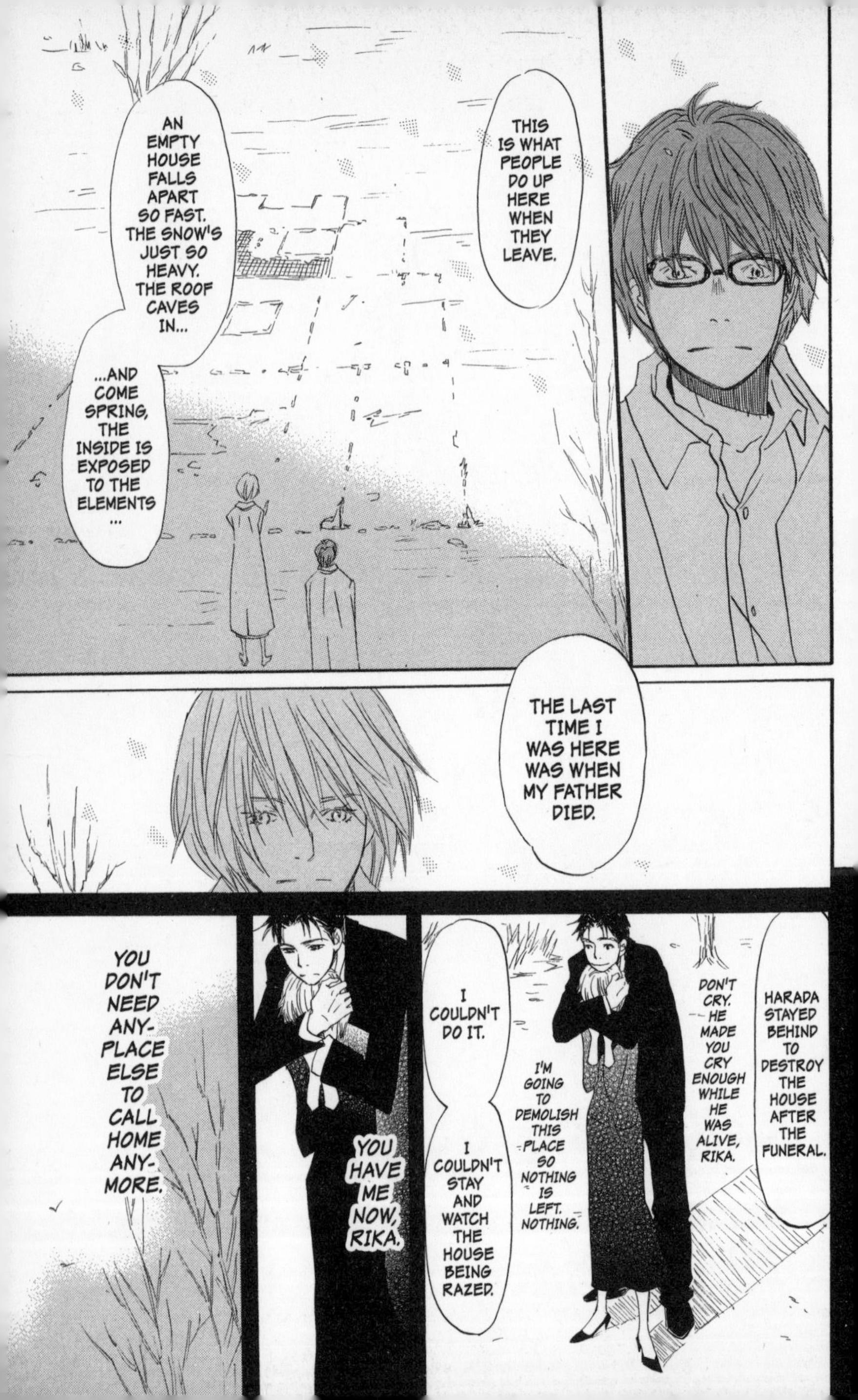
THIS IS WHAT PEOPLE DO UP HERE WHEN THEY LEAVE.
AN EMPTY HOUSE FALLS APART SO FAST. THE SNOW'S JUST SO HEAVY. THE ROOF CAVES IN...
...AND COME SPRING, THE INSIDE IS EXPOSED TO THE ELEMENTS...
THE LAST TIME I WAS HERE WAS WHEN MY FATHER DIED.
HARADA STAYED BEHIND TO DESTROY THE HOUSE AFTER THE FUNERAL.
DON'T CRY. HE MADE YOU CRY ENOUGH WHILE HE WAS ALIVE, RIKA.
I'M GOING TO DEMOLISH THIS PLACE SO NOTHING IS LEFT. NOTHING.
I COULDN'T DO IT.
I COULDN'T STAY AND WATCH THE HOUSE BEING RAZED.
YOU HAVE ME NOW, RIKA.
YOU DON'T NEED ANY-PLACE ELSE TO CALL HOME ANY-MORE.

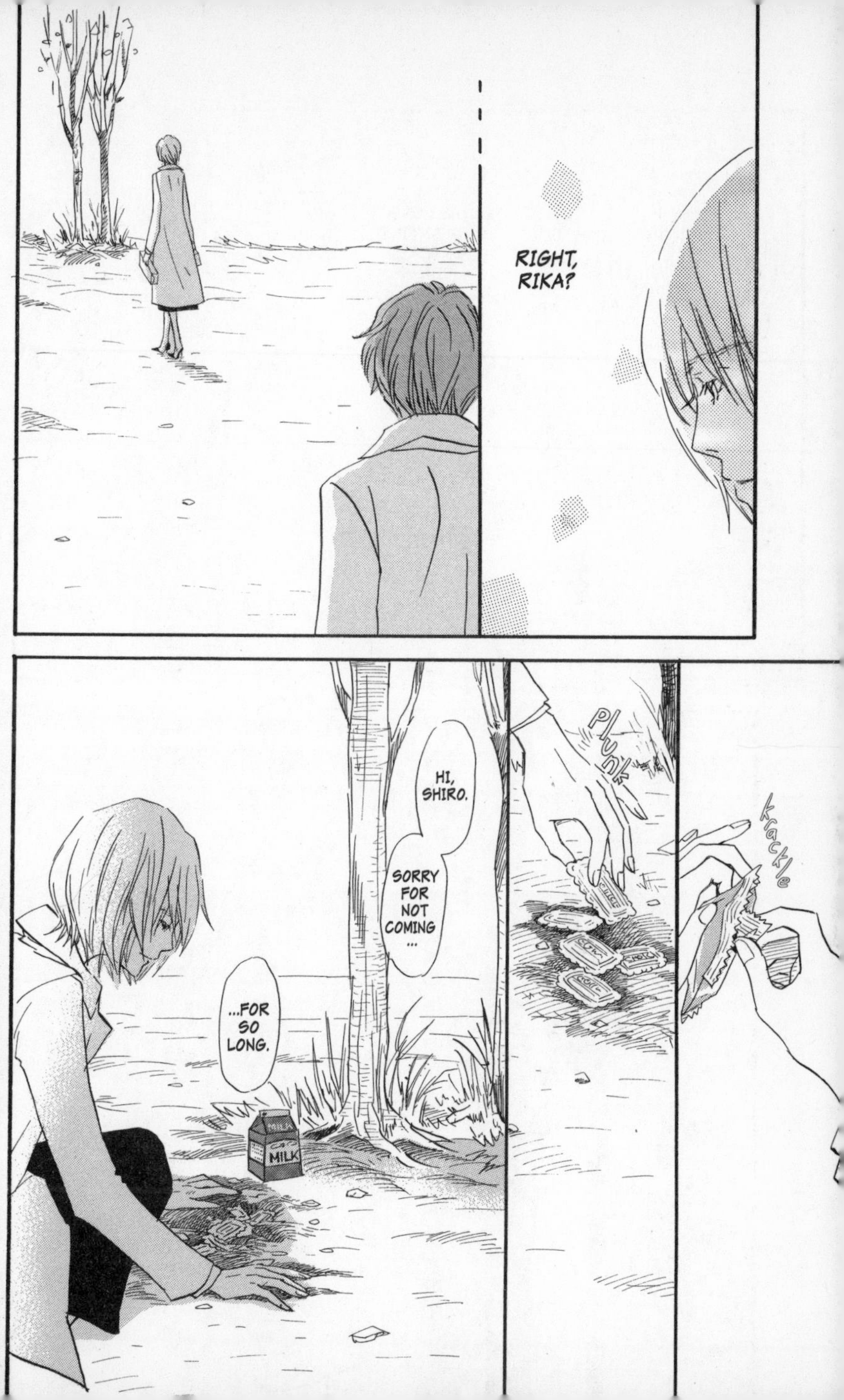
RIGHT, RIKA?
krackle
Plunk
HI, SHIRO.
SORRY FOR NOT COMING ...
...FOR SO LONG.
MILK

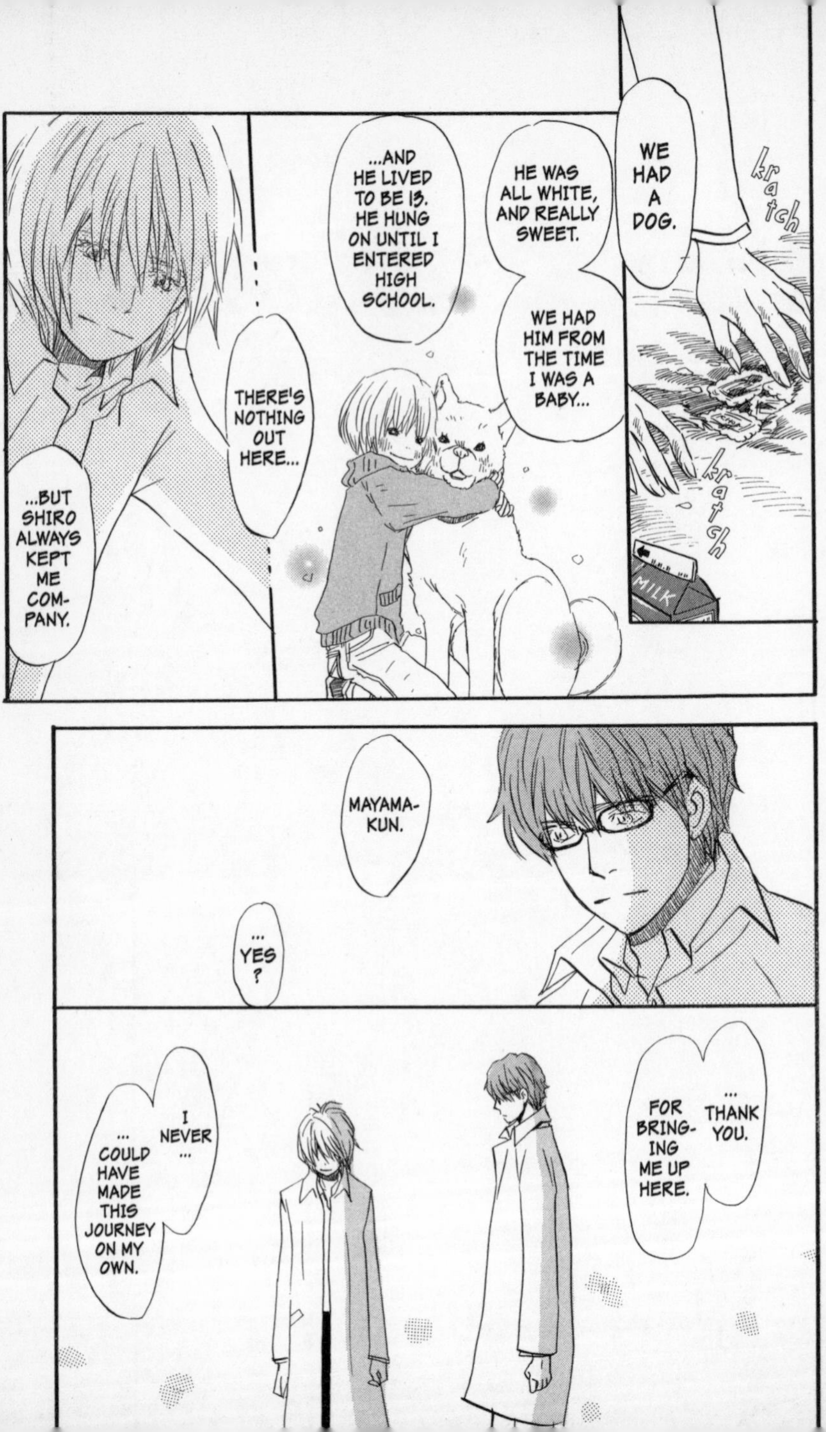
WE HAD A DOG.
kratch
kratch
MILK
HE WAS ALL WHITE, AND REALLY SWEET.
WE HAD HIM FROM THE TIME I WAS A BABY...
...AND HE LIVED TO BE 13. HE HUNG ON UNTIL I ENTERED HIGH SCHOOL.
THERE'S NOTHING OUT HERE...
...BUT SHIRO ALWAYS KEPT ME COMPANY.
MAYAMA-KUN.
...YES?
...THANK YOU.
FOR BRINGING ME UP HERE.
I NEVER...
...COULD HAVE MADE THIS JOURNEY ON MY OWN.

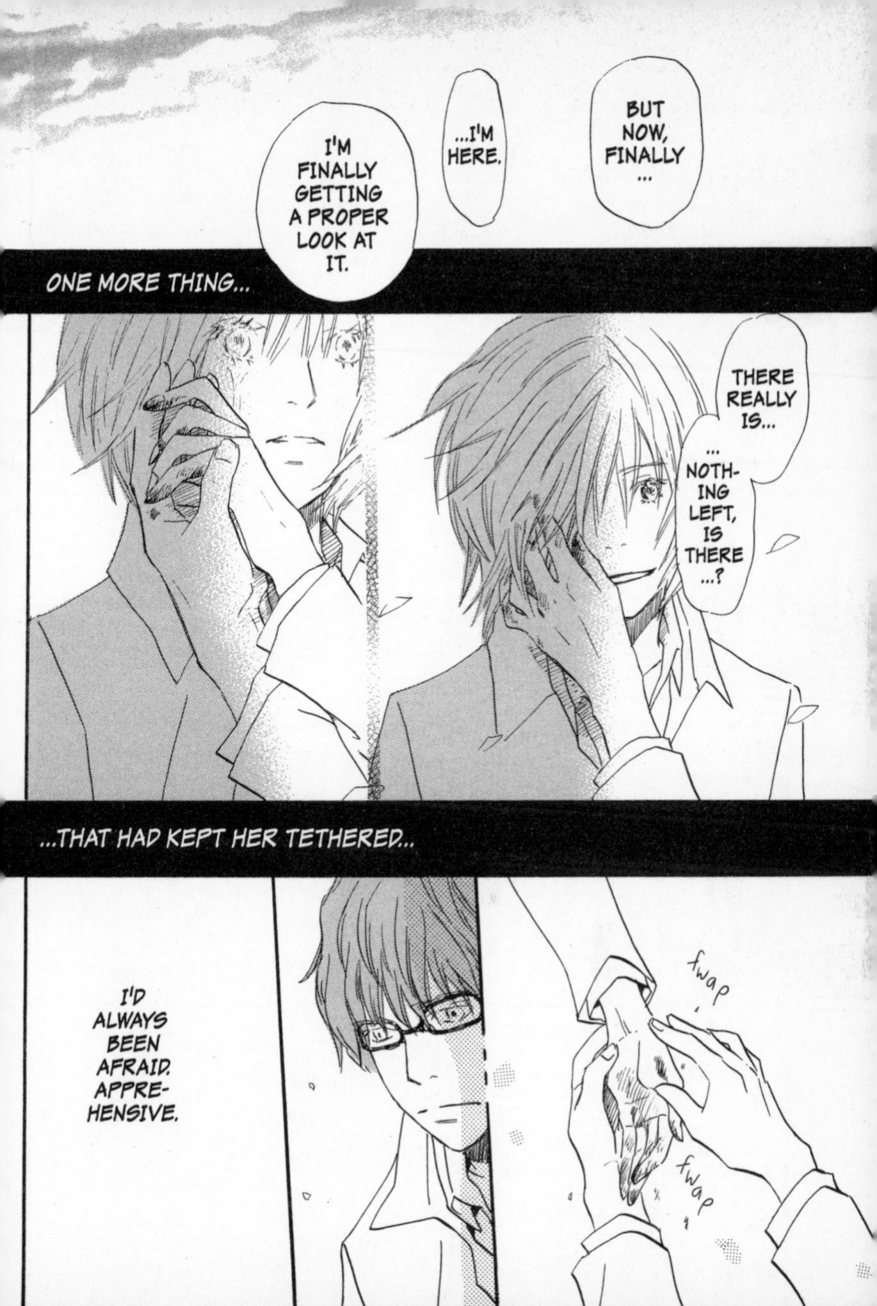
BUT NOW, FINALLY ...
...I'M HERE.
I'M FINALLY GETTING A PROPER LOOK AT IT.
ONE MORE THING...
THERE REALLY IS...
... NOTHING LEFT, IS THERE ...?
...THAT HAD KEPT HER TETHERED...
fwap
fwap
I'D ALWAYS BEEN AFRAID. APPRE-HENSIVE.

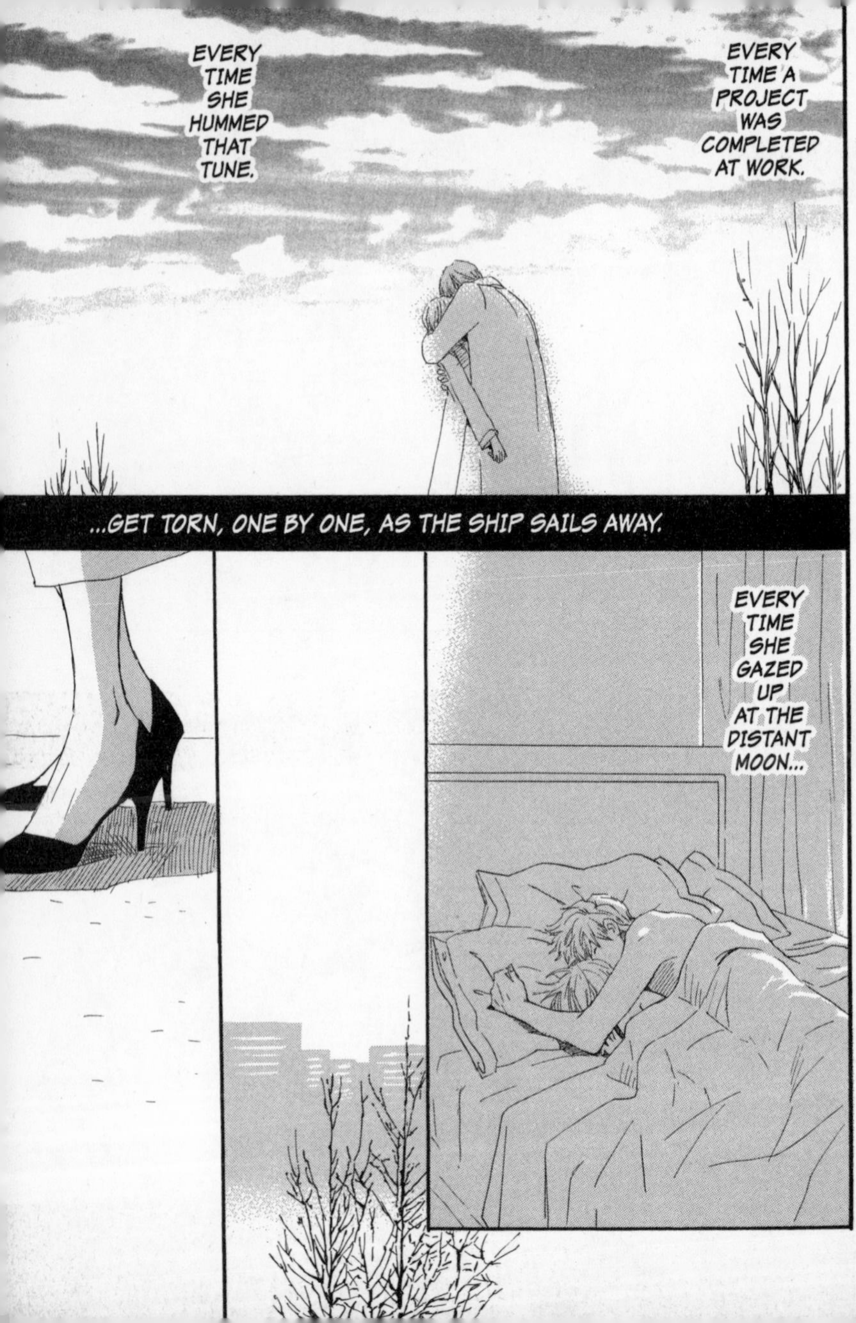
EVERY TIME A PROJECT WAS COMPLETED AT WORK.
EVERY TIME SHE HUMMED THAT TUNE.
...GET TORN, ONE BY ONE, AS THE SHIP SAILS AWAY.
EVERY TIME SHE GAZED UP AT THE DISTANT MOON...

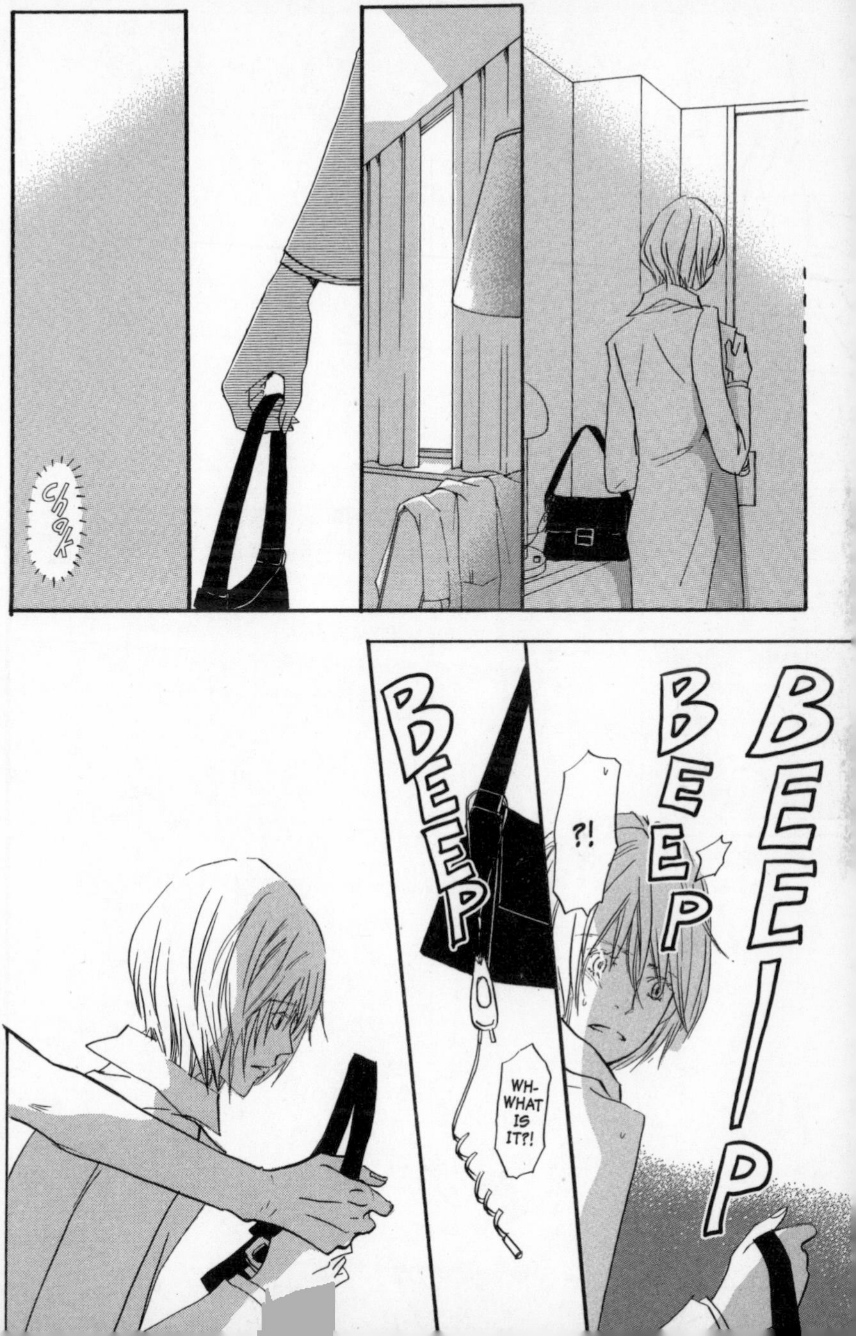
chak
BEEEP
BEEP
?!
BEEP
WH- WHAT IS IT?!

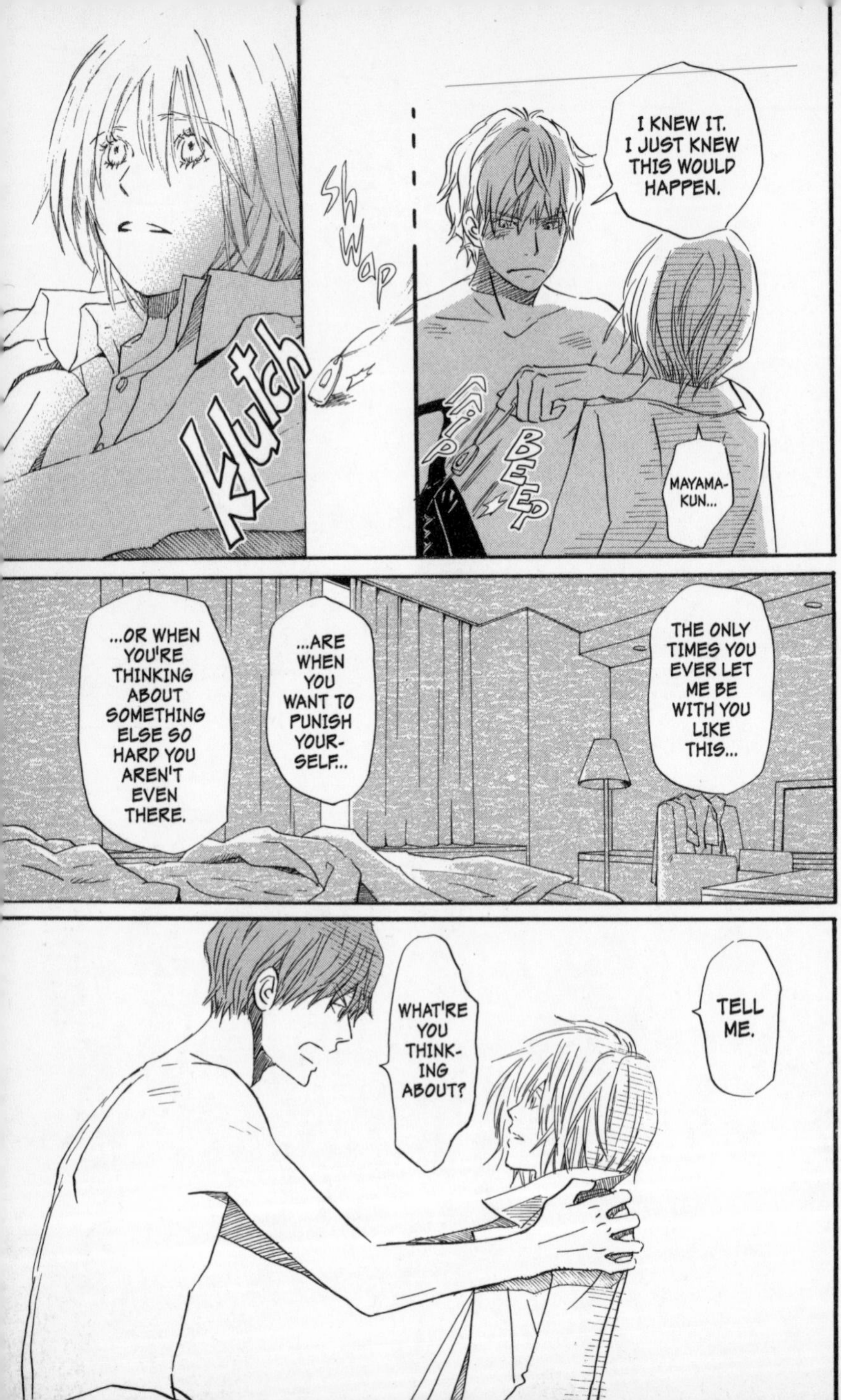
I KNEW IT. I JUST KNEW THIS WOULD HAPPEN.
MAYAMA-KUN...
BEEP
Shwap
Klutch
THE ONLY TIMES YOU EVER LET ME BE WITH YOU LIKE THIS...
...ARE WHEN YOU WANT TO PUNISH YOURSELF...
...OR WHEN YOU'RE THINKING ABOUT SOMETHING ELSE SO HARD YOU AREN'T EVEN THERE.
TELL ME.
WHAT'RE YOU THINKING ABOUT?

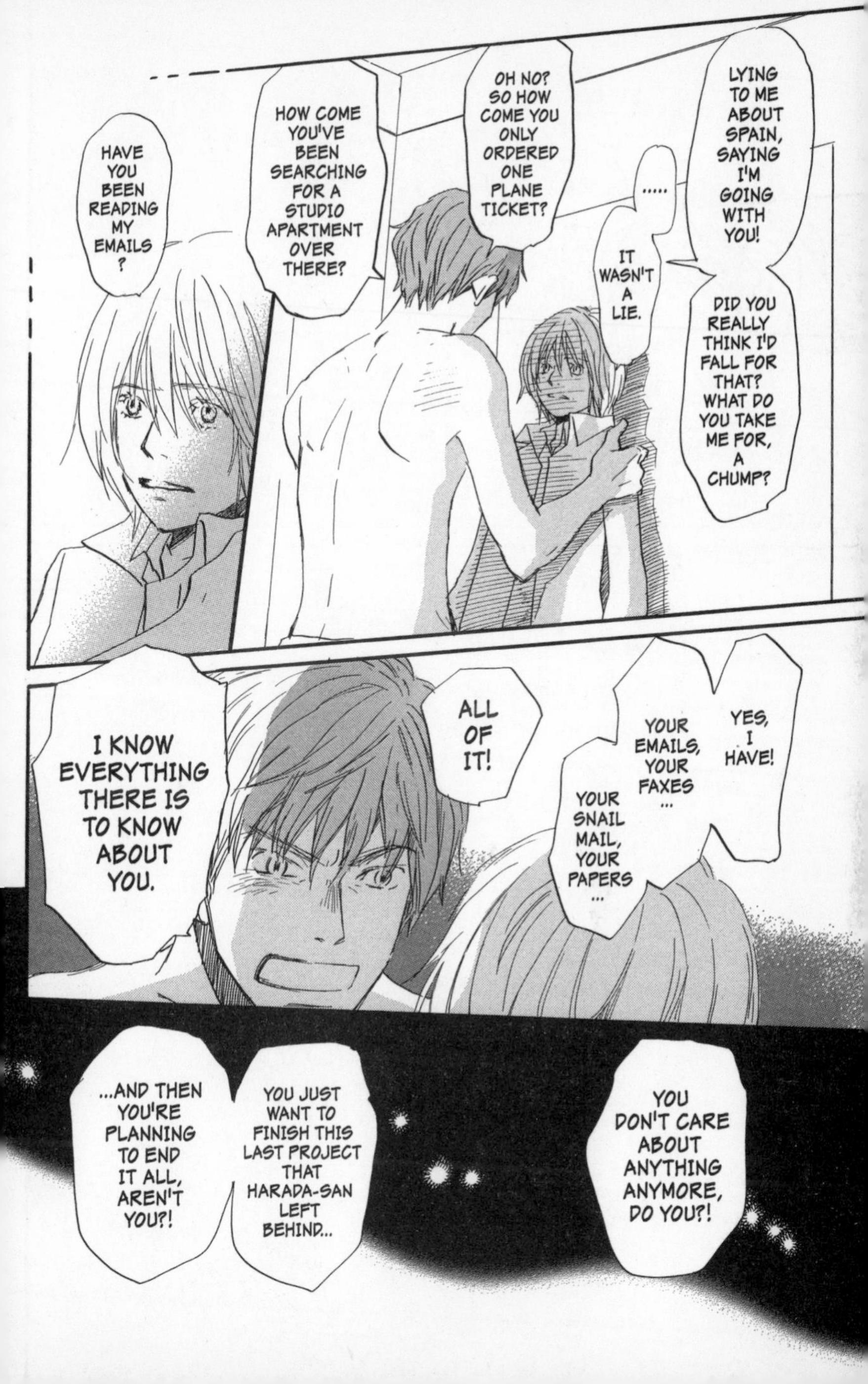
LYING TO ME ABOUT SPAIN, SAYING I'M GOING WITH YOU!
DID YOU REALLY THINK I'D FALL FOR THAT? WHAT DO YOU TAKE ME FOR, A CHUMP?
.....
IT WASN'T A LIE.
OH NO? SO HOW COME YOU ONLY ORDERED ONE PLANE TICKET?
HOW COME YOU'VE BEEN SEARCHING FOR A STUDIO APARTMENT OVER THERE?
HAVE YOU BEEN READING MY EMAILS?
YES, I HAVE!
YOUR EMAILS, YOUR FAXES...
YOUR SNAIL MAIL, YOUR PAPERS...
ALL OF IT!
I KNOW EVERYTHING THERE IS TO KNOW ABOUT YOU.
YOU DON'T CARE ABOUT ANYTHING ANYMORE, DO YOU?!
YOU JUST WANT TO FINISH THIS LAST PROJECT THAT HARADA-SAN LEFT BEHIND...
...AND THEN YOU'RE PLANNING TO END IT ALL, AREN'T YOU?!

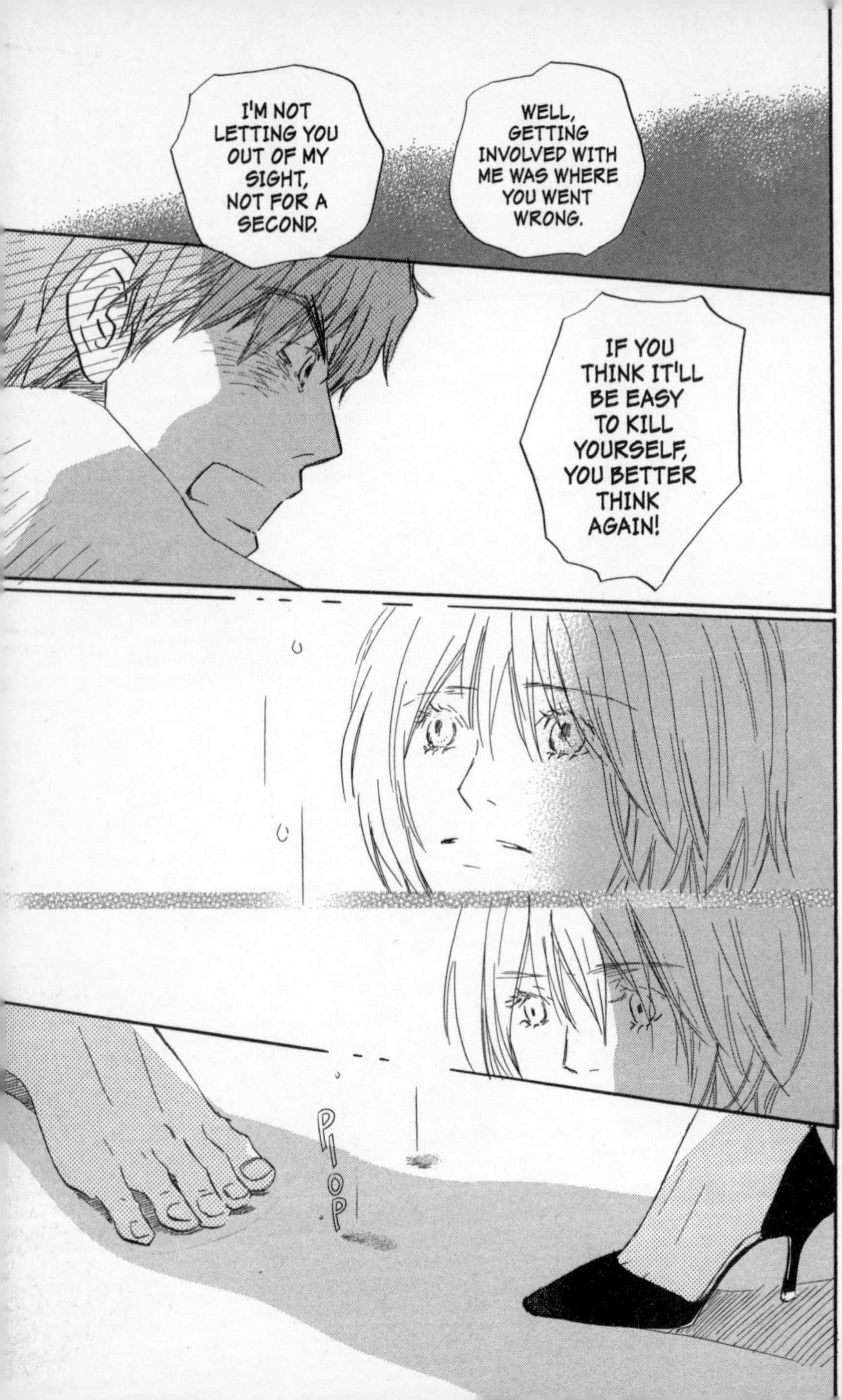
WELL, GETTING INVOLVED WITH ME WAS WHERE YOU WENT WRONG.
I'M NOT LETTING YOU OUT OF MY SIGHT, NOT FOR A SECOND.
IF YOU THINK IT'LL BE EASY TO KILL YOURSELF, YOU BETTER THINK AGAIN!
PLOP

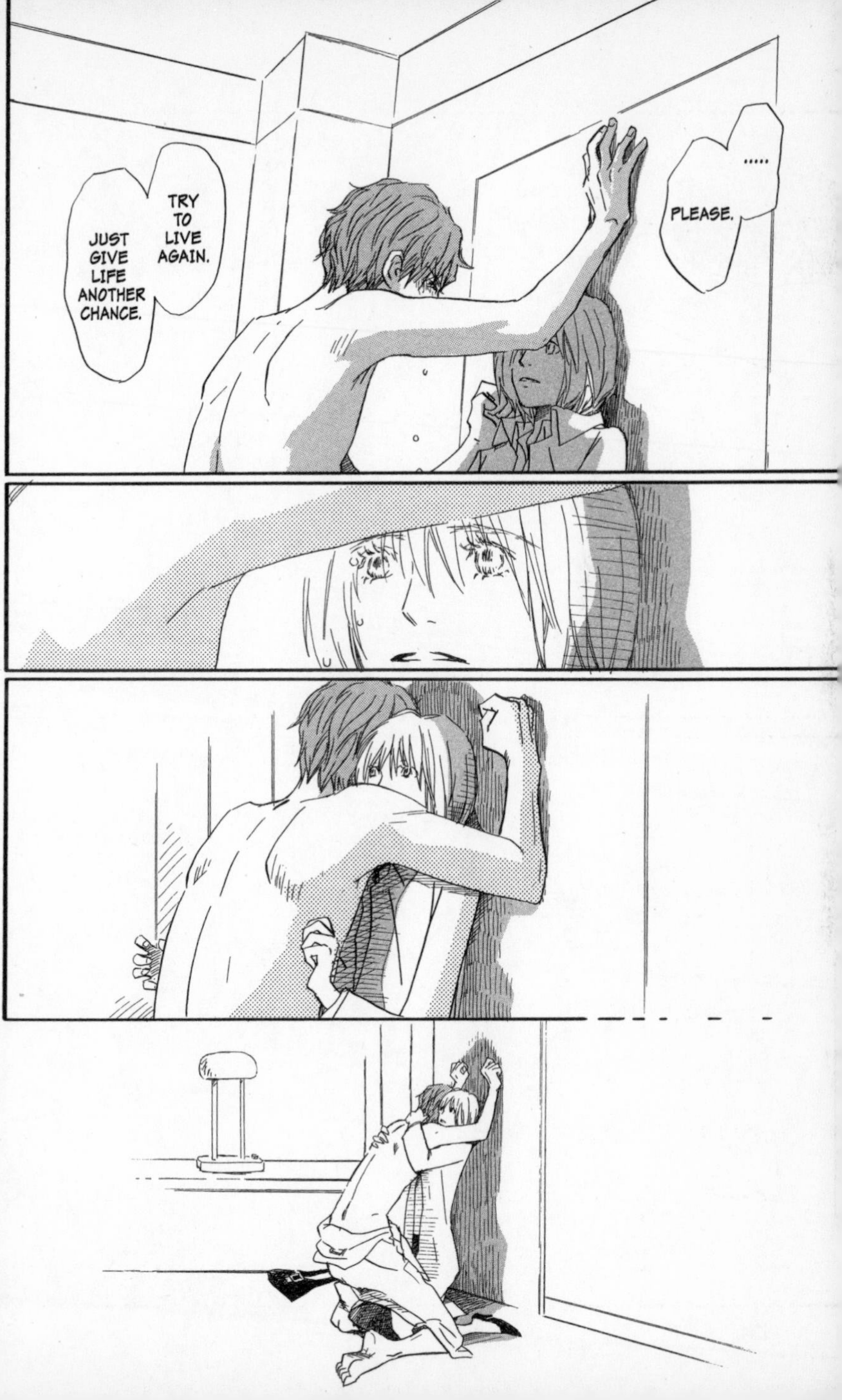
.....
PLEASE.
TRY TO LIVE AGAIN.
JUST GIVE LIFE ANOTHER CHANCE.

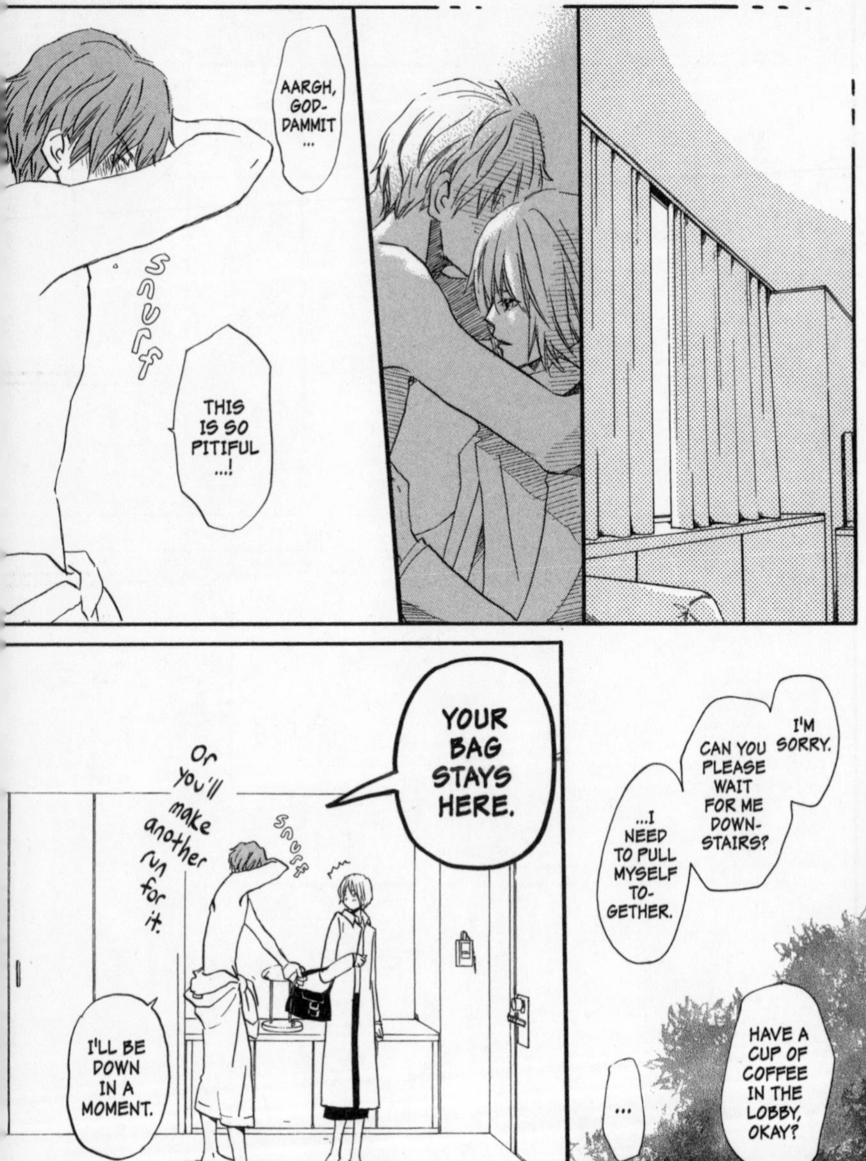
AARGH, GOD-DAMMIT ...
Snurf
THIS IS SO PITIFUL ...!
I'M SORRY.
CAN YOU PLEASE WAIT FOR ME DOWN-STAIRS?
...I NEED TO PULL MYSELF TO-GETHER.
HAVE A CUP OF COFFEE IN THE LOBBY, OKAY?
...
YOUR BAG STAYS HERE.
Or you'll make another run for it.
Snurf
I'LL BE DOWN IN A MOMENT.

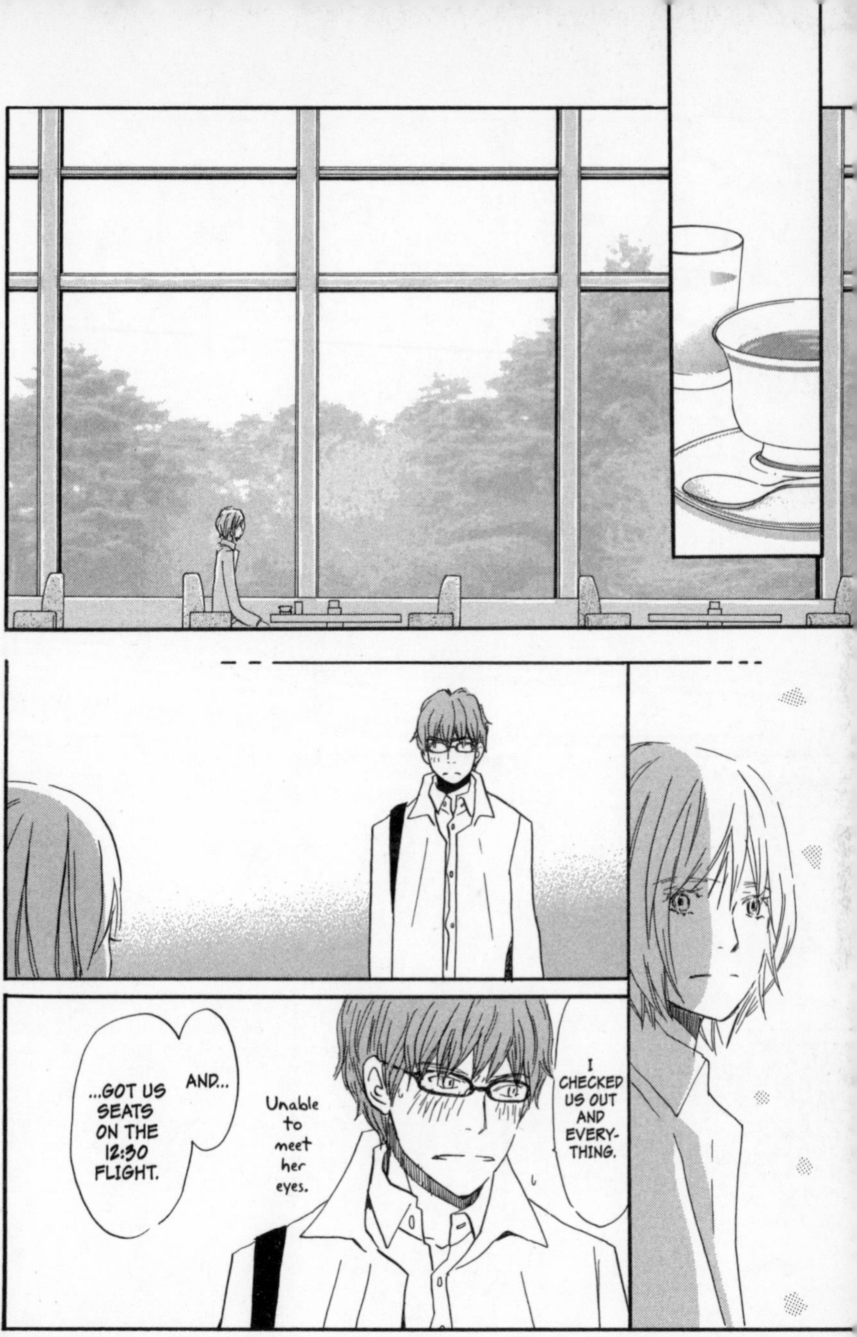
I CHECKED US OUT AND EVERY-THING.
Unable to meet her eyes.
AND...
...GOT US SEATS ON THE 12:30 FLIGHT.

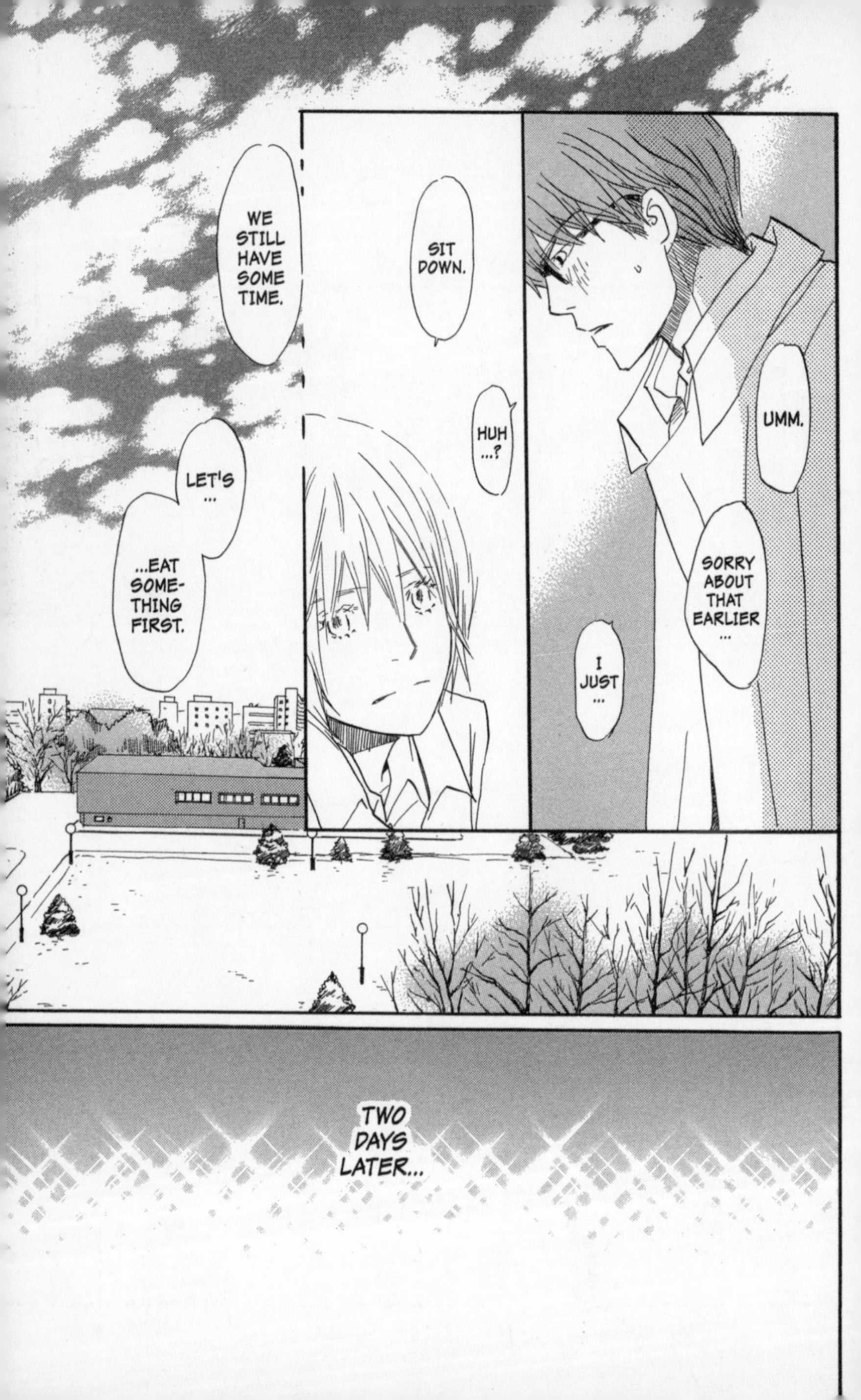
UMM.
SORRY ABOUT THAT EARLIER...
I JUST...
SIT DOWN.
HUH...?
WE STILL HAVE SOME TIME.
LET'S...
...EAT SOMETHING FIRST.
TWO DAYS LATER...

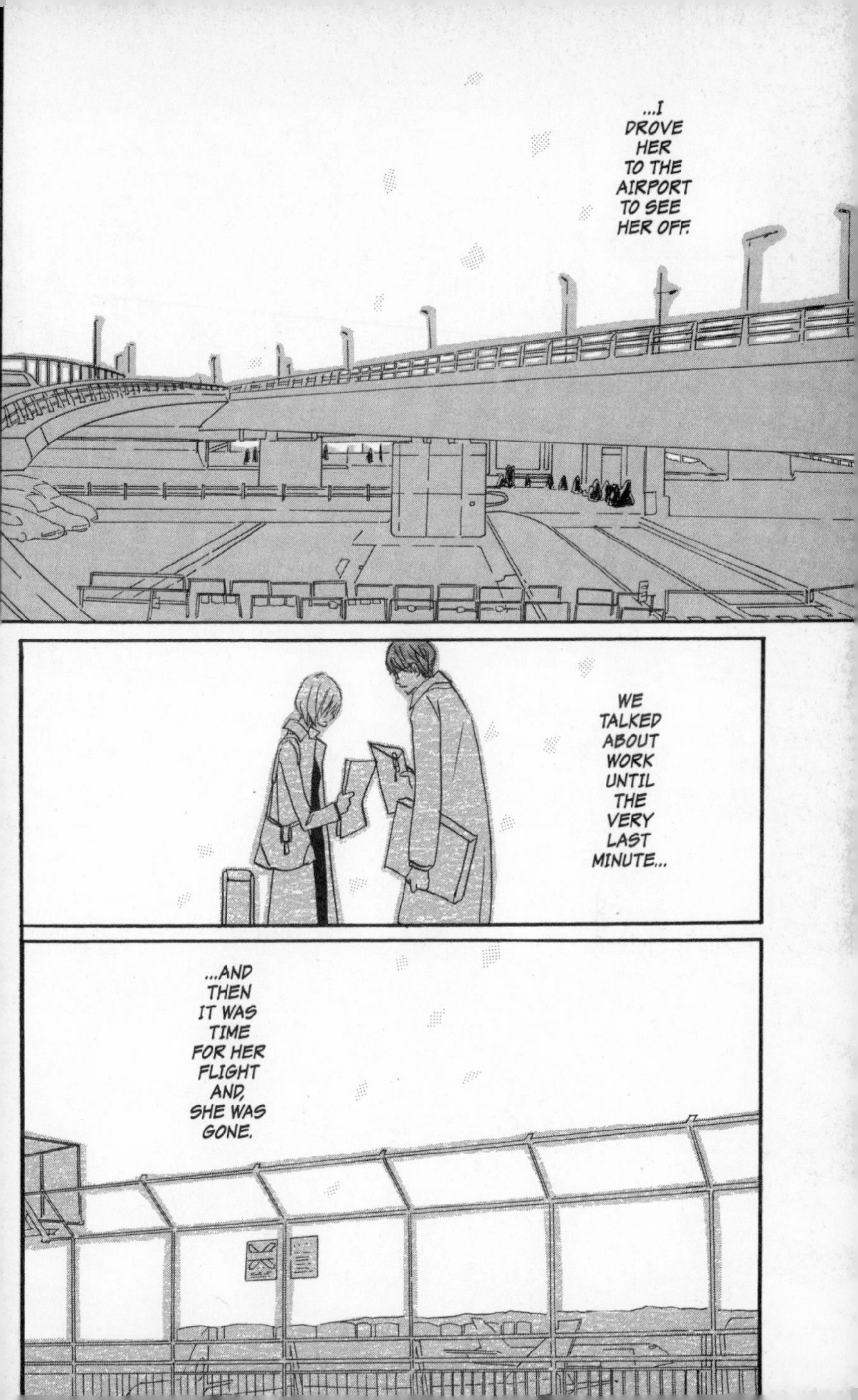
...I DROVE HER TO THE AIRPORT TO SEE HER OFF.
WE TALKED ABOUT WORK UNTIL THE VERY LAST MINUTE...
...AND THEN IT WAS TIME FOR HER FLIGHT AND, SHE WAS GONE.

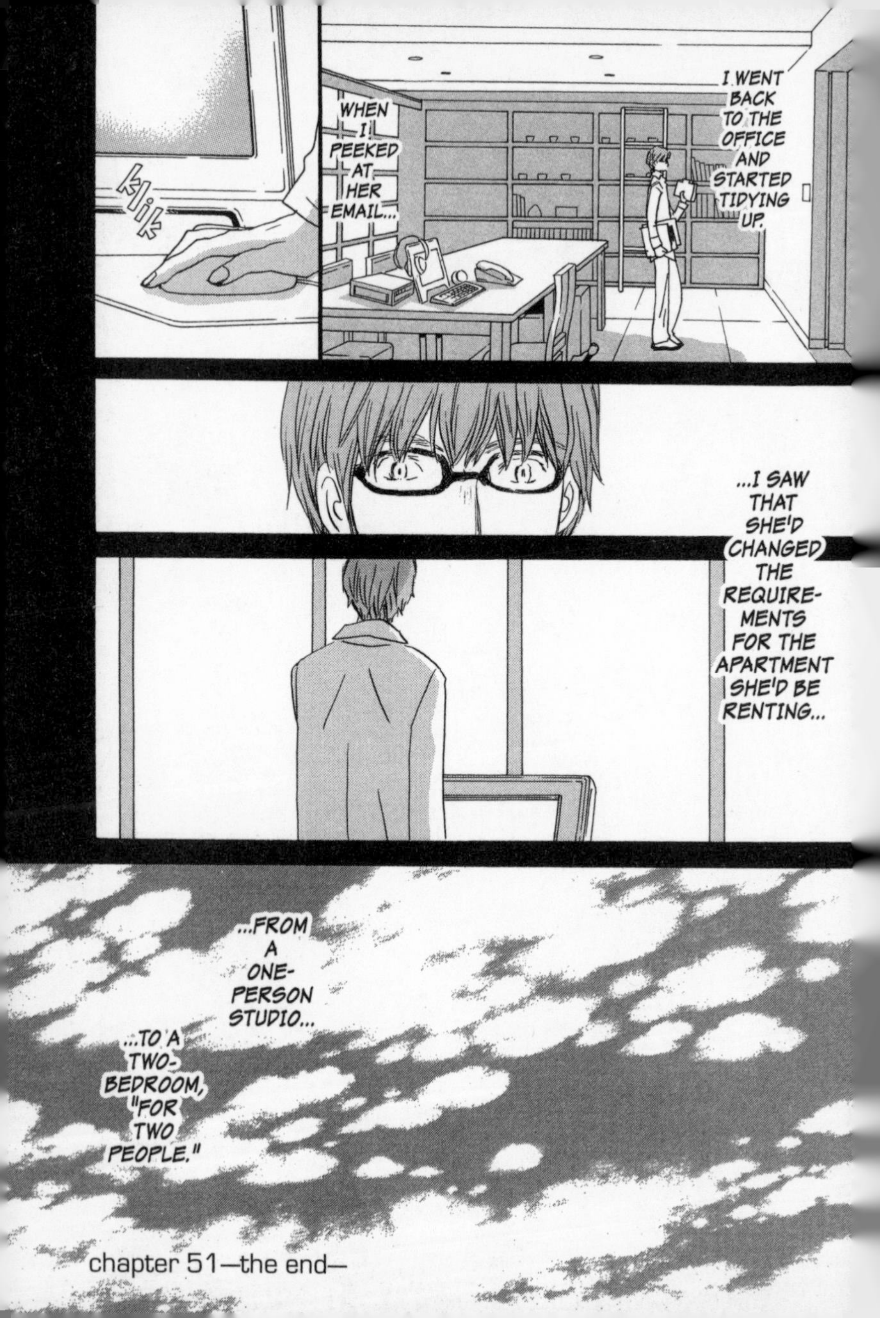
I WENT BACK TO THE OFFICE AND STARTED TIDYING UP.
WHEN I PEEKED AT HER EMAIL...
klik
...I SAW THAT SHE'D CHANGED THE REQUIRE-MENTS FOR THE APARTMENT SHE'D BE RENTING...
...FROM A ONE-PERSON STUDIO...
...TO A TWO-BEDROOM, "FOR TWO PEOPLE."
chapter 51—the end—

Rough sketches for color illustrations

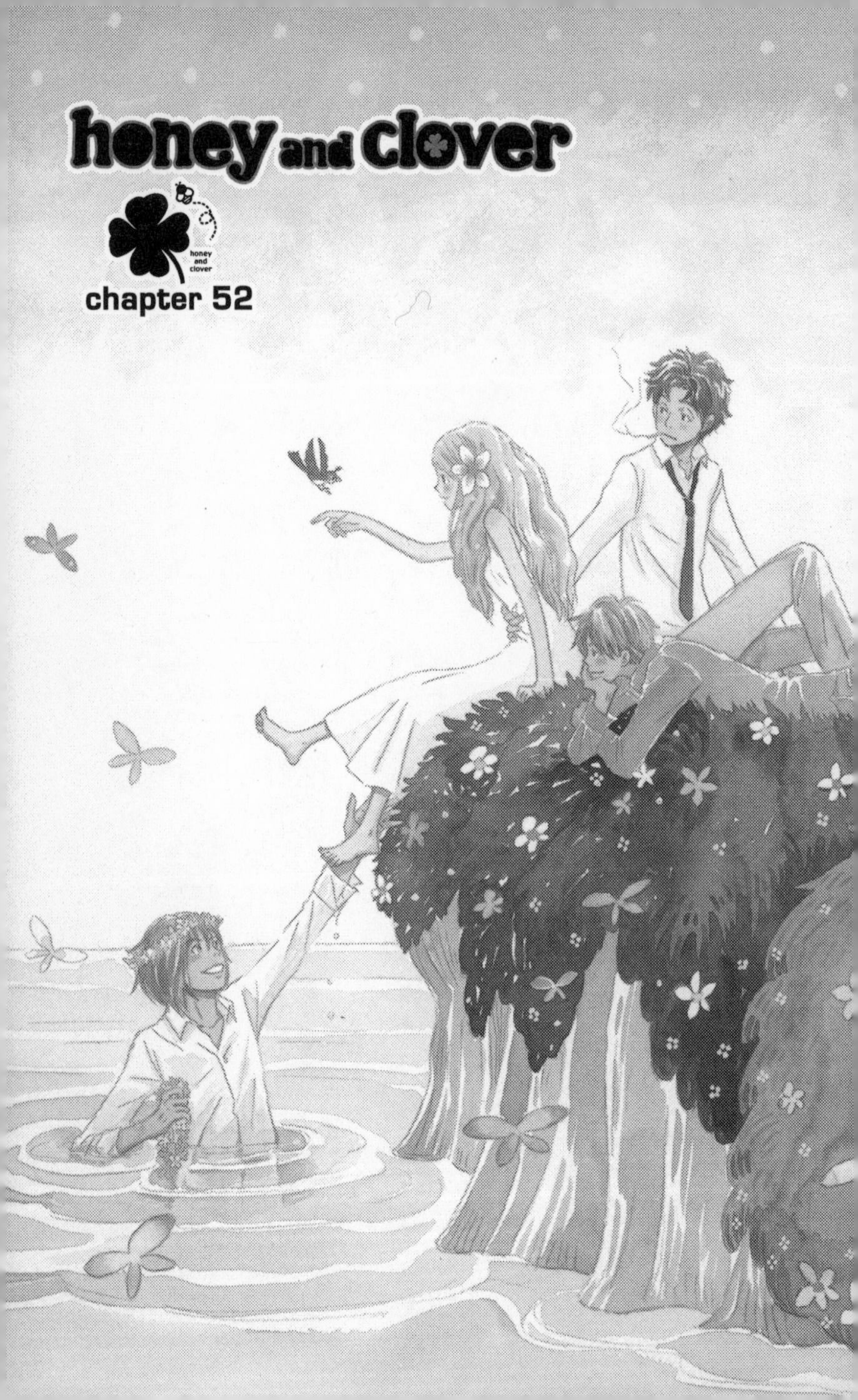
honey and clover
honey and clover
chapter 52

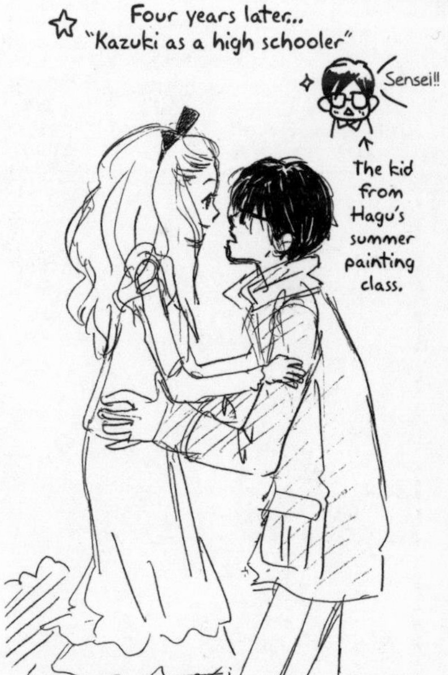
☆ Four years later...
"Kazuki as a high schooler"
Sensei!!
The kid from Hagu's summer painting class.

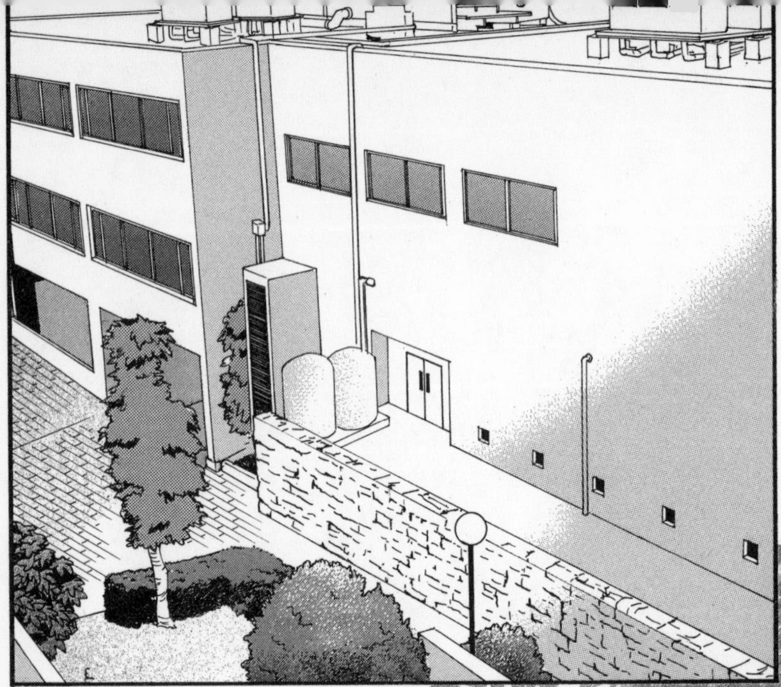

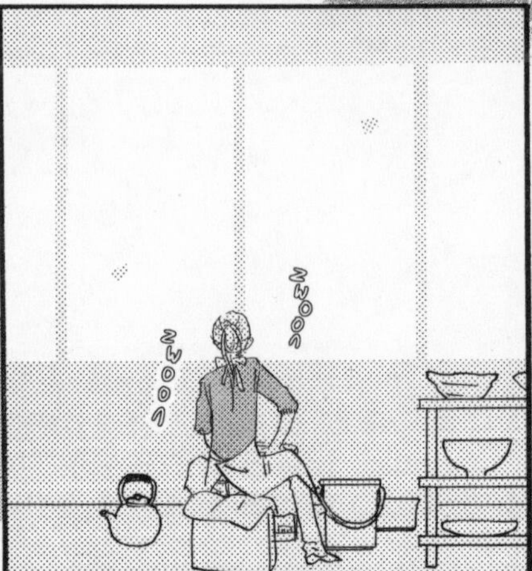
ZWOON
ZWOON

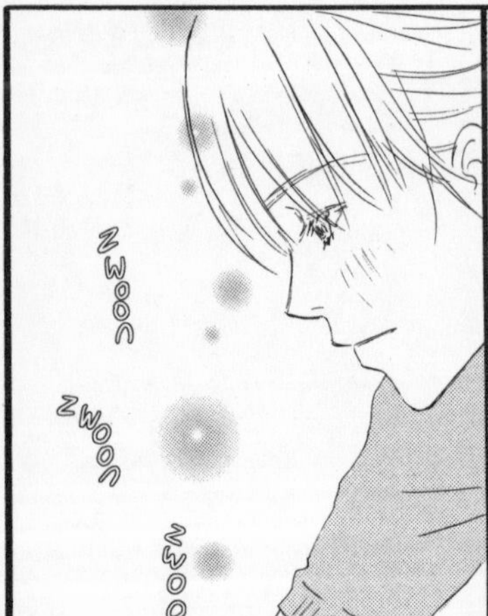
ZWOON
ZWOON
ZWOON

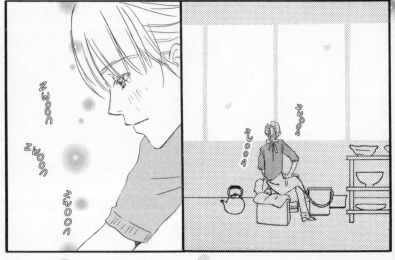

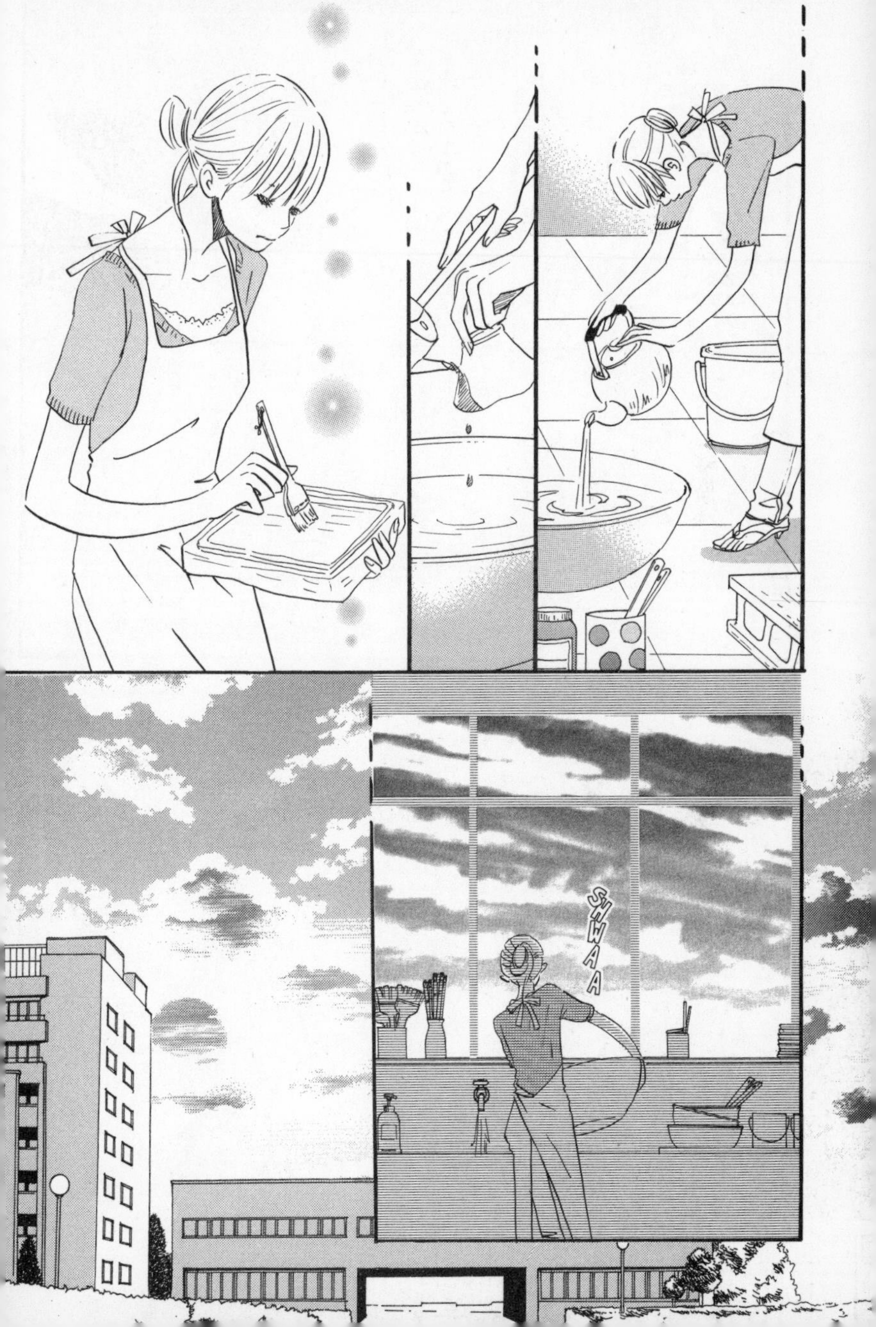
SHWAA

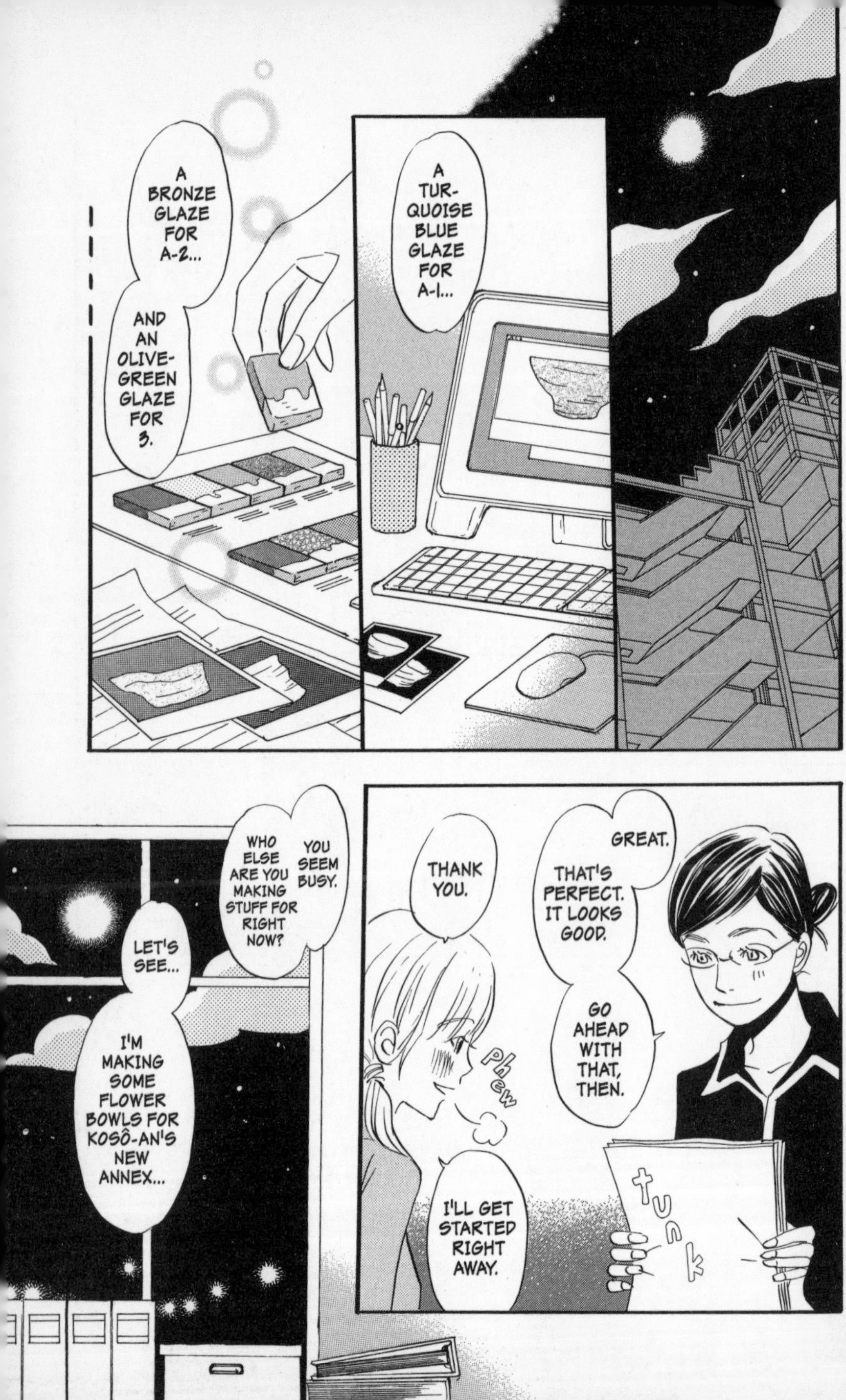
A TURQUOISE BLUE GLAZE FOR A-1...
A BRONZE GLAZE FOR A-2...
AND AN OLIVE-GREEN GLAZE FOR 3.
GREAT.
THAT'S PERFECT. IT LOOKS GOOD.
GO AHEAD WITH THAT, THEN.
THANK YOU.
Phew
tunk
I'LL GET STARTED RIGHT AWAY.
YOU SEEM BUSY.
WHO ELSE ARE YOU MAKING STUFF FOR RIGHT NOW?
LET'S SEE...
I'M MAKING SOME FLOWER BOWLS FOR KOSÔ-AN'S NEW ANNEX...

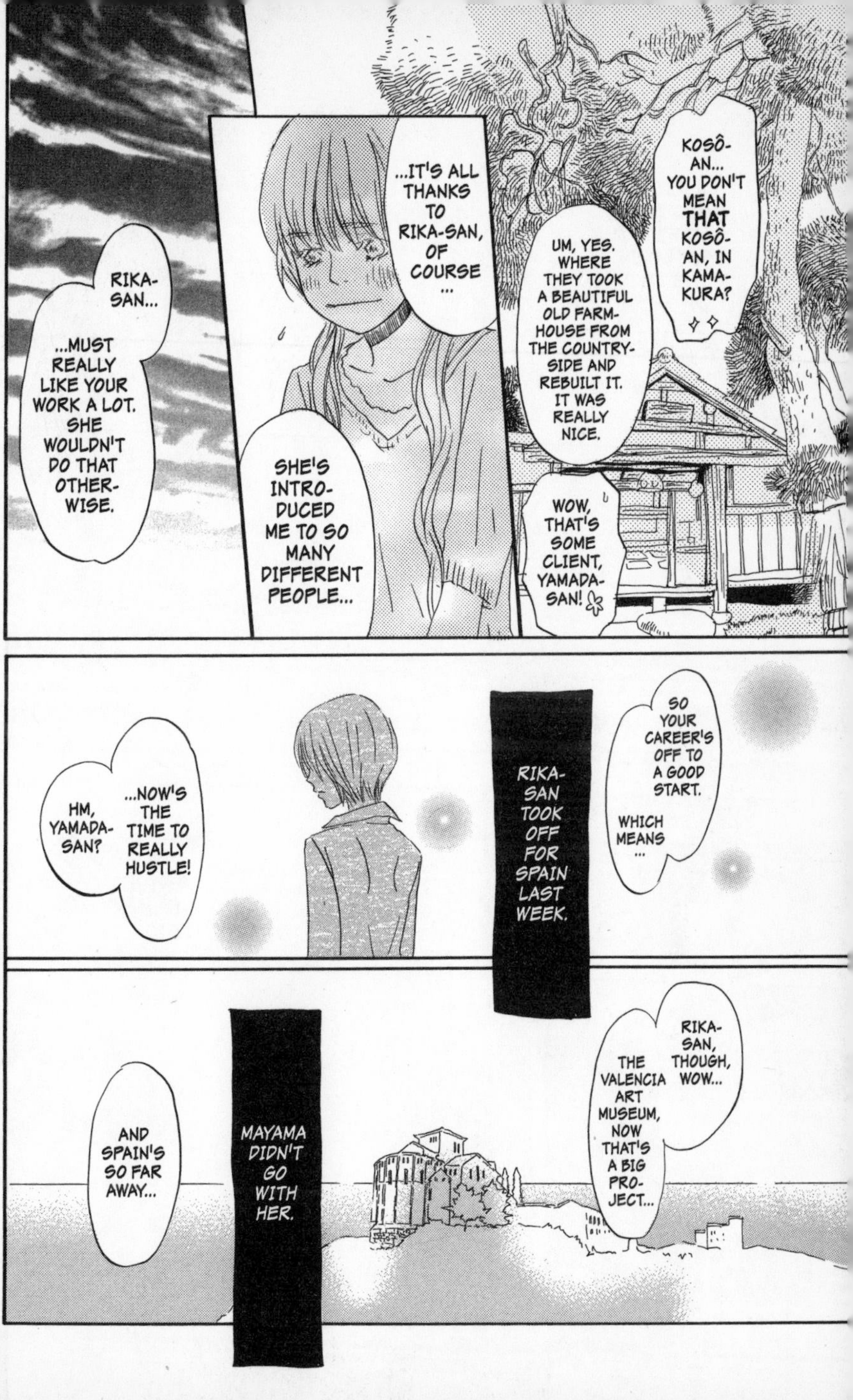
KOSÔ-AN... YOU DON'T MEAN THAT KOSÔ-AN, IN KAMAKURA?
UM, YES. WHERE THEY TOOK A BEAUTIFUL OLD FARMHOUSE FROM THE COUNTRYSIDE AND REBUILT IT. IT WAS REALLY NICE.
WOW, THAT'S SOME CLIENT, YAMADA-SAN!
...IT'S ALL THANKS TO RIKA-SAN, OF COURSE...
SHE'S INTRODUCED ME TO SO MANY DIFFERENT PEOPLE...
RIKA-SAN...
...MUST REALLY LIKE YOUR WORK A LOT. SHE WOULDN'T DO THAT OTHERWISE.
SO YOUR CAREER'S OFF TO A GOOD START.
WHICH MEANS...
RIKA-SAN TOOK OFF FOR SPAIN LAST WEEK.
...NOW'S THE TIME TO REALLY HUSTLE!
HM, YAMADA-SAN?
RIKA-SAN, THOUGH, WOW...
THE VALENCIA ART MUSEUM, NOW THAT'S A BIG PROJECT...
MAYAMA DIDN'T GO WITH HER.
AND SPAIN'S SO FAR AWAY...

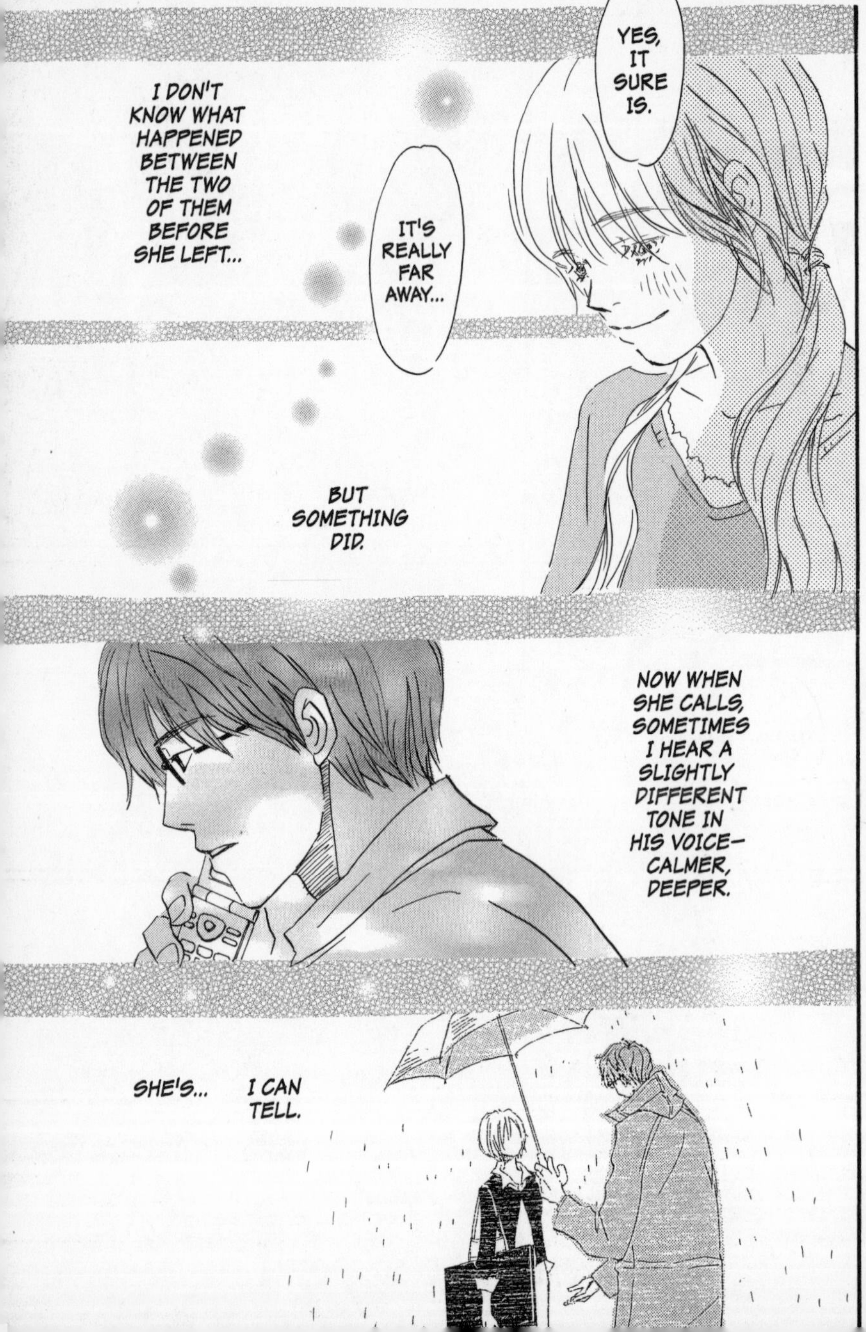
YES, IT SURE IS.
IT'S REALLY FAR AWAY...
I DON'T KNOW WHAT HAPPENED BETWEEN THE TWO OF THEM BEFORE SHE LEFT...
BUT SOMETHING DID.
NOW WHEN SHE CALLS, SOMETIMES I HEAR A SLIGHTLY DIFFERENT TONE IN HIS VOICE—CALMER, DEEPER.
I CAN TELL.
SHE'S...

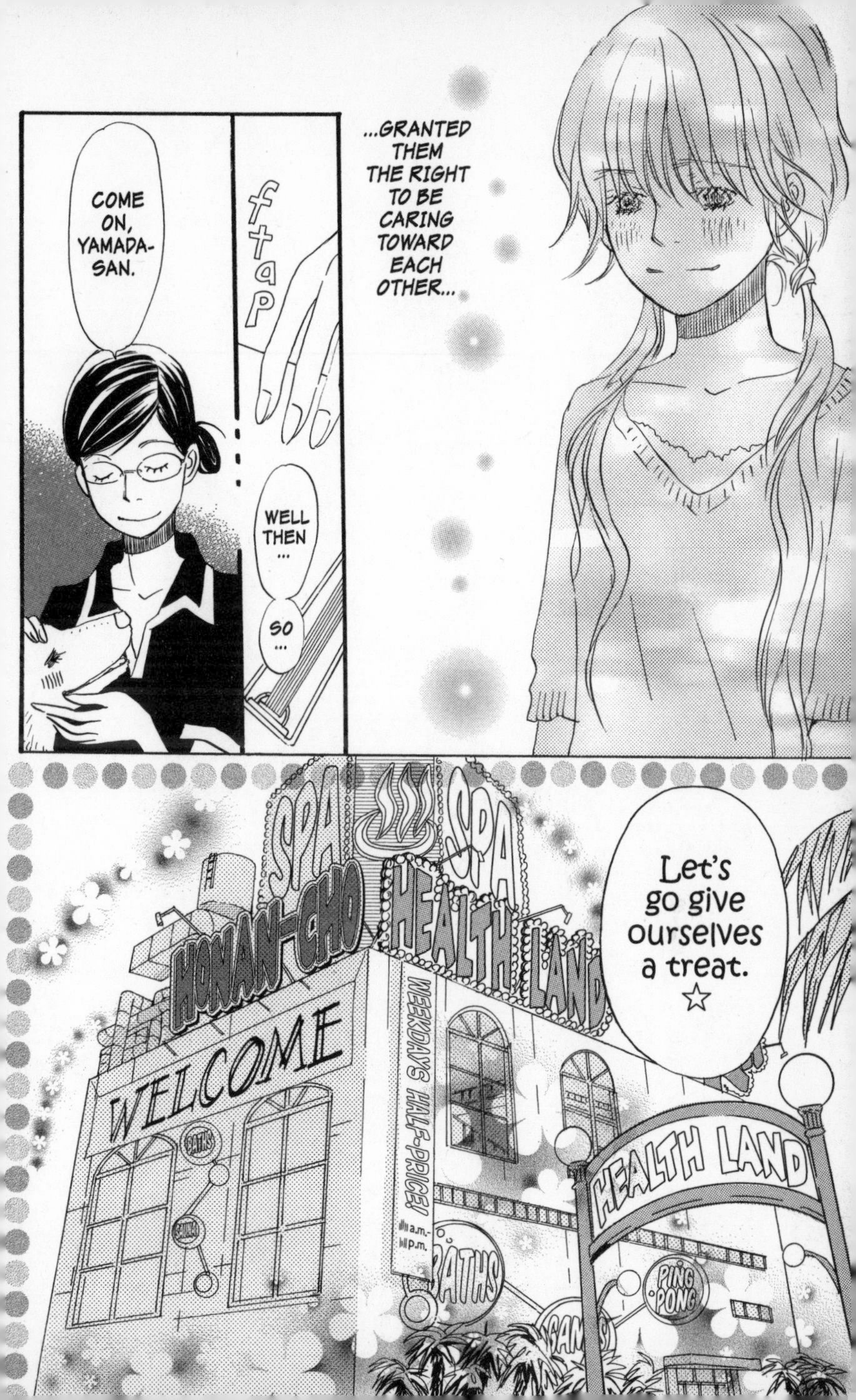
...GRANTED THEM THE RIGHT TO BE CARING TOWARD EACH OTHER...
ftap
WELL THEN ...
SO ...
COME ON, YAMADA-SAN.
Let's go give ourselves a treat. ☆
SPA
SPA
HONAN-CHO HEALTH LAND
WELCOME
WEEKDAYS HALF-PRICE!
BATHS
HEALTH LAND
PING-PONG

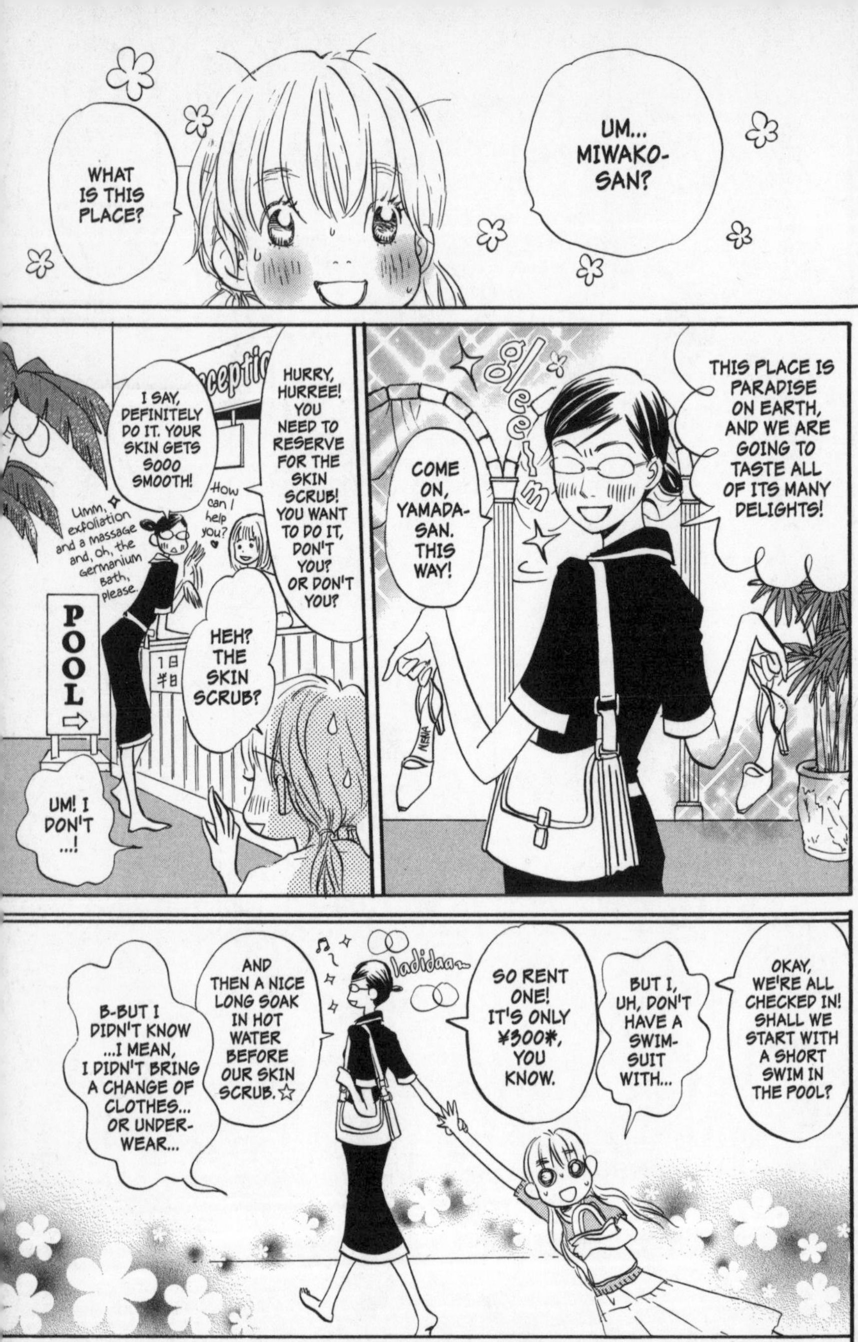
UM... MIWAKO-SAN?
WHAT IS THIS PLACE?
THIS PLACE IS PARADISE ON EARTH, AND WE ARE GOING TO TASTE ALL OF ITS MANY DELIGHTS!
gle~m
COME ON, YAMADA-SAN. THIS WAY!
HURRY, HURREE! YOU NEED TO RESERVE FOR THE SKIN SCRUB! YOU WANT TO DO IT, DON'T YOU? OR DON'T YOU?
I SAY, DEFINITELY DO IT. YOUR SKIN GETS SOOO SMOOTH!
How can I help you?
Umm, exfoliation and a massage and, oh, the Germanium Bath, please.
POOL
HEH? THE SKIN SCRUB?
UM! I DON'T ...!
OKAY, WE'RE ALL CHECKED IN! SHALL WE START WITH A SHORT SWIM IN THE POOL?
BUT I, UH, DON'T HAVE A SWIM-SUIT WITH...
SO RENT ONE! IT'S ONLY ¥300*, YOU KNOW.
ladidaa
AND THEN A NICE LONG SOAK IN HOT WATER BEFORE OUR SKIN SCRUB.☆
B-BUT I DIDN'T KNOW ...I MEAN, I DIDN'T BRING A CHANGE OF CLOTHES... OR UNDER-WEAR...

*$2.95

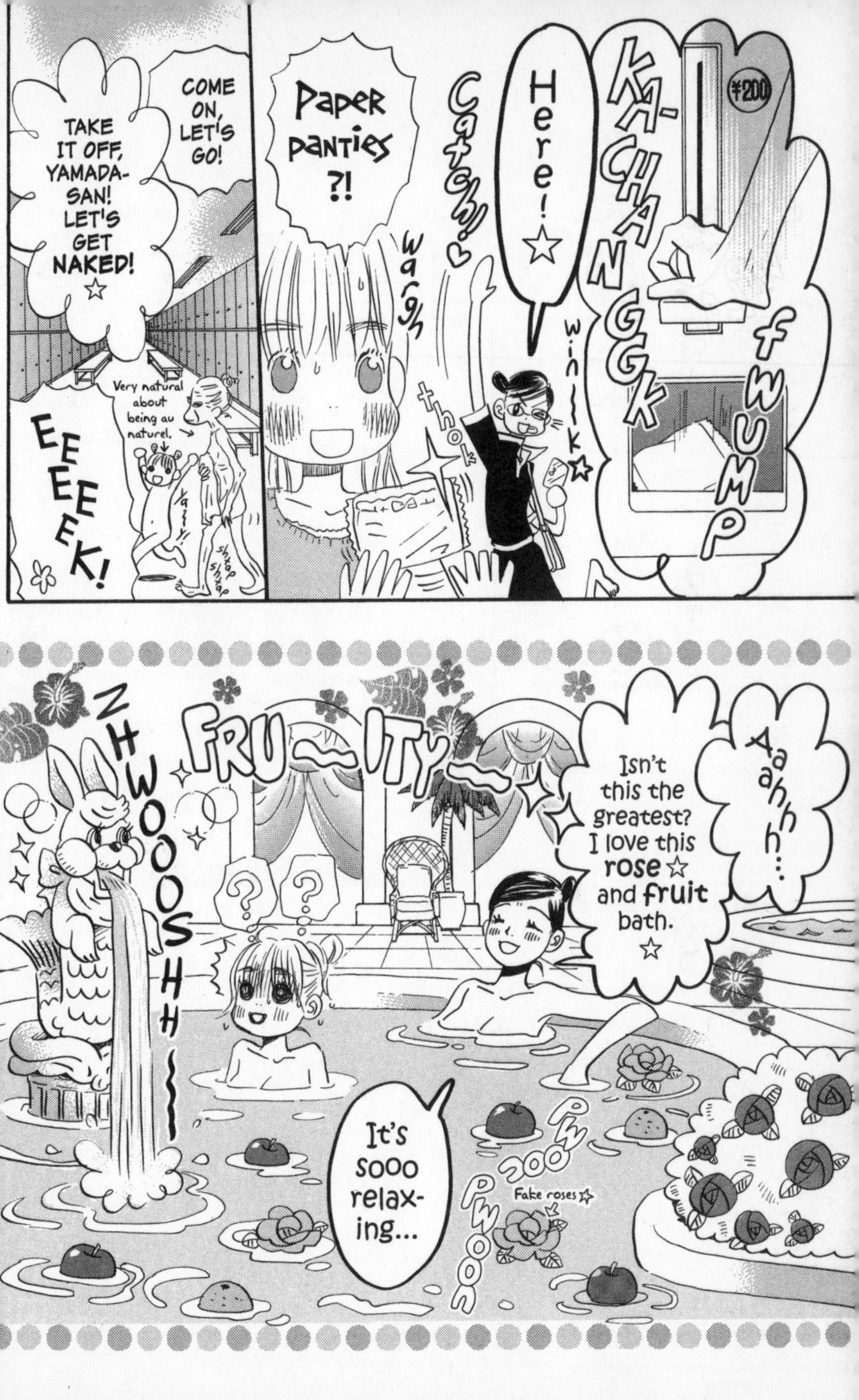
KA-CHANGGK
fwump
Here! ☆
win~k☆
Catch! ♥
Paper panties ?!
wargh
thok
COME ON, LET'S GO!
TAKE IT OFF, YAMADA-SAN! LET'S GET NAKED! ☆
Very natural about being au naturel.
EEEEEK!
shtap shtap
Aaahhh...
Isn't this the greatest? I love this rose☆ and fruit bath. ☆
FRU~ITY~
ZHWOOOOSHH~~
It's sooo relaxing...
Pwoon pwooon
Fake roses☆

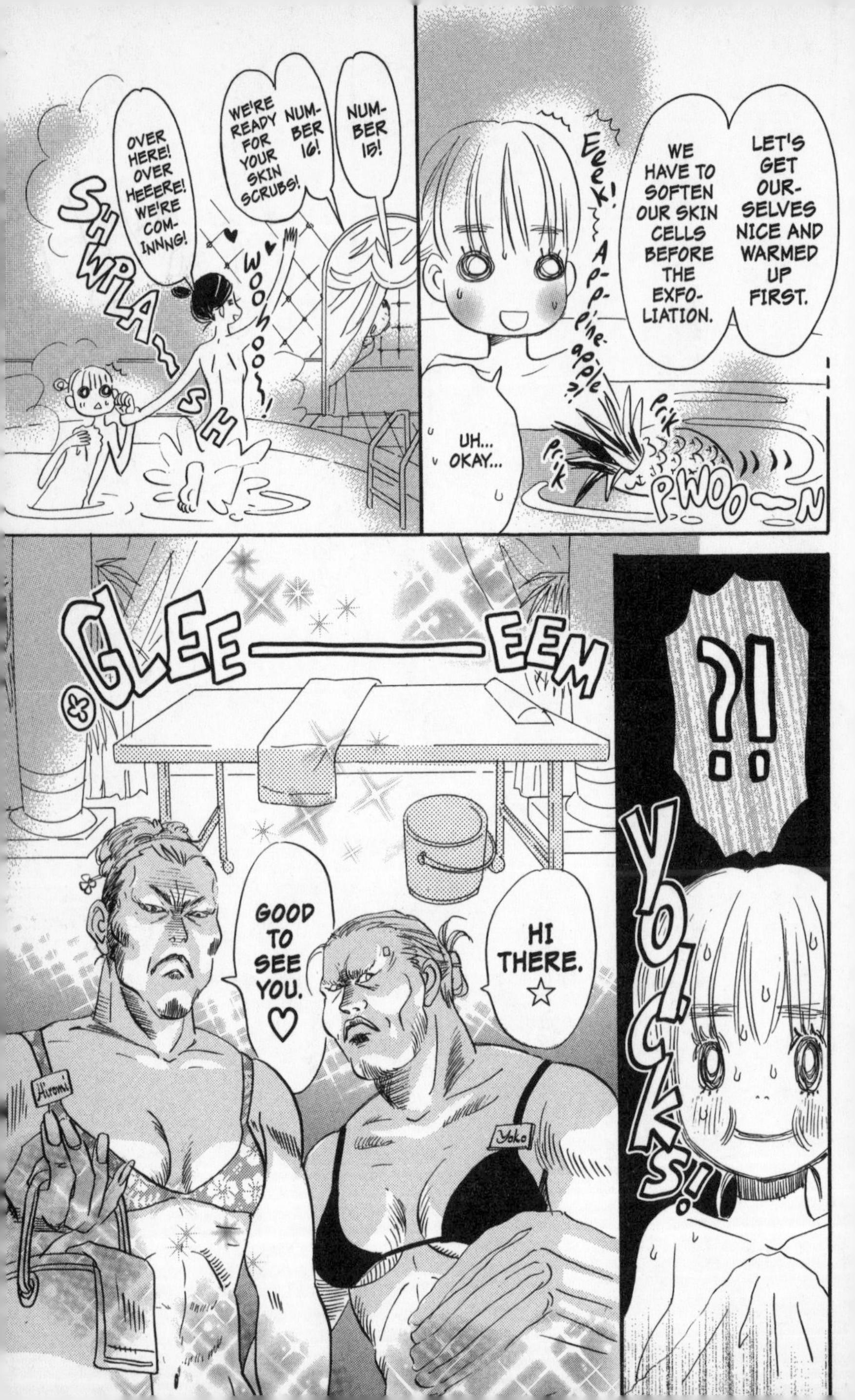
LET'S GET OURSELVES NICE AND WARMED UP FIRST.
WE HAVE TO SOFTEN OUR SKIN CELLS BEFORE THE EXFOLIATION.
Eeek! App-pine-apple?!
Prik Prik
PWOO—N
UH... OKAY...
NUMBER 15!
NUMBER 16!
WE'RE READY FOR YOUR SKIN SCRUBS!
OVER HERE! OVER HEEERE! WE'RE COMINNNG!
WOOHOO~!
SHWPLA~SH
?!
YOICKS!
GLEE—EEM
HI THERE. ☆
GOOD TO SEE YOU. ♡
Hiromi
Yoko

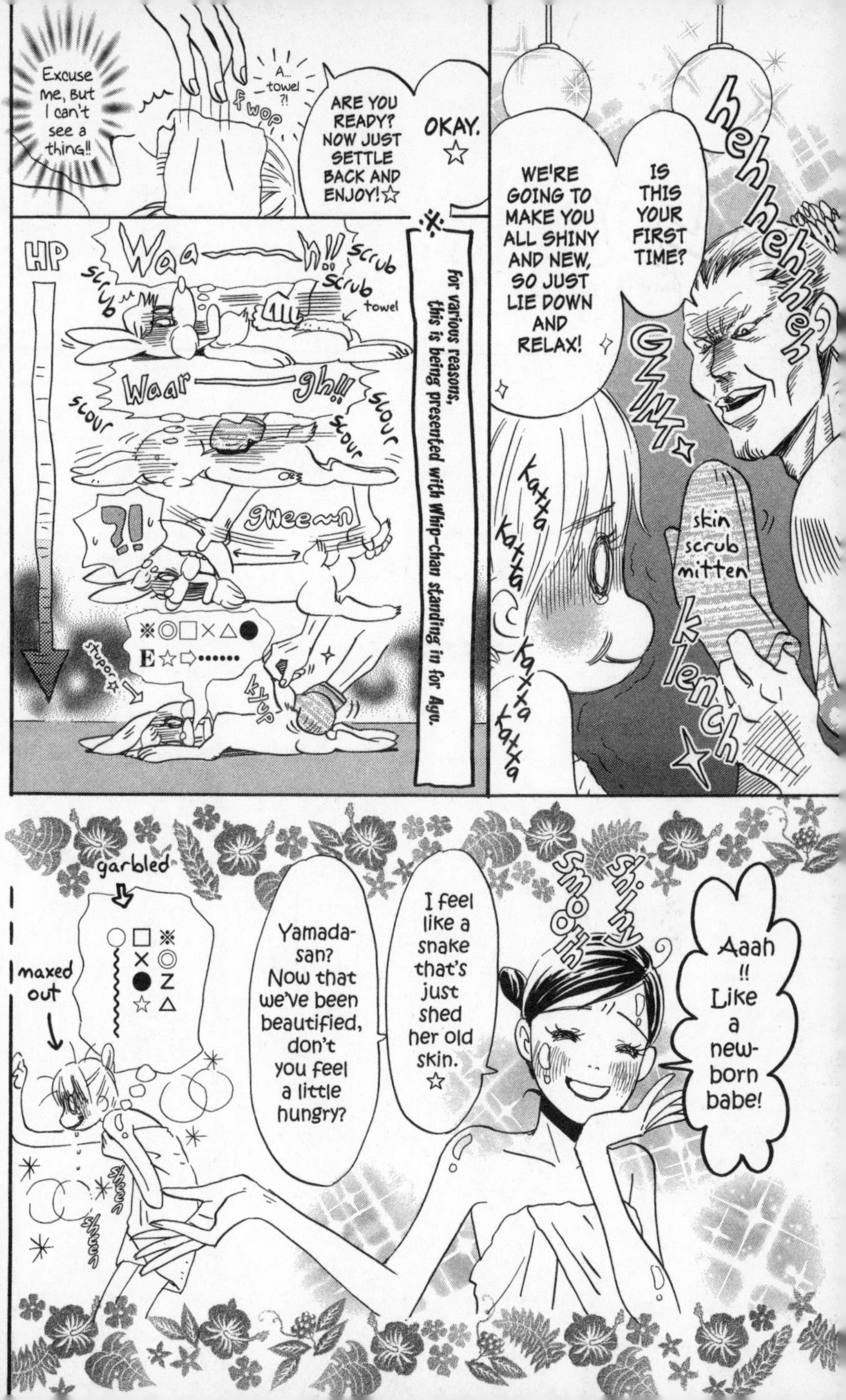
hehhehheh
IS THIS YOUR FIRST TIME?
WE'RE GOING TO MAKE YOU ALL SHINY AND NEW, SO JUST LIE DOWN AND RELAX!
GLINT
skin scrub mitten
klench
Katta katta katta katta katta
OKAY. ☆
ARE YOU READY? NOW JUST SETTLE BACK AND ENJOY!☆
A... towel ?!
fwop
Excuse me, but I can't see a thing!!
※ For various reasons, this is being presented with Whip-chan standing in for Ayu.
HP
Waa—h!!
scrub scrub scrub
towel
Waar—gh!!
scour scour scour
?!
gwee~n
※◎□×△●
E☆⇨......
stupor☆
kyup
Aaah!! Like a newborn babe!
Shiny
Smooth
I feel like a snake that's just shed her old skin. ☆
Yamada-san? Now that we've been beautified, don't you feel a little hungry?
garbled
○□※ ×◎ ●Z ☆△
maxed out
sheen sheen

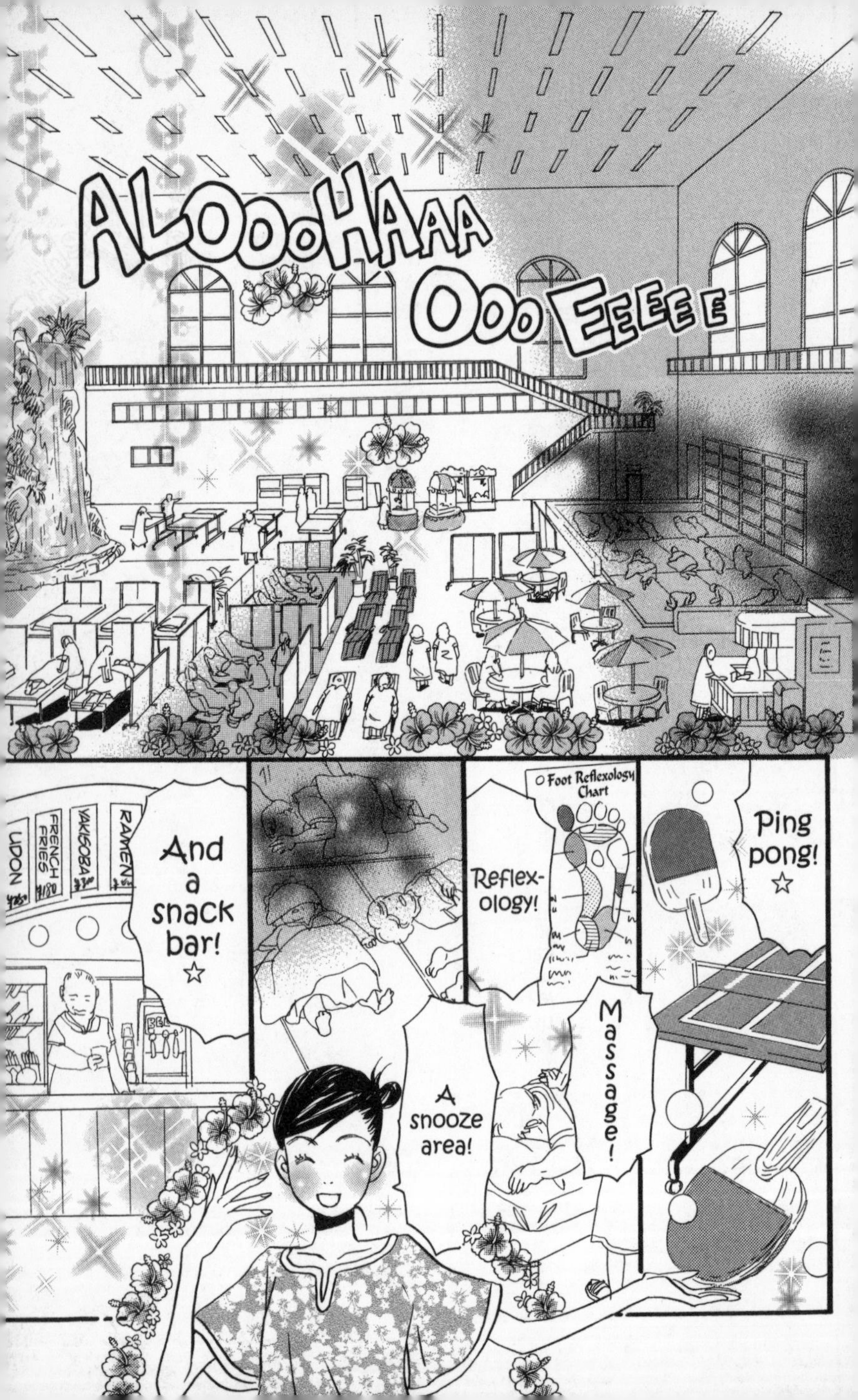
ALOOoHAAA OOo EEEEE
Ping pong! ☆
Foot Reflexology Chart
Reflexology!
Massage!
A snooze area!
RAMEN
YAKISOBA
FRENCH FRIES ¥180
UDON
And a snack bar! ☆

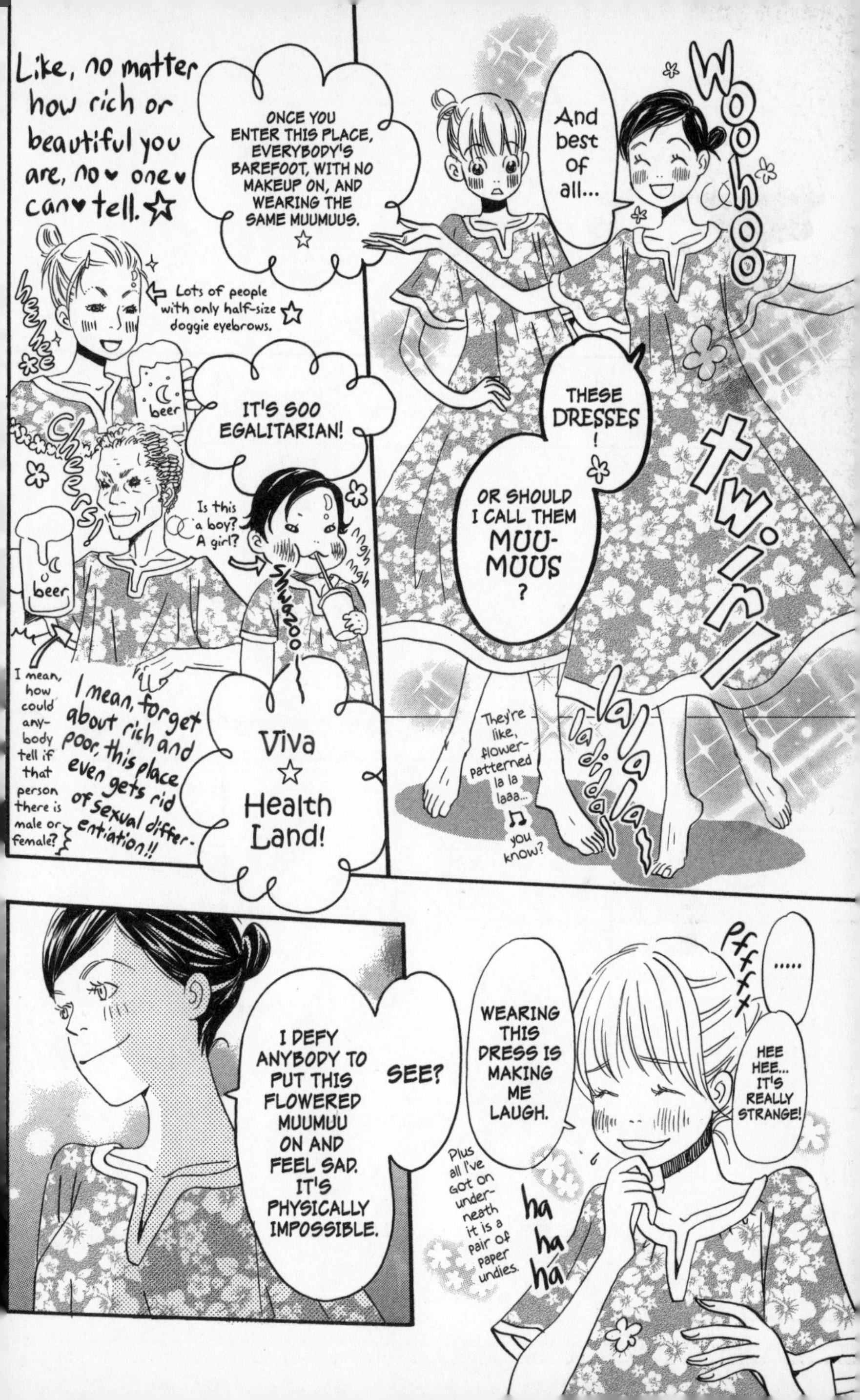
Woohoo
And best of all...
THESE DRESSES!
OR SHOULD I CALL THEM MUU-MUUS?
twirl
la la ladi da la
They're like, flower-patterned la la laaa... ♫ you know?
ONCE YOU ENTER THIS PLACE, EVERYBODY'S BAREFOOT, WITH NO MAKEUP ON, AND WEARING THE SAME MUUMUUS. ☆
Like, no matter how rich or beautiful you are, no♥ one♥ can♥ tell.☆
hee hee
Lots of people with only half-size doggie eyebrows. ☆
beer
IT'S SOO EGALITARIAN!
Cheers!
Is this a boy? A girl?
ngh ngh
shwazoo
beer
Viva ☆ Health Land!
I mean, forget about rich and poor, this place even gets rid of sexual differ-entiation!!
I mean, how could any-body tell if that person there is male or female?
Pfffft
.....
HEE HEE... IT'S REALLY STRANGE!
WEARING THIS DRESS IS MAKING ME LAUGH.
Plus all I've got on under-neath it is a pair of paper undies.
ha ha há
SEE?
I DEFY ANYBODY TO PUT THIS FLOWERED MUUMUU ON AND FEEL SAD. IT'S PHYSICALLY IMPOSSIBLE.

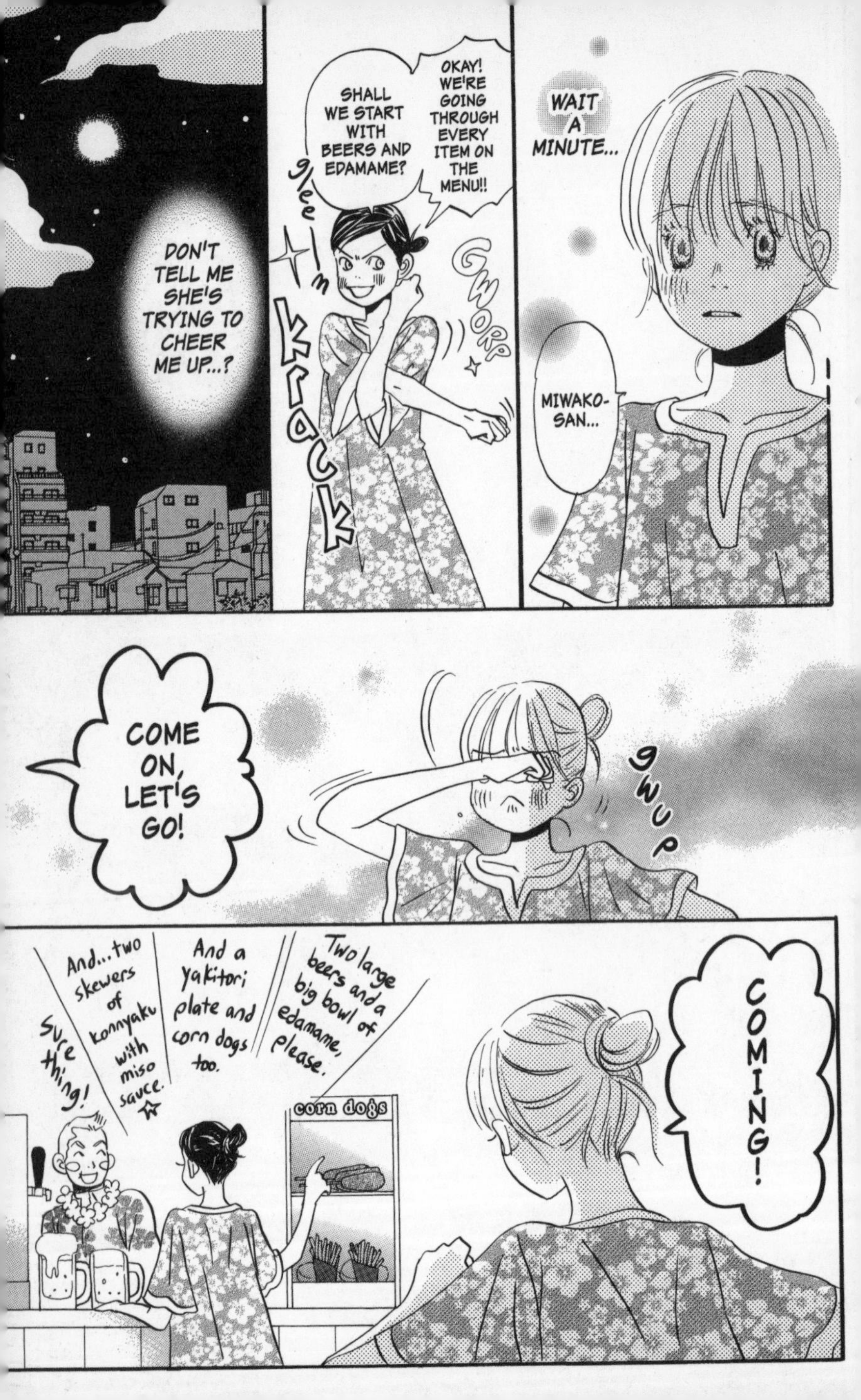

WAIT A MINUTE...
MIWAKO-SAN...
OKAY! WE'RE GOING THROUGH EVERY ITEM ON THE MENU!!
SHALL WE START WITH BEERS AND EDAMAME?
GWORP
glee-m
krack
DON'T TELL ME SHE'S TRYING TO CHEER ME UP...?
GWUP
COME ON, LET'S GO!
COMING!
Two large beers and a big bowl of edamame, please.
And a yakitori plate and corn dogs too.
And...two skewers of konnyaku with miso sauce.
Sure thing!
corn dogs

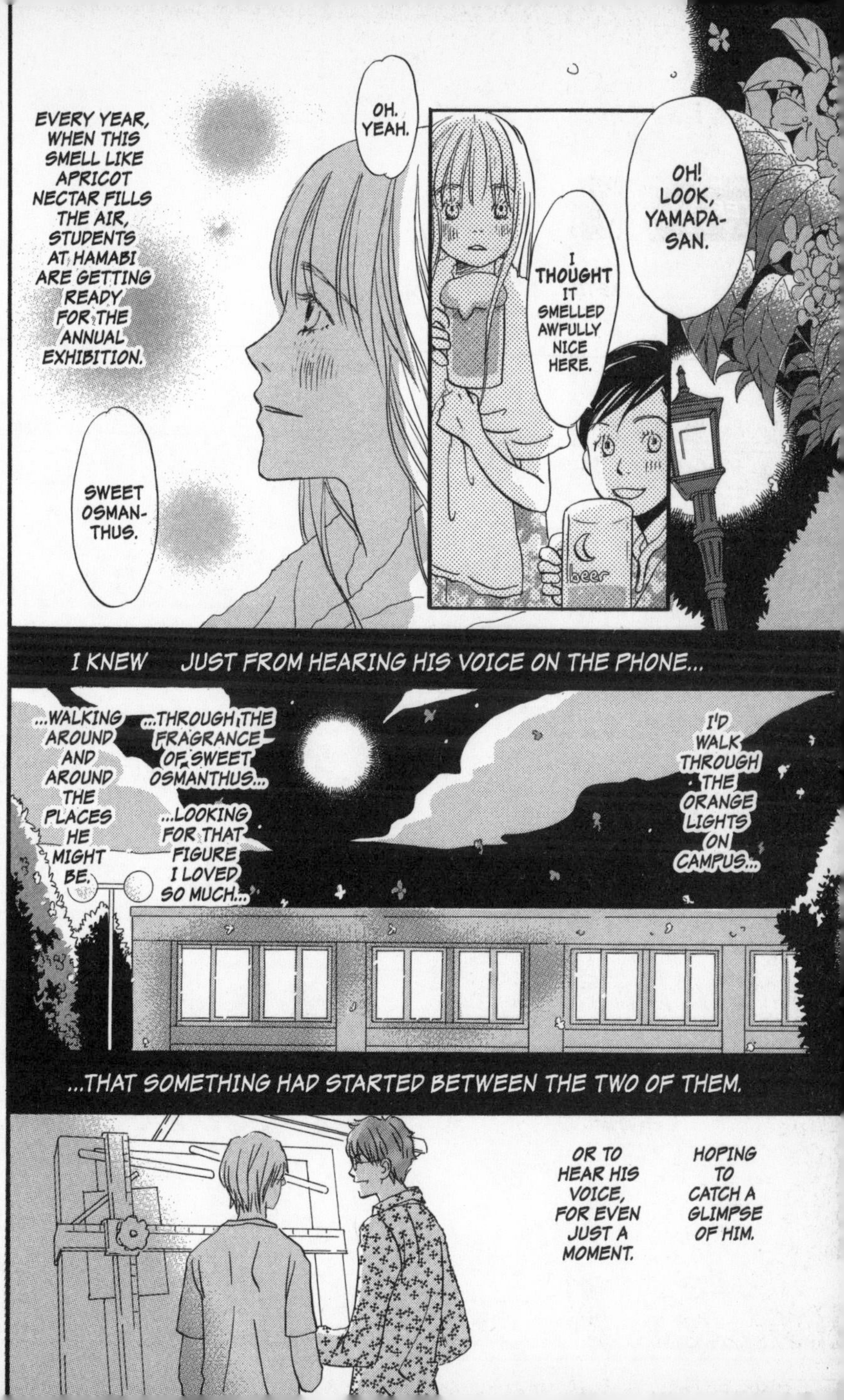
OH! LOOK, YAMADA-SAN.
I THOUGHT IT SMELLED AWFULLY NICE HERE.
OH. YEAH.
EVERY YEAR, WHEN THIS SMELL LIKE APRICOT NECTAR FILLS THE AIR, STUDENTS AT HAMABI ARE GETTING READY FOR THE ANNUAL EXHIBITION.
SWEET OSMANTHUS.
I KNEW JUST FROM HEARING HIS VOICE ON THE PHONE...
I'D WALK THROUGH THE ORANGE LIGHTS ON CAMPUS...
...THROUGH THE FRAGRANCE OF SWEET OSMANTHUS...
...LOOKING FOR THAT FIGURE I LOVED SO MUCH...
...WALKING AROUND AND AROUND THE PLACES HE MIGHT BE.
...THAT SOMETHING HAD STARTED BETWEEN THE TWO OF THEM.
HOPING TO CATCH A GLIMPSE OF HIM.
OR TO HEAR HIS VOICE, FOR EVEN JUST A MOMENT.

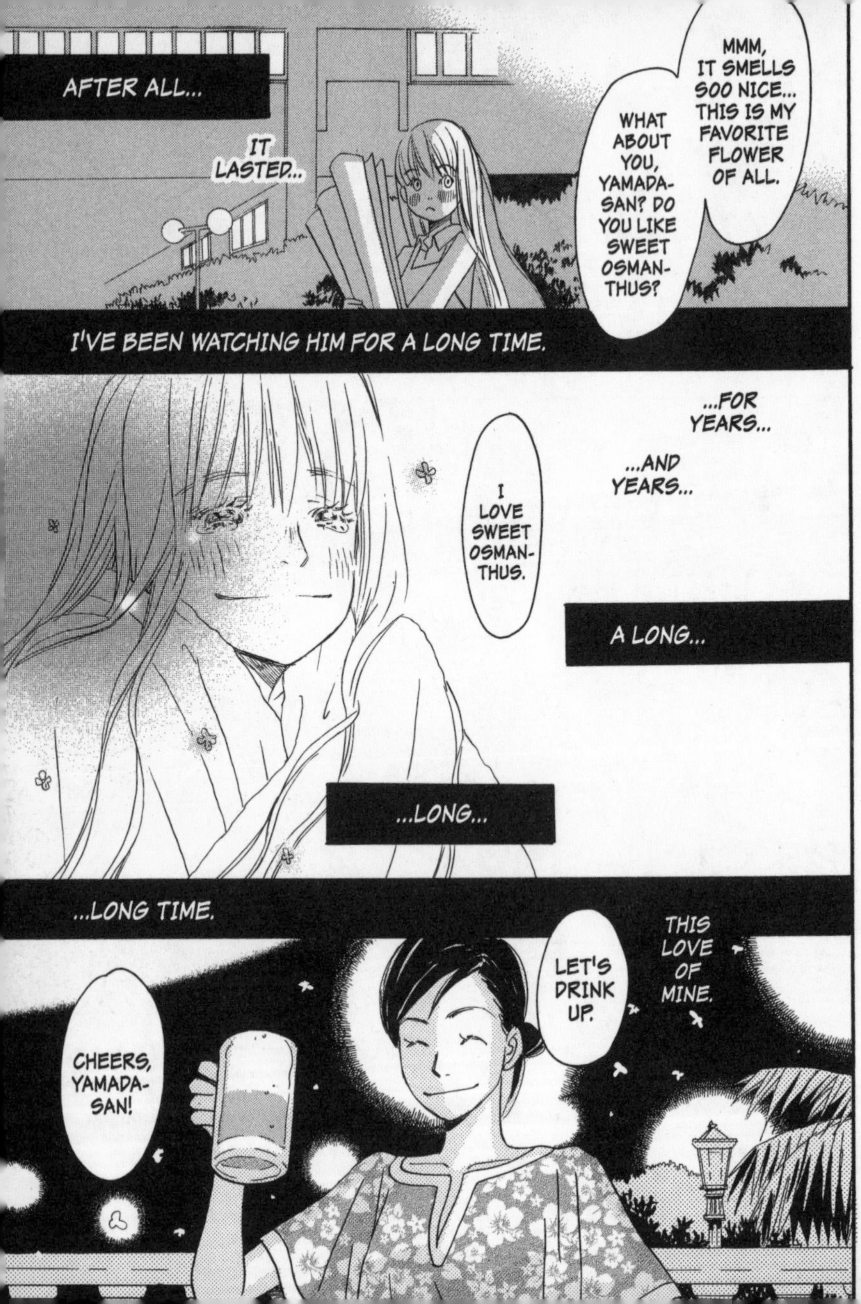
MMM, IT SMELLS SOO NICE... THIS IS MY FAVORITE FLOWER OF ALL.
WHAT ABOUT YOU, YAMADA-SAN? DO YOU LIKE SWEET OSMANTHUS?
AFTER ALL...
IT LASTED...
I'VE BEEN WATCHING HIM FOR A LONG TIME.
...FOR YEARS...
...AND YEARS...
I LOVE SWEET OSMANTHUS.
A LONG...
...LONG...
...LONG TIME.
THIS LOVE OF MINE.
LET'S DRINK UP.
CHEERS, YAMADA-SAN!

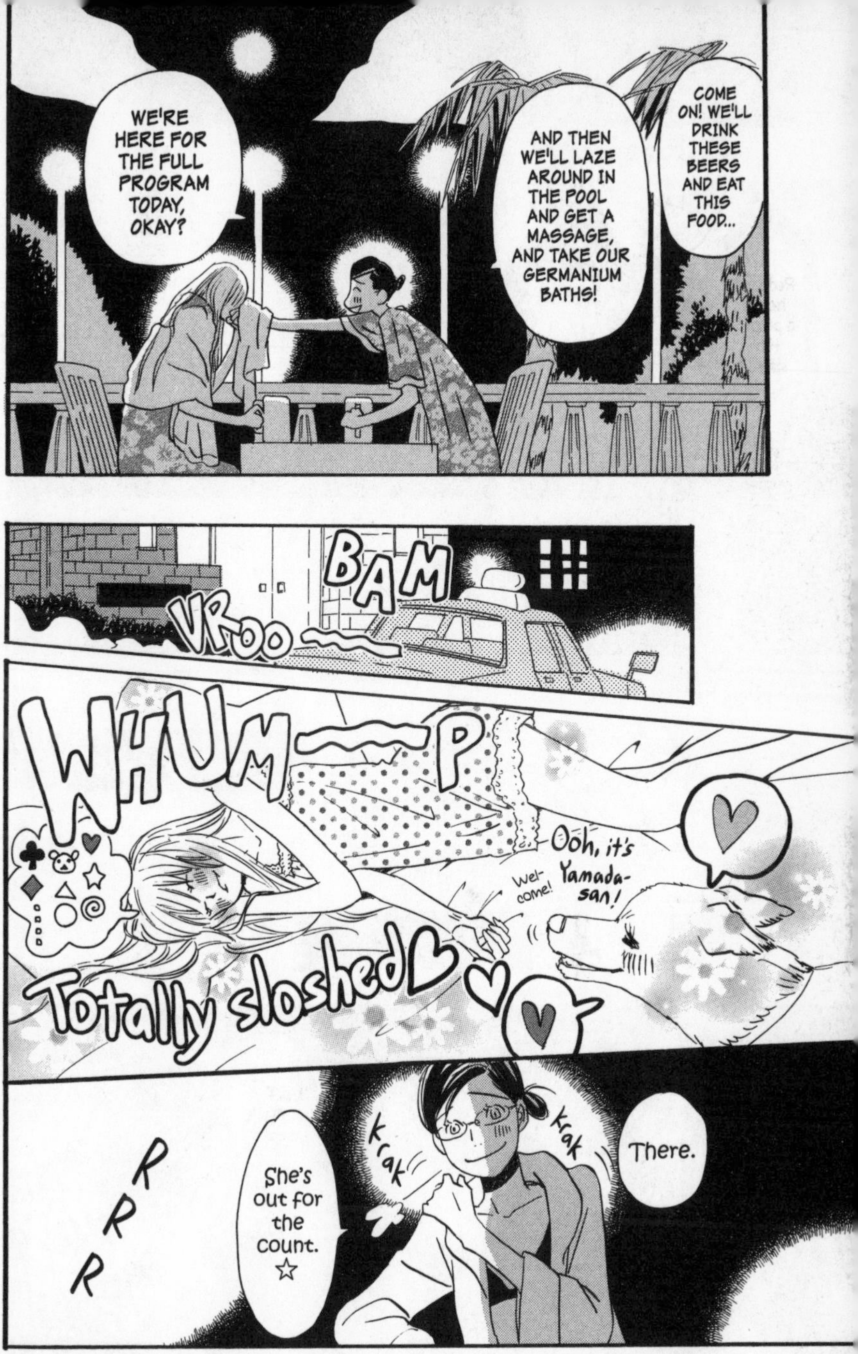
COME ON! WE'LL DRINK THESE BEERS AND EAT THIS FOOD...
AND THEN WE'LL LAZE AROUND IN THE POOL AND GET A MASSAGE, AND TAKE OUR GERMANIUM BATHS!
WE'RE HERE FOR THE FULL PROGRAM TODAY, OKAY?
BAM
VROO~~
WHUM—P
Ooh, it's Yamada-san!
Wel-come!
Totally sloshed♥
There.
krak krak
She's out for the count. ☆
RRRR

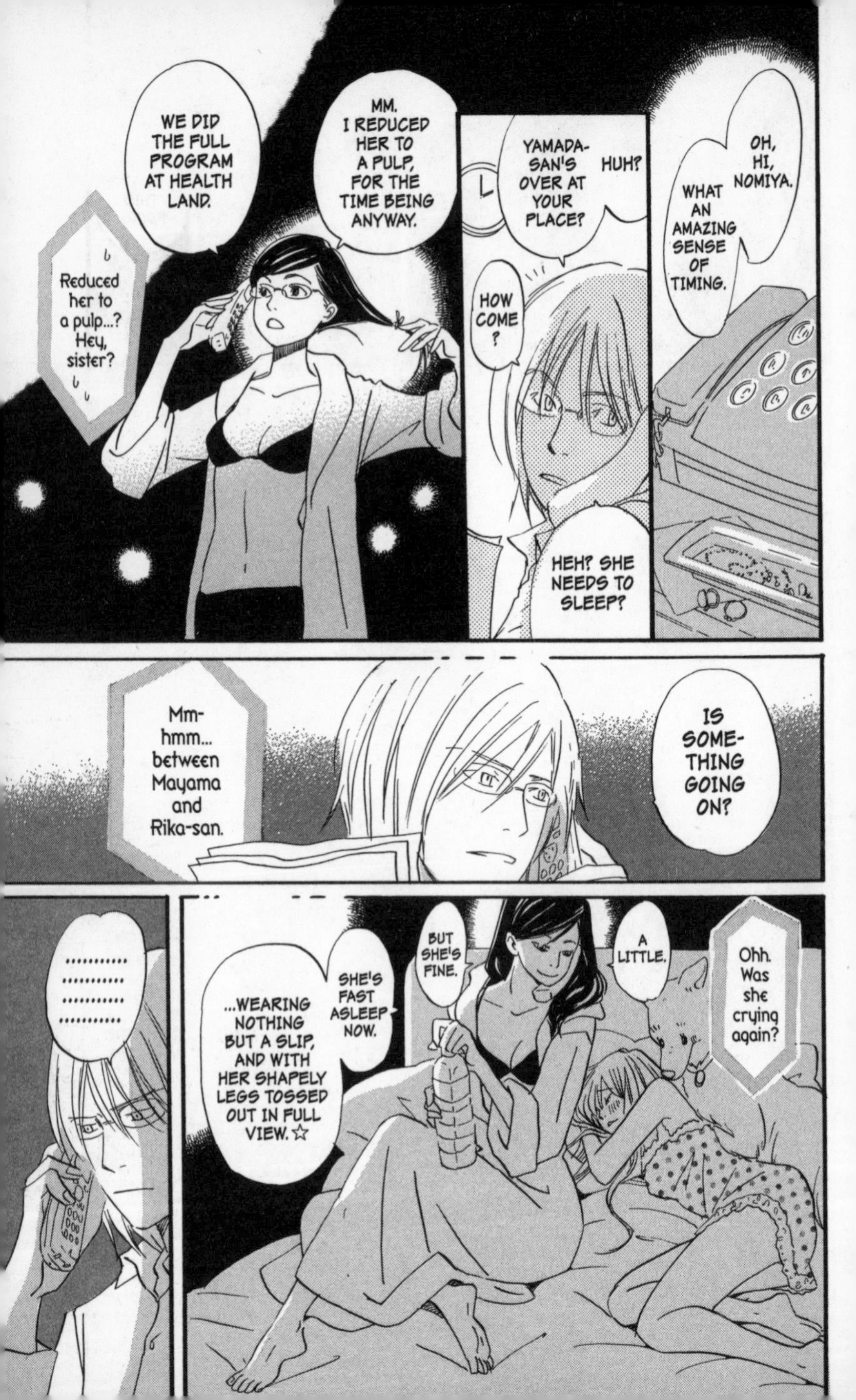
OH, HI, NOMIYA.
WHAT AN AMAZING SENSE OF TIMING.
HUH?
YAMADA-SAN'S OVER AT YOUR PLACE?
HOW COME?
HEH? SHE NEEDS TO SLEEP?
MM. I REDUCED HER TO A PULP, FOR THE TIME BEING ANYWAY.
WE DID THE FULL PROGRAM AT HEALTH LAND.
Reduced her to a pulp...? Hey, sister?
IS SOMETHING GOING ON?
Mm-hmm... between Mayama and Rika-san.
Ohh. Was she crying again?
A LITTLE.
BUT SHE'S FINE.
SHE'S FAST ASLEEP NOW.
...WEARING NOTHING BUT A SLIP, AND WITH HER SHAPELY LEGS TOSSED OUT IN FULL VIEW. ☆
....

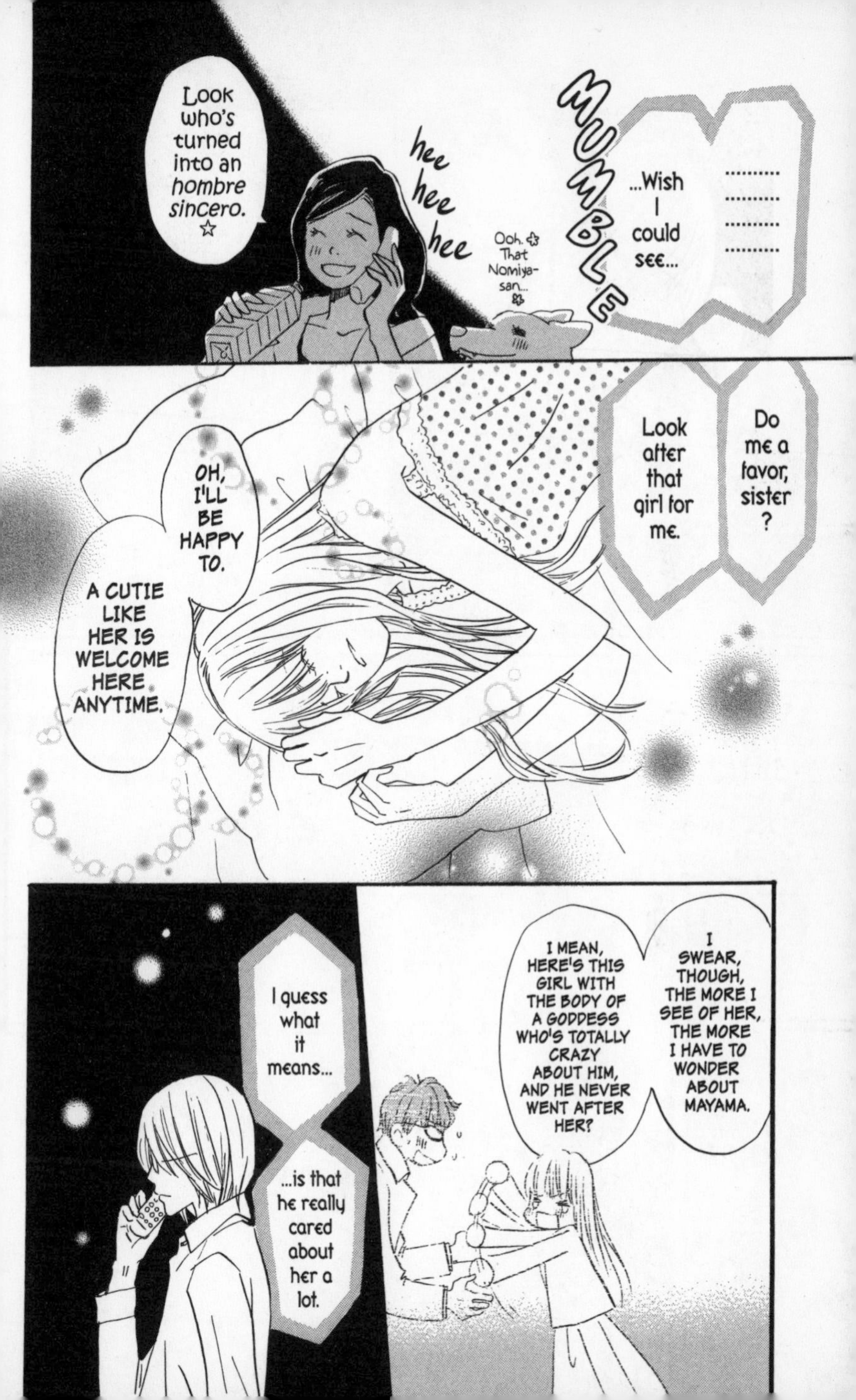

....
...Wish I could see...
MUMBLE
Ooh. ✿ That Nomiya-san... ✿
hee hee hee
Look who's turned into an hombre sincero. ☆
Do me a favor, sister?
Look after that girl for me.
OH, I'LL BE HAPPY TO.
A CUTIE LIKE HER IS WELCOME HERE ANYTIME.
I SWEAR, THOUGH, THE MORE I SEE OF HER, THE MORE I HAVE TO WONDER ABOUT MAYAMA.
I MEAN, HERE'S THIS GIRL WITH THE BODY OF A GODDESS WHO'S TOTALLY CRAZY ABOUT HIM, AND HE NEVER WENT AFTER HER?
I guess what it means...
...is that he really cared about her a lot.

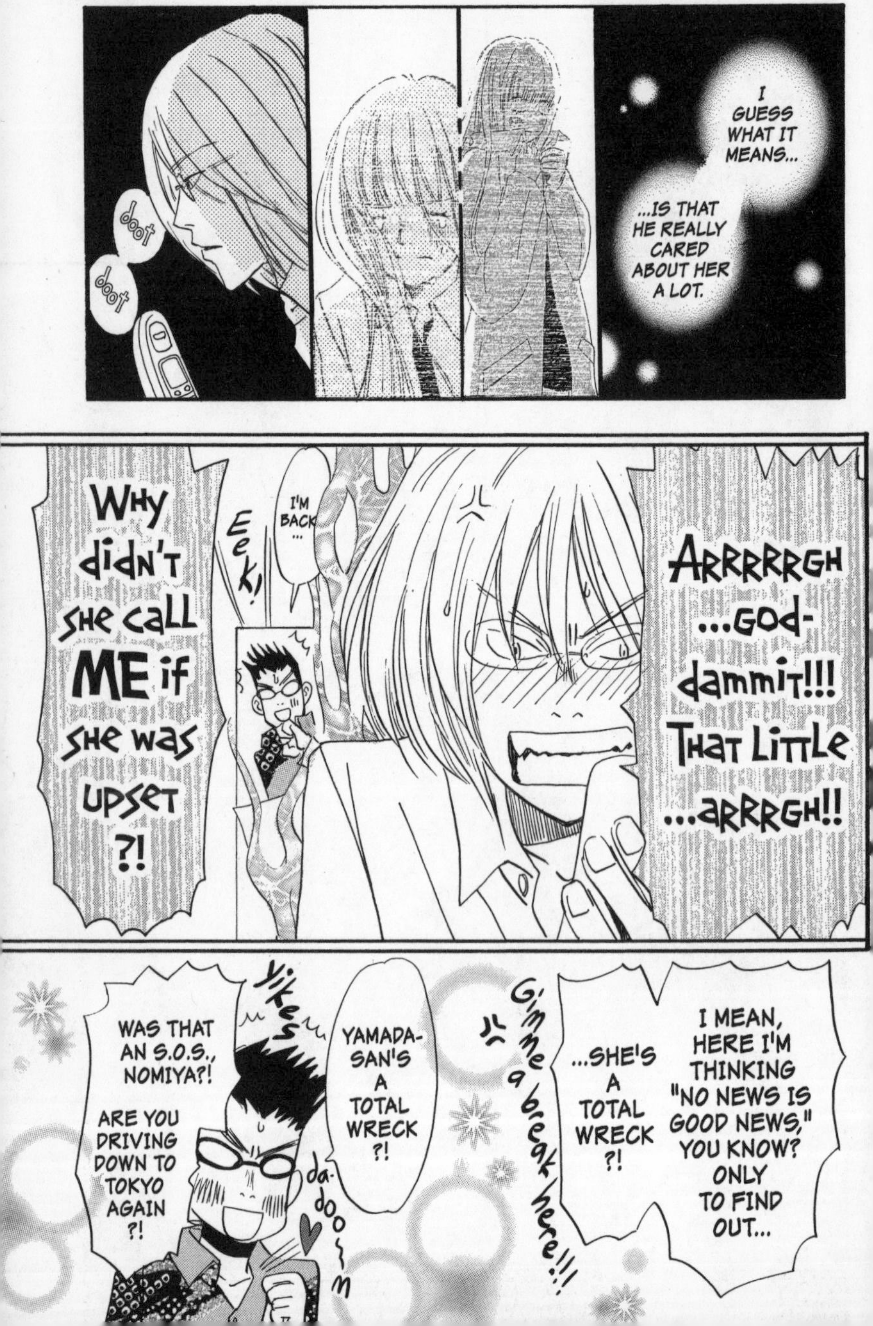
I GUESS WHAT IT MEANS...
...IS THAT HE REALLY CARED ABOUT HER A LOT.
doot
doot
ARRRRRGH ...GOD-DAMMIT!!! THAT LITTLE ...ARRRGH!!
I'M BACK...
Eek!
Why didn't she call ME if she was upset?!
I MEAN, HERE I'M THINKING "NO NEWS IS GOOD NEWS," YOU KNOW? ONLY TO FIND OUT...
...SHE'S A TOTAL WRECK?!
Gimme a break here!!!
YAMADA-SAN'S A TOTAL WRECK?!
Yikes
WAS THAT AN S.O.S., NOMIYA?!
ARE YOU DRIVING DOWN TO TOKYO AGAIN?!
da-doo~m

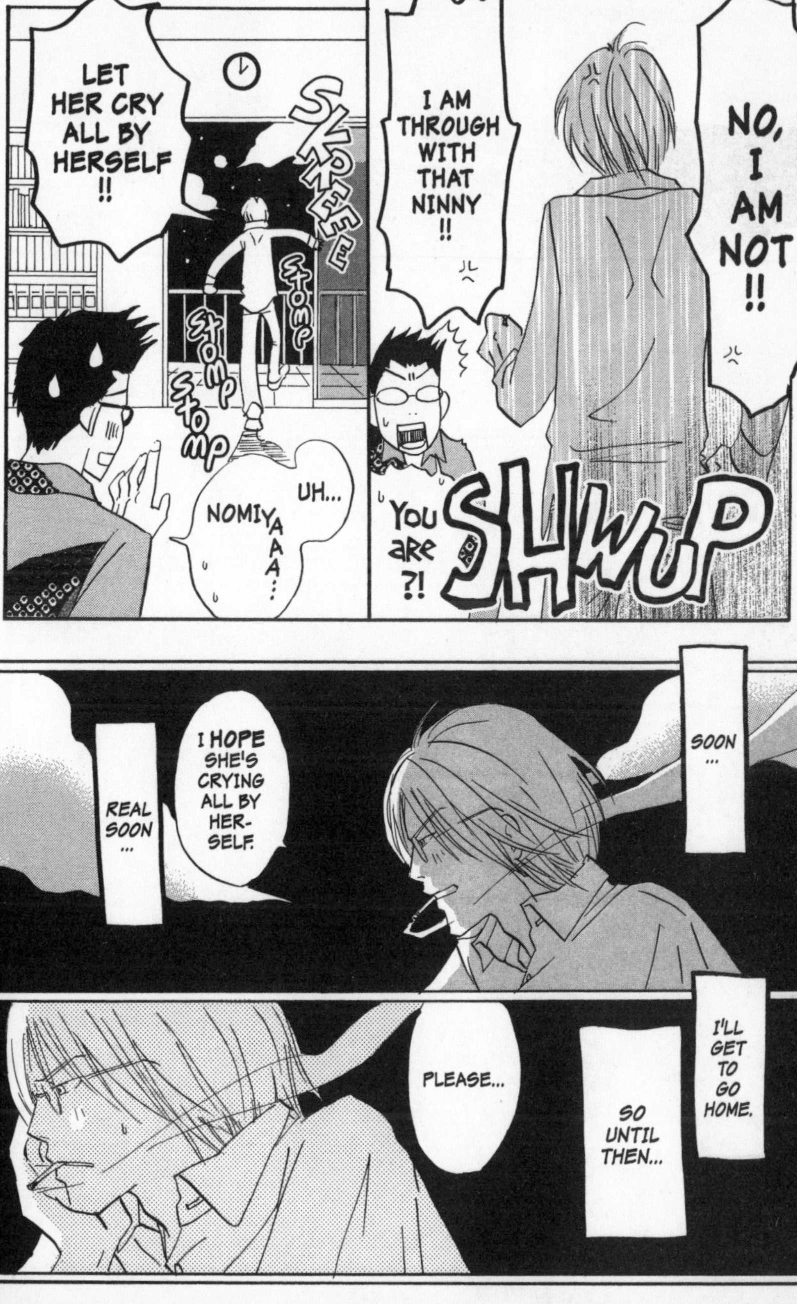
I AM THROUGH WITH THAT NINNY!!
NO, I AM NOT!!
SHWUP
You are?!
SKREEE
LET HER CRY ALL BY HERSELF!!
STOMP
STOMP
STOMP
STOMP
UH...
NOMIYAAAA...
SOON...
I HOPE SHE'S CRYING ALL BY HER-SELF.
REAL SOON...
I'LL GET TO GO HOME.
SO UNTIL THEN...
PLEASE...

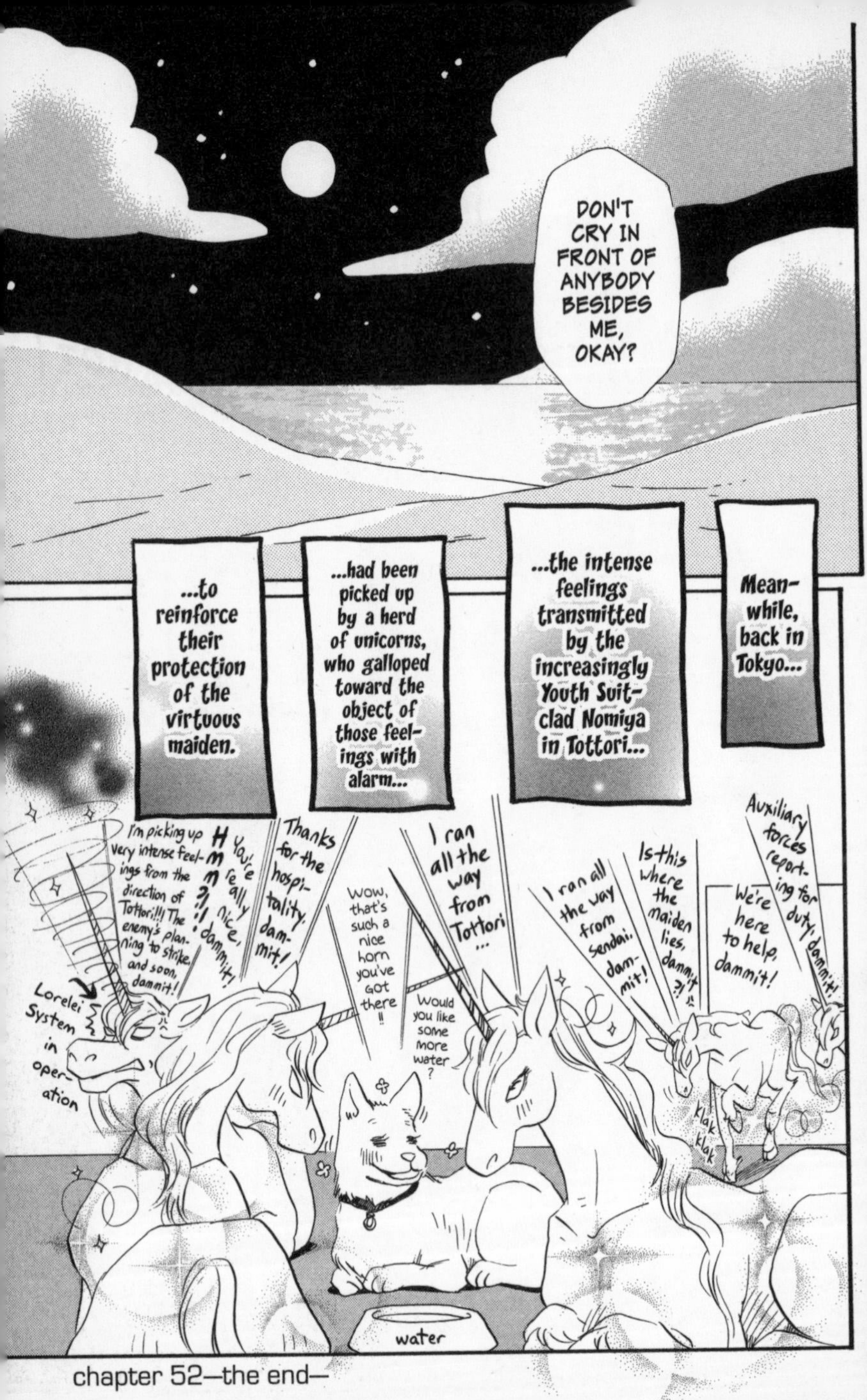
DON'T CRY IN FRONT OF ANYBODY BESIDES ME, OKAY?
Mean-while, back in Tokyo...
...the intense feelings transmitted by the increasingly Youth Suit-clad Nomiya in Tottori...
...had been picked up by a herd of unicorns, who galloped toward the object of those feel-ings with alarm...
...to reinforce their protection of the virtuous maiden.
Auxiliary forces report-ing for duty, dammit!
We're here to help, dammit!
klak klak
Is this where the maiden lies, dammit?!
I ran all the way from Sendai, dam-mit!
I ran all the way from Tottori...
Would you like some more water?
Wow, that's such a nice horn you've got there!!
Thanks for the hospi-tality, dam-mit!
You're really nice, dammit!
Hmm?!
I'm picking up very intense feel-ings from the direction of Tottori!!! The enemy's plan-ning to strike, and soon, dammit!
Lorelei System in oper-ation
water

chapter 52—the end—

Cowgirl ✦Ayu✦

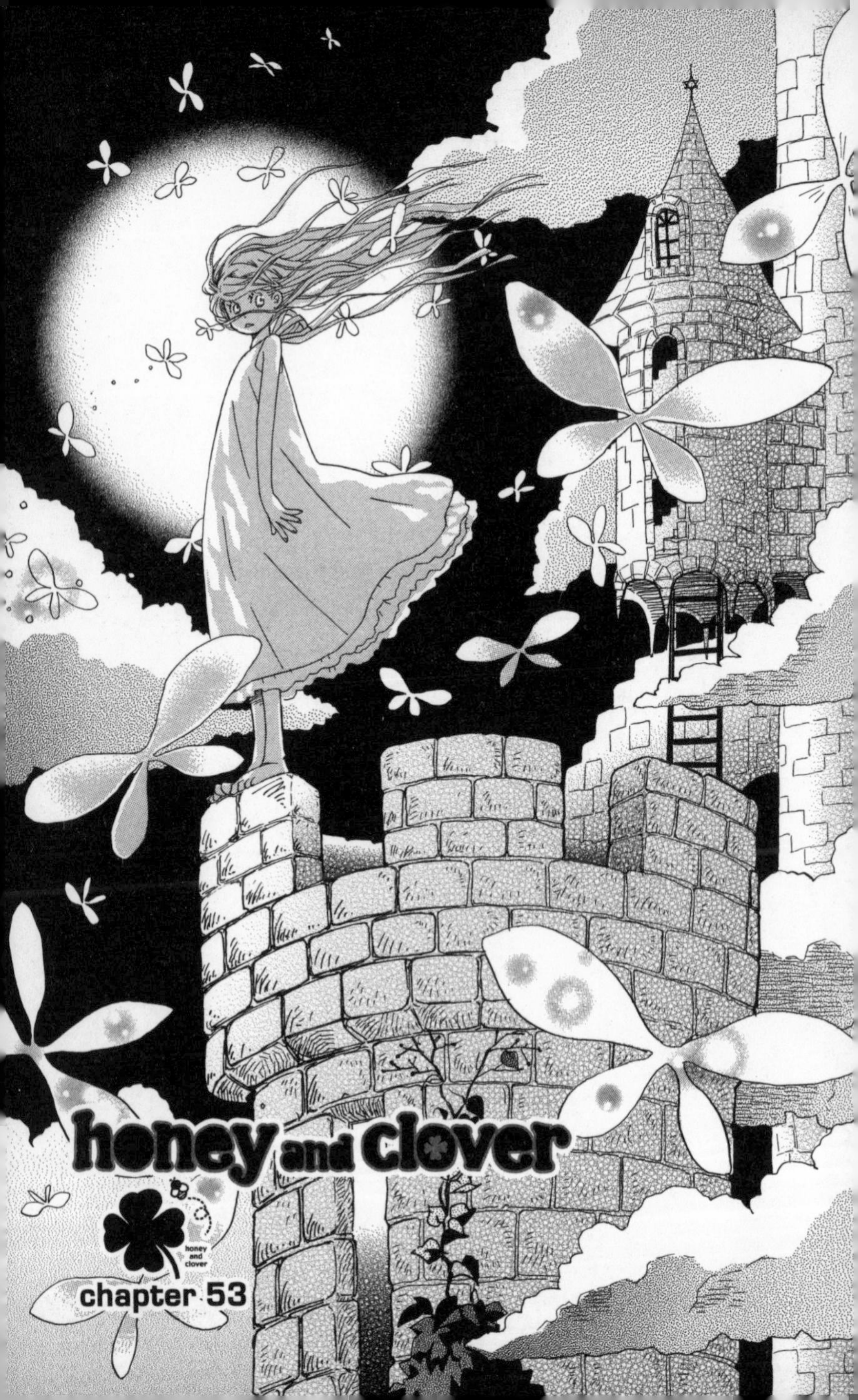
honey and clover
honey and clover
chapter 53

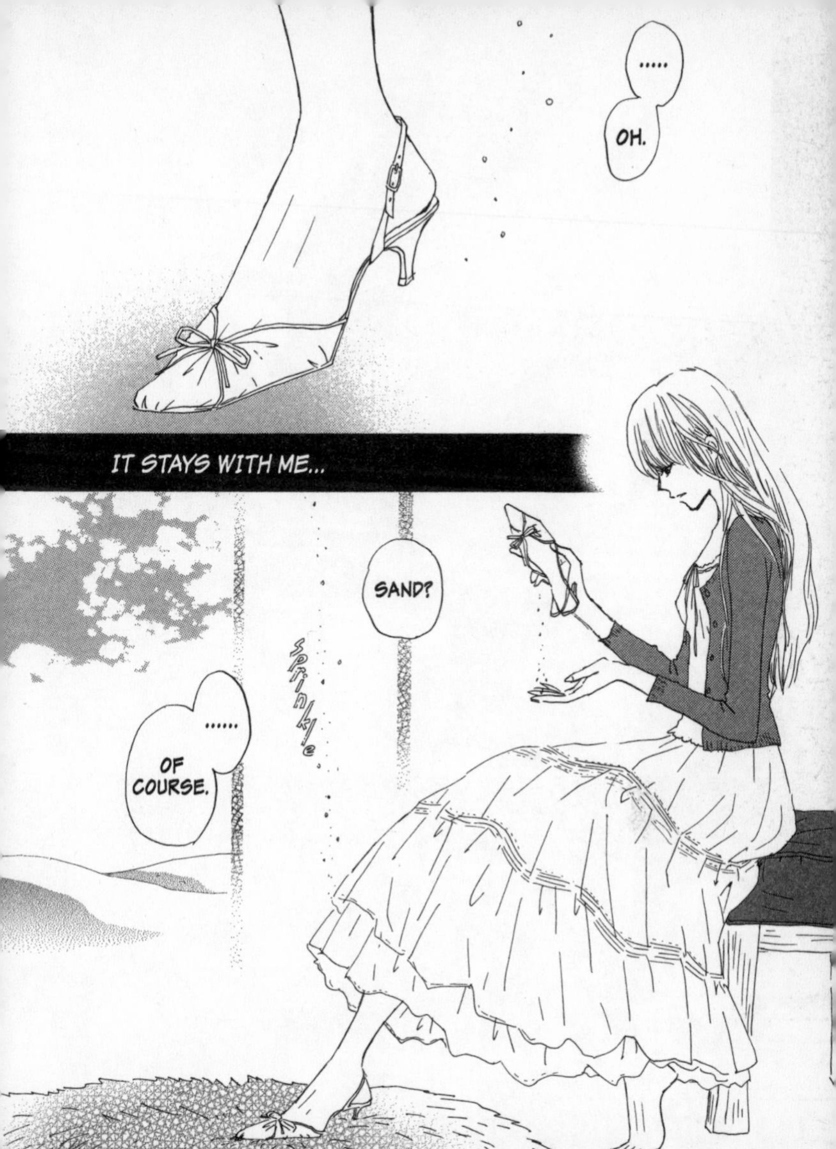
......
OH.
IT STAYS WITH ME...
SAND?
sprinkle
...... OF COURSE.

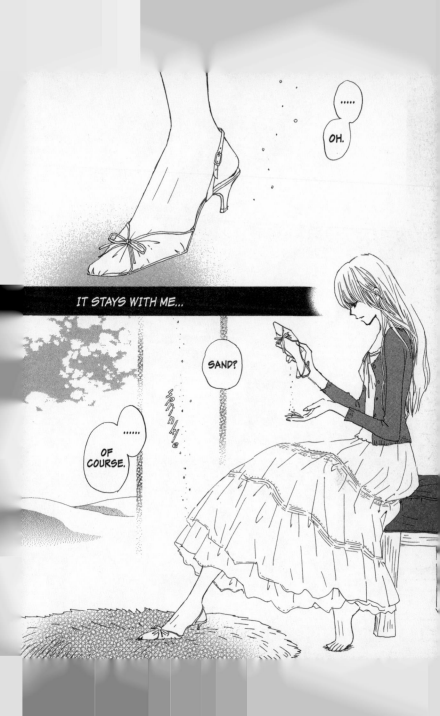

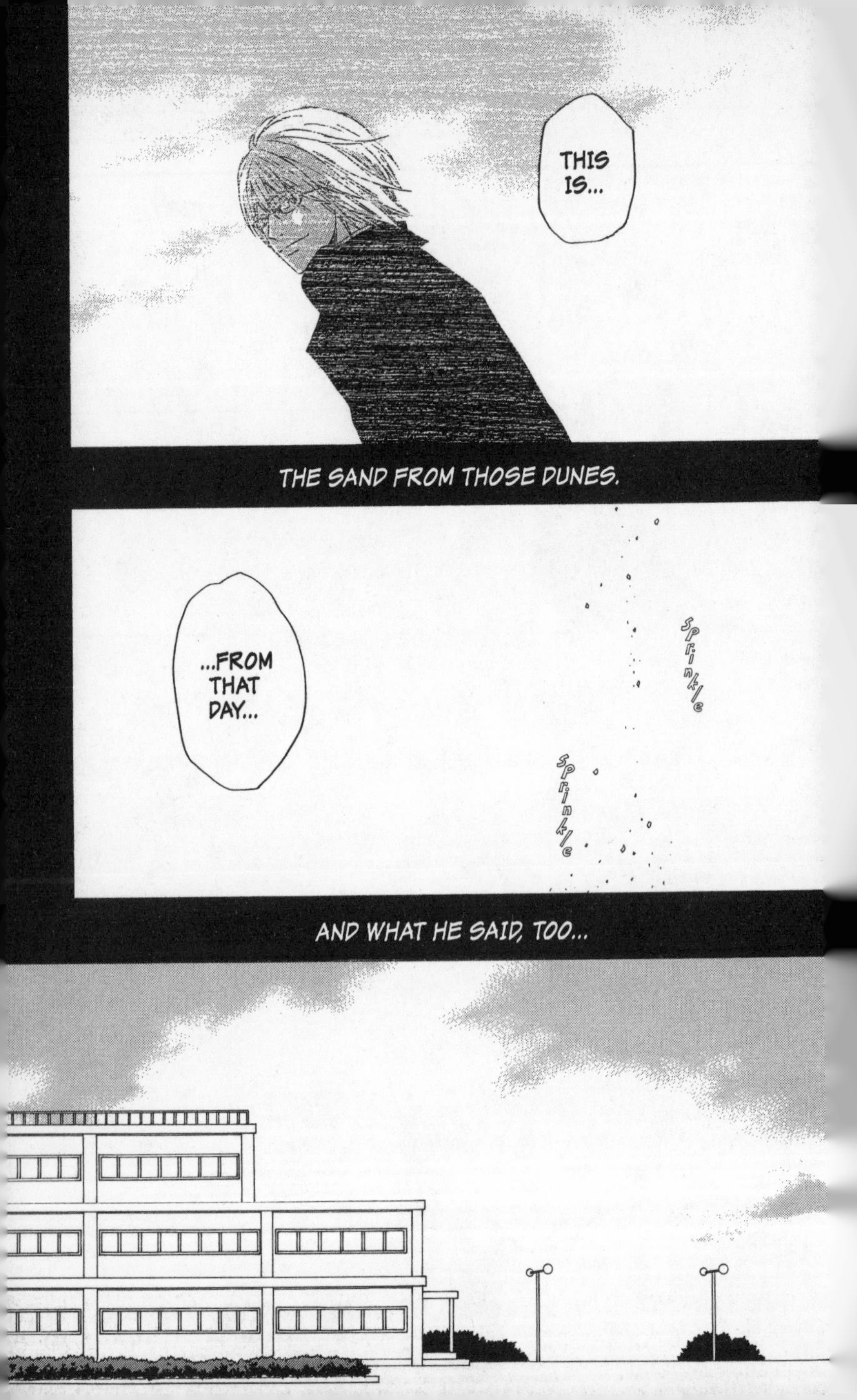
THIS IS...
THE SAND FROM THOSE DUNES.
...FROM THAT DAY...
Sprinkle
Sprinkle
AND WHAT HE SAID, TOO...

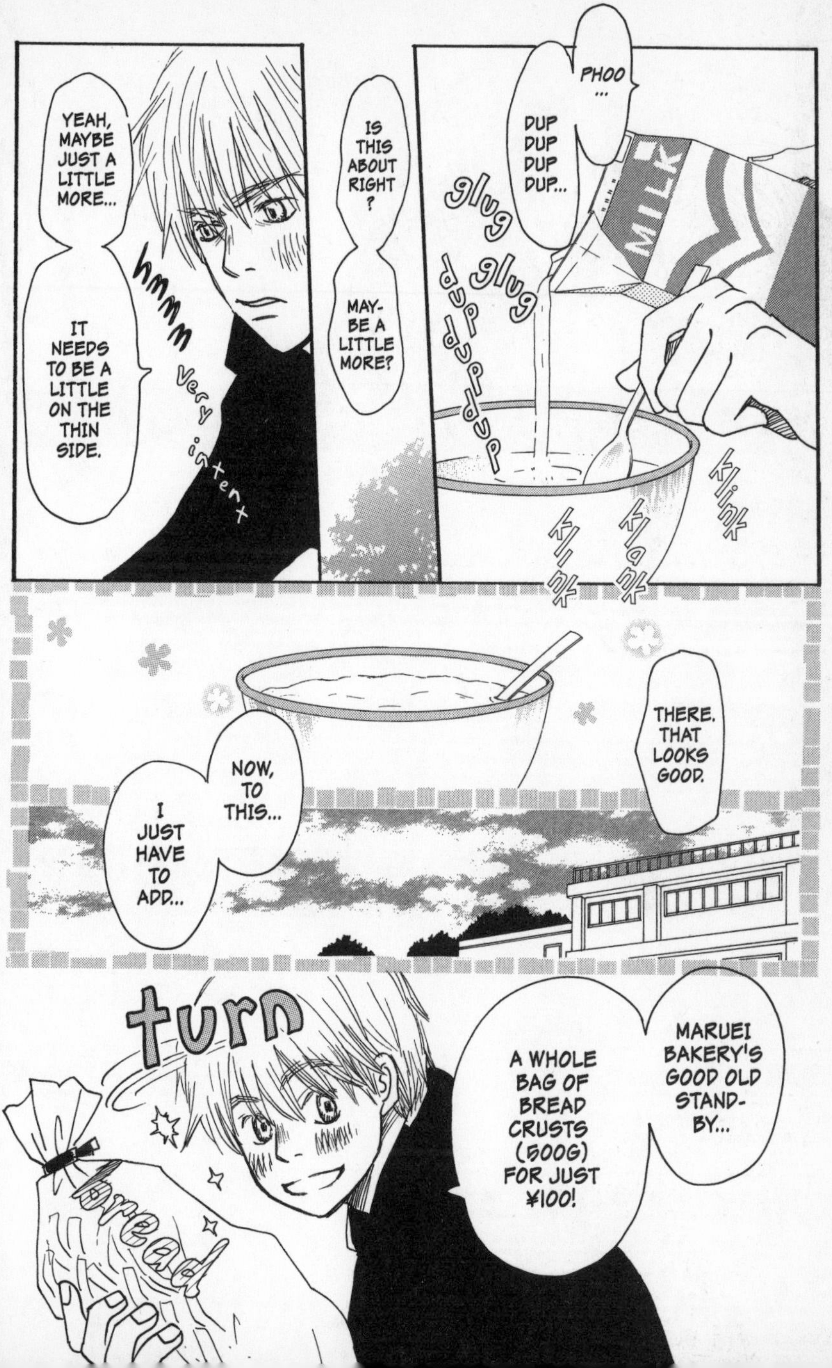
PHOO ...
DUP DUP DUP DUP...
glug glug
dupdupdupdup
klink klank klink
IS THIS ABOUT RIGHT?
MAY-BE A LITTLE MORE?
YEAH, MAYBE JUST A LITTLE MORE...
IT NEEDS TO BE A LITTLE ON THE THIN SIDE.
hmmm
very intent
THERE. THAT LOOKS GOOD.
NOW, TO THIS...
I JUST HAVE TO ADD...
MARUEI BAKERY'S GOOD OLD STAND-BY...
A WHOLE BAG OF BREAD CRUSTS (500G) FOR JUST ¥100!
turn
bread

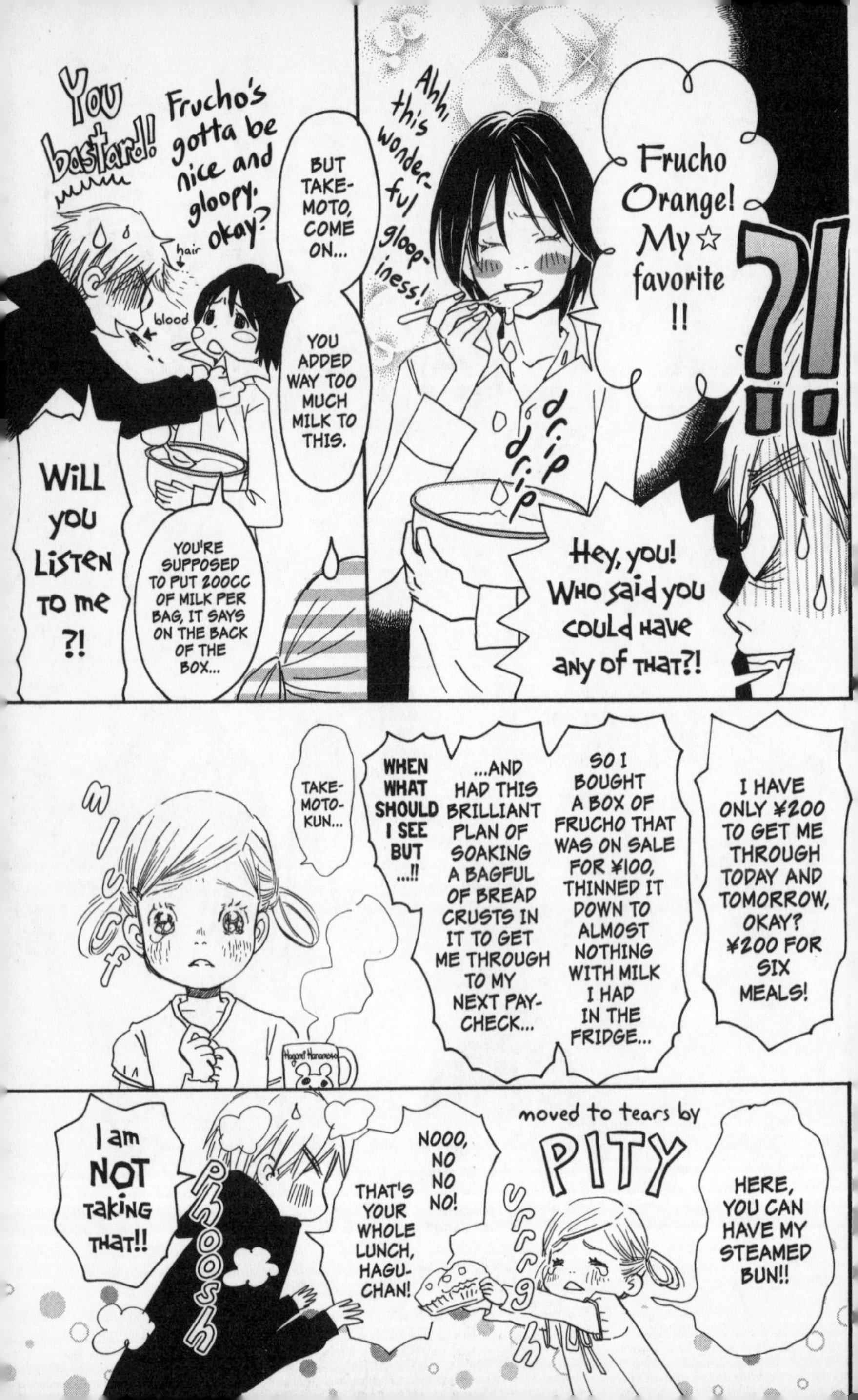
Frucho Orange! My☆ favorite !!
Ahh, this wonderful gloopiness!
?!
drip drip drip
Hey, you! Who said you could have any of that?!
BUT TAKE-MOTO, COME ON...
Frucho's gotta be nice and gloopy, okay?
You bastard!!
hair
blood
YOU ADDED WAY TOO MUCH MILK TO THIS.
YOU'RE SUPPOSED TO PUT 200CC OF MILK PER BAG, IT SAYS ON THE BACK OF THE BOX...
Will you listen to me ?!
I HAVE ONLY ¥200 TO GET ME THROUGH TODAY AND TOMORROW, OKAY? ¥200 FOR SIX MEALS!
SO I BOUGHT A BOX OF FRUCHO THAT WAS ON SALE FOR ¥100, THINNED IT DOWN TO ALMOST NOTHING WITH MILK I HAD IN THE FRIDGE...
...AND HAD THIS BRILLIANT PLAN OF SOAKING A BAGFUL OF BREAD CRUSTS IN IT TO GET ME THROUGH TO MY NEXT PAY-CHECK...
WHEN WHAT SHOULD I SEE BUT ...!!
TAKE-MOTO-KUN...
moved to tears by PITY
HERE, YOU CAN HAVE MY STEAMED BUN!!
urrrgh
NOOO, NO NO NO!
THAT'S YOUR WHOLE LUNCH, HAGU-CHAN!
I am NOT taking that!!
phoosh

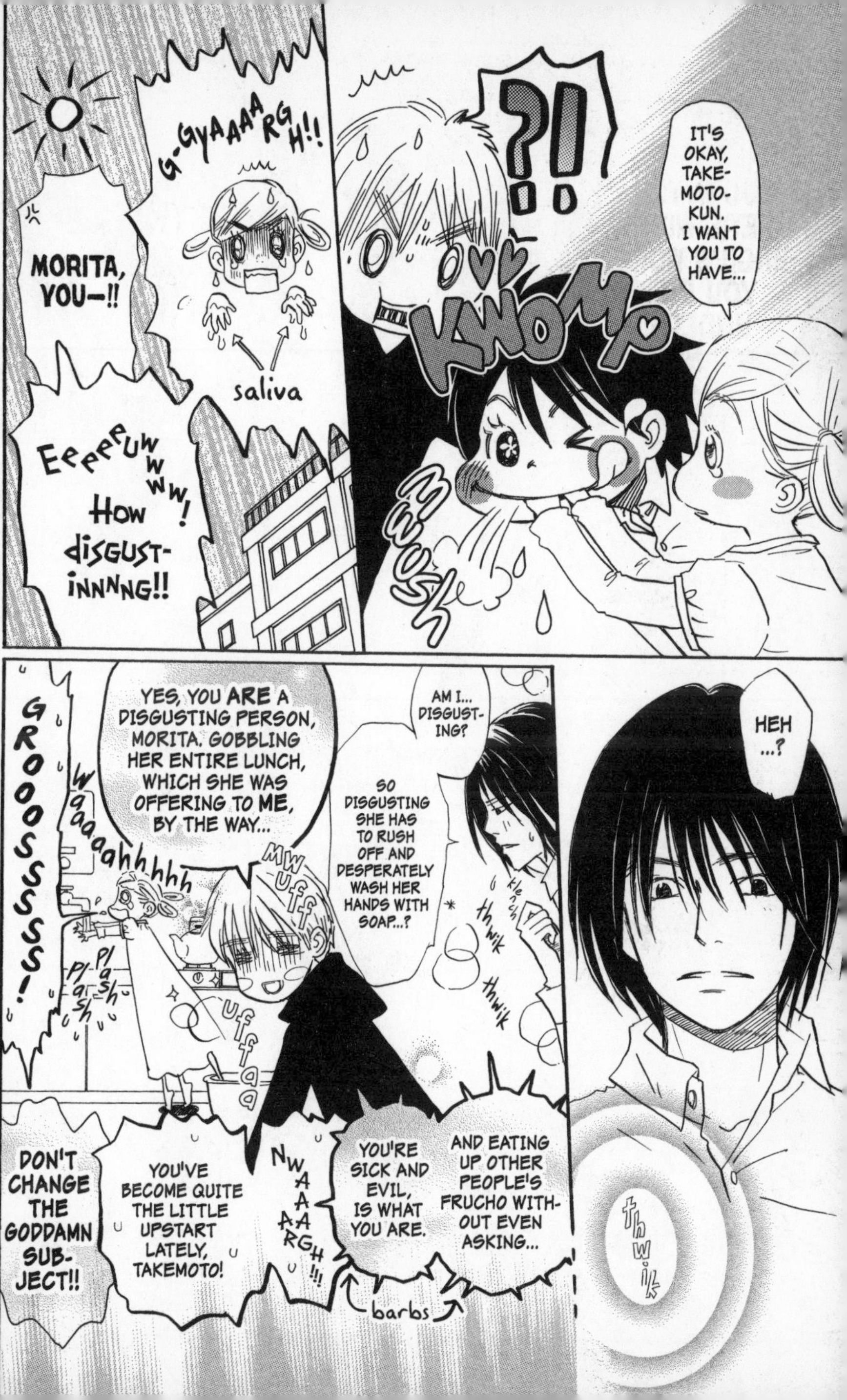
IT'S OKAY, TAKEMOTO-KUN. I WANT YOU TO HAVE...
?!
!!
KNOMP
MWUSH
G-GYAAAARGH!!
MORITA, YOU-!!
saliva
Eeeeeuwwwww! How disgust-innnng!!
HEH ...?
thwik
AM I... DISGUSTING?
SO DISGUSTING SHE HAS TO RUSH OFF AND DESPERATELY WASH HER HANDS WITH SOAP...?
kle-nch
thwik
thwik
YES, YOU ARE A DISGUSTING PERSON, MORITA. GOBBLING HER ENTIRE LUNCH, WHICH SHE WAS OFFERING TO ME, BY THE WAY...
MWUFF
Uffaaa
Waaaaahhhhh
Plaash
Plaash
GROOOSSSSS!
AND EATING UP OTHER PEOPLE'S FRUCHO WITHOUT EVEN ASKING...
YOU'RE SICK AND EVIL, IS WHAT YOU ARE.
barbs
NWAAAAARGH!!!
YOU'VE BECOME QUITE THE LITTLE UPSTART LATELY, TAKEMOTO!
DON'T CHANGE THE GODDAMN SUBJECT!!

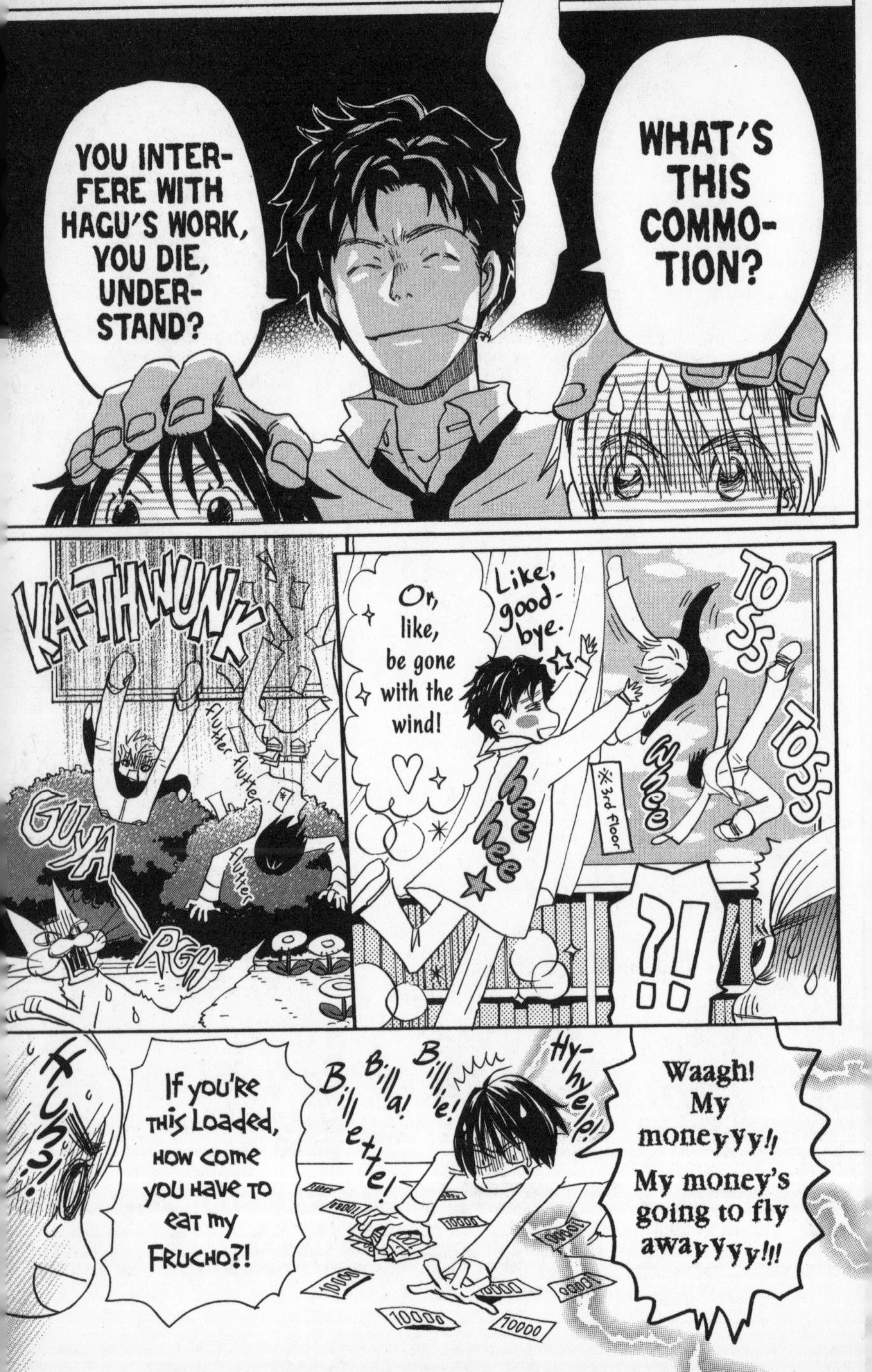
WHAT'S THIS COMMO-TION?
YOU INTER-FERE WITH HAGU'S WORK, YOU DIE, UNDER-STAND?
TOSS TOSS
whee
※3rd floor
?!!
Like, good-bye.
Or, like, be gone with the wind!
hee hee
KA-THWUNK
flutter flutter
flutter
GUYA
RGH
Waagh! My moneyyyy!! My money's going to fly awayyyy!!!
Hy-hyelp!
Billie!
Billa!
Billette!
If you're this Loaded, how come you have to eat my Frucho?!
Huh?!

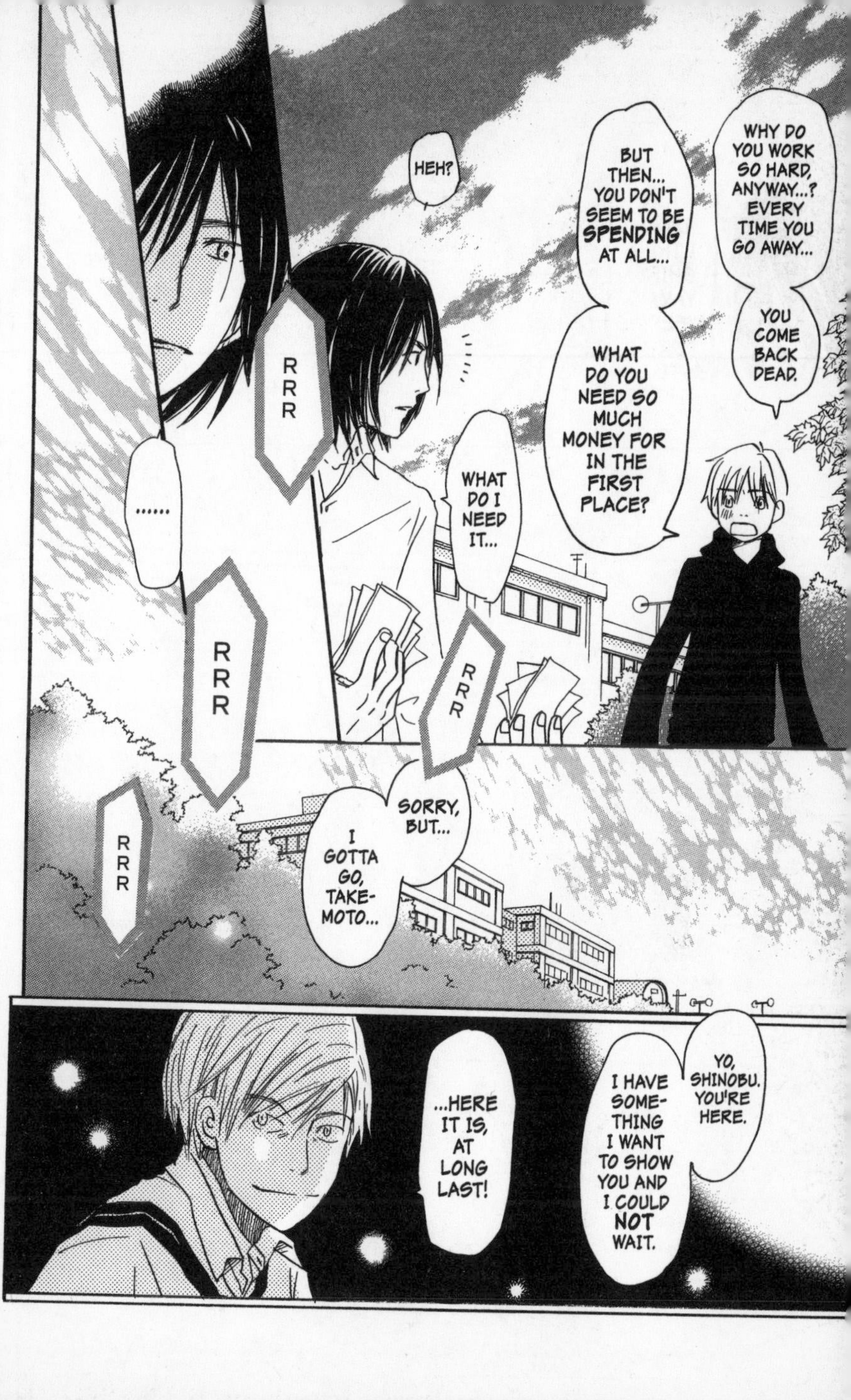
WHY DO YOU WORK SO HARD, ANYWAY...? EVERY TIME YOU GO AWAY...
YOU COME BACK DEAD.
BUT THEN... YOU DON'T SEEM TO BE SPENDING AT ALL...
WHAT DO YOU NEED SO MUCH MONEY FOR IN THE FIRST PLACE?
HEH?
WHAT DO I NEED IT...
RRR
......
RRR
RRR
SORRY, BUT...
I GOTTA GO, TAKE-MOTO...
RRR
YO, SHINOBU. YOU'RE HERE.
I HAVE SOME-THING I WANT TO SHOW YOU AND I COULD NOT WAIT.
...HERE IT IS, AT LONG LAST!

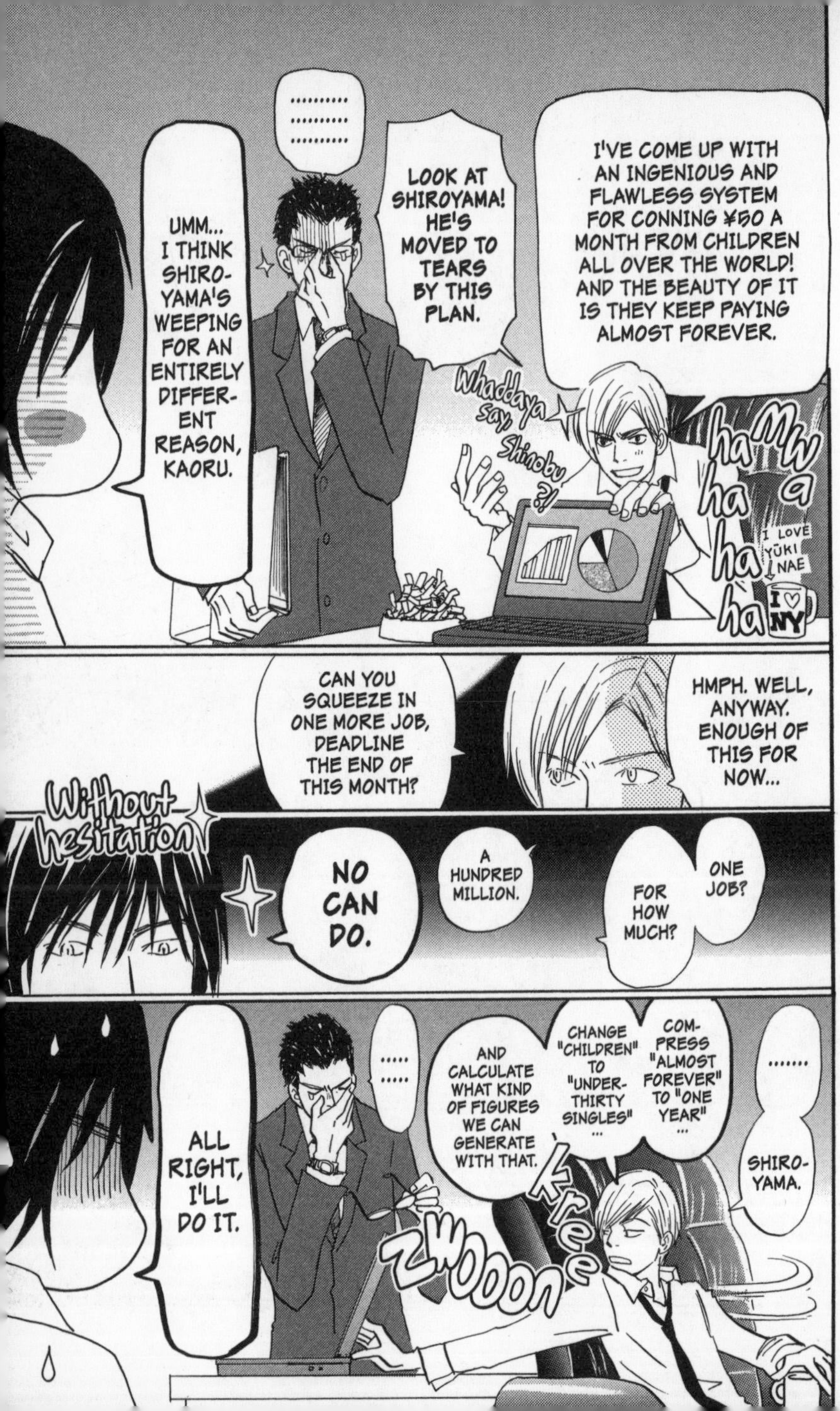
I'VE COME UP WITH AN INGENIOUS AND FLAWLESS SYSTEM FOR CONNING ¥50 A MONTH FROM CHILDREN ALL OVER THE WORLD! AND THE BEAUTY OF IT IS THEY KEEP PAYING ALMOST FOREVER.
Whaddaya say, Shinobu?!
Mwa ha ha ha ha ha
I LOVE YŪKI NAE
I ♥ NY
LOOK AT SHIROYAMA! HE'S MOVED TO TEARS BY THIS PLAN.
....
....
....
UMM... I THINK SHIRO-YAMA'S WEEPING FOR AN ENTIRELY DIFFER-ENT REASON, KAORU.
HMPH. WELL, ANYWAY. ENOUGH OF THIS FOR NOW...
CAN YOU SQUEEZE IN ONE MORE JOB, DEADLINE THE END OF THIS MONTH?
ONE JOB?
FOR HOW MUCH?
A HUNDRED MILLION.
NO CAN DO.
Without hesitation
SHIRO-YAMA.
....
COM-PRESS "ALMOST FOREVER" TO "ONE YEAR"...
CHANGE "CHILDREN" TO "UNDER-THIRTY SINGLES"...
AND CALCULATE WHAT KIND OF FIGURES WE CAN GENERATE WITH THAT.
kree
ZWOOOON
.....
.....
ALL RIGHT, I'LL DO IT.

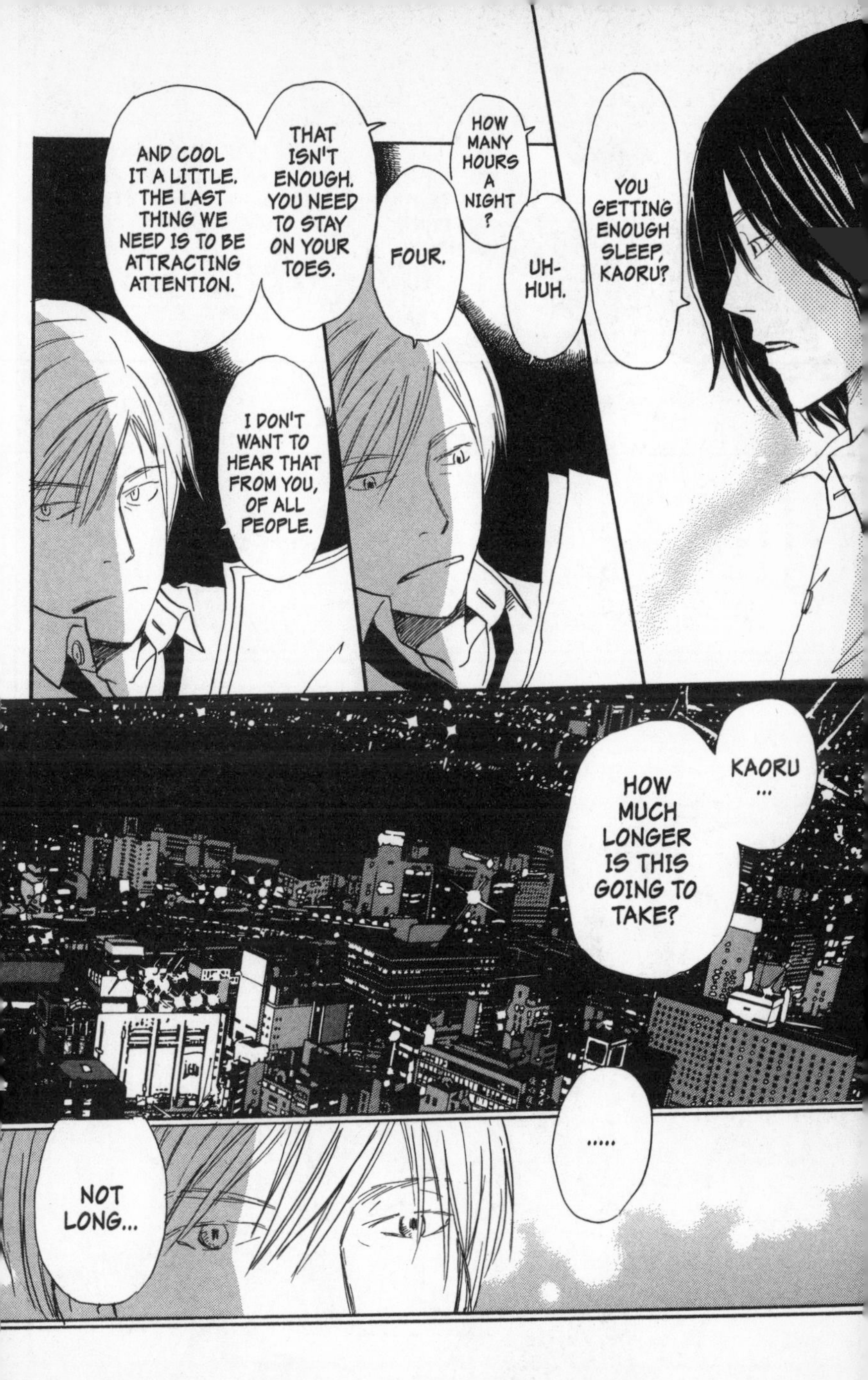
YOU GETTING ENOUGH SLEEP, KAORU?
UH-HUH.
HOW MANY HOURS A NIGHT?
FOUR.
THAT ISN'T ENOUGH. YOU NEED TO STAY ON YOUR TOES.
AND COOL IT A LITTLE. THE LAST THING WE NEED IS TO BE ATTRACTING ATTENTION.
I DON'T WANT TO HEAR THAT FROM YOU, OF ALL PEOPLE.
KAORU...
HOW MUCH LONGER IS THIS GOING TO TAKE?
.....
NOT LONG...

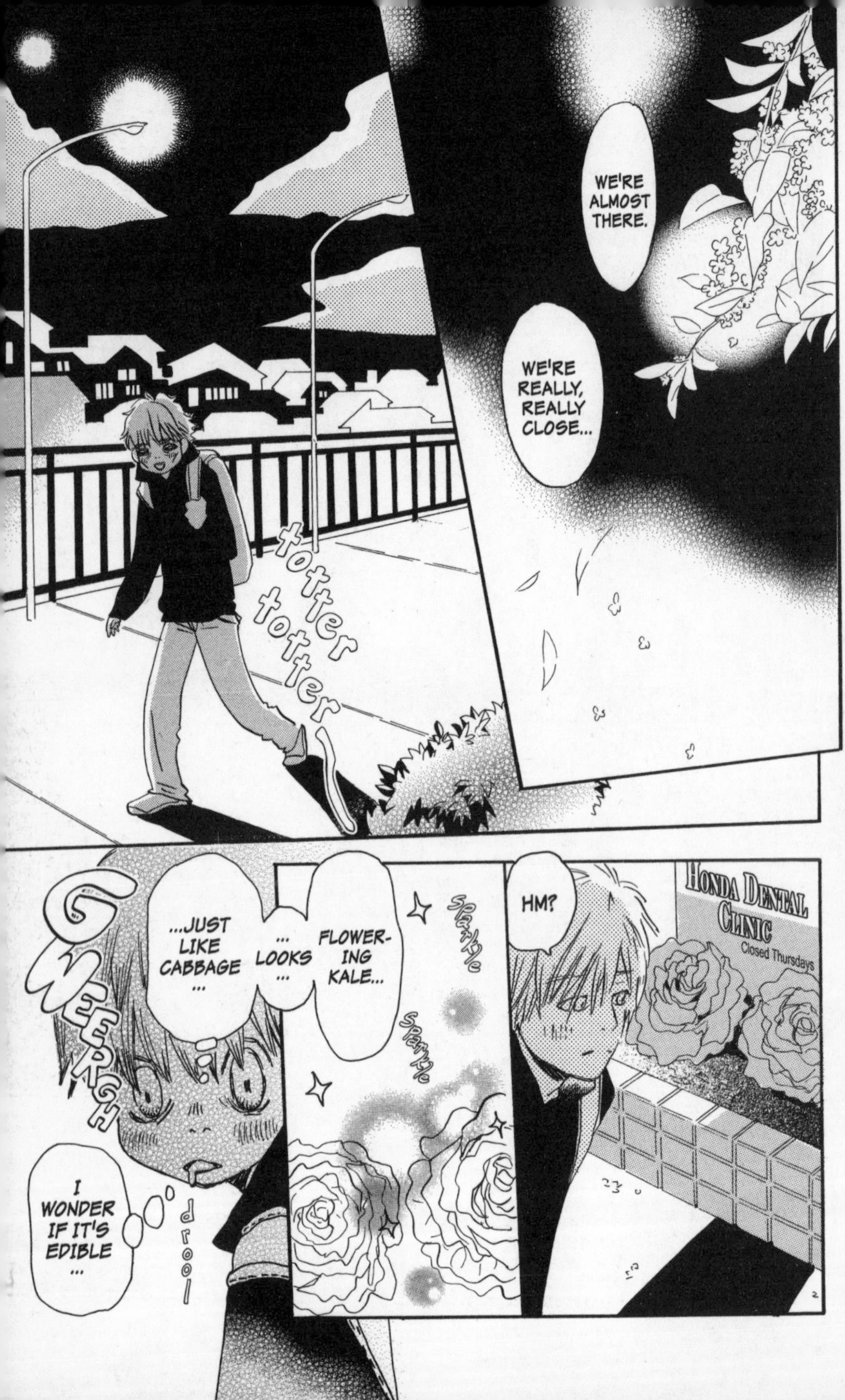
WE'RE ALMOST THERE.
WE'RE REALLY, REALLY CLOSE...
totter totter
HM?
HONDA DENTAL CLINIC
Closed Thursdays
FLOWERING KALE...
... LOOKS ...
...JUST LIKE CABBAGE ...
sparkle
sparkle
GWEERGH
I WONDER IF IT'S EDIBLE ...
drool

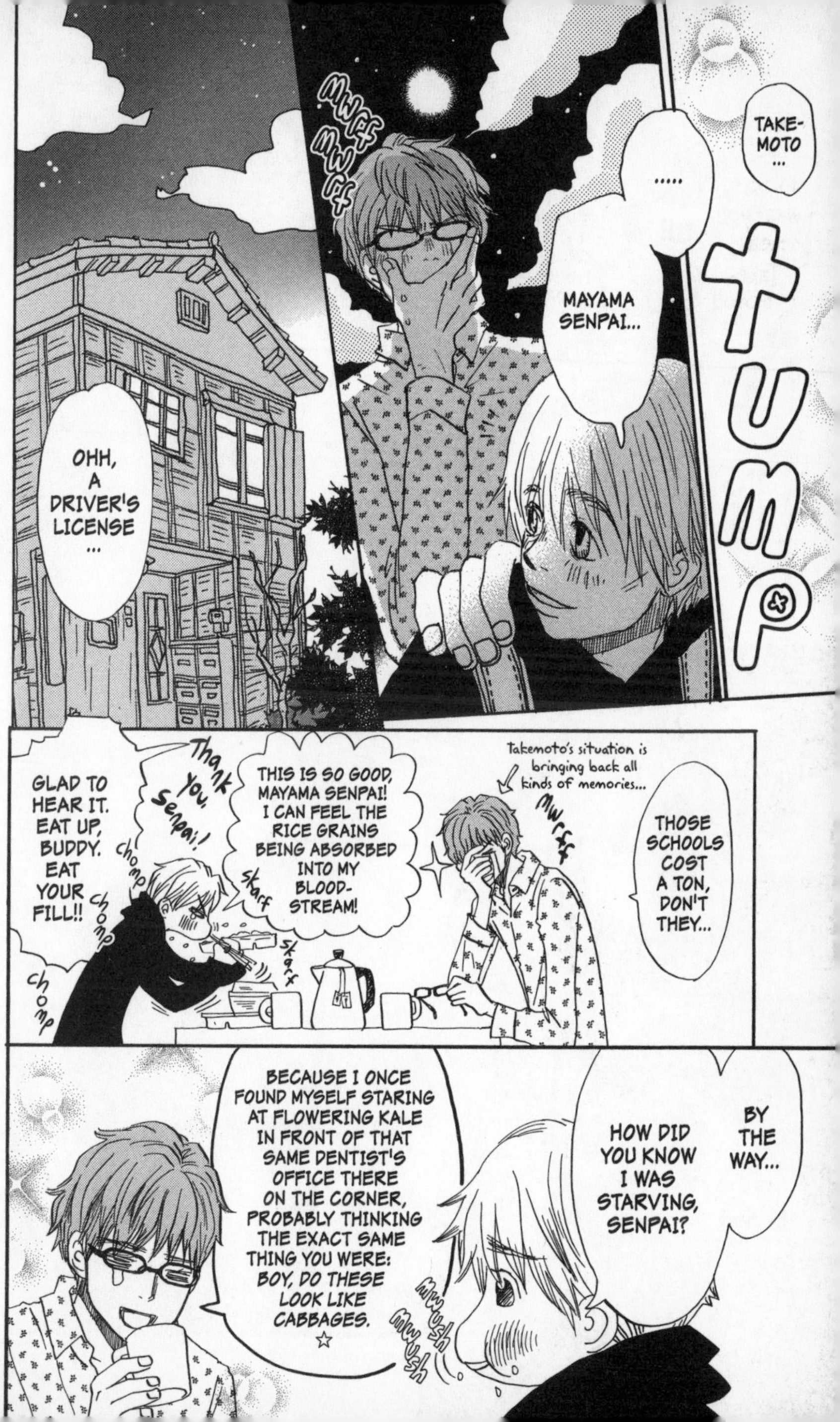
TAKE-MOTO ...
.....
MAYAMA SENPAI...
THUMP
OHH, A DRIVER'S LICENSE ...
THOSE SCHOOLS COST A TON, DON'T THEY...
mwrff
Takemoto's situation is bringing back all kinds of memories...
THIS IS SO GOOD, MAYAMA SENPAI! I CAN FEEL THE RICE GRAINS BEING ABSORBED INTO MY BLOOD-STREAM!
skarf
skarf
Thank you, Senpai!
chomp
chomp
chomp
GLAD TO HEAR IT. EAT UP, BUDDY. EAT YOUR FILL!!
BY THE WAY...
HOW DID YOU KNOW I WAS STARVING, SENPAI?
mwush
mwush
BECAUSE I ONCE FOUND MYSELF STARING AT FLOWERING KALE IN FRONT OF THAT SAME DENTIST'S OFFICE THERE ON THE CORNER, PROBABLY THINKING THE EXACT SAME THING YOU WERE: BOY, DO THESE LOOK LIKE CABBAGES. ☆

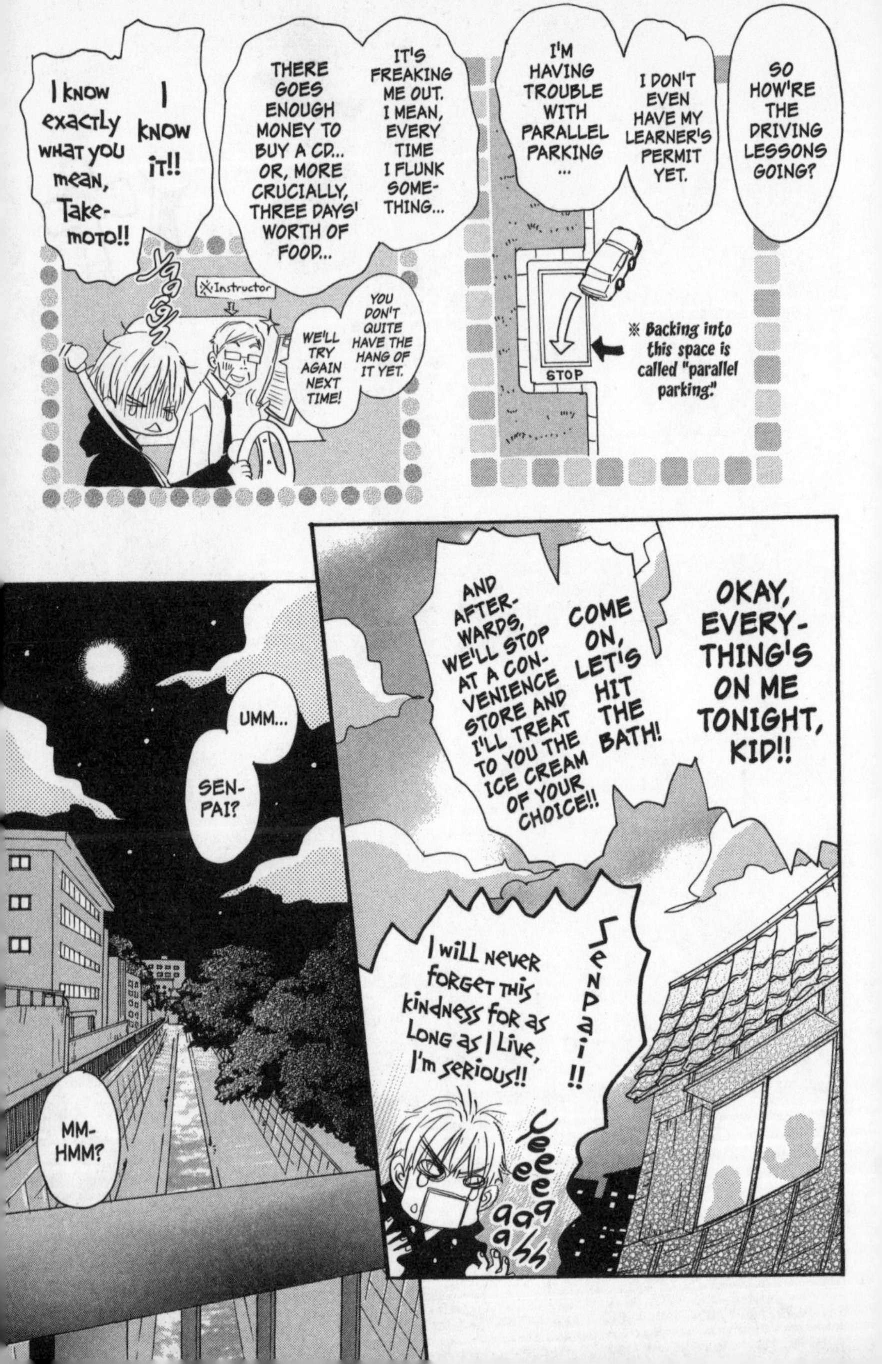
SO HOW'RE THE DRIVING LESSONS GOING?
I DON'T EVEN HAVE MY LEARNER'S PERMIT YET.
I'M HAVING TROUBLE WITH PARALLEL PARKING ...
STOP
※ Backing into this space is called "parallel parking."
IT'S FREAKING ME OUT. I MEAN, EVERY TIME I FLUNK SOMETHING...
THERE GOES ENOUGH MONEY TO BUY A CD... OR, MORE CRUCIALLY, THREE DAYS' WORTH OF FOOD...
I KNOW IT!!
I know exactly what you mean, Take-moto!!
YOU DON'T QUITE HAVE THE HANG OF IT YET.
WE'LL TRY AGAIN NEXT TIME!
※Instructor
Yaagh
OKAY, EVERY-THING'S ON ME TONIGHT, KID!!
COME ON, LET'S HIT THE BATH!
AND AFTER-WARDS, WE'LL STOP AT A CON-VENIENCE STORE AND I'LL TREAT TO YOU THE ICE CREAM OF YOUR CHOICE!!
Senpai!!
I will never forget this kindness for as long as I live, I'm serious!!
Yeeeeaaaahh
UMM...
SEN-PAI?
MM-HMM?

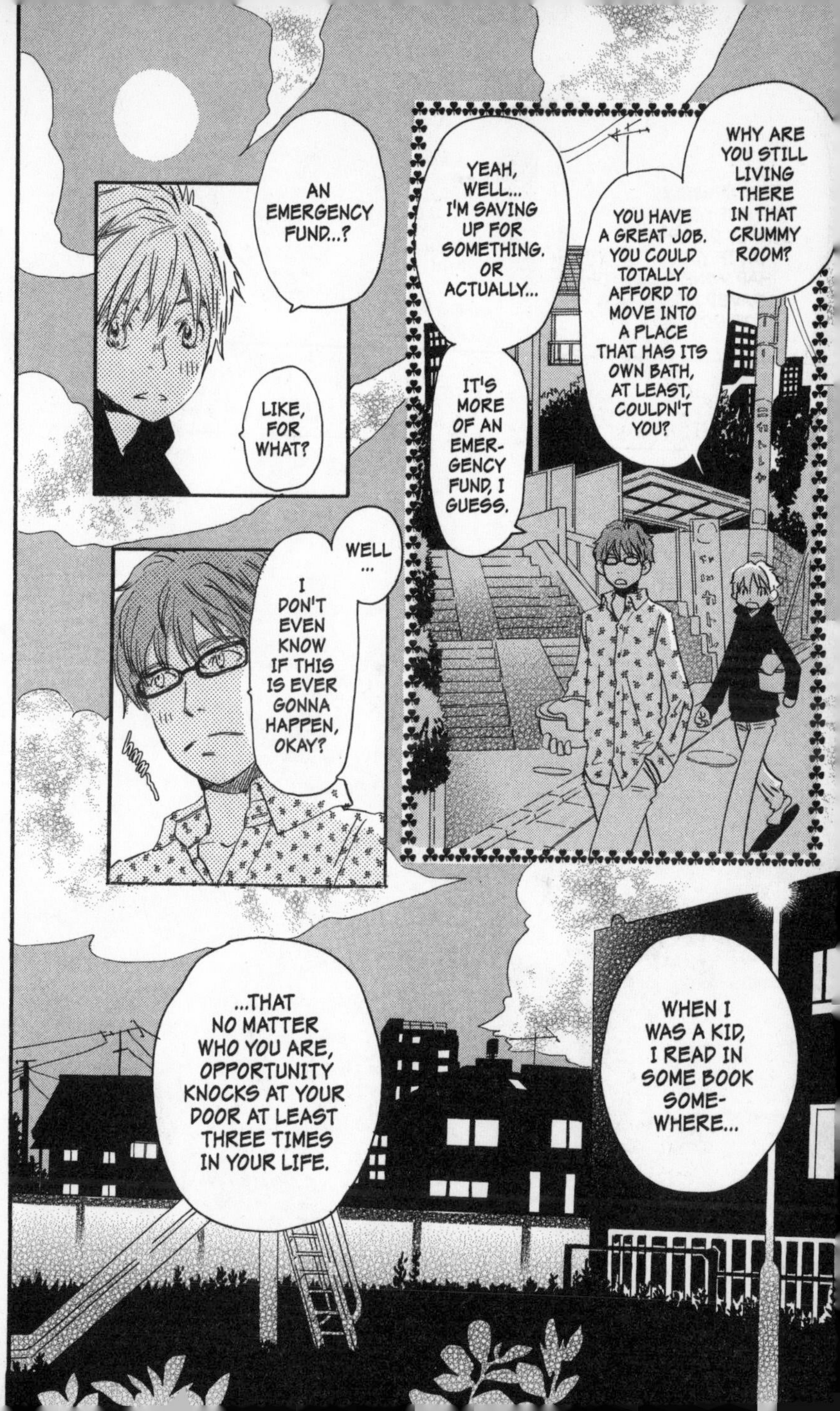
WHY ARE YOU STILL LIVING THERE IN THAT CRUMMY ROOM?
YOU HAVE A GREAT JOB. YOU COULD TOTALLY AFFORD TO MOVE INTO A PLACE THAT HAS ITS OWN BATH, AT LEAST, COULDN'T YOU?
YEAH, WELL... I'M SAVING UP FOR SOMETHING. OR ACTUALLY...
IT'S MORE OF AN EMERGENCY FUND, I GUESS.
AN EMERGENCY FUND...?
LIKE, FOR WHAT?
WELL...
I DON'T EVEN KNOW IF THIS IS EVER GONNA HAPPEN, OKAY?
hmm~
WHEN I WAS A KID, I READ IN SOME BOOK SOMEWHERE...
...THAT NO MATTER WHO YOU ARE, OPPORTUNITY KNOCKS AT YOUR DOOR AT LEAST THREE TIMES IN YOUR LIFE.

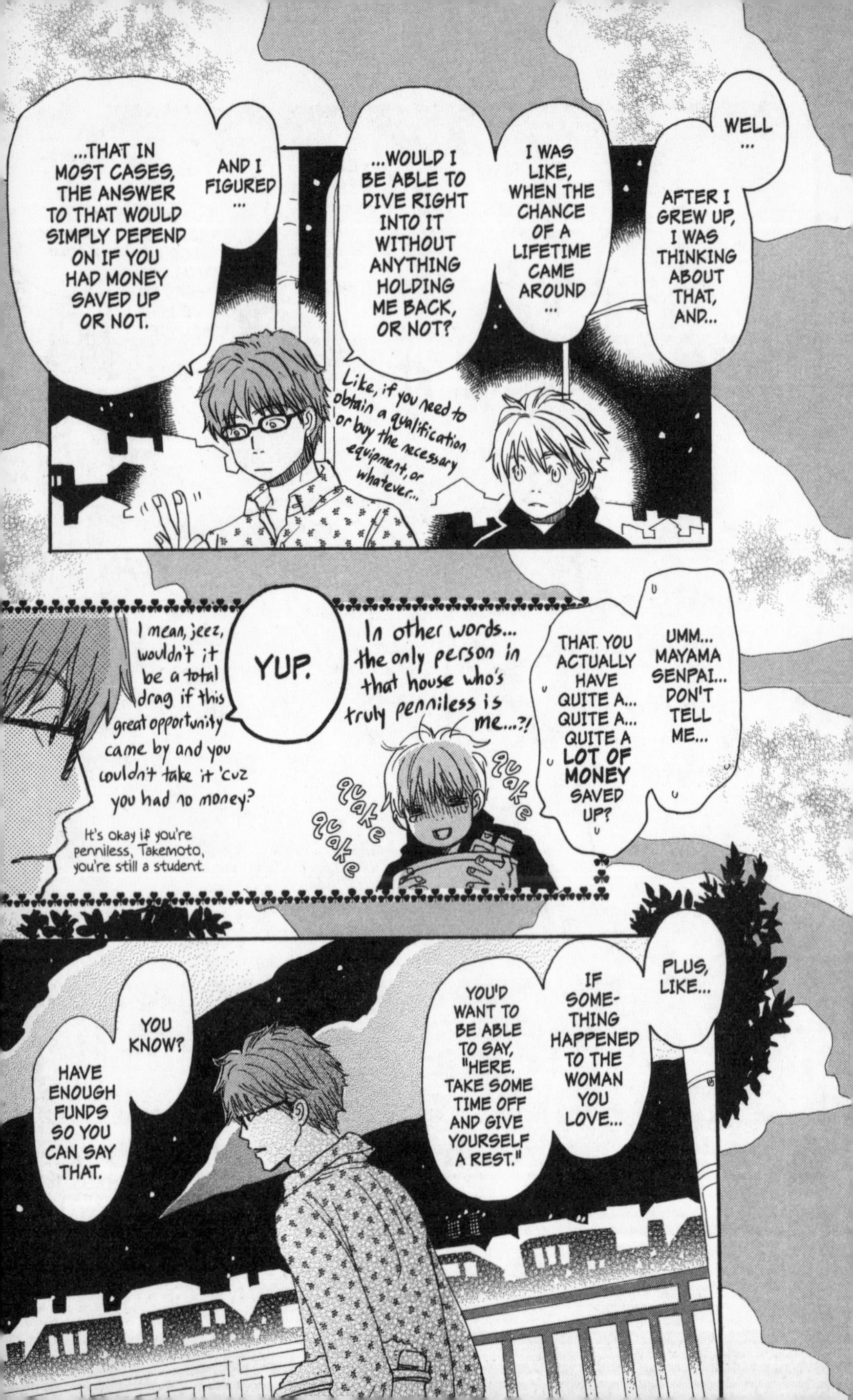
WELL ...
AFTER I GREW UP, I WAS THINKING ABOUT THAT, AND...
I WAS LIKE, WHEN THE CHANCE OF A LIFETIME CAME AROUND ...
...WOULD I BE ABLE TO DIVE RIGHT INTO IT WITHOUT ANYTHING HOLDING ME BACK, OR NOT?
Like, if you need to obtain a qualification or buy the necessary equipment, or whatever...
AND I FIGURED ...
...THAT IN MOST CASES, THE ANSWER TO THAT WOULD SIMPLY DEPEND ON IF YOU HAD MONEY SAVED UP OR NOT.
UMM... MAYAMA SENPAI... DON'T TELL ME...
THAT YOU ACTUALLY HAVE QUITE A... QUITE A... QUITE A LOT OF MONEY SAVED UP?
In other words... the only person in that house who's truly penniless is me...?!
quake quake quake
YUP.
I mean, jeez, wouldn't it be a total drag if this great opportunity came by and you couldn't take it 'cuz you had no money?
It's okay if you're penniless, Takemoto, you're still a student.
PLUS, LIKE...
IF SOME-THING HAPPENED TO THE WOMAN YOU LOVE...
YOU'D WANT TO BE ABLE TO SAY, "HERE. TAKE SOME TIME OFF AND GIVE YOURSELF A REST."
YOU KNOW?
HAVE ENOUGH FUNDS SO YOU CAN SAY THAT.

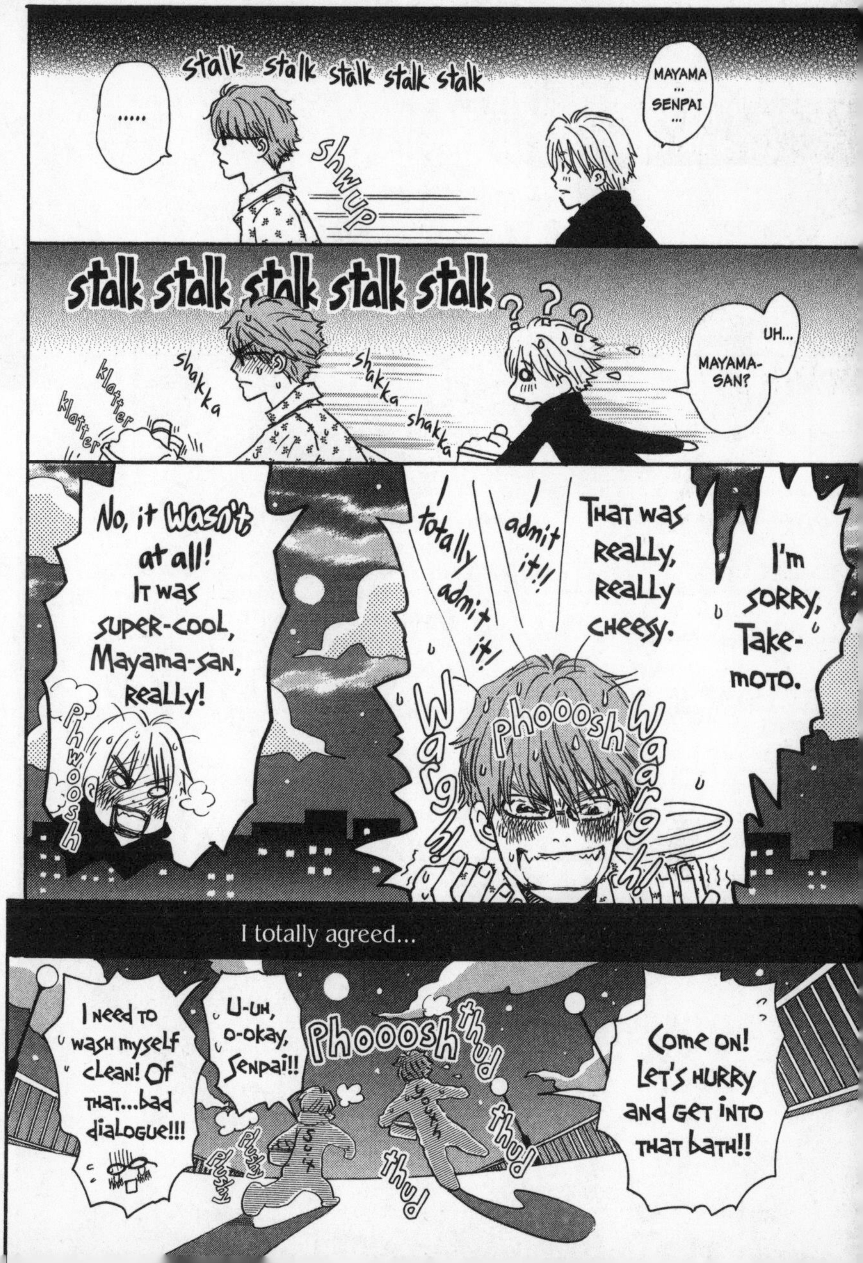
MAYAMA... SENPAI...
stalk stalk stalk stalk stalk
shwup
......
UH... MAYAMA-SAN?
shakka
shakka
stalk stalk stalk stalk stalk
shakka
klatter klatter
I'm SORRY, Take-moto.
THAT was REALLY, REALLY CHEESY.
I admit it!!
I totally admit it!
Waargh!
phoooosh
Waargh!
No, it wasn't at all! It was super-cool, Mayama-san, really!
Phwoosh
I totally agreed...
Come on! Let's hurry and get into that bath!!
thud
thud
thud
Phoooosh
U-uh, o-okay, Senpai!!
I need to wash myself clean! Of that...bad dialogue!!!

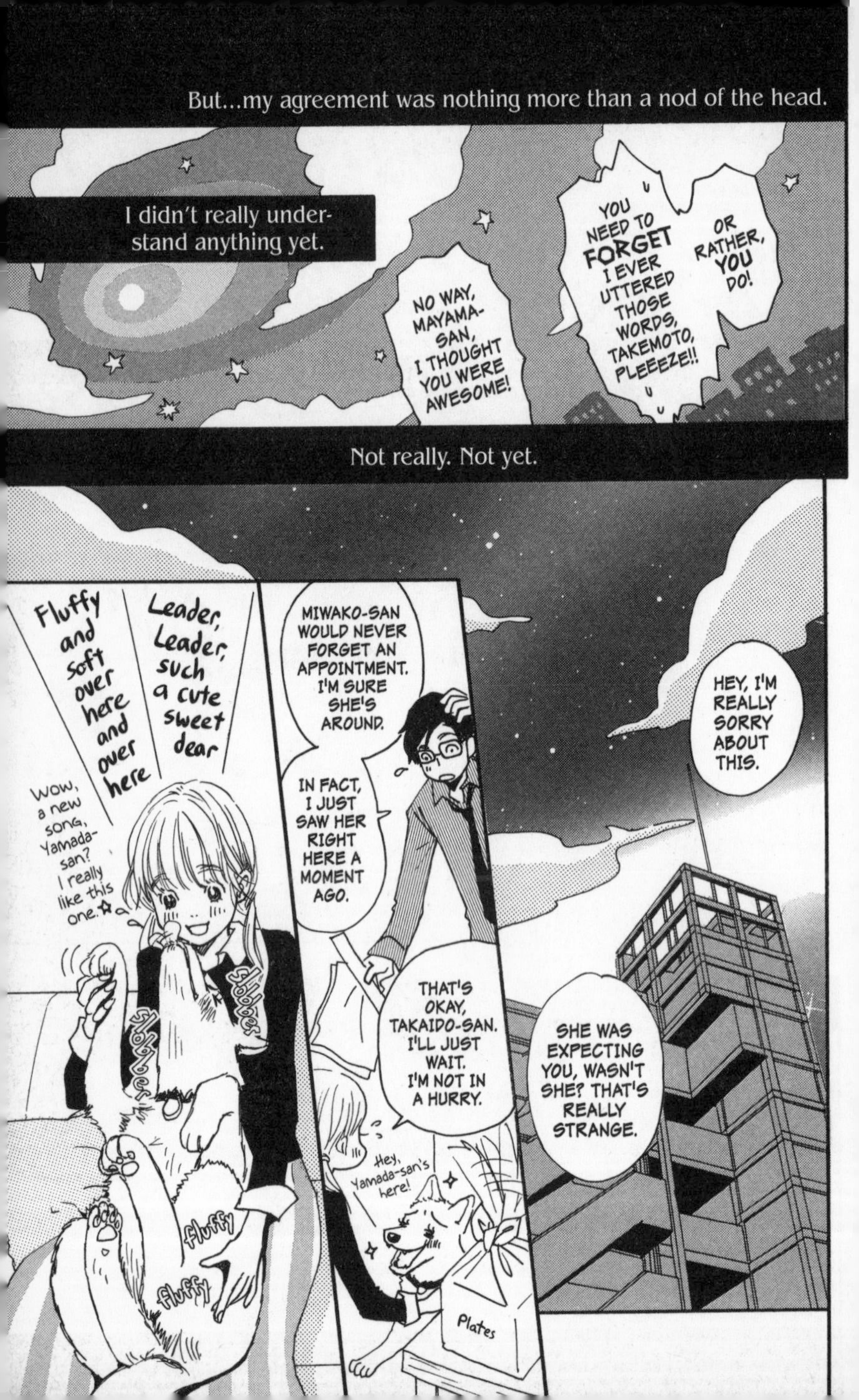
But...my agreement was nothing more than a nod of the head.
OR RATHER, YOU DO!
YOU NEED TO FORGET I EVER UTTERED THOSE WORDS, TAKEMOTO, PLEEEZE!!
I didn't really understand anything yet.
NO WAY, MAYAMA-SAN, I THOUGHT YOU WERE AWESOME!
Not really. Not yet.
HEY, I'M REALLY SORRY ABOUT THIS.
SHE WAS EXPECTING YOU, WASN'T SHE? THAT'S REALLY STRANGE.
MIWAKO-SAN WOULD NEVER FORGET AN APPOINTMENT. I'M SURE SHE'S AROUND.
IN FACT, I JUST SAW HER RIGHT HERE A MOMENT AGO.
THAT'S OKAY, TAKAIDO-SAN. I'LL JUST WAIT. I'M NOT IN A HURRY.
Hey, Yamada-san's here!
Plates
Leader, Leader, such a cute sweet dear
Fluffy and soft over here and over here
Wow, a new song, Yamada-san? I really like this one. ✩
Slobber
Slobber
fluffy
fluffy

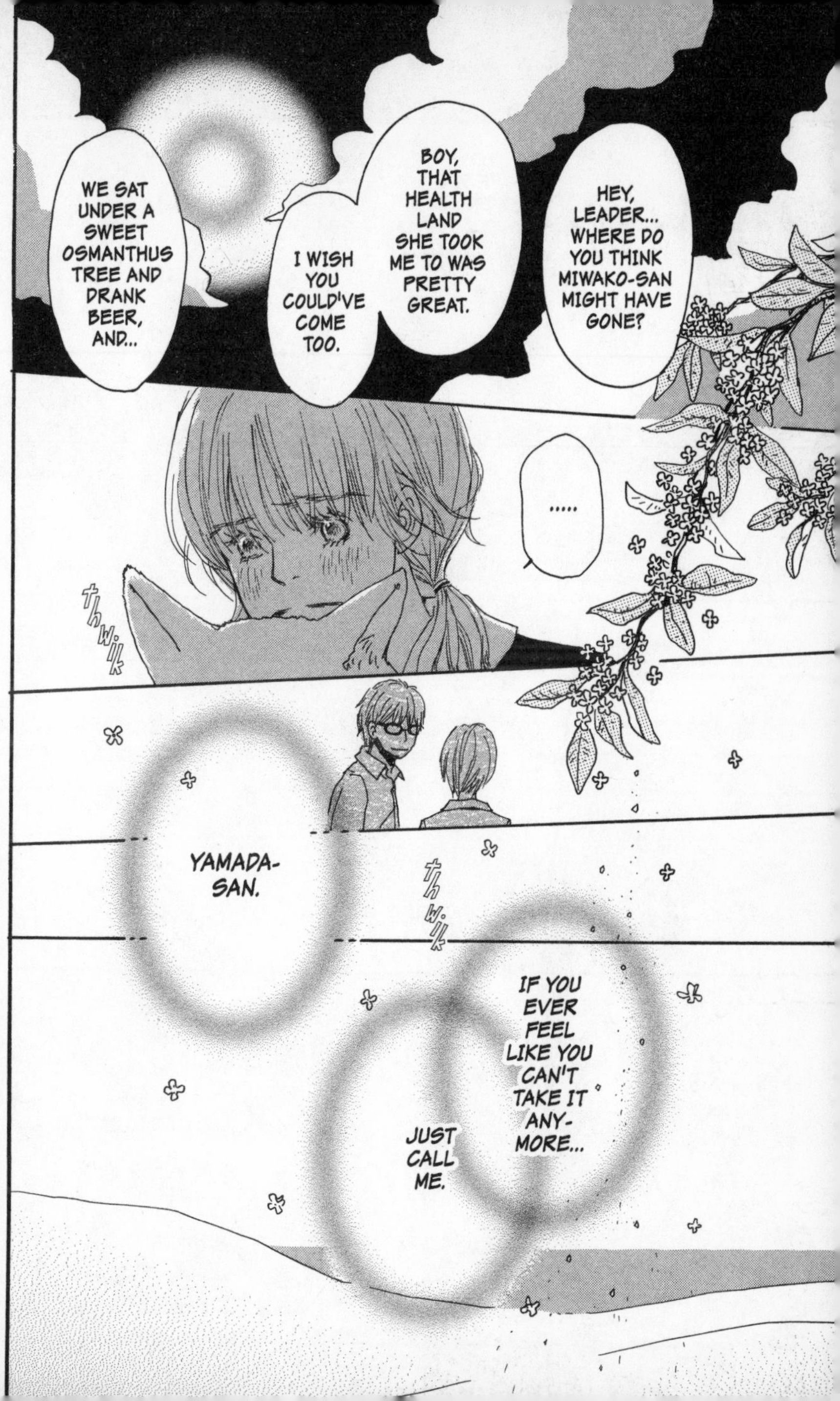
HEY, LEADER... WHERE DO YOU THINK MIWAKO-SAN MIGHT HAVE GONE?
BOY, THAT HEALTH LAND SHE TOOK ME TO WAS PRETTY GREAT.
I WISH YOU COULD'VE COME TOO.
WE SAT UNDER A SWEET OSMANTHUS TREE AND DRANK BEER, AND...
.....
thwik
thwik
YAMADA-SAN.
IF YOU EVER FEEL LIKE YOU CAN'T TAKE IT ANYMORE...
JUST CALL ME.

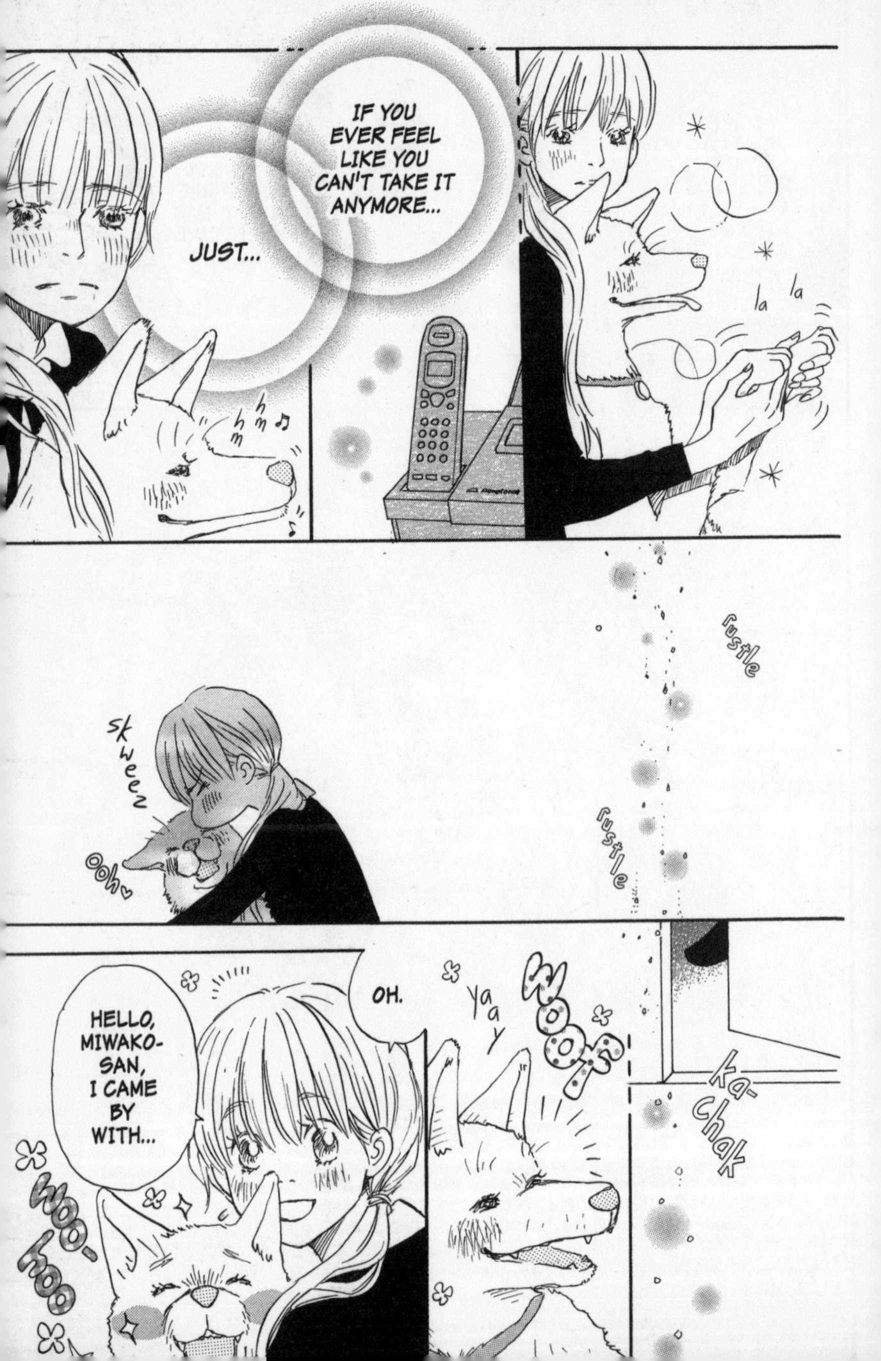
IF YOU EVER FEEL LIKE YOU CAN'T TAKE IT ANYMORE...
la la
JUST...
hm hm m
rustle
rustle
skweez
ooh
ka-chak
woof
yaay
OH.
HELLO, MIWAKO-SAN, I CAME BY WITH...
woo-hoo

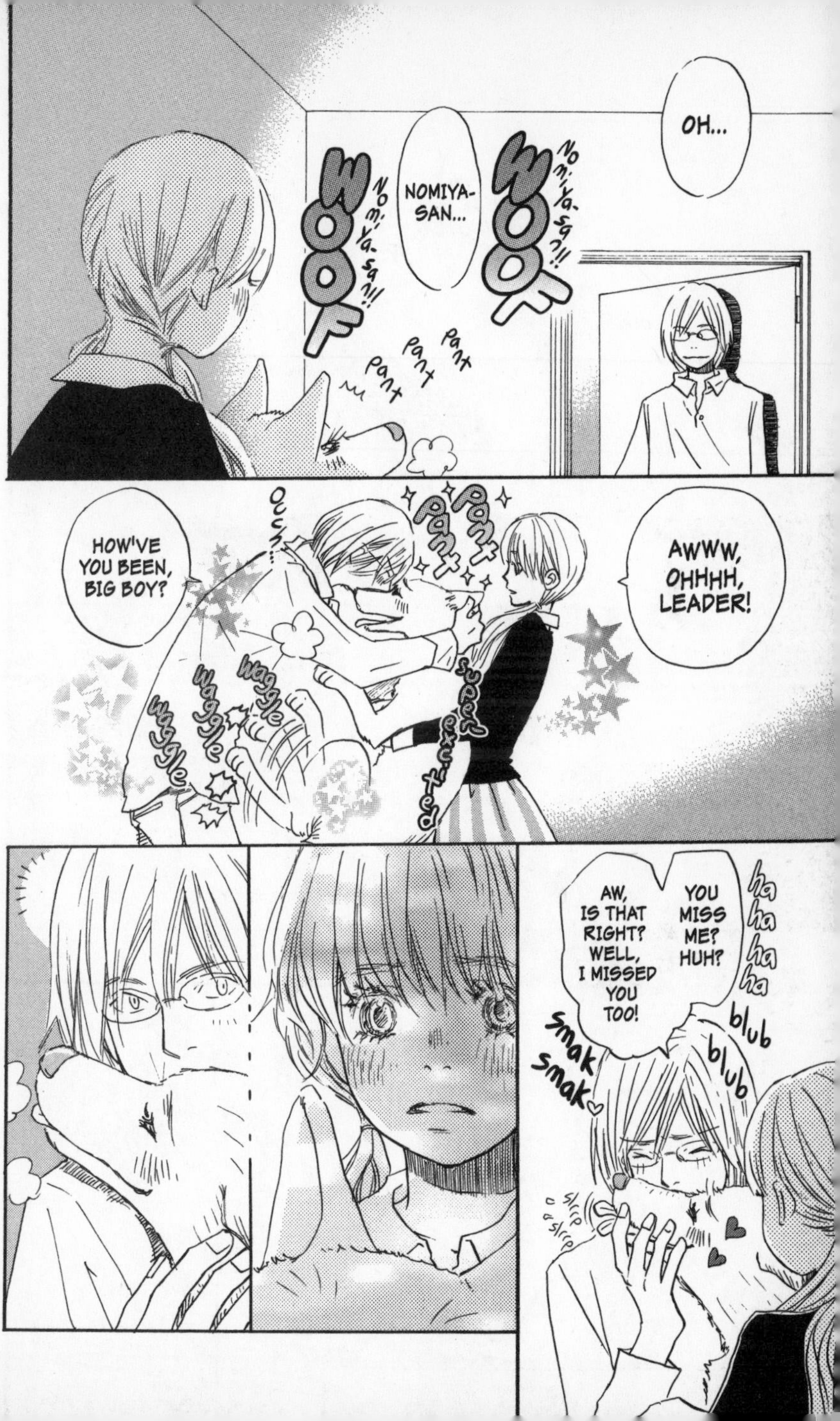
OH...
WOOF
Nomiya-san!!
NOMIYA-SAN...
WOOF
Nomiya-san!!
pant pant pant
AWWW, OHHHH, LEADER!
Pant Pant
super excited
Ouch...
HOW'VE YOU BEEN, BIG BOY?
waggle waggle waggle
YOU MISS ME? HUH?
AW, IS THAT RIGHT? WELL, I MISSED YOU TOO!
ha ha ha ha
blub blub
smak smak
slrrp slrrp

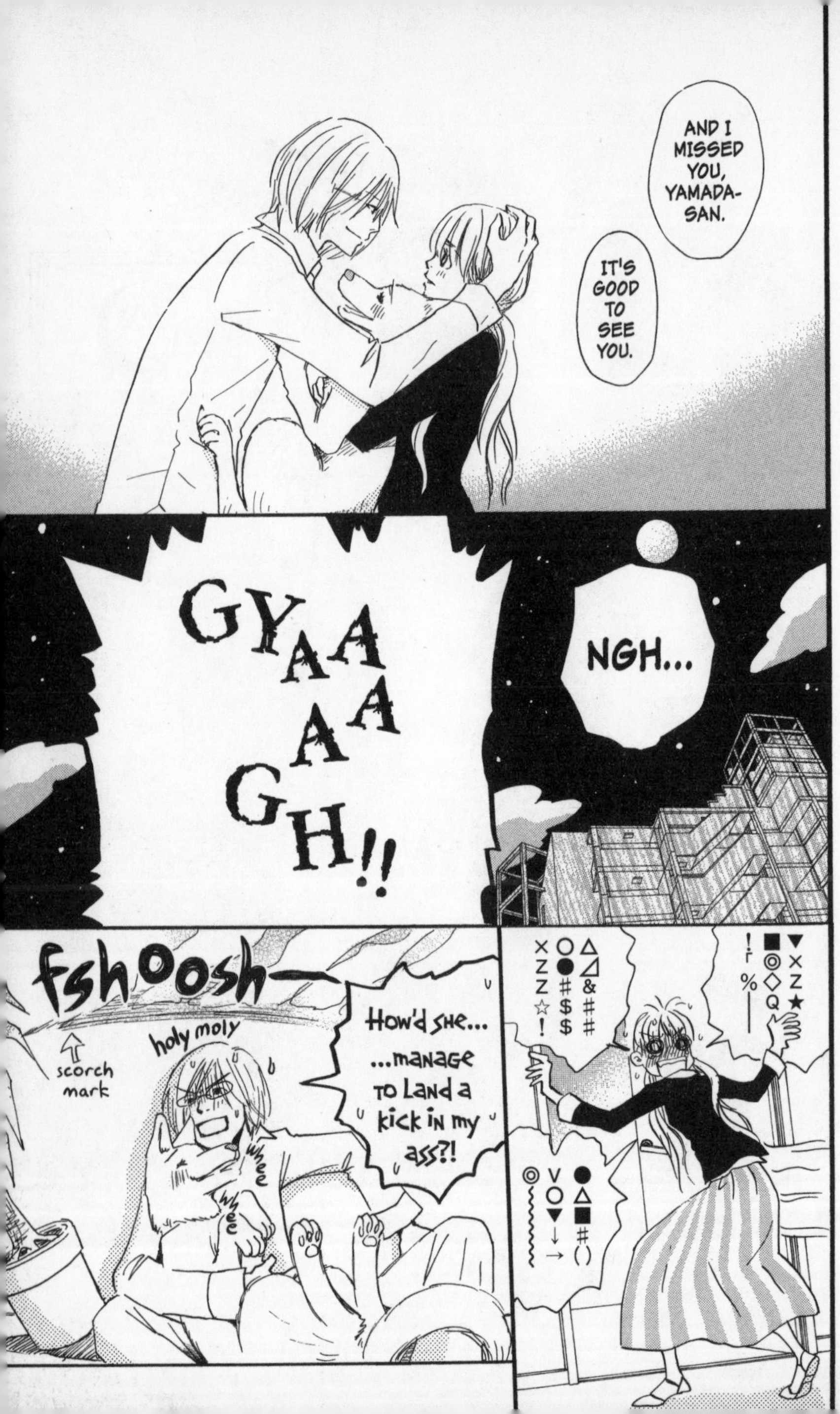

AND I MISSED YOU, YAMADA-SAN.
IT'S GOOD TO SEE YOU.
NGH...
GYAAAAGH!!
fshoosh—
holy moly
scorch mark
How'd she... ...manage to land a kick in my ass?!
whee whee

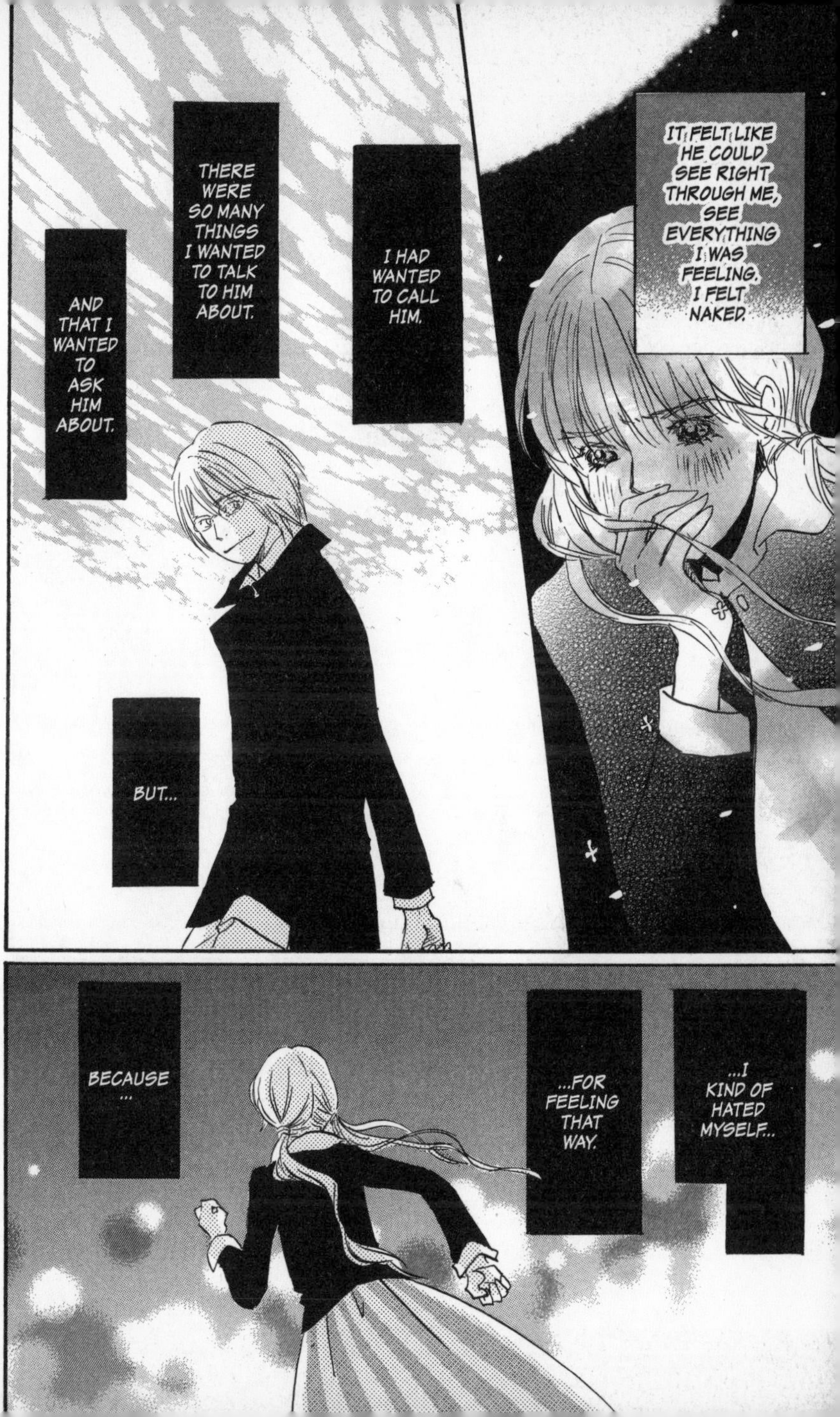
IT FELT LIKE HE COULD SEE RIGHT THROUGH ME, SEE EVERYTHING I WAS FEELING. I FELT NAKED.
I HAD WANTED TO CALL HIM.
THERE WERE SO MANY THINGS I WANTED TO TALK TO HIM ABOUT.
AND THAT I WANTED TO ASK HIM ABOUT.
BUT...
...I KIND OF HATED MYSELF...
...FOR FEELING THAT WAY.
BECAUSE ...

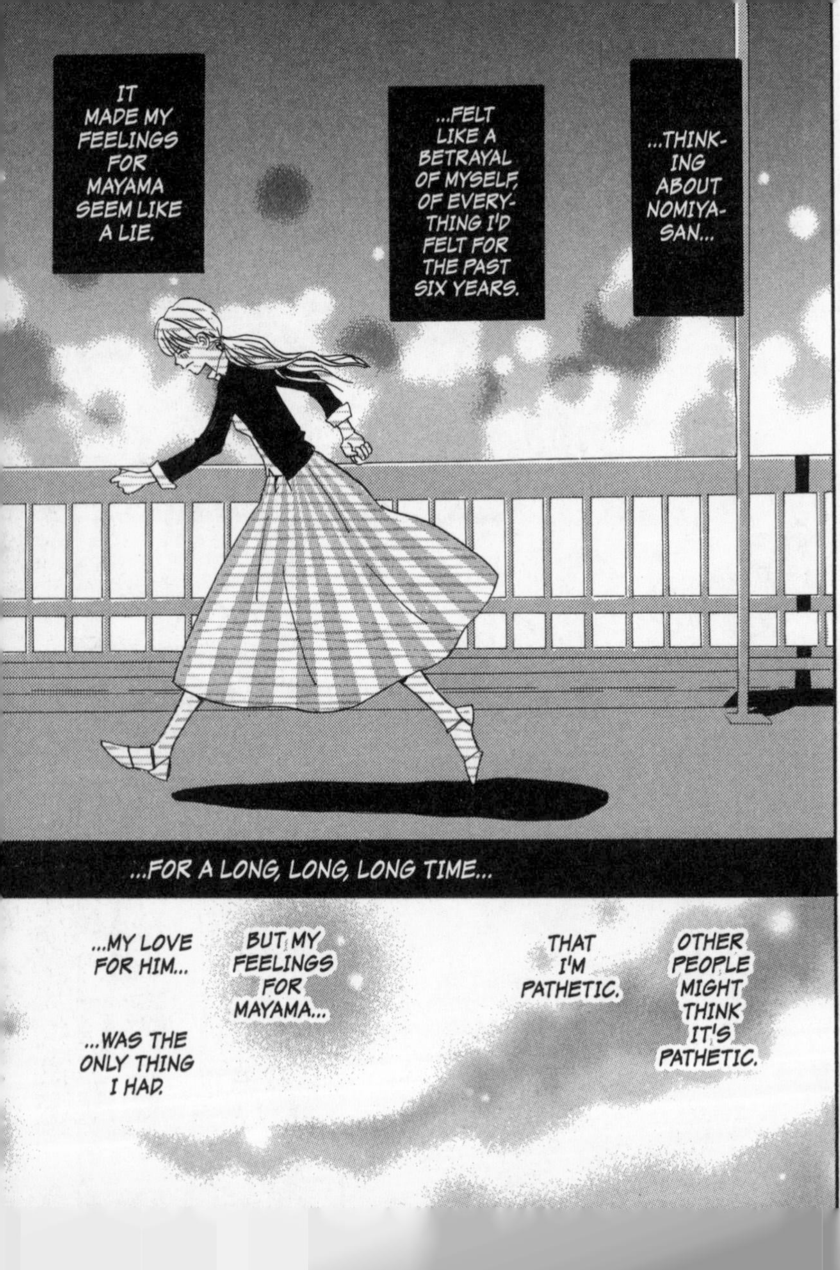
...THINKING ABOUT NOMIYA-SAN...
...FELT LIKE A BETRAYAL OF MYSELF, OF EVERYTHING I'D FELT FOR THE PAST SIX YEARS.
IT MADE MY FEELINGS FOR MAYAMA SEEM LIKE A LIE.
...FOR A LONG, LONG, LONG TIME...
OTHER PEOPLE MIGHT THINK IT'S PATHETIC.
THAT I'M PATHETIC.
BUT MY FEELINGS FOR MAYAMA...
...MY LOVE FOR HIM...
...WAS THE ONLY THING I HAD.

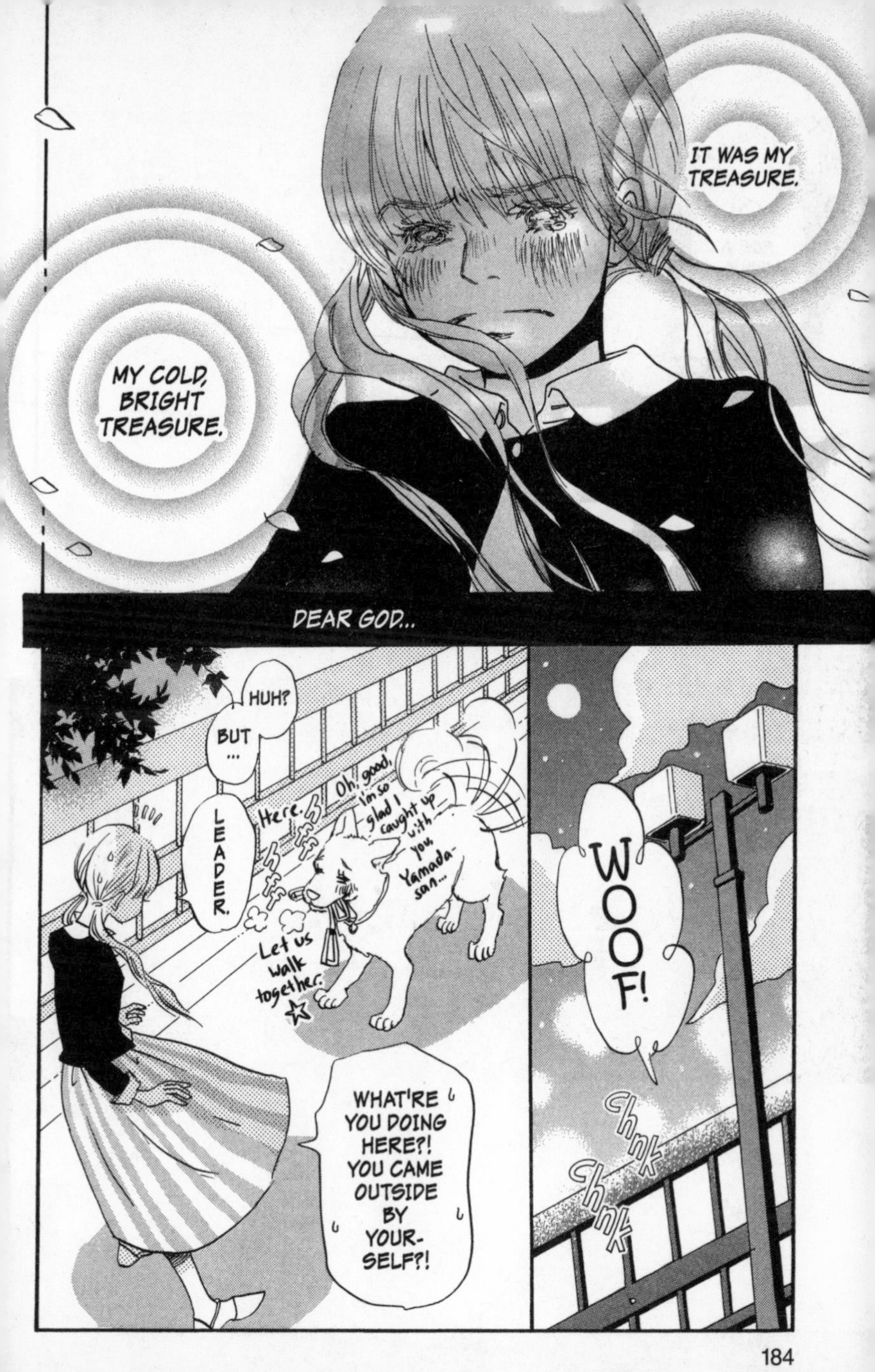
IT WAS MY TREASURE.
MY COLD, BRIGHT TREASURE.
DEAR GOD...
WOOF!
Chnk
Chnk
HUH?
BUT ...
LEADER.
Here.
Oh, good, I'm so glad I caught up with you, Yamada-san...
Let us walk together. ☆
WHAT'RE YOU DOING HERE?! YOU CAME OUTSIDE BY YOUR-SELF?!

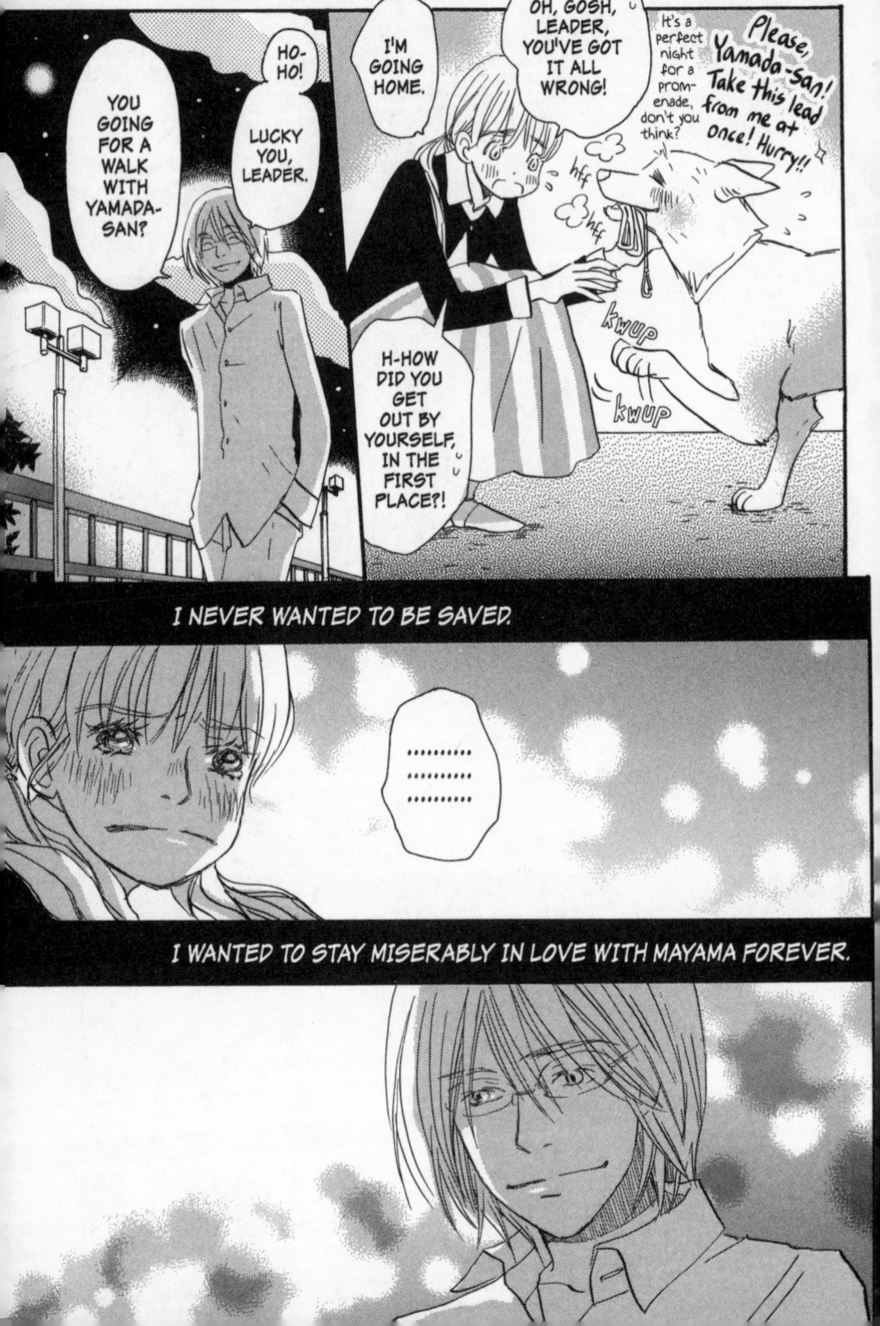
Please, Yamada-san! Take this lead from me at once! Hurry!!
It's a perfect night for a promenade, don't you think?
hff
hff
OH, GOSH, LEADER, YOU'VE GOT IT ALL WRONG!
I'M GOING HOME.
kwup
kwup
H-HOW DID YOU GET OUT BY YOURSELF, IN THE FIRST PLACE?!
HO-HO!
LUCKY YOU, LEADER.
YOU GOING FOR A WALK WITH YAMADA-SAN?
I NEVER WANTED TO BE SAVED.
....
....
....
I WANTED TO STAY MISERABLY IN LOVE WITH MAYAMA FOREVER.

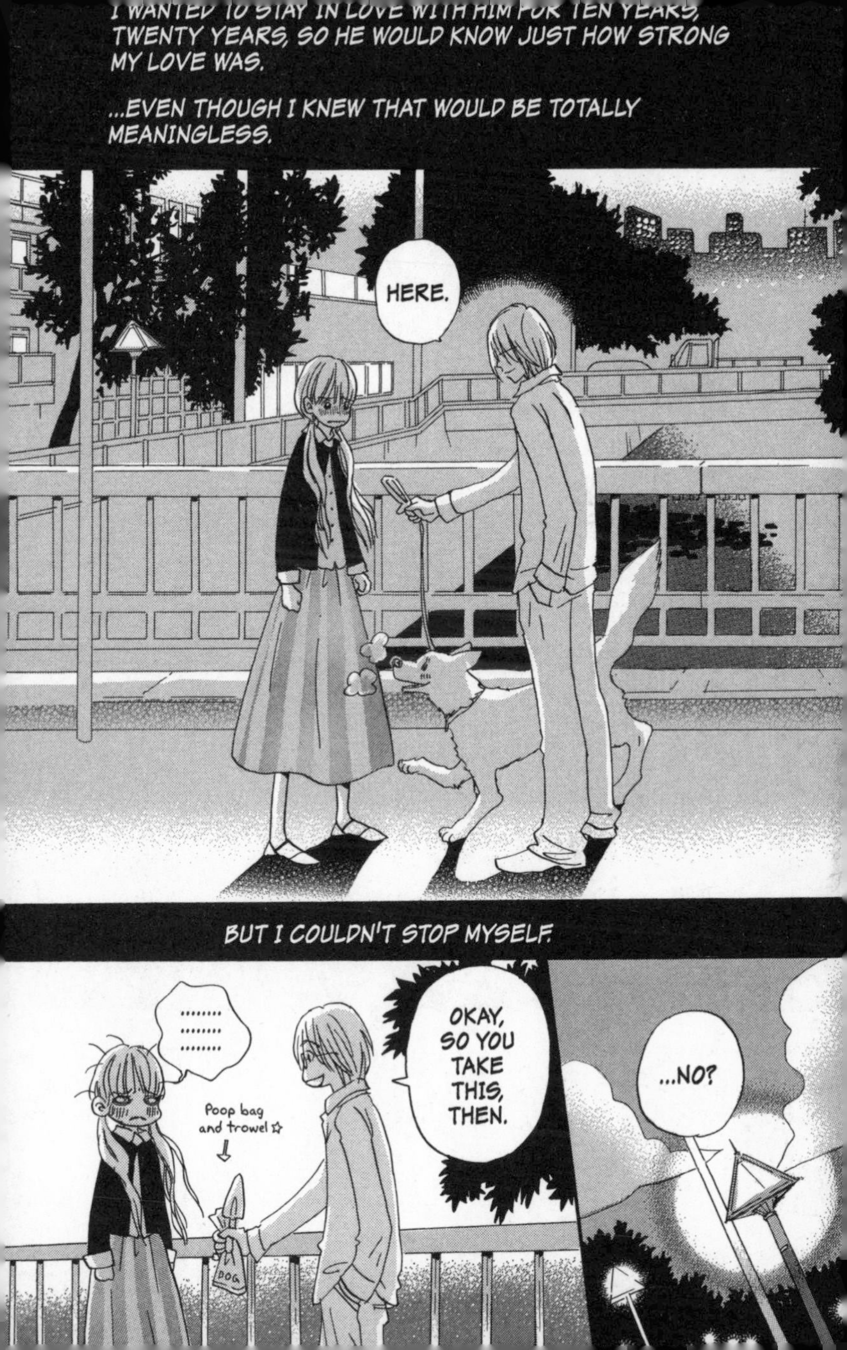
I WANTED TO STAY IN LOVE WITH HIM FOR TEN YEARS, TWENTY YEARS, SO HE WOULD KNOW JUST HOW STRONG MY LOVE WAS.
...EVEN THOUGH I KNEW THAT WOULD BE TOTALLY MEANINGLESS.
HERE.
BUT I COULDN'T STOP MYSELF.
...NO?
OKAY, SO YOU TAKE THIS, THEN.
....
Poop bag and trowel ☆
DOG

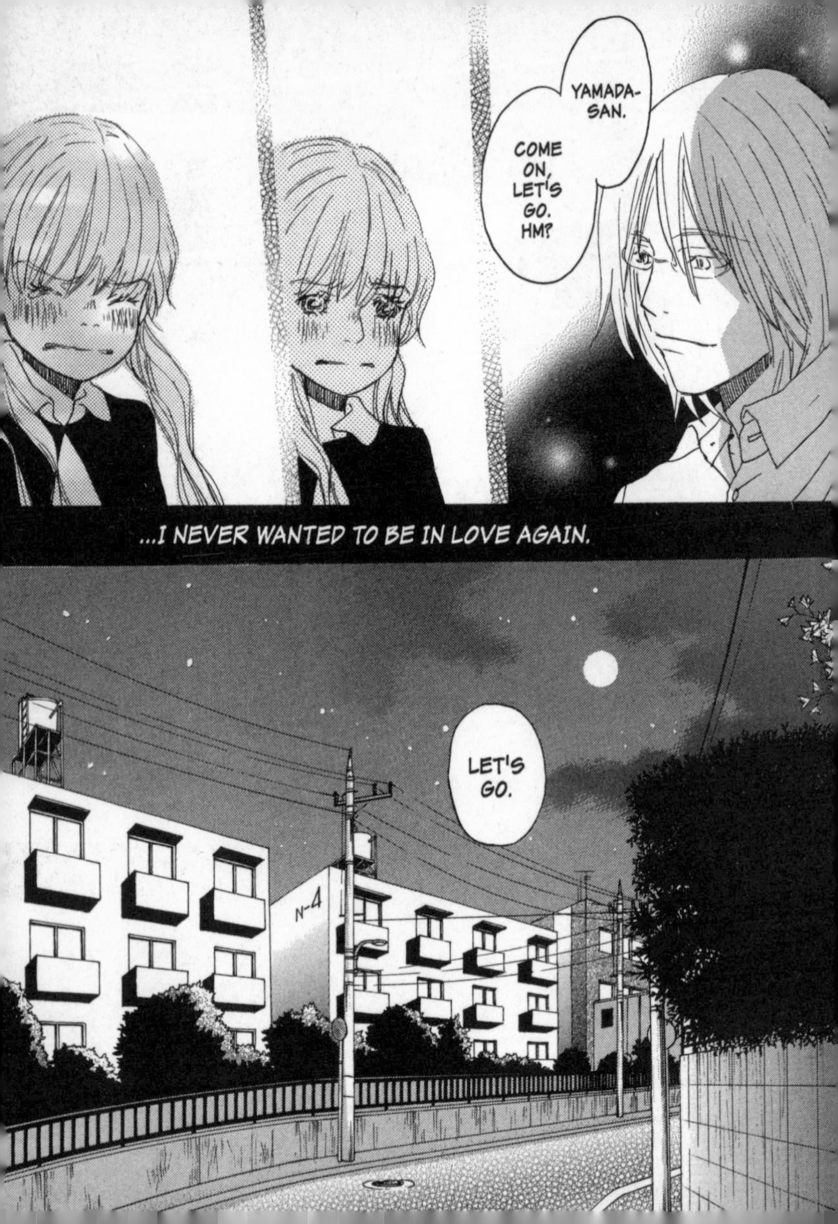
YAMADA-SAN.
COME ON, LET'S GO. HM?
...I NEVER WANTED TO BE IN LOVE AGAIN.
LET'S GO.

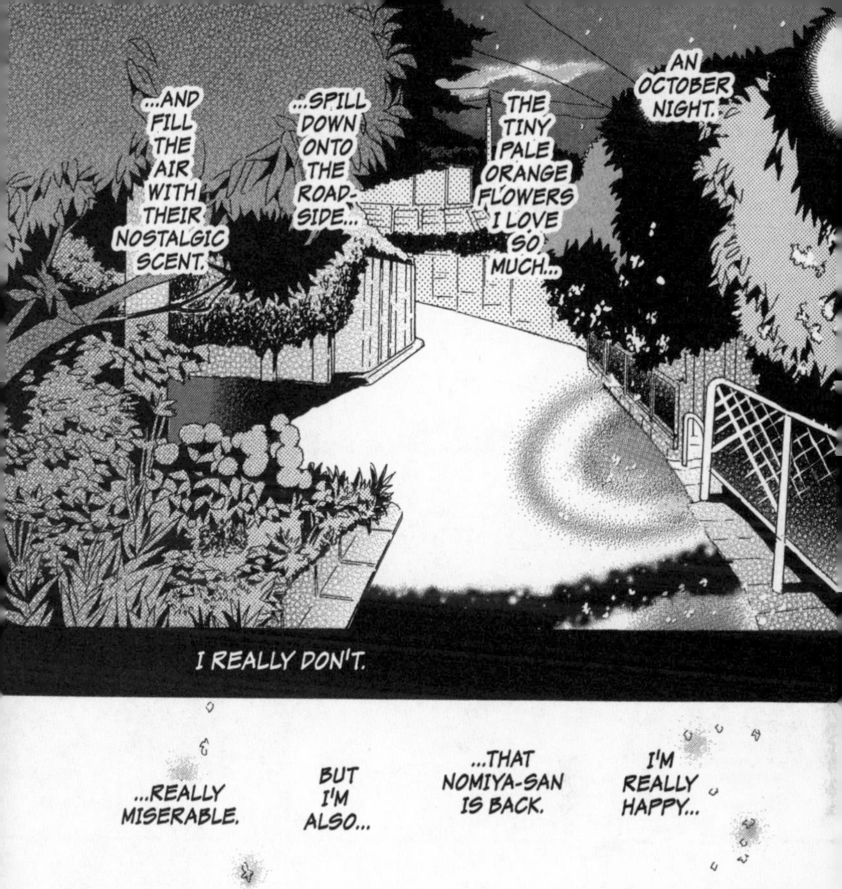
AN OCTOBER NIGHT.
THE TINY PALE ORANGE FLOWERS I LOVE SO MUCH...
...SPILL DOWN ONTO THE ROAD-SIDE...
...AND FILL THE AIR WITH THEIR NOSTALGIC SCENT.
I REALLY DON'T.
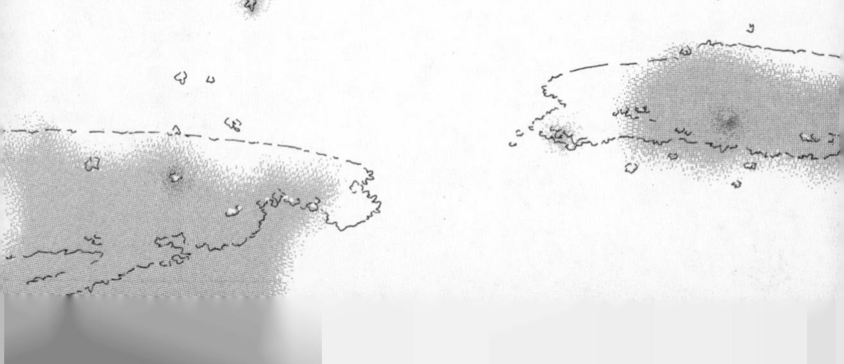
I'M REALLY HAPPY...
...THAT NOMIYA-SAN IS BACK.
BUT I'M ALSO...
...REALLY MISERABLE.

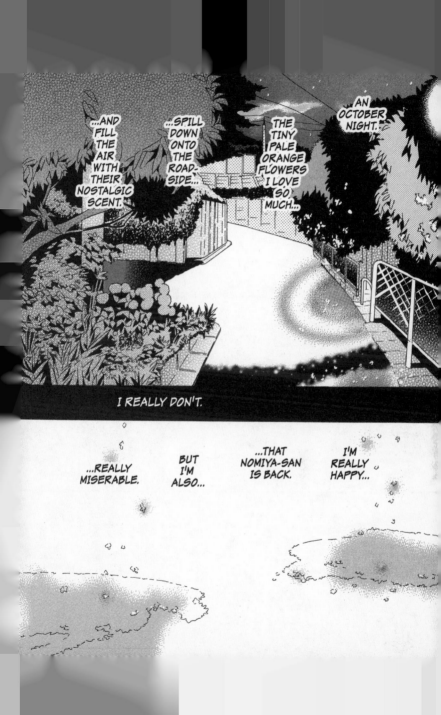

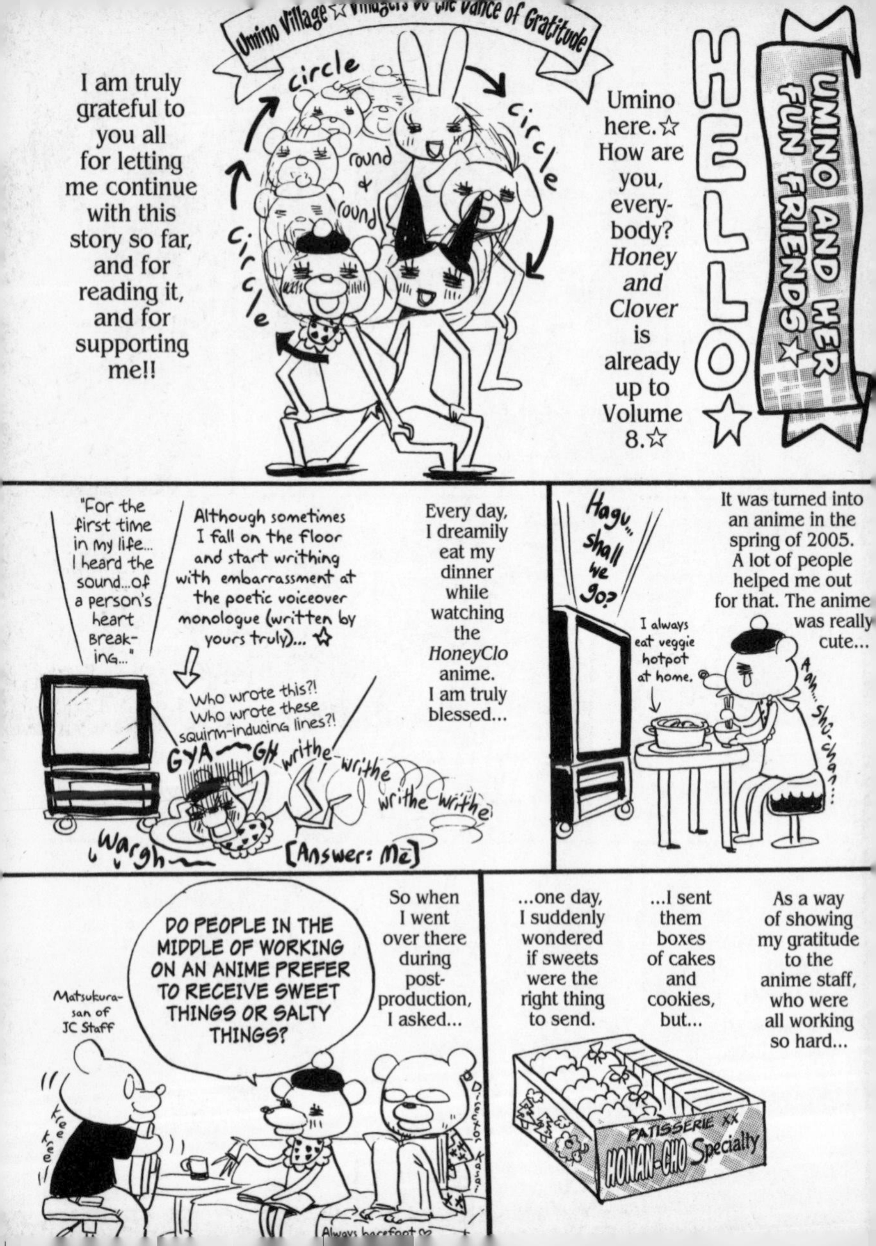
UMINO AND HER FUN FRIENDS☆
HELLO☆
Umino here.☆ How are you, everybody? *Honey and Clover* is already up to Volume 8.☆
Umino Village☆Villagers Do the Dance of Gratitude
circle
circle
round & round
circle
I am truly grateful to you all for letting me continue with this story so far, and for reading it, and for supporting me!!
It was turned into an anime in the spring of 2005. A lot of people helped me out for that. The anime was really cute...
Hagu... shall we go?
I always eat veggie hotpot at home.
Aah... Shu-chan...
Every day, I dreamily eat my dinner while watching the *HoneyClo* anime. I am truly blessed...
Although sometimes I fall on the floor and start writhing with embarrassment at the poetic voiceover monologue (written by yours truly)...☆
"For the first time in my life... I heard the sound...of a person's heart break-ing..."
Who wrote this?! Who wrote these squirm-inducing lines?!
GYA—GH
writhe writhe writhe writhe
Wargh—
[Answer: Me]
As a way of showing my gratitude to the anime staff, who were all working so hard...
...I sent them boxes of cakes and cookies, but...
...one day, I suddenly wondered if sweets were the right thing to send.
PATISSERIE XX
HONAN-CHO Specialty
So when I went over there during post-production, I asked...
DO PEOPLE IN THE MIDDLE OF WORKING ON AN ANIME PREFER TO RECEIVE SWEET THINGS OR SALTY THINGS?
Matsukura-san of JC Staff
kree kree
Director Kasai
Always barefoot♡

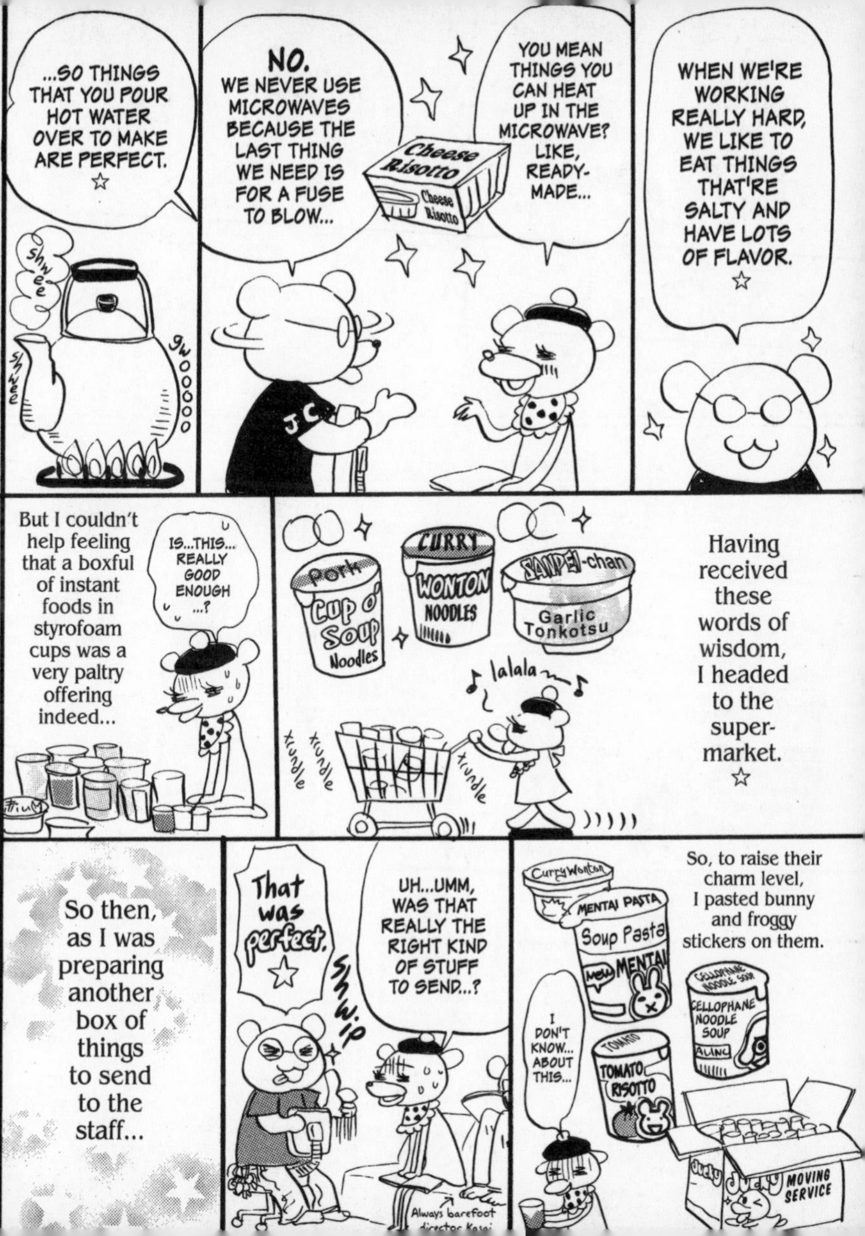
WHEN WE'RE WORKING REALLY HARD, WE LIKE TO EAT THINGS THAT'RE SALTY AND HAVE LOTS OF FLAVOR. ☆
YOU MEAN THINGS YOU CAN HEAT UP IN THE MICROWAVE? LIKE, READY-MADE...
Cheese Risotto
Cheese Risotto
NO.
WE NEVER USE MICROWAVES BECAUSE THE LAST THING WE NEED IS FOR A FUSE TO BLOW...
J.C.
...SO THINGS THAT YOU POUR HOT WATER OVER TO MAKE ARE PERFECT. ☆
shwee
shwee
gwoooooo
Having received these words of wisdom, I headed to the supermarket. ☆
CURRY WONTON NOODLES
SANPEI-chan
Garlic Tonkotsu
Pork Cup o' Soup Noodles
lalala
xrundle
xrundle
xrundle
But I couldn't help feeling that a boxful of instant foods in styrofoam cups was a very paltry offering indeed...
IS...THIS... REALLY GOOD ENOUGH ...?
So, to raise their charm level, I pasted bunny and froggy stickers on them.
Curry Wonton
MENTAI PASTA
Soup Pasta
MENTAI
CELLOPHANE NOODLE SOUP
CELLOPHANE NOODLE SOUP
TOMATO
TOMATO RISOTTO
MOVING SERVICE
I DON'T KNOW... ABOUT THIS...
UH...UMM, WAS THAT REALLY THE RIGHT KIND OF STUFF TO SEND...?
That was perfect. ☆
shwip
Always barefoot director Kasai
So then, as I was preparing another box of things to send to the staff...

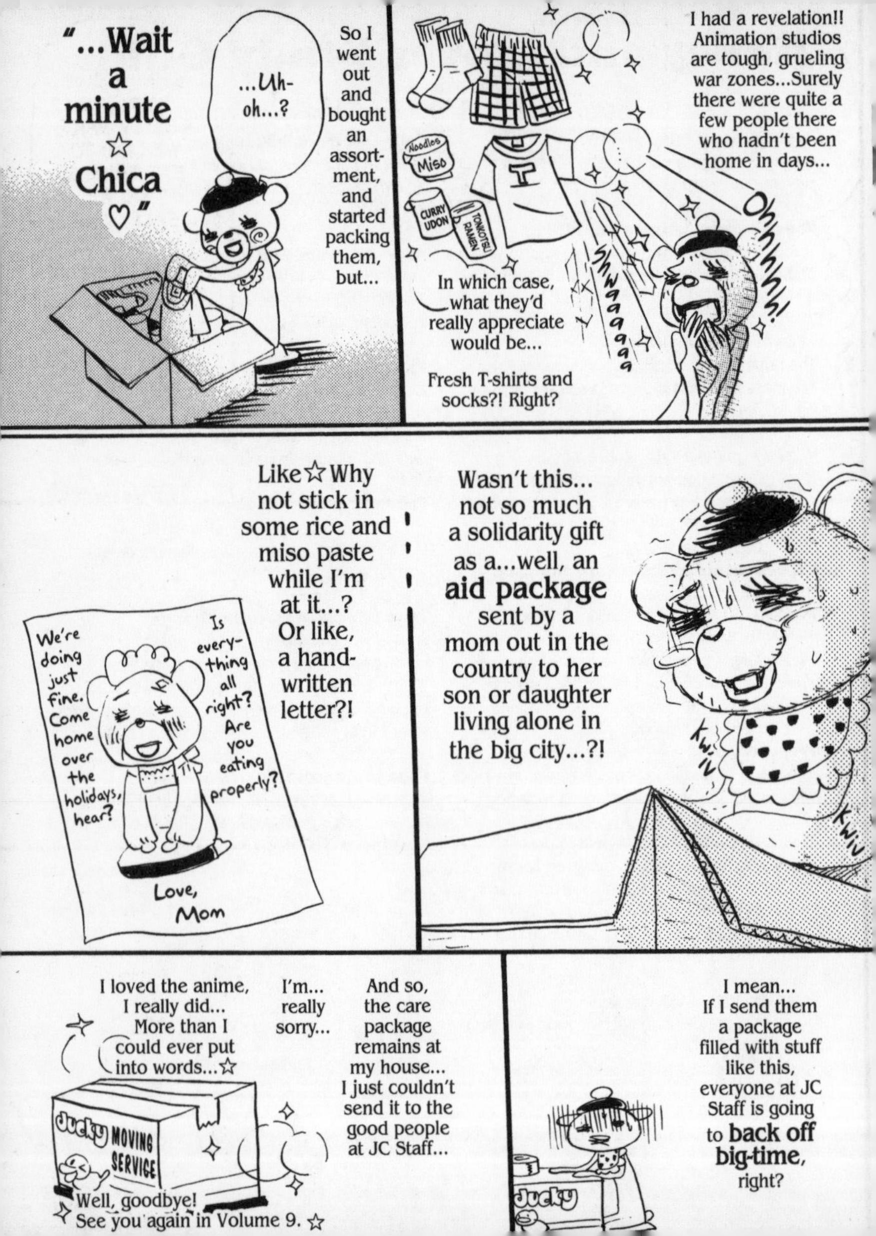
I had a revelation!! Animation studios are tough, grueling war zones...Surely there were quite a few people there who hadn't been home in days...
Ohhhhhh!!
Shwaaaaaaaa
Noodles Miso
CURRY UDON
TONKOTSU RAMEN
T
In which case, what they'd really appreciate would be...
Fresh T-shirts and socks?! Right?
So I went out and bought an assortment, and started packing them, but...
...Uh-oh...?
"...Wait a minute ☆ Chica ♡"
Wasn't this... not so much a solidarity gift as a...well, an **aid package** sent by a mom out in the country to her son or daughter living alone in the big city...?!
Kwiv
Kwiv
Like☆ Why not stick in some rice and miso paste while I'm at it...? Or like, a hand-written letter?!
Is everything all right? Are you eating properly?
We're doing just fine. Come home over the holidays, hear?
Love, Mom
I mean... If I send them a package filled with stuff like this, everyone at JC Staff is going to **back off big-time**, right?
Ducky
And so, the care package remains at my house... I just couldn't send it to the good people at JC Staff...
I'm... really sorry...
I loved the anime, I really did... More than I could ever put into words...☆
Ducky MOVING SERVICE
Well, goodbye! See you again in Volume 9. ☆

Honey and Clover Study Guide

Page 28, panel 5: Katsu-don
A bowl of rice topped with deep-fried breaded pork cutlets, eggs and sauce.

Page 37, panel 3: Izumo Grand Shrine
The oldest Shinto shrine in Japan and dedicated to the god of marriage, Ôkuninushi no Okami.

Page 45, panel 4: Hokkaido
The northernmost and second largest of the Japanese islands. It is also the coldest of the islands.

Page 49, panel 2: Otaru
A port city located northwest of Sapporo. It's known for its many historic buildings, cobbled streets and oil lamp–lined canal.

Page 69, panel 2: Tottori attractions and specialties
Yamazaki is listing off the things Tottori Prefecture is known for. The sand dunes are Japan's largest, stretching ten miles from east to west. Jinpûkaku was built in 1907 for the crown prince's visit to the area. *Koen dango* are a type of rice flour dumpling tinted three colors. The award-winning actress Sayuri Yoshinaga starred in the movie *Yumechiyo Nikki*, which partially took place in Tottori.

Page 105, panel 3: Cassiopeia Express
A two-story train that runs between Tokyo and Sapporo in about 17 hours. It only offers private berth rooms (in Suite, Deluxe or Twin class), and travelers can have dinner in the dining car or their rooms.

Page 106, panel 1: Sapporo
The capital of Hokkaido and the fourth-largest population in Japan.

Page 142, panel 1: Kamakura
A city in Kanagawa, about 24 miles south of Tokyo. It was the main city of Japan during the Kamakura era (1185–1333).

Page 151, panel 5: Edamame
Fresh soybeans boiled in the pods and salted. They are often served as a bar snack or appetizer.

Page 151, panel 5: Konnyaku
A type of plant gelatin made from the plant of the same name (*Amorphophallus konjac*). It has little taste of its own, so it's most often flavored with other ingredients or served with sauce.

Page 152, panel 2: Osmanthus
Osmanthus fragrans. An evergreen shrub native to Asia, its blossoms have a peach or apricot scent.

Page 165, panel 1: Frucho Orange
A take on a popular instant dessert that involves adding milk to the contents of a packet to create something similar to yogurt or instant pudding. Normally, one would need to mix in only a single serving's worth of milk.

Page 169, panel 1: Yuki Nae
A Japanese actress who has appeared in such films as *Letters from Iwo Jima*, *MPD Psycho*, *Ultraman* and *White on Rice*.

Thanks to the *Honey and Clover* anime version being made, I've gotten to know a lot of people. I'm slowly making some more friends too. Maybe in a few years I'll finally be able to sing the song that goes "I wonder if I can make a hundred friends" without getting all teary-eyed!!

-Chica Umino

Chica Umino was born in Tokyo and started out as a product designer and illustrator. Her beloved *Honey and Clover* debuted in 2000 and received the Kodansha Manga Award in 2003. *Honey and Clover* was also nominated for the Tezuka Culture Prize and an award from the Japan Media Arts Festival.

HONEY AND CLOVER
VOL. 8
Shojo Beat Manga Edition

STORY AND ART BY CHICA UMINO

English Translation & Adaptation/Akemi Wegmuller
Touch-up Art & Lettering/Sabrina Heep
Design/Yukiko Whitley
Editor/Pancha Diaz

VP, Production/Alvin Lu
VP, Publishing Licensing/Rika Inouye
VP, Sales & Product Marketing/Gonzalo Ferreyra
VP, Creative/Linda Espinosa
Publisher/Hyoe Narita

Printed in Canada

Published by VIZ Media, LLC
P.O. Box 77010
San Francisco, CA 94107

10 9 8 7 6 5 4 3 2 1
First printing, December 2009

www.viz.com
www.shojobeat.com

RATED T+ FOR OLDER TEEN

PARENTAL ADVISORY
HONEY AND CLOVER is rated T+ for Older Teen and is recommended for ages 16 and up. This volume contains adult situations.

ratings.viz.com

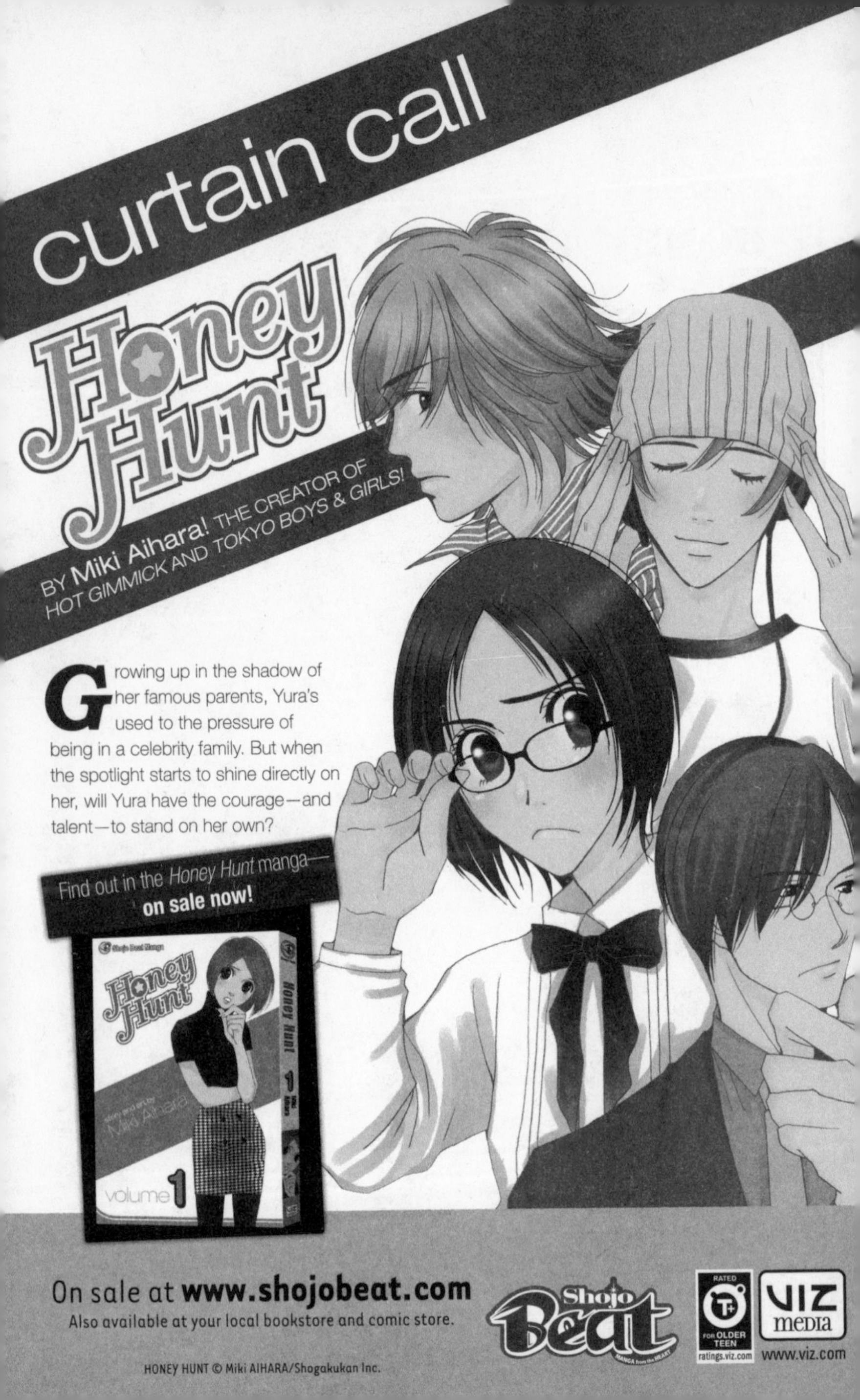
curtain call
Honey Hunt
BY Miki Aihara! THE CREATOR OF
HOT GIMMICK AND TOKYO BOYS & GIRLS!
Growing up in the shadow of her famous parents, Yura's used to the pressure of being in a celebrity family. But when the spotlight starts to shine directly on her, will Yura have the courage—and talent—to stand on her own?
Find out in the Honey Hunt manga—
on sale now!
Shojo Beat Manga
Honey Hunt
story and art by
Miki Aihara
volume 1
On sale at www.shojobeat.com
Also available at your local bookstore and comic store.
Shojo Beat
MANGA from the HEART
RATED
T+
FOR OLDER TEEN
ratings.viz.com
VIZ media
www.viz.com
HONEY HUNT © Miki AIHARA/Shogakukan Inc.

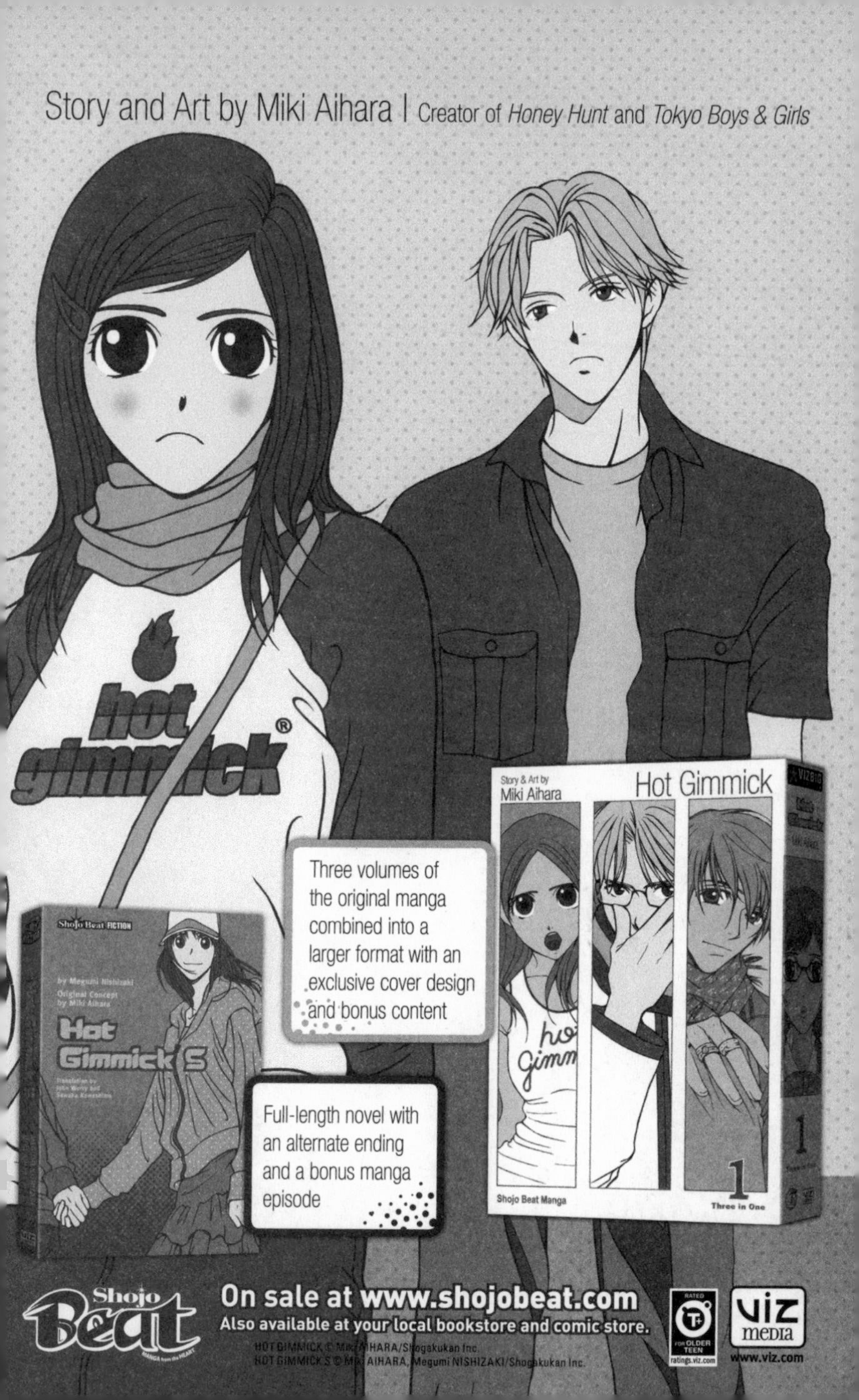
Story and Art by Miki Aihara | Creator of *Honey Hunt* and *Tokyo Boys & Girls*
hot gimmick®
Story & Art by
Miki Aihara
Hot Gimmick
Shojo Beat Manga
1
Three in One
Shojo Beat FICTION
by Megumi Nishizaki
Original Concept
by Miki Aihara
Hot Gimmick S
Three volumes of the original manga combined into a larger format with an exclusive cover design and bonus content
Full-length novel with an alternate ending and a bonus manga episode
Shojo Beat
On sale at www.shojobeat.com
Also available at your local bookstore and comic store.
HOT GIMMICK © Miki AIHARA/Shogakukan Inc.
HOT GIMMICK S © Miki AIHARA, Megumi NISHIZAKI/Shogakukan Inc.
RATED T+ FOR OLDER TEEN
ratings.viz.com
VIZ media
www.viz.com

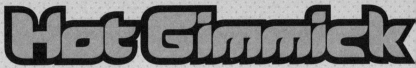

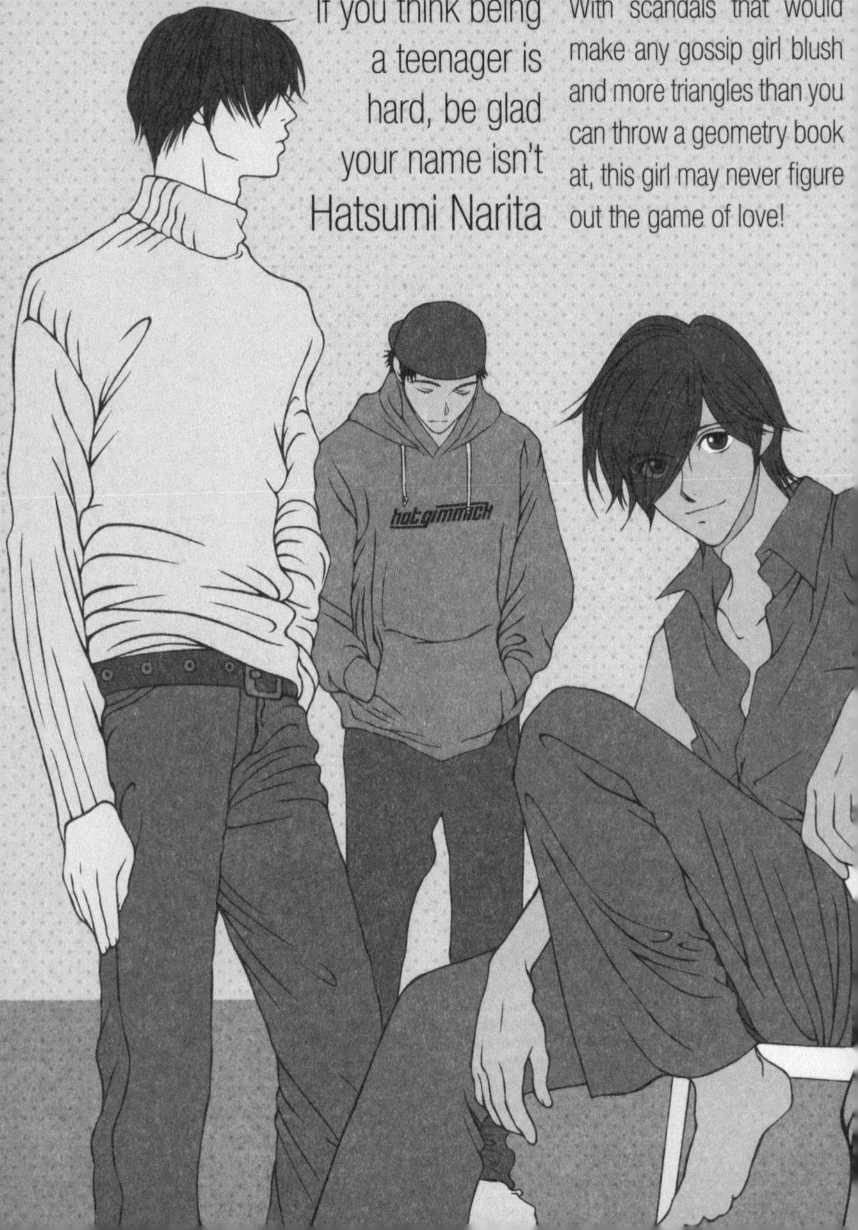
hotgimmick

LAND OF *Fantasy*

MIAKA YŪKI IS AN ORDINARY JUNIOR-HIGH STUDENT WHO IS SUDDENLY WHISKED AWAY INTO THE WORLD OF A BOOK, *THE UNIVERSE OF THE FOUR GODS.* WILL THE BEAUTIFUL CELESTIAL BEINGS SHE ENCOUNTERS AND THE CHANCE TO BECOME A PRIESTESS DIVERT MIAKA FROM EVER RETURNING HOME?

THREE VOLUMES OF THE ORIGINAL *FUSHIGI YŪGI* SERIES COMBINED INTO A LARGER FORMAT WITH AN EXCLUSIVE COVER DESIGN AND BONUS CONTENT

EXPERIENCE THE BEAUTY OF *FUSHIGI YŪGI* WITH THE HARDCOVER ART BOOK

ALSO AVAILABLE: THE *FUSHIGI YŪGI: GENBU KAIDEN* MANGA, THE EIGHT VOLUME PREQUEL TO THIS BEST-SELLING FANTASY SERIES

Tell us what you think about Shojo Beat Manga!

Our survey is now available online. Go to:

shojobeat.com/mangasurvey

Help us make our product offerings better!